THE EVANGELICAL FAITH

Other Books by Helmut Thielicke:

Between God and Satan

A Little Exercise for Young Theologians

Out of the Depths

The Silence of God

The Hidden Question of God

The Evangelical Faith, Volume I

THE EVANGELICAL FAITH

by Helmut Thielicke

Translated
and edited by
Geoffrey W. Bromiley

Volume Two:
*The Doctrine of God
and of Christ*

William B. Eerdmans
Publishing Company   Grand Rapids, Michigan

Translated from the German edition *Der Evangelische Glaube*
© Helmut Thielicke, J. C. B. Mohr (Paul Siebeck) Tübingen 1973

Library of Congress Cataloging in Publication Data

Thielicke, Helmut, 1908-
The evangelical faith.

Translation of Der evangelische Glaube.
Includes bibliographical references.
CONTENTS: v. 1. Prolegomena: the relation of
theology to modern thought-forms. — v. 2. The
doctrine of God and of Christ.
1. Theology, Doctrinal. I. Title.
ISBN 0-8028-2342-4 (v. 1)
ISBN 0-8028-2343-2 (v. 2)

Editor's Preface

In this second volume of *The Evangelical Faith,* **Helmut Thielicke** takes up the first two articles of the Creed. He relates these to the general theme of revelation by seeing in the Father the origin of revelation and in the Son its form. Included in the treatment of God the Father are valuable discussions of faith and its relation to word, history, and experience, of the place of God in modern thought, of the personhood of God, of the Trinity, and of the word as law and gospel. The approach to Christology is not through the two natures but through the three offices, so that the atonement and the resurrection can be treated as well as the traditional, if less important, christological themes of the virgin birth, the descent, and the ascension.

The general approach enables the author to display once again a basic orthodoxy in lively and thoughtful interaction with contemporary theological discussion. When Thielicke describes his theology as evangelical, he obviously does not take the term in the narrower sense which it often bears in the English-speaking world. The duty of the theologian, as he sees it, is not simply to repeat or defend the formulations and interpretations of the past. At the same time Thielicke does not construe the term so broadly as to allow a wholesale reconstruction in which the gospel itself is no longer apparent in any meaningful way. His aim in this evangelical dogmatics is to state the gospel that does not change in language and concepts that do. This is an undertaking of peculiar delicacy, and it is hardly to be expected, or perhaps even desired, that readers either right or left should agree with all that is suggested or concluded. Yet a careful and critical reading might well lead to that better understanding of content or expression which will further the cause of authentic evangelical theology.

In this volume of the English edition, as in the first, some passages have been slightly condensed, especially the longer footnotes and those passages which in the German edition are set in fine print. Nevertheless, the text of the original is offered here with no substantial abridgment, alteration, or excision.

G. W. Bromiley

Pasadena
Advent, 1976

Contents

General Plan of the Third and Final Volume

PART THREE: The Present and Future of Revelation: The Holy Spirit

A. The Power of Presentation

B. The Form of Presentation: The Church

C. The Exclusiveness of Presentation: The Gospel
and World Religions

D. The Culmination of Presentation: The Eschaton

Is it not much too arrogant and hazardous to try to build a system today, instead of setting up some forward posts or erecting huts and emergency quarters?

The reader may be sure of my understanding if he regards a book like this as a venture which comes very close to the limits of what is nowadays permissible, or if indeed he thinks these limits have been overstepped. Subjectively this became clear to me as, along with the joys of discovery, the present work also seemed to me continually to be attempting too much. The tempting question whether I should not capitulate arose in no small part from the present college situation, which leaves little space for research and teaching and constantly threatens to sap our resources for any large-scale enterprise. The greatness of the theme itself, of course, provided the more important impulse for a defeatist mood. In an age of radical questionings and confusing controversies, trying to raise up the skyscraper of a doctrine of God and of Christ easily arouses doubts as to one's own courage. I will try to explain, then, why in spite of all these obstacles I have addressed myself to the present task.

First, I must dampen certain expectations. Although a systematic exposition of Christian doctrines will be attempted, I dare not say quite so cheerily as the preface to Volume I might suggest that a "system" is being propounded. I have the feeling that I can speak only of studies of some of the central points in such a system. If I were to discuss all the *loci* of classical dogmatics in the detail I am permitting myself, a whole series of volumes would be needed, and even then it would probably remain unfinished like the unique work of Barth, if I may compare small things with great.

If I have decided to tackle the totality of Christian doctrine and abandon the modern style of treatment, this is because the one-sided fixations of recent theological history disturb me. From a rather introverted concentration on hermeneutical and methodological questions, thematic attention has abruptly switched to a theology of exclusively social and even social-revolutionary interest. Once again, then, we find the familiar swing of the pendulum. Observing this violent oscillation I cannot escape the question whether it is really possible to do "theology" from positions of this kind. Is not a great deal necessarily lost with so restricted a focus? I thus came to see it as my task to contemplate again the totality of that which the certainty of our faith includes. Even if this attempt can enjoy only limited success, and even if it leaves my flanks exposed to the critics, then even as a spur my effort might still render the service of a correction or even perhaps an invitation for fresh orientation to the totality of faith's heritage.

In view of the first volume of the work, it is hardly necessary to offer the assurance that I am not taking refuge in a theological ivory tower remote from the age. Discussion of modern forms of thought will provide lively dialog in the spheres of the doctrine of God and of Christ as well. One can hardly deal with such matters without justifying the credibility of theological statements for the modern mind with its attachment to empiricism and its constant suspicion of ideology and metaphysics. Dialog of this kind will naturally be unfruitful if representatives of this mind are found only in contemporaries outside, and it is not recognized that as a theologian I stand also in solidarity with the current sense of immanence, and that I can win through to faith only as I wrestle with this sense. Conceptually these problems will intensify in the sphere of Christology, where slow advance can be made only as we engage in close combat with all types of existentialism, historicism, and other attempts to manipulate the spirit of the age. Here, then, epistemological reflection will be required for the sake of intellectual credibility. It cannot be left out, for even if we take refuge in paradoxical statements—"he whom the whole universe could not contain lies in Mary's bosom"—we still have to find a basis for these, too. If something is incomprehensible and resists every attempt at expression, we must try, at least, in Kant's sense to comprehend the fact of this incomprehensibility.

When I said a few lines back that I must rest content with studies of the central points in such a system, there were various reasons for this modesty.

For one thing, I saw that I could not aim at equality of treatment, because some problems seem to me to be particularly important in the context of modern theological discussion and these demand fuller exposition. Among these we may number in the present volume the complex of problems relating to God, the dialectic of law and gospel, and Christology. Even within these areas, however, some things will be emphasized while others are disregarded.

Again, in my *Theological Ethics* I have already said many things that also belong in a dogmatics, e.g., about creation and sin. From the dilemma thus posed I have sought a way out in compromise. I have kept in mind the contours of a complete system and tried to make them clear to the reader. But I have not filled in the details at every point, sometimes being content merely to give brief indications. Thus I have not included a chapter about man, since the *Ethics* presents a comprehensive anthropology. What I say about man in the present work is not a self-contained section, as in the *Theological Ethics,* but is integrated into other thematic spheres. For this reason I hope that readers will treat the ethical and dogmatic works as a corpus whose individual parts supplement one another.

Along these lines, as a supplement to Christology, I may refer especially to the chapters on justification and sanctification (ThE, I, § 213-689; E.T. I, pp. 52-451) and on the anthropological background of the doctrine of justification, particularly on controversial aspects of creation, the first estate of man, the fall, and the concept of grace (ThE, I, § 690-1440; E.T. I, pp. 147ff.).

In spite of this, I must agree with potential critics if they feel that the absence of special chapters on creation, sin, anthropology, and other classical themes is more than an architectonic loss. Above all, I do not want to be classified with theologians who have no feeling for creation, whether this be due to an ideology of escape or of sanctification, or for whom the fall is not a reality which serves as an antidote against utopian dreams and illusions of progress. The reader who is indulgent enough to include the *Theological Ethics,* especially the first volume, in his survey of my theological enterprise will perhaps understand that it is through fear of quantitative excess that I do not repeat what I said there simply to meet the requirements of architectonic symmetry, much as I too respect these. References to the *Theological Ethics* will be given so that what is left out here may be easily found. I have also been at pains to relate the two volumes of the dogmatics in the same way.

To give the reader some idea of the planned completion of the present effort in systematics, I have included in the table of contents an outline of the third and final volume.

Many reviewers of the first volume—if this observation may be permitted —have stated that what is being offered here is a theology of the Holy Spirit or of the third article of the creed. This is correct insofar as the approach is concerned. The point of my debate with various hermeneutical ideas is that they have renounced the testimony of the Holy Spirit or not done sufficient justice to it. No small part of my own deliberations has been devoted to the attempt to expound the nature of this testimony. The pneumatological approach may be seen again in the present volume, all the *loci* being handled in terms of the presuppositions worked out in the first volume. In the doctrine of God and of Christ, of course, this is more implicit than explicit. While it is in keeping with my intentions to pursue every theological discussion *sub specie* of the third article, I feel that I should be misunderstood if regarded as projecting a theology of the Spirit. In my view, linking the nominative "theology" with a genitive is a serious mistake, whether the reference be to a theology of the Spirit, a theology of the facts, or indeed a theology of revolution.

The author cannot conclude this preface without expressing pleasure that in the troubled seventies of the present century there is still the possibility— and a publishing house is still willing to take the risk—of presenting to the contemporary world a broad exposition of the problems of the Trinity and Christology, thereby helping it to find traces of lofty ideas in basic formulae of the history of early dogma. These ideas are lofty not merely because they embrace an exalted theme but also to the extent that they enclose and provide for our own ideas, which are often so arrogant and think themselves to be so emancipated. The ancient doctrine of the Trinity is not just reflection; it is also prophecy.

Among my assistants I wish to give special thanks to Uwe Böschmeyer and Joachim Sach for help with the Subject Index, and not for this alone, but also because the vital fellowship of life and work which unites us has about it something most exhilarating for theological endeavor. During the reading of the proofs I was lecturing for some time in America, so that unfortunately I was not able to scrutinize every chapter personally.

Abbreviations

ApolCA	Apology of the Confession of Augsburg
CA	Confession of Augsburg
CD	Karl Barth, *Church Dogmatics,* ed. G. W. Bromiley and T. F. Torrance (1936ff.)
Cl	Otto Clemen, *Luthers Werke in Auswahl* (1925ff.)
Denz.	Heinrich Denzinger, *Enchiridion Symbolorum,* Editio XXXIII
ETh	*Evangelische Theologie, Monatsschrift,* ed. E. Wolf (Munich)
GV	Rudolf Bultmann, *Glauben und Verstehen* I-IV (1933ff.); E.T. *Faith and Understanding,* I (1969)
Inst.	Calvin's *Institutes* (the reference is to the last edition of 1559 unless otherwise indicated)
KD	*Kerygma und Dogma. Zeitschrift für theologische Forschung und kirchliche Lehre,* ed. W. Joest (Göttingen)
KM	*Kerygma und Mythos,* ed. H. W. Bartsch (1951ff.); E.T. R. H. Fuller (London, 1953)
LCC	Library of Christian Classics
LThK	*Lexikon für Theologie und Kirche,* ed. J. Höfer and K. Rahner (from 1957)
RE	*Realenzyklopädie für protestantische Theologie und Kirche,* 3rd ed., ed. A. Hauck (1896ff.)
RGG² ᵃⁿᵈ ³	*Die Religion in Geschichte und Gegenwart,* 2nd ed., ed. H. Gunkel and L. Zscharnack (Tübingen, 1927ff.); 3rd ed., ed. K. Galling (1957ff.)
SBAW	*Sitzungsberichte der Heidelberger Akademie der Wissenschaften, Philos.-histor. Klasse*
Stud. gen.	*Studium generale. Zeitschrift für die Einheit der Wissenschaften . . .* (Heidelberg)
TDNT	*Theological Dictionary of the New Testament,* ed. G. Kittel and G. Friedrich, tr. G. W. Bromiley (1964ff.)
ThBl	*Theologische Blätter,* ed. Hermann Strathmann (Leipzig)
ThE	Helmut Thielicke, *Theologische Ethik* I-III (1951ff.); E.T. (altered and abridged) *Theological Ethics* (1966ff.)
ThEx	*Theologische Existenz heute*
ThLZ	*Theologische Literaturzeitung,* ed. K. Aland (Berlin)
WA	*D. Martin Luthers Werke.* Kritische Gesamtausgabe (Weimar, 1883ff.)
ZEE	*Zeitschrift für evangelische Ethik,* ed. W. Schweitzer (Gütersloh)
ZNW	*Zeitschrift für die neutestamentliche Wissenschaft*
ZThK	*Zeitschrift für Theologie und Kirche,* ed. G. Ebeling (Tübingen)

All ungodliness arises out of a false confusion or a false separation of creative and creaturely being.   FRANZ VON BAADER

Of all boldly ventured existences, can there be one that is more radiant and brave? We come up against our limits and penetrate the unknown.
                                                                    RAINER MARIA RILKE

It is one of the hardest things for a thoughtful man that, seeing among those who do not see, he has to live through the course of a historical process whose ineluctable outcome he has long since clearly perceived. In these circumstances the time of the error of others, of their false hopes and blind mistakes, is very long.

CARL J. BURCKHARDT
on Tocqueville

Part One

THE SOURCE OF REVELATION:
GOD THE FATHER

Preliminary Methodological Note

Any attempt to work out a dogmatic system faces the difficulty that no progressive sequence of thought can be developed in which one thing follows
on another. Such a sequence would presuppose that there are first principles
from which deductions may be made. Principles of this kind have sometimes been presupposed in theological or philosophical thought, as in the
Reformed doctrine of the decrees or Hegel's concept of the absolute spirit,[1]
but the result has always been that the dynamism of the salvation event has
yielded to a reference system of timeless truths. Instead of being able to
make theological statements in a developing sequence of this kind, a theological system finds itself under the constraint of having to say everything
at once. It also forms an organism whose members are in mutual relationship. Thus the doctrine of creation cannot be expounded without some consideration of its connection with Christology and eschatology, so that continual anticipations are required. Similarly eschatology has to be constantly
looking back to creation and Christology.

Nevertheless, the discursive character of thought, to which theological
reflection is also subject, means that we have to divide that which is for
faith an indivisible whole. The different aspects of this whole have to be considered separately. This does not mean that the whole is to be developed
in terms of its parts but rather that in everything that is said about the parts
we are already confronted with the whole.

In view of its structure, theological thinking is in some sense an "alien"
medium into which statements of faith must be transposed. In virtue of the
autonomy of the structure of thought there will always be refractions of that

---

[1] We may refer in this connection to later orthodox Calvinists such as Beza, Peter
Martyr, and Zanchius. These men base their radicalized doctrine of predestination
on God's *potentia absoluta,* which as the supreme cause makes predestination into
determination and allows salvation history, including the fall and redemption, to be
deduced causally from the primal decrees of this omnipotent God. The ground is
thus prepared for later Deism.

which the system seeks to apprehend. Theological history offers a rich store of such refractions. Reason, even theological reason, proves constantly unfaithful to its true function of being an organ of perception and allows the principles of its thought to master what is thought. Orthodox theology expressed this revolt of the means of thought by speaking of a transition from the organic use (perceptive reason) to the normative use (controlling reason).[2]

For this reason theology is always an undertaking of fallen man. The sinfulness of man finds expression in the given structural realities of his functions of thought. This does not mean, of course, that it is better not to attempt a theological examination of faith, thereby safeguarding faith against refraction. Faith's claim to the whole man entails a claim to his acts of thought. The only point is that theology is not a sacred affair. It needs forgiveness in the same way as all else that man does. Being at the same time both righteous and a sinner applies also to the act of theological thinking. This act is not justified by what man is and thinks in present reality but by that toward which he looks and behind which he constantly lags in his *de facto* state.

Because the whole of the theological organism remains indivisible and must be seen in its various aspects only by reason of the discursiveness of our thought, the placing of the specific dogmatic themes or *loci* is in most cases a matter of individual discretion. Thus the doctrine of holy scripture as the source of all theological knowledge might theoretically be put first as a prolegomenon. We do not follow this course, however, but place this doctrine among the themes of the third article, the doctrine of the Holy Spirit. It will be shown later why we select a trinitarian introduction to the material and thereby follow the order of the Apostles' Creed.[3]

---

[2] D. Hollaz, *Ex. theol.,* p. 71; J. A. Quenstedt, *Syst. theol.,* I, 42. Cf. the theological critique of reason in ThE, II, 1, § 1321ff.

[3] References to this ordering of the material may be found already in Volume I (Chapters VII-XI).

A. *Revelation as the Self-Disclosure of God*

I

The Problem of the Concept of Revelation

The concept of revelation is not a specifically Christian concept. It belongs to the general world of religion. This world abounds in references to theophanies, auditions, visions, miracles, and other intimations of deity. The receiving of such intimations is usually bound up with a claim to authority and not infrequently with a supposedly exclusive possession of truth. The one to whom the revelation is given is called to be a mediator to others and holds a privileged position in relation to what has been revealed to him. The claim of the Christian religion to absolute truth—to use the loaded phrase of Hegel—has thus to compete with many rivals. Neither revelations nor the claim to exclusiveness is peculiar to Christianity. This thesis spells many dangers for theology. Those who give the concept of revelation a dominant place in their dogmatic system, as we are doing, have to be on guard against the possibility that they will make a general religious phenomenon out of faith and its object.

Furthermore, a general concept of revelation such as theology usually employs cannot easily be based on biblical usage. A concordance quickly shows that both the verb "to reveal" (which noticeably predominates) and also the noun "revelation" refer to individual instances of the divine speech and action. The revelation of God in the form of Christ is an event or active occurrence in this sense (Luke 17:30; John 21:1, 14; Galatians 1:16; Colossians 3:4; 2 Thessalonians 1:7; 1 Peter 1:7, etc.).[1]

If, however, the term "to reveal" denotes actual intimations of God, it does not refer in summary form to a reality which in principle, e.g., in the form of polarities of time and eternity or God and the world, escapes or

---

[1] Cf. the Arts. *apokalýptein, gnōrízein, dēloún* in TDNT; W. won Loewenich, *Was heisst Offenbarung?* (1938); R. Bultmann, "Der Begriff des Wortes Gottes im NT," *Glauben und Verstehen* (GV), I (1933), pp. 268ff.; E.T. *Faith and Understanding* (1966), pp. 286ff.

even resists apprehension in human experience. As a summary reference of this type the concept of revelation is the result of an abstraction which plainly bears the signature of subsequent reflection.

Historically the term "revelation" assumes a dominant position only at a later stage, i.e., in the age of orthodoxy. The Enlightenment makes the concept a favorite theme of its attacks and challenges it in a rich variety of forms. The theologies of the past two centuries have attempted—again with very different nuances—to rehabilitate the concept.

Although the concept of revelation as a summary designation of *the* self-disclosure of God is a later product of reflection, this cannot mean that continuity with the usage of the Bible is broken or that a principle has replaced an active event. Theological reflection of this type is in fact formally necessitated by the actual self-manifestations of God. The question has to be considered why God's reality expresses itself in these specific words which transcend all human speech, or why God's reality manifests itself in signs,[2] i.e., in acts which, being part of the special salvation event, are not simply enfolded in the continuity of immanent processes. The acts of God's self-disclosure do in fact call for reflection on the question to what extent there is manifested behind these acts a dimension of reality which belongs only to God and to what extent this reality lies beyond the horizon of human reality and human experience.

A way is thus opened up which leads from simple reception of the divine self-disclosures to reflection on them and hence to the formation of a general concept of revelation. He who experiences God in action is apprehended by him as a whole, in the sphere of action (i.e., love) and also in that of reflection. In this latter sphere the problem at once arises how revelation and reason, or grace and nature, are related to one another and whether or how far they stand in mutual correlation.

This transition from an actual to an abstract use of the concept of revelation, in which it denotes the dimension of the divine reality which escapes human experience, may be seen even in Romans 1:18ff. This may not be clear at first glance. For it seems in the first instance that the reference is not to an actual event of revelation but to God's ontic revelation in the works of creation. At the same time, even if from a different angle, the original actuality of revelation may also be perceived. It occurs on the part of man, who constantly stands in a relation of opposition to the truth. For the fact that he does not see God's invisible being, his eternal power and deity (Romans 1:20), is not due to the limitation of knowledge, as Kant understands the matter. Failure to accept the revelation of God has its basis rather in that man has surrendered himself to untruth, that he has no longer praised God, that he is not grateful to him (1:21), that he no longer understands himself in his creatureliness (Romans 3:4; Ephesians 4:25), and that he loves darkness more than light (John 3:19). The actuality of man is that he rejects God's revelation and can no longer understand the here

---

[2] *Térata kaí sēmeía*, Acts 2:43, 5:12; 6:8; 14:3; Romans 15:19; Hebrews 2:4.

and now as the definitive and real, as that wherein he truly hears God's Word, as the field on which he really does God's will (R. Bultmann, "Die Frage der natürlichen Offenbarung," GV, II [1952], p. 94). This negative side of human existence and conduct is then brought into relation to something that God does. As man opposes truth, God withdraws from him his revelation in creation. He delivers him up (*parédōken,* Romans 1:24, 26) to his opposition to the truth and hence hardens him in error.

This passage of Romans contains, then, hints of the more developed concept of revelation. It points to the dimension of divine reality which is beyond the horizon of human experience. To adopt a modern phrase, one might say that Paul refers to God here as a Wholly Other who is not to be found in the here and now. To that degree his concept of revelation does in fact denote the special dimension of God's reality. On the other hand, this does not imply an ontological interest in which the "being" of God is set over against the "being" of man and from the inadequacy of both it is deduced that the revelation of God is closed to man. While Paul does in fact speak of this inadequacy, in so doing he refers to the actuality of an event of revelation and concealment. God proffers himself in the works of creation. Man refuses to accept him. This refusal is confirmed by his being delivered up (*parédōken*).

Here, then, we have a model of the movement from an actual event of revelation to the concept of revelation, including the implied statement about the dimension of the divine reality. The change is made, however, without any abandoning of the reference of the resultant statements to the event of revelation and concealment.

Naturally the transition from the actuality of the event of revelation to reflection and the formation of general concepts does not take place all that smoothly. Nor does it guarantee material identity in the new mode of expression. For reflection makes use of forms of perception and categories which belong to our world of objective experience. Even the vocabulary it employs contains words which already have specific content.[3] The possibility arises, then, that the mode of statement will cause the object of statement to undergo a mutation, or, in other words, that there will be a revolt of the mode of statement. The self-assertion of man in face of the claim revelation makes on him can take this form of resistance too. The sin of being in untruth does not have the form of an open repudiation of God. It can express itself in structural stifling of the Word, like the thorns which choke the Word in Luke 8:7.

This can easily take place in the transition from the actuality of the event of revelation to the stage of reflection. It has in fact taken place more than once. The further the concept of revelation moves away from its original reference of actuality, the more it takes on dubious features. It becomes formally weak and ambivalent. It is often confusing and unsettling. It generalizes differentiated matters, covers over genuine antitheses, and engen-

---

[3] Cf. Volume I, pp. 78, 125ff.

ders sham problems.[4] One of the perversions which results is that revelation increasingly takes on static characteristics and alienates itself in consequence from the original reference of actuality. The age of orthodoxy offers an example. Here general revelation becomes a state of revelation, a static transparency of the created world,[5] while special revelation comes to be equated with the given thesaurus of holy scripture. Thus the active *fieri* of revelation yields to the static *propositum* of a given document.[6] The act of inspiration disappears in the product in which it is also conserved.[7]

A given and static document of revelation which transcends the normal speech and processes of the world necessarily gives rise to the question how it actualizes itself for me and how it may be appropriated by me. Hence the original reference of actuality, which has been increasingly denied, returns in a new way and in the form of a question and challenge. When revelation takes on a static character, and constitutes an alien body in the world of experience, the result in the next age is that the problem of appropriation becomes the dominant question, as it still is even to our own day.[8] Lessing and Schleiermacher make this plain. This actualization of the second degree, however, must be differentiated strictly from the genuine actuality of the event of revelation.

Originally it denoted a powerful experience of faith. Its later form in the post-orthodox period arose out of a desire to overcome doubt. The empirical approach to the world, and the understanding of this as a self-sufficient domain, brought under increasing suspicion the possibility of understanding a specific nexus of events, and the record of these events, as a transcendent exception. Hence the question of the actualizability of revelation is a later echo, filtered through multiple reflection, of that which was once its true actuality and which signified the events that holy scripture, in notable fashion, expresses for the most part by verbs.

Nevertheless, in spite of the change in the understanding of revelation, one element is always preserved at least in intention. When revelation is discussed, the permanent factor is that something comes to man from without, that he can only receive it, that he does not himself produce it. This is true even when, as in early apologists like Justin Martyr and Tatian, revelation is simply a higher form of what is accessible to the human logos, or even when, as in Lessing, revelation is conversely an anticipation of what reason can achieve by its own independent development.[9] Hegel and Schlei-

---

[4] G. Gloege, RGG³, IV, 1611.

[5] The possibility of proofs of God, as this is accepted in scholastic ontology, has its basis in this principle.

[6] J. Gerhard, *Loci theol.*: Holy scripture is the Word of God (i.e., revelation) set forth in the holy scriptures.

[7] Schleiermacher has this in mind when in the second of his *Speeches*, within the framework of Romantic subjectivity, he describes holy scripture as the hardened form of what was in its original state flowing lava.

[8] Cf. Volume I, pp. 38-55, *passim*.

[9] Cf. H. Thielicke, *Offenbarung, Vernunft und Existenz. Studien zur Religionsphilosophie Lessings*, 5th ed. (1967).

ermacher, too, intend at least to maintain in their concept of revelation this element which comes from outside.

Hegel in his *Lectures on the Philosophy of Religion* (E.T. 1895), Part III, says that revealed or positive religion comes or is given to man from without. Schleiermacher, too, posits as the basis of the Christian religion a divine impartation and manifestation which is different from all that we may discover for ourselves, receive from tradition, work out by thought, or learn from others. What we attain on our own can never be described as revelation (*The Christian Faith* [E.T. 1928], § 10).

Certainly both Hegel and Schleiermacher are adopting here an ambivalent position. This is why we had to say that they only *intended* to maintain the character of revelation as something that comes from outside. They did not do this in fact. In Hegel the absolute comes in historical form as a positive religion and to that extent it comes to man from outside. On the other hand the finite consciousness is aware of its identity with the absolute Spirit. God as self-consciousness knows himself in a consciousness which is different from himself. This is God's consciousness both in itself and also for itself inasmuch as it realizes its identity with God (II, p. 327). This identity, however, is mediated through the negation of finitude. Although, then, revelation seems to be something that comes from outside, and consequently forms no part of what man himself can achieve or produce, it is not transcendent to the degree that the finite consciousness understands itself in its identity with this which comes from outside.

The same applies to the divine impartation and manifestation which comes from without in Schleiermacher. To the extent that the figure of Christ is its content, this becomes an encounter of man with his identity. To be sure, the revelation which has taken place in Christ cannot be explained in terms of the content of the circle of human life to which it belonged. It is a creative divine act (*The Christian Faith,* § 93). Nevertheless, there is fulfilled in this act the concept of man as the subject of the divine self-consciousness. This takes place through the prototypical significance of Christ which expresses in the true sense the being of the concept itself (*ibid.*). This means that in Christ the original of man as the bearer of unbroken God-consciousness becomes fully historical, so that each historical moment bears the original within itself (*ibid.*). To this degree man recognizes again his own identity, or, if we will, the oughtness of his being, in the revelation in Christ. In virtue of the prototypical significance of Christ the concept of the human encounters man as historical being. At this point being is congruent with the concept of it and, as it were, completely fills the concept.

It is with good reason, then, that we speak of the ambivalence of the concept of revelation in Hegel and Schleiermacher. Revelation here undoubtedly comes to me from without, but it loses this element of the without. It has to some extent a Socratic significance. It releases man's self-recognition of his true identity. In both men, therefore, we find a certain analogy to Lessing, for whom revelation plays the role of a precursor and pacemaker.

Revelation does indeed come from outside. It says to man something that he cannot—yet—know on his own. But as an act of Socratic instruction it releases this knowledge. In our view, a qualification is thus demanded. In all these cases the character of revelation as something which comes from outside is maintained only conditionally. Its true transcendence is in fact overthrown.

The external factor, which the concept of revelation seeks to speak to even in its broken forms, is undoubtedly one of the distinctive elements which constantly recur in the biblical understanding of revelation. From Kierkegaard to Otto and the earlier Barth the author of revelation has not incorrectly been called the Wholly Other in virtue of this factor. He is the one who lies beyond the continuity of the world and hence also the activity of human perception.

Just as revelation itself, or the claim to have a revelation, is not a monopoly of Christian faith, so this element of a coming from outside cannot be regarded as exclusive to Christianity. Many parallels in religious history testify to the contrary. The Hellenes, Egyptians, and Indians claim that many mysteries and cults originally came down from heaven or were made known by deity in a way that lies outside the nexus of human things.[10] The history of religion offers a rich assortment of examples of auditions, visions, and various manifestations of deity in the phenomena of nature and history.[11] In face of these analogies the unique factor in the Christian understanding of revelation is not to be sought in the formal processes of revealing but solely in the content of what is disclosed.

What is dubiously called the absoluteness or exclusiveness of Christian revelation cannot be based on formal criteria but only on the self-evidence of what is attested here. Formal criteria could be oriented only to a generally acceptable (or supposedly generally acceptable) schema of verifiability which is already present and which has thus to be applied to revelation. But this would rule out in advance any possibility of revelation advancing on its own behalf the criteria appropriate to it, and refusing to subject itself to pre-existent external criteria. When it bears witness to what no eye has seen, nor ear heard, nor has it entered any human heart (1 Corinthians 2:9), this saying can mean only that the eye, ear, and heart do not have suitable criteria. If they did, something would have entered them. When we have the criteria for something, this no longer stands over against us in silence and the void. We are always dialogically open to it. We are presumptive partners. Our existence is already the prolegomenon of a text for whose exposition preparation has been made in us.

The doctrine of the Holy Spirit in Volume I has already shown us that according to the Christian understanding this existence is not so unbrokenly

---

[10] Schleiermacher, *The Christian Faith*, § 10, Postscript.

[11] H. Kraemer, *Religion and the Christian Faith* (1956); G. van der Leeuw and A. J. Arberry, *Revelation and Reason in Islam* (1957); G. van der Leeuw, *Der Mensch und die Religion* (1941).

open and that it is not so completely ready for revelation. For epistemologically this doctrine tells us that revelation does not consist merely in the content which it attests but also in the mode by which this content is made accessible. The witness of the Spirit is to the effect that from the very first man encounters God's revelation in the Word, and also in creation, without understanding it, and that in the form of obduracy he seeks to maintain the status quo of his rebellious existence (Mark 4:10-12; Isaiah 6:9f.). God needs to make this self-disclosure accessible in and of itself in order that it may enter into the eye, ear, and heart. This simply means, however, that God controls the criteria in virtue of which he can be regarded as credible in his self-manifestation. To that degree the witness of the Spirit maintains the impossibility of verifying revelation with the help of preexistent formal criteria.

There is more to it, however, than the renunciation of these formal criteria and a reference to the content of revelation. For if the content of revelation is simply stated generally and in bulk, it does not bring to light in any way the particularity of revelation. The requirement of obedience and the divine government of history, the ten commandments and the cultic law, certainly belong to this content, but like much else they lie within the sphere of religious analogies and hence they do not have the accent of uniqueness. What is meant by content in the strict sense, only the author of revelation himself, the one who discloses himself, can really be. The "what" at issue here is in truth a "who."

This applies in all strictness. Negatively it means that the more precise content of revelation does not consist of the works of the author of revelation as those are set forth in nature and history. We are not dealing with indirect manifestations but with a direct self-disclosure. In this sense revelation does not disclose a transparency of nature; hence it does not include a corresponding view of nature as revealed.

Psalm 104 does not address nature but the Creator himself: *"Thou* art clothed with honor and majesty, who . . . stretchest out the heavens like a curtain" (vv. lf.). Nor is the Thou of this Creator known from nature. He is known from the Word by which he proclaims himself directly. Nature in its indirectness is ambivalent. It does not make God manifest. It envelops him in mystery. In the majesty of its forms it may well show forth eternity but it is also a parable of the corruptible, of the blatantly non-eternal, which sinks into nothingness when God withdraws his breath (Psalm 104:29). Along with the trees of the Lord which are full of sap and the cedars of Lebanon which he has planted (v. 16), we also find the grass which perishes and which thus denotes the mortality rather than the glory of created things (Psalm 37:2; 90:5; 103:14f.; Isaiah 40:6f.). Grass bears witness to both life and death (Psalm 104:14; Matthew 6:30; Isaiah 15:6; James 1:10). It thus represents the ambivalence of all created forms and of all indirectness in which God appears.

The same applies to the manifestation and concealment of God in history.[12] Here again God is not set forth directly so that one can grasp him. The course of historical events as we see them is inscrutable, e.g., in relation to guilt and punishment. If the Wisdom literature and sayings influenced by it often link their summons to fear of the Lord and obedience with the promise of a reward,[13] rather along the lines of the proverb that honesty is the best policy, the afflictions described in Job or Psalm 73 present us with a rationally insoluble problem, namely, that of reconciling the divine over-ruling of history with the complete absence of any such relation, and hence of bringing it out of its obscurity (Psalm 73:12, 16). The Lord of history is not in fact manifest in his works. On the contrary, he is hidden in these works, so that faith in him can consist only in the protest of a Nevertheless against what the senses see and what reason recognizes to be the law operative in events of this kind (Psalm 72:23ff.).

God shows himself, not in what is mediated through history, but only in wonders that defy understanding.[14] He shows himself only where he makes himself known directly in a very special revelation of judgment and salvation (cf. Exodus 2; 12; 14; Hebrews 11:23ff.). Even here, however, God is not identical with his works and cannot be grasped in them. Even signs and wonders can let him slip and become an empty husk for unbelievers: "Thy way is in the sea, and thy path in the great waters, but thy footsteps are not known" (Psalm 77:19). Even at this point there is no revelation in the sense of an equation of God and his works. Even in express forms of his action the distinction remains between what God is and what he does, so that his presence in his acts may escape the view of human eyes.

All this points to the fact that we can speak of revelation in the strict sense only when the author of revelation manifests himself in, if we will, "absolute directness," i.e., only when he is identical with the mode of his manifestation. This holds true, however, only of his Word. God is his Word, or, better, he makes himself identical with it (John 1:1). In the word of his self-presentation ("I am who I will be," Exodus 3:14), in the word of the covenant ("I am the Lord your God," Exodus 20:2; Deuteronomy 6:4; cf. Exodus 3:15; 6:2), and in the word of salvation and judgment as it is laid upon the prophets, he makes himself directly present. He is wholly in his Word. Even when the reference is to his glory (*kabod*), name (*shem*), or countenance (*panim*), he is attested as the one who presents himself in his Word.

Only in the light of this does his work in history become plain, so that believers do not have to meet what they cannot understand negatively with the Nevertheless of defiance, but can now meet it in the name of him whom they know and from whom they can infer the saving theme in all his direction of history, even when he and the theme are not to be discerned in detail.

---

[12] Cf. ThE, II, 1, § 2084-2331.
[13] Cf. G. von Rad, *Die Weisheit in Israel* (1970), pp. 170ff.; E.T. *Wisdom in Israel* (1972), pp. 124ff.
[14] Bultmann, "Die Frage der natürlichen Offenbarung," GV, II, p. 102.

For the man to whom God is present in the immediacy of his Word, even the unrecognizability of his presence is still presence—a presence which is not seen but which is grasped in a faith that trusts in God himself and God alone.

God's true presence, then, is to be sought in the incarnate Word, in the manifestation of Jesus Christ. Here is the mirror of the fatherly heart (Luther) and hence the Father himself. Even under the cover of the cross, even in the alien form of the suffering, death, and lowliness of the Son of God, even under apparent concealment, God is present in the directness of his form as the Word. For the lowliness of this manifestation is the form of his self-emptying love. This is his very nature. It is God himself.

II

Negative Delimitations of the Concept of Revelation

1. OVER AGAINST THE UNDERSTANDING OF REVELATION AS A SUPERNATURAL INVASION

In the previous section we have disputed the possibility of defining revelation with the help of formal criteria and argued instead that the self-presentation of the author of revelation is the point of revelation. This means the elimination of two interpretations of revelation which have taken various forms in the history of theology. On the one hand we reject any attempt to understand revelation as essentially and centrally a supernatural invasion. On the other hand we reject any attempt to interpret it as a product or culmination of the nature of man. In both of these understandings we have classic instances of what have been called formal criteria.

First, then, the essence of revelation is not to be seen in its specific mode as a supernatural event.

If revelation is the self-disclosure of God, we should not allow natural etymological associations to make us think of the unveiling of something hidden, of the impartation of a knowledge of higher worlds,[1] and of the corresponding extraordinary disclosure of what is concealed by way of oracles, miracles, and so forth, with such experiences as self-forgetfulness, ecstatic rapture, asceticism, and a secret discipline as the appropriate responses on man's part.[2]

Quite apart from the fact that fixation on the supernatural form of revelation obscures the distinctive element in the biblical understanding of revelation—we shall deal with this later—our main objection is that it leaves no place for the real intention of this revelation. In revelation, as the Bible understands it, man, either as the covenant people, the community, or the individual, is called into a personal relation with God. But this aspect can-

---

[1] Cf. R. Steiner, *Wie erlangt man Erkenntnisse der höheren Welten* (1920).
[2] As an example of subjective states of this kind the way in which Mohammed received his revelations is interesting; cf. C. M. Edsman in RGG³, IV, 1598.

not be kept to the fore when stress is laid either exclusively or even predominantly on the supernatural form of the impartation. In these circumstances revelation becomes the exclusive privilege of those who are supernaturally addressed in this way and made the subject of ecstatic rapture or charismatic distinction. The mass of ordinary, noncharismatic men cannot be the subject of revelation. Hence they are not called into a direct relation of personal fellowship with the God who discloses himself. Normal men are represented by the select group of charismatics. They thus delegate their immediacy to God, which cannot be delegated according to biblical thinking, since it constitutes what is most proper to man and is the basis of his alien dignity.[3] Their own relation to the one who is revealed and who reveals himself is made indirect. They have to entrust themselves to, and rely on the sponsorship of, those who have been given a mediatorial function, whether they be individuals or institutions, e.g., an organized church which dispenses salvation.[4] In this way personally appropriated faith yields to the blind adoption of presuppositions that are subject to the guarantees of others and hence bear heteronomous features. There thus arises what Herbert Braun calls an "advance"[5] or what Roman Catholic dogmatics calls implicit faith.[6]

2. OVER AGAINST THE UNDERSTANDING OF REVELATION AS AN ENHANCEMENT OF NATURE — A CRITIQUE OF NATURAL THEOLOGY

As revelation is not to be regarded as essentially a supernatural invasion, and as it is not therefore to be brought under a formal criterion, we must also maintain that it cannot be defined by the contrary method. This method consists in viewing it as an impartation by which what is known naturally is caught up, completed, and enhanced. This is how natural theology arises in the broadest sense of the term.[7] The problem with natural theology is that it regards human nature as a foundation which is in accordance with creation and cannot be challenged. In virtue of its origin and intactness it does not stand in any contradiction to what revelation imparts no matter how it be defined. Between natural reason and any kind of supernatural revelation there can thus be at most only a quantitative and not a qualitative difference, i.e., to the extent that revelation can extend the sphere of action of natural reason. Even then what it imparts can be integrated into the schema which reason has established, e.g., when it proclaims the postulates of the existence of God, of immortality, or of the relation between guilt and punishment.

---

3 Volume I, p. 133; ThE, I, § 1084ff.; E.T. I, pp. 220f.

4 This is especially clear in the anthroposophist R. Steiner.

5 Cf. Volume I, pp. 160ff.

6 Ritschl, *Fides implicita* (1890); cf. Volume I, pp. 124, 155.

7 What can only be sketched here has been dealt with more explicitly elsewhere; cf. "Kritik der natürlichen Theologie," *Theologie der Anfechtung* (1949), pp. 14-49; and also the discussion of the Thomistic *natura-gratia* scheme in ThE, I, § 172ff., 1880ff.; E.T. I, pp. 200f., 388ff.

In this process the postulates are surreptitiously made into conditions of what is acceptable as revelation. They become criteria of verifiability. He who controls these criteria then controls proleptically what is subjected to them. The pre-understanding which is set up by reason for this purpose not only precedes revelation in time but also has the power of material postulation. Hence it exercises material and normative control over what can be generally regarded as valid revelation or kerygma.[8]

This is how reason tends to stake a prior claim to the sphere of revelation and to establish preconceptions in it. The premise is thus established on which Lessing can advance his thesis that revelation does not say anything new in principle, nor can it tell us anything that is beyond the grasp of reason, but reason has the power, by what is of course a slower route, to perceive finally what revelation is already proclaiming in mythological cipher. In principle, then, revelation is superfluous, although pragmatically it is useful, since it acts as a pedagogic aid and pacemaker and thus accelerates the process of mere self-development. Once the initial stage is over, we thus have the dominion of pure reason. This will finally dominate the field and will be liberated from the rivalry of a claim to revelation.

This presentation presupposes the idea of the intactness of human nature and hence also the intactness of natural reason. Even Thomas, however, deviated from this idea of intactness when he spoke of the condition or concrete state which governs man as he now is.[9] This opens the way, at least, to Paul's thesis in Romans 1:18ff. Man does not in virtue of natural reason receive the revelation of God in creation, let alone, one might add, the supernatural or special revelation in the Word. His failure to do this does not rest, according to Paul, on any epistemological incapacity of natural reason but on the present condition, the pressure of the actual state, in which natural reason finds itself. This state is characterized by the fact that man no longer understands himself in his creatureliness. He does not praise God nor give him thanks. He does not acknowledge him as that which is over him. The desire for self-assertion which is expressed herein leads to the result that in his religions he strives after self-activity and makes himself the central point of the cosmos.

Thus God, instead of being for man the norm of his self-understanding and conduct, is assigned only the function of confirming man's own existence. Man is no longer the image of God and God is no longer the criterion of his existence. On the contrary, God is made in the image of man. Man changes "the glory of the uncorruptible God into an image made like to corruptible man . . ." (Romans 1:23; cf. 4:15ff.). God, and hence also his revelation, becomes a function of human existence, not a norm. He becomes an echo of the voice of man, a projection of what man hopes and wishes and also fears. This provides the starting-point for the criticism of

---

[8] Cf. the discussion of Bultmann in Volume I, pp. 55ff.

[9] This limitation (cf. *Summa Theologica*, I, q. 1, a. 1) was omitted in Cap. 2 of Vatican Council I; cf. Denz., 3005.

human religion, and of Christianity as a religion,[10] which culminates in the left-wing Hegelian (Feuerbach) and especially the Marxist contention that religion is to be diagnosed as ideology, i.e., as an echo and reflection of the life-process.[11]

The important thing in this criticism of religion is not the epistemological argument that it involves a process of projection and thus results in our deceiving ourselves about supposed transcendental realities. Much more important is the Pauline-type assertion that man's desire to assert himself is the decisive impulse. Since in Marxism man is determined by a social and economic situation, the form of his self-assertion has to take on corresponding features. Religious ideology serves the dominant class by stabilizing the status quo in its interests and preserving their monopoly. Religion is thus misused as the "opium of the people."[12] It is a means of anesthetizing which hampers the will of the oppressed to assert themselves while leaving free rein for that of the oppressors. Primarily, then, the point of projection is pragmatic rather than epistemological. Its purpose is self-assertion. Luther already brought this to our attention in his criticism of religion.[13]

Among the objects of this criticism is to be numbered the natural religion of the Enlightenment. Lord Herbert of Cherbury offers a typical sketch of this in his *De religione Gentilium* (1705). Cherbury's aim is to find alongside and within the positive religions a nondogmatic religion of reason, which derives from man's nature, and which is at once the goal toward which the positive religions are finally moving and also the original root from which the different religions stem. Cherbury sees that he is fighting here on two fronts, first against the authoritative claim of the "accidental" historical religions, which are only later and situational variations on the original religion, and secondly against the modern movements of empiricism, scepticism, and nominalism. (In the name of these Locke in his famous *Essay* takes issue with Cherbury's idea of a native religion which is part of the nature of man; cf. I, 3, § 15ff.)

To establish a natural religious truth which is completely independent of revelation, authority, and experience, Cherbury appeals to the Stoic view, which was known to him through Cicero. According to this view there are common notions which embrace the ontic logos of the world and also the subjective logos of our faculty of knowledge. Truth may be perceived only

---

[10] Cf. in this regard Barth, Bonhoeffer, Bultmann, and van der Leeuw; the bibliographical survey in U. Mann, "Theologie der Religionsgeschichte," *Lutherische Monatshefte*, 3 (1946), 6, pp. 250ff.; H. Vossberg, *Luthers Kritik aller Religion* (1922); W. Holsten, *Christentum und nichtchristliche Religion nach der Auffassung Luthers* (1932); also M. Buber, *Chassidische Botschaft* (1952), pp. 14f.

[11] Cf. the discussion of the concept of ideology in ThE, II, 2, § 154ff.; E.T. II, pp. 26ff.

[12] Herder uses this phrase first, e.g., in criticism of the doctrine of reincarnation. It is then taken over by Hegel and the left-wing Hegelians. Cf. E. Benz, "Das Anliegen der Menschheit und die Religionen," Stud. gen., 15 (1962), p. 767.

[13] Cf. Ficker ed., II, p. 72 on Romans 3:5; WA, 19, 709; E.T. LCC, XV, pp. 66f.

on the basis of the correspondence between the divine reason in the universe and our cognitive reason. If this correspondence is presupposed, we must also be able to discern it within the rich variations in the world of religion. Here, too, it is that which is common in the midst of the variations. It makes itself known as the universal consensus. This original element which always remains the same, this primal natural religion, has five features (common notions): priority (this thought recurs in the later idea of a religious *a priori* in Troeltsch, A. Nygren, and R. Otto; cf. Volume I, p. 308, n. 55); independence; universality; certainty; necessity and common consent. On the basis of these criteria five basic truths are constructed which are part of the *a priori* legacy of human nature and may be seen in all the variations which the play of history brings into being. Only those who hold these basic truths are in contact with religious truth and thus have autonomous and—to use a later phrase—adult knowledge. These basic truths are (1) the existence of a supreme being, (2) worship of this supreme being (in independence of the multiplicity of associated ceremonies), (3) piety and virtue as the moral core of this worship, (4) sorrow for mistakes and vices, and (5) future reward and punishment in accordance with present conduct.

This concept of a natural religion displays all the symptoms to which we have referred.

First, it helps to confirm the way in which man understands himself and in so doing it brings to light the element of self-assertion. Rational man, like later existential man, wants to be sovereign in his own world. With the help of a process of projection he thus makes God a function in his system of norms. God is an objectification of what each of us says by way of self-definition. Second, the method with whose help this self-objectification is achieved is subject to a particular mistake to which no less a thinker than Schleiermacher has drawn attention. Natural religion thinks that it is original, preceding all the positive manifestations of religious history, but in fact the exact opposite is the case. It is a later and secondary distillation of the positive religions and is a mere abstraction. Hence it cannot be the basis of a religious communion. It is simply that which can be abstracted from all the higher religious communions, being present in all but taking different forms in each (*The Christian Faith*, p. 48). Now it is true that Schleiermacher follows a similar path with his own idea of what is original. He finds revelation in a primary release of pious affections which does not itself derive from anything else (pp. 49f., and cf. the second of his *Speeches*). But this is another story. He is simply seeking the unconditioned original element in subjectivity rather than in a demonstrable system of basic truths.

From what has been said, it is evident that the idea that revelation completes and enhances nature is wrong to the extent that nature is simply seeking approval for its own self-completing and self-enhancing. By means of its principles of reason it regards itself as the norm by which to test the truth of a claim to revelation and in so doing it already undermines this claim in practice. It may do this by testifying that the revelation is to be found already in the original nature of man, and by thus deriving it from itself. It may do it by interpreting revelation as merely the mythical and hence dispensable cipher of its own understanding of truth. It may do it finally by rejecting the claim at the very outset as heteronomous and finding in it the optical illusion of a process of projection. The motive of self-assertion, as we have seen, lies behind all these ways of undermining and contesting the claim of revelation.

At best, then, the understanding and recognition of revelation in the name of the idea of completing and enhancing nature will be transitory. It forms a longer or shorter interlude whose backward limit is the as yet unbroken "orthodox" authority of revelation and whose forward limit is the complete overthrow of this authority in the name of the autonomy of reason.

While the interim lasts, the idea of an analogy between God and man lies behind the concept of completion and enhancement. Only because this analogy obtains can a common plane be found on which completion and enhancement are possible and revelation and reason can recognize themselves in each other.

The Christian understanding of revelation tells us, however, that this analogy has been broken. It has yielded to the diastasis of darkness and light (John 3:19). Instead of being open to God, man is now curved in upon himself. Loss of this analogy, which is to be understood as an event, as the basis of a new and perverted state of being, is also loss of knowledge, i.e., loss of the possibility of knowledge of God.[14] God is an adequate object of knowledge only to himself. Knowledge of God arises only as God's self-knowledge (1 Corinthians 2:11b). Revelation, then, can mean only that by virtue of his self-disclosure God gives man a share in this knowledge of himself. To this degree it implies a form and content of impartation which in principle are beyond the grasp of human nature and hence cannot be regarded as a supplementing or enhancing of human nature. "God dwells in the light which no man can approach unto" (1 Timothy 6:16). The encounter of reason and revelation can no longer make possible a simple recognition of the one in the other. Reason, in the name of the condition of being which it represents, has to make a decision either to let itself and its condition be radically reoriented by revelation[15] or to harden itself obstinately against it. That revelation will overcome this rift with reason is the eschatological hope.[16]

If revelation evades the various attempts of nature, and hence also of reason, to master it; if it will not let itself be either resisted as heteronomous or integrated as analogous, this does not mean that it stands unrelated to the self or that the testimony of the Holy Spirit, in the power of which the word of revelation causes itself to be appropriated, simply replaces, without any connection, whatever presuppositions of understanding the self brings

---

[14] Cf. Volume I, Chapter VIII.
[15] Cf. the teaching on the Holy Spirit in Volume I, Chapter IX.
[16] Cf. G. Gloege, Art. "Offenbarung," RGG³, IV, 1611.

with it. If this were so, it would mean either that revelation would come to us as a heteronomous tyranny which must be accepted blindly and in servile obedience, or that the new creation which is effected by the Spirit would have the form of a creation out of nothing, no part being left at all for the old self. A mere mention of these two errors will suffice to show their theological absurdity.

Our present task, then, is to elucidate the relation between revelation and the human self. In so doing we shall take up what was said in the teaching about the Spirit in Volume I and develop it with special reference to the doctrine of revelation.

III

The Dialectical Relation between the Self-Disclosure of God and Reception by the Human Self

Revelation and Subjectivity, Word and Faith

1. NATURAL THEOLOGY ONLY IN RETROSPECT OF FAITH — AGAINST TILLICH'S PRINCIPLE OF CORRELATION AND ALTHAUS' DOCTRINE OF PRIMITIVE REVELATION

The relation between revelation and the human self is not to be understood as a completing and enhancing. Hence it is not to be regarded as rectilinear but dialectical. This means that features which appear to be antithetical coincide in it. But the form of this coincidence cannot be brought within a closed system of rules with a demonstrable function. Automatism of this kind is ruled out by the fact that the author of revelation discloses himself in free address. The form of this event is historical. It does not follow natural or technological law.

The dialectical character of this relation of revelation and the self finds typical expression in the account of Paul's conversion in Galatians 1:11ff. On the one hand the revelation of Jesus Christ to Paul is a completely new thing which does not arise out of the previous stages in his life and stands in no psychologically assessable relation to them. The gospel which is imparted as revelation in this way has not been received or learned from any man. It also stands in discontinuity with that part of life which comes to us from outside by encounter (1:12, 16). As with the prophets, God himself prepares his instrument in the contingent, creative Word.

It is to this same action of God which comes into the nexus of events, and hence cannot be derived from it, that Paul is pointing when he refers to creation. As God once pronounced the *fiat* which caused light to shine, so by his self-disclosure he has brought light into our hearts and enlightened us by "the knowledge of the glory of God in the face of Jesus Christ" (2 Corinthians 4:6). The accounts of Paul's conversion in Acts also use this motif of light and thereby echo again the creation event (Acts 9:3; 22:6; 26:12). In terms of the apocalyptic view of history, a new thing has now burst into the process of the old history. The incursion of the future world has begun.

Nevertheless, although the creative intervention of God stands in no demonstrable continuity with events on the secular plane, whether historical or psychological, some preparation in the life of Paul may be discerned in retrospect. He himself alludes to it. This is not, of course, a preparation in the sense that experience of Christ derives from it, that it is a result, and that revelation is just a mythical way of describing it. It is a preparation in the sense that Paul achieves a maturity and comes to a specific hour in his life which might be regarded as a "condition" and "disposition" for receiving the revelation. The terms condition and disposition leave the concept of revelation protected in two ways against the misunderstanding that it is the result of a given state of existence or of a specific constellation of circumstances.

They do this first to the extent that they for their part are not to be regarded as having evolved by immanent processes but have been brought into being by God himself. (For not just revelation itself but also the conditions for its reception acquire their significance from a reference to creation and the creative Word.) Second, the word "condition," as distinct from "cause," does not say that something has to happen but that it can happen. It denotes, not the necessity of a result, but the possibility of an event.[1]

Along these lines the law, which made Paul kick against the pricks (Acts 26:14), was for him a pedagog to bring him to Christ (Galatians 3:24). As Paul followed the way of the law to the limit (Acts 23:6; 26:5; Romans 10:2f.; Galatians 1), the end and destruction of this way became the condition of the new thing which intervened. It was not a result at the end of this way. If we want to talk of results of the way of the law, the alternatives are either doctrinaire hardening such as is found in the Talmud, or, to apply Hegel's principle of dialectical reversion, a libertinistic overturning of the law. That the revelation of Christ comes is in no sense implied in this way. It has its basis strictly in the miracle of the divine self-disclosure, which cannot be postulated. Nevertheless, this miracle does not begin only with the event of revelation. It begins with the positing of a prior history, i.e., of conditions. The concept of the new presupposes the old—what is past (2 Corinthians 5:19). Light shines in the darkness, which is dispelled by it (1 John 2:8; Revelation 21:1, 4).

In this sense the beginning of the new thing that God does is linked to the end of the way of law (Romans 10:4). If this new thing is to be understood as gain, necessarily what was there before must be understood as loss and even as refuse (Philippians 3:7ff.). The backward look is integral to

---

[1] We have already referred (Volume I, pp. 79, 104) to an analogous situation in the relation between the Logos of John's Gospel and the Stoic concept of the logos. We have here a preparation in the field of concepts (J. Maritain) which, inasmuch as the idea of the logos had already been tossed around for a long time in Stoic philosophy, gave rise to an intellectual disposition or condition, so that revelation and its linguistic elucidation could enter into a situation which was already ripe.

this understanding because only the state of redemption can provide a standard by which to measure the state of being bound and unredeemed, and only the entry of light can show the extent of darkness (1 Corinthians 4:5). The old way does not seal off itself, as an existential form of natural theology likes to think, suggesting that man perceives that this way leads only to despair, that he can thus see, and indeed is forced to see, his unredeemed state, and that he thus calls out for redemption.

K. Heim, for example, with the help of existential analysis seeks to force on us the alternative of meaninglessness or Christ, desperation or redemption. Bultmann's prior explanation of existence, which holds that natural man and his philosophical self-understanding can perceive nothingness, self-alienation, and enslavement to what we meet with, presses us hard in the direction of the same alternative. We have a homiletical form of the same idea when the preacher in the first part of his address paints the darkness of the world in the blackest possible colors, presenting a sorry picture of all secular matters, in order to "warm up" his hearers for the message of salvation.

Although the futility of the way that is followed can be seen only in a backward glance which discloses revelation and the spiritual wonder of the new creation, insight into this futility, into the "refuse" aspect, is prepared on the way itself and can thus be a disposition for receiving the new thing. The one who experiences resurrection from the dead must first have tasted death and traversed the way of death (although naturally this does not mean that he can know the mystery of this death in advance, Acts 26:8f.). When mention is made of the forgiveness of sins, this stands in dialectical relation to what is already known of good and evil and of self-alienation even though we cannot as yet attain to its understanding as "sin."

The opposite, however, is also true. When the question of the relation between the self and the external world is raised (as in Descartes in the form of radical doubt), the question of God is also put (as Descartes again saw very clearly when he tried to relate the self and the external world by way of proof of God). For God is the comprehensive factor which relates the self to the created world and which places the created world at the disposal of the self as an object of knowledge and cultivation. Here again, however—and this is what Descartes did not see—the God who reveals himself does not stand related to the original question in a continuity which can be understood along the lines of completion and enhancement. If this continuity is espoused in the sense of Descartes, and the concept of God is constructed in terms of the original question, it can never contain a portrait of the Father of Jesus Christ nor the content of revelation. As the abstract idea of an absolute, it can never form the schema into which the God of revelation must be integrated. The schema of this pre-understanding will have to be broken[2] once it has performed its service and been an effective disposition for the "receiving" of the higher answer.

---

[2] Cf. Volume I, pp. 140ff.

Other illustrations may easily be given of this type of disposition and the transcending of it. Thus man may be terrified by the threat of non-being which is implied in his finitude. The encounter with the self-revealing God, who raises from the dead and calls things which are not as though they were (Romans 4:17), bears an obvious connection with this experience of finitude.

It will be apparent to the reader that at this point we are adopting, but also radically reconstructing, a statement of Tillich's. In his exposition of the principle of correlation Tillich tells us that when the concept of God appears in correlation to the threat of non-being which lurks in existence, then God has to be called the infinite power of being which resists the threat of nothingness (*Systematic Theology,* I [1951], p. 64). Understood thus, the correlation between the self's experience of existence and experience of the God of revelation contradicts, in the immediacy of its continuity, that which we have tried to express by the concept of the dialectical element in this relation. For this reason we have to bring two criticisms against Tillich.

First, the correlation rests on two experiences of being of which the first— the threat of non-being—leads to a forced question whereas the second—as experience of the God of revelation—has the character of an answer. If, however, the two experiences are then related as question and answer,[3] the dialectic between them ceases, yielding to immediacy in the sense of enhancing and completing. For a concept of being forms here the bracket which encloses the experience of self and the experience of God. Hence the concept of being which is presupposed in this way prejudges what the being of God has to mean. Theology thus becomes ontology, even though a subtle thinker like Tillich naturally has at his command several correctives which enable him to break the schema and exploit chance inconsistencies.

Second, the character of revelation as a direct "answer" is called in question to the extent that the presupposed question lying in human existence is not direct. For, as we have already stated, the experience of non-being and finitude does not express itself merely as a threat which raises the question of true being. Surrendering in advance to its threatening character, it constantly becomes the very opposite of a feeling of being threatened, namely, the state of euphoria which says: "Let us eat and drink; for tomorrow we die" (Isaiah 22:13; 1 Corinthians 15:32). During this eating and drinking joy and pleasure in life are triumphant, so that the sense of being threatened is suppressed and no question is raised. One might also mention the escape in activity and work, which can be very productive. Part of man's instinct of self-preservation is that he does not give free rein to the melancholy of an existential sense of menace. Before it develops he transforms it into its opposite, namely, into a means of achieving mastery over life. If the Gentiles of Romans 1:18ff., who held down the truth in unrighteous-

---

[3] Cf. *op. cit.,* p. 61, where Tillich argues that theology formulates the questions enclosed in human existence and that it formulates the answers that are given in the divine self-declaration by adducing the questions that lie in human existence.

ness, had been asked about their feelings about life, they would certainly not have replied that they were in despair and saw themselves in need of redemption. They would have made it known that they were well enough satisfied with their manufactured idols, with their four-footed, creeping, and flying animals, with their ideologies and world-views. The *fact* that they were living under stress and strain, and that despair was the impulse that gave birth to euphoria, would have become plain only later in the light of their encounter with the God of revelation. Only in the light of the answer which is contained in this revelation does the question contained in the earlier state of existence become evident and urgent. Then, and only then, may it be seen in retrospect as a disposition which the author of revelation placed at the disposal of his self-revelation and which he brought on the scene as the pre-history of his creative Word. Even his delivering up to constraint and futility (the *parédōken* of Romans 1:24, 26) belongs to the pre-history of revelation which he has shaped as a disposition.

P. Althaus has tried to express the correspondence between the self and revelation by the concept of primitive revelation (*Die christliche Wahrheit*, I [1947], pp. 43ff.), for which there are parallels in the thought of E. Brunner and also, along different lines, in A. Schlatter. The original aim and concern here is to find the place in human existence where God's revelation addresses us and to set up antennae by which it may be received. If the issue, as in Brunner, is that of "contact," this is not meant in the sense of continuity between the self and revelation, as in the completing and enhancing which we have discussed above. Instead, reference is made along Pauline lines to the inexcusability of man (Romans 1:20) when he fails to see his creatureliness and his alienation from what he was created to be, or rather, when he suppresses the knowledge of this. Human guilt and alienation, against which the message of the forgiveness of sins stands in relief, can be discussed seriously, however, only when God's reality, offer, and command are declared to man first, and declared in such a way that man ought to be aware of them, guilt arising when he is not in fact aware of them (*op. cit.*, p. 51).

Thus far Althaus sticks closely to Paul. Later, when by the Spirit the Word has been revealed to him, man recognizes that this Word has had a pre-history with him (what Althaus calls primitive revelation), that it presupposed the disposition or conditions for its acceptance. Only in the retrospective glance of faith is the dialectic of the relation of the self and revelation set up. Only when the Christian looks back from the fact of the miracle of his calling does he see that this miracle blocks the demonstration of any continuity (cf. Volume I, pp. 184ff.). He sees that it was God who used and indeed posited these presuppositions. To this extent the history of the old Adam has come to a complete end. Continuity between the old and the new has ceased.

Does Althaus stop at this retrospective glance, however, or does he mean much more by his primitive revelation? In fact he means a good deal more. Faith is certainly the work of God in man, the miracle of his Holy Spirit (*op. cit.*, p. 52). To this degree continuity with the old man is severed. Hard by this insight, however, and with no theological connection, Althaus finds in the NT the thesis that failure to believe in Christ makes a man guilty, so that he is paradoxically responsible if the testimony of the Holy Spirit is not granted to him.

Althaus tries to solve this problem with the help of another nuance in his doctrine of primitive revelation. This is a treacherous nuance. It is to the effect that there is a demonstrable, rectilinear, and to that extent nondialectical relation between primitive revelation and the revelation of the Word, between the knowledge of God and Christology. Because man knows of God through God's original manifestation, he cannot be blind to Christ (*ibid.*). There is a bridge here which anyone can see and cross. Man should recognize the deity of Christ's Word because he has once heard God's voice. In this sense he must recognize God in Jesus (*ibid.*).

Primitive revelation as Althaus understands it makes of the new thing of the miracle of the Spirit a process of anamnesis which stands in a relation of continuity to the old existence. This construction is possible only if the primitive revelation makes itself known in some other way than by the retrospective glance of faith. If it arose only out of this retrospective glance, it could no longer stand on its own feet and show itself to be an independent declaration of God. It could speak only in connection with what faith has to proclaim. Even the revelation of God in creation—primitive revelation—could declare itself only as the one addressed is looking back, so that for him the primitive revelation and the revelation in Christ are effected together.

If, however, the link between the two is understood in such a way that there can be an effect of anamnesis, the primitive revelation is noetically as well as ontically the first, and hence the revelation in Christ completes and enhances it. In simplified form this means that if primitive revelation is elucidated by an analysis of nature, being, and history, and succeeds in causing man to say A, then he can also be compelled to utter the christological B, i.e., to experience the effect of anamnesis.

The theological construction is consistently developed in such a way that it moves from below to above or from what comes first in time to what follows. This is possible, however, only on the assumption that from the outset, and not just in the retrospective glance of faith, we can see traces and even massive evidence of the God who discloses himself in nature and history. This relative independence of primitive revelation, in terms of which all else is expounded, although naturally with the help of the Holy Spirit and the additional Word that God has spoken, may be seen in several forms in Althaus, especially in his doctrine of the orders (cf. *Theologie der Ordnungen* [1935]). If the orders are understood as a more or less intact remnant of creation, and hence as plain footprints of God, necessarily this type of theology is temporarily rendered defenseless against the doctrine of natural revelation and providence as it arises in the ideology of Nazism. This is the only possible explanation of Althaus' consent to the *Ansbacher Rat-schlag* of 1934 (cf. on this ThE, II, 2, § 3095ff.; E.T. II, pp. 446f.).

2. INSTANCES OF THE DIALECTIC OF NATURAL KNOWLEDGE AND REVELATION — THE TRANSFORMATION OF THE WORDS LIFE, MEANING, AND TRUTH[4]

Although there is, then, an affinity between revelation and the given experi-ence of existence, no continuity can be demonstrated between them. Reve-lation does not disclose something which simply develops what was already present in germ, so that to validate itself it can and should appeal to this prior element. Instead, it both adopts and also rejects, since as the Word of fulfilment it sets up a new creation.[5] To bring out this discontinuity be-tween the old man and the new we have spoken of the dialectical relation in which revelation stands to the prior factor of the old existence. These earlier experiences, we have found, are not a fixed and static schema in which that which comes in revelation is located and into which it can be integrated. On the contrary, the schema itself is altered. Hence in the field of force of revelation the very terms which we use to express our earlier experience are also altered. (We have already stated that these terms have to repent and be baptized.) Three typical modifications of this kind may be briefly dealt with here.

1. What we call life is only a distorted shadow of what revelation pro-claims, gives, and promises as new life. The substitution of the word *zoe* for the word *bios,* which does not occur in the NT, and for *psyche* in the sense of vitality, is simply an etymological sign of this. We have here a true change into another genus.[6]

Our natural life is enclosed by finitude. The history of human life is a his-tory that is subject to death (Job 14:1f.). The fundamental sense that this life is a broken one comes to expression in many symptoms, and especially in the concern to win incorruptibility for that which is corruptible, not to let all trace of our life on earth be obliterated by the aeons. This attempt is the spur to doctrines of immortality.

Procreation can also be motivated in part by the desire to live on in other beings. Another sign of the sense of the fragmentariness of all life may be seen in that awareness of finitude also unleashes the impulse to taste pre-cious life to the full, not merely by enjoyment (1 Corinthians 15:32), but also in creative activity which is accompanied by the knowledge of death. We are only young once. Youth and beauty perish. These sayings are indica-

---

[4] The terms dealt with here will be discussed from another angle in the doctrine of God; cf. Chapter VI, 2.

[5] On this problem of point of contact and rejection cf. Volume I, esp. Chapter VIII.

[6] *Zoe* is the life by which we live, *bios* the life which we live; H. Cremer, *Biblico-Theological Lexicon of NT Greek,* 4th English ed. (1892), p. 270.

tions that life is a preparation for death and that awareness of death does not have to be associated with the imminence of the last hour. The consciousness of being hemmed in by swiftly passing time is the force which produces achievement. The *kairos,* the fruitful moment, the chance, will not come again. The intensity of life-fulfilment engendered by the absurd finitude of our existence is one of the normative themes in the work of Albert Camus.

A final symptom of our awareness of finitude, and hence of the brokenness of our lives, may be mentioned. It is the riddle of human death. As Hoche says, it is a strange thing that although man knows that the cessation of all life around him, and as far back as he can see, is a supreme and pitiless law, nevertheless he finds it very hard to adjust to this personally. The idea that the vast subjective world which he carries within him, and which lives only once in this form, will just be wiped out, is for him an intolerable one. It is intolerable that he should fall by the wayside while others march on chatting as though nothing had happened. The force of this feeling defies all logic.[7] Just because the death of man ends something unique and does not simply give another form to what is readily exchangeable, as in nature, it is torturing and incomprehensible. Its inscrutability is thus grounded in what is specifically human in man, in that which distinguishes him from nature, in that which the biblical story of creation expresses by the Thou-address that lifts him out of the sphere of all other creatures (Genesis 1:28; 2:16ff.). Death can certainly be explained and grasped as an objective biological process. But it cannot be understood if this term, according to the customary distinction,[8] is applied to the understanding of personal life. Hence the very mode of cognition which is adapted to give insight into human existence lets us down when it comes to the decisive existential factor, namely, the finitude of this existence and its subjection to death.

In nature, as one might say in this sense, life is round and comprehensible. It constantly renews itself, coming to manifestation in ever new examples. This is possible because the examples simply manifest the general and do not have the quality of the unique or specific. Hence contemplation of the self-renewing life of nature—the leaves fall but come again—offers no consolation to man. "For there is hope of a tree, if it be cut down . . . but man dieth, and wasteth away" (Job 14:7, 10). The very greatness of human life entails its misery. Because it contains something unique, its appointed end brings the experience of brokenness, and not just its own brokenness, but the brokenness of its relation with other unique beings, the breaking off of the relations which for their part have a share in this uniqueness. Seeing that death brings out the misery of human life as the

---

[7] E. Hoche, *Jahresringe* (1936), p. 292.

[8] E.g., in modern hermeneutics. Cf. H. Dilthey, "Ideen über eine beschreibende und zergliedernde Psychologie" (1894), *Ges. Schriften,* V (1961), pp. 139ff.; J. Wach, *Das Verstehen* (1926ff.); K. Jaspers, *Allgemeine Psychopathologie,* 4th ed. (1946), pp. 250ff.

reverse side of its greatness, one can understand that it contains within it the sting of an incomprehensible contradiction.

This sting seems also to affect the relation of this finite life to the Creator. Is not he the one who called the uniqueness of human existence into life? Can and should the wrath of God, on whose account we perish (Psalm 90:7; cf. Genesis 3:19b, 22), allow death to become a final separation between human life and the life of God? Can and should the exclusive uniqueness of the link between God and man become an ultimate victim of death? Does not the severing of this link call in question the very relation between God and man and pose the problem of theodicy, since it seems to be God himself who abolishes the relation, revises his creation program, and allows nothingness, from which he took created being, to reign again? "Thou destroyest the hope of man" (Job 14:19c): thou, and thou alone. In this accusation of God by Job there also shines out in the world of OT faith a first signal of the coming hope of resurrection. God must still desire the work of his hands if this is not to sink back into non-being. For "thou shalt call, and I will answer thee" (Job 14:15). My life will rise above its brokenness, not because it is immortal, but because it lives by the faithfulness of God.

It is no wonder, then, that man suppresses the signs of the brokenness of his natural life. This suppression may be seen not only in the refusal to talk about death, especially before the dying, but also in the banishing from public view of sickness, age, and the close of life, and their consignment to the esoteric world of hospitals, institutions, and cemeteries.[9] An even deeper form of this suppression tries to blunt the sting which causes the pain of human finitude, namely, the fact that a unique personality comes to its radical end in death. It accomplishes this decisive elimination by thinking of death as an objectifiable biological process which undoubtedly happens to others, as we can see, but which does not apply to my own end or to the dimension of the personal.[10] Another possibility is to subsume one's personality into the anonymity of the impersonal or the suprapersonal, where death bears no relation to a specific, unique life, but is just an effect of sickness, and is thus understood as a general and not a particular biological process. In this way man does not think, or tries not to think, of his own death. This is merely a part of general dying. When the personal spirit has been abandoned, he can no longer "give up his spirit."

This is why Rilke prays in his *Stundenbuch*: "O Lord, give each his

---

[9] Forest Lawn is a good example of the pseudo-lyrical playing down of death; cf. my analysis of the American situation in *Gespräche über Himmel und Erde* (1964), pp. 253ff.; E.T. *Between Heaven and Earth* (1965), pp. 183ff.

[10] Cf. Tolstoy's story "The Death of Ivan Ilyitch" in *Master and Servant* (1906). Pyotr Ivanovitch speaks here of three days and nights of dreadful suffering followed by death, which might strike him at any moment. But then in some way he is helped by the everyday thought that it would be Ivan Ilyitch who would be stricken, not himself. He himself would not and could not be stricken. This consoles him, as though death concerned only Ivan Ilyitch and were completely alien to him.

own death, the death which proceeds from the life in which he had love, meaning, and need" (86). The classical depiction of this depersonalizing of death is to be found in *Malte*. Here distinction is made between the little death which belongs to no one in particular, but is part of the general sickness, and the great death which is that of an individual, which "ripens" in the individual and hence shares in his uniqueness. The defused little death is portrayed in macabre visions of mass dying as on a production line in which individual death does not matter. Even the desire for an individual death gets rarer each day. Soon it will be as rare as an individual life. The death which is died is that of the sickness one has; since all sicknesses are now known, it is also known that the various lethal terminations belong to the sicknesses and not to the sick; the sick have, as it were, nothing to do (V, 13).

The knowledge of death as well as its suppression is thus a sign of the brokenness of our life. The message of the new life which is given by God undoubtedly relates to this preceding sign. It might even be said that this message would be without content and would lead nowhere if it did not hit the nerve which that brokenness contains within itself as a question. But it does not strike this nerve in such a way that it simply offers a variation on the preceding understanding of life, e.g., by giving the promise of continuation to finitude and survival to mortality (*athanasia*). Instead of this variation on what remains the same, and instead of the related possibility of integrating the message of the new life into the schema of the old understanding, the preceding concept of life is qualitatively altered and transported on to a new plane. This takes place so fundamentally that the new life is not simply an answer to the question contained in the earlier understanding, for the direct correlation of question and answer would be another form of continuity. The new life is something more and different. It transcends any question that could be put in terms of the old understanding. To that degree it rises above the former questioning. In its "whence" as well as its "whither" the new life differs from the old, so that the link between them, manifested in the common word *zoe,* is a constantly self-nullifying likeness.

Thus the "whence" of both indicates an infinite qualitative distinction to the degree that the new life derives from the Spirit and is from above, whereas the old life is grounded in the flesh and has its origin below (John 3:6; 8:23; Romans 8:13). For this reason the new cannot develop out of the old. It is the product of a new generation and birth of the Spirit (John 3:5). Nicodemus asks how these things can be (John 3:9). He is inquiring about the continuity of the two forms of life. But he is given no answer, and this is in fact the only relevant answer, since it brings into relief the miracle of the Spirit.

The "whither" of the new life points to the same basic distinction from the old life. It focuses on the one who carries his people through death to the life of the resurrection, so that they live even though they die (John 11:25f.; 14:19; Romans 8:13; 1 Peter 4:6). No quality intrinsic in or imparted to the old life makes possible the new form of life. It derives exclusively from the altered "whither" to which human destiny is now oriented. It is life with Christ (Romans 6:8). Hence it is life by faith in him (Romans 1:17). This life that is set on Christ persists through the death of the old life (Romans 14:8). For fellowship with the risen Lord does not break off.[11] The change of the form of life can be understood so radically that even the identity of the man who undergoes this change becomes questionable: "I live, yet not I, but Christ in me" (Galatians 2:20).

The existence set up by the new "whence" and "whither" is not just newly posited in the world of death. It also survives all perishing in this world. It thus transcends the limit of death. Hence the predicate "eternal life" denotes not just qualitative distinction in the midst of the corruptibility of the flesh but also quantitative survival after death. This is so because the risen Lord does not forsake his people. The fellowship that has been established is not going to break off. Job's indefinite wish is thus fulfilled. The old life does not have anything *proper* to it out of which this quality of survival might develop. Everything here is finite and corruptible. Ideas of immortality, including the Platonic *athanatos,* are thus brought under judgment.[12] What we are dealing with is the *alien* factor of the divine address and the faithfulness of God which will not leave his people in death.[13]

In retrospect of the new life which is wrought by the Spirit the question contained in the old life is thus both adopted and also revised. God is not just the answer to the questions implied in our finitude. He is also the one who questions these questions and, of course, the answers which we give to them within the framework of our finitude. As the competence of the old questions is restricted or overthrown, new questions arise and with them new actualities and priorities (Luke 10:42). The previous concept of life is baptized into a death, so that it is not permissible to point to an objectifiable continuity between the natural man and the spiritual man.[14]

2. Not just the understanding of life, but all the basic concepts of human existence participate in this dialectic of adoption and transformation. Since the outlines of the dialectic have become clear from the example of the concept of life, we need refer only briefly to the two other instances.

---

[11] Cf. Paul Gerhardt's "Auf, auf, mein Herz, mit Freuden."

[12] This judgment is sounded forth in Marlowe's *Faust* when after twenty-four years of the pact with the devil Faust is afraid of immortality. He asks the hills to fall on him, the earth to swallow him up, the cosmos to be dissolved in him. Immortality without the grace of God is hell.

[13] Cf. Luther: "Wherever and with whomsoever God speaks, whether in wrath or grace, that same is immortal. The person of God who speaks and the Word of God show that we are creatures with whom God will speak immortally and to eternity" (WA, 43, 481). The concept of immortality undergoes a radical transformation here. It becomes the very opposite of the traditional idea of immortality.

[14] On the understanding of death and life, and the change in this understanding, cf. my *Tod und Leben. Studien zur christlichen Anthropologie,* 2nd ed. (1946); E.T. *Death and Life* (1970).

A second concept which is set in the zone of tension is that of meaning. The question of meaning is the question of the significance of human existence, and hence of history too, for the totality of being. This differentiates the question of meaning from that of ends. The end relates only to specific pragmatic goals and hence normally to the utility of things and the appropriateness of functions. Hence it is possible that the proximate end might be called in question by the less proximate or ultimate end. What is tactically suitable might be strategically useless or even hurtful. What is technically useful, e.g., television, might be valueless in relation to the higher ends it is supposed to serve, e.g., when it transmits banalities or ideologically twisted information or when it is used foolishly.

The question of the meaning of life, however, is more than that of the final end. For the latter will never be more than a summation and harmonization of all the partial ends. It can thus rest only on the conformity of the functions we discharge. The meaning of our life, however, is more and other than the sum of the ends attained by this life or its functions. As life is more than food (Matthew 5:25), so it is more than functions.

For this reason the question of the meaning of life often reaches its critical and even desperate stage when the sham consolation offered by end-directed and successful functions fails because the functions themselves fail, e.g., with entry into old age. The question what meaning life had in its achievement stage, and what meaning it can have now—what sense is there in eternal creating if what is created is swept into nothingness?—finds its point in the difference between end and meaning. Since life does not consist only in its functions, and for this reason, according to Kant, is an end in itself as personal life, and should never be the mere means to an end, meaning is not identical with the end which its activities serve.

Meaning as distinct from fulfilling ends implies direct evidence of the relation which personal existence, which is subject to no end, stands to its final ground. Since this ground, as the ground of meaning, is God himself, since he is not objectifiable, not even as the ultimate end, within the hierarchy of ends, the affliction of homelessness and exposure remains, so does also the assault of the absurdity of a Sisyphus existence (Camus).[15] It remains even if perceived meaninglessness and the inward-looking abyss of nothingness (Nietzsche) do not result in crippling and resignation but increase the intensity of life (Camus, G. Benn). The man who objectifies himself, being hemmed in by causes and ends, sees himself as a small and insignificant unit in the infinitude of causal series,[16] or as a mere nothing in the vastness of the cosmos,[17] and he experiences the anxiety of an awareness which stimulates thought in a dark universe.[18]

---

[15] As Thornton Wilder puts it in his *Eighth Day of Creation,* only understanding of the whole can bring happiness.

[16] K. Heim, *Leitfaden der Dogmatik* (1923), pp. 3ff.; cf. Volume I, pp. 87f.

[17] I. Kant, *Critique of Pure Reason* (E.T. 1929).

[18] Cf. Teilhard de Chardin as quoted by M. Susmann, *Ich habe viele Leben gelebt* (1964), p. 184.

The crisis of meaning has another aspect. Evidence of relation to the ground of meaning is sought not merely from the standpoint of our personal existence which transcends all functionality. It is sought also from the standpoint of the interrelationship of historical events. In the name of the ground of meaning which is supposed to give evidence of itself, the postulate is advanced that Schiller's thesis, namely, that world history is world judgment, ought to be in force, that the connection between guilt and punishment or merit and reward ought to be perceptible as metaphysical justice, and hence that the meaning of the whole process ought to be apparent. It is hardly necessary to give examples of the fact that this meaning is constantly challenged by apparent contingency and chance, even among the righteous.[19] Here again the experience of meaninglessness thrusts us out into open country. It discredits all individual experiences of meaning and gives them the appearance of purely accidental coincidences.

If God discloses himself as the living ground of meaning for all being, whether in nature or history, whether for the individual or the whole process within history, then this revelation of meaning cannot be a completing or enhancing of individual insights, so that the whole panorama of meaning is now displayed on a cosmic scale. The manifestation of the whole is rather an eschatological revelation which the historical world of death cannot produce from within itself. The whole in its total sweep and compass remains hidden from view. Of a piece with this is the fact that faith in God is also faith against appearances. We are theologians of the cross and not of glory.[20] Just as the new life is powerful in the world of death ("even though we die"), so God as the ground of meaning is powerful in the experience of meaninglessness.

The crisis of meaning which arises out of our experience will not be solved, then, by the meaning of experienced events becoming manifest or the emerging of continuity between the old experience and the new. Faith is not an insight into the nexus of meaning which enables us to speak in terms of a Because and which thus achieves continuity with our causal thinking. Instead, it finds itself referred to a Nevertheless. "Nevertheless I am continually with thee . . ." (Psalm 73:23).

Here again we find the infinite qualitative distinction of the concept of meaning. We do not know meaning; we believe in him who knows meaning. Hence meaning does not manifest itself with demonstrable evidence. It remains under the cover of the cross (*sub tecto crucis*). It is grasped only in a faith which is immediate to him who fixes our destiny but only mediate, in a relation of Nevertheless, to destiny itself.

There is, then, no web of meaning which embraces both experience and

---

[19] Cf. the problem of Job, Psalm 73, etc.

[20] Cf. Luther's *Heidelberg Disputation of 1518* (WA, 1, 353ff.). On this cf. W. von Loewenich, *Luthers theologia crucis,* 2nd ed. (1933), pp. 21ff.; K. Stürmer, *Gottesgerechtigkeit und Gottesweisheit* (1939); P. Althaus, *Die Theologie M. Luthers* (1962), pp. 34ff.; E.T. 1966, pp. 25ff.; W. Joest, *Ontologie der Person bei Luther* (1967), pp. 118ff.

faith, both natural knowledge and revelation. The dialectical relation to which we have referred applies here too. Revelation takes up our question of meaning, but also revises it. The validity of the revision rests only on its own ground, which is found only by faith. It cannot be known as an answer in terms of the prior form of the question, for it undergoes a change into another genus. As a relevant direct answer it will be despised as folly (*mōria,* I Corinthians 1:21, 25, 27). The term "meaning" has also to repent and be baptized into death.

3. With the terms life and meaning we offer truth as our third illustration of the dialectical relation between revelation and the knowledge that precedes it. Here again that which revelation imparts does not signify a development of the spermatic logos in which we have our particular understanding of truth. Instead, we ourselves in our relation to truth are transformed by the Word and Spirit and come to have a share in the "being" in truth within which the voice of truth may be heard (John 18:37). Here, then, is no *a priori* concept of truth which as a constant and unchanging schema can embrace both our natural knowledge of truth and also the truth of God. We have dealt with this point in Volume I.[21]

The dialectic at issue reflects the problem Barth brought to our attention when he set his analogy of faith over against the analogy of being. The difference in solving the problem, which will be obvious to any student of Barth's writings, need not be dealt with here. For pertinent literature cf. F. Flückiger, "Analogia entis und analogia fidei," Stud. gen. (1955), 2, pp. 678ff.; G. Söhngen, "Analogia entis oder analogia fidei?" *Die Einheit in der Theologie* (1952), pp. 235ff.; E. Przywara, "Analogia entis in analogia fidei," *Antwort, K. Barth zum 70. Geburtstag* (1956), pp. 266ff.; H. G. Pöhlmann, *Analogia entis und fidei* (1965).

The fact that no continuity can be shown between the prior concepts of life, meaning, and truth and the corresponding concepts in revelation is related to the character of the Word in and by which the self-disclosure of God takes place. It is not just a signifying word which works in a given and ongoing schema of understanding; it is rather an active word which posits a new creation by the power of the *pneuma.*[22]

3. IMPLICATIONS FOR THE RELATION OF REVELATION AND FAITH

a. Faith and Word

The Word of God is different and stands outside the natural nexus of words just as God himself is different and is not a secular object. The fact that God identifies himself with this Word and pours his whole self into it (John 1:1c), so that he is not another, hidden God with another will behind

---

[21] Cf. pp. 202ff.
[22] Cf. Volume I, pp. 155ff.

his revelation, means that God in his essence wills to exist for us, is the author of a history with us, and is thus Immanuel. For this reason his Word represents him. It always bears an address. It thus has a partner in view to whom it is directed. It expresses God as he is and always will be (Exodus 3:14f.). It bears witness who God is for me now and always will be. The Word is the presence of God and also the promise of his future presence, i.e., of his ongoing identity as Immanuel. The Word is that wherein God binds himself and it is thus a synonym for his faithfulness.[23]

On my side, then, faith corresponds to this Word. Faith means that I trust this Word. Faith means here confessing the promised faithfulness of God. It thus means letting God be my God.[24] In this way the alienation of my emancipation is overcome. It gives place to a new conformity with God.

To this schema belongs the specific understanding of faith as this is expressed in "righteousness by faith alone" (Romans 3:28). I am righteous in faith inasmuch as by it I am conformed to the nature and the will of God. Putting my trust in the faithfulness of God manifested in Christ, I let God be my God and grasp the new conformity which I am offered. Whereas the attempt to fulfil the law brings "nonconformity," I now act in conformity with God. I no longer set God below my own conception of a principle of righteousness. I no longer serve idols. Within the framework of this principle I no longer make myself an independent partner nor imagine that I can manipulate God.

Luther in his *Commentary on Romans* tested this view of conformity by the extreme thought of resignation to hell. Even if God were to consign me to hell in spite of my justifying faith, I should still have no doubts. Otherwise this would be a sign that for me faith is only a device of my salvation egoism with whose help I calculate on achieving certain effects, in exactly the same way as the one who banks on his legal righteousness. What faith has really meant for me will be brought out with this consignment to hell. If I still praise God in hell, I let him be my God with final consistency and I thus take seriously what faith ought to be from the very outset. In this case, however, God cannot leave me in hell. He has to draw me to himself. For with my praise in hell I achieve the conformity which he wants of me. In the deepest depths I am conformed to him. Cf. Ficker ed., II, 217, 27f.; E.T. LCC, XV, p. 263.

Since faith is trust in God's presence in his Word, this Word is, as it were, the "thing in itself," as Hans Iwand puts it in a daring but significant phrase.[25] This means that we cannot look beyond it, whether in the

---

[23] H. Iwand, *Nachgelassene Werke,* I (1962), p. 200.

[24] The correspondence between faithfulness and faith is so radical that Paul, as is well known, can use the same word *pistis* for both. Similarly the genitive *Christou* or *theou* can in this connection vacillate between a subjective genitive and an objective genitive, e.g., Acts 3:16; Romans 3:22; Galatians 2:16, 20; Ephesians 3:12; Philippians 3:9; James 2:1, etc.

[25] *Op. cit.,* p. 200.

sense of seeking dimensions in God—a kind of dark margin[26]—which are not in congruity with his Word, or by seeking data, objectifying sections of history, with whose help this Word can be confirmed.

Rejection of this mistaken question lies in the background when Jesus speaks against seeking after signs. To seek after signs is to want to see instead of believing. It is to want certainty instead of assurance.[27] The impression made on the senses by seeing, however, touches only the periphery of our existence whereas faith ventures all and is a reaction of the center of existence, the heart. Hence the man who asks for a sign is not concerned about Christ himself or fellowship with the one who is present in him. He is concerned about the fleeting impression (John 6:26). Faith, which replies to God's faithfulness with trust in his Word, grasps the constant element in this faithfulness. In contrast sight and feeling, which avoid this venture and build on the apparently solid foundation of what is perceived and can be controlled, commit themselves to that which has gone the very next moment and is dissolved by new impressions.

Just as miracle is relativized when with its help we try to get behind the Word and to evade faith, so there can be no possibility of finding objectifiable history behind the Word. If we try to view the event of the resurrection in its historicity apart from faith in the risen Lord, if, for, example, we need to verify faith by the empty tomb, we find nothing. It is striking in this regard that the first news of the resurrection does not come from official recorders but from those who stand in a relation of faith to the person of him who rose,[28] and who have ventured their own persons on him, i.e., committed themselves to discipleship.

The history of God with his covenant people cannot be isolated in its being as such, or presented as the sum of facts that either offer confirmation or raise questions. It remains always a history which is interpreted in the light of faith. This history cannot be made into a supposedly objective history apart from faith—not, at any rate, to the degree that what emerges explains or even validates its interpretation as salvation history. To be sure, the faith which discovers and hands down this history has also been received

---

[26] The *extra Calvinisticum,* to which we have often referred (Volume I, pp. 292ff.), does not seek an *extra verbum* or *extra incarnationem* in this sense. Its point is to avoid identifying God with his act of revelation in such a way as to produce a static immanence of God. Hence the subject of revelation must always transcend the act. God is the one who resolves on condescension and accepts it. To that extent he is above it; he transcends it. Hence the subject who transcends revelation is not a dark margin pointing to an alien and hidden God distinct from his revelation. The fact that God in his sovereignty decides to be Immanuel and wills to be the Lord of the first commandment explains his revelation and is thus in line with it.

[27] Matthew 12:38f.; 16:1; Mark 8:11; Luke 11:16, 29, 39; John 4:48, etc.

[28] Cf. Chapter XXX, 2.d, and also the author's "The Resurrection Kerygma," *The Easter Message Today,* ed. M. Barth (1964), pp. 59ff.

from history. Even if the Moses stories were purely legendary,[29] they would still go back to historical experiences which could be interpreted as examples of divine guidance or as salvation events. The fact that they were interpreted in this way, and reached us only in this interpreted form, could be possible only because they manifestly contained the Word. In them the one who has presented himself in the Word by his messengers either made himself known or was remembered. Only in this sense does the history become a medium in which God announces himself and by which he makes and fulfils his promises, presenting and even correcting what is understood as promise in the light of new historical experiences.[30]

Historical events can be understood as examples of divine guidance or as salvation events only *in actu,* i.e., only by those to whom they happen. Judgment and grace as historical experiences can be told only by those who undergo them, only as penitence and praise, only in the Nevertheless of faith as regards the present and the expectation of fulfilled promise as regards the future. To seek historical facticity as such at a historical distance and with disinterested objectivity, and in so doing to cherish the expectation that this will furnish a basis for faith and a diagnosis of salvation events, is to come under the verdict of trying to get behind the Word by seeking after signs, and hence of evading the faith which is engendered by this Word.[31]

On man's side faith is the response to both the Word and also the history which contains it. We can go behind the Word neither as it is spoken nor as it comes to historical fulfilment. What is seen, and to that extent experienced, as a confirmation of the Word, cannot serve as a basis for it nor as a basis for faith in it. This experience of reality itself stands in the light of the Word. Miracle, as an extraordinary form of historical experience, is elucidated by the Word, not *vice versa.*[32] Only as elucidated event does it become anamnesis of the Word and to that degree its confirmation (Acts 2:22). Without the elucidating Word miracle is as silent as any other event. It can even be performed against God. Taken alone, then, it is empty and carries no message. When filled out with a self-selected meaning it can even be a temptation (Deuteronomy 13:2-4; Matthew 24:24; 2 Thessalonians 2:8f.; Revelation 13:13).

The spiritual circle of the Word and faith cannot, then, be entered from outside. This is again connected with the character of the Word as active Word. The Word is a truth which itself creates the conditions under which

---

[29] Cf. K. Koch, "Der Tod des Religionsstifters," KD (1962), 2, pp. 100ff., esp. 104ff., but also in criticism F. Baumgärtel, KD (1963), 3, pp. 223ff. On the theological importance of the problem cf. also R. Hermann, "Offenbarung, Wort und Texte," ETh (1959), 3, pp. 99ff., esp. 109ff.

[30] Cf. O. Cullmann, *Heil als Geschichte* (1965), esp. pp. 70ff.; E.T. *Salvation in History* (1965), esp. pp. 88ff.

[31] This is the dubious element in F. Hesse, "Die Erforschung der Geschichte Israels als theologische Aufgabe," KD (1958), pp. 1ff., and "Kerygma oder geschichtliche Wirklichkeit?" ZThK (1960), pp. 17ff. Cf. G. von Rad's position in *Theologie des AT* (1957), II, pp. 8ff.; E.T. 1965, cf. pp. vff.

[32] Cf. the author's essay "Das Wunder," *Theologie der Anfechtung* (1949), pp. 94ff.

it discloses itself, namely, the being in the truth of which the Fourth Gospel speaks.

The faith which effects this being in the truth and thus gives rise to conformity with the will of God is not, then, an act of man or a position which he himself adopts.[33] It is engendered by the Word and by the creative work of the Spirit within it.[34] "Faith cometh by hearing" (Romans 10:17). What is thus heard does not return empty (Isaiah 55:11). It works, accomplishes, and creates.

This relation of Word and faith implies two things for the understanding of revelation.

First, revelation does not take place merely on the event side of an external history. It is not just what we usually call the mighty acts of God.[35] It also takes place as appropriation, as the miracle of hearing and understanding which overcomes hardening (Matthew 13:15; Acts 28:27, etc.) and opens deaf ears. It is closed to the wise and prudent, i.e., to the initiative of intellectual work (Matthew 11:25-27). Where the reception of revelation takes place in the consciousness, it is extolled as the miracle of an experience that we cannot control (Matthew 16:17). This miracle in virtue of which the Word opens itself to hearing and appropriation is performed by the Spirit of God who dwells in the Word (1 Corinthians 2:7-16). The Spirit brings it about that man can break out of the prison of the world and let God's saving work take place in him. What takes place *on* him, and only then and to that extent *in* him, he cannot understand in terms of himself because his alienation from God renders him unable to let God's Word be manifest to him. His closedness is overcome, and what is not at his disposal is made accessible, in the way that we have shown. God causes man to participate in the knowledge of himself. Only he himself can do this. Hence he alone is the subject of the knowledge of God.[36] Only the Spirit searches out the deep things of the Godhead (1 Corinthians 2:10).

This is why the Spirit of God performs the miracle of appropriation, grants participation in the self-knowledge of God, and gives faith the form of this participation. Revelation takes place here in the form of being revealed, of the ability to hear, and to that extent of appropriation.

Second, this experience that takes place to us and in us, this entry into our consciousness as we may now put it,[37] makes it apparent that faith is something that has been effected. It is a new creation by the Spirit. This means that it is not grounded in itself. It cannot be understood as an inner light after the manner of mysticism or enthusiasm. It relates to the external

---

[33] On the misunderstanding of faith as a work cf. Volume I, p. 158, n. 10.

[34] We may again refer to the idea of the "mathematical point" as a description of faith and its determination by the Word; cf. Volume I, p. 129.

[35] Acts 2:11. For the event side cf. Stephen's address in Acts 7:1ff.

[36] 1 Corinthians 2:11; cf. Volume I, p. 207.

[37] We may put it thus because there can be no further question here of the theology of consciousness which we had to reject earlier; cf. the concept of Cartesian theology in Volume I.

reality of a salvation event which is there apart from it and before it. Being able to hear comes after what is to be heard. It is not simultaneous with it. For faith to arise the Christ event and declaration of this event must have already taken place. These are contemporaneous with me, for God encounters me today, here and now,[38] and I see myself in the rich young man and the woman who sinned much. The faith of the Syro-Phoenician woman and the Capernaum centurion is always held up before me as a present possibility. But this today, here and now, is simply the reproduction of a once, of the mighty acts of God. It is the present (prolepsis) of the future for which we wait in the name of the promise. Both the once and the future are already before us. They are given, and given in advance, to faith. The community consists of those who remember and wait.

In his debate with the enthusiasts, and especially with Carlstadt's relativizing of the external word and sacramental sign, Luther in his sacramental teaching increasingly stresses the externality of the salvation event to which faith relates as to something already there. The object of faith is outside the heart. Faith appropriates this external factor. It is indeed that which takes place in the heart. But it cannot arise out of the heart. It is effected by the external factor; cf. Luther's *Sermon on the Body and Blood of Christ,* WA, 19, 482, 15ff., and on this W. Joest, *Ontologie der Person,* pp. 414ff.

What does it mean, however, that the space between the once and the future is abolished and that, while the Word remains external and is a given factor, it also draws near and enters the heart (Romans 10:8)?

This making present is also the work of the Holy Spirit. It is another form of what we have called the miracle of appropriation. We do not have here a cooperation with man with whose help man accomplishes a kind of actualization of the once and the future. We do not need to go up to heaven to bring Christ down (Romans 10:7). We are not dealing with a Platonic heaven in which Christ dwells and from which we have to bring him concretely into the here and now. To *make* Christ present would be a righteousness of our own works and not an invocation of him who is already present here and now for me and who will conform me to himself if I accept his being for me in faith.[39] Nor do we need to go down into the depths to bring up Christ from the dead (Romans 10:8). This means that he is not a part of the history which takes place in death's field of force, so that the once is now the dead past. When we think of the great characters of history we think of dead people. When we set them in analogy to the present and try to enter into dialog with them, we have to go back in our minds (to go down into their depths) and bring them back in an actualization. Actualizing recollection is in fact cooperation. In Christ's case, however, things are different. Another has brought him from the realm of the dead. In his origin and also in his exaltation he is not tied to history in the sphere of death.

He is present in Word and Spirit and does not need to be made present

---

[38] Cf. Althaus, *Die christliche Wahrheit,* I, pp. 37f.
[39] Cf. Iwand, *op. cit.,* p. 193.

as he would have to be if he were in heaven as a timeless idea or in the depths of history as a form of the past. Faith grasps him as the one who is present in history. He is presented to faith in history just as surely as he once lived. As the one he was he makes himself manifest as the one who is present and who will come (Revelation 1:4). Faith is not the power which makes him present; it is the point at which his presence breaks through.

Faith belongs to the salvation event, for it is brought about by the Spirit as an act in which something becomes manifest to me. Without faith that which is declared would be silent. It would be of no avail. It would become for us the judgment of hardening. Nevertheless, even as this salvation event it is not of equal rank with the "mighty acts of God" on the event side of history.[40] For these acts are set before it and remain so for all time.[41] They are and remain that to which faith relates and that which brings it into being through the testimony of the Holy Spirit which presents them, thus adopting faith for its part into the series of those "mighty acts."

The relation of Word and faith, then, can be thought of only as one in which the Word has undisputed primacy. This is inseparably related to, and even identical with, the primacy of history as a salvation event, i.e., revelation outside me. Here the table is spread to which I am invited as a believer (Matthew 22:1-14). In this salvation event the covenant of God with his community is decreed. Faith is only the counter-signature to God's signature which is attached already. It is simply a ratification. It does not simply take what is already present into itself, so that a theology of consciousness might arise. Nor does it make it present, so that it might become an act of hermeneutical cooperation. It is integrated into the salvation event as a last member.[42]

Faith, then, does not believe in itself. It cannot be an end in itself or a goal. It is thrown back on that which is already given. It believes in this. This is what engenders it by the miracle of the Spirit.

The implied difference between reception of the salvation event into the consciousness and the opposing integration of ourselves into the salvation event finds some analogy in Kierkegaard's distinction between religion A and religion B.

In the first, God, or the eternal, is immanent in man. Hence its only presupposition is human nature in general (*Concluding Unscientific Postscript* [1941], pp. 493ff.). The first presupposition of the concern to find God here is thus the *via dialectica,* the way of self-annihilation, resignation, and a total sense of guilt. This is one form of cooperation as man's contro-

---

[40] As against some statements in the Tübingen faculty's *Für und wider die Theologie Bultmanns,* 2nd ed. (1952), p. 32.

[41] "For all time" means that there is no moment when faith absorbs the proddings of the divine Word and becomes capable of independence, as Schleiermacher thinks in the *Speeches* (religious man can finally write his own holy scriptures) or Lessing in the *Education of the Human Race* (revelation trains man in emancipated autonomy).

[42] Cf. G. Bornkamm, "Mythos und Evangelium," ThEx, N.S. 26, p. 25.

versy with himself. We thus have a direct inwardness which because of its directness Luther would arrange under the theology of glory.

In religion B, however, what edifies man is something outside the individual. The individual is edified, not by finding the relation to God inside himself, but by relating himself to something outside himself to find edification (*ibid.*, p. 498). The paradox, and insoluble dialectic, is that the apparently aesthetic relation in which the individual stands to something outside himself, at what seems to be a distance, has to be an absolute relation to God (*ibid.*). This relation is grounded, then, in mediation and a mediator, i.e., Christ. That which is outside the self, preceding inwardness and appropriation and remaining in dialectic with it, gives rise to a paradox that cannot be overcome.

b. Faith and History

If revelation is Word as history, mediated verbally and historically, the relation between revelation and faith may also be presented as the relation between faith and history. The connection between them will be dealt with under various aspects, e.g., in the doctrines of the Trinity, of law and gospel, of salvation history, etc. It is of a piece with the incarnation of the Word as the center of the gospel that no dimension of faith does not in some way involve the question of history. Christian theology is always and everywhere a theology of facts.[43] In the discussion which follows we shall be dealing only with one very special aspect of the relation between faith and history.

In the preceding subsection it might have seemed that the Holy Spirit with his positing of the new creature is relevant only for the individual and works only vertically from above in the punctilinear here and now, so that there is little connection with the horizontal line of the course of history.[44] Nevertheless, we have given indications that the spiritual Word is mediated historically and meets us in the mighty acts of God, in the tradition which expounds them, in the commissioned words of "holy men of God" (2 Peter 1:21), and finally in the Son (Hebrews 1:2). This reference of faith to historical mediation comes to light especially when we emphasize that the salvation event, as the nexus of God's words and acts, has already taken place, and comes before faith both chronologically and also materially.

Along with this reference of faith to the historical givenness of revelation,

---

[43] We have shown already, e.g., in Volume I, pp. 266ff., that "fact" cannot mean a finding of historical research which may be reached and objectified outside faith.
[44] Some serious critics have made this point in relation to the doctrine of the Holy Spirit in Volume I. The author sees that this impression could be left, and why it could. He would point out in defense that the volume was essentially a debate with Cartesian theology or theological existentialism. This trend, however, is oriented to the individual in Kierkegaard's sense and to that degree bears an individualistic stress. When the debate is conducted on this level, it is thus unavoidable that the focus should be on this individualistic aspect.

faith also finds itself referred in a second sense to history and therewith to the dimension of the supra-individual.

The word received in faith is not just history. It also makes history. Primarily, of course, it makes church history by calling, gathering, and separating the community, and by working in its institutionalizing. But it is also at work in secular history. The Christian west is only one among many concepts which express this constructive working of the Word in the world. A long list would be needed to illustrate effects of this type in detail. In it we should surely have to include the theological background of modern democracy along with the ideas of freedom and personhood which govern it.[45] The antidote to the totalitarian claim of the state, which includes a claim to dominion over souls, is also connected with the Christian background.[46] Impulses toward social reform and revolution are also inconceivable without this basic theological element in view of the idea of humanity which is at work in them.

This holds good in spite of the incontestable argument that the nineteenth-century church resisted the idea of a fourth estate and largely opposed the changing of the status quo by either reform or revolution. Even the humanist and humanitarian intention which is proper to Marxism is unthinkable without the background of the image of God according to the Judeo-Christian tradition. It is bitterly ironical that atheists rather than Christians have accepted the theme of humanity which was entrusted to faith and which became part of the atheist tradition through the mediation of faith.

The Creator Spirit who is at work in the Word is thus creative not merely to the degree that he transforms man, individual man, into a new creature, but also to the degree that he fashions order, structure, and historical form, that he embodies himself in them, and that he molds things through this renewed historical mediation. Political and social structures can also be forms of this work and witness.

In this context we shall dwell for a moment on the primary operation of the Word, i.e., on the rise of the church.[47]

The church stands at the intersection of the two relations of faith to history to which we have alluded. On the one side the church as a kind of institutional symbol represents the divine act of salvation which is a given for faith. Through the church we receive the Word which brings faith, for it is there before our faith. It is believed as the Spirit is who works through it.[48] On the other hand, while we receive the Word in the church, the church

---

[45] Thus U. Scheuner in F. Karrenberg, ed., *Evangelisches Soziallexikon* (1954), col. 986, argues that modern theories of the state, in view of their common use of theological concepts, cannot be understood apart from their theological background. On this whole problem cf. ThE, II, 2, esp. § 1347ff.; E.T. II, esp. pp. 210ff.

[46] Scheuner, *op. cit.,* col. 987; ThE, II, 2, § 294ff., 332ff.; E.T. II, pp. 46ff., 53ff.

[47] As regards the share of the Word in the fashioning of historical structures we may refer to the whole of ThE, esp. II, 2 and III.

[48] Cf. the third article of the Creed.

receives itself from the Word as the fellowship of believers. The Word makes history, church history. This implies the corporeality and visibility of the church in concrete institutional form.

A feature of Luther's doctrine of the church is that he locates it at this point which we have called the intersection of two lines. The church is the work of the Word and it also works in the name of the Word and to that extent takes form.

As regards the first point, it is not believers who assemble or associate (cf. the fourth of Schleiermacher's *Speeches*) in the name of faith or their own piety that constitute the heart of the church, but the Word of the gospel. All the church's life and substance is in the Word of God (*Ad librum . . . Catharini . . .* , WA, 7, 721, 12). The rock Christ on which it is built is this Word. Even its description as the communion of saints points to this basis in the Word and begetting by the Word (WA, 7, 709, 25; 712, 40). For the saints are not holy by intrinsic piety. Their holiness is the justifying Word. It is thus outside them (cf. *Lectures on Hebrews, WA, 57, 215, 1*). The object of faith, which is the salvation event of the given Word, is outside the heart (*Sermon on the Sacrament of the Body and Blood of Christ, WA, 19, 482, 15*). For this reason the church cannot arise out of faith insofar as this is socially active. It arises out of that in which faith believes. It is grounded in and called forth by that which is outside it. (Cf. W. Kreck, "Christus extra nos und pro nobis," ThLZ [1965], pp. 641ff.) To this degree it is the work of the Word (WA, 7, 743, 7).

The second point is that the church which is called forth thus is a historical reality and not what Melanchthon calls a *Platonica civitas* (Apol. CA, VII, 20). It demands concrete form and corporeality. The Word of God cannot be a written gospel which the individual accepts in isolated confrontation. It has to be preached. It must be a vocal gospel (WA, 7, 721, 15). This Word is thus heard in common and those who are assembled by it are seen as a community. The community is a form in this world. It is thus the visible church. (This term may be used here so long as it is not taken in the sense of Melanchthon's contrast between visible and invisible with its idealistic implication but in the sense of Luther's contrast between visible and hidden (cf. Elert, *Morphologie des Luthertums,* I [1931], p. 229; E.T. *The Structure of Lutheranism* [1962], p. 261). Apart from faith the church is hidden because the mystery of its form cannot be perceived, not even in the habit of holiness in its members. For this mystery is grounded in the Word which is its basis and which discloses itself only to faith. Even faith itself cannot fix the limit of the church by setting visible boundaries, e.g., members who obviously have true faith and members who obviously do not. Revelation of what the ontological church is, is always an eschatological act. Only in the last judgment will distinction be made between the sheep and the goats (Matthew 25:32f.).

This is why the marks of the church are also its constitutive factors, namely, preaching the Word and administering the sacraments (CA, VII). These marks are living and concrete; they can be heard and seen. But what they are essentially as that which is heard and seen, and what validates them as the work of the Spirit, escapes hearing and seeing and is reserved for faith. The second point at issue, then, stresses the concrete form of the church as it is fashioned by the Word.

If we take seriously the corporeality of the church, we must also take seriously the institutional problems posed by this corporeality. Not to regard the institutional element, i.e., matters of structure and constitution, as part of the church[49] would lead to Platonic and docetic spiritualizings which would deny to the Word its incarnation and its assumption of historical form.[50]

If the Lutheran tradition has relativized constitutional and ceremonial questions and granted them no divine right,[51] this does not imply that the corporeality of the church must be distinguished from the idea of it or that it has an inferior character. (The change in intellectual climate is shown by our having to use idealist terminology to describe this view.) The concreteness of form manifested in the institutional side is intrinsic to the church, for the Word was made flesh and is a Word that acts, entering history and making history.

If something has to be relativized here, it is not the fact of institutional form but the form itself. It is a relative matter whether the form is synodal or hierarchical, whether it is that of a national church or a free church, whether it involves taxes or offerings, whether it uses this or that liturgical pattern. In all these matters there is historical and situational elasticity. But the elastic and variable forms relate to one and the same constant, namely, the historical assumption of form by the Word. One might say that the fact of this assumption belongs to the essence of the Spirit-effected Word while its manner is left to the judgment of those who believe in this Word.

If we say that this judgment is made by reason, which interprets changing situations and considers the related questions of ecclesiastical structure, this does not mean that we are leaving the judgment to "free-floating" reason. The reason in question is a hearing and receiving reason which within its own sphere and competence receives the Word into the current situation and tries to find a suitable institutional setting for it. To that extent it is always ready to make appropriate revisions.

No matter whether we are thinking of the form or forms of the church or the historical impact of the gospel in political and social structures (e.g., democracy), we are always dealing here with the end of the ways of God in corporeality.[52] The creative work of the Creator Spirit does not take

---

[49] Cf. the chapter on the theological problems of church law in ThE, III, esp. § 1637ff.

[50] Cf. my discussion of the charismatic concept of the church in R. Sohm and the personalistic concept in E. Brunner, ThE, III, § 1611ff.

[51] ThE, § 1661ff.; 1694ff.

[52] Cf. F. C. Oetinger, "Leiblichkeit ist das Ende der Wege (Werke) Gottes," *Werke*, I, 3, pp. 27f., 196, 439, 442; E. Zinn, *Die Theologie des F. C. Oetinger* (1932), p. 152.

place only vertically from above[53] nor merely in individuals. Its historical mediation also has the form of mighty acts and the message of those whom it commissions. It thus seeks embodiment as historical form and reality.

We thus have the self-witness of the Creator Spirit and his assumption of form on the horizontal level of history. (This is expressed in the Decalog in the promise annexed to the fifth commandment [Exodus 20:12], and the wisdom literature is full of similar references.) Biblically the ongoing way of God in history is demonstrated especially by examples of the opposite. Thus when man resists God and perishes on the vertical dimension by confusing Creator and creature, he blocks the assumption of form by God's Word in his history and instead introduces perversions, dissipations, and the forces of opposing forms on the horizontal level. The tower of Babel is the classic illustration (Genesis 11:1-9; cf. Exodus 20:5; Jeremiah 31:28ff.; Ezekiel 18:5-20; Romans 1:26-32).

What theological rank are we to accord to these assumptions of form by the Creator Spirit in the horizontal operations, and especially the structures, of history? Does God enter equally into these historical mediations? For example, is democracy an institutional form of the Word of God? Is socialism Christianity in action? Is the concept of humanity which lies behind such things a distillation of the gospel?—rather after the manner of Lessing when he calls the eternal pure gospel of reason the epitome of Christian revelation. Has God taken form in all these things? Has a second source of revelation sprung up in addition to the Word? Has this source replaced the Word so that we no longer need it?

If so, we should be back at Hegel, who views history as a self-representation of the Spirit and who thus identifies the Spirit ontologically with his form (cf. Volume I, pp. 259ff.). Against this Kierkegaard rightly protested. Some theologians who in no sense belong to Hegel's school still follow this line which leads to identification of the Spirit of God with the secular forms that are assumed. Thus for R. Rothe the church makes itself superfluous as the Word penetrates the world and Christianizes it structurally (*Die Anfänge der christlichen Kirche* [1837], p. 81; *Theologische Ethik,* 2nd ed. [1867], V, p. 379; cf. ThE, II, 2, § 4070ff.; E.T. II, pp. 576ff.). We find the same tendency in the theocratic ideas of A. A. van Ruler (cf. *The Christian Church and the OT* [1955; E.T. 1971]; cf. ThE, II, 2, §

---

[53] This phrase of the early Barth rests on Kierkegaard's idea of the moment. This in turn is a protest against Hegel's dissolving of the Spirit in the horizontal process of history and the related depersonalizing of the individual in his unconditionality and his quality as a decision-maker (cf. ThE, II, 1, § 75ff., 79ff.). With this reference the phrase is obviously justified, for it characterizes the work of the Word and Spirit of God as one which is not identical with the continuity of the historical process nor deducible from it. Apart from this reference, however, phrases like "vertically from above" and the "wholly other" seem to stand in antithesis to the assumption of form and hence to have a docetic thrust, as E. Bloch rightly urges against Barth and Bultmann in his *Atheismus im Christentum* (1968), pp. 69ff., 72ff.; E.T. 1972, pp. 42ff.

4275ff.; E.T. II, pp. 604ff.). A Deutelmoser even tries to interpret Luther along these lines (*Luther, Staat und Glaube* [1937]; cf. ThE, I, § 1814, 1828; E.T. pp. 370, 374).

Two important objections may be raised against these identifications of God's Spirit and historical form. We shall develop them with democracy as a model.

First, historical form, e.g., the democratic structure of society, is ambivalent in itself. Hence historically mediated acts of God need the immediacy of the Word to reveal their background. As salvation event, history is plain only when interpreted. Only through the Word does it acquire a kerygmatic quality,[54] just as the historical events narrated in the OT become salvation event only through kerygmatic interpretation.[55]

This means concretely that if the spiritual Word has invested itself in the political structure of democracy, it does not automatically continue to live in it in such a way that the structure itself now has a function of proclamation. If the Word that has become indirect in the structure is not elucidated by the direct Word of proclamation, it remains silent, just as the proclaimed Word, if it does not constantly relate to the being of man in the world and its structures, remains empty. In these circumstances democracy can be understood only as a technique of exercising power (with the help of controls and a division of powers). The underlying knowledge which is imparted to it by the Word, namely, the knowledge of fallen man who is corrupted by power, and corrupted absolutely by absolute power,[56] and who has thus to be protected against a totalitarian power state, merges into the background and is lost to sight.

Also lost is the basic democratic recognition of the personal dignity of man, the dignity which has its source in the freedom of the Christian man, his emancipation from bondage to the law and servile fear. If the message is not proclaimed that man is called by his name (Isaiah 43:1), that he has thereby the accent of unconditionality, and that for this reason he can never become the means to an end or a particle in a collective, then in the long run the humanity will be lost to which democracies appeal with their programs of reform. In place of the unconditionality of human worth, there will be advanced either latently or as an open platform the thesis of man's pragmatic utility, e.g., his functional value in the process of production.[57] The driving wheel of humanism in the machinery of modern Christian culture might continue to turn for some time, and the Word from which this distinctive definition of man derives might continue as a distant and hazy

---

[54] Reinhold Niebuhr attempts this type of theological interpretation of democracy, e.g., in *The Children of Light and the Children of Darkness* (1945). For a similar attempt cf. ThE, II, 2, § 54-131; E.T. II, pp. 12-21.

[55] We recall the debate between F. Hesse and G. von Rad.

[56] Lord Acton; cf. ThE, II, 2, § 1108; E.T. II, p. 173.

[57] This decisive modification may be seen already in many forms, e.g., in the question what patients are worth treating in some costly medical procedures; cf. the author's *Wer darf leben?* (1970).

memory under the slogan of humanity. But the motor itself has been shut off if the proclaimed Word no longer supplies the motive force for human dignity and no longer speaks of man's greatness and misery. For it is man's greatness and dignity that constitute together the background of the democratic structure. Democracy is here only an illustration and represents many structural phenomena in political, social, and cultural life.

We shall refrain from giving a list of these phenomena[58] and simply cling to the decisive point that God's Word and Spirit, while they produce concrete historical forms and institutional structures, do not enter into these forms in such a way that the living voice of the Word can be dropped and institutionally supported preaching can take its place. The institution which is not elucidated and interpreted by the direct Word remains ambiguous and hence its proclamation cannot be heard.

Second, insofar as structures are not seen in their relation to the Word, they are also silent to the degree that three things might happen.

(a) They might take on the character of law, i.e., become an uncontested rule which men obey. In this way they no longer allow the gift and promise to shine through. Instead they become a dividing wall which shuts off that which ought to shine through. We find this kind of walling off in the history of the OT law. Originally it stood under the rule of the first commandment and thus enabled us to see the author of the law. But in later casuistry and rabbinic exegesis it lost this ability and became an end in itself. Its basis in the divine covenant and its function as a self-presentation of Yahweh were no longer perceived. This degenerate law, which had turned into its opposite, is the *nomos* which Paul describes as the antithesis of the gospel and the power of death (Romans 7:11; 2 Corinthians 3:6; Ephesians 2:1; Colossians 2:13).[59]

(b) By reason of the law of historical inertia and the nature of man, institutions might become as it were "second nature" to man, i.e., something traditional which he takes for granted. He will then wear them, not like clothes which he chooses, but like his skin which is part of himself.[60] The resultant indifference is another mode of the silence in which the structures hide when the question of their determination is no longer posed.

(c) A third form of silence is when an attempt is made to overcome the emptying of institutional structures in legalism and the indifference of second nature by filling them with a self-selected meaning, e.g., by ideologizing them and making them into pragmatic-synthetic constructs. When this is done, the walling off is complete.

---

[58] If we were to give a list, freedom would figure high on it. Freedom lives by the power to be free and the definition in the name of which it is lived. Without this "word" background it becomes a slogan of libertinism and a synonym of caprice. Cf. the author's essay "Was heisst Freiheit," *Der Einzelne und der Apparat,* 2nd ed. (1966), pp. 51ff.

[59] Cf. on this Chapters XV and XVI.

[60] This is the attitude which Nietzsche fights with his concept of critical history, *Vom Nutzen und Nachteil der Historie . . .* (1873/74); cf. A. de Tocqueville.

The decisive conclusion to be drawn from all this is that the Word, insofar as it produces historical forms, never identifies itself with these forms. It never makes them "disciples." It does not ordain them to an independent preaching office.

We thus have a modulated echo of conclusions already reached in Volume I.[61] The Creator Spirit at work in the Word never integrates himself into what is created. He always remains in juxtaposition as the *alienum* or *extra me* of the Word that is continually said to me afresh. Hence the Spirit is never a created impulse in creatures.[62] He is a person as in the trinitarian tradition and thus stands over against human persons. This is why traditional doctrinal formulations never say that we "have" the Holy Spirit. The Spirit remains the object of prayer: "Come, Creator Spirit."

The relation between the Spirit and the self is a model for the relation between the Spirit and the institution. This relation never has the form of integration. Hence everything depends on keeping the distinction in view. The Creator never becomes creature and the Spirit never becomes historical form.

For this reason, too, the structures can never be converted, as a theology which has degenerated into sociology is obviously maintaining when it regards the kingdom of God as a utopian form of world conditions in which hunger, injustice, and repression are overcome and conformity with the will of God is thus achieved. Even if their utopian unreality be disregarded, one may still say of these structures that without the Word they are prey to the various forms of silence which we have just outlined.

Undoubtedly the Word and Spirit of God press for historical form and we are thus under commission to change the structures of the world and their organization in accordance with the principle of love.[63] Creative love consists not merely of charity extended to the Thou of the human brother but also of attempts to change the structures and the corresponding organization of society. If, as Marx rightly perceived, a specific social system leads to mass misery, loving concern for the afflicted masses must drive us primarily to change the system. (Whether this is done by reform or revolution is in this context a secondary question.) This means that love cannot work only on the individual level of the diaconate. It must also relate constructively to the general format of the world. To that degree it has a prophylactic side which is supra-individual and organizational.

In this respect the atheistic criticism which appeared in a Moscow newspaper was right when it said that the modern church may no longer be compared to a pillar of fire which goes before mankind and leads it to its highest goal. It is more like an ambulance bringing up the rear and picking

---

[61] Pp. 131f., etc.

[62] CA, II, 6.

[63] We are consciously opposing here the concept of the kingdom of God advanced by Ritschl in his *Christliche Lehre von der Rechtfertigung und Versöhnung*, 3rd ed. (1889), III, p. 12; E.T. *The Christian Doctrine of Justification and Reconciliation* (1900), p. 10.

up the wounded (cf. H. F. Steiner, *Marxisten-Leninisten über den Sinn des Lebens* [1970], p. 254).

The relation of love to the structures of life cannot be contested. Love has to be active not merely at the personal level but also at the material level, i.e., in politics, society, economics, and so forth. Nevertheless, the change which is to be brought about can never be a conversion. In their new form the structures—like any worldly form or event, including miracles—will still be equivocal.

This may be seen already in the fact that attempts at changing structures may be made from many different standpoints. Marxists, Moslems, and neo-pagans of every kind can want them as well as Christians. Conversion belongs only to the individual, to the man who is called by name. In the name of this conversion of his, the individual will then will what God wills, namely, that the world should be different from what it is, that there should be achieved provisionally and symbolically that which as God's kingdom transcends the form of this world—the kingdom in which the old has gone, pain is no more, and there will be no more sorrow or death (Revelation 21:4).

Since the changing of the world begins with the changing of man, it is putting the cart before the horse to make the structural alteration of the world a primary or even an exclusive goal without this initial step. In the Bible the world is always regarded as a macrocosmic gradation of the human heart in which the new creation must begin even though it cannot stop there.[64] Only when the Word and Spirit are admitted into the heart as the strategic point of the cosmic nexus is a place found for the promise that they will also work at the reconstruction of the world and its structures.

Along these lines Paul does not attack the institution of slavery or try to initiate changes in social structure in the name of the gospel. Instead he brings the slave Onesimus to conversion and sends him back to his former master Philemon as a "brother," thus undermining the institution.[65] Only when the change in world structures begins at this point with the changing of the heart by the Word and Spirit will the link be upheld between the structures that are to be changed and the Word. Only then will there be preaching about the determination of these structures and their relation to the salvation event. Only then will interpretation be possible. Only in this way will the structures remain transparent and not be reduced to silence. To leave out man's conversion in the name of converting the structures would mean changing the world into an empty bureaucratic and institutional apparatus. The political situation today, as K. Jaspers forthrightly puts it,[66] demands

---

[64] Cf. ThE, I, § 2144ff.; E.T. I, pp. 434ff. We again recall the lines from Francis Thompson's poem *The Heart*: "Our towns are copied fragments from our breast,/ And all man's Babylons strive but to impart/The grandeurs of his Babylonian heart."

[65] ThE, II, 1, § 2057ff.

[66] *Die Atombombe und die Zukunft des Menschen* (1958), p. 356.

more than ever the new birth of man, and Jaspers calls on the churches to begin their message at *this* point.

We feel that we are misunderstood if this stress on the person rather than the structure is taken to imply that men in their totality must be converted, or, in more secular terms, must find their way to a new consciousness, before the new spiritual situation can objectify itself structurally and institutionally.[67] Now it is true that as a rule social and political structures can show a measure of historical durability only when the consciousnes of those affected by them stands in some correspondence to them. When this is not so, they are an external shackle, and being ill-adapted they will be rejected as alien at the first suitable opportunity. (At this institutional level, too, there is a limit of tolerance.) Nevertheless, the opposite experience must also be taken into account.

It is possible that new structures may for their part alter the consciousness of men and hence men themselves. While it is hazardous to introduce a democratic system prematurely, i.e., without considering the ripeness or maturity of those concerned, it can also happen in some instances that the democratic system will teach maturity and bring ripeness. Appropriate social legislation can also engender respect for the human and to that extent help to produce a new consciousness. Hence Kohnstamm is undoubtedly right when he argues that structures can change men and even make them open to fellow-men whom they have not thus far recognized as neighbors.

It would also be a mistake, however, to think that the causal sequence of person first and then structure can simply be reversed. We have to ask rather who it is that is pressing for structural change, who perhaps wants this structural change first, possibly as an immediate revolutionary act, and who is not prepared to change the consciousness first and hence to create the spiritual disposition for the new structures. Surely of the initiator or initiators at least we have to say that they can want the structural changes only because *their* consciousness at any rate has reached a stage which makes them capable of their structural postulates.

It may thus be assumed that changed structures can change men. The experience of history supports this. Nevertheless, it must also be said that for their part the revolutionary or reforming pioneers are already changed or converted personally before they think out their program of structural change and especially before they put it into practice.

This means, however, that in the minds of these elite there must have been formed a view of the relation between person and structure. In other words, there must have developed a specific understanding of man which has normative significance for this relation. This understanding might imply a view of man in which man is respected in his unconditionality, or, in Kantian terms, in his significance as an end in himself. Or it might imply a view of man in which he is evaluated as a mere functionary and hence

---

[67] This is the objection raised by Max Kohnstamm, "Person und Struktur," ZEE (1970), against my essay "Können sich Strukturen bekehren?" ZThK (1969), 1.

pragmatically. Dependent on this alternative is whether man is made for the sabbath (the institution) or the sabbath for man (Mark 2:27). Here too, then, whether unwittingly or explicitly in the program, the answer to structural questions depends on the prior understanding of the human person. Even in remote utopian dreams the form of the structures is determined thereby. We shall either have functional structures that serve man or an apparatus which is an end in itself and in relation to which man functions merely as an impotent and unwilling participant.

Christian proclamation and Christian theology have thus to put both to their partners in debate and also to themselves the question who or what man is, or, more precisely, what is the basis of his existence, the Word or the structures.

c. Faith and Experience[68]

Already at the beginning of this volume we have pointed out that faith is always to be characterized not merely by what it is "in" but also by what it is "against." It is a nondoubting of what is not seen (Hebrews 11:1). It is an affirmation against appearance, against experience, against the trend of natural knowledge, even though it is itself integrated into a new mode of knowledge. Why the "in" and "against" are so closely tied together, and by this tie constitute the essence of faith, should become clear as we go along.

If faith does not come from experience, if it is the mark of the new creation which takes man out of his self-enclosed being and his riveting to the phenomenological, this means that conflict with experience arises. This conflict takes on the character of temptation or trial. The struggle between the spiritual man and the natural man never ends. The end of the struggle remains an eschatological promise (Romans 7:24f.; 1 Corinthians 13:12; 15:57).

To say this is to say also that the conflict is not between believers and champions of reason. It is not a merely external conflict. Temptation does not just come from outside. It arises on the field of faith itself, for the believer himself is also, in personal union, a subject of experience and of rational reflection. Because he is this subject, non-experience of God, and the tension in which the God who is hidden under the cross stands to all rational postulates, is for him a real trial. The believer himself is the field of battle. The "against" as well as the "in" of faith is actual in him.

We shall now attempt a brief survey of that "against" which faith believes. We shall also ask how the antithesis of faith and experience is to be explained. We shall thus seek its origin.

---

[68] On what follows cf. W. Elert, *Morphologie*, I, pp. 15ff.; E.T. pp. 17ff.; W. Joest, *Ontologie der Person*, § 3; B. Lohse, *Ratio und Fides* (1958); ThE, II, 1, § 1321-1368.

Now we have already shown[69] that the question of temptation arises out of the experience of history as well as what we call experience of life. What is observed here in history seems not to be consonant with a God of righteousness and love. Hence the question of theodicy arises, and this denotes a questioning of God. The "higher thoughts" which may make such odd things as the suffering of the good and the prosperity of the wicked intelligible in the self-consciousness of God are certainly not "our thoughts." Where we can only trust, we want to understand and we cannot console ourselves with the "hereafter" for which understanding is reserved (John 13:7).

The temptation arises, then, that our thoughts are not content to be trusting and waiting thoughts but ascribe to themselves normative rank. This normative claim finds expression in the conditions which we impose on the deity of God. If there is a God, we say, then he must not allow this or that and he must act thus and thus. The strategy of the tempter counts on there being behind the piety of Job conditions of this kind—conditions in which the deity of God is integrated into the norms of human ideas of righteousness.

If such conditions rule our consciousness and also our pre-reflective feelings about life, this is based on the fact that our reason fashions certain postulates of God. Hence it also forms certain postulates of the acts which agree with this postulate of God. In other words reason, on the basis of its own inventory of norms, tells God who he has to be and how he must act.

Luther has this in view when he says that if the light of reason wants to explain for itself the acts of God it is blind and stupid. For in its dealings with God reason can only suggest to God what is valuable and good, and as it judges, so God must act (*Genesis Lectures* of 1527, WA, 24, 272, 18ff.).

The temptation against which one must believe does not properly arise, then, because God's thoughts are "higher" but because the autonomy of reason is not prepared to give up its normative rank or to renounce the role of being itself the criterion of those higher thoughts. The role which reason assigns itself here reflects exactly the role which man assigns himself over against God. He wants to know good and evil so that he may be as God (Genesis 3:5).

Temptation is thus a sign that God refuses to correspond to the image which man's autonomy makes of him. The pain of temptation intimates the contradiction of God against the congruence with our wishes which we ascribe to him. To believe against temptation, then, can only mean justifying the contradiction of God against our autonomy.

If the gap between what we want God to be and what he is becomes actual already in the experience of the cosmic process, it becomes sharper once the image of God is thematized. The question here is whether the

---

[69] The question will be raised again when we deal with the question of God in Chapters IV-VIII.

Christian view of God does not contradict itself to the degree that rationally intolerable antinomies are concealed in it. Does not the omnipotence of God mean that our condition has its origin in him and not in us? Yet does he not summon us to responsibility? Is there not an equally significant contradiction between the fact that we have a servile will on the one side and yet that we are faced with a demand, i.e., that we *ought* to be, without being *able* to be?

Luther wrestles with this in his *De servo arbitrio*. How is it possible to demand the impossible? (God demands . . . impossible things, WA, 18, 107, 33). If man is a bad tree, how can good fruits be required from him? (WA, 1, 224, 13). Up above, God works with the help of the evil, as in Judas. He sets it in his service. He rides the lame horse and cuts rotten wood. (God works in and through the evil, WA, 18, 109, 27.) Cf. the account of this problem of the "impossible" demand and the related responsibility in ThE, I, § 1394ff., esp. 1438; E.T. pp. 290ff., esp. 297.

The process of thought within which these antinomies necessarily arise is as follows. God is identified with a normative concept like omnipotence. The necessary relation between Creator and creature is deduced from this. To the total omnipotence of the Creator there has to correspond the total impotence of the creature. Total impotence, however, means the negation of any subjectivity and hence of any responsibility. If the Almighty issues commands that call for decision, this presupposes on the part of those to whom it is put the subjectivity which is ruled out from the very outset by the concept of omnipotence. Antinomy thus arises. This finds classical formulation in the song of the old harpist in Goethe's *Wilhelm Meister:* You bring us into life, let the poor man become guilty, and then deliver him up to pain, for all guilt avenges itself on earth.

This antinomy, and the temptation it engenders, have the same foundation as that which we have just laid down. Reason posits an axiomatic view of omnipotence and with the help of it shapes its view of God. It does not let the meaning of omnipotence be defined by God himself, so that we shall learn what it is from his conduct and the original sense will be changed accordingly. It defines God with the help of the concept already at its disposal. Hence the so-called antinomy arises out of the same autonomy of reason which we observed in its postulate of a course of history that runs according to the norms of reason and right.

The resultant temptation cannot, then, be overcome by a rational adjustment of the antinomy but only by bringing its basis to light and then asking what omnipotence will mean if it is defined, not by reason, but by God.

This question can be answered only by referring to the I who is made known in the self-disclosure of God. The fact that God is radically above us or our radius of possible action, and that his claims extend into the sphere of the impossible, is close to the further fact that we owe ourselves totally to him. Christian theology has always anchored the element of ·the total in its understanding of creation by speaking of creation out of nothing (*ex nihilo*).[70] When creation myths understand God as a kind of artist (*technites*) who fashions the world out of existent material, man can be only partially and not totally responsible. The forces of guilt and the tragic entanglements which afflict him can be traced back to the cosmic material, which is often regarded as under a curse, and which determines the immobile situation of human existence, so that man cannot be held responsible for it. In this way much guilt is transformed into fate. Guilt becomes tragic. Man can be responsible in the sense of accounting or imputation only to the degree that he moves freely on this immobile plane of existence. Hence he is responsible, not in his being, but only in his actions, and even this only to the extent that existent being has no determinative significance for his actions.[71]

All this changes fundamentally when God is understood, or causes himself to be understood, as the Creator out of nothing. This rules out all possibility of dividing the I into an inferior sector, which is determined by the original matter of the world, and a higher stage of personality which is set up above matter and is an area for the responsible exercise of freedom. To the Creator out of nothing I owe myself totally. As I have received myself wholly from him, no dimension of the I being excluded, so I must give myself back wholly to him.

Only in this framework do the radicalizations of the law of Moses in the Sermon on the Mount make sense. In other words, only then are they without antinomy, as is expressed in that not just the part of the I which is endowed with will, but my whole being, even to the thoughts of the heart, is claimed for God (Matthew 5:21-48). Or to put it in yet another way, it is apparent here that man's reply: I ought, but I cannot, contains no inherent contradiction and hence does not refute the intelligibility of this kind of imperative.

Here, then, the concept of omnipotence is defined by God to the degree that his being and conduct are normative for its understanding. The concept of omnipotence ceases to be a cipher that reason invents for the first cause or prime mover, i.e., for a reality which makes an impotent and non-autonomous effect of everything that it produces. Instead, the term omnipotence can be only a description of the being and conduct of God himself. But this being and conduct are characterized by the fact that (1) God in creating out of nothing is not tied to any pre-existent matter but has power over matter too, and that (2), again in sovereign freedom and hence in virtue of omnipotence, God calls a creature to be his partner and counterpart, and addresses it as Thou (Genesis 1:28f.; 2:16), thus endowing it with personal responsibility.

As this creature, man, sees himself thus before God in both nature and

---

[70] ThE, I, § 712-762 and 1330-1353; E.T. I, pp. 279ff.
[71] Cf. Kant, who uses the term predispositions to describe the immobile basis of the ego which is not subject to responsibility (*Religion within the Limits of Reason Alone*, pp. 21ff.; on this cf. ThE, I, § 1612ff.).

destiny, as it realizes that it is created by God, judged by him (i.e., brought into responsibility), and also loved by him, there arises the faith which maintains itself against temptation. This triumph over temptation is achieved because the autonomy of reason is broken and the antinomy which it produced in the concept of God is overcome. The resolution of the antinomy, and the defeat of the temptation which it causes, is not then an epistemological phenomenon. It is an existential event.

Man does not reach a better view of God which dispels the fog of the antinomy. On the contrary, man sees himself brought into the truth to the degree that he lets the truth of his being be defined by God. The self-revealing God reveals man. In this disclosure of his being man does not simply confess that he has *done* this or that which he should not have done. He confesses: I *am* a sinful man (Luke 5:8). He does not see himself as under orders only in the free sphere of his autonomy. He sees himself claimed in the very being which he has been loaned by God and which is now required of him. He has to say I before God in this dimension of his existence and not just in the sphere of mobile action.

Hence his natural rationality, like his natural experience of God, is called in question. In the name of this questioning faith believes against the temptation which, e.g., in the form of the antinomy mentioned, necessarily results from the autonomy of rationality and experience.

The inadequacy of what reason says about God, compared to what faith confesses about him, may be seen in philosophy as the representative of reason. Luther constantly finds new phrases in his attempt to express this inadequacy.

Only the external side of reality is the theme of reason.[72] Within this dimension of reality which is offered to the senses reason can find its way about with the help of its conclusions.[73] It is thus restricted to what may be seen of phenomena here and now. In this zone, as Luther points out in the *Genesis Lectures* of 1535,[74] reason can perceive formal and material causes. It can portray things phenomenologically and relate them causally. But it cannot see the efficient and final cause of the phenomena thus displayed before it. Hence their origin and meaning are hidden from it.[75] This means that God, who is their origin and meaning, is also hidden from it, if by God we do not understand a general idea of the ground of the world along the lines of Aristotle's prime mover, but if we view him in relation to phenomena and wish to say how far he is the efficient and final cause of the course of history and its enigma. Should reason attempt this, then as post-Kantian critics we can point out that it is becoming a dogmatic metaphysics, and no matter whether the term God is used, as in Hegel, or not used, as in

---

[72] This external side is called the sphere of things visible and apparent, e.g., WA, 3, 508, 1ff.
[73] WA, 39, II, 5.
[74] WA, 42, 93, 14ff.
[75] Cf. for the most important references Joest, *op. cit.*, pp. 89-95.

Marx, it is inventing a cosmic formula which will elucidate the basis, goal, and meaning of all immanent being and occurrence.

Whether reason stops at formal and material causes, or whether it illegitimately tries to grasp the efficient and final cause, either way its situation will lead to temptation when what it knows, or thinks it knows, comes into collision with faith in the God of the Bible.

If reason is content with its immanent horizon of knowledge, it seems to be offering a negative report on the existence and rule of God. This is partly because the basic meaning of things, and indications of the divine background of being, are outside its grasp, and partly because the nexus of the being and occurrence of world phenomena can be explained without the help of the hypothesis of God, so that this hypothesis is not needed.

If, however, reason moves beyond this horizon and becomes a dogmatic metaphysics, it becomes an opponent of faith to the degree that the picture of the ground of the world which it produces cannot be harmonized with the hidden and revealed God as the Bible bears witness to him—as it bears this witness by speaking of his heart, his will, his freedom, and his higher thoughts. The biblical and historical God of Abraham, Isaac, and Jacob stands in irresolvable tension with the God of the philosophers (Pascal).[76]

If one asks how this tension arises and why reason is in no position to perceive God as the basis, meaning, and goal of world occurrence, an important negative point must be made first. It is not enough to adduce epistemological reasons for this limitation of reason, as Kant does.[77] Reasons of this kind can relate only to the immanent structure of reason and establish only the fact that the modes of perception and the categories of the human power of knowing bind reason to the sphere of objectifiable experience. Theology, however, views reason predominantly in its connection with the conditions of human existence. As we have seen, Paul already points out in Romans 1:18ff. that the existential state of human self-assertion leads man to hold down or repress the truth of God in unrighteousness. Reason as the organ of knowledge which has to do with finding the truth is never isolated, then, but is always to be seen in conjunction with the existence within whose framework and in whose name it acts.

Roman Catholic as well as Reformation theology refers to this even though it does so in another schema of thought. Thus Vatican I distinguishes between the intrinsic possibilities of reason and those which can be achieved under the conditions of man's present state of existence.[78] Lutheran orthodoxy makes a distinction between reason before and after the fall and also between the reason of the natural man and that of the regenerate man.[79] For Luther himself there is along these lines a close connection between

---

[76] Cf. the chapters on the doctrine of God.

[77] Cf. the discussion of Kant in the chapter on the "theological criticism of reason" in ThE, II, 1, § 1321-1368.

[78] Cap. 2, Denz., 1786. Cf. J. Maritain, *An Essay on Christian Philosophy* (1955), pp. 62ff.

[79] J. Gerhard, *Loci theol.*, II, 37.

reason and will. If reason is incapable of the knowledge of God, this is not just in virtue of its natural disposition but in virtue of its deficient goodness of will,[80] i.e., its existential reference.[81] To this degree reason belongs to the flesh;[82] it is not a timeless *a priori* capacity. It is bound up with the history of man. Thus it shares the fall with him, "holds down in unrighteousness," provides man's autonomy with arguments, and does not think that it needs redemption.

Insight into these relations is one reason why Luther does not attribute sin in Platonic fashion to the sphere of the sensual libido but finds it active in the sphere of the spirit too, so that flesh denotes both the sensual and the spiritual, i.e., the whole man as he now is.[83] Reason, then, is not to be viewed as independent of the subject of the acts of knowledge which it performs. To that extent reason shares in the history of man.

In terms of the doctrine of justification one might say that since the person qualifies the works, the same applies to acts of knowledge. For knowing is also a work in which the person who achieves it expresses—and betrays—himself. If the person is autonomous, asserts himself against God, and persists in this emancipated being for self, the activity of the reason is qualified thereby and confirms and hardens the person in this curving in upon itself. Thus reason sees only what it wants to see, what serves the self-will of man, and what opens up the possibility of self-affirmation.[84] This applies at least to the sphere of the metaphysical speculations of reason in which it exceeds its competence and grapples with the efficient and final cause. In this case the final reality which reason proclaims is only an objectification of its own desires and an exaltation of the creature, which decks it out with divine attributes and makes it a false god. Here Luther anticipates the formulations of Feuerbach.[85] The *persona* of the man who has fallen from God determines here too the *opus* of the capacity for knowledge and involves it in the fall.

It is no surprise, then, that reason, being grounded in an alienated existence, necessarily sees as a contradiction and even an absurdity the God who does not originate in its speculations but who manifests himself to it as the wholly other. Even the believer does not escape the temptation which comes to him from the zone of his rationality. For as the old Adam is the

---

[80] Lohse, *op. cit.*, p. 29.

[81] It is typical of Luther, in distinction from the Scholastics, especially Occam, that he does not regard the will as a partial capacity, and hence does not differentiate it from the intellect and action, but makes it the representative of the whole man and his state of existence; cf. WA, 3, 30, 9.

[82] The flesh is the whole nature of man with reason and all his powers; WA, 40, I, 244, 17.

[83] We do not find sin in the skin and hairs, but in the reason and will; WA, 18, 782, 14; cf. Lohse, *op. cit.*, p. 71, n. 3.

[84] Lohse, *op. cit.*, p. 71.

[85] Cf. the exposition of the first article of the creed in the Larger Catechism, esp. 18-23; H. Vossberg, *Luthers Kritik aller Religion* (1922); W. Holsten, *Christentum und nichtchristliche Religion nach der Auffassung Luthers* (1932).

persistent object of his struggle and is bound to him by a *simul*,[86] so the old reason is his constant adversary. Its attempt to portray God as nonsensical, contradictory, absurd, and even hostile, engenders a temptation which it is the task of faith to overcome.[87] The distorted ideas of God which are fostered all involve contradictions, e.g., between the God of omnipotence and the God of unconditional demands, or insoluble tensions, e.g., between law and gospel and judgment and grace, not to speak of the incongruence between the God of faith and the postulated God of the philosophers. All these aspects under which God seems to be impossible, especially in his radical requirement, are simply reflections of the impossible situation in which reason for its part finds itself. (So Luther in the third disputation against the antinomians.) This impossibility of reason lies in the fact that it acts autonomously as the advocate of the emancipated creature and thus curves in upon itself.[88]

If the activity of rational knowledge is to be characterized as a work, and if it thus receives its quality from the subject who performs it, then the close connection between knowledge and justification is plain. For in this area, too, the rule holds good that a new beginning cannot consist in amendments and exercises in works, i.e., in a reform of the rational capability. If works, including the activity of knowledge insofar as it relates to the efficient and final cause, are simply objectifications of ourselves, then exercises in them can only deal with symptoms and cannot alter the person as the one who does them. For good works do not make a good man; a good man does good works. Change cannot be brought about, then, merely by correcting the operation of a defective state of existence. It can come only through the new birth of the person who exists in alienation and who is thus alienated in reason too. New birth means being brought to the level of rationality. It is a redemption to objectivity.[89] Objectivity here is (1) a restriction of reason to its proper object, to its own sphere of competence, or, as Luther puts it, to the area of formal and material causes. It also means (2) that redemption from fear and hope, or, better, from false fear and false hope, confers soberness and protects the reflections of reason from slipping into illusory aspirings.

Reason itself, of course, cannot find its own way back to this objectivity. It remains tied to the vicious circle in which it moves. Even its struggle for soberness would be a form of work-righteousness which cannot succeed.

---

[86] R. Hermann, *Luthers These "Gerecht und Sünder zugleich"* (1930); G. Dehn, "Der neue Mensch," *Theologia viatorum* (1939).

[87] In *De servo arbitrio*, etc. Luther can say that without the gospel this temptation leads to despair, hatred of God, and blasphemy; WA, 18, 631, 14; 5, 622, 33. For God seems to be a liar whose assurances are false; WA, 43, 241, 13f. Cf. also Luther's wrestling with the *Deus absconditus* and on this W. von Loewenich, *Luthers theologia crucis*, pp. 21ff.

[88] God does not demand impossibilities; man falls into them through sin; WA, 39, I, 515, 16.

[89] Cf. Volume I, pp. 332ff.

For it strengthens rather than obviates the defective state of existence which gives rise to it. The regeneration of existence, and hence of alienated reason, takes place only as the relation between God and existence is changed. This change consists in the fact that reason no longer controls the relation and thus makes it representative of the God of the philosophers. God himself now determines who he will be for man, i.e., that he will manifest himself as the God who is near, as the God who loves and forgives, as Immanuel. This is offense and folly for reason (1 Corinthians 1:18ff.). For the God whom reason postulates is the God of glory and majesty.[90]

Where God manifests himself in his love, however, he is the lowly one. In solidarity with those to whom he draws near in love he conceals himself in the suffering form of the Crucified. In the cross his judgment goes forth on all the autonomous grasping of man and his reason. Hence the cross is nonsense to reason, although in truth it is the wisdom of God by which he gives the lie to our sham wisdom. In the crucified Christ, then, is true theology and knowledge of God.[91] The cross is not the dissolving of knowledge by a faith which for its part is without knowledge. Faith for the first time opens up true knowledge by relating itself to the self-disclosure of God and letting itself be led into all truth (John 16:13) and also true knowledge of the world, by its liberation from fear and hope and its redemption to objectivity.

To sum up, if faith is faith "against" as well as "in," this rests on the fact that it is engaged in a constant struggle between the old man and the new and that the old Adam has to be "drowned" afresh every day.

Paul expresses this struggle between the old man and the new especially by his combination of the indicative and the imperative (ThE, I, § 314ff.; E.T. I, pp. 83ff.). There are, of course, passages in Paul (e.g., Romans 6:12-18; 8:4; 1 Corinthians 6:12; Galatians 5:16, 24f.) in which, if we take them in isolation, the state of the new existence might also seem to be a perfect inherent quality. On the basis of these passages the holiness movements (cf. C. Finney and O. S. von Bibra) deny that there is an ongoing struggle between the old man and the new, while Osiander, and more recently A. and T. Schlatter with rather different presuppositions, attack Luther's thesis of "at once both righteous and sinner." On this debate and our reasons for taking the contrary view cf. ThE, I, § 482-551, esp. 510ff.; E.T. I, pp. 78ff.

Since the old man is the one who wants to control himself, he can achieve his autonomy only by controlling God too, whether by denying him and making himself the lord of immanence,[92] or by fashioning him in his

---

[90] Cf. the concept of *theologia gloriae* in Luther's *Heidelberg Disputation of 1518*. The concept denotes what Pascal has in view with his God of the philosophers.
[91] *Heidelberg Disputation of 1518*, WA, 1, 362, 13; cf. Sermon II on the Passion (1518), WA, 1, 340, 35: All wisdom and truth shine forth in the suffering and dying Christ.
[92] Cf. Volume I, pp. 316ff.

own image and saying that creaturely powers and ideas are ultimate reality. The tool he uses to achieve this self-determination is reason.

Strictly speaking, of course, there is no such thing as reason in the sense of a neutral, timeless, *a priori* faculty divorced from the actual state of man's existence. There is either reason which serves this self-determination and furnishes arguments for it or reason which is redeemed from this intention, brought to itself, and restored to objectivity. To this extent reason is not timeless and *a priori* but historical, at least insofar as it relates to the determination of ultimate reality and goes beyond the sphere of reference allotted to it.[93] If we speak of the reason which is the basis of man's autonomy we have in view the old reason, or the reason of the old man, to the extent that this determines the basis, goal, and meaning of existence itself. Hence the epistemological activity of man and his reason has the theological character of a work. As such it is an expression of his present state of existence. It is clear, then, in what way human knowledge forms part of the question of justification.

The temptation which is posed by Adamic reason forms the front "against" which faith believes. It believes against it because it knows him who at the cross of Christ judges all human autonomy but who at the same cross draws near to the one who is in the grasp of this autonomy and opens up new horizons to him.

---

[93] The same impossibility of depicting reason as a neutral faculty which embraces all states of man's existence may be seen when an attempt is made to portray conscience as an all-embracing authority which may be viewed intrinsically. In Luther conscience is characterized as the conscience of either the old man or the new, and hence as an afflicted or a comforted conscience. Cf. the penetrating study by G. Jacob, *Der Gewissensbegriff in der Theologie Luthers* (1929); also ThE, I, § 1441ff.

B. Revelation as a General Pointer to the Question of God. On the Relevance and Validity of Theos in Theology. What Does it Mean to Talk about God?

Bibliography: A. Antweiler, *Unendlich. Eine Untersuchung zur metaphysischen Wesenheit Gottes* (1934); K. Barth, CD, I, 1, Index "God"; H. Braun, *Gesammelte Studien zum NT und seiner Umwelt* (1962); E. Brunner, *Die christliche Lehre von Gott, Dogmatik*, I, 3rd ed. (1960); E.T. 1949; R. Bultmann, "Welchen Sinn hat es, von Gott zu reden?" GV, I, 3rd ed. (1958), pp. 26ff.; E.T. pp. 53ff.; H. Cremer, *Die christliche Lehre von den Eigenschaften Gottes* (1897); G. Ebeling, "Weltliches Reden von Gott," *Wort und Glaube* (1960), pp. 372ff.; E.T. *Word and Faith* (1963), pp. 354ff.; also "Elementare Besinnung auf verantwortliches Reden von Gott," *ibid.*, pp. 349ff.; E.T. pp. 333ff.; W. Elert, *Der Kampf um das Christentum* (1921), cf. Index "Gottesbewusstsein," "Gottesglaube," "Gottesgedanke," p. 510; J. G. Fichte, *Über den Grund unseres Glaubens an eine göttliche Weltregierung* (1798); F. Garigou-Lagrange, *Dieu. Son existence et sa nature*, 11th ed. (1950); H. G. Geyer, "Gottes Sein als Thema der Theologie" in *Jesus Christus im Zeugnis der heiligen Schrift und der Kirche*, Beihefte zu ETh, 2 (1936), pp. 3ff.; G. Gloege, "Der theologische Personalismus als dogmatisches Problem," *Heilsgeschehen und Welt*, I (1965), pp. 53ff.; F. Gogarten, *Die Frage nach Gott* (1968); H. Gollwitzer, *Die Existenz Gottes im Bekenntnis des Glaubens*, 4th ed. (1965); S. Holm, "Gott und die Werte" in J. C. Bock, *Die Rolle der Werte im Leben* (1969): A. M. Horvath, *Studien zum Gottesbegriff* (1954); W. Joest, *Ontologie der Person bei Luther* (1967); E. Jüngel, *Gottes Sein ist im Werden*, 2nd ed. (1967); K. Koch, "Der hebräische Wahrheitsbegriff im griechischen Sprachraum" in H. R. Müller-Schwefe, ed., *Was ist Wahrheit?* (1965), pp. 47ff.; H. Kössler, Art. "Neuzeitlicher Atheismus, philosophisch," RGG³, I, 672; H. J. Kraus, "Wahrheit in der Geschichte" in Müller-Schwefe, *op. cit.*, pp. 35ff.; B. Langemeyer, *Der dialogische Personalismus in der evangel. und kathol. Theologie der Gegenwart* (1963); M. Löhrer, "Dogmatische Bemerkungen zur Frage der Eigenschaften und Verhaltensweisen Gottes," *Mysterium salutis*, II (1967), pp. 291ff.; F. Mildenberger, "Überlegungen zum Gottesbegriff," ZThK (1965), pp. 458ff.; H. Mühlen, *Der Heilige Geist als Person* (1963); W. Pannenberg, "Die Frage nach Gott," *Grundfragen systematischer Theologie* (1967), pp. 361ff.; E.T. *Basic Questions in Theology*, II (1970), pp. 201ff.; also "Der Gott der Hoffnung," *ibid.*, pp. 387ff.; E.T. pp. 234ff.; L. Pinomaa, "Der Zorn Gottes," *Zeitschrift für systematische Theologie*, 17 (1940), pp. 587ff.; E. Przywara, *Was ist Gott?* (1947); K. Rahner, "Theos im NT," *Schriften zur Theologie*, I (1962), pp. 91ff.; E.T. *Theological Investigations*, I (1961), pp. 79ff.; C. H. Ratschow, *Gott existiert* (1966); J. Ratzinger, *Einführung in das Christentum*, 5th ed. (1968), esp. pp. 73ff.; E.T. *Introduction to Christianity* (1969), esp. pp. 67ff.; J. A. T. Robinson,

Honest to God (1963); R. Röhricht, "Der Name 'Gott'" in B. Lohse and H. P. Schmidt, eds., *Leben angesichts des Todes* (1968) pp. 171ff.; J. P. Sartre, *L'être et le néant* (1943); E.T. *Being and Nothingness* (1956), pp. 557ff., esp. p. 566; M. Scheler, *Der Formalismus in der Ethik und die materiale Wertethik*, 4th ed. (1954), pp. 403ff.: also *Die Stellung des Menschen im Kosmos*, 2nd ed. (1947), pp. 84f.; E. Schillebeeckx, "Das nicht-begriffliche Erkenntnismoment in unserer Gotteserkenntnis nach Thomas v. Aquin," *Offenbarung und Theologie* (1965), pp. 225ff.; F. K. Schumann, *Der Gottesgedanke und der Zerfall der Moderne* (1929), esp. pp. 316ff.; H. Symanowski, *Post Bultmann locutum, Diskussion zwischen Gollwitzer und Braun* (1965); P. Tillich, *Systematic Theology*, I (1951), esp. pp. 163-289; also *The Courage to Be* (1952); cf. also the death of God theologians J. Altizer, W. Hamilton, P. van Buren, G. Vahanian. as listed in Volume I, pp. 223f.

IV

The Problem

In what we have said so far about revelation, a subject of revelation has always been presupposed. Implicit reference has been made to the author of revelation. To this degree revelation is always a historical event. To put it negatively, revelation cannot be understood in terms of a timeless state of revealedness, as some nuances of the word "truth" suggest to the degree that they present truth as disclosure. Revelation in the biblical sense refers instead to an act of disclosure and hence to a subject which performs this act.

What does it mean, however, to talk about God along these lines? Obviously today this question is often left unanswered. Even in the sphere of Christian theology an aversion against theism may be seen in many circles.[1] On the other hand there is still talk of the content of revelation. What is said is the relevant question. There are specific criteria, e.g., existential or ethical, by which to answer it. So long as the focus rests on this issue of the material validity of revelation or the kerygma, it seems unnecessary to assume that there is a specific subject of revelation. Hence the question of its author is superfluous. The validity of the Pythagorean theorem is not affected by the fact that Pythagoras was the first to state it and was thus its author. Concentration on the question of what is relevant for me or what applies unconditionally to me or what finds self-attestation in the data seems in fact to dispense with the question of the subject of these relevant things or these data. Moreover, the question of the subject might signify an attempt at reassurance. One's own criteria and judgment are perhaps felt to be inadequate in relation to these relevant things or data. There is a desire to

---

[1] Cf., e.g., Volume I, pp. 163f.

find assurance by authoritarian confirmation. We must ask about God himself or a God, so that a *Deus dixit* will lend certainty to that which is dubious. Appealing to metaphysical props of this kind is considered a sign of immaturity.

Hence even a theologian who calls himself a Christian may nowadays speak of the death of God without feeling that he has made a declaration of bankruptcy.[2] On the contrary, he does so with the sense of being liberated for adult confrontation with the thing at issue in the supposed *Deus dixit*. He thinks he sees that this can stand in its own right and by the insight which it confers. Validation by a *Deus dixit* is no longer needed.

The challenging of God does not rest merely on the argument that the kerygma can stand on its own evidence and that we no longer need to seek the subject or a divine guarantee. This argument joins hands with certain general feelings which may be found also in the spheres of science and our understanding of the world.

Like other spheres which are ruled by immanent autonomies, e.g., politics and economics, science finds no place for the hypothesis of God (Laplace). It fundamentally rejects transcendental interventions and the author of such interventions. In the more general religious and philosophical sphere, too, the concept of God is no longer self-evident in the way it used to be. "The Almighty who so wondrously reigneth" but who fails to act when he sees the suffering of the innocent[3] is now called in question. Camus expresses the mood of the age very accurately with his concept of the absurd.

We thus see a distinctive reversal of prior approaches. Whereas previously the existence of God was accepted without question and doubt arose as to the validity and function of the figure of Christ, the opposite is often true today. As a paradigm of human existence enclosed in finitude and ambivalence, Christ is accepted without question as self-evident, but God is set in the dubious light of a theistic preamble (Braun).[4] With all the greater urgency, then, the question arises what meaning it can have to talk about God, and especially about God as the subject of revelation.

The secular and theological questioning of God to which we have referred need not result, of course, in radical atheism. As church history often shows, it may also express itself in such a way that the concept of God is retained but a change of function takes place under cover of the concept. God comes to be understood as a cipher for something else. This something else which he first mediates ends up by dissolving and completely replacing him.

Thus God for Kant is a term for the unconditional validity of moral laws. In Tillich he is a symbol for being itself. Since he is universal essence it is a mistake to speak about God as existing or to ascribe individual being to him (*Systematic Theology*, I, pp. 235f.). He is the union of that which

---

[2] Cf. Volume I, pp. 221-311.
[3] Volume I, p. 225.
[4] Volume I, pp. 160ff.

splits up discursively into the antithesis of essence and existence. Tillich denies using God merely as a cipher for something else. He denies it quite expressly when he uses symbol instead of cipher. Symbol certainly implies that something else is in view and that the *de facto* form of the image or concept is "improper" (cf. K. D. Nörenberg, *Analogia imaginis* [1966]). In this regard Tillich says that the statement that God is being itself is not symbolical. It does not point beyond itself. It says what it means directly and properly (*op. cit.,* I, p. 238). Nevertheless, we must insist that Tillich views God as a cipher, as the very fact that he is a synonym of being shows. (This need not contradict what Tillich actually says. For him being itself is the real thing beyond which one cannot point. Of being itself we may naturally say that there is no "something else" for which it might have the significance of a mere cipher.) For Ernst Bloch, God as an objectified hypothesis (*Das Prinzip Hoffnung* [1959], p. 1408) represents the hope of the kingdom, which transcends all social utopias and signifies the ontological primacy of the future. This heteronomy immanent in the concept of God is radically abolished already, Bloch thinks, in the theology of the NT community, being replaced by the thing itself, i.e., the absolute future, which he describes as a dubious cipher. It may be said generally and basically that where the concept of God serves as a cipher, the thing of which it is a cipher eventually takes its place. To that degree it has only interim significance, and has done its work when people learn to read the secret writing and can thus integrate what is read into texts which they have been able to compare on their own.

In Lessing's *Education of the Human Race* this process is classically prefigured. God is an educator who makes himself superfluous, not just because people learn what he has imparted and hence do not need him any more, but also because they come to know his methods.

It thus takes on the rank of a thesis when the point is made that wherever God is a cipher and represents something other than himself, he becomes redundant and is set aside by this other after the act of reading the cipher. Where the term God tells us only what the world in principle can tell itself, and where it simply represents this word propaedeutically, at bottom it tells us nothing.

In the light of this, two questions call for consideration.

First, where are we to find that which is proper to God and which cannot be identified with anything else, not even with Tillich's being itself, so that the interchangeability of the concept of God with any other concept is blocked?

Second, what is the way between the Charybdis in which God means something but *only* means something, so that as a cipher he must be dissolved by what he means, and the Scylla in which he is declared to exist only in the form of a proposal and therefore of a doctrinaire premise? These are the problems we must now tackle.

V

The Modern Crisis in the Concept of God[1]

The scientific atheism to which we have referred and which rules out in principle transcendent direction or intervention, using instead the closed immanence of the world as a presupposition, has been given classical formulation by Bonhoeffer. In his view—and in this he follows Laplace—God is not to be thought of as the one who fills in the gaps in our imperfect knowledge. If we adopt this apologetic strategy, we condemn belief in God to a lingering death. For since the boundaries of knowledge are constantly being extended, God is constantly being pushed back. He is thus in continual retreat. Hence we ought to find God in what we know rather than in what we do not know, in solved questions rather than unsolved questions.[2] Faith in God needs to be thought out afresh on the assumption that man has now come of age and is autonomous. It needs to be adjusted to the new situation. It is absurd to try to show the world come of age that it cannot live without God as a tutor.[3] It has long since shown that it can do so very well, so that the attempt to demonstrate the opposite is reactionary. It resembles a mistaken effort to put an adult back in the age of puberty.[4]

Bonhoeffer's polemic is illuminating from the negative standpoint. It constitutes a powerful warning against trying to put belief in God in an asylum of ignorance or to confine it to borderline experiences. Nevertheless, its positive implications are not clear, and this lack of clarity can lead interpreters into all kinds of escapades. What does it mean to find God in what we know? What does it mean to approach even biblical materials from the standpoint of man come of age and to subject them to secular interpretation? In other words, how is God to be experienced positively in

---

[1] Cf. Volume I, Part II. Our deliberations there are now presupposed and in part recalled.
[2] *Widerstand und Ergebung*, 8th ed. (1958), pp. 210f.; *Letters and Papers from Prison*, 3rd ed. (1973), p. 311.
[3] *Ibid.*, p. 216; E.T. p. 326.   [4] *Ibid.*, p. 217; E.T. p. 327.

the new and changed situation? We are thus brought back to our original question: What does it mean to talk about God at all? What content or meaning resides in the term?

Bonhoeffer's negative thesis is right enough. A specific form of apologetic which began in the Enlightenment and reached its last great representative in Karl Heim has undoubtedly come to an irreversible end. This apologetic attempt to resist God's expulsion in the name of closed immanence rather than finding God a place and discovering indications of his presence within this immanence has been on the scene for a long time and has some notable achievements to its credit.

The climax of this apologetics was reached with the physico-theology of deism. Here the self-resting finitude of the world was seen under the sign of a teleology running through all being. To the logos of knowing corresponded the logos of being, which for its part was grounded in the thoughts and plans of God. The danger of an expulsion of God from this nexus and hence of his denial came here in the sphere of empirical detail. For in this sphere phenomena were constantly encountered which seemed to be either meaningless or superfluous and which thus challenged the teleological conception. What meaning could deep-sea fish have if man as the telos of creation never saw them? This was the question of the worthy Gottfried Ohnefurcht Richter in his weighty *Ichthyotheologie* (1754). Questions of this kind pressed the deistic apologetic hard. For if a single blatantly antiteleological phenomenon cropped up even in minutest detail, this meant that the divine world-logos was not in force. To that degree observation of such a phenomenon, no matter how trivial in itself, could lead to the bankruptcy of this theology. This is why the physico-theologians had to produce proofs of God from fish, minerals, and so forth. This is why they had to deal with exceptional phenomena. For it was these that threatened a crisis in teleology. Thus Richter was happy to be able to reply that deep-sea fish moved the sea with their tails and thus prevented it from becoming a fetid pond. They had, then, a productive function in creation.

This deistic defense against a retreat of God from immanence is distinguished from later apologetic efforts by its philosophical presupposition. Whereas today the cosmic nexus with its unbroken autonomy brings theology under assault and temptation, for deism the autonomy of the world (in the form of teleology) was the element of comfort which bore testimony to God and confirmed him in his immanent presence. In this case the accidental factor that cannot be integrated into the whole poses the theological threat. Apart from Richter's book cf. along these lines Barthold Heinrich Brockes, *Irdisches Vergnügen in Gott, bestehend in physikalisch- u. moralischen Gedichten*, 9 Books (1721ff.), and on this A. Brandi, *B. H. Brockes* (1878); Bernhard Nieuwetyts (Bernard Nieuwentijdt), *Rechter Gebrauch der Welt-Betrachtung; zur Erkentnis [sic] der Macht, Weisheit und Güte Gottes, auch Überzeugung der Atheisten und Ungläubigen* (1747) (translation of *Het regt gebruik der werelt beschouwingen*); Friedrich Christian Lesser, *Lithotheologie, das ist . . . geistliche Betrachtung der Steine, also abgefasst, das daraus die Allmacht, Weisheit, Güte und Gerechtigkeit des grossen Schöpfers gezeigt wird* (1735).

In distinction from this the nineteenth-century apologetic was in the main provoked by the timespan and regularity of evolution as this was brought to light by geological and biological research and brought to popular attention especially by Darwin and Haeckel. The apparent discrediting of the biblical creation story by science was probably not the primary cause of offense here, though this could, of course, take on independent rank, especially where the biblical view of the world was defended against Copernican astronomy. The central point of contention in this regard was Joshua's command to the sun to stand still (Joshua 10:12), and the Berlin pastor Gustav Knak in 1867 could reply to a synodal question whether he believed this with the affirmation that he did and that there could be no other view of the world than that of the Bible (cf. Wangemann, *Gustav Knak* [1879], 3rd ed. [1895], pp. 359ff.).

More basic if not unrelated was the blockade which a regular and progressive evolution seemed to set up against the creative and providential intervention of God. If, of course, this blockade was really in force and only the regularity of immanent forces held sway, then obviously God became irrelevant and his non-existence could be asserted. As regards the creation of the world in six days, the reply to the "challenge" was to view the six days as symbolical periods whose real form as geological ages did not alter in the slightest the fact that God spoke his creative "Let there be" (cf. A. Hengstenberg, *Buch des Glaubens* [1867], pp. 400ff.). Heinrich Kurtz went even further and tried to find in the biblical account a period of time which would allow for the geological ages. He did this by interposing a fall of angels between Genesis 1:1 and 1:2; this led to the *tohu vabohu* of v. 2 (Elert, *Kampf*, p. 230).

More serious, however, was the false apologetic switch in relation to the Darwinian theory of evolution. On this theory the regular continuum of evolution implied cosmic immanence and thus seemed to leave the Creator God without any function. In face of this no attempt was made to make the permanent significance of God intelligible in terms of the new situation. Instead an attack was launched on the idea of closed immanence under the rule of law. This meant, however, that the empirical data which as the basis of the evolutionary continuum supported the theory of descent had to be denied. This in turn meant engaging in scientific controversy, which could obviously be done only with the inadequate resources of the dilettante. Thus Hermann Werner, "Die Zweckmässigkeit in der Natur," *Zeitfragen des christlichen Volkslebens,* III, 4 (1878), called attention to phenomena which defied causal-mechanistic explanation, e.g., the peculiar properties of water which enable ice to float, or the relation between the height of land and the depth of the sea (cf. Elert, *Kampf*, pp. 235f.). It was not at all difficult for Darwinians to oppose to this obsession with teleology the factors which count against design and look odd or even fatal in a world which is viewed as God's creation, e.g., organs or organisms which serve no purpose and the processes of waste and destruction in nature.

Even the distorted popular view that Darwin was teaching a descent of man from monkeys did not induce contemporary apologists to attempt a Christian anthropology which would make the basic difference between man and animals its major theme. Instead we find once again an empirico-immanent disputing of the facts and a preoccupation with the "missing link" in the evolutionary chain from animals to man, the idea being that this would scientifically disprove the fateful continuum.

All such apologies involve both improper means and improper objects. They cannot bring out what is distinctive in God, for they do not transcend the level of the empirical sciences. They are unable for this reason to bear witness to transcendence. They themselves move only on the empirical level and hence they remain within the jurisdiction of the opponent whom they are fighting.

While nineteenth-century apologetics, faced by modern science,[5] was unready to accept the thesis of a closed system of natural forces, while it attempted, then, to find discontinuities in which it could locate God and his working, the situation underwent a basic change. What Bonhoeffer has said along these lines simply represents a pointed formulation of theses which describe the theological understanding of the world before and after him and to which one may ascribe the rank of a common opinion.

As distinct from nineteenth-century apologetics, self-resting finitude (Tillich) now forms the starting-point for almost all theological reflection not only in the biblical sphere but also in dogmatics and ethics.[6] Hence it can no longer be an aim of theology to contest the heuristic principle underlying all science or to break open the cosmic nexus in order to find a place for God. Gogarten has provided this new approach of theology with a special nuance by claiming that Christianity itself has engendered secularization and with it the thesis of closed immanence.[7]

Making common cause against the apologetic attempt to find traces of God and places for him within immanence, Karl Barth has rejected the idea that natural man may find any demonstrable point of contact for faith in reality.[8] Already in his *Epistle to the Romans* he espouses the view that all talk about God outside Christianity is a dubious form of religion, i.e.,

---

[5] We find the same procedure in relation to history, e.g., when in face of the disputing of miracles, especially after D. F. Strauss, no fundamental consideration was given to the nature of miracles but instead an attempt was made to establish the historical reliability of the accounts of miracles, especially the resurrection stories; cf. F. L. Steinmeyer, *Apologetische Beiträge* (1866ff.); on this whole subject cf. the chapter "Die Apologetik als Versuch zur Rettung der Synthese" in Elert, *Kampf*, pp. 214ff.

[6] On ethics cf. the discussion listed in ThE, III, General Index, p. 941 under "Eigengesetzlichkeit."

[7] Cf. Volume I, pp. 326ff.

[8] Cf. his *Nein* in answer to E. Brunner, ThEx, No. 14 (1934); *Natural Theology* (1946).

of human self-deification. In Christian proclamation the one who is addressed is man self-enclosed in immanence and hence "god-less" in the full sense of the term. This means that there can be no preliminary apologetic field which can serve as the site for a first act which will break the bonds of immanence by argument and hence create in the hearer the presupposition of his ability to hear.

In Bultmann's hermeneutics the immanentist presupposition of modern science and history is the decisive theological premise. It constitutes the criterion which enables him to distinguish between that which is kerygmatically relevant on the one side and historically conditioned statements about transcendent interventions, miracles, and mythologoumena on the other. Rejection of all efforts to indicate the presence of God and his revelation in historical immanence leads Bultmann to the conclusion that not only is the historical facticity of what happened a matter of indifference, so that critical erasures of gospel records do not affect the relation between the kerygma and faith, but that to insist on the historical accuracy of the records is indeed to provide an illegitimate support for faith.

In the same sense G. Ebeling finds the significance of historical research, which rests on the principle of immanence, in the smashing of all the supposed historical assurances which make the decision of faith dispensable. He thus set it in immediate connection with the reformation doctrine of justification:[9] "As everywhere in reformation theology, so here in relation to history the Yes to uncertainty is simply the reverse side of the assurance of salvation *sola fide.*"[10] It is highly paradoxical that an attempt is made here to become uncertain and hence to achieve the exact opposite of what research is all about.[11]

Even if faith is made so uncertain that it regards any historical demonstration of its object as an illicit prop and hence as unbelief, this trend of thought shows at least how radical a break has been made with earlier apologetics. God is now no longer inserted into laboriously opened rents, gaps, and discontinuities in observable immanence. No demonstrable places are sought for God in the world, whether in nature or history. A closed world-continuum is accepted along the lines of the working hypothesis of science and the modern sense of things. This is made the starting-point of theological thought. Modified in this way, the question of God becomes the question whether and how far that which is attested concerning him in the Bible has unconditional relevance for man enclosed in his immanence. Does

---

[9] "Die Bedeutung der historisch-kritischen Methode für die protestantische Theologie," *Wort und Glaube* (1960), pp. 1ff., esp. 43ff.; E.T. *Word and Faith* (1963), pp. 17ff., esp. 55ff.

[10] *Ibid.,* p. 45; E.T. p. 57.

[11] On this cf. E. Reisner, "Hermeneutik und historische Vernunft," ZThK (1952), p. 233; H. Diem, *Dogmatik,* II (1952), pp. 83f.

it change his understanding of himself, summon him to decision, and qualify his existence?[12]

We ask, however, whether the absolute paradox of this nondemonstrability can really become a ground of faith. Does not faith become here a leap in the void in response to a random call? And if I do really hear in the no-man's-land of history a voice which cannot be identified as to time or space, but which summons me and is unconditionally relevant to me, may not that which I receive be expressed in other terms, e.g., as a secular philosophy of existence or a Socratic appeal, so that it belongs to immanence and can be integrated into it? But if so, may it not and must it not be a matter of indifference what voice speaks here or even whether it speaks at all? What this alleged voice says might just as well be spoken by man himself.[13] Can faith really be grounded thus? Can it have a basis of such sort that it decides for an offense which stands outside, and unrelated to, all that affects man in his immanence? For a plenitude of factors affects him here: the sequence of the generations, sexual love, hunger and anxiety, hope and longing, the threat and the endowment of nature, human communication and human enmity, the justice and injustice of human structures, and much else. Can that which affects me unconditionally be unrelated to that which also affects me even if only conditionally? Without such a relation would we not have a new Docetism, a ghostly sham-corporeality of that which seems to address me kerygmatically but calls me away from any reference to immanent reality? Is not that an absolute nonhistoricity which reduces man to his individual and even solipsistic existence and thus makes the question of God irrelevant compared to the interweaving of existence into the natural *bios* and historical structures?[14]

One thing is sure. The relevance of the question of God can be indicated only by seeing God, the one who affects me unconditionally, in a relation, however this be defined, to that which affects me conditionally. Provisionally it may be left open whether the two forms of "affects me" are understood along the lines of an analogy, whether the "unconditionally" is viewed as a quantitative enhancement of the "conditionally" or whether it is distin-

---

[12] ". . . In what does this faith believe when all historical ground has been cut away from under it? It believes in the kerygma which encounters it in the gospel, or, more accurately, in encounter with the kerygma and in face of its absolute nondemonstrability it decides against the offense and for the faith which qualifies existence afresh" (Diem, *op. cit.,* p. 84).

[13] Cf. the debate with Bultmann in Volume I, pp. 55-65, 68ff., 110ff. Along these lines K. Jaspers, in a discussion with the author, suggested that the Christian element in Kierkegaard, as in Lessing's understanding of revelation, does not point to a basis outside the self or the world but is to be understood as merely a cipher for a general understanding of existence, and to that extent has an existentialist-philosophical character.

[14] Cf. the critical words of O. F. Bollnow to the effect that before the unconditional radiance of one's own existence the whole world sinks into a background devoid of meaning ("Existenzphilosophie," *Systematische Philosophie* [1942], p. 356).

guished from it qualitatively and is perhaps even to be understood as *totaliter aliter*. At this stage in our train of thought the only important thing is the postulate that there has to be a connection beween the two forms if God is not to be levelled down to docetic irrelevance. The objection to a certain form of theism, which pushes God off into transcendence and leaves him unconnected with all that belongs to this world, so that he is not the basis of a "conviction" but only a doctrinaire authority (as a given)—this objection is right negatively when it criticizes the absolute discontinuity in which the God of this theism stands to the phenomena of immanence. The resultant talk of the death of God, i.e., of his complete irrelevance, overshoots the mark, of course, for only the God of this type of theism is dead, only a questionable image or concept of God dies.[15]

The idea that there has to be a relation between what affects me unconditionally and what affects me conditionally if credible witness is to be borne to God's immanence forms the basis of Tillich's principle of correlation.[16] Here, however, the word "relation" is not used in the sense suggested above. It is limited to the references posited in Tillich's ontology. Thus God, as we have pointed out already in another connection,[17] is presented as the infinite power of being when seen in his correlation with the threat of non-being that lies in existence. He is presented as the basis of courage when set in relation to anxiety as awareness of finitude. Tillich is concerned, then, to bring out the way in which the concept of God actualizes itself for us so that it affects me and overcomes its fatal role as a purely doctrinaire assertion. Is it adequate, however, to restrict these actualizing relations to existential things such as anxiety, the threat of non-being, the experience of absurdity, and so forth? Should not these references to the question of God be extended to historical structures such as politics, economics, and society if God, or the concept of God, is to affect man in the complex concreteness of his existence and not just in his inner life? In this sense it ought to be possible to consider "theo"-logically the problem of transplants of organs, the artificial prolongation of life, the right of political resistance, the death penalty, partnership in industrial management, the problem of political systems, and many other things, showing that the question of God is competent in these areas too. If we cannot make it clear that historical structures have their center in the *humanum* and that human existence as thus structured experiences the relevance of God in all its dimensions, then we shall always remain under the jurisdiction of theistic Docetism.

How are we to show this aspect of the relevance of God, however, if we do not demand a theologizing of the sciences and historical structures and are not so bold as to reverse the universal secular axiom, i.e., the axiom

---

[15] Cf. the chapter on the death of God in Volume I, pp. 221ff.
[16] *Systematic Theology*, I, p. 61; cf. Volume I, pp. 47ff.
[17] Chapter III, 1.

according to which knowledge and mastery of the world can be achieved only on the presupposition that we start with self-enclosed immanence?[18] If we are not prepared for this, what is the meaning of the actuality of the concept of God?

From another angle, then, there arises the repeated question what it can mean to talk about God under the conditions mentioned.

Basic and theoretical acknowledgment of the idea just presented, that the concept of God finds actualization only in reference to the other actualities of existence, has hardly ever been contested even though for the most part this acknowledgment is only proclaimed in a general way or is subjected to existential restriction. E. Brunner has it within the framework of his well-known idea of a point of contact, P. Althaus in his notion of primal revelation, R. Bultmann in his theory of pre-understanding in virtue of which philosophy too is aware of the ambiguity and inauthenticity of existence (cf. the essay "Das Problem der 'natürlichen Theologie' " in GV, I, pp. 297f., 311; E.T. pp. 316., 329.). Even Barth in his *Epistle to the Romans,* where one would least expect it, points to connections of this kind (cf. W. Pannenberg, *Grundfragen systematischer Theologie,* pp. 366f.; E.T. *Basic Questions,* II, pp. 207.).

---

[18] The author has attempted an interpretation of the world along these lines in his ThE. What we are thinking out *here* is the possibility of this attempt from the special standpoint of the concept of God.

VI

Negative and Positive Aspects of the Idea of God

Having presented the problem, we must now list on the one side what the question of God cannot mean (the negative aspect) and on the other side what it can only mean (the positive aspect).

1. THE NEGATIVE ASPECT

1. The question of God is wrongly put if one asks about God along the lines of a purely traditional and received theism. In this case the fact of God is understood as given in advance, and the question of God can only be that of what we are to hold or believe about him in terms of common sense. Since the question of God as thus posed does not find actualization in personal encounter, in personal hearing and experience of the self-declaration of God, an answer to its theistic form is possible only as one takes over from others not only the idea of God but also a more precise description of his nature. The sources from which one receives these are tradition and a Christian background. There thus arises the host of Christian fellow-travellers, of nominal Christians, of those who are formally baptized, of conformists. The reasons for fringe membership may be the conformism which according to the law of least resistance simply goes along with a traditional trend and is equally prepared to abandon it at once if the wind changes. Or it may be a pragmatism which without the least personal concern for the question of God regards the respecting of religious beliefs and customs as useful, since with their help, it is calculated, one can exercise power, establish authority, and make men amenable to rule. Along these lines the postulate can be adopted that religion must be upheld among the people.

The pragmatic and conformist misunderstandings of the question of God rest on the presupposition that it does not apply existentially and will do so all the less the more its purpose is perceived.[1] Hence the religion bound up with this idea of God can be manipulated pragmatically, and it will always give rise to nominal Christianity and will constantly lose credibility as a result. The situation of the national church in secularized society offers a gruesome model.

2. The question of God is wrongly put if it does not imply the questions which are our own questions, i.e., when it is put in terms of what was once an actual question: How may I find a gracious God? or when it arises out of experiences of reality which are no longer our own experiences.

This applies in the case of the orthodox doctrine of general revelation.[2] The modern experience of reality as it finds expression in philosophy and poetry is much too ambivalent, and much too drastically marked by the sense of absurdity, to be either ready or able to trace or recognize the footprints of God in the sphere of natural or historical experience. Thus Camus has the physician Rieux say that he could not forgive God for letting innocent children suffer. Death of God theology says that no one after Auschwitz can sing "who so wondrously reigneth." Mistaken though this statement may be, it is grounded in the experience of the indetectability and absence of God. When faith in God persists in face of this experience of reality, and finds traces of God retrospectively after the manner of the analogy of faith, it is always based on original and personal experiences of God and is not fashioned out of an existing experience of reality, at any rate in the sense that this experience carries with it traces or evident indications of God. Borderline experiences of this kind may well actualize the *theme* of the God question. Because of their ambivalence, however, it is an open question whether they will result in acceptance or rejection, in prayer or in cursing, or even in pure indifference.[3]

When we made the demand earlier that there must be correspondence between that which affects us unconditionally and that which affects us conditionally if the relevance of God is to be perspicuous, this correspondence cannot be constructed in such a way as to produce a natural theology or to make God a deduction from our experience of reality. As we stated in the first chapter, faith is not just faith in but also faith against. It defies the elements in natural experience which seem to constitute a refutation of God. This is why the problem of theodicy that finds expression in Psalm 73:1ff. and Psalm 77:19 stands closer to the modern relation between encounter with God and the experience of reality than does the natural theology of orthodoxy.

3. The question of God is wrongly put if God is equated with a dimen-

---

[1] The (varied) interpretation of religion as the discovery of a purpose, in Feuerbach, Nietzsche, and Marx, shows to what extent disinterest increases with the degree of perception, even to the point of polemical alienation.

[2] Cf. the definition of Calov in *System. Vit.*, according to which general or natural revelation is through the light of nature and the effects of God visible in the natural realm; cf. C. A. Hase, *Hutterus redivivus,* 5th ed. (1842), p. 61.

[3] Cf. Volume I, pp. 227f.

sion of being as its ground. This happens when he is interpreted as the author of divine commands (Kant) or as a cipher for the unconditionality of moral duty. In such cases he can claim only interim validity, which is contrary to the divine majesty. He is rendered superfluous by the awakened sense of autonomy. God is similarly equated with a dimension of being when he is regarded as the basis of utopian hope (Bloch) or the fulfilment and unity of history (Tillich).

Whenever the unconditioned is identified with something conditioned, no matter how eminent, the conditioned emancipates itself as an idea which can be concocted of itself and which can thus be interpreted atheistically, i.e., without the help of the hypothesis of God. A vacuum is then left by the evacuation of the hypothesis of God.[4] God (in distinction from a mere hypothesis of God) obviously transcends the possibilities of a religion which arises out of the sacral and numinous transfiguration of partial spheres of life. When something creaturely is identified with the Creator, we do not arrive at God but at an idol representing deified reality. The idol, however, is overtaken by the twilight of the gods when the deified dimension of reality shows itself to be a factor with its own specific worth, when it is seen to be something which can stand alone in its own immanent strength and which does not need that numinous enhancement. Apollo must vanish from the scene when the knowledge and wisdom he seemed to give become autarchous. The Delphic oracle is rendered superfluous when the future can be calculated rationally and can even become the subject of a special study.

4. The question of God is wrongly put, finally, when the *question* of God implied in human existence is changed into an *answer* according to the analysis in Romans 1:18ff. The question of God implied in human existence means that man becomes an open question to himself. He constantly faces the problem why he is here, what will become of him, and what he will make of himself. In distinction from the animal, man is not a being whose entelechy develops automativally out of itself.[5] On the contrary, he must inquire into his destiny. He is thus a question to himself. He must gain (or venture) the answer or he may miss it.[6] To this degree man is always an open possibility. Fulfilment of this possibility can never be fully presupposed in a given form. Man's identity is not simply there in such a way that it can be read off in a given form of existence.[7]

The same applies to humanity in general. The goal of hope in which it reaches identity with its destiny coincides directly neither with what has been attained in the present nor with what is projected for the future. What

---

[4] Bloch, *op. cit.*, p. 1529.

[5] Cf. Schiller's *Über Anmut und Wurde* (1793). Schiller argues that in animals and plants nature directs as well as grants the determination but in man it only grants it and leaves the fulfilment to man himself.

[6] Cf. Heidegger's discussion in *Sein und Zeit* and our own debate with Gehlen and Schelsky in Volume I, pp. 253f.

[7] Max Frisch constantly centers on this questions of identity in his journals and poems.

has been or can be attained can in principle be surpassed like any social utopia. This is true even of an attained classless society.[8] Hence man is a being which in principle reaches out beyond what he has become and now is. His identity remains a hope. He is constantly mounting up to it as something which is not yet here, which has always still to come in its fulness.[9] The principial "not yet" of man bears the implication that he basically transcends himself.

If God is regarded as the representative of this transcendence—and we may very provisionally and formally say that Christian proclamation sees him in this framework—this means that he encounters us within our natural consciousness as the object of this question about ourselves, as the basis of questioning of our state. Hence it comes about that when God encounters us truly in his self-declaration he "uncovers"[10] the questionability of human existence, radicalizes it in the law, and presents himself as the answer to it. Since God, however, is not just a cipher for the answer to this question which is ourselves, since he does not simply enter in as the postulate of an answer—such a postulate would always be fashioned in advance by the constellation of the question—and since he uncovers and radicalizes the question which is ourselves in a way that we ourselves cannot do, the question which is ourselves is always an open question within the sphere of our natural horizon. It even remains a question that we cannot understand and that withholds its basis from us. Only the answer, which is God, establishes the question, i.e., gives it its basis.

Along these lines the question of God is wrongly put when it thinks it is itself capable of an answer, and when it forestalls its own radicalizing with this answer, thus posing itself as a purely provisional and limited question. Paul interprets idolatry from this standpoint in Romans 1:18ff.

God is "manifest" to the Gentiles, and is so in answer to the question contained in the works (*poiêmata,* v. 20) of creation, including man himself. This question, however, is not an "open" one. It has been answered in advance. Hence it cannot reach the depths suggested by it. It is answered in such a way that the creature "man" does not stand by that which transcends it and indeed raises the question for it. This creature resists the Creator and denies God. It does so by not being ready to understand itself in its creatureliness. It will not give God praise and thanksgiving (v. 21). It refuses to acknowledge the one from whom it receives its identity, who gives it its destiny, from whom and to whom it "is." Instead man tries to go it alone. He curves in upon himself. He gives to the question posed in him, the question which he himself is, the answer which lies along the line and within the framework of the question perceived. This answer is not God. It is the idol, the likeness (*homoíōma,* v. 23), the exaltation of the creaturely in the form of "birds, four-footed beasts, and creeping things."

---

[8] Bloch, *op. cit.,* pp. 1410-1413.
[9] Sartre, *op. cit.,* p. 128.
[10] So the earlier Barth in *Christliche Dogmatik* (1927), p. 74.

Man, then, does not expect an answer which will transcend the question, which will surprise him as something unexpected, as the Wholly Other, and which he could not give himself and thereby set himself in a new light. He makes his own reply, and it is one that rivets and secures him in his existence thus far, in his old existence. God does not reach him in the form of the counter-question: "Adam, where art thou?" which would radicalize his questionability and in the light of the answer lay bare its basis. He reaches him in masked and distorted form as the idol, as a bit of man's own creaturely reality, which upholds, confirms, and secures him.

God himself, however, remains outside this creature-idol relation. The religion which arises in this manner is the anamnesis of a question which is posed by the true God of human existence but which has been falsified. It has been falsified because man has given the answer of his own choosing to his questionability and because he has missed the point of the questionability in so doing, namely, that it was designed to make him open to insight into its basis and to the answer which was already present, and was meant to be given him, in this basis. Instead, man has imprisoned himself in himself. He has desired to be alone with himself and creation. He has not been ready to let his questionability become a possible calling in question by confrontation with the living God who as Creator has set him in existence and who thus has a total claim to him. Deified creatures, in contrast, do not call him in question. They are flesh of his flesh and spirit of his spirit. The identical thing cannot call itself in question. Commanding and judging can come only from outside, from that which is transcendent. To this, however, man has refused praise and thanksgiving. He has thus negated it as that which is above himself and everything creaturely.

God himself, however, remains outside the creature-idol relation inasmuch as he gives up (*parédōken,* vv. 24, 26) the man who has falsified his questionability to the decision which he has made for himself. He lets him bear the consequences of the falsified question. He delivers him up to the fateful answer by which he has ruined the openness of this question (vv. 24ff.). The perversion of the vertical relation which causes an exchanging of Creator and creature brings about a horizontal perversion, namely, a chaotic confusion of the orders of the world when they rest upon themselves and are detached from the basis which transcends and sustains them.

Thus God remains the answer to the falsified question even when he yields, lets loose, and retires.[11] He remains this answer even in the form of the wrath of God.[12] He retains the sovereignty of one who even in silent indulgence controls that to which he gives free rein and then gives it his meaning and answer, namely, the meaning and answer of judgment. God remains outside the creature-idol relation even as he lets it take place as Lord and Judge, and thereby transcends it.

God, then, is the answer to the question contained in human existence

---

[11] Cf. Léon Bloy's phrase: "Dieu se retire" (Volume I, pp. 231, 318).

[12] *Orgḗ theoú,* 1:18.

in a basic way and not in such sort that this answer is identical to the one that man himself gives, be it ever so pious or religious. Indeed, since man's own answer conceals his questionability and shuts him off from the appointed openness, it intensifies, if one might put it thus, the transcendence of God, for this becomes a withdrawn transcendence which is no longer manifest to man but veiled from him.[13]

In this case, then, the question of God is wrongly put insofar as the question of God contained in human existence is changed into an answer and is thus suppressed as a pure "question."

Perhaps the theological value of Camus lies in the fact that he wishes to abide in answerless openness and prefers absurdity to sneaking through to an answer which supposedly makes sense of things. Does this mean that Camus breaks solidarity with the mass of men and thus escapes the verdict of Romans 1:18ff.? Might it not rather be that the absurdity which first comes up as a necessity is secretly changed into a virtue, a new invention of meaning in the negative mood, so that we again have an answer in highly dialectical form? This consideration may at least be allowed as an expression of uncertainty.

2. THE POSITIVE ASPECT

This aspect, and therewith the legitimate question of God, is achieved when the understanding of what I mean by the word "God" is certainly related to the given realities or even the deficiencies of human existence but when, far from being exhausted by these, it also transcends them. The fact that the reality denoted by "God" cannot be confined to any immanent relation is emphasized even by the concept of analogy in Roman Catholic theology. Thus the Fourth Lateran Council points out that in the relation between Creator and creature dissimilarity, i.e., transcendent otherness, always preponderates over similarity.[14]

Since there can be no thoroughgoing analogy between the question of the unconditional that is contained in human existence and the answer to this question which is denoted by the word "God," it is impossible to equate God with answers whose material consists in creaturely references, e.g., to fellow-humanity or to historical laws such as are found in Schiller's statement that world history is world judgment or in Hegel's dialectic of history. If this is done, the referent of the likeness is absolutized and God becomes a mere cipher for what the creature can itself draw out of the relation of immanence.

Some illustrations will now help us to see why the reality that we call "God" transcends all immanent relations, can never be identical with them, and, unlike them, can never be objectified.

---

[13] *Tó gnōstón toú theoú phanerón*, 1:19.
[14] Cf. Denz., 432; G. Söhngen, *Die Einheit in der Theologie* (1952), p. 237; E. Przywara, *Religionsphilosophie katholischer Theologie* (1927), p. 23.

a. God and Meaning[15]

If one asks after God in the expectation of finding in him the point where the riddles, contradictions, and nonsensicalities of history, and therewith our own existence, are resolved, it is a mistake[16] to see in God merely a representation of this sought-after meaning and in the kingdom of God a mere representation of the sought-after unity and coincidence of the historical process, or, in other words, the being which embraces all divergent being. Unity of this kind can also be thought of as an idea, as in Hegel's concept of reason in history. I may even make the idea of unity a heuristic viewpoint for my own contemplation of history and with the help of it try to gain control of the empirical world.[17] These ideas may not be demonstrable empirically. They may work as functional categories of the mind. Or, like Kant's idea of the supreme good, they may be the object of eschatological hope. Nevertheless, these ideas, including that of the unity of history, still come under the autarchy of reason and hence they do not need the hypothesis "God." If the word "God" adds something of its own and is not just a synonym of the unity of history and its basis of meaning, this can only mean that while it is these "too" it adds something more and different and is not exhausted by them.

But what is this extra element and how can we show its relevance? How can I be made to understand that this extra element is not just a dispensable mythical husk of which the kernel is the enclosed idea, e.g., that of unity, and hence a possession of reason?

The idea of a unity of history, of a basis of meaning, no matter whether this idea be a regulative idea of reason or a utopian idea such as that of a classless society, takes from man what we may call his nondefinability. Defining that unity of history, I deny man's openness to historical possibility and integrate him into the process of history as the bearer of a necessary and definable function. Man is no longer one who grasps himself but one who is grasped by the goal of history. Instead of deciding for himself, and being himself in the venture of decision, decision is made concerning him. He knows what he is and will be. As the Hegelian-Marxist model has it, his freedom is no more than insight into this necessity. One might add that this entails depersonalizing. We are justified in saying this, since the concept of person represents the openness of the human possibility and therefore man's destiny of grasping himself in freedom.

We are thus faced by a dilemma.

On the one hand, to be able to exist historically, we must ask about the

---

[15] Cf. Chapter III, 2 on life, meaning, and truth in connection with the concept of revelation.

[16] We have in mind the thesis of Tillich that "if the notion of the Kingdom of God appears in correlation with the riddle of our historical existence it must be called the meaning, fulfilment, and unity of history" (*Systematic Theology*, I, p. 64).

[17] We are using "ideas" here in the sense of Kant's transcendental regulative judgments which are contained in the unity of the mind.

unity and meaning of history so that we may orient and shape ourselves thereby and not be betrayed into a chaotic and formless nexus in which we simply move as helpless objects.[18] On the other hand, an answer to the question as posed thus sets us in a state in which we are robbed of the presuppositions on which we posed the question of unity and meaning. For it robs us of the possibility of understanding human existence as an open, personal existence which involves decision.

The very thing in the Word of God that goes beyond the unity and meaning of history and cannot be imprisoned in these concepts opens up for us a meaning of history which does not make us an impersonal function but sustains us in the unconditionality and openness of our history.

We are not definable inasmuch as "the world knoweth us not, because it knew him not" (1 John 3:1). We exist as a relation to God. We thus resist definability as God does. Only God himself defines us. We are known in him (1 Corinthians 13:12). Hence "it doth not yet appear what we shall be" (1 John 3:2). Our life "is hid with Christ in God. When Christ, who is our life, shall appear, then shall ye also (in that which you truly are) appear with him in glory" (Colossians 3:3f.; cf. Philippians 3:21).

That it has not yet appeared what we shall be, that our Now is still hidden as regards its Whither, proves that we stand before an open possibility and that we cannot be defined, and robbed of our openness, by the necessity of a process in which we exist as mere elements and functions. The relation which defines us is not to an immanent entity, whether it be nature, above which we lift up ourselves, or society, of which we seek to be useful members, or an idea, for whose realization we expend ourselves. A relation of this type makes us a mere function. It makes us the means to an end. It deprives us of our unconditionality.[19] The unconditionality of man is maintained only when he himself is related to the unconditional, which is not exhausted by any immanent connection even though it be present in this and indeed sustains it. Only in relation to the unconditional which we call God does man's existence attain to the "infinite reality" of which Kierkeguard speaks.

Caution is naturally demanded here. For the concept of the unconditional which we have introduced and which prevents the word "God" from having a purely immanent reference, although it obviously has a correlation to everything immanent, can again for its part become a synonym for the word "God," so that it exhausts this term and thus makes it interchangeable and replaceable. The God in mind would then be, in Pascal's phrase, the God of the philosophers, the logos structure of the cosmic nexus which upholds and conditions all occurrence as its basis of unity, while itself remaining

---

[18] Cf. Theodor Lessing, *Die Geschichte als Sinngebung des Sinnlosen,* 4th ed. (1927).

[19] On human existence as a relation cf. ThE, I, § 690ff.; E.T. I, pp. 147ff.; II, 1, § 1168ff., 1251ff.; and the quotation from Kierkegaard's *Sickness Unto Death* in ThE, I, § 460; E.T. I, pp. 167f.

unconditioned. In this way we should be brought face to face with the same calamity as we noted earlier. The idea "God" would merge into another entity, in this case the unconditioned, and could be correspondingly dissolved by it.

The statement "it doth not yet appear what we shall be" contains, however, the antidote to this equation of God with the philosophical idea of the world logos or the unconditioned. It does so in two respects.

First, the unconditioned one (not the unconditioned) knows who we are. He is not what we know or can think of as a postulate. He is the one who knows us and thinks of us. He knows us in love and is opened up to us in freedom. Unlike the interchangeable God of the philosophers, God is not the unconditional world logos who simply upholds the cosmic nexus, holds it together, and functions in it as a coincidence of opposites. He is understanding, love, and freedom. He thus stands over against us as a person.[20] This means that with the word "God" something is said which cannot be comprised within the idea of the unconditioned. It tells us that the unconditioned one, in distinction from what we call the unconditioned, does not degrade creaturely existence into something conditioned but confers on it the dignity of partnership. He who loves creates his image (Genesis 1:26f.) and counterpart. In distinction from stars, plants, and animals, which are simply objects of his "Let there be," man is called to the freedom of partnership. He is addressed as Thou and given commands and goals (Genesis 1:28f.; 3:3, 9). He is given the destiny of a subject which can decide between obedience and disobedience, which can stay in covenant with God or leave the covenant, which can fulfil its destiny or fail to do so.

If God is understanding, love, and freedom, the background and basis of the world is not the unconditioned but a person who grants personality, who does not just condition but wills unconditionally, who does not integrate man as an element into the cosmic nexus and subject him to its mediacy but calls him out and grants him the immediacy to itself that the God of the philosophers denies, substituting for it the mediacy of a definable function.

What we have thus called the transcendent element in the word "God," the element in it which also escapes synonymity with the unconditioned, means that in the word "God" we can see the coincidence of antitheses which reflection acting on its own has to regard as irreconcilable.

For with it we express the fact that God is to be understood both as the meaning and unity of the cosmic process and also as the one who sustains human existence in its openness. "It does not yet appear what we shall be," but we shall know it "as we are known by him."[21]

Again, if the word "God" means that the background and basis of the

---

[20] We shall deal later with the concept of person in relation to God.
[21] Cf. also the chapter "Der Gott des Glaubens und der Gott der Philosophen" in Ratzinger's *Einführung*, pp. 103ff., esp. p. 122; E.T. pp. 94ff., esp. pp. 111f.

world is understanding, love, and freedom, this also implies that the meaning and unity of the cosmic process are indeed provided in God, so that he is in fact the point where what is divergent coincides, and is consequently unconditioned, but that they cannot be objectified in a universal formula. Being and occurrence as they concretely encounter me cannot be expressed in a formula which is under my control. As we have seen, the mark of the biblical experience of God and the world is precisely the fact that, e.g., suffering Job fails in every attempt to construct such a formula or to live and think in the name of the premise that the course of the world is just and hence doing of the right will be rewarded (Job 1:8ff.). Similarly the poet of Psalm 73 does not succeed in harmonizing the contradictions of the world which lie in the fact that the wicked triumph and the righteous go under. The failure to achieve such a formula, and the absence or rejection of God when he is identified with it, make the course of the world appear to be absurd and meaningless to human cognition, or at the very least inscrutable and unfathomable. In spite of this appearance and the failure of our cognition, however, the meaningfulness of the ground of the world is not disputed here. Noetic renunciation of sensory knowledge goes hand in hand with the confession of faith that ontically there is meaning in the world. The impossibility of making world occurrence intelligible by bringing it under a formula and establishing the statement: "Because . . . therefore this is so and this happens"—this impossibility is accompanied by the confession of the righteous: "Nevertheless I am continually with thee" (Psalm 73:23).

How is this hiatus to be explained?

If the background and basis of being that we call "God" is understanding, love, and freedom, then knowledge and meaning are hidden here and in him. Not we alone are known; meaning is known too. We may thus recall, against a wider horizon, a statement we made earlier. We ourselves do not know meaning; those who think they do, as we have seen, dissolve the personal element in the necessity of processes and make it a factor in them. We do not know meaning; we believe in him who knows it.

This cannot simply imply that for knowledge of meaning we substitute (mere) belief in meaning. If this were so, faith would be the provisional pre-stage of knowledge. Faith, then, would be understood, not as trust, but as mere conjecture and therewith as deficient knowledge. What we really mean by "God" is that we stand to him, as the one who understands and loves, in a relation of trust, and that this trust implies the assurance that knowledge of the meaning that is unknown to us is hidden and safe in him. The one who understands and loves is the one who calls what is not into being (Romans 4:17) and thus gives shape to his thoughts in it. Because these thoughts are his and not ours, because they are higher than our thoughts and different from them (Isaiah 55:8), we trust that thoughts (and not nonsensicalities) rule the world—but not our thoughts. Hence there is no reason in history if we mean that our reason participates in it and, in Hegel's phrase, the finite spirit knows its knowledge as the absolute spirit.[22] Just because another knows and thinks here, we have access to this thought and knowledge by way of trust in their subject, by way of trust in this other.

It might be suspected that in this interpretation of the word "God" an attempt is being made to overcome a specific difficulty of thought with the help of more or less refined speculation. We are referring to the problem which consists in the fact that on the one hand we have to put the question of the unity and meaning of the world for the sake of our personality but that on the other hand we eliminate this personality if we think we have found an answer to the question in some cosmic formula, i.e., a materialistic or idealistic or similar answer. Might it not be that the idea of God is an attempt to reconcile what seems to be irreconcilable?

This suspicion would be confirmed if the idea of God arose in an attempt at interpretation of the world, or even of human existence, as a supporting theoretical construction. All that interpretative exertions of this kind can ever produce is the God of the philosophers, i.e., the God who does not transcend the defined idea of the basis of the world but merges into this idea. In contrast, our own attempt to interpret the word "God" in terms of the meaning and unity of world occurrence is made with reference to the God of the Bible, who is basically different from that idea.

If we describe this God by such terms as understanding, love, and freedom in order to emphasize the aspects which distinguish him from the God of the philosophers, this already suggests that the God who is understood thus has not arisen as the regulative idea in an interpretation of the world. But how, then, do we come to have faith in this God?

We shall have to give a more detailed answer to this question in our discussions of the name and the person of God. For the moment we may provisionally reply as follows.

This faith arises through the immediacy and evidence of the self-disclosure that we call "revelation." God makes himself known in his glory (Exodus 33:12ff.). He manifests himself by name at the burning bush (Exodus 3:13ff.). He appears in the form of Christ and makes him his mirror (Luther). Whenever the Bible speaks of this God, he discloses himself as the one who addresses man and the cosmos in every dimension. We know this only from the prior encounter. Hence all the reflections with whose help we interpret world occurrence and our own existence according to the light thus manifested[23] are triggered by this prior encounter and are definitely subsidiary to it. Hence Israel understands its history as a series of experiences of God. In the perplexities of the moment it recalls the mighty acts (Psalm 77:12). When the present is inscrutable it finds comfort in looking back at past guidance. What cannot be understood at the time may be

---

[22] *Philosophie der Religion, Werke* (1832), XI, p. 122; E.T. *Lectures on the Philosophy of Religion* (1895), I, p. 205.
[23] "In thy light shall we see light" (Psalm 36:9).

grasped in retrospect (John 12:16) and will certainly be understood in the hereafter (John 13:7).

Hence faith leads to understanding and offers an interpretation of the world even though the fact that God's thoughts are higher constantly sets a limit to the attempt to achieve a full theological explanation and to merge the thoughts of God into our own thoughts again. When understanding of the world and history arises in this light it is not a conjecturing or resolving with the help of an idea of God misused as a cosmic formula. No, when this understanding takes place, signs and signals are given to us. Only in the sanctuary does the psalmist come to see that the distribution of rewards and punishments is not wholly inscrutable in this world, but that foreshadowings of divine judgments are set before our eyes (Psalm 73:17ff.) or a divine purpose is signalized (John 9:3).

If it is asked, with some exaggeration, whether we do not have a process of deduction here, the only answer can be that, if so, it is not after the style of natural theology. We do not arrive at God by observation of nature and history. If the doubtful idea of a deductive process may be provisionally accepted, the movement is from an encounter with the God who discloses himself, and the light achieved in this encounter, to the way in which we are to understand the world created and directed by God, to what may be held concerning its order and disorder, its nexus of guilt and fate, and remarkable men like Cyrus and Nebuchadnezzar. Only in the framework of this "deduction" does the question become an urgent one why the reality that we call "God" can never be identical with an idea or an immanent entity, and why that in God which transcends all being and value makes it possible for us to overcome the difficulty of thought to which we referred, namely, that of conceiving of the unity and meaning of world processes without eliminating the personal, unconditional, and subjective aspects of human existence. Our answer is as follows. We do not know meaning but we believe in him who does. We believe in him, not because interpretation of the world forces this speculative possibility of interpretation on us, but because of his own self-disclosure in whose light we see the world with new eyes.

b. God and the Good

To the question of the good, too, there can be no answer which presents God as a purely synonymous term for the good. Here again there has to be a transcendent element which is not exhausted by the idea of the good.

In Matthew's version the rich young man asks Jesus about the good: "What good thing shall I do, that I may have eternal life?" (Matthew 19:16). He is given the answer: "Why askest thou me about the good? One alone is the good" (19:17).[24] Is God here simply the answer to the question of the good, so that he is no more than the good, and the rich young man

---

[24] Cf. Mark 10:18 ("There is none good but one, that is, God") and Luke 18:19.

is really referring to him with his question about the good? Is God a mere personifying, not to say mythifying, of the norm of the good?

If so, then again God could be dissolved in this norm once it is mastered by man's autonomous insight. In this story, however, even the very wording shows that God is more and other than the mere norm of the good. The text brings out the difference by two essential nuances.

First, God is not the good in the neutral sense of a norm but the good in a personal sense, the "good one." The predicate "good" denotes an accident or quality of his person and it does so in such a way that here and here alone, in and in relation to him, is it posited (only one is good). This means that the good does not exist apart from him and cannot be known apart from him. It is not a universally valid norm which is accessible to all. It can be defined only in connection with this person, i.e., "God." As God is not generally accessible, but must reveal and manifest himself[25] if his presence is to be imparted to us, so the good that is defined in him is from the very beginning, i.e., our "natural" beginning, concealed from us, being made known to us only in the self-disclosure of God.

The second nuance in the text is related to the first.

If the good in view can be defined only in terms of the person to which it is constitutively related, then one can no longer say that God is good because he corresponds to a prior norm of the good that may be perceived apart from him. One must say instead that what is good is essentially defined by God himself, so that it is characterized as the good in the personal rather than the neuter sense.[26] In illustration of what is meant by the concept of the "good one" we may think of the self-emptying of God,[27] of his love, of his being there for man.[28]

This reorientation of definition corresponds exactly to the change that we noted in the early Apologists in relation to John's Gospel.[29]

Apologists like Justin and Tatian view the logos as an entity which pervades all being and which is thus accessible to the *nous* of the philosophers. Christ is then described as a representation of this world logos. He validates himself by this representation of his. Through it he becomes the Son of the God of the philosophers. He is accessible to speculative reason in the same way as the cosmic logos is. But whereas here Christ is defined by the logos, the precise opposite takes place in John's Gospel. The Logos in John is the Word that is spoken by God and incarnated in Christ (John 1:1ff.). It is tied to it once and for all (*eph hápax*). Only here is it to be found and only here, by its self-disclosure, may it be perceived. Who (not what) the Logos is, is defined by Christ, or, more precisely, by the incarnate Logos, by a

---

[25] Isaiah 29:14; Matthew 11:25ff.; Luke 10:21; John 17:25; 18:37.

[26] The distinction reminds us of the problem of the good in the debate between the Thomists and Scotists; cf. ThE, I, § 1869ff.

[27] John 3:16; Romans 5:8; 8:32; 1 John 4:9.

[28] Only secondarily does what is usually treated under the heading of God's attributes come into consideration.

[29] Volume I, p. 126.

person in whom God manifests himself and is present. What is true of the Logos in relation to Christ may also be said of the good in relation to God.

The way in which God escapes equation with a general and prior norm of the good must now be explained more closely. A mere reference to the fact of it hardly suffices. For the extra element which in the word "God" says more than a mere norm of the good can express might be merely a mythological margin that says nothing. If so, it might be better to cut off this margin so that the norm can be seen as a pure and unencumbered ethical quantity. The question thus arises what is the significance of the element in the word "God" which transcends the norm of the good and resists its equation with this norm.[30]

Two aspects are to be noted.

(1) *The Antithesis of God to the Polarity of Good and Evil*

In the ethical sphere the good encounters us only within the polarity of good and evil. To will or even to think the good is not to will or think the evil, and hence to see the good as the opposite of the evil.

This integration of the good into the polarity of good and evil may be seen already in the fact that we can understand every ethical imperative only as a protest. Man ought not to be as he is. What he should be is always thought of as what he should not be. It is a controversy of man with the way he is. The laws of the Decalog bring out very strictly this character of imperatives as a protest, for they are for the most part formulated negatively: "Thou shalt not. . . ." They relate to the man who has the fall behind him and who has to be told: "You ought not to be as you are."[31]

This negative tendency also finds a plain enough emphasis in the categorical imperative of Kant. The personhood of man finds expression in his refusal to accept himself as he is, in his fight against the rule of impulse, eudaemonism, and *laissez-faire*. Indeed, the very sign of his humanity is that he is involved in this conflict against himself. The greater the intensity of this civil war, the more human he is.

How can we think of God, however, in terms of the presupposed polarity of good and evil?

We see again at this point what we have already seen earlier. Whenever God is integrated into a given schema, there is assigned to this schema outside God the role of the true *ens realissimum,* while God sinks to the level of a purely mythical term for this *ens* and sooner or later proves to be superfluous.[32]

For on the one side God will be viewed as a representation of the good as it is defined in terms of this polarity. In this case evil is an opposing power existing independently alongside him. Along the lines of Marcion

---

[30] For what follows cf. also Volume I, pp. 138ff.

[31] On the negative structure of the Decalog cf. ThE, I, § 2163ff.; E.T. I, pp. 440ff.

[32] Cf. the previous chapter and also the interpretation of Kant and Heine in Volume I, pp. 266-275.

God is a cosmic party but not an all-encompassing pantocrator. Like Odin in relation to Loki, he is interwoven into the polar law of the structure of being. He is simply one element in this dialectic. He is the God of Plato who as a *technites* shapes the material set before him but has to accept, without being able to control it, the autonomous, refractory, and evil element in this material. He can no longer be thought of in any case as the biblical Creator who creates out of nothing[33] and to that extent knows nothing which is there outside him or before him, with which he has thus to reckon, and by which the law of his action will be in part decided.

On the other side—this is the second possibility—God will be viewed as a representation of the polarity of good and evil itself, i.e., the point of indifference of both the polar entities. In this case he is the personification of the principle of teleology which indwells the polarity. The evil is regarded as a productive transition (Hegel) to the good and even as a stimulus which calls for decision and thus makes the good possible for the first time. In this sense is not Goethe's Mephistopheles a part of the power which always wills the evil and always achieves the good? Is he not given to Faust because man so easily becomes inactive and needs a companion who will charm, and work, and accomplish things as the devil? Along the same lines, did not Schiller view the fall as the most fortunate act in world history, since it rescued man from the animal twilight of paradise and made decision possible for him, thus placing at his disposal the *conditio sine qua non* of his humanity? Did not the prodigal son, in the version according to André Gide, need the far country in order to pass through the productive polarity of good and evil and win through the alienation to the good of his identity?

When God is thus equated again with a general idea—this time the teleology of good and evil—he is made subordinate to an *ens realissimum* which is stronger than he is and which finds him a place in the nexus of being only as a secondary being or even as a mere cipher of the nexus. Again, therefore, it must be said that the God of the Bible does not fit into this schematization nor yield to this subsuming. Far from God being the point of indifference between good and evil, the wrath of God burns against evil. This evil is not overcome, as in Gide's version of the prodigal son, by being manifested in its creative finality but by being unmasked without excuse as evil and then being pardoned and overcome in love (Luke 15:20f.).

No matter how God may be brought into equation with the polarity of good and evil, whether he be identified with the good as the positive aspect or merged into the polarity itself, the sum does not work out. The God of the Bible cannot be brought into any congruity of this kind. The elements which rise above it are all too evident.

But in what way does he rise above it and what is the significance of the transcendent elements?

The God of the Bible relativizes the polarity of good and evil, or, better,

---

[33] ThE, I, § 712-762, 1330-1353; E.T. I, pp. 279ff.

he judges it, instead of being integrated into it. What we mean by this is as follows.

When God creates out of nothing, then the man created by him belongs to him totally and must give himself back to him as he has received himself from him. If he has alienated and falsified himself, he can no longer refer by way of extenuation to realities which are taken from God's creative act and which thus exist apart from the guilt of man. For example, he cannot refer to matter, which drags him down and through no fault of his own poisons his existence. Nor can he refer to the blighting forces of fate which indwell the world from the very outset, as in the myth that the world is made out of the corpse of the murdered giant Ymir.[34] Instead man is totally guilty before God.

Seeing himself placed thus between good and evil, he discovers the evil in himself as something which God indubitably has not called forth out of nothing. Mephistopheles is not God's creature. God does not will evil. Man may oppose that which he ought to be to evil, as Kant does, but evil is in himself. He is constitutionally tied to it. His acts may be an unbroken protest against it. Yet that against which he protests is part of himself. He has to say to it: I am it.

For a brief moment Paul can say experimentally: Here I am and there is the evil in me, there is the sin in my members. For an instant he presents sin almost as a mythical entity with which he finds himself confronted and which is not himself.[35] His true self is simply that in him which does not will sin but resists it. If he still does this thing he does not will (Romans 7:15ff.), it seems to be a force outside himself which he does not control and which he cannot be responsible for mastering. He finds evil within himself, but for a moment it seems to be the partisan of another and alien power which has infiltrated his self. Yet only for a moment, for the passage concludes with the words: "O wretched man that I am! Who shall deliver me from the body of this death?" (7:24). Here Paul is again saying "I" to himself and describing his own body as the vessel in which evil is contained. The temporary distance between himself and the evil he notes in himself is solemnly closed again. He is compelled to identify himself with this evil, or, more accurately, he would have to do so were victory not given to him by Christ, had he not become a new creature thereby and thus achieved a new identity.[36]

The radicalizations of the Mosaic law in the Sermon on the Mount show that I have to say "I" to the potential evil which lurks within me. If we are angry with our brother without a cause and he is conciliatory, part of us, or we ourselves in this part, turn aside from God (Matthew 5:21ff.). If we look on a woman to lust after her, we emancipate ourselves from the

---

[34] Cf. ThE, I, § 1339ff.
[35] *Hē oikoúsa en emoí hamartía* (Romans 7:17, 20); *tó nómō tês hamartías tó ónti en toís mélesín mou* (7:23).
[36] Romans 7:24b; Galatians 2:20; 2 Corinthians 5:17.

divine order even though we go no further and do not commit adultery (5:27ff.).

It is not possible, then, to say "I" only to the ethical and higher self, i.e., to the self which in mind and act says Yes to the good. That against which I protest in mind and act, that which as the thought of the heart lies beneath the zone of conscious control,[37] also belongs to me. Before the one who created the world out of nothing I cannot appeal to a fate outside myself or blame God himself as the first cause.[38] Potential evil, far from being material for the fulfilment of duty, far from being productive, is also part of myself. It prevents me from belonging wholly and entirely to the one to whom I owe myself wholly and entirely. There can be no more question of my commitment to him with all my heart and soul and mind (Matthew 22:37; Deuteronomy 6:4).

Here, then, the polarity of good and evil is finally called in question. When confrontation between good and evil takes place, full commitment to God and the integrity of creaturehood are already shattered. If I see myself in God's light, I am startled by the dark possibilities that I find in myself. For in this light I learn my true identity. The self-identification into which I am forced is first an annihilating work of the law. It is judgment. I must also say "I" to that in me which God does not will and in which I have departed from him.

On the other hand, if the polarity of good and evil becomes the *ens realissimum* in God's place, that self-identification cannot be authentically radical. I identify myself only with myself as the moral subject of my disposition. The result is that I must set the potential evil in me in the distant sphere of what does not belong to me. It is an inheritance over which I have no control. It is the baneful work of environment. It is destiny in one form or another. It is, as Kant would say, an inclination which I do not have to impute to myself and to which I need not say "I."[39] The dominion of the polarity of good and evil implies that certain dimensions of the I are ethically sundered from the person. This prevents what we have described as radical self-identification.

The biblical story of the fall contains some underlying hints of this.

In this story it is the serpent who brings knowledge of good and evil and whose victory establishes the polarity (Genesis 3:5). In his uprightness as he comes from the creative hand of God man is oriented totally to God. He lives and moves and has his being in God in original integrity. The hour when autonomy awakens and emancipates itself from God's embrace has not yet struck. He still addresses God in eternal liturgy. Knowledge of good and evil is not yet relevant, for evil has no actuality. Only when man touches

---

[37] Matthew 15:19; Mark 7:21; Luke 9:47; cf. also Romans 2:15.

[38] Adalbert Stifter in his *Bunte Steine* (short story *Zuversicht*) has shown poetically how the unconscious tendencies of the I also belong to the I.

[39] On Kant's doctrine of inclinations cf. ThE, I, § 1612ff.; *Geschichte und Existenz*, 2nd ed. (1964), pp. 68ff.

the tree of good and evil and rejects the divine prohibition does knowledge of good and evil arise and the polarity come into force. This means that the knowledge arises at the moment when evil actualizes itself and man turns from his Maker. Knowledge of good and evil is achieved, not theoretically, but in the act. This means that it can be had only as man abandons his creaturely integrity and delivers himself up to contradiction.

In a kind of prophecy in reverse the historicity of man is thus seen here to be one which now takes place within the framework of the polarity of good and evil. But this present state or nature of man is also totally challenged. Does not that which we venture to call polarity and the productiveness of antithesis carry a dark shadow with it at the same time? Is not man seen to be bound and chained to this polarity? Can he really overcome himself and become another man? Can he ever break free from the evil in himself even when he opposes it in the name of moral imperatives? Will not this dark sign of an alien power always cling to him and prevent the emergence of a new and utopian man? Is it not, for example, a sinister token that man can call war the father of all things, indicating thereby that he can reach his best achievements only in frustration and that he needs antitheses, including that which is dubious and evil? Along the same lines is it not also a dark sign that egoism is the most elemental driving force of history and to that extent of progress too, although not only of progress?

It is evident here that the word "God" says something more and other than the idea of the good, and to what extent it does this. God calls in question what man means by the good, for he shows how questionable is the framework within which this good occurs, and strips it of the idealizing which makes the polarity of good and evil a vital and creative impulse of being and exalts it as a teleological principle.

The reference, however, is not just to the law by which God challenges the good and its framework. At issue, too, is the gospel in which he introduces the new form of the good. This new form is the reawakening of lost integrity. It is offered in love as the fulfilment of the law.[40]

He who loves is whole in the act of his loving. No dimension of his ego has to be overcome in protest. To this extent promptitude and spontaneity are proper to love, as Luther puts it. If it is also true of this love that "I have not already attained . . . but I follow after, if that I may apprehend that for which also I am apprehended by Christ Jesus" (Philippians 3:12), still the new integrity of love is given as a promise and the story of the fulfilment of this promise has already begun its course. I am already apprehended by Christ. This is why I for my part can apprehend. I am loved and therefore I can love (1 John 4:19).

The reference to my being apprehended indicates the basis of this possibility of love and hence the new integrity. This love does not have its origin in an ethical act by which I wrest it out of myself. If it did, it would be

---

[40] Romans 13:10; cf. Matthew 19:19; 22:34-40; Mark 12:31; Galatians 5:14; James 2:8.

located in the very place where it obviously does not belong, namely, in the relation of good and evil, and therefore in man's conflict with himself, in the contradiction which the new integrity does not resolve. In fact, however, this love arises as a response and reaction of man to a love which lays hold of him (1 John 4:10). If one might speak in this way, it is the subjective reflection of the fact that God has become for us in Christ a lovable object.[41]

Here, then, the word "God" with its transcending of the idea of good in polarity offers us a glimpse of the true nature of man, of the overcoming of his alienation, of his new integrity. This occurs in the message of a God who discloses himself to me as love and thereby makes possible my love in return. Total questioning is thus replaced with a new and total Yes which we also call justification. That which transcends the good in this understanding of the word "God" points, then, to the totality of my self which without God, as the polarity of good and evil shows, slips into the "necessity" of contradiction which is then idealized as a "virtue" and made a substitute for the lost totality.

The transcendent element in the word "God" has a final implication for the good. The love which is won from me and which leads to the new integrity refers me also to my fellow-man. Love of God and love of neighbor are indissolubly related. To confess Christ is to recognize in the man who needs me Christ himself encountering me here and now; it is to understand the call of love as a claim of faith.[42] This means that the good in this turning to our fellows can never become an independent enterprise which is detached from faith in God, at least so long as we understand our acts to be "Christian." As a believer I see Christ in my fellow-man. Even though he is alien to me and does not kindle my sympathy, I see in him one whom God seeks with the same love as he seeks me, whom he forgives as he forgives me (Matthew 18:21ff.), who is bought at a price as I am (Romans 14:15; 1 Corinthians 8:11).

My fellow-man is thus changed for me. He becomes the bearer of an alien worth which is given him by God and which lifts him above all mere usability, including the ethical. I am not there for him in order that he may be there for me (Matthew 5:46f.). Nor do I turn to him with a view to self-actualization and self-fulfilment.[43]

In this respect, too, God as the lord of neighborly love constantly transcends the ethical motive and the good intended in it. He does so because, by loving first, he grants to fellow-man as my neighbor a meaning which qualifies my natural love in a new way and makes it impossible that God should be dropped out in some, possibly later stage of this natural love.

---

[41] Apol. CA, III, 8.

[42] Ratzinger, *Einführung*, p. 167; E.T. p. 154.

[43] Everywhere apparent in the new humanism of Wilhlem von Humboldt is the idea that all ethical motivation is oriented to the realization of one's own entelechy; cf. his letters.

In other words, it is impossible that faith in God should lead me to this form of humanity and then drop out in favor of atheistic humanism—a humanism which is governed by some general proclamation of human worth. Another way of putting it is to say that dogmatics and ethics are inextricably intertwined. Faith cannot be dissolved by fellow-humanity, for the meaning of fellow-man has its ground in this faith and the word "God" constantly defines the word "fellow-man" in its true sense.

This, then, is the element in the word "God" which transcends all else that is meant by the good, including concern for one's fellow-man.

(2) *The Antithesis of God to the Principle of Achievement*

The element in the word "God" that transcends the good manifests itself not only in that God remains outside the ethical relation of good and evil, but also in that I can never reach God if I seek him in terms of the good. To understand this, we must return to the story of the rich young man.

We have seen already that it is God he is seeking when he asks about eternal life, since this life is life in fellowship with God. He expects this question to be answered when he finds the good which, when it is done, accomplishes union with God (Matthew 19:16ff.). Most striking is the way in which Jesus makes it clear at this point that the question as posed misses God altogether, or, better, that God stands apart from this line of questioning and transcends it.

At first, of course, Jesus seems to deal with the question on its own level. He answers the question of the good by referring to the commandments: "If thou wilt enter into life, keep the commandments" (19:17). When the man answers that he has already done this, and wants to know what is still missing (v. 20),[44] it is apparent that he has followed the ethical path in vain, not finding the goal he seeks. The fact that Jesus clearly evokes this admission of failure shows that his reference to the way of the commandments was meant "Socratically." It provoked awareness of the uselessness of this way.

Why is this way futile? Why does it not lead to God?

The answer is provided by the demand of Jesus: "If thou wilt be perfect, go and sell what thou hast, and give to the poor, and thou shalt have treasure in heaven" (v. 21). But "the young man went away sorrowful: for he had great possessions."

With his demand for the selling of everything Jesus destroys as it were the way of the commandments or the ethical way. He does this again in a "Socratic" manner, forcing upon the rich young man an experiment in thought. In other words, the demand makes him ask what degree of unconditionality eternal life and God have for him. Has he merely a philosophical interest so that he can accept it if this is not satisfied? Does he experience

---

[44] The Marcan version tells us that after this reply "Jesus beholding him loved him" (Mark 10:21).

an unfulfilled void in his life which troubles him but which is not intolerable? Or is the young man in his search for God concerned about a question of destiny and existence *par excellence,* so that his enterprise is one by whose success or failure he stands or falls? Only if the question is meant in this radical way has he really asked about God. Only thus has he understood God and the gaining of eternal life to be the one thing needful (Luke 10:42) without which his life will be no less than total shipwreck. If this is not the case, however, God is for him the object of only one question among many others, and he is thus regarded more "incidentally" as a kind of eleventh commandment alongside the familiar ten commandments. Evidently he has an additional commandment of this kind in view when he asks about other forms of the good which will go beyond his existing list of duties.

The young man's decision in which of these ways he is asking about God, whether radically or incidentally, or even not at all—this decision clearly has to be made once Jesus tells him to sell all that he has. The experiment of thought which this forces on him, and which will necessarily bring to light the quality of his question about God, takes the following form.

The young man has to say what is more important for him, his possessions, prestige, culture, and life-style, or the question of eternal life and hence the question of God himself. If he loves his wealth more, or, in other words, himself, then *de facto* he has not even put the question of God. On the way proposed, then, he can find no answer to the question he has not put. He did not have in mind the good which he seemed to be asking about. He meant it only as an ethical quantity which could be enhanced by greater effort. He did not have in mind the authentic good as it may be seen when defined by God, namely, self-sacrifice, being there for others in an unconditional and unreserved sense.

The one who talks to Jesus here is not ready for this kind of self-sacrifice. Hence he went away sorrowful, for he had great possessions. He had tried to ask about the good and God in such a way as to avoid this readiness for self-sacrifice. Hence he did not really put the question at all. He was confounded, not because no answer was given, but because he never even posed the right question.

According to God and according to what the word "God" means, I can obviously ask the question only on two conditions.

First, I must have in mind, not the good which naturally suggests itself when I understand it as a kind of ethical quantum along the lines of a principle of ahievement, but the good as it is in and through God: One alone is good.

Second, I can put the question of the good—this good and therefore God—only in a radical way, i.e., not in uncommitted even though serious curiosity, but with the unconditional readiness and commitment which regards God as the one and all: "And ye shall seek me, and find me, when ye shall search for me with all your heart" (Jeremiah 29:13; Deuteronomy

4:29). If God is love, he can accordingly be asked after only in the same situation of love and sacrifice. This is not possible, however, if the heart is divided and the will split. I cannot love both God and mammon (Luke 16:13). I cannot love both God and myself. For precisely this reason the Gentiles of Romans 1:18ff. failed to put the real question about God. They had adequate speculative resources. But they focused on themselves and hence they did not glorify God nor were they thankful. Theology, in which the issue is *theos,* can be pursued only with a specific orientation of existence. Only the who "is" of the truth, i.e., who wills God unequivocally, hears the voice.

3. RESULTS AND EVALUATION: THEOLOGICAL STATEMENTS REGARDING THE TRANSCENDENCE OF GOD

First, God transcends the norm of the good.

The question of the good leads into the void if it starts with the assumption that God is identical with the good I have in mind, or is just a cipher for it.

Second, insight into the good which is God is not at our disposal.

I do not have at my disposal the true good which is God himself and which transcends any good that I may have in view. If God himself is the good, I learn the good only if he discloses himself to me. God's self-disclosure, however, can never mean only that a doctrine of his being and nature is imparted to me. When it takes place, it means that my existence is brought into the truth and undergoes transformation to self-sacrifice and openness to God.

Biblically this miracle of change is described as the work of the Spirit of God. For this Spirit not only reveals what flesh and blood cannot tell itself (Matthew 16:17) but also confers the mind which opens me up to what is revealed. The Spirit brings about the miracle of the new birth (John 3:3, 5), effects a new creation (2 Corinthians 5:17), and places in a new life (Romans 7:6). He thus accomplishes an ontic and not just a cognitive changing of life.[45] This new existence which I do not control is characterized by the fact that my concern is for God alone, that I want him unconditionally, that I can thus have him in view and aim at him with my question, whereas otherwise I would pass him by and understand him as the cipher of a norm, value, or end of my own existence.

Third, the interest of religious man in God is open to question.

The fact that the new mind is not under my own control implies that the question of eternal life and therewith of God remains problematical if it is merely the question of natural man or an expression of his religious interest. Our discussion of the story of the rich young man has shown this. Because he was finally asking about God from within an attitude to life

---

[45] This is why the breath of God (*ruach*) is presented as creative and life-giving: Genesis 2:7; Wisdom 15:11; Psalm 104:29f.; Ecclesiastes 12:7, etc.

which prevented him from really having God in view, he missed him. He did so unavoidably because the natural constitution of our existence does not allow us to escape the dominion of self and self-love and therefore permits us to ask only about a God who is reconcilable with this self-love, who does not challenge it, who does not, as the unconditioned, summon me out of the conditions of my previous existence. To this extent "with men this is impossible" (Matthew 19:26). God himself is the possibility which breaks the compulsion here.

Since man's basic aim is self-confirmation, human religion involves deification of the creature, which illegitimately makes itself out to be God. The God who is thus taken out of the creaturely sphere and serves as its cipher is the desired God cut to human size, fitting smoothly, causing no pressure, and sparing us any radical questioning. For a reality identical with itself—in this case the reality of the creaturely sphere—cannot call itself in question.[46]

Fourth, a rational account of the difference between God and norms is not a proof of God.

It might be asked whether there is any point in demonstrating the content of the word "God" in a general way. Is not this content revealed only when the Godward mind, which we cannot control, is present, or, better, becomes an event?

This question is justified to the degree that God cannot be demonstrated outside the mind which thus eventuates itself. This impossibility finds reflection in the failure of the so-called proofs of God. The impossibility has a deeper basis than the epistemological one (in the Kantian sense). It is connected with the fact that the existence which emancipates itself from God is inadequate when faced with God's reality and is thus robbed of the reality of its own being. This is why the question underlying the proofs of God misses God. (Anselm says this very plainly in what is wrongly called his proof of God.)[47]

Elucidating the meaning of the word "God" apart from this inadequacy (and therefore generally) can only mean, then, bringing to light the difference between God and all other concepts, including that of meaning or of the good.

This does not have to imply that in this framework we can speak only negatively of God and hence say no more than what he is not. Instead we can consider the significance of the fact that there is this difference. We have done this in relation to the distinction between God and meaning or the good as we can understand them, and we have tried to show to what extent meaning and the good do not answer man's question about that which transcends him but fix his gaze solely upon himself.

---

[46] On this point cf. Luther's Larger Catechism, First Commandment. On the understanding of religious man expressed here cf. H. Vossberg, *Luthers Kritik aller Religion* (1922), and E. Wolf, "M. Luther," ThEx, No. 6; also the author's essay: "Kritik der natürlichen Theologie," *Theologie der Anfechtung* (1949), pp. 14ff.
[47] Cf. Volume I, pp. 276ff.

Reflected in the difference between God and these values and norms is another difference, namely, the gap between man's awareness that he is a being which rises above itself, which will not accept its given status, which must take itself in hand and try to develop into something, and man's other awareness, which is suppressed according to Romans 1:18, that the goals which he has selected do not transcend him, but are taken from his own given reality, so that they are idols, deified creatures, which function as a religious superstructure.

These differences may well be the object of a general deliberation and their significance may be pondered. To this extent they are legitimate as reflections on the meaning of the word "God." They are one of the many forms under which the believer bears witness to the logos of his hope and develops it as logos (1 Peter 3:15f.), trying to make it clear to every man[48] and not just Christians or fellow-believers to what extent his talk about God is responsible talk, or, as one might put it, to what extent he truly thinks about the word "God" and does not simply use it unthinkingly as a traditional cliché.

This is all that this general reflection on the word "God" can seek to do. Giving a logos for the word "God" in this way is not a proof of God. Even if this logos is cogent, its cogency is simply that of a Christian idea of God. Hence we have only a shadow of the reality. It is still an open question whether this idea of God, this representation of transcendence, has any corresponding reality. Do we have here the Immanuel, the God for me, to whom I may turn with all my heart and trust?[49] Decisive access to God is present only when we have something more and other than mere insight into the meaningfulness of the concept, only when we have what we have called the mind that the Spirit has conferred on our existence.

All the same it is a constant and important task to clarify the meaning of the word "God" conceptually in the vestibule of faith. Only thus can he who speaks about God in proclamation and confession make it clear that what is at issue is neither a private revelation nor a mere repetition of traditional jargon. Both these would necessarily block any readiness to listen and would simply convince the hearer of the irrelevance of such God-talk. On the other hand, he who speaks about God as indicated will find himself in solidarity with all thinking people as he renders to himself and others the logos of his talk.

Fifth, God's question about us is the important one rather than our question about God.

That God is different from, and transcends, all the norms and values to be found on the line of our questioning is manifested by the structure of most of the conversations of Jesus. When questions are put to him, whether it be the question of eternal life, the question who is the greatest (Mark 9:33ff.; Matthew 18:1f.), whether taxes should be paid to Caesar (Mat-

---

[48] *Pantí tô aitoúnti*, 1 Peter 3:15f.
[49] Cf. Luther's Larger Catechism, First Commandment, 13f.

thew 22:15ff.), who is my neighbor (Luke 10:29, 36), or how often we should forgive others (Matthew 18:21ff.), a direct answer is seldom if ever given. If it were, such an answer would stand under the control of a given and as yet unredeemed line of questioning. Since this would be the line of questioning of the "old" existence an answer within its framework could not bear appropriate witness to God. Hence instead of a direct answer we usually find a counter-question, as in the story of the rich young man according to our interpretation. This counter-question, which does not have to be formulated externally as such, but may be Socratically indirect, has the function of bringing something to light. It shows the inappropriateness of the disposition of existence out of which the original question springs. First, then, the question as put is corrected. This happens when man comes to know himself as one who is questioned by God. The original question: "Where is God?" is replaced by the counter-question, or rather the prior question: "Adam, where art thou?" (Genesis 3:9).

Sixth, the task is that of finding the ground of the ungroundability of God.

If in virtue of that which differentiates him from immanent norms and values God is the ground of all things, he himself can have no ground. In face of this aspect reason is reduced to silence, since it is deprived of its function of finding grounds. Nevertheless, the aspect itself is not irrational. For it may be shown that if an entity exists that is the ground of all things there is nothing with whose help this entity can itself be grounded.[50] An appeal can also be made to the understanding to meditate on this entity. We are confronted with this appeal when that which we can grasp in our immanent relations of grounding does not do justice to man as a self-transcending being, when it makes him instead a function of these relations and thus robs him of his unconditionality.

Even if all this is only the obscure sign of a distant power, the sign is still set up. When we deal with God's revelation or self-disclosure, however, the obscure sign is replaced by the word "I am" and the questionable good by him who is good. This is why the divine commandments find their one and final basis in the statement which follows each individual decree like a liturgical litany: "I am the Lord your God" (Numbers 19:2, 4, 10, 14, 18, etc.). The author of the law does not vindicate himself by the meaningfulness of his laws. The laws have their ground and vindication in their ungroundable author.

This is where the leap is made over the barrier that has been set up between the norms, values, and gods of human religion and the self-disclosing "I am" of God. All reflection on the meaning of the word God can only center on this barrier and hence on that which is separated and yet at the same time connected by it.

Seventh, all the concepts that we use in relation to God (logos, person, substance, etc.) are inadequate.

---

[50] Medieval and older Protestant scholasticism brings this to expression in the concept of the aseity of God.

The most important result of our deliberations is as follows.

Although God stands in relevant relation to human existence in all its dimensions, although something is learned from him about the meaning of being and history, although, as the good one, he makes himself known in his relation to the good, although he has to do with our love and freedom, nevertheless he is not identical with any one of these dimensions but is qualitatively and infinitely distinct from them.

Christian theology has always been brought up sharp against this distinction by the fact that none of the concepts which we use to describe God, and especially the Trinity, is really adequate to do the job. This is why concepts like logos, nature, person, and substance have had to undergo a change of sense, their meaning being received from the one they are seeking to describe and express. This means that the doctrine of God cannot be worked out deductively, in the sense of deducing the personality of God from the prior concept of person, or the monotheistic structure of the Christian belief in God from the prior concept of substance. The normative use of such terms would lead only to the God of the philosophers and rob even him of those elements which transcend a purely speculative extension of our own experience of the world. The terms referred to above are rather given a ministering function and directed to an instrumental use. As we have seen already in the case of the Johannine logos, they must shed their original meaning and take up into themselves a new thing which their primary sense could not foresee.

All the same, the new definition which they receive in relation to the word "God" is not unrelated to their original meaning. Thus the meaning of the Stoic logos is taken up into the new Johannine definition of the logos. If this were not so, if the concepts had no affinity at all to what they come to mean theologically and christologically, then they would be freely exchangeable, no articulate terms would exist at all, and free rein would be given to glossolalia or dadaism.

It might be said, then, that the language of faith adopts the vocabulary already fashioned for it by the theater,[51] philosophy, and popular usage.[52] It makes use of what is there. But the terms have to be baptized, they have to undergo conversion, before they can carry out the service assigned to them.[53] This is why God cannot be subsumed under any pre-existing concept. It is one of the reasons why the Bible speaks of the "name" of God instead of the "concept" of God. For the name, denoting the person, expresses uniqueness. It even expresses exception to the extent that the one

---

[51] Cf. person, Latin *persona*, Greek *prósōpon*, the actor's mask, or role.

[52] Ratzinger, *Einführung*, p. 129; E.T. p. 118.

[53] In his essay "Die Struktur der dogmatischen Aussage als ökumenisches Problem," KD (1957), pp. 251ff., E. Schlink speaks of the doxological character of the Christian use of concepts. Being given the task of praise and being totally absorbed in this new intention, the concepts offer up the creaturely content which previously governed them. When the creaturely content of terms like love, righteousness, and wisdom is referred to the eternal being of God, it undergoes a mutation.

who bears it cannot be subsumed under a species but is himself with no possibility of mistake or exchange. (We shall return to this later.)

The mere concept "God" tells us nothing in and of itself. It is theologically empty. As we have seen, it might be used to denote a numinously enhanced creaturely reality. What we have called the difference between God and every creaturely reality does not have to be part of the mere term "God." It is by no means obvious whether an unconditional relation to God is expressed thereby or merely the mechanical continuation of a pious tradition.[54] In *this* sense Tillich is surely correct when he says that it can be atheism to maintain God's existence as well as atheism to deny it.[55]

Eighth, we note that it is a duty, and yet also a danger, to ask about God's relevance.

As we have seen in the first volume, this question is posed in more recent theological discussion by the fact that in some circles there is an almost exclusive interest in demonstrating the relevance of God. This is usually done by establishing the human, social, and more broadly ethical affinity of the word "God." Lest the term should become a mere cliché, an uncritically adopted assumption, God is no longer accepted as a personal other, e.g., the one to whom prayer is addressed,[56] but is equated with immanent relations, especially with other men. It is believed that along such lines the name "God" can be made intelligible for the famous modern man who will accept only immanence. New possibilities are thus opened up for this name. The difference is smoothed over out of missionary interest.

It has to be said, however, that an irresponsibly high price is paid for this smoothing over, namely, no less a price than surrender of the true point of the word "God" in the Christian sense. The result is a relapse into paganism, into the deification of creaturely relations. An easy path is thus made available for the achievement of secularism. Fellow-humanity symbolized by the concept of God has only to be read according to the straightforward text of reason to make the symbol unnecessary. When theology says only what the world can say to itself, it says nothing. The feet of those who will remove it are already at the door. To put it in popular language, the attractive wrapping which is designed to push the concept of God and lead to a boom in sales simply shows that what we have is a clearance sale at reduced prices.

The word "God" lives not only by its affinity to all creaturely dimensions but also by its difference from them. When the affinity is overlooked we have a docetically weakened theism or the cliché of a dead but dragged out tradition. When the difference is suppressed, we have a transitional stage to the autarchy of self-enclosed and truly atheistic secularism—a stage during which journalists and intellectuals admire the candor and avant-gardism of

---

[54] Cf. the polls which indicate that the majority of people believe in the existence of a supreme being.

[55] *Systematic Theology,* I, p. 237.

[56] Cf. Volume I, pp. 111ff., on P. M. van Buren and H. Braun.

those who talk along these lines. The momentary shock caused by the message of a secular, all too secular God soon passes. After paying brief attention, a world which can understand itself without this God engulfs him in silence. What is self-evident is soon played out.

Concluding Note: Can Certainty of God be Reached Through the Feeling of Inadequacy?

Röhricht (*art. cit.,* pp. 175ff.) rightly has some objections against Bonhoeffer's thesis that God is to be found, not in borderline situations or in deficiencies, but in the center and fulness of life. If, he says, man lives in distorted time, unremovable guilt, finite power, and the certainty of death (p. 175), this reality which is apparently filled out in this way is the questionable thing for him. Can he, then, really hear the word of God without borderline experiences (p. 177)? Does not experience of God correspond to this experience of deficiency? Do we not see the element of affinity very clearly at this point? One can agree with this only if one adds what is implicit, although not explicit, in Röhricht, namely, that this sense of lack does not have to lead to God in every case. This may be seen from Camus' experience of the absurd and even more plainly perhaps from Ernst Bloch, who says that everything that now is is deficient, since it can be excelled and surpassed in the name of utopia or the principle of hope. This, however, does not lead to God as the hypostasis of a most perfect being or the positive counterpart of the lack. It leads to the positing of a utopian end and hence to the translating of the most perfect being into time, or rather the end time.

The experience of deficiency is thus ambivalent. As a borderline experience it may be either open or closed to God. It may seem to be open to him but in reality be closed. This is so in the case suggested by Bonhoeffer when we think we should deprive this world of its light in order to make the heavenly Jerusalem shine out the more brightly, or when we strike up laments about this world as a vale of tears in order to make heaven seem all the more desirable. This is misleading, for the God who is smuggled thus into the darkened world can easily become the expression of a wish or dream and can thus be interpreted according to the illusion theory of Feuerbach.

Theologically, then, the experience of lack is to be construed in the very opposite way. What is truly unsatisfying about human life is known only from experience of the fulness of God. When I know God as he is present in Christ, I know the fulness of love and I thus know also the basic lovelessness and selfishness of human existence. From this knowledge of God I learn the connection between power and love and herewith the opposite picture of their separation as the history of the world everywhere presents it.

When, however, God is brought into relation with experience of the deficiency of human existence, this is not altered by addition and correction but by the transforming of man into a new creature and his acceptance of the promised and proffered regeneration (Röhricht, p. 177). Adding, correcting, and supplementing are my own action. Transformation, however, has to be done on me.

VII

The Personality of God

1. THE PROBLEM OF THE CONCEPT OF PERSON AS A THEOLOGICAL CATEGORY

From what has been said thus far, the use of the concept of person for God, or his description as a personal God, is suggested for two negative reasons and has thus occurred already in our deliberations.

The first of these negative reasons is that the concept of person forms a good barrier against ideas, postulates, and the like out of which the God of the philosophers is constructed.[1] Intrinsic to the idea of person is the principle that it involves an individuality that cannot be subsumed. The question naturally arises—and we shall soon have to discuss it—whether the use of the concept in relation to God does not raise difficulties of its own in other respects. For instance, does not individuality imply limitation and thus do violence to the deity of God?

The second negative reason why the use of the concept of person for God is suggested is, as we have seen, that God is never just the answer to human questions. In disclosing himself, he sets up the existential position for the question regarding him. He brings us into the truth, and raises new questions with the new creation. Hence the who and what of God can hardly be expressed in any other way than by the word "person." For as person he is never a mere object, e.g., the object of our asking, thinking, hoping, or postulating. He is also the working and self-revealing subject. Only with the help of the concept of person does it seem that we can express the fact that God is understanding, freedom, and love. Negatively, this means that God is not a first cause which lends the character of a mere effect to his work. Instead, he is the Creator who gives the creature man his own being, and confers on him the destiny of being a counterpart who is capable of decision and can either grasp his destiny or miss it.

---

[1] Thus Barth notes that the idea of the personality of God is "a product of the battle against modern naturalism and pantheism," CD, I, 1, pp. 350f.

The concept of person which is thus suggested will naturally pose its own problems, as we have said. This is why Tillich thinks we should avoid speaking of the personal God and speak instead of the ground of being. In the light of our previous deliberations on the question of God, there can be no denying that the concept of person has its dubious aspects when it is applied to God.

Thus we have shown that the term "God" can never be the synonym of another word (e.g., norm or value), since it always transcends such words. This means, however, that the same difficulty arises in relation to the word "person." Any equation of God and person, or any attempt to make the human person a model in thinking of God, is thus ruled out from the very outset. Equations of this kind would again make God an image of the creaturely in the sense of human religion or idolatry. Depicting God as an old man with a long beard is only an extreme instance or caricature of what can take place along these lines. If God's personal character is defined by the model of man the verdict of anthropomorphism cannot be averted.

We may thus say at once that just as Christ can be defined in terms of the logos concept but also himself determines the content of the concept, so God is not to be defined in terms of a given concept of person. On the contrary, the word "God" gives the concept of person a new thrust once the concept is impressed into the service of describing the nature of God. It, too, is baptized, as we put it earlier.

We shall thus take two steps in our further deliberations. We shall first consider the positive and then the negative fitness of the concept of person in statements about God.

2. THE POSITIVE AND NEGATIVE AFFINITY OF THE WORD "PERSON" IN DESCRIPTION OF GOD

a. The Positive Aspect

That the word "person" has a certain fitness in statements about God may be suspected already from the fact that some theologians are so emphatic in banishing it from this field. We refer, for example, to the theological representatives of right-wing and left-wing Hegelianism, A. E. Biedermann[2] and D. F. Strauss.[3]

If God is thought of as absolute spirit, for whom finite spirit is only a transition in the process of self-knowledge, the concept of person or personality can only be the expression of an inferior or inadequate religious idea. Since Hegel puts finite and absolute spirit in some sense on the same line, i.e., that of the process of self-development, he works out the classical schema of thought within which God is integrated with the human concept and

---

[2] *Christliche Dogmatik* (1869), § 618, 715f.
[3] *Die christliche Glaubenslehre*, I (1840), § 33, pp. 502ff.

thus ceases to transcend it. Rejection of the concept of person commends itself to him for this reason.

In fact, whenever God is spoken of as a person, that in God which transcends all concepts comes to expression.

(1) God's personhood implies that he cannot be the object of our thinking—so-called natural theology leads to human religion—nor can he be the object of our ethical concern along the lines of the question of the rich young man: 'What good thing shall I do, that I may have eternal life?' For this concern leads to work-righteousness as a form of self-confirmation. Instead God is a free subject who causes us, who works in us, who can thus bring us into the truth in which we can hear his voice and conceive of him, and who can direct our willing and doing to himself (Philippians 2:13).[4]

This means that the concept of person offers here only one aspect of its significance for use in description of the nature of God. In its totality it is not congruent with (or normative for) what is meant by the word "God." For this reason Barth rightly contends for a limited use of the concept of person when he says that the real issue is not that God is or has personality but that God is the One who loves. What must be affirmed is not that God is person but what specific person he is. This is the one necessary thing even when the terms person and personality are not used at all.[5]

On the other hand, one need not be afraid of using the personal attribute so long as it is realized that no more is being done than in the use of any theological terms. The language of theology makes use of the available vocabulary (in the form of an instrumental use). In so doing it does not let the original content of the terms become dominant or normative. God is a free subject turning to us freely in love. Insofar as it denotes this, the term person may be employed.

(2) Another element in the content of the word "person" is also serviceable. By nature person always includes relation to a Thou, to another personal being. In older trinitarian ontology the term "person" thus served as a corrective to the idea of substance and to the substantial unity of God expressed thereby.[6] Genesis 1:26 brings out this relational character of the word "person" when it has God speak in the first person plural and in the form of a dialog: "Let us make man." This "we" also forms the framework of Johannine Christology.[7]

When the Johannine Christ says: "The Son can do nothing of himself" (5:19, 30), he hereby describes his person as pure relationality to the Father. Indeed, the very terms Father and Son already imply this relation. The Father is Father only insofar as he is related to the Son and *vice versa*. Neither is centered in itself as substance and entelechy. Each is there for

---

[4] Cf. Barth, CD, I, 1, pp. 138f.
[5] CD, II, 1, pp. 296f.
[6] This is finely worked out by Ratzinger, *Einführung*, pp. 142ff.; E.T. pp. 130ff.
[7] *Ibid.*, p. 145; E.T. pp. 132f.

and to the other. For this reason the term substance with its monological character is not adequate to describe the relation of God and Christ as the unity of the divine essence. The oneness of the two[8] is misunderstood if it is viewed merely as the static unity which is implicit in the term substance when this alone is used.

This is where the concept of person comes in with its corrective function. Just because the Son is only to the Father, not therefore standing in or centered on himself, but finding himself in constant self-giving, he is one with the Father and lives a dialogical and not a monological life.

The concept of person, however, plays a part not merely in this intra-trinitarian relation but also in regard to man. In correspondence with the oneness of Christ with the Father, Jesus in the high-priestly prayer asks also that his own may be one with one another in him (John 17:11, 21f.). Again, as Christ can do nothing without the Father, the same applies to his own: "Without me ye can do nothing" (15:5). They, too, do not stand in themselves. They are to him and from him. This is precisely and solely what is meant to be expressed by the concept of person insofar as person always implies a being in relation to the Thou.[9]

Even when the word "person" is used for God himself, the relational aspect is still claimed. God determines himself as Immanuel, i.e., as God for man, for his people, and for the world.[10] In the first commandment he makes himself known as "my" Lord and God.[11] He is the Lord of the covenant, freely establishing it (diatheke), and not functioning merely as the partner in an agreement (syntheke) which exists independently of him and apart from him.[12]

The fact that God freely turns to man and enters into covenant with him, becoming Immanuel and not keeping anything back (in Luther's sense), finds expression supremely in his speaking, in his sending forth his word, and his doing this in free sovereignty. "He is the Lord of the wording of His word."[13] When he causes his word to become flesh, his condescension, his dialogical solidarity with man, reaches its height. Because he thus meets us in the word, and enters his word, he makes those whom he addresses capable of words. He makes them responsive. He gives them responsible existence. He commands them to give this response by showing trust and obedience and also by making reply in prayer and worship: "Seek ye my face" (Psalm 27:8).

W. Herrmann points out that this "responding" means God wants vocal

---

[8] "I and the Father are one," John 10:30; 14:5-11.
[9] The Lutheran doctrine of the communication of attributes gives extreme expression to this relational character of the concept of person; Volume I, pp. 292ff.
[10] As regards the world cf. John 3:16f.; 12:47; 8:12; 9:5; 2 Corinthians 5:19; 1 Timothy 1:15; 1 John 4:14.
[11] Althaus, "Gottes Gottheit als Sinn der Rechtfertigungslehre Luthers," Theologische Aufsätze, II (1935), pp. 1ff.
[12] O. Procksch, Theologie des AT (1950), p. 92.
[13] Barth, CD, I, 1, p. 139.

rather than silent worship. If we are confident that God is present, we can address him in truth, and we should do so if we are not to suffer serious harm. To interiorize God's reality and not address him opens up a rift in man which will lead to dissolution of the inner life, i.e., the personal existence of man which is initiated by God through his word (Art. "Gebet," RE, IV, p. 387).

In emphasizing the dialogical and relational element in the concept of person, we realize that this, too, does not give an adequate account of God's being and nature. In christological debates this comes to expression in that although God, as we said, enters his word, he is not exhausted by it nor shut up within it. If he were, this would again mean that he makes himself superfluous and dissolves himself in another, as many theologians think he merges into the neighbor. In contrast, we must insist that God in free sovereignty, as the Lord of the wording, resolves on dialog, speech, and openness to man as Immanuel. He is thus more than the relation, and transcends it, for he always remains the free subject of his resolve, never becomes its captive, and can therefore keep silence or withdraw (Deuteronomy 31:18; Job 13:24; Proverbs 1:28; Jeremiah 14:8f.; 15:18; 23:23, etc.). Calvin expressed this ongoing transcendence in his statement that God is always *eksarkos* too and never just *ensarkos*. For him the incarnation of the Word is a personal act of constant self-giving and never a fixed ontological status. Cf. the so-called *extra Calvinisticum* in Inst., II, 13, 4 and II, 14, and on this Volume I, pp. 292ff.

The fact that man achieves dialogical existence through the word of God (Buber) directs our gaze once again to the personal element.

Through the word God and man are related as I and Thou, i.e., as persons. Human personality finds its basis here. What other basis can it have but this relation to the inviolable majesty of God through whose word it is itself made capable of words?[14] When today we express by the concept of personality the unconditionality of man which distinguishes him from things and animals, which makes him inviolable, and which prevents him from being made the means to an end, the rank of the *humanum* proclaimed herewith has its basis in what the *imago Dei* passages of the OT say about man's participation in the majesty of God.[15] When this alien dignity of man, his existence in relation to God, is forgotten, the infinite worth implied in the concept of person yields to his exploitability, his degradation as a mere functionary, and his self-alienation in terms of pure instrumentality.

Even when the modern understanding of the person derives, not from the Bible, but from Greek antiquity and its understanding of the person as individuality, we still find a reference to the gods and not just to the idea of a self-grounded and autonomous entelechy. In Greek antiquity, too, man regards himself as theonomous. Homer calls men mortals (*thnetoi*). The relation which defines them is not to the animals, as in modern thought,

---

[14] Cf. Pannenberg, *Grundfragen*, pp. 328f.; E.T. *Basic Questions*, II, pp. 227f.
[15] ThE, I, § 800, 806ff.; E.T. I, pp. 160ff.

but to the gods as the immortals (*athanatoi*). One may compare Pindar's warning not to try to become Zeus, since only what is mortal befits mortals (V. Isth. 13f.). Odysseus speaks to the same effect in Sophocles' *Ajax* when he tells the stricken Ajax that all who live are no more than phantoms and empty shadows (125ff.). Aeneas again is not a hero who emancipates himself from the gods. He does not defy the powers, as Goethe put it. In Vergil he is the "pious Aeneas" who just because he subordinates his personal will to his destiny becomes the ancestor of Rome (Franz Altheim, "Von den Ursachen der Grösse Roms" in H. Oppermann, *Römertum* [1962]): "Because thou bowest to the gods, thou rulest. Here is always the beginning and the end" (Horace, Ode 6). Finally Plato sees man set in the same relation. In the *Laws* (716c) he refutes the famous statement of the Sophist Protagoras that man is the measure of all things, arguing in reply that the measure of all things is God (W. Jaeger, *Paideia,* I [1936], pp. 382ff.; cf. also K. Ringshausen, "Der Humanismus in der Erziehungs- und Bildungskreise der Gegenwart," *Veröffentl. Nr. 48 der Ev. Akademie Hessen-Nassau* [1962], pp. 13ff.). The modern humanism which has developed out of the concept of person cannot be understood apart from this origin and background.

(3) Another content of the word "person" has already been indicated by our observation that the person can never be equated with a concept but resists this. This can be illustrated from the sphere of human relations.

A person's identity is obscured if he is given a purely material reference, as when people speak of "the appendix in room 197," "manpower," or the like. When a person is subsumed under a concept or reduced to a stereotype,[16] he is robbed of the individual being which cannot be equated with an immanent entity or made anything other than it is.[17]

H. Braun, who obviously thinks that the concept of person is a modern one with no basis in the Bible and hence inadequate as a description of God, once thought that he could embarrass L. Goppelt in a radio discussion by asking him to translate the word "person" in Hebrew. Without the slightest hesitation, however, Goppelt suggested the Hebrew word *shem*, i.e., "name."

It is, in fact, a noteworthy point that persons have names which express their unique identity. The identity denoted by the name forbids definition by anything else, e.g., a concept. We all know how awkward it is[18] when we

---

[16] M. Frisch points out that the commandment not to make graven images does not apply only to God. God is the living element in man which cannot be pinned down. To make an image of man is an offense from which we suffer and which we commit in return except when we love (*Tagebuch 1946-49,* Knaur Bd. 100, p. 30). We miss the mark in any case, for man as a living being is constantly changing. A fixed image contradicts self-fulfilling and changing life (*Santa Cruz,* p. 53). There is a constant danger of breaking the mystery and also a danger of coming to a premature halt (*Tagebuch,* p. 34). Stiller, too, admits that he has no words for the reality (*Stiller,* 1965, p. 65, cf. also p. 114).

[17] As noted, this is the reason why Hegel cannot finally conceive of personality. It is "only" a transition in the process of the world spirit.

[18] Cf. Röhricht, *art. cit.,* p. 178.

have to give "definitions" of a man and thus identify him by something
that is purely external. This involves definition in an intolerably specific
way. He must be characterized merely by what has come to light in an inter-
view with him in a very limited space of time. Might he not have been different earlier and might he not become different yet again later? Might he not
have presented himself in a very different light to others, e.g., his mother,
loved ones, associates at work, or competitors, so that the partial impressions cannot be brought into congruity? Any attempt to identify a man
with his role or subsume him under a concept leads necessarily to the falsifying of his uniqueness. This uniqueness always contains a transcendent element, a free possibility which cannot be pinned down.

The name expresses this transcendent content. It eludes any concept.
The concept is always a fixed designation. It encloses a thing, or process,
or idea, or norm in a meaning which it itself prescribes and fixes. The name,
however, is not a designation of this kind. In itself it tells us nothing. When
I do not know a man or have heard of him only from accounts, I can get no
conception of him merely from his name. When I am discussing somebody
with others and they tell me whom he married and what happened to him,
this becomes very boring, for the names alone mean nothing. Sometimes
descriptions may be added to names to bring out some aspect of those who
bear them, e.g., Pippin the Short, or Charles the Great, or Hilda the Red.[19]
The name can be filled out and interpreted, however, only by its bearer.

To be sure, as I meet people I constantly find myself categorizing name-
bearers by fixed concepts. This man is a typical manager, another is an
ambitious type, yet another a phlegmatic type. In stereotyping them thus,
I bring them under concepts which do not do them justice. I deprive them
of the possibility of being themselves, and of representing that transcendent
element which consists in development and presents different aspects to
others, "to the ship as coast and to the land as ship" (R. M. Rilke).

Only the name, then, can do justice to the being of the self in its inex-
changeability. The name-bearer is not defined; he is introduced and he
presents himself. This means that he opens up a history with himself by
showing or concealing what he really is, so that this actually is in either
case the relevant point. By merely telling us his name, as in a telephone
directory, he tells us nothing about himself.

The name in its uniqueness[20] is thus a privilege of the person and ex-

---

[19] This does not rule out the fact that in the Bible the name may be originally
given as a designation, e.g., Jesus in Matthew 1:21, Simon Peter in Mark 3:16,
and cf. Matthew 16:18; Luke 9:54f.; Acts 4:36; 13:8; Philippians 2:9. The same
is true of names like Abraham, Isaac, Israel, Jacob. It applies especially when
names are changed, as in Genesis 17:5, 15; Ruth 1:20. This does not mean, however, a full equation of the person with what the name designates. Nor does it
preclude the name's being characterized by its bearer.

[20] This uniqueness is not destroyed even though we bear common surnames like
Smith. If these surnames pose a threat to uniqueness it can be reversed by less
usual first names or even by the use of irony to denote the distinction between
personal originality and the common name.

presses the fact that this person cannot be reduced to a common denominator or equated with anyone else.[21]

Names also serve to identify people in personal relations. This does not mean, of course, that the name discloses the mystery of another person. It simply denotes that this or that person is here or is under discussion. Who this person is can be disclosed only as he makes himself known.

From the fact that names have this function in personal relations one may understand why names are usually given by others. Even if persons do sometimes name themselves, it is not for their own sake but for the sake of others. This function of the name also corresponds to the nature of the person, for the person exists in communication, in being for the Thou, not solipsistically for itself.

These characteristics of the name enable us to understand why the name of God stands representatively for his personality and why in some dimensions of its meaning the word "person" can be used to describe God. When God indicates his name, he shows that he is not to be located in a nexus of being, as though there were something all-embracing in which he could be integrated or something higher and general under which he could be subsumed. He makes himself known as the unique One who has no other gods beside him (Exodus 15:11; 23:13; Psalm 86:8; 96:4f., etc.).[22] He also makes himself known as the One who wills to be Immanuel, who demands obedience and wills to be involved. In short, he binds himself to man in address and answer, in the interchange of person and person.

This is the point of the declaration of God's name at the burning bush in Exodus 3:14, when God discloses himself as Yahweh: "I will be who I will be." That this giving of the name does not have the significance of self-definition, and cannot, therefore, be an antipersonal act, is shown by the fact that this name in no way ties God down either in nature or conduct. Everything is left "open," as H. J. Kraus says. He himself will make it plain in the future who he is and will be. I will be—but it is still to be revealed who I will be. There is thus expressed here the freedom of this self-revealing God for the future self-disclosing and self-imparting which will take place in history.[23] If the name were meant as a concept embracing the nature of God, we should have definitive information with this self-declaration. Instead, the name simply denotes the one with whom we have to do or who is under discussion. It leaves it for him to disclose himself. It leaves it for him to interpret his name by what he makes known by word and work in his self-disclosure. The only definitive thing that this name Yahweh lays down is that this self-disclosure and self-impartation will follow, so that Yahweh has at his command an incalculable multiplicity of ways of acting

---

21 Number is always less than word, and word than name; cf. E. Rosenstock-Huessi, *Die Sprache des Menschengeschlechtes*, I (1963), p. 48, cited by Röhricht, *art. cit.*, p. 180, n. 13.
22 Cf. Volume I, pp. 92ff.
23 H. J. Kraus, "Wahrheit in der Geschichte" in Müller-Schwefe, *op. cit.*, p. 38.

and working.[24] In this sense W. Eichrodt believes that "I am" and "I will be" are the same as "I am for you." The being in the name of Yahweh is to be construed, not as being in itself, but as being for.[25]

How little the name Yahweh has here the function of defining and pinning down may be seen from two other aspects.

First, Yahweh's self-naming as "I will be who I will be" is not self-naming in the sense that he lets himself be grasped in the form of an image, likeness, or concept. From that standpoint we have concealment and the refusal of a name. When Moses asks: "Behold, when I come unto the children of Israel, and shall say unto them, The God of your fathers hath sent me unto you; and they shall say to me, What is his name? what shall I say unto them?" he receives no true answer, or at any rate not the answer which the question of the name implied. For the desire of Israel was to know the name so as to have it, to apprehend it. In rejection of this desire the name of Yahweh might even have a tacitly ironical sense: "I am who I am—there!"[26] If we want to keep in line with modern OT scholarship and see a future in the name Yahweh, we might express the irony of this refusal of a name as follows: You will see from the history inaugurated by me who I am and as whom I shall make myself known.

Does Yahweh accept, then, the question as to his name? When he answers: "I will be who I will be," is this really a name at all, a name which stands in some analogy to the names of the gods and which might be listed along with others in a catalog of the gods? Is it not rather a rejection of any apprehension by name and instead a promise, a promise which leaves everything open and thus permits a mosaic of the image of God to be formed? Is not everything suspended on the future possibilities of God which he reserves for himself, so that he alone knows himself and will declare this knowledge only with his deeds and works?

As with the concept "person," "name," too, when it is referred to God, is not a synonym for him which tells us all about him. The name, too, is wrapped in a final inappropriateness, so that God escapes and transcends it. The name, too, even if on another page, shares the ambivalence of all concepts that try to embrace God's nature and subsume him under something higher. That the name can be judged, too, as an attempt to lay hands on God finds expression in the refusal to give a name. The Elohist obviously knows how names can be misused in magic, how knowledge of a name confers the power to control it, how with its help authority can be exercised over what is named, and how incantations and charms can arise in consequence.[27] For this reason the transcendence of Yahweh will not let itself be reduced to a name.

---

[24] *Ibid.*

[25] *Theology of the OT,* I (E.T. 1961), p. 190. In the name Yahweh the name of God means being "present" (in the sense of a presence which blesses and afflicts). The emphasis is not on inactive but on active existence.

[26] Cf. Ratzinger, *Einführung,* p. 94; E.T. p. 86.

[27] Kraus, *loc. cit.;* cf. Barth, CD, II, 1, pp. 60f.

We find similar refusals elsewhere. When Jacob wrestled with God at the ford Jabbok he asked: "What is thy name?" But God refused: "Wherefore is it that thou dost ask after my name? And he blessed him there" (Genesis 32:29). Yahweh is known, not by his name, but by his blessing.

Similarly when Manoah asks the angel of the Lord what is his name, he meets with this repulse: "Why askest thou thus after my name, seeing it is secret?" (Judges 13:17f.).

Second, the refusal of Yahweh to let his name be a means of grasping him conceptually may be seen from the mutation this name undergoes in the Septuagint. Here the name suffers alienation by being made into an ontological concept of being. "I will be who I will be" means here "I am he who truly is."[28] Thus the refusal of a name, which safeguards the mystery of Yahweh and points forward to future revelations, gives place now to conceptual definition. This definition integrates the nature and essence of God into a nonhistorical ontological understanding. It subsumes God. Even if name, which as distinct from concept has a certain appropriateness in relation to the personal, is not exempt from the possibility of alienation, this alienation becomes utter distortion once name for its part has to take over again the functions of concept.[29]

b. The Negative Aspect

Our attempt thus far to elucidate the meaning of the word "person" in description of God has brought us up continually against the limitation of the possibilities of the term. As we have seen, it can even take over the functions of a concept and thus become incapable of expressing what we mean when we speak of the personal God. For what we intend by this is that God turns to us freely, addresses us in his word, and thereby discloses himself, and that in so doing he causes us for our part to share in the dignity of the personal, making us I to the divine Thou. If this and this alone is meant when we speak of God as a person, it is plain that only some aspects of the meaning of the word "person" can apply to God. In other words, the term is not a conceptual framework in which God can be put. Its function is to serve, and it can do this only with certain elements of its total signification.

When we consider the question in what respects the word "person" is inadequate and falls short when used in description of God, we may note— and this should occasion no surprise—that the inadequacy is always apparent when, instead of being defined by God, the term is used to define God and thus becomes impermissibly normative.

In more recent philosophy a classical instance of this alien normative

---

[28] *Egố eimi ho ốn.*
[29] For similar mutations in the Septuagint cf. K. Koch in relation to the concept of truth, in Müller-Schwefe, *op. cit.*, pp. 47ff., esp. 58ff.

use of the term person is to be found in M. Scheler. In his ethics (*Der Formalismus in der Ethik*) the word "person" is defined in advance in a blatantly nonrelational way, so that no I is expressed nor is there any reference to a Thou or to the world outside. Hence God can be a person but not an I, since there is for him neither Thou nor outside world (p. 404). Even though God is described as free personal will, he is still not an I which turns to a Thou in love but is understood as a power of spontaneity which has to be distinguished from the Greek Heimarmene as the universal power of fate and blind necessity (*Das Ewige im Menschen,* II [1923], pp. 204f.). When Scheler calls the person the center of action in which the Spirit appears in finite spheres of being, there is again no reference to a Thou. I-Thou relations to God in the sense of Lord and servant or Father and child (including the divine sonship of Christ) have thus to be given their ultimate basis in a philosophical consideration of the relation of man (*Die Stellung des Menschen im Kosmos,* pp. 39, 89f.). Scheler certainly finds personality in God. But this is no cause for rejoicing, since we do not find the very thing that we think is denoted by the words "personal God," i.e., his self-declaration as an I and his self-disclosure in relation to man. We necessarily miss this, for God here is not the model according to which person is to be defined. Instead, an ontologically constructed concept of person is the model which serves as a norm for the philosophical idea of God. Scheler does not contest the application of the concept of person to God; he exacts too high a price.

If, then, we begin with an existing concept of person which serves as a criterion, we miss the God of the Bible. We do so because—and Fichte was right here—"personality and consciousness . . . cannot be conceived of apart from limitation and finitude."[30] An infinite person is thus a contradiction in terms.[31] Communication between I and Thou is possible only because we are limited. We talk to each other because we do not know what the other will say. We work together because limits are set for our own activity and ability. We investigate because our knowledge is partial. We are constantly striving because we never reach the whole. We sense the ethical imperative because we are not congruent with the picture of what we ought to be. The personal life of man can be imagined only on the condition of the limits and barriers between the I and the Thou, the I and the world, the real and the ideal.

This line of thought is what impels Tillich to argue against the symbol of a personal God and to describe it as misleading.[32] God cannot be *a* person. The personal element in him is that he is the ground of all personhood and bears in himself the ontological power of the personal. Otherwise, in

---

[30] *Über den Grund unseres Glaubens an eine göttliche Weltregierung* (1798). This article started the atheism debate.

[31] Röhricht, *op. cit.,* p. 185.

[32] *Systematic Theology,* I, pp. 244f.

virtue of the limitations of the person, we make him an individual[33] and hence *a* being instead of being itself.

What remains, however, if along the lines of Tillich God is simply all-embracing being and not the personal counterpart he determines himself to be? Can the biblical symbol of the "heart" of God be used for being? Can the ground of the world as thus described be thought of as love and understanding? Does the depth of being *speak?* Tillich excludes the word "person" from his depiction of God because in his understanding of being he sets forth an ontological system in which the words "person" and "God" represent specific but very different aspects of being. The terms are thus brought into a fixed relation to one another and set at a fixed distance from one another. Under the rule of the system it is impossible that the content of the word "person" should be defined by God and that some aspects of its content should be serviceable in this definition.

When the word "person" has this function of service, it is even possible, biblically, that the "individual" aspects contained in it should be brought into use. This happens, for example, when God does not just call himself the ground of being from which all gods and powers derive and which embraces them all—and where do we find this anyway?[34]—but when he delimits himself from the gods and the powers as though he had limits of this kind. He is "to be feared above all gods" (1 Chronicles 16:25; Psalm 96:4); he is (comparatively) greater (Exodus 15:11; 18:11; Psalm 72:18f.; 86:8, etc.); among the gods there is none like him (Psalm 86:8); he triumphs over them (1 Kings 18:21-40); he is their judge (Psalm 82:1). Even when he is exalted above all the gods as the one and only God (Deuteronomy 32:39; 1 Corinthians 12:16), he still shows himself to be God in comparison and hence leaves a third term between himself and the gods. Certainly there is a grain of irony in this. For the common element which God seems to establish between himself and the gods for the purpose of comparison is only on account of our all too human conceptions. From God's own standpoint the gods are nothing (Jeremiah 10:8; 16:19; Isaiah 41:29), so that it is nonsensical to speak of God's privileges in relation to them or even to call him the only one to whom the title "God" really belongs.

This simply confirms the fact that the word "person" relates to our ideas and that it simply contains aspects of meaning which can be used within this framework. Even this is possible, however, only if one keeps in mind the purpose for which these elements are brought into service, so that steps are taken to avert any revolt of means, and the concept of "person" is excluded from any normative role.

Typical of this purely instrumental signification of the concept of "person" is its use in the doctrine of the Trinity. Here it does not refer to God as such—this comes only with the nineteenth century—but applies to the

---

[33] If possible the shadowy concept for an "absolute individual," *ibid.*
[34] Colossians 1:16 can hardly be taken in this sense.

trinitarian figures of Father, Son, and Holy Spirit. The only elements implied in the word "person" that are used here are the relational and dialogical elements. The trinitarian controversies between Modalists, Monarchians, and Subordinationists all arose basically because there was on the one hand an attempt to see autonomy in the persons, and this threatened to produce tritheism or a hierarchy, while on the other hand the aim was to prevent this distortion and to use the concept of "person" in a statement which would express both the unity and also the plurality of God. For the way in which the dogma utilizes terms without feeling subject to them K. Rahner has coined the pregnant expression "speech-control" ("Was ist eine dogmatische Aussage?" *Schriften zur Theologie,* V [1962], pp. 67-72; E.T. *Theological Investigations,* V [1966], pp. 42ff.).

The principles which we have thus worked out, and which must be normative in the theological use of the word "person," may now be summed up as follows.

When we describe God as person this cannot mean that we apply to him a concept of person which is modelled on man or which is taken from general ontology. The truth is the very opposite. The self-disclosing divine I makes the human Thou its personal counterpart. As the human idea of person can offer only partial aspects of meaning for a description of God, the converse is also true. The way in which we describe God as personal, or as the personal God, can itself apply only in part to the way in which we call man a person. In this regard it must also be maintained that the personhood of God has ontic primacy over that of man.

We may thus venture the formulation that when we speak of God as person we do not mean this anthropomorphously. On the contrary, we mean it theomorphously when we speak of man as person.

Related hereto is a final point. If the word "God" cannot be fitted into any proposed understanding of the term, if it transcends all concepts and norms, including those that relate specifically to itself, and if it thus refuses to be a cipher for anything outside itself, then we can understand the dominant biblical form of speaking about God, namely, its proclamation of God in history, in declaration of the salvation event, in stories. The course of history, which opens up constantly into a future that is ever new, makes it apparent that the name of God cannot be contained. We have here the space and time of the possibility which this name always opens up and keeps open. God comes forward and discloses himself but he also steps back and guards his secret. He is both revealed and hidden here at one and the same time. "Thy way is in the sea, and thy path in the great waters, and thy footsteps are not known" (Psalm 77:19; cf. Exodus 33:23).

This noncontainment, this openness to possibilities, is a mark of the revelation of God. It corresponds exactly to what the name Yahweh implies with its "I will be what I will be." God is to be found in the work and action which he reserves for himself in freedom, which is thus his possibility and his alone, and which can never be absorbed into the necessity of a concept or into a philosophy of the course of history.

For this reason all the events recorded in the Bible are at one and the same time both prophecy, i.e., a reference to the future possibilities of God which are his affair, and also a reference to the noncontainment and incomprehensibility of the present. This is why we do not have God as an idea but hear about him and receive him in the form of stories. We do this as we make what has happened present by remembrance (Exodus 12:26; 13:14; Deuteronomy 6:20). We do it as we are mindful of his mighty acts (Acts 2:11). We do it in hope, trusting his promise and looking ahead to his open possibilities. These possibilities, however, do not mean leaps in the dark, for God will be the same to all eternity (1 Peter 1:25; 2 John 2; Hebrews 13:8), and with every new step he is the God who manifested himself in the burning bush.

VIII

A Polemical Conclusion:
Transcendentalism in the Question of God

THE REVERSION OF THEOLOGY TO METAPHYSICS

How Does So-called Christian Atheism Arise?

No matter how we have approached the question of God thus far, from the standpoint of word, name, or person, the God of the Bible has always met us as the Immanuel who encounters man, discloses himself to him, and communicates with him. He is the God who leaves the other world and comes to this world. When we speak of him, therefore, we cannot describe him as he is ontically in himself, as the supreme being, but only as we see him in this relation of his to this world. Since he is the reality which determines our existence, we can speak of him only by speaking of his word which is addressed to us and his work which is directed upon us.[1] Christ, too, is not accessible to us as he is in himself, but only in his benefits, i.e., in his history as this is oriented to us.[2]

If God is thus understood as the reality which radically determines my existence and my being in the world, then it is possible in principle for me to grasp this relation of God and the world at either end when I begin to speak of God. I may thus begin with the question of God itself and then move on from this to the world and existence as they are determined by him. Or I may take the opposite course, beginning with anthropology or cosmology and then going on to understand man and his world in their determination by God. When the believer speaks about himself, this has to mean that he

---

[1] R. Bultmann, "Welchen Sinn hat es von Gott zu reden?" GV, I, p. 36; E.T. p. 63. Cf. also Bultmann's quotation from W. Herrmann, *Die Wirklichkeit Gottes* (1914), p. 42: "We can tell about God only what he does to us."
[2] We recall the well-known saying of Melanchthon in the 1521 *Loci*: "To know Christ is to know his benefits."

speaks about his determination by God. The question who I am is the same as the question who God is for me.

It is well known that in Luther's view of God this relation is the key. He is thus describing this relation when he is talking about God. This is why, in his exposition of the first commandment in the Larger Catechism, he has the following question and answer: "What does it mean to have a God or what is God? A God is that by which we are provided with all good things and in which we have a refuge in all troubles," so that "only the trust and belief of the heart makes either God or idol."[3]

Starting with trust and belief, i.e., with an anthropological datum, seems especially to characterize theologians who are concerned about the problem of appropriation and who raise the question how the thought of God, faith, and religion can be integrated into the consciousness and brought into harmony with the conditions of our understanding.[4]

This kind of tendency or approach increases in urgency as this world emancipates itself and is understood as self-resting finitude. The result is that everything that transcends the world and consciousness comes under the verdict of being an object of dogmatic metaphysics and hence of being part of a process of thought outside the bounds of verifiability. This difficulty, it seems, can be overcome only if we succeed in detaching God from his transcendence and finding him in his relation to existence and within immanent realities. If theology can be given a demonstrable place in anthropology and cosmology and perhaps understood as a function of these, then the suspicion is removed (or at least lessened) that the word "God" is simply a doctrinaire positing, whether in a metaphysical game or for some pragmatic reason. In attempted integration of this kind welcome aid is obviously extended by the theological consideration just adduced, namely, that God is to be found in a constitutive relation to man's existence and his being in the world.

We are well aware of the degree to which Schleiermacher introduces the thought of God with the help of an existential element, i.e., the feeling of absolute dependence. The term God indicates the whence of our impressionable and self-acting existence.[5] Similarly the qualities which we ascribe to God denote special features in the way of relating the feeling of absolute dependence to him.[6]

---

[3] Cf. also WA, 56, 234, 4: As a man is in himself, so is his God.

[4] In Volume I we dealt with these theologians from the standpoint of their Cartesian starting-point, pp. 38ff.

[5] *The Christian Faith* (E.T. 1928), § 4; cf. Volume I, pp. 44f., 303ff.

[6] *The Christian Faith*, § 50. Cf. the typical statement of J. C. K. von Hofmann: "I, the Christian, am the real material of knowledge for myself, the theologian" (*Der Schriftbeweis*, I, 2nd ed. [1857], p. 10). G. Wobbermin speaks to the same effect when defining his religio-psychological method: "On the basis of the transcendental inquiry into the conditions of grasping a religious object, the historical constructs in which the religious consciousness of men has objectified itself must be analyzed in terms of their specifically religious core and content" (*Systematische Theologie nach rel.-psychologischer Methode*, I, 2nd ed. [1925], p. 388).

It is unmistakable that the Copernican revolution of Kantian epistemology exerts an influence here: we can make valid statements only about objects of our experience. Objects of experience, however, have to be things which correspond to the structure of our theoretical or practical consciousness or which are formed in part by this structure. Hence we do not see things as they are in themselves but only things which are refashioned by our forms and categories of apprehension.

This transcendental principle of Kantian epistemology is now applied to the thought of God, so that R. Seeberg[7] and E. Seeberg[8] can speak of a religious transcendentalism in which, supposedly after the manner of Luther, religious objects are defined by the way in which man appropriates them noetically and practically. We thus have here a correspondence between the reality that encounters us and the mode of our perception and conduct. Since God's being in itself is outside this correspondence it is beyond our epistemological grasp, like Kant's "thing in itself." As in Luther religious objects are accessible to us only to the extent that they are palpably related to our consciousness and condition, so this transcendental concept of the being of God in some sense anticipates Kant, so that Luther is almost viewed as Kant's forerunner.[9]

Here, then, the self-disclosure of God, which occurs in relation to man and makes all statements about God into statements about this relation, gives rise to the attempt to understand the relation as a transcendent ontological nexus which constitutes the horizon of our experience and which makes the conditions of our consciousness and situation normative for what we call the object of our faith. Luther's theology thus becomes a preliminary form of Kantian transcendentalism or, in the terminology of Volume I, of Cartesian theology. It seems obvious that we have here a distorting mutation. But where does the mistake lie?

This type of transcendentalism reaches its culmination in G. Ebeling.[10]

Ebeling develops the theological principle of transcendentalism out of Luther's opposition to the metaphysical concept of substance. In this polemic a radical change occurs in the concept of substance and hence also in the understanding of ontology. The substance of a thing is no longer what it is in itself but the relation in which it stands to man. More precisely, substance is what the thing means for the man who handles it, or what he takes it to be as he understands himself in his relation to it.[11] According to this relational structure of thought the being of things is thus determined by the manner of man's dealings with them, just as the being of man is de-

---

[7] *Lehrbuch der Dogmengeschichte*, IV, 1, 4th ed. (1933), pp. 47f., 156f.

[8] *Luthers Theologie*, I (1929), pp. 109ff.

[9] R. Seeberg, "Zur Rel.-philosophie Luthers," *Zeitschrift für Philosophie und philosophische Kritik*, 164 (1917), p. 91.

[10] One might also mention Gogarten, who expresses the relational element through the idea of the personal. Cf. on this G. Gloege, *Heilsgeschehen und Welt*, I, pp. 61ff.; B. Langemeyer, *Der dialogische Personalismus*, pp. 145ff.

[11] "Anfänge von Luthers Hermeneutik," ZThK, 48 (1951), p. 192.

termined by that with which he has dealings, on which he relies, and which he fears.

Whether in respect of the ontology of things or the ontology of man, what substance is will thus be decided by these dealings, by "meaning for," and hence by an existential reference.[12] The category of this existential relation to the object is represented in Luther by the terms *uti* and *usus*—Ebeling bases this on the 1531/35 *Commentary on Galatians*.[13] There is a striking linguistic parallel to this in Thornton Wilder's *Eighth Day of Creation* when we are told never to ask a man what he believes but what he uses, since belief is a dead word and brings death with it.[14] Only when there is use do we stand in a true living relation to a thing. Only in use is understanding tested.[15]

This interpretation of Luther, which is influenced by Kierkegaard's idea of the "existing thinker," is correct enough insofar as it describes Luther's attack on the Aristotelian idea of substance and emphasizes the relational character of Luther's own theological approach. Problems arise, however, when we investigate the positive foundations of this relational ontology and ask whether Luther's statement that God and faith belong together[16] can be understood in terms of reciprocal dependence or can be used as a shibboleth for transcendentalism in Luther.

When Ebeling erects upon this relational foundation the thesis[17] that theologically we cannot separate God, the world, and man, or treat them apart, but can speak of them only in a single nexus of reality, this is again true enough insofar as the mutual relation is concerned. But the fundamental theological question also comes to light in this thesis. For the problem is how the relation arises. By whom or what is it caused? Can we, like Ebeling, speak of a single nexus of reality which is structurally determined by the relations of God, the world, and man? Is this nexus of reality understood here as a nexus of being which is to be defined ontologically and within which God has his place, so that he is enclosed within something higher and all-embracing? If so, does not this nexus and reality have again the character of a substantial and static nexus which can be distinguished from the similar Aristotelian conception only to the extent that its elements consist, not of substantial monads, but of relations? Might there not have taken place here a new, if latent, subversion by metaphysics?

The decisive question on which everything depends is thus the question of the basis of the relational nexus. Does this basis consist of a universal be-

---

12 *Ibid.*

13 In his doctrine of the triple use of the law (cf. Ebeling, *Wort und Glaube* [1960], p. 60; E.T. *Word and Faith*, p. 71), Luther says that force lies in the use of things, not in things themselves (WA, 40, I, 174, 25).

14 Cf. p. 240.

15 Ebeling, *loc. cit.*

16 This is the basic statement on which Wobbermin's transcendentalism rests.

17 "Theologie und Wirklichkeit," *op. cit.*, p. 202; E.T. "Theology and Reality," *Word and Faith*, p. 200.

ing beyond which one cannot go, or does it consist in the fact that the nexus of relations has been set up by the self-disclosure of God and hence by his freedom? Do all the relations between God, the world, and man derive from the fact that God wills to be relational, that he thus resolves on a history with man, that he speaks to him and has dealings with him instead of remaining the silent ground of the world? Or do they derive from the relational structure of being itself as reason thinks it can explain it in speculative apprehension?

It is easy to see that the different answers to this question will give rise to two principially different theologies, or, better, to theology on the one side and metaphysics on the other. (One may regard as metaphysics of this kind some forms of a theological existentialism which subsumes God under his significance for existence and thus makes him a God in relation instead of accepting his resolve to be this as the basis of this mode of being beyond which one cannot go.

A certain intellectual affinity of Luther to Occam has constantly suggested that Luther should be interpreted along the lines of the transcendentalism treated above. For according to Occam we see things, including God, only in the reflex of our consciousness, and hence in relation to this. In Occam this has nothing whatever to do with the fact that by virtue of his self-disclosure God has accommodated himself in his word to the receptive capacity of our consciousness. Instead, the relation between God and consciousness arises out of the structure of the consciousness itself, so that the relational nexus is posited and grounded in it rather than God. Universals, including God as the supreme universal, have no independent ontic significance outside the mind. They are simply the reflex of the consciousness to something outside which provokes it; cf. P. Boehner, ed., *Ockham, Philosophical Writings* (1957), esp. here *Summa totius logicae*, I, cap. 14f.; cf. W. Joest, *Ontologie der Person*, pp. 68ff.

This brings us already to the critical point in theological transcendentalism. It consists in the misuse of a legitimate theological premise. God's being there for me, his secularity, is used to erect a metaphysical schema of the God-world relation which can stand only in an ontological framework which embraces both God and the world. Hence God does not just come within the God-man relation, i.e., for my consciousness insofar as he discloses himself to me. He is absorbed into it. To speak of God thus means to speak in a very definite way of the world, man, and reality in general. God becomes the cipher for an understanding of reality. In keeping with this, revelation is simply an elucidation of reality and especially of existence.

Revelation is no longer the invasion of a supernatural set of events and facts. It is simply a new qualification of existence by disclosure of the relation to God. In contrast, we ourselves have tried to make it plain[18] that revelation consists of more than a new illumination of reality. It points to a

---

[18] Cf. the debate with Cartesian theology in Volume I.

new source of light. It is thus in fact a datum outside the mind and outside the world.

As we have tried to show in this chapter, the disclosure of a new source of light does not mean that we see or ever could see the sun directly. This would simply blind us and would be a mistake. God as he is in himself does not offer himself to us as an object. In fact he appears to us only in that which is lit up by this source of light and which it warms and changes. We see ourselves in our old being and our new being. We see the act of change which takes place between the two. We see history and nature afresh. We see God in the reflection of what he does. We see the light in the reflection of what it shines upon. Paradoxically what has taken place would not be seen if we were to interpret this kind of illumination as the aspect of an eternal view in general and if we were not to ask how and through what the possibility of this aspect arises, namely, that the light has risen upon us and that we may say to him who causes it to rise: "In thy light we see light" (Psalm 36:9).

In this connection it is absolutely crucial to differentiate between the noetic and the ontological aspects.

Noetically, as the transcendentalists rightly saw, God comes to me only in the reflection of our reality. This is related to the self-disclosure of God in virtue of which he wills to be my God, God in the world, God in relation. As the God of Abraham, Isaac, and Jacob, to cite Pascal, he is fundamentally different from the God of the philosophers, who seek him as the supreme being and as being in itself. Noetically I have Christ, I have God, only in his benefits, in his history with me. But I have him thus only as I ontologically supplement this noetic aspect by the certainty that God is more than these benefits. He is more than they because he is subject in relation to them. He puts his condescension into effect freely and voluntarily. Unlike the God of the metaphysicians or Pascal's philosophers, he cannot be shut up in the necessity of a process of self-development. It is not that he "exists" or "is" in this history of his. The fact that the sun arises is an unquestionable miracle—it did not need to shine. It is a miracle, too, that we may see ourselves and this world afresh in this transforming light. Hence we cannot simply speak of a nexus of reality in which God, the world, and existence stand in mutual relations. We cannot take account only of that which is illumined. A *sine qua non* of appropriate theological speech is that we should speak also of the source of light itself and of the reason for its shining. The former course would give us only a cosmology and anthropology influenced by Christian ideas. The latter gives us "theo-logy" which has for its part cosmological and anthropological implications.

What might at first glance seem to be a hair-splitting distinction is shown to be a very serious one by its results.

After a period of secularized theology we can see today where the noetic aspect of a Christian interpretation of the world leads. God is exhausted in this world, in the act of faith (or, more sharply if also more maliciously, in the habit of belief), and in the attitude of general fellow-humanity. He thus becomes a cipher for something else. But once the true significance of this something else is perceived, it can stand on its own material evidence and will no longer need a cipher.

There can thus arise, and will necessarily do so, an absurd construct such as "Christian atheism." When what we have called the noetic aspect is absolutized, and when God becomes a synonym for a specific understanding of the world, revelation can no longer be the active self-disclosure of God but is reduced to a mere "being manifest," revelation without revelation, illumination without a source of light, disclosure without the self-disclosing subject.

Is it not as a safeguard against this attempt, not to see God in his willed relation to the world, but to imprison him in this relation, that the Bible refers in many ways to God's transcendence over the world? Thus he is more than either heaven or earth, and the heaven and heaven of heavens cannot contain him (2 Chronicles 2:3; 6:18; 1 Kings 8:27). He is also more than faith. Faith simply means that I anchor myself in the salvation event which he brings to pass and of which he always remains the subject.[19]

Theological transcendentalism is a secularized version of the doctrine of the incarnation. It starts with the basic Christian fact that God has freely determined himself as Immanuel, as God for me, and that he has given himself to the solidarity of a history with man. The miracle of this free resolve, grounded in his own will, gives place, however, to the relation which results therefrom. The background of this relation is forgotten and it becomes itself a principle of relationism.

A consequence of this conception is the inclusion of God in an all-embracing nexus of being (relationally understood) and his reduction to its cipher as himself an immanent principle. "Atheistic" theology is the logical consequence of this transcendentalism. If this is recognized to be an error, what one should contest is not the final symptom but the original transcendental schema.

The development of this schema is a process which takes many forms in the history of theology. It may be seen whenever a principle is distilled out of the active history which God has inaugurated, so that a basic mutation takes place and theology reverts to metaphysics. In its early stages the mutation is very hard to detect. Yet the tiny difference at the outset becomes bigger and bigger until finally, as today, God is divested of his transcendence in the name of relational thinking and he becomes the synonym of an immanent understanding of the world.

To illustrate the alternatives one might take the doctrine of the divine attributes as a model.

When we speak of the God of revelation we can also speak of his attributes only in terms of revelation. When revelation tells me that God speaks to me and acts on and with me, the word "attribute" can denote, not a constituent of God in himself, but only the nature of God as it is declared in

---

[19] H. J. Kraus, in Müller-Schwefe, *op. cit.*, p. 42.

his speech and action. Hence attributes such as his omnicausality, eternity, immutability, omnipotence, omniscience, etc., are to be expounded as modes of his historical relation to the cosmos and man. This can be done, however, only if the word "attribute" has a different sense as the mode of the subject who resolves upon these forms of relationship. When we confess the aseity of God we also bear witness to the aseity of his attributes and hence to their basis. This basis, which lets God be what he wills to be, lies outside the God-man relation, or is not, at least, exhausted in it. If this basis and background is overlooked, the attributes of God are made, as in Schleiermacher, into a cipher for the way in which I interpret certain phenomena of the consciousness, in this case the feeling of absolute dependence (*The Christian Faith,* § 50).

As Schleiermacher puts it here, the qualities which we attribute to God do not denote anything special in God but only something special in the way in which we relate the feeling of absolute dependence to him. Not to do injustice to Schleiermacher, we must acknowledge that serious questions of interpretation arise in respect of this statement. Even if he is not speaking of the attributes of God himself, of what is special "in" God, but only—epigrammatically—of the attributes of the relation of our consciousness to him, it is surely obvious, in spite of a common line of exposition, that for him God is not just the reference point of the consciousness posited by the latter itself. The stress on the consciousness in his doctrine of the attributes is occasioned by his controversy with speculative metaphysics and its doctrine of a God in himself. As there is for Schleiermacher no doctrine of a God in himself, so there is for him no doctrine of the consciousness in itself. He is referring always to the pious self-consciousness of the Christian which is posited by God the Creator and which is freed by God the Redeemer for personal reality (M. Redeker, *F. Schleiermacher* [1968], p. 217). To this extent knowledge and will as a fulfilling of our self-consciousness are not in the last resort founding functions of the human spirit but founded functions (p. 228). When Schleiermacher speaks of the pious self-consciousness he has in view a reference which God has set up and he thus sees sharp differences between his own teaching and the speculative concern which begins with the autarchy of the consciousness; cf. G. Ebeling, "Schleiermachers Lehre von den göttlichen Eigenschaften," *Wort und Glaube,* II (1969), pp. 310, 313. Even if this be true, however, the misunderstanding of Schleiermacher as an anthropocentric theologian of consciousness strengthens considerably the tendency to subsume the reality of God under relationism and finally to reduce it to a mere description of the reality of the world itself.

C. Revelation as a Word which Posits History. God's Being within Historical Revelation. Preliminary Note: The Creative and Active Word

Creation comes into being through the divine fiat: "Let there be." It thus derives from the creative Word which God not only speaks but "is" (John 1:1). This Word is creative because it calls forth out of nothing (Romans 4:17).[1] God is this Word because he gives himself in it and declares himself to be the God who discloses himself and who opens himself up to his creation.

This ontic Word which calls into being also calls into understanding and thus has a noetic side. It is the Word of proclamation which addresses me. When the Creator has spoken his "Let there be," he speaks to Adam and gives him the command and the promise. In both cases the Word is the same but in different forms, just as it is the same Spirit who hovers over the beginning of creation (Genesis 1:2), who calls Adam into being (2:7), and who finally makes the last Adam a life-giving Spirit (1 Corinthians 15:45). One might put it this way: The Word which effects creation also expounds it. What derives its nature from word can be disclosed only by word. The Word of creation and the Word of proclamation belong together.

Negatively this means that there is no access to creation apart from the Word. If this is attempted, the image of God is formed in accordance with that of creation. Instead of creation being the likeness of God, God becomes the likeness of creation. "The incorruptible is only a likeness" (Nietzsche). The hour of the gods strikes, or the hour of a philosophy that defines ultimate reality by the world, sets up a world-view, and either makes God its postulate or eliminates him.

Positively the implication is that the Word can be known only by the Word. If God is disclosed in the Word, the only way to him is via the Word. Luther's familiar saying that it is the person that does the works, and qualifies itself thereby, is true here also. I can understand the work of cre-

---

[1] This is why the Bible, as is well known, uses for "create" the term *barah*, which is reserved for God alone and differentiated from all artistic fashioning.

ation only in terms of the person of the Creator—the Creator who presents himself in his Word with a repeated "I am" and "I do."

Both forms of the Word are characterized by the fact that they are active and not just indicatory or interpretative Words.[2] In relation to the Word of proclamation in particular what we said about its expository function should not lead to the misconception that it merely interprets creation. As we said in Volume I, the indicatory or interpretative Word has validity only as facticity is enclosed in the act-word. It brings about regeneration and the new creation.[3] In it there is accomplished the miracle of the Spirit which initiates a being in the truth in which the voice of Christ can be received (John 18:37; cf. 3:21) and which leads to a new attitude to existence that can distinguish between what is of God and what is of self (John 7:17). Hence hearing, perceiving, understanding, and self-opening, too, are not just noetic functions which have their origin in the spontaneity of our consciousness. They are effects of the transforming Spirit-Word[4] which brings in a new being and by way of it renews the consciousness. To borrow a term from a completely different sphere, the consciousness here is in fact the superstructure of this new, created being.

To this degree the Word of God here too is more than an interpretative Word which simply extends the horizon of my understanding and gives me better insights into the depth of being. What is effected by it cannot be described in quantitative categories. Christian love is not "greater" than natural love. It is different from it. No comparative can assess the new obedience in relation to the old. It has a qualitatively new basis. Christ is not more perfect than other great men. He has a different origin. The same applies to the new hearing and receiving. This does not rest on enhanced alertness or a refining of the organ of spiritual reception. It rests on a mighty act which opens blind eyes and deaf ears[5] and removes the stones and thistles that choke the seed of the Word (Matthew 13:3-23). At every point we are dealing with the miracle of the Spirit who creatively calls something new to life.

The ontic Word of creation and the noetic Word of proclamation have, therefore, a decisive thing in common. They are both act-words in which God brings forth something new. They do not work along evolutionary lines in the sense that the world "develops"[6] out of what precedes, nor in the sense that the new is included in the continuity of human existence as a deepening or extension, so that, Socratically, it performs only the function of releasing what is already there.

Related hereto is the fact that the Word, thus qualified, is not enlightenment but act. It is a synonym for the "wonderful works of God" (Acts 2:11). This Word goes forth, then, in the form of events. It incarnates itself in history. It is salvation history. It thus chooses the form of stories to mani-

---

[2] Cf. Volume I, pp. 155ff.   [3] *Ibid.,* p. 156.   [4] *Ibid.,* pp. 129-218.
[5] Matthew 13:13-15; Mark 4:12; 8:18; Luke 8:10; John 9:39; 12:40; Romans 11:8.
[6] Here lies the critical question which has to be put to Teilhard de Chardin.

fest itself. The "I will be who I will be" discloses himself in the form of sequences of events, of judgments and deliverances, of foreshadowings of the incarnation and the incarnation itself. All these events are marked by their word-character. They say something. But what they say is present only within the Word of proclamation which changes existence and enables us to receive the one who utters his Word here and who is indeed this Word. Only to this extent are the events manifest as salvation history, as the sequence of covenant events. Only to this extent—to the extent that they present the history from the standpoint of the person who achieves it—are they accepted as the ways in which God discloses himself as the one who is disclosed in the Word, as Immanuel, as the one who addresses man.

When we speak of God along these lines we can thus have in view only the Lord of history, or, more precisely, the one who from the hour of creation to the last judgment enters into a history with man. To enter into this history, to summon man to divine likeness, to suffer in him, to let him go into the far country, to visit him and call him back, and to accept full solidarity with him in the incarnate Word—all this cannot mean that this kind of history is simply the accidental outgoing of a substance that cannot in any way be affected itself thereby. It can imply only that by nature and being God himself is in all this, that he resolves without reservation to be God in relation, and that he gives himself totally and holds nothing back (Luther).

Even Luther's many-faceted concept of the *Deus absconditus*[7] does not mean that behind and apart from his manifestations God is very different and we do not know him. It simply means that God maintains the awesome mystery of his divine majesty. Part of this is that we can never find out why he decides to be God in this way, why he makes himself God in relation, and why in particular he takes the path of abasement and the cross which seems to be the reverse of deity.[8] The *Deus absconditus* is not, then, a dark margin which might hold painful surprises and which has to be accepted in blind faith along with the aspects of God on which light has been shed. No, the unknown in God does not differ from what we find in the *Deus revelatus*. It belongs to God in relation. But in this context it passes our understanding. The gap, therefore, is not in the being of God but in our understanding which cannot and should not grasp the mystery of God.

Hence we are not to fix our gaze on the naked majesty of God. We are to flee from the *Deus absconditus* to the *Deus revelatus* in order to replace the darkness that might lead us astray by the light which allows us to see God as he is.[9] This makes sense, however, only if it be presupposed that God is wholly in his Word, that he himself is present in the incarnate Word,

---

[7] Cf. Fritz Blanke, *Der verborgene Gott bei Luther* (1928).

[8] Cf. the *Heidelberg Disputation of 1518;* W. von Loewenich, *Luthers theologia crucis,* 2nd ed. (1933), pp. 21ff.; P. Althaus, *Die Theologie M. Luthers* (1962), pp. 34ff.; E.T. 1966, pp. 25ff.

[9] Cf. WA, 14, 299, 20; 29, 223, 15; K. Holl, *Gesammelte Aufsätze,* I, 6th ed. (1932), p. 77; ThE, I, § 290, 606; E.T. I, pp. 67ff., 118ff.

that he is in no way different from this, and hence that he holds nothing back. What he says takes place and becomes an event (Psalm 33:9); what he speaks with his mouth he fulfils with his hand (1 Kings 8:24). This unity of speech and action, which shows that his word is word-act, is grounded in the fact that he invests himself, and hence pours out himself, in the relationship posited by his words and acts. This self-involvement finds biblical expression in the fact that God's heart, or innermost personal core, has a part in these words and acts and discloses itself therein.[10] When the Johannine Christ says that he and the Father are one, that the Father is seen in him (John 12:45; 14:9), and hence that his words and acts are those of the Father (14:10), this shows us in the fullest possible way that God is no other than the one whom we encounter in his Word and its incarnation. He *is* the one who has entered into a history with man. To quote Pascal again, he *is* the God of Abraham, Isaac, and Jacob,[11] not the God of the philosophers. To this extent he is not a supreme being in abstraction from his will and word and work. He *is* in his historical being for me, in extreme alienation, in the crucifixion of Christ, with regard to which Johann Rist bewails the death of God himself. To this extent God's being is in his becoming; it is not in a being in and for itself apart from and behind this becoming.[12]

Jüngel (*ibid.,* pp. 2ff.) is right, then, when he takes issue with Gollwitzer's distinction between the essence of God and the will of God (*Die Existenz Gottes im Bekenntnis des Glaubens,* pp. 148f., 175; E.T. *The Existence of God as Confessed by Faith,* pp. 185f., 217), expressing the fear that with this essence which is separated from God's will a space might be left for a metaphysical hinterland in the being of God whose relation to God's historical work of revelation is one of indifference (p. 6). As a disciple of Barth, Gollwitzer should obviously be on guard against any analogical deductive movement from God's self-disclosing personal being in the encounter of I and Thou to the essence of God. The only possible movement here is from the self-disclosure of God in word and act to the will of God, so that from God's being, understood as revelation, in the mode of being of a subject in history, no conclusion can be reached analogically regarding the essence of God in the sense of a state, a being of God in and for himself, but only regarding the nature of his will. That is, from the will of God in its historical manifestation one may infer the eternal will of God as the will of his free love (Gollwitzer, *op. cit.,* p. 149; E.T. pp. 185f.; Jüngel, *op. cit.,* p. 6).

What Jüngel finds in Gollwitzer is the very thing which we have tried to avoid in our own argumentation, namely, the idea that apart from his self-disclosure, his being as God in relation, God is a different God, so that there is a metaphysical hinterland which lies outside God's self-definition.

The so-called Calvinistic *extra* (cf. Volume I, pp. 292ff., 374f.) poses a

---

[10] Cf. Jeremiah 31:20; Lamentations 3:33; Hosea 11:8; 1 Samuel 2:35.

[11] *Mémorial* (1654).

[12] E. Jüngel, *Gottes Sein ist im Werden.*

problem, of course, once we see God's essence and his will in unison as Gollwitzer does not do. For there is a point at which God obviously transcends his condescension and his being for me, so that he is not subsumed under this but is *Logos eksarkos* as well as *Logos ensarkos*. We fix our sights on this point when we see that God's self-revelation as God-for-me is not a kind of self-evident emanation from his essence or a constitutionally determined secularization. In it we see rather the free sovereignty of his will and the free resolve of his love to condescend to us. To this extent, and to this alone, God as the subject of his condescension transcends this condescension, just as the person who performs works is distinct from them. This element of transcendence, however, does not permit us to differentiate God's essence from his will. For the will determines the essence as self-opening and self-disclosing love. Wherever God's will manifests itself in words and works, he *is* in his essence too. His being enters, then, into historical becoming. This is why talk about God is "worldly" talk about God; God himself is in view in the reference to the world. One cannot talk about God without the world being present in some way, not, of course, as an unfortunate necessity, but in virtue of the fact that talk about God is directed to the world if it is proper talk about God, since God himself addresses the world, comes to it, and to that extent belongs to it; cf. G. Ebeling, "Weltliches Reden von Gott," *Wort und Glaube,* p. 377; E.T. p. 359.

Christian doctrine has traditionally dealt with God's relation to himself, which means, according to what we have said above, his relation to himself as the subject of revelation and the author of his word and work, under two main heads and with various differentiations, namely, under the heads of the doctrine of the Trinity and the distinction of law and gospel. We shall now try to work out what is to be said on these topics.

IX

The Trinity of God

Bibliography: 1. Dictionaries: O. Kirn, Art. "Trinität," RE, XX, p. 111; H. de Lavalette, H. Rahner, J. Felderer, W. Braunfels, W. Dürig, Art. "Dreifaltigkeit," LThK, 2nd ed., III, p. 543; W. Breuning, H. Geisser, Art. "Trinitätslehre, wissenschafts-theoretisch," LThK, X, p. 360; C. M. Edsman, P. Meyer, F. H. Kettler, E. Schlink, M. D. Beck, Art. "Trinität," RGG³, IV, 1023.

2. Dogmatics: P. Althaus, *Die christliche Wahrheit*, 3rd ed. (1952), p. 689; K. Barth, CD, I, 1, 2nd ed. (1974), pp. 348ff.; E. Brunner, *The Christian Doctrine of God*, I (E.T. 1949), pp. 205ff.; F. Diekamp-K. Jüssen, *Katholische Dogmatik*, I, 13th ed. (1958), p. 265; W. Elert, *Der christliche Glaube* (1940), p. 241; J. Ratzinger, *Einführung in das Christentum*, 5th ed. (1968); E.T. *Introduction to Christianity* (1969); M. Schmaus, *Katholische Dogmatik*, I, 6th ed. (1960), pp. 291ff., 324ff.; G. Thomasius, *Christi Person und Werk*, esp. II (1857); W. Trillhaas, *Dogmatik* (1962), p. 107; O. Weber, *Grundlagen der Dogmatik*, I, 3rd ed. (1964), pp. 386ff.

3. Monographs and Essays: C. Andresen, "Zur Entstehung und Geschichte des trinitar. Personbegriffs," ZNW (1901), p. 1; F. C. Baur, *Die christliche Lehre von der Dreifaltigkeit (geschichtl. Entwicklung)*, I-III, pp. 1841ff.; H. G. Geyer, "Gottes Sein als Thema der Theologie," *Beiträge in Jesus Christus im Zeugnis der heiligen Schrift und der Kirche*, Beihefte zur ETh, 2 (1966), pp. 3ff.; H. Gollwitzer, *Die Existenz Gottes im Bekenntnis des Glaubens*, 4th ed. (1965); E.T. *The Existence of God as Confessed by Faith* (1965); H. Gollwitzer and W. Weischedel, *Denken und Glauben. Ein Streitgespräch* (1965); J. Hessen, *Hegels Trinitätslehre* (1922); L. Hodgson, *The Doctrine of the Trinity*, 6th ed. (1960); W. Joest, *Ontologie der Person bei Luther* (1967); E. Jüngel, *Gottes Sein ist im Werden*, 2nd ed. (1967); W. Kasper, *Das Absolute in der Geschichte (Schellings Tr.-Lehre)* (1965), esp. pp. 266ff.; G. Kretschmar, *Studien zur frühchristlichen Trinitätstheologie* (1956); F. K. Mayr, "Trinitätstheologie und theologische Anthropologie," ZThK (1971), 4, pp. 427-477; F. Mildenberger, "Überlegungen zum Gottesbegriff," ZThK (1965), pp. 458ff.; H. Mühlen, *Der heilige Geist als Person* (1963); A. Peters, "Die Trinitätslehre der reformatorischen Christenheit," ThLZ (1969), 8, p. 561; K. Rahner, "Der dreifaltige Gott als transzendenter Urgrund der Heilsgeschichte" in J. Feiner and M. Löhrer, eds., *Mys-*

terium salutis, II (1967), pp. 317-401; also "Bemerkungen zur Gotteslehre in der katholischen Dogmatik," *Catholica,* 20 (1966), pp. 1ff.; C. H. Ratschow, *Luth. Dogmatik zwischen Reformation und Aufklärung* (1964ff.); L. Scheffczyk, "Lehramtliche Formulierungen und Dogmengeschichte der Trinität," *Mysterium salutis,* II, p. 146; M. Schmaus, *Die psychologische Trinitätslehre Augustins* (1927); M. Tetz, *F. Schleiermacher und die Trinitätslehre* (1969); P. Vanier, *Théol. trinitaire chez St. Thomas d'A.* (1953); C. Welch, *In This Name. The Doctrine of the Trinity in Contemporary Theology* (1952); W. Weischedel, see Gollwitzer.

THE PROBLEM WHICH LEADS TO THE DOCTRINE OF THE TRINITY

The fact that we are not dealing with the doctrine of the Trinity independently, but within the framework of the doctrine of the Word that posits history, has programmatic significance. To put it in the words of W. Herrmann, whom we are not, of course, following in this dogmatics, the doctrine of the Holy Trinity does not serve as a basis of faith but belongs to the circle of concepts of faith. These concepts become necessary only when the true basis of faith—the Word of God that posits history—comes into contact with the categories of our consciousness and thus forces reflection upon us. So long as we try to think of God as the supreme being the categories of our consciousness compel us to think of this supreme being in terms of an all-embracing unity. (This is why terms like the supreme being, the supreme good, aseity, etc., are used in description of the divine essence.) How is this to be harmonized, however, with the fact that in the Word which posits history God posits what is outside himself, sets up a counterpart, clearly breaks up his unity into plurality and even antitheses, and tolerates alongside or outside himself a fallen world of guilt, suffering, and death? How can the unity of God be understood as anything else but a static and unmoved homogeneity? But the world that we know is in movement, in history. And the doctrine of the Word of this God that posits history tells us that God is the initiator of history.

How is this conceptual difficulty to be solved, or, if it is not soluble, how is it to be explained as a necessary impasse of thought? In other words, how can the fact that God permits history, and is himself in becoming, be brought to expression without doing violence to the unity of God and dissolving it in the plurality of the process thus inaugurated? In simplified and more popular form, what we are asking is how the means of thought can safeguard monotheism and prevent a slide into polytheism or pantheism.

In this form the problem arises not only in religious history in general but also in the christological debates of the early centuries. The doctrine of the Trinity was the answer. This doctrine has then, as we shall try to show, the significance of a conceptual aid in relation to a problem which crops up with revelation, i.e., with the Word that posits history.

The word "aid" might sound derogatory and therefore inappropriate unless it be added at once that the doctrine is a reflexive tool which Christian consensus views as unavoidable if the problem of the one God which revelation poses is to be mastered.

The statement that the doctrine of the Trinity masters a problem is, of course, unsatisfactory. For it might suggest that a logical riddle is solved speculatively and given a rational explanation. Notwithstanding all the energy and acuteness of thoughts expended on this doctrine, there can be no question of this. When one surveys the earlier history of trinitarian theology and the conflicts between the Alexandrians and the Antiochenes, between modalists, subordinationists, monarchians and many other groups, the formula which was eventually adopted is obviously not the solution of a problem. It shows that all the previously advocated solutions are facile attempts to set aside the mystery of God and to make it accessible to reason. Everything is as it were seized and explained when God is viewed in the Origenistic sense as the primal unity which develops and breaks up into antitheses, or when, as among the subordinationists, Christ as the incarnate Word is detached from his unity with God and grouped with what is human and creaturely.

Strictly speaking the doctrine of the Trinity does not solve a problem. It recognizes that all solutions are inadequate because in arrogant autonomy they dissolve the mystery of God. As Ratzinger felicitously puts it, the doctrine of the Trinity demonstrates the pathlessness of all other paths and is thus to be understood as a rejection of every desire to penetrate the divine mystery.[1] It protects this mystery and wards off illegal attacks. Its concern is to show that the incomprehensible is in fact incomprehensible, and yet to do so in such a way that it does not become a mere refuge of ignorance but is seen to be the incomprehensible of this God who discloses himself in the Word. This concern, then, necessitates a powerful effort of thought. It has to accept formulations which will inevitably seem to be absurd to anyone who does not have the pre-rational experience of faith. For faith alone triggers the generative impulses which produce these formulations. The formulations themselves are a manner of speaking which is aware of its limitations and which constantly resists ignorance of these limitations or rational comprehension of the mystery. To this extent the doctrine of the Trinity is in fact a statement of limitation, a gesture of rebuke which is also a reference to the ineffable.[2] It does not belong to the sphere of definitions, which presuppose the possession of concepts.

When we say that the doctrine of the Trinity is a conceptual aid or a concept of faith, this does not imply any reduction of its importance. Certainly it is not the basis of faith, as though the trinity of God had to be present to the consciousness with intellectual clarity for a man to come to faith in

---

[1] *Einführung*, p. 133; E.T. p. 121.
[2] *Ibid.*

the God who has disclosed himself in the incarnate Word.[3] Instead, it is the subsequent product of a discussion which our consciousness must conduct with itself when it finds itself confronted with this divine self-disclosure. The so-called heresies which are attacked by the doctrine of the Trinity may take historical form but they are in fact no more than an objectification of various solutions that suggest themselves to our consciousness. This is true at any rate if, like the classical heretics of the early period, we believe that the consciousness is furnished with intellectual ability, readiness, and openness in respect of the revelation which confronts it.

We intend no disrespect to the importance of the doctrine of the Trinity when we call it an aid, for we are expressing the conviction, which we shall have to support with further arguments, that the trinitarian doctrine of God is the only one among all the conceivable possibilities of thought which can think of God as the subject of the Word that posits history, as the author of revelation, without surrendering the mystery or falling victim to the danger of seeking rational mastery over it. To this extent, even though the doctrine is not the basis of faith, but "only" a concept of faith, it still has dogmatic rank.

We shall now attempt a first attack on the problems which beset a formulation of the doctrine of the Trinity. We shall do so by considering its threefold structure in terms of the question how far the "collision" of revelation with our consciousness finds expression in it.

If God is God in relation, if he determines himself as such in the unity of his essence and will, then numerous problems arise, some of which we have touched on already. Only if we keep these problems in view can we keep track of the thematic point in the church's struggle for the doctrine of the Trinity. Once this thematic point is lost to sight we are left with a bundle of metaphysical speculations, and often the concepts begin to dance around or play leapfrog with one another. This happens especially when we come up against an autonomous intellectual development such as might seem to be initiated by the ontological schema of thought of patristic Christology. Within this framework an attempt is made to harmonize the substantial unity of God with the fulness of his willed, dynamic and personal developments. This mistaken interpretation leads finally to a boring interplay of new conceptual emanations which are pathogenetically self-produced. To avoid it, we shall concentrate on the problems indicated above, in which the theme of the doctrine of the Trinity arises.

If God is thus God in relation, or, more precisely, if he wills to be this and consequently is so, since will and being are identical in him, the question immediately arises in what relation God as the one who resolves stands to this resolve of his. The point of the question is the implication of the rela-

---

[3] This is why we cannot go along with J. Gerhard when he says that no one can be saved without a knowledge of the doctrine of the Trinity (*Loci theol.*, III, 209ff.

tion. The questions which then come to actualization in the doctrine of the Trinity may thus be sketched as follows.

The relation is primarily God's relation to his Word. For the Word is the means or vehicle by which God enters into relation to man. The Word is by nature an addressed Word. Hence he to whom it is directed belongs to it as its object. To that extent God's self-disclosure in the Word means that God binds himself to man and enters into relation with him.

When this Word becomes flesh and personifies itself in Christ, the new question arises whether the Word is God himself, so that God is no longer distinct from it but is totally within it. Is it theophany? Are God and Christ one in the sense that we have here identity? Or has the Word parted from God and emancipated itself from him, so that Christ belongs on the side of the creaturely and as most holy man is the final culmination of creaturely man or a supreme example of this man (Schleiermacher)?

These questions obviously do not result merely from a logic which thinks it is compelled to harmonize the idea of God's unity with the kind of development which takes place by the Word's going out and especially by its incarnation. They are posed supremely by interpretation of the christological texts in the NT. For the relation of Christ to God displays a provokingly open structure. Differentiations are assumed which allow us to speak neither of identity nor of difference. The Johannine Christ certainly says: "I and the Father are one" (John 10:30) and: "He that hath seen me hath seen the Father" (14:9), but nowhere do we find identity expressed along the lines of sayings such as: "The Son is the Father," or: "The Father is the Son."

The openness of the relation finds expression above all in the twofold solidarity of Christ with the Father and with man.

On the one hand he is the mediator because he represents God. He stands on God's side and causes him to meet us in himself. In him the secret which was hidden from the beginning of the world is revealed (Romans 16:25f.). With this divine aspect of Christ, which for the moment we shall deliberately speak of in an indefinite way, there is related the eternal present that is also predicated of him. This embraces past and future. It culminates in what is said about his pre-existence and in the intimation of his *parousia*.[4] The redemptive significance of Christ would not hold up if he were confined with us inside the limits of guilt and death and were thus unable not only to restore the lost relation to God but to be this relation in person.

On the other hand he is a man as we are and is tempted as we are (Hebrews 4:15). He stands on our side too. He speaks to his Father in prayer as to another. He struggles to be in harmony with his will (Luke 22:42). He bewails his dereliction by a Thou from whom he is at a distance (Matthew 27:46). We see expressed here the solidarity of Christ with us as a fellow-man. But this solidarity is, of course, relativized again and

---

[4] John 8:58; Ephesians 3:9; Colossians 1:16; Matthew 10:23; 24:30; 25:31; Acts 3:20f.; 1 Corinthians 4:5; 15:23; 1 Thessalonians 4:15ff.; 2 Thessalonians 2:1ff.; etc.

hence it is open in this regard. His very human temptation is mysteriously different from the vacillation between God and Satan which makes it the mark of human existence, for it takes place "without sin" (Hebrews 4:15). Again, although he teaches us to pray "Our Father," he never includes himself with us in this "Our Father." His own relation to the Thou of the Father is different from ours.

There thus arises the question of this relation of God to his Word, to his incarnate Word. How can the concept of the one God be linked with this figure which lives among us as God's alter ego?

Again, if God's Spirit is the life-giving, transforming, and creative Spirit which posits history, how are we to define his relation to the transforming God on the one side and the transformed creature on the other? Is he identical with God, so that he is God in action and consequently God himself, God in his confrontation with the creature? Or is he that in the creature which fills it with power and is integrated into it? Is the Spirit a created motion in things?[5]

Here again one has to decide how God's unity is to be harmonized with his movement outward. Here again the point is that this movement outward, in the gifts of the Spirit no less than in Christ, can be thought of neither as abstract identity nor as separation and creaturely otherness.[6] The doctrine of the Spirit has thus to be elucidated as follows. The Spirit is God's creative working for and in us. Yet he is not exhausted in this for and in us. He does not let himself be absorbed in it. He does not secularize himself. He remains over us. It is certainly God himself that gives himself in the Spirit, works through him, and makes himself present in him. Yet because he does this in freedom and not, e.g., under the compulsion of an emanation or a process, as in the case of Hegel's world spirit, he is more than his work. In other words, the God who resolves on action transcends God in action.

All these problems which center on the relation of God to his movement outward, to his Word and Spirit, force us in the direction of an understanding which the trinitarian formula presents as an intellectual possibility. They also suggest all the alternatives mentioned, all the possibilities and impossibilities of solution in the various modifications of the trinitarian model, especially in the christological controversies which preceded the final formulaation of the dogma of the Trinity. What we said above about the incarnate Logos applies to this whole complex. The problems which lead to the doctrine of the Trinity do not arise merely under the pressure of the threadbare logic which has to harmonize the unity of God with his movement outward. The problems are not self-generated. They are always stimulated by the salvation event which is recorded in the Bible. Here is God in action, moving outward, revealing himself, and positing history. He is this God as God the Creator who summons the world and man within it into encounter with

---

[5] *Motus in rebus creatus,* CA, I, 6.
[6] The latter misunderstanding is refuted in the above quotation from CA, I, 6.

himself. He is this God as God the Redeemer who in the incarnate Word enters into solidarity with his creatures. He is this God as God the Holy Spirit who makes himself present to us in the creative work of his Word. These three stages of the salvation event which is attested in the Bible encounter us as the simultaneity of the one God who encounters us. In the threefoldness of the forms of encounter we are always dealing with the one God.

Whenever the threefoldness is eliminated or reduced to unity the result is a loss of history. That is, God is no longer understood as one who works personally and remains superior to his works. If he is viewed merely as the Creator, idolatry arises. The creaturely product of his outward movement acquires autonomy alongside him. The dimensions of the world or of worldly things achieve numinous rank and are sacralized, whether in the form of fetishism, polytheism, or, nonreligiously, ideologizing.

If God is isolated as the Redeemer, the figure of Christ is detached from the Trinity and a broad range of distortions is made possible. On the right one might find a christomonism which presents redemption without reference to the created world. This results in an ecclesiastical ghetto in which the world is abandoned and a rival spiritual world is set up. Or it might result in a form of theocracy or christocracy in which the gospel is made into a law or a principle by which to shape the world. On the left Christ can be detached from the nexus of salvation and made into "the finite at its highest" (Jean Paul), the original or prototype of man, and hence the norm of the creaturely world which this has produced from within itself.

Finally, if God the Holy Spirit is taken alone, a broad range of philosophical and religious conceptions again results. This reaches from the cult of supremely religious man in pentecostal movements to Hegel's reason in history which exhibits the world spirit in its evolution.

The God of the Bible, however, cannot be had in this kind of isolation. This is not merely because such isolation carries with it a transposition of Creator and creature. It is also because the history with man that God has inaugurated, the Word of God that posits history, is in such circumstances replaced by the history which is undertaken and written by man himself, while God becomes a timeless idea or an entity which was long since subsumed under its effects.

The doctrine of the Trinity resists all the various distortions of this kind. It fulfils the function of a defensive formula. It is the guardian of what the biblical salvation event attests in its fulness, namely, that God is he who discloses himself in freedom, that he is the same at every stage of the salvation event: God the Creator, God the Redeemer, and God the Holy Spirit, and that in all this he is not the timeless God of an idea but the acting God who posits history and brings himself into history. The doctrine of the Trinity safeguards this actuosity of God and it also safeguards his majesty, which as the one God transcends all the modes of his movement outward. It safeguards all this, we say. This means that it expounds but does not explain the essence of God as it is thus declared. In expounding it, it also spells out what the Word seeks to tell us about God in action and it wards off all threats to this Word from autonomous speculation. In not explaining it, it lets the mystery stand. The freedom from out of which God wills to be the one he is remains inscrutable. This freedom can only be worshipped.

X

The Doctrine of the Trinity as a Defensive Formula: A Safeguard against Speculative Ideas of the Divine Unity and Singularity

Now that we have shown what problems lead to the doctrine of the Trinity, our best course is perhaps to consider typical attempts which have been made to understand the unity of God and his self-revelation apart from the doctrine of the Trinity, which means, in dogmatic history, prior to the rise of the dogma of the Trinity. Understandably this question arises for the most part in christological contexts. For it is here that one must ask very definitely whether and how the deity of Christ or the Logos can be reconciled with the unity of God and what intellectual precautions must be taken lest there be a relapse into polytheism. From this angle the doctrine of the Trinity, which we earlier called an intellectual aid, constitutes a defensive formula within which the positions which are being refuted may be plainly descried.

The same type of structure occurs in confessional statements which combine the positive "we confess" with a negative "we condemn." It should be noted that the position or positions to which the anathema applies provide the occasion for the explication of the doctrine and thus discharge the creative function of a challenge (cf. Volume I, p. 120).

In virtue of the polemical character of the trinitarian formula we ought to give some concrete representative models of what we have already described in principle as contrary positions. In so doing we shall not follow any chronological order nor shall we attempt a general historical survey. Our selection is governed by the need to offer systematic examples.

Origen as an Initial Model

The classical representative of an attempt to think out the unity of God abstractly, and to integrate existing trinitarian gropings into this speculative concept of unity, is Origen.[1] One can hardly say this, of course, without

---

[1] Tertullian seems to have been the one who coined the term *trinitas*. Origen develops and modifies some essential insights of Tertullian.

being guilty of simplification. For in spite of the polished logic and architectonic breadth of his thought, Origen is not a systematician in the sense that he deductively develops a single principle and then refashions heaven and earth in the autarchy of his speculation. Even while he proceeds speculatively and systematically he seizes on the *logos spermatikos* in every construct of thought around him. He is a genius at integration.

The Bible has a place in his total thinking. This thinking is thus subject to various corrections which prevent it from becoming the mere outpouring of an isolated speculative thinker. Considerable discrimination is needed, therefore, when a full-scale presentation of Origen's own thought is the goal. Within the terms of reference of our special investigation, however, we take the liberty of speaking of an abstract idea of unity which governs Origen's doctrine of God and to that extent is challenged by the trinitarian aspect of the dogma. Expounding Origen in this way is justified only by the conviction that the idea of unity is the true problem in Origen's thinking and that our special inquiry allows us to concentrate on this difficulty.

A system such as that of Origen, which tries to harmonize a monistic foundation with a duality or plurality of concrete phenomena, is usually characterized by three-stage construction.

First (1) we have the primal self-grounded unity of God which unfolds itself. Then (2) the independent developments emancipate and alienate themselves. Finally (3) the alienated forms return to God's primal unity. This is the same three-stage structure as that which governs Hegel's monistic thinking and whose dialectic frees the monon from being static and sets it in a process of movement.

The first stage of God's self-unfolding, in which his being in himself enters the movement of a cosmic drama, is the coming into being of the Son and the Spirit. Apparently, then, there is the initiation of a trinitarian event. Why "apparently"? On this view there is in God no event which posits something new in the historical sense and to that extent engenders change. Hence for Origen even the biblical terms "Son of God" and "generation" stand under the verdict of anthropomorphism, for they are taken from the structural sphere of the changing history of man. In the Logos, who is only improperly called the "Son of God," we have rather a comprehensive term for the ideas of the world contained in God, i.e., divine thoughts which fill God's thinking in eternal immutability, in an eternal present.

There thus arises the problem how this statically conceived being of God in himself can become a being outside himself in spite of its immutability. How can it bring into being the movement of occurrence which we see around us and in us? The ontological axiom which explains this transition consists in the thesis that in God thinking and creating are one and the same. What God thinks is at the same time willed by him. What he wills is at the same time done by him. More precisely, one ought to say that it is already done even as he wills it. Even more strictly one must go further. For if one says: "God wills," this might be construed in the sense of an act of will which would replace prior resolves and hence imply change. But this would contradict the immutability of God's being in himself. This self-actualizing will, then, is not an act. It must be viewed as a timeless state. In a rather daring phrase etymologically, it is eternal "wilfulness." There was thus no time when the Son was not generated, for time is a medium of change. The eternity of the Logos corresponds to the eternal willing of God. Hence it is impossible to conceive of a time when the Son and the Spirit did not exist.[2]

Historically we are close here to the complex of Neoplatonic emanation theories. These are prepared at most to speak of the movement which comes forth from the divine substance without attaching any historical character to it. For if the divine substance overflows, first in the form of Son and Spirit and then in that of the world, we have only a change in the aggregate state of the substance and its own immutability is not affected. (We are selecting a physical comparison to illustrate the co-existence of identity and fulness of forms.) The concept of emanation, then, determines the structure of the trinitarian, or, more accurately, trinity-like statements.

On the one hand, if the Son is the outflowing of the divine glory, the Logos will have the same substantial quality as the Father. What emanates shares the same essence as its source. On the other hand, it suffers some reduction as compared with the ground of emanation. Geometrically, it is further from the center of the divine substance. It lies on the periphery. Since the Pneuma proceeds from the Father and the Son, its emanative place is even further from the source than that of the Logos. With some boldness one might say that we have here the same kind of reduction as we have in a copy compared with the original. At any rate, the Logos is not self-grounded—this applies only to the Father as the original divine substance. The Logos is generated and derived.

Naturally the speculative attempt to relate identity and gradation leads to statements which are full of tension even to the point of self-contradiction. Thus we find a co-ordination of the thesis that Father and Son are one in an eternal communion of substance with the thesis that the Son is other than the Father. It is not surprising, then, that champions of the *homoousios* as well as subordinationists were tempted to appeal to Origen. His monistic thinking seemed to offer similarities to both the opposing positions.

That we have in Origen an early form of the trinitarian theses, even if distorted by his monistic thinking, is supported by the fact that he does not bring the world into his process of emanation in the same way as he does the Logos and the Pneuma. A clear break occurs after he has allotted the Spirit his place. Intrinsically, of course, his thinking carried with it a tendency to continue the emanations and to give the world a part in the consubstantial communion. Was he prevented from taking this course by the corrective influence of the biblical word, since the resultant pantheism

---

[2] *Ouk éstin, hóte ouk ên.*

would stand in diametrical opposition to this? Did this word bring about dualistic modifications in his schema?

Naturally the monistic principle is still significant in his view of the material world. This world cannot be regarded merely as the opposite of God, since it derives from the divine monad. For Origen it is in fact full of traces of the Spirit and is by no means mere *hyle* alien to the Spirit. The fallen world of contradiction acquires features of alienation from the Spirit only in time, i.e., outside God's immutable remoteness from time. Here, then, something new does actually take place. It results from the ambivalence of the freedom imparted by God. This is on the one side the supreme mark of the rational creature. On the other side, however, it represents a deficiency. It permits men, angels, and demons to be no longer self-evident transitional stages of emanation. It is a power of possible alienation. Hence the origin of the world—the fall is regarded as pre-temporal—can be understood as also the beginning of the divine judgment. In this sense Origen combines his monistic idea of emanation with the dualisms which are implied in the biblical view of the fallen world, of history on this side of the fall, and of the salvation event.

We said earlier that the dogma of the Trinity has the intellectual function of safeguarding the unity of God in his movement outward and of bearing witness to the modes of his presence or immanence in the salvation event fulfilled in creation, redemption, and self-presentation. We must now state that Origen does not do justice to this intention of the doctrine. His monistic thinking centers on God in himself who as substance stands outside the movement of the trinitarian God of the Bible. In contrast, the movement to which the Trinity bears witness can be understood only as a history "in" God. (This "history" is completely different from what we usually understand by human history,[3] but no other term is at our disposal.) In virtue of this history God determines himself as Immanuel, i.e., as the one who as Creator, Redeemer, and Holy Spirit wills to be there for man and presents himself totally in this being there for him; he is not also some other apart from it.[4]

Although the term history is inadequate in this context, we are compelled to use it because we have to speak about a willed self-determination of God if we are to understand him as person, as "heart." This manner of speaking, far from being anthropomorphic, is the only appropriate one if we are not to fall victim to thinking in terms of impersonal substance and then viewing God's outward movement as automatic emanation along the lines of Origen. In place of the automatic process implied in the very nature of substance the biblical God displays a will which is motivated by love and which ad-

---

[3] Theologically this refers only to events between the fall and the judgment; cf. my *Geschichte und Existenz*, 2nd ed. (1964).

[4] "His Word is so much the same as he is that deity is wholly in it and whosoever has the Word has the whole deity. . . . In God the Word does not bring with it only a sign and picture but the whole nature, and hence it is just as fully God as he whose image or Word it is" (Luther, *Kirchenpostille*, 1522, WA, 10, I, 1, 186ff.).

dresses itself in freedom. Will and freedom, however, stand in some analogy to history, so that with reservations the term may be used here.

Naturally Origen, too, speaks about God's will. This will is identical with his doing. But "will" is used improperly here for a different kind of willing, since it has no freedom. The necessity of the emanative process has God will what he has to will in the sense of the necessary overflowing of his glory. The God of Origen no more makes resolves than does later the God of Spinoza, who is equally subject to the law of development. This God cannot love either. He cannot decide against himself, as the author of the gospel does against the author of the law. He cannot "repent." He cannot cast off his immutability (Exodus 32:14; Jeremiah 26:13, etc.). The dogma of the Trinity, however, is formulated within an understanding of God whose whole point is the free self-determination of God and the resolve of his love, so that the reference is, in the full sense of the word, to the "God of history." Only on the basis of this free resolve of God's will to be the God who is for us—the God who turns to us in love—are we required to recognize the same God in all the forms of his turning, in creation, redemption, and self-presentation, and to think of this God in all these forms as the same God (Hebrews 13:8). What unites deity in the distinction of the modes of being is not the atomon of substance and the "God in himself" denoted thereby, but the love of the "God for us," or, more precisely, the free resolve of this God to be the loving God.

The system of Origen, which vacillates as we have seen between monotheism and pantheism, was characterized by a unity of the divine essence which had been thought through with the help of the concept of substance. It was thus compelled to see a diminution of being in the Son and Spirit or Logos and Pneuma. In contrast, other christological views are essentially controlled by their absolutizing of one of the aspects that we find in Origen. For the purpose of our systematic inquiry it will be enough if we simply consider the polar extremes of this early thinking. For it is these primarily which throw down the challenge that the dogma of the Trinity takes up and in face of which it has the significance of a defensive formula.

Subordinationism and Adoptionism

The emphasis may be placed on the unity and singularity of God, as among adoptionists and subordinationists of various kinds. In this case, to grant Christ at the same time the significance of express deity will be a contradiction which involves the threat of ditheism. The tendency, then, is to separate the Son from the Father and to set him on the side of the creature, even though he is regarded as the supreme culmination of creation.

The separation of Christ from the Father, which is even equated with the distinction between creature and Creator in Arius, may be worked out (1) in the form of subordinationism. On this view Christ as a subordinate divine being can claim pre-existence but only as the first creature among equals. (This is why Arius, in contrast to Origen, can say that "there was when he was not.") As the perfect pre-existent creature of God he does not have the same honor as God. It is along these lines that an attempt is made to deal with the difficulty of doing justice to God's being in Christ (2 Corinthians 5:19) while in no way damaging the divine singularity and unity. The question arises, however, as to the price which has to be paid for this solution to the difficulty.

The distinction between God and Christ can take (2) the form of adoptionism. On this view God imparts his Spirit to the chosen man Jesus, lifts him out of the purely human sphere, and at the same time makes him the most fully human of all men. The time at which this impartation of the Spirit takes place need not concern us in this context. It might be found in the resurrection, the baptism, or even the miraculous birth. The common factor in each case is that for the sake of the divine unity and singularity the figure of Christ is placed at the head of a creaturely hierarchy.

No matter which of the two alternatives be adopted, what is sacrificed is no less than the gospel of Christ as the effective Redeemer. Christ is still the one who reveals and reflects God. He is still the privileged object of divine address. But he is imprisoned with us in finitude, even though this finitude might be extended to cover various stages of pre-existence. Insofar as he represents God to man and man to God he is certainly a mediator. But he is so only in an ontological sense as the figure in whom divine and human attributes merge for our noesis. He is not the one in whom we have to do with God. He is a delegate. He has a ministerial office. The sovereign has given him this. He is the latter's representative or vice-gerent. But we do not hear God when we hear him nor does God hear us when we speak with Christ. In adoptionists and subordinationists the possibility of retaining God's unity and singularity carries with it the cost that while we may conceive of God we can no longer "have" him (at least directly). In modern terms, we can think of him theoretically but he is taken from us existentially. We are cut off from him in the sphere of our finitude.

When the Nicene Creed in its trinitarian formulae says that Christ was begotten of the Father, not made (*genitum, non factum*), that he is of one substance with the Father (*consubstantialis Patri*), and that by him all thing were made (*per quem omnia facta sunt*), these statements are directed against an understanding of Christ which sets him on the side of creaturely finitude and denies the real presence of God in him. If the confession that he is begotten, not made, is a statement of great linguistic daring which skirts the limits of the mythological, it is made in order to put Christ on the side of the Creator rather than in creaturely juxtaposition to him.

Excursus on Schleiermacher, Ritschl, and the Theology of Revolution as Later Variants

We have taken the views described above as models because the main elements in them recur constantly in the course of the history of theology.

We may simply recall here some of the later instances, namely, in the systems of F. Schleiermacher and A. Ritschl.

In Schleiermacher Christ is the perfect image of man in historical form (*The Christian Faith*, § 93). He is the example of man at the height of his potential. If he is like all men in the identity of human nature, he differs from all men in the force of his God-consciousness (§ 94). The unbrokenness of this consciousness, which distinguishes him from men, is also the way in which there is an undivided being of God in him (§ 94). The being of God in Christ is thus a being conscious. The undividedness of this consciousness which wholly fills him, and which stands in decisive contrast to the broken and particular consciousness of others, does not alter, however, the fact that this is still a creaturely consciousness. Only in degree and not in principle does it transcend that of other men. By the creative divine act from which it derives, the concept of man reaches its supreme limit in him as the subject of God-consciousness (§ 93, 3). He thus has the rank of an archetype, for the archetype expresses the very being of the concept (§ 93, 2), i.e., the concept of man in respect of the God-consciousness which constitutes him in his humanity.

The work of the Redeemer is understood along the same lines. In him God does not encounter us himself or in person. He does not bring us into direct fellowship with himself. Hence the redeeming activity of Christ can consist only in his bringing us into a certain conformity with himself. He gives us a share in his exemplary representation of true man with unbroken God-consciousness. The Redeemer takes up believers into the force of his God-consciousness and this is his redeeming activity (§ 100). He does this work with the aim of engendering a spontaneity of the God-consciousness in us, so that we do not follow him as a stranger but become identical with our own authentic being. This is the help he gives us. The act of the Redeemer becomes our own act (§ 100, 1).

Here, then, God does not come into our finitude in person, as the incarnation bears witness (John 1:14). He chooses the one and only man to be his representative. This man, however, is shut up with us in finitude, whereas God in his transcendence is above it. If there is still verbal reference to the "divine" character of Christ, this is dialectically justified only to the extent that (as Hegel might put it) quantity changes into quality. The specific quantitative measure with which Christ exceeds the human order of magnitude through the unbrokenness of his God-consciousness changes into the quality of the divine, i.e., of a perfect conformity with God.

When Schleiermacher takes the being of God in Christ to which the gospel of the incarnation testifies, and changes it into Christ's being conscious of God, he finds a solution to the difficulty with which the doctrine of the Trinity wrestles, namely, the problem how faith in the one and only God can be reconciled with the fact that God as this one and only God comes into a specific here and now of finite history, is wholly present in Christ, alienates and humbles himself in him, and yet is still himself in all his fulness. This problem, which the doctrine of the Trinity expounds rather than solves—for to try to solve it would be to force the incomprehensible into our comprehension—no longer presents itself to Schleiermacher. For if the ontic relation of God and his incarnate Word is incomprehensible, the same does not apply to the noetic possibility of conceiving of a perfect God-consciousness and of God's being in this consciousness. Once the goad which provokes the trinitarian reaction is taken away, the dogma of the Trinity necessarily becomes an embarrassment for Schleiermacher. He puts it in a kind of siding at the end of his *Christian Faith,* and one easily detects how futile is his attempt to find any remnant of point or meaning for it.

Using different terms, Ritschl too finds the divinity of Christ, not in God's being in him, but in the exemplary representation he gives of true man. The attribute of divinity sums up his grace and fidelity in the fulfilment of his calling and the superiority of his spiritual self-determination to the particular and natural motives which the world offers (*The Christian Doctrine of Justification and Reconciliation* [E.T. 1900], p. 463). This marks him as *sui generis* (p. 465). To this extent, as in Schleiermacher, he stands above the level of empirical humanity.

Here too, then, God himself does not meet us in Christ. As Redeemer, Christ is not God's personified address to us. Justification and the remission of sins, which are the central content of his redeeming work, simply signify the fact—and this again reminds us of Schleiermacher—that something changes in the human sphere. Separation due to guilt feelings and mistrust is purged away and transformed into the fellowship of confidence in God and peace with him when the conduct of the exemplary man Christ becomes our example (p. 534). It is not that God himself arises over us as the sun of righteousness and makes this rising his deed and resolve, but rather— if we may use the same metaphor—that this sun shines over us with eternal immutability. It is simply hidden from us by our unbelief and sense of guilt. Our subjective ethical state is like a fog. It causes clouds to come between the sun and us. Hence the sun is concealed. But the cause of the cloudiness—our own subjective ethical state—is removed by the example of man which we are given in Christ. We can thus see that which was always and unchangeably there, namely, the sun, the loving God. The NT, however, never presents the loving God as an eternal and timeless state of the Father which is simply concealed from us. It speaks about God's love only as an event on which God resolves in his freedom and which becomes a reality in Christ. Whereas in the NT something takes place in and from God, in Ritschl the only happening is on man's side. God in himself is frozen in timeless immutability. One might say that he becomes the eternal principle of love.

When we compare Ritschl's ethical attitude with Schleiermacher's God-consciousness, we see at once how similar is the structure of thought in the two authors. In both we have variations on subordinationist and adoptionist themes. Only man, not God, is historical. To use the categories of Volume I of the present work, we have here two examples of the Cartesian approach. The "I am" of man is the dominant note. Theology is controlled, not by the history of God with man, his self-disclosure as Father, Son, and Holy Spirit, but by the history of man's relation to the idea of God, the arising, obscuring, and re-arising of this idea as these come about through the state of man's consciousness or his ethical situation.

Ritschl, too, is thus able to evade the problem which leads to the doctrine of the Trinity. The doctrine has just as miserable an existence in him as it does in Schleiermacher.

The modern theology of revolution offers a primitive and almost pathologically distorted variant of the same patterns of thought. Its serious initial question need not be discussed here. But its christological implications—we can hardly refer to the role of trinitarian doctrine as such—are most important in this context. God's being in Christ is completely irrelevant. The only relevant thing is the significance of Christ as an example of and for man. Yet even this example is relevant only insofar as Christ is constantly opposed to the present structure of the world, the establishment and its manifestations. It is relevant only insofar as Christ does not fit in with the world as it is, but shakes its foundations in revolutionary protest.

Here the distance between God and Christ is so radical that the question of God is lost to view altogether. Even subordinationism is beside the point, for the one to whom Christ is subordinate is irrelevant. Christ is the representative of the absent God; he causes the one who commissioned him to be forgotten. We are at home with Christ. It is no surprise that the slogan "death of God" synchronizes very noticeably with this theology of revolution (cf. Volume I, pp. 219ff.). What we suggested by way of criticism of early Christian subordinationism and adoptionism, namely, that on these views God no longer encounters us in person through Christ and we are thus shut up in our finitude, is now carried to its most radical conclusion. The caricature of Christ, which in various forms can discharge the function of a teaching model, very quickly fulfils its task and can be dispensed with, like the God whose temporary representative he once appeared to be.

Literature on the theology of revolution includes H. E. Tödt, "Revolution als neue sozialethische Konzeption" in T. Rendtorff–H. E. Tödt, *Theologie der Revolution* (1968); H. E. Tödt, "Bedeutung und Mängel der Genfer Weltkirchenkonferenz," ZEE (1967), 1, pp. 2ff. (with bibliography); H. D. Wendland, "Kirche und Revolution," *Appell an die Kirchen der Welt,* 2nd ed. (1967); R. Shaull, *Encounter with Revolution* (1955); H. Krimm, "Theologie der Revolution?" *Deutsches Pfarrerblatt* (1968), 2, pp. 37ff.; J. Moltmann, "Gott in Revolution," *Ev. Kommentare* (1968), 10, pp. 565ff.

We now need to take stock of the situation.

Our task has been, and is, to consider systematically early one-sided extremes in trinitarian thinking and therewith to recognize the problems which led to the answer in the doctrine of the Trinity. The system of Origen has been the plan by which we have taken our bearings. The extremes referred to may be regarded as one-sided emphases on elements which are

united in the complex syntheses of Origen. Along these lines the subordinationists and adoptionists absolutize the idea of God in himself, trying to
safeguard his unity and singularity by putting Christ on the creaturely side—
with a rich scale of nuances—instead of thinking of Father, Son, and Holy
Spirit as the one self-revealing God.

Modalism and Its Implications

The other alternative, which is taken by the modal monarchians, thinks in
terms of an unbroken identity of Son and Father, and indeed in a prolepsis
of the trinitarian formula, of God, Logos, and Pneuma. The reduction in
the being of the Logos which necessarily results from an emanative or
subordinationist understanding is to be avoided here without affecting the
unity of God. At first glance it might seem that what we have is simply an
abstract game. A synthesis is reached, with all its nuances, between an
ontologically static concept of God in terms of substance and the dynamic
of God's self-unfolding in history. Closer investigation, however, shows that
this conception has extraordinary significance for the future. Elements of
it may be found even in the latest offshoots of a secularistic philosophy.

Sabellius, the high priest of extreme modalism, finds in the Father, Son,
and Holy Spirit only three different forms of the self-disclosure of the one
divine essence (*tres modi apparitionis*). If they are called persons (*prósōpa*)
this bears no relation to the modern understanding of person as a separate
and self-grounded individual. What is meant is the mask of the Greek
theater through which the voice of the one who wears the mask sounds
forth (*personare*="to sound through"). Strictly speaking, then, the three
figures of the Trinity are not "figures" but simply different modes in which
the one identical figure of God comes to expression. These modes are to be
linked with three acts in the cosmic drama which are controlled by the
three masks: creation and the law as the period of the Father, redemption
as the period of the Son, and the community as the period of the Holy
Spirit.

The concept of person, understood thus as a mode of expression or of relating to man, is to be regarded as an intellectual aid which is again
designed, although along different lines from the positions discussed earlier,
to make possible the harmonizing of God's unity and singularity with his
movement outward and the dynamic multiplicity of his historical presence.
Once more, however, it must be asked what price has to be paid for this
attempt to make the mystery of God comprehensible by subjecting it to
smooth logical calculation.

A first point is this. In the modalists, unlike Origen, the three modes in
which the one God appears do not come into being by derivation from the
implications of the divine substance. To use the terminology of Kant, the
system of Origen consists of a summation of analytical judgments and
tautologies. All that is stated basically—apart from the biblical correctives
to which we referred—is what the concept of the divine substance contains

by way of potential expressions. The concept has only to be analyzed and its explication alone will lead us to the Logos, the Pneuma, and ultimately the creation of the cosmos. What is ontically emanation in Origen is noetically deduction and explicatory analysis. Hence all the operations of thought have their source in one reality or monon, i.e., in the divine substance.

In the modalists, however, a completely new element enters in—one might almost speak of a foreshadowing of the modern period—to the extent that a hidden dualism comes into play. The theater, whose dramatic roles and masks acquire great importance here, rests on the duality of actors and spectators. The former act and speak while the latter see, hear, and understand. The words and acts of the players are addressed. Hence those to whom they are addressed—the spectators—have a role too. The whole complex of the theater cannot be understood unless account is taken of the questions, the categories of thought, the pre-understanding, and the receptive ability of the spectator. (A history of the theater will necessarily be incomplete if it deals only with plays, the understanding of parts, and matters of decor and direction, but ignores the temporally conditioned consciousness of audiences in different ages and disregards the interaction between text and production on the one side and contemporary expectations of the parts and message on the other.)

The spectator who sees God play his three roles, each in a different act, but all merging into one another, is man. As we have seen, man too, as a spectator, has his own part. He thus helps to shape the structure of the play. For the three modes of appearance plainly denote a relation. They are the way in which God encounters our consciousness in the multiplicity of his utterance. Indeed, one might say that they are the way in which our consciousness reacts to the historical self-disclosure of God. We seem to see different figures behind the "Let there be" of creation and "Thou shalt" of the law, behind the incarnate Word of love, and behind the pentecostal founding of the community. Various divine characters seem to fill the stage. But when the consciousness begins to reflect on the matter, it sees through the optical illusion and has to say that all the time there was only one actor playing different parts and wearing different masks.

In face of this fascinating explanation we are forced to applaud but we must criticize too. We have to applaud because modalists always find the same God in the different forms and behind what seem to be the very divergent stages of salvation history—one need only think of God as author of both law and gospel. The fact that this can happen is a sign that while God appears in the reflection of our consciousness and it is the discursive structure of our thinking which divides the one divine figure into the plurality of its modes of appearance, there is more to it than this, for the consciousness is not productive here. It does not invent this divine masquerade itself. Instead it is reproductive. It reacts. Modalists are convinced that what appears as roles and masks goes back to something which really encounters us, with which our consciousness is confronted, feeling its impact and finding responses engendered to it within itself. In this process the one beam of light breaks up into the spectrum of various colors but the unity of its operation is still perceived. We are certainly imprisoned in the laws by which our consciousness functions. As Kant would say, we cannot see the thing in itself directly. We can see it only as it is refashioned by our forms of perception and the categories of our consciousness. Nevertheless, even in the "prison" of the structure of our consciousness we are affected by something from outside. Hence the operation of the consciousness is not productive but reproductive.

Modalists assume, then, that we are not dealing with hallucinations but with God himself, and that this one God uses various roles and masks to accommodate himself to our consciousness.[5] In metaphorical terms, we cannot get out of Plato's cave in which we see only the shadows of true reality, or phenomena as they are filtered through our own situation and consciousness. But God can come into the cave from outside and manifest himself in the mask of the shadow. While we cannot move out, God can come in with his signs. In modalism, then, man in spite of his imprisonment in the consciousness does in fact stand over against God and not just himself. He has to do with God.

In applauding modalism for this, we do not forget that criticism is in order too. The God presented here is a static God in himself who remains in inaccessible transcendence. Movement and historical life are breathed into him only by the consciousness. By means of its discursive structure the consciousness can know the one only in its multiplicity. One might say—and perhaps one has to say—that it is God who brings himself into historical movement by this consciousness. Nevertheless, even if this is so, the theatrical aspect comes to the fore again. God only "plays" a dynamic role. He achieves movement by exchanging masks. In himself, however, he remains in the background, unknowable and inaccessible. He does not invest himself in his personae. We do not have him totally and directly in the encounter with Christ and the reception of the Pneuma. To return to the metaphor of the cave, we encounter only his shadows. We are still tied to reactions of our own consciousness. We know that he produces these but we do not know how he is or who he is. Christ is simply the echo which an indeterminable voice draws from the walls of our finitude. We remain imprisoned in this finitude. Christ is not the incarnate one who comes into this finite history, so that God himself is present in it.[6] God does not invest himself in an event. Although in a different way from that found in Origen or the subordinationists, he is not a God who in freedom resolves on

---

[5] To cite a modern variation on this idea, we are reminded of Lessing's view that the divine educator uses mythical imagery or rational directness as the state of the consciousness requires. Cf. the author's *Offenbarung, Vernunft und Existenz. Studien zur Religionsphilosophie Lessings*, 5th ed. (1967).

[6] Even the extreme form of patripassianism, in which the Father himself suffers and dies, cannot rescue the incarnation. This doctrine is a product of the immanent logic of the modalistic principle. If Christ is simply a mask of God, this means that

gracious address and is present in person in the act of this turning to us. Christologically speaking, he is not "in Christ." The God in himself who is thought of monistically in Origen is here the same God in himself but now transposed into the dualistic thinking which arises out of the relation between the "affecting" transcendent God and the "receiving" consciousness of man.

The question of the doctrine of the Trinity is thus raised, and it is raised in such a way that the doctrine must be worked out as a defensive formula if God is not to be known only in his unity and singularity (as among modalists as well as subordinationists) but the church is to bear witness to his free resolve to be Immanuel and to be this God of ours in the salvation history of creation (Father), redemption (Son), and the imparting of his presence (Spirit). To put this anti-modalistically, the stations of salvation history are not inauthentic modifications of the one God shaped by our consciousness. Based on the free resolve of God, they are condescensions in which he is present "in person" as the one and total God.

In the doctrine of the Trinity, then, "in person" does not mean in a mask or inauthentically. It denotes the real disclosure of the heart of God.[7] Under the pressure of the defense required at this point the word "person," which is taken from the Greek theater, acquires a new content and becomes synonymous with membership in a koinonia. The term is baptized. Hence a long history is started which leads finally to the modern understanding of person although not without the retention of certain basic elements in the trinitarian concept.

Excursus on the Consequences in Religious Relativism, Consciousness Theology, and Historical Materialism

In modalistic monarchianism one may detect the first signs of a theological trend which manifests itself in various ways through history and which takes on some extreme forms in its secularized offshoots. This trend is characterized by the fact that increasing worth is ascribed to the human consciousness in theology. Whereas the Platonic idea reveals itself, but the consciousness can develop no activity of its own but must win through to theoria in order to break free from the activity which is directed on shadows, on this view the consciousness is a factor which cooperates actively in the encounter with the self-revealing God. This is a revolution in intellectual history comparable to that in art when Apollodorus of Athens and Agatharchos of Samos discover perspective and thus begin to portray

---

God himself is the player in the death and passion. He is the *player*. This means that we have here the inauthenticity of a role whose significance remains radically different from the true and realistic solidarity of Christ, who in suffering, temptation, and death exposes himself to the full pressure of human life.

[7] Cf. Chapter VII on the personality of God.

objects, not in isolation as in Egyptian art,[8] but in their relation to the spectator and as they are shaped by this relation. One might say similarly of the position of the modalists that in it the Trinity is a matter of perspective. It is the way in which God's self-manifestation is reflected in the consciousness of the spectator. It is the way God orients his mode of appearance to this relation.

For reasons of space—another book would be needed—we cannot pursue the historical development of the co-operative function of the consciousness. We can only sketch some instances which confront us today, and will continue to do so.

First, it may be stated generally that when modalists set up periods of salvation history on a trinitarian model (creation and law, redemption, and impartation of the Spirit), then in spite of appearances to the contrary their concern is not with the God who comes into history but with the history of the human consciousness as it reflects on God. The theatrical simile of the role and the mask offers an illuminating illustration of this. The actor never enters totally into his role. Identification has its limits. He stays on the outside and is in part a spectator of himself. Otherwise the torments of soul which he depicts would destroy him. Similarly the stages in salvation history which represent the persons of the Trinity in the mode of temporality are not, as we have seen, historically formed modes of being of God himself. They are the history of relations in which the human consciousness has a normative and co-operative share.

To the extent that the I and I-consciousness are emancipating themselves in the modern era,[9] their normative role is increasing within the relation of God and man.

For Lessing, who might be taken as a representative of the Enlightenment, the rational consciousness with its derived truth of reason is the criterion of possible certainty even in the sphere of revelation. For Kant the structure of our rationality (in both the theoretical and the practical sense) forms the horizon of our experience, so that God becomes a magnitude which transcends experience and which thus comes into view only with indirect certainty as a mere postulate.

A mark of the complex and comprehensive structure of Schleiermacher's system is that it is governed by modalist as well as subordinationist characteristics. All the dimensions of revelation as they are developed in the trinitarian formula are here discussed in terms of the way they impinge on the sense of absolute dependence. The consciousness is thus the criterion of the relevance of any dimension of revelation. That which cannot be developed in terms of the consciousness counts as theologically irrelevant.

---

[8] Cf. E. Brunner-Traut, "Die Darstellungsweise der ägypt. Kunst—ein Wahrheitsproblem," *Universitas* (1953), pp. 481ff.; W. Wolf, *Das Problem des Künstlers in der ägypt. Kunst* (1951). On the anthropological significance of perspective cf. ThE, III, § 3285ff.

[9] Cf. what is said about Descartes and Kant in Volume I (see the Index), and also the analysis of secularism, esp. pp. 265ff.

In Christology statements about Christ's pre-existence and eschatological statements fall into this category.[10]

The enhanced rank of the relation to consciousness may be seen especially in the theological existentialism of the middle part of the twentieth century. The content of my faith now has to be something which is in harmony with the state of my consciousness, which links up with my pre-understanding, e.g., with such existential things as anxiety, care, guilt, or alienation, and which is subject to what my consciousness accepts as the normative criteria of verifiability.[11] There thus arises a tendency to introspection, i.e., to concentration on the structure of consciousness and the hermeneutical possibilities enclosed in it.

Under the dominion of a consciousness which is increasingly thematized in this way, theology threatens to move over conceptually into the field of anthropology. If in the first stage the consciousness was a mere criterion of the possibility of appropriating revelation, this criterion surreptitiously changes into a normative principle which prejudges what may be considered as possible truth about God. The final result is the fully emancipated and completely autonomous consciousness of a radical secularism.

In the terminology of Lessing one might describe the process as follows. The consciousness is at first given pushes in the right direction by revelation. But when it has been helped to independence it no longer needs these outside interventions. When this final stage is reached, a reversal takes place. Previously, in the modalist stage, God seemed to reflect himself in the consciousness with the help of his masks. But now the consciousness reflects itself in the ideas of God that it produces. This leads finally to Feuerbach's theory of projection, which is not limited to its first statement, but can and will be found in constantly new forms. One of these forms—although only one—is to be found in Nietzsche's *Will for Power,* which carries the necessarily self-developing anthropocentric conception to its extreme limit. As he puts it, meaning, even the meaning described mythically in the concept of God, is necessarily perspective, perspectivism, in virtue of which every center of power constructs all the rest of the world in terms of itself.[12]

The initial modalist relating of the consciousness to God can be carried even further. We shall choose two representative forms of this development.

1. When the consciousness becomes the key point of reference from which we take our bearings on all relations in this world and the world above, one cannot stop at the trinitarian problem. Not just the Father, Son, and Holy Spirit are modes of God's self-reflection in the consciousness as Sabellians aver. The consciousness does not have to do merely with the God of Christianity. If this path is taken, it leads us into the broad field of religious history. What is to prevent us from understanding all religions, and

---

[10] In his early work *Die Mystik und das Wort,* 2nd ed. (1928), E. Brunner refers to the "eschatological lacuna" in Schleiermacher.

[11] Cf. Volume I, pp. 55ff., on Bultmann.

[12] *Wille zur Macht,* 78, 430.

not just the trinitarian faith of Christians, as modifications of the one God reflecting himself differently in different states of the consciousness?

Schleiermacher, whose thinking has a bewildering range of color, championed this position, especially in his early years. The fifth of his *Speeches* says that there is one religion, but that this one religion has to individualize itself and hence it is to be found only in the plural, as the multiplicity of positive historical religions. But why is there this drive for individualization? The individual factor in religion arises as an individual view of the universe by free selection becomes the central point of all religion to which all else is related (*Speeches on Religion* [E.T. 1958], pp. 222f.). But the individual view, which particularizes the original "one" that is unavailable as such, is simply the consciousness. (In this regard we have to remember that in Schleiermacher consciousness is not limited to reflection or even rationality but embraces a general sense of existence—another inadequate term—which includes that which in an age of depth psychology we usually call the unconscious.) On the basis of its individual components and characteristics this consciousness reacts in different ways to religious affections. Hence different articulations of religion arise. We find monotheism, polytheism, and pantheism according to different views which a particular consciousness derives from the universe and to which it then extends exclusiveness. The different religions are not really mutually exclusive, although they often think they are by reason of their imprisonment in a particular view. In reality—to put it in modern terms—they are complementary. Only when taken together do they constitute the totality of religion, which is split into many different aspects by the various forms of the consciousness. The substitution of complementarity for exclusiveness is necessarily bound up with a principle of toleration. The "one" religion cannot be grasped by me. It is an inaccessible "in itself" like the God of the modalists hidden behind his masks. But I believe that it exists. Knowing the "that," I have at my disposal the critical principle which relativizes the religions for me or helps me to understand them as a mosaic. The truth of my religion, then, is not an alternative to that of others. I accept other religions along with my own, since they contain a supplementary element.

Even Christ as the center of the Christian religion comes under this relativity. (This is true at least in the *Speeches*. In *The Christian Faith* and the sermons at Trinity Church in Berlin the situation is different; cf. the Advent Sermon on Matthew 21:9 in *Predigten*, II, pp. 5-20.) In Christ the idea of religion finds exemplary expression. He shows that everything finite needs higher mediations to come to the Godhead (*Speeches*, p. 246). This idea underlies what we have called the complementary relation of the religions. Here, too, what is separated must be referred to its basis of unity by mediation. Even as the personified principle of mediation, however, Christ is not the only representative of religion. He never claimed to be the only object of the application of his idea or to be the only mediator (*Speeches*, p. 248).

Although Christianity is closest to religion, then, it shares the lot of particularity, and hence it cannot reign alone as the only form of religion. Accordingly it is provisional and not definitive. Christ himself never tired of pointing to the truth that should come after him (*Speeches*, p. 249).

In his comparatively unknown but recently republished essay *On the Difference between the Sabellian and the Athanasian Ideas of the Trinity* (1822) (cf. M. Tetz, *F. Schleiermacher und die Trinitätslehre*, pp. 37ff.), Schleiermacher expressly takes up the cudgels on behalf of Sabellian modalism. His statement that the Trinity here relates only to different modes and circles of divine activity (*op. cit.*, p. 88) reminds us not only of his own presentation of the doctrine but more especially of his doctrine of the divine attributes, for these, as we have seen, do not denote something special in God but only something special in the way of relating the feeling of absolute dependence to him (*The Christian Faith*, § 50; cf. § 30, where the same principle is applied to all doctrines). We are not dealing, then, with an ontic pleroma of the Godhead itself but with the reflection of the Godhead in our consciousness, which causes it to appear multiple. In just the same way the one Pneuma divides into the many charismata on encountering and uniting with man and his consciousness (p. 80). Each charisma is thus a prosopon of the Pneuma (p. 85).

In this regard Schleiermacher is simply a representative of many understandings which in different ways represent complementarity under the guiding concept of the relation of the deity and religion to the consciousness. One of the clearest examples of this trend is E. Troeltsch.

In Troeltsch the principle of individuation leads to religious relativism and a kind of interdependence of all religions. What links him with the Schleiermacher of the *Speeches* is that in Troeltsch, too, the fragmentary character of individual religions arises in virtue of a suspected if not accessible "one religion." Troeltsch himself does not use this term for the comprehensive entity. He says rather that the Christian religion relates to a common goal the individual impulses and intimations that we feel when we test the religions in terms of the powers revealed in them (*Die Absolutheit des Christentums und die Religionsgeschichte* [1912], p. 87). What Schleiermacher calls the one religion is the ultimate common goal in Troeltsch. In our limited consciousness this common goal finds only particular reflection and hence it leaves only fragmentary deposits in the religions.

For Troeltsch, as for the modalists, the final goal which is hidden behind the modes (or masks) of its expression is beyond our grasp. It can be sensed. We know that it exists. Since it is not available as a criterion, however, we cannot show with strict certainty whether Christianity is the highest point, beyond which we cannot go (*ibid.*, p. 90). We can only state empirically, with the consciousness as a subjective correlate, that Christianity must be accepted not merely as the climax but as the point of convergence of all knowable trends in religious development (p. 90).

It may thus be maintained that the modalist initiative of seeing God reflected in the consciousness, and of finding different roles in this reflection, has in the long run had implications not merely for the Christian understanding of God but also for the understanding of the religions, i.e., in the form of the principle of complementarity. What applies first to the modes or roles or masks of God applies later to the religions. God is not fully in any of the modes. Similarly the one religion is not fully in any of the religions. The individualized forms and roles are relative to our reproductive or even productive consciousness. We confront ourselves rather than ultimate truth. Ultimate truth is still wrapped in inaccessible transcendence.

Yet religious relativism and the principle of individuation and complementarity in the sphere of religion are not the only implications of the modalist initiative. It also contains the possibility of certain mutations. It can be turned on its head in just the same way as the dialectical materialism of Marx turned the philosophy of Hegel on its head. The following question will show how this may happen.

Might it not be that what appears to be God's history, and what we proclaim to be a mere drama, a play of a higher order, is in fact the true and authentic history? Might it not be that the background God whom Sabellius proclaimed is himself a mere mask or postulate of thought which falsely seems to be the reality?

When we consider the various possibilities which this type of question opens up, we might conclude that the distinction on which modalism is based cannot be sustained, namely, the distinction between an eternal and immutable background God on the one side and his historical modes on the other. In this case it might be that God exists only in the historical process, that he himself is this process or historical development, and even that through its stages he comes for the first time to himself, to his pleroma. This is precisely what we find in Hegel's doctrine of the self-development of the Spirit.

If God as Spirit is called the Triune in Hegel (*Lectures on the Philosophy of Religion* [1832; E.T. 1895], III, p. 25), this means that the Spirit's self-development or coming to himself takes place in three stages. The eternal and absolute Idea is first (1) God in and for himself in his eternity before the creation of the world and apart from this. Then (2) it steps out of itself in the form of the created world and this creation is in the first instance something other that is posited outside God. But (3) it is essential to God that he should make sure of this alien other which is posited outside him. As the Idea has fallen away from itself, it must take back to itself what has fallen away and bring it back to its truth (*op. cit.*, III, p. 1). The trinitarian structure of the divine being (Idea or Spirit) is not restricted, then, to its inner divine constitution, its being in itself. The trinitarian element is also a paradigmatic law of being. It characterizes the universal process of occurrence. This is inevitable, since God here is in himself history, event, process, and development.

The modalist construction is stood on its head now because what the monarchian God was doing with his left hand—staging the play of history and presenting himself under different masks—has suddenly become his own authentic being. God "is" himself history. He "is" himself the developing one. One might describe the mutation as follows. For modalists God "seemed" to be historical but it could not be said that he "was." His appearing to be so was a noetic phenomenon—the reflection of his being in our consciousness. In Hegel, however, God's historicity, his being in process, is ontological. The being of God, his "is," comes to expression in his historicity. As the meaning of history God neither precedes nor transcends it. He is identical with it. To put it in the language of Christian dogmatics, Creator and creature are not only not separated from one another, as the concept of creation out of nothing so radically implies.[13] The Creator does not even exist prior to the creature. He has his existence in the creature and comes to self-actualization only through created being.

In the process of thought which, with mutations and yet with ongoing identity, leads from the modalists to Hegel, one may note a final mutation which seems to exhaust the possibilities contained in the process.

If God is a process in Hegel, this means that God constantly differentiates himself from himself and becomes an object, but that in this distinction he is absolutely identical with himself (*op. cit.,* II, p. 327). He becomes an object or eventuates himself when in the process of self-development he presses beyond unconscious nature and reaches the stage of consciousness. Here thought of God arises and hence he becomes an object. But there is no effective separation of subject and object at this point. For the finite consciousness knows God only insofar as God knows himself in it (II, pp. 327f.). Hence the finite spirit does not meet the absolute Spirit as another outside itself. Instead, when the absolute Spirit or divine Idea distinguishes itself from itself in the finite spirit, it also remains identical with itself. It has to do with itself as this other. There is thus a close relation between the fact that the absolute Spirit thinks itself in the finite spirit and the fact that the finite spirit knows itself as absolute Spirit. This means that man as finite spirit does not have the initiative in his thinking. He does not produce his thoughts. He is simply the place or medium where or whereby the absolute Spirit thinks itself.

At this stage in our deliberations we may use another question as we try to feel our way toward the final possibility in this process of thought. The question is this: How is it that Hegel fell victim to the same illusion that the modalists did in his view? The modalists believed that God is immutably transcendent and therefore that he never enters history, which is only his play. Hegel, as we have seen, reversed this view and developed the thesis that God "is" only in the historical process and that he is identical with this process. Our question is, however, whether Hegel might not have been subject to a new illusion. Is it not conceivable that the absolute Spirit who in the process of self-development goes through the stage of finite consciousness, and comes to know himself therein, is an illusion which in reality the finite consciousness itself has generated? If so, the finite consciousness is not a mere transition or a mere accident of the absolute Spirit.

---

[13] Cf. Volume I, pp. 88ff.; ThE, I, Index: "creation ex nihilo."

It is authentic reality as compared with the unreality of the world-spirit.

If, however, one reverses Hegel's position, does not another step have to be taken? Does not one have to ask whether the finite spirit for its part is not produced, whether it is not an original magnitude but one that is caused and functional? May not that which we call finite spirit be dependent on material constituents of reality, e.g., on our physiology,[14] or on economic situations, or social structures?

It will undoubtedly be no surprise to the reader that in these questions we have in mind the reversal of Hegel's philosophy in the dialectical materialism of Karl Marx and also in the various ideas of the left-wing Hegelians, e.g., Feuerbach and D. F. Strauss. If the final synthesis of all being in the form of Spirit existing in and for itself no longer precedes the historical process, then the finite consciousness necessarily sees itself challenged to produce the synthesis itself and to program itself and its own future. If pure form or *eidos* in the sense of Aristotle is no longer behind me and no longer directs me, if the divine Idea in Hegel's sense is no longer at the back of me, realizing itself through me, if I no longer fulfil this, then I simply have the future ahead of me as a task. Apart from Marx, who takes this view, Sartre might also be mentioned here. For Sartre man does not have at his disposal the legacy of an end (*telos*) which actualizes itself in him as entelechy. He is a blank page which must inscribe itself and give itself its own norms and future.[15]

As we follow the modalist train of thought to its ultimate limit,[16] we may see negatively what rank is ascribed to the doctrine of the Trinity. The unity of God is upheld in his movement outward, in creation, redemption, and the impartation of the Spirit. It is confessed that in all forms of his self-disclosure we have to do with the one and total God, with the God who in all forms of his self-divesting wills to be there for us, and is there for us, as Immanuel.

Whenever the unity and singularity of God are thought of in themselves, and the triunity of the divine being is thus dissolved, whether it be through the modalist idea of masks or through viewing triunity as a mere step to the creaturely, an inevitable slide takes place into theologies which can no longer grasp the salvation event fulfilled in creation, redemption, and the impartation of the Spirit. Either the true God remains transcendent and inaccessible, so that the incarnation has no point, or else God is detached from what he has perhaps begun as the initiator. In the end, what we find in this process are not theologies at all but metaphysical constructions or ideological programs in which this world is an area from which God is banished and which is governed by his succesor, man.[17]

---

[14] On the thesis that man is (*ist*) what he eats (*isst*) cf. J. Moleschott, *Blätter für lit. Unterhaltung*, No. 269, Jahrg. 1850, p. 1082.

[15] Cf. on Sartre ThE, I, § 1969ff.

[16] The author is pleased to note that Ratzinger has a very similar presentation in *Einführung*, pp. 129-132; E.T. pp. 118-121.

[17] Cf. Volume I, pp. 238ff.

Our purpose has been to bring out the significance of the doctrine of the Trinity first of all in this indirect method. This method is best able to correct the initial impression that the trinitarian and christological debates usually make—and this not merely on tyros, such as theological students—namely, that of engaging in abstruse quibbling with the help of a very inadequate ontological schema of thought. By working out the final implications of some of the more prominent theses of early trinitarian thinking we have been able to show that the original minute differences widen later like a stork's beak. In this way their full significance is brought to light.

In the dogma of the Trinity the fathers recognized the full weight of the differences. Their formulae were not meant to make the incomprehensible comprehensible or to define it in formulae. They were designed to show that we cannot take any of the ways that try to make the incomprehensible comprehensible and are ready to sacrifice essential elements of the faith in order to attain this comprehensibility. The reason for the cautious punctiliousness of the formulae is not to be sought in a passion for definition nor in an arrogant cocksureness of thought but in the experience of children who have been burned or who know that even a small step in the wrong direction can plunge us off the knife-edge which we have to traverse at this point.

In a work devoted to systematics we do not have to work our way through all the tangled forest of dogmatic history. It is easy to see, however, that the method used here might be applied to almost all the positions which have been taken in the battle for the dogma of the Trinity. We must be content with a few typical examples which bring out the questions that surround the dogma and which show what consequences ineluctably follow when damage is done to the foundations of the trinitarian structure.

XI

The Aim and Mode of the Trinitarian Statement

THE AIM OF THE STATEMENT

We have now considered the forces which produced the doctrine of the Trinity. We have also noted the serious results which follow if the doctrine is either evaded or weakened. In so doing we have already described implicitly the positive significance of the doctrine. Its intellectual function, as we have seen, is to safeguard the unity and singularity of God in his movement outward and yet at the same time bear witness to the salvation event which is fulfilled in creation, redemption, and self-presentation as modes of his presence, immanence, and identity.

The doctrine is a defensive formula which is aimed against two opposite heresies. It is aimed against an abstract in-himselfness of God which sets him in unknowable transcendence and which can thus understand his historical manifestations, i.e., what is called the salvation event, only as an inauthentic playing of roles. It is also aimed against the very different deformation of the Christian understanding of God in the form of the dissolution of the Creator in the creature. The variations on this dissolution cover a wide spectrum. They range from the interpretation of Christ as a created religious man (Arius) to the changing of God into a historical process (Hegel) and finally to the complete emancipation of this process (Marx).

One might say, then, that the positive meaning of the doctrine of the Trinity is to be found in its presentation of God as the Lord of salvation history and of history in general. It does this on the one hand by distinguishing God from his self-disclosure. The Son and Spirit as modes of this self-disclosure are presented in the form of distinct persons. Hence God is never swallowed up in the salvation event and the latter can never achieve autonomy or finally emancipate itself from him. On the other hand the doctrine of the Trinity bears witness to the fact that God is identical with himself in his self-disclosure. He is the same God in his movement outward

(Isaiah 41:4).[1] This finds expression above all in the christological section of the trinitarian formulae.

In Christ, in the incarnate Logos of God, we have to do with God himself. He himself is our Redeemer in Christ. If this were not so and Christ were only a creature, then Christ would not have the saving authority which is mighty over death and sin.

For, as Luther says, we can be helped out of our dreadful fall into sin and eternal death only by an eternal person who has power over sin and death to destroy them and to give righteousness and eternal life instead. No angel or creature could do this. It had to be God himself.[2]

What calls thus for theological reflection, demanding a theologoumenon which is not itself the revealed kerygma but a necessary form of meditation on it, does not have its origin in the kind of speculative impulse which may well underlie some part of the so-called proofs of God. It derives exclusively from the fact that God is to be confessed in his relation to the salvation event, and that we have to say both that he is in it and also that he is not exhausted by it, that he gives himself to it totally and yet that he does not give himself up to it. What the doctrine of the Trinity is seeking to say may be expressed both abstractly and also christologically.

Abstractly it is trying to formulate the interrelation of God's transcendence and immanence without losing either dimension. God is he who discloses himself to us, who creates, upholds, and redeems the world. He is thus the God who condescends to immanence, who commits himself to it, who enters into a history with us. To that extent we have him in his immanence. At the same time, however, he maintains transcendence. For God is he who wills this condescension of his in freedom. He resolves to create the world and to be the gracious God. To that extent, while he enacts the process of the salvation event and history, even entering the process in the incarnate Word, he does not "become" the process. This ontological difference between God's being and his being in the world we describe as the element of ongoing transcendence. At the same time the two terms immanence and transcendence are obviously unsuitable here. The logical exclusiveness in which they stand to one another breaks down the moment they are related to God. They are thus inadequate means whereby to describe the mystery. They fail to make it plausible.

The christological way of expressing the relation of God to his self-disclosure, or of the Father to the Son, runs into the same difficulty. The Johannine Christ says that to see him is to see the Father (John 14:9), or that he and the Father are one (10:30), but he never says that the Father is the Son or that the Son is the Father. We "have" the Father in the Son, for God is present in the salvation event which mediates the Son to us. But it cannot be said that the Father "is" this event or that the Father "is" the Son.

---

[1] Cf. also the familiar stanza of H. Claudius which speaks of changes in the world and the nations while God himself, in whose hands they lie, remains the same.
[2] WA, 21, 511.

In leaving a distinction open here, the doctrine of the Trinity shows us clearly what is at issue. We have to express God's presence in his self-disclosure, in his history with us. We have to safeguard his being as God for us, as Immanuel. This being of God has in fact to be watched over, or, better, human thought itself has to be on the watch when it deals with this mystery of God. The history of the doctrine of the Trinity, or the trinitarian debates, concessions, and distortions, has shown us plainly how human thought, when left to its own devices, either inclines to an abstract and non-historical divine transcendence or dissolves God's being in the immanent processes of occurrence.[3]

From all this one may see that the doctrine of the Trinity does not try to penetrate the mystery of God speculatively, and that even what seems to be over-subtle and sophistical in it is not basically addressed to the mystery itself in an attempt to break it but to the human thought which constantly wants to lay hold of this mystery.

The doctrine of the Trinity, as we have said, is a defensive formula, and we can express this aspect more precisely by saying that it defends the mystery of God against ourselves to the extent that, if we are left unchecked, we continually incline to modalistic, tritheistic, Hegelian, or dialectical-materialistic aberrations. Being left unchecked means positively being abandoned to the autonomy of our own thinking and its underlying axioms, while negatively it means losing sight of the fact that God may be perceived by us only in his self-disclosure or the salvation event ("he that hath seen me hath seen the Father"), but that he cannot be perceived by us as the one who resolves on this in free condescension. The oscillation between the divine comprehensibility and incomprehensibility, by which the doctrine of the Trinity is determined, shows us how emphatically it leads us to worship the mystery of God instead of trying to master it. As Melanchthon tells us, we are to worship the mysteries of the Godhead aright rather than searching them out.[4] The doctrine of the Trinity ensures a place for thinking in which worship is possible. It prevents the sanctuary from being secularized into a laboratory. To protect thinking from itself, however, demands a prodigious amount of thinking.

This is why theology reaches its highest measure of reflection in the doctrine of the Trinity. At the same time it is clear that the trinitarian debates with their sharp conceptual distinctions show that they are concerned not merely about the mysteries of the Godhead but also about the experiments in expression which constantly attract human nature and in which it is represented by reason. In this regard the early formulations of the doc-

---

[3] The trinitarian statements of the Confession of Augsburg indicate this problem, especially on the christological side. The concept of "person" is used here to express the difference between God and his self-disclosure. As the Confession says, this term does not express a part or quality in another (which would mean identity of Father and Son or God and revelation) but that which subsists itself (i.e., in itself as its own center of action) (CA, I, 4).

[4] *Loci* (1521).

trine of the Trinity are surprisingly prophetic. In them we find not only an intimation of, but also an incomparable remedy against, almost every possible experiment of this kind, including modern secularization.

Just because an effort of thought is needed, however, even in the self-limitation of thought, we must now turn to some of the difficulties and contradictions which this particular task of thought seems to pose. Primarily we are confronted by the logical problem of thinking of the divine Trinity as a unity. The question is, then, that of the identity of God.

THE MODE OF THE STATEMENT

As regards the question of identity, we recall that the various modalistic theories were controlled primarily by a concern to safeguard God's unity and singularity conceptually and hence to remove the difficulties of thought to which we have referred. Such a safeguard seemed to be offered by the view that the threefold form of the divine manifestation is in fact only an appearance and does not apply to the divine essence. We thus meet with the three forms only as masks on the periphery of the divine action. The fear that the divine essence would otherwise be divided, and polytheism would result, was not entirely unfounded. Polytheistic ideas were not uncongenial to the thinking of antiquity.

This is demonstrated by the actual rise of tritheistic heresy in the sixth century under Justinian I. Its main proponent seems to have been John Philoponus, an Alexandrian philosopher. It was almost impossible to think of trinity as unity in God within an Aristotelian framework of thought. The Aristotelian concept of substance necessarily seemed to demand the idea of an abstract atomistic unity. In fact Peripatetic philosophy, to whose tradition John Philoponus belongs, understood hypostasis as atomon. Hence John's doctrine of the Trinity, as developed in his work *The Arbiter or On the Unity,* postulates three mutually exclusive essences sharing the same divine *ousia,* just as the many individual men share the same *ousia* of humanity.

I thought it might be useful to quote this example of tritheism here because it actualizes two points that have constantly occupied us in our discussion thus far. First, one may see in it what might be called the self-jeopardizing of human thinking. The autonomy of any scheme of thought that we may claim can have implications which run contrary to the original intention of our statement, in this case the intention of demonstrating the unity of God within the three forms of his self-disclosure. Secondly, one may see what efforts the doctrine of the Trinity has in fact made in order to counteract the systematic thrust of thought and to protect the true aim of its statement.

The difficulty of being able to conceive of the unity of God in the various forms of his movement outward is due in the main to the prevailing models of the thinking of antiquity.[5] In Eleatic a-cosmism, e.g., Parmenides, the multiplicity of things merges into the universal one. This alone has being, while the multiple is mere appearance and an unreal reflection of the ground of being understood as undivided unity. In the Neo-Pythagoreans of the first century, especially Apollonios of Tyana, the primal essence is an unbroken monon which causes to emanate from itself the duality of spirit and matter and then the multiplicity of material things. For ancient thought—examples could easily be multiplied—plurality and division always represent a reduction of being in comparison with the original one. The influence of this approach may still be seen in Augustine when the divine Spirit is for him absolute unity, the one, the true, and the good.[6] Even today in scholastic ontology W. Kern can still find the thesis of antiquity that multiplicity implies non-being or that it represents imperfection or a deficient mode of being restricted to what is finite.[7]

Trinitarian theology, then, means no less than a revolutionary liberation from this ancient mode of thinking. It opposes to it the thesis that there is distinction of divine persons in the "one" God. But this plurality in God cannot denote imperfection or a diminution or restriction of being.[8]

Before we consider how the logical difficulty inherent in this thesis (the one is also the many) can be overcome, we may take a look at its important ontological implications. In fact it carries with it a completely new approach to cosmological and anthropological thinking. If God as the ground of being is many, and if his deity is in no way despoiled by the incarnation of the Word, then this necessarily means also that finite being as the image of God[9] is fulness and multiplicity, and that the material structure of things which brings about this multiplicity no longer stands under the curse of the negation or diminution of being.[10] If matter is disparaged, as in Plato, there can be mathematical truth only in the nonmaterial realm of the idea. This is why there is no place for physics. Physics is mathematics applied to the world of matter. It can arise only in relation to the heavenly bodies, which are not regarded as material bodies but as gods. Just because their courses follow geometrical patterns they are not subject to the fate of reduction of being which governs material things. If Galileo can turn confidently to the empirical world, and seek mathematical relations and courses in it too

---

[5] On what follows cf. W. Kern, "Einheit in Mannigfaltigkeit . . ." in H. Vorgrimler, ed., *Gott in Welt*, I (Festgabe K. Rahner, 1964), pp. 207ff.; E. Coreth, *Metaphysik* (1961), pp. 205ff.; Bruno Schulz, *Einfachheit und Mannigfaltigkeit* (1938).

[6] *De lib. arb.*, II, 7ff.

[7] *Art. cit.*, p. 209.

[8] *Ibid.*, p. 207.

[9] The concept of the image of God in no way implies a specific understanding of the analogy of being; cf. ThE, I, § 700ff., 763ff., 829ff., 948ff.; E.T. I, pp. 150ff., 152ff., 171ff., 195ff.

[10] Cf. K. Rahner, "Zur Theologie des Symbols," *Schriften zur Theologie*, IV, pp. 275ff., esp. 281; E.T. *Theological Investigations*, IV (1966), pp. 221f., esp. 226f.

and not merely in the upper world of ideas, it is because in his day true being is no longer limited to the ideal "one" of origin but the quality of being can now be ascribed to the sphere of the material and its multiplicity as well. Flesh, history, and finite reality have been rescued from their former disparagement by the Logos that has come into them. They have now become dimensions in which truth is and which can thus be objects of scientific inquiry. As image they share the essence of supreme truth, the truth of God himself. The being of God is, no doubt, totally different from finite reality,[11] yet not as the undivided one in contrast to plurality, as antiquity believed. At this point trinitarian distinction in God lends a new quality of being to what is created and finite. The disparagement which previously afflicted material multiplicity is lifted.

One may thus say that trinitarian thinking was not without influence on the new understanding of the empirical world which is the presupposition of the rise of modern science.[12]

There still confronts us the logical question. How can we hold together the unity of God and the distinction of the persons of the Trinity without falling into polytheism or tritheism?

In fact, we can no longer conceive of the unity of God in terms of the ancient ontology which starts with the concept of the atomon and hence makes multiplicity into an absolute alternative. To overcome the division into unity and multiplicity we have to use personal categories rather than ontological categories. Love as a personal category binds that which is distinct to unity without swallowing up the distinctness of that which binds itself in love.

As noted in the chapter on the doctrine of God, the application of the concept of person to God suggests this kind of unity in love. In principle person cannot be understood as absolutely singular or purely one. Person is oriented to fellowship or word. This at any rate is the specific element in the concept of person—in distinction from others that are inappropriate—which supports its application to God. The application, however, is itself a derived one, and Tillich may well be right when he says that God was first called person only in the nineteenth century on the basis of Kant's distinction between nature, which is ruled by physical laws, and personality, which is ruled by moral laws.[13] The original connection between God and person was different; the intratrinitarian relations as such were called persons. This is what made it possible, however, for God himself later to be described as person, i.e., as a Thou, as the subject of the Word, as the object of prayer and trust, as the one who discloses himself for fellowship. For without the earlier trinitarian use of the concept there would have been

---

[11] Cf. what is said about creation out of nothing in ThE, I, § 712ff., 1330ff.; E.T. I, pp. 279ff.

[12] For a fuller discussion of this point cf. Volume I, pp. 332-336. The point here is that redemption brings release in relation to the world and thus opens up the possibility of objectivity.

[13] *Systematic Theology,* I, p. 238.

serious obstacles in the way of calling God person—the very obstacles which Tillich himself so strikingly presents. For does not person suggest individuality and limitation? When used of God, does it not ascribe to him qualities which are completely incompatible with his deity? Since God is the ground of the personal, and since he carries its ontological power within himself, how can he himself be a person? Do we not have to say, then, that the symbol "personal God" is a misleading one?[14]

Now we have to agree with Tillich that the idea of the personal God can in fact be misleading, especially when theism stylizes God as a perfect heavenly person or a personalized supreme good. Nevertheless, it seems to us to be a mistake to allow the abuse to drive out the proper use in relation to the description of God as person. To do this is to make possible what is at least an equally bad mistake, namely, that of understanding God as an a-personal supreme being.

If the application of the concept of person to God does not have to lead to the mistakes that Tillich fears, this is due to the earlier thinking about person in the trinitarian discussions. For here the very things which chiefly seem to disqualify the term for use in relation to God are irrelevant. When the trinitarian figures, or dimensions, of Father, Son, and Holy Spirit are said to be persons, the term "person" does not carry the encumbrance of being a description of finite individuality limited in time and space. As we pointed out in the doctrine of God, and as we can now see at a more basic level, the understanding of person here is not modelled on that of human personality. If it were, God would be simply a supreme magnification of the human person and hence its enlarged projection. The real truth is the very opposite. Our understanding of the human person must be modelled on the prior trinitarian understanding of the person, even though only some of its features may be transferred to man.

The fact that in trinitarian thought we have a distinctive concept of person which is not tied to individual limitation may be seen at various points.

First, the unity and singularity of God transcend singular and plural and thus burst through the ancient concept of substance. I and Thou are already contained in them. Along these lines the fathers did not see in the saying in Genesis 1:26: "Let us make man," a plural of majesty but a reference to the personal structure of God which is developed in the doctrine of the Trinity. The same applies to the communion in God expressed in Psalm 110:1: "The Lord said unto my Lord" (cf. Matthew 22:44).

Second, the concept of person in its trinitarian use brings out what it means that God is love (1 John 4:16), and that his unity is not, therefore, that of the atomon substance but a personal communicative We. What does this imply?

If the predicate of being "is" can be used of God in such a way that it may be said that God *is* love, this means that the word love says everything about God that can ever be said about him. His love, however, is

---

[14] *Ibid.*

there bodily in the Son, in the incarnate Word (John 3:16). The Revealer and the Revealed are thus a unity. The statement that God is love points to the unity of the communicative We. In other words, since the saying: "God is love" is christological in 1 John, it tells us that God is in himself the one he is for us in Christ. To put it negatively, God in himself is not other than the one who encounters us as the self-revealing one. The being of God does not have a dark and unknown margin which does not come to expression in the appearing of Jesus Christ. God is love in his very essence and not just in his manifestation as the one who loves in his relation to us.

The NT expresses the fact that God is in himself the one who loves by saying that he loved the Son before the foundation of the world (John 17:24; cf. Ephesians 4:1). This means that God's love is not a particular event which is triggered by the world. He does not love only from the time there is a world (E. Brunner). He is love from all eternity in himself. Hence the unity of God is defined as love, as the fellowship of Father and Son, and therefore as personal. All the trinitarian definitions suggest this personal form of unity. The term "Father" implies already a relation to the "Son" and *vice versa*. Similarly the Pneuma implies outgoing and self-imparting. God *is* love, Word, Spirit.

The same must be said of Spirit as is said of love. Spirit is from the foundation of the world. As God is not just love only from the time there is a world, so he is not just Spirit from the time there is a world. He is Spirit in himself. This needs to be said in opposition to enthusiasts who regard the Spirit as something to be embraced and appropriated by man, as a created movement in us, and hence as a creaturely entity. If in contrast the doctrine of the Trinity defines the Spirit, not as *dynamis,* but as the third person of the Godhead, it sets him first at the side of God (John 4:24) and Christ (2 Corinthians 3:17) and only secondly does it relate him as person to us, so that while we may pray for his coming (*Veni, creator Spiritus*) we can never annex him to ourselves as a possession or quality (cf. CA, I, 6).

Third, the doctrine of the Trinity expresses God's unity in such a way that the communion of love between the three persons is not understood as eros, i.e., as the tense and polar relation of independent entities, but rather as a being from and being to the other. This comes out most clearly in the christological part of the doctrine, which also seems to call the unity of God most sharply in question. We already touched on being to the other when we dealt with the statement that God is love: God's being is self-giving. Being from the other, i.e., from the Father, occurs time and again in the sayings of the Johannine Christ about himself.

When we try to define the I of Christ in terms of these statements we reach very paradoxical conclusions. This I of Christ lives by its basis, i.e., the Father. Hence it cannot be defined as self-grounded entelechy in Aristotle's sense. Its basis is a relation: openness to the Father. Christ does not seek his own will but the will of the Father (John 5:30; 6:38). This is his primal uniqueness which distinguishes him from every human creature and in face of which every human I is seen to be an alienation, a fall from its own origin. One might almost venture to say that the impressed, vital, and self-developing form, the germlike self-grounded entelechy, does not let man be himself in his authenticity but emancipates him from this self; it is born of flesh (John 3:6) and to that extent has lost its authentic self. Jesus Christ, however, being from the Father, is also wholly himself. Hence the communion of persons, illustrated here by the relation of God the Father and God the Son, does not eliminate the unity and singularity of God. It is the trinitarian interpretation of this unity.

For this reason we can speak of the I of Christ only in paradoxes. His I is also his non-I, since he lives by the will of the Father. This paradox finds direct expression in what he says about himself: "He that believeth on me, believeth not on me, but on him that sent me" (John 12:44); "He that hath seen me hath seen the Father" (John 14:9); "My doctrine is not mine, but his that sent me" (John 7:16). Augustine reflects on the paradox in his exposition of this final verse.[15] Is it not absurd and against all logic, he asks, to say that what is mine is not mine? (Does not this make a the equivalent of non-a?) But if we examine the Johannine saying more closely, Augustine thinks, we come up against its decisive presupposition, namely, that Christ identifies himself with his word and doctrine. He "is" his word. This sheds light on our exposition of the dialectic of I and non-I in the Johannine Christ. If his doctrine is not his, but his that sent him, this means that "I am not just I, I am not just mine, but my I is that of another."

---

[15] *Tractate on John's Gospel*, 29, 3. I owe this important reference to J. Ratzinger, *Einführung*, p. 149; E.T. p. 137.

XII

Anthropological Perspectives of the Doctrine of the Trinity

The statement quoted at the end of the last chapter, like all trinitarian statements, has important anthropological implications. In this passage Augustine indicates these when he sees the paradox of the union of I and non-I reflected in man too: "What belongs to thee as thine so much as thyself? And what is so little thine as thyself?"[1] This saying, which in a surprising way reminds us of the problem of identity in Max Frisch,[2] points out that on the one side the I is the thing most proper to me, for I alone can have it. I am an underivable subject. Hence, as the phenomenon of responsibility shows, I cannot trace back myself to any entity outside myself. I am my own first cause.[3] On the other side, my subjectivity does not mean that I called myself into life or posited myself as the one I am. I am simply confronted with my whence and whither. I did not choose myself. In respect of what is most myself I am thus "thrown" (Heidegger) or "absolutely dependent" (Schleiermacher). I live between two mutually exclusive possibilities of self-understanding which logically can merge into one another very smoothly but which are both supposed to solve the mystery of human existence.

The one possibility is that of the self-creator.[4] This self-creator is the unrestricted subject. He is not under subjection to any createdness. He posits himself. He controls no less than his own existence. In hybrid form he thus moves on to equality with God. He wants to be as God. The other possibility is the direct opposite. Man abandons his being as subject. He views himself as an object and as the product of forces outside his own

---

[1] *Quid tam tuum quam tu, quid tam non tuum quam tu?* (*loc. cit.*).
[2] Cf. Volume I, p. 252. Cf. also Bonhoeffer's poem: "Who am I?" in *Letters and Papers from Prison*, 3rd ed. (1973), pp. 347ff.
[3] The story of the fall shows this, for Adam cannot blame Eve nor Eve the serpent; cf. my *Wie die Welt begann*, 3rd ed. (1963), pp. 175ff.
[4] Cf. on Jean Paul in Volume I, pp. 236ff.

personality: other men, circumstances, the nexus of events, constitutional endowment, impulses and the like.[5]

In face of these things man sees himself as one who is irresistibly compelled against his will, so that he is unburdened of responsibility. In this case he falls below the level of his humanity to that of the animal which is ruled by instinct and cannot attain to subjectivity. His freedom[6] sets him in the paradoxical situation of having to choose responsibility without having chosen himself to be his most proper self and yet also to be from another. From this situation stems the whole problem of the nature of identity. The heart of this problem is the mystery of the person, which sees that it is posited, but which within this being posited has then to posit itself, so that it is responsible for itself, not merely for what it does, but for what it makes of itself.

The doctrine of the Trinity anticipates again this paradox of being a person both in its christological and also in its pneumatological aspects.

(1) Christologically the point is that Christ is on the one hand supreme subject and has incomparable authority. Although assailed and tempted,[7] he is master of himself in virtue of his authority and can thus ask: "Which of you convinceth me of sin?" (John 8:46). Paradoxically, however, this rank of subjectivity is based on the fact that his identity is not grounded in himself; his statements about himself in John's Gospel can be put in the epigrammatic form: What is mine is not mine but the Father's.

The prototypical statements which are made therewith concerning personality are also characterized by another element which should not be overlooked.

If in all statements about the personal I determination by a non-I also occurs ("I have not chosen myself, posited myself, or called myself into existence"), then the trinitarian statements about the Son show that the decisive thing is what I understand this determinative non-I to be. If I regard it as a creaturely entity, e.g., a cluster of circumstances, or men who influence me, or the drive which impels me, this understanding of the non-I pushes me into self-alienation and robs me of my identity as a person. We have seen how I lose my subjectivity this way and become the mere effect of a cause coming upon me from outside. I sink below the level of humanity, as we put it. But if, as in the statements of the Johannine Christ and the general trinitarian understanding of the person of Christ, God himself is the non-I which posits the person and gives it its own life, will, speech, and action, then the person is wholly itself in being God's, and its word is its own as God's word. If the essence of one's own existence is grounded in

---

[5] Thus Kant constantly asks whether and how far man is determined by his inclinations; cf. ThE, I, § 1612ff.; *Geschichte und Existenz,* pp. 74ff.

[6] Freedom brings it about that as compared with animals man is deficient in instinct and the resultant determination; cf. Herder in the *Ideen* and more recently Gehlen and Schelsky. Cf. Volume I, pp. 253ff.

[7] Matthew 4:1ff.; Mark 14:36; Hebrews 4:15. We shall deal with this more fully in Part II.

God, it is the more its own the more it is God's, and it has itself when it has itself from God. To be permeated by the being and will of God is the supreme possibility of identity.

(2) Pneumatologically, too, the doctrine of the Trinity refers us to the problem of personality and identity. As we pointed out in Volume I,[8] the spiritual word is not an interpretative word but a creative act-word. It establishes the new creature which is radically different from the old Adamic existence. But since the Creator Spirit sets man in his determination by God, he does not lead him away from himself or alienate him. On the contrary, he brings him to himself and enables him to achieve his own identity.[9]

Once we are aware of the nature of the person as it is anticipated in the doctrine of the Trinity, we find it in many places in the NT. Human existence is a being in or sharing in, e.g., a being in the flesh or a being in the Spirit (John 3:6; Romans 8:13), a being in the truth or in untruth (John 3:21; 18:37). The address on the vine in John 15:1ff. shows that only the branch which remains in the vine is itself; cut off from the vine it withers. Finally, in a climax which is supremely paradoxical Paul discusses this problem of identity in Galatians 2:20. Here the old or former I disappears. It is replaced by being in Christ. But being in Christ denotes my own true identity. "I live, yet not I, but Christ liveth in me." Since conformity is achieved with the true and proper determinative ground of my life, I am wholly myself thereby. My humanity is rescued from its alienation and finds itself. As God orders me to himself in Christ and by the Holy Spirit, my existence is heteronomized. I am no longer deflected from myself and mine. I come to myself for the first time. I find the *autos* that God meant me to be. I am freed for authentic autonomy. Loving God, I achieve a spontaneity which opens up for me free and to that extent autonomous turning to God.

The prodigal son in the parable of Jesus, who wants to be a self-developing subject, and who thus goes off on his own into the far country, falls victim to alienation and thus loses both his freedom and himself. He finds himself only when he comes to have his life from his father in a new way, not in servile obedience as before, but in the filial love of the one who has returned home.

---

[8] Pp. 193ff.
[9] Cf. Volume I, pp. 155ff.

XIII

The Dogmatic Rank of the Doctrine of the Trinity

We have stated that the doctrine of the Trinity is a real doctrine, even a defensive formula, and not kerygma in the strict sense. In other words, it is not the object of faith but the reflection of faith on its object.[1] Faith reflects here in such a way that it regards the God who discloses himself as one and the same in the modes of his self-disclosure, i.e., Father, Son, and Holy Spirit. On the one hand it does not regard him as an abstract unity of substance in a transcendent "in himself," while on the other hand it does not identify him with the act of his self-disclosure and integrate him into the historical process. (We have offered examples of both alternatives in the corresponding models from the Modalists to Hegel.) The doctrine of the Trinity has, then, an apologetic or defensive character. It is a "provoked" doctrine. It is the response to a challenge. This applies at least to its developed form as this finds expression in concepts like *homoousios* or *persona* or in a christological phrase like *genitus, non factus*.[2]

The two points, first that the Christian belief in God is threatened by the two possibilities of misunderstanding, and second that the first steps can be taken on these false paths without being easily detected, help us to understand why trinitarian reflection has to make some very difficult conceptual distinctions. These operations of thought are needed if the narrow ridge is to be discerned which leads between the two theological abysses. We are really dealing with abysses here, with serious possibilities of falling, for thinkers want to master the mystery of God, to make it comprehensible,[3] and to integrate it into ontological, historical, and other schemes of thought.

If, however, the trinitarian understanding of God watches over that which faith believes, namely, that God is one and the same in the forms of his

---

[1] Cf. M. Kähler, *Die Wissenschaft der christlichen Lehre* (1893), p. 316.

[2] "Begotten, not made" (Nicene and Athanasian Creeds).

[3] M. Kähler, *op. cit.*, p. 317. Kähler issues a warning against trying to use the more precise definition of the triune personality of God for the purpose of achieving further knowledge of the Godhead.

self-disclosure, the doctrine of the Trinity is also more than just a subsequent theologoumenon. One would have to allow that an added reflection or concept of faith[4] might be variable, exchangeable, or time-conditioned. Theological schools and systems are obviously subject to the changes and chances of history. If in contrast the doctrine of the Trinity is a dogma, this is a true indication of the fact that faith is expressing itself here in a valid, adequate, and inalienable form. The doctrine of the Trinity, we insist, is not as such the object of faith but a separate reflexive way in which faith relates to its object and which is demanded by the only too imminent possibilities of unbelief and betrayal. This reflection then, in contrast to other theological deliberations, stands in a constitutive relation to faith and to that extent it has dogmatic rank.

This distinctive relation between faith and the form of reflection which is unique because indissolubly ordered to it,[5] must now be stated with greater precision. We shall attempt this clarification in two stages.

First, the doctrine of the Trinity is not the object of faith, and is not part of the kerygma that generates faith, as a naive faith is both possible and in fact widespread. This naive faith can say that the God who is present in Christ, and who reveals himself in the Word and Spirit, is the Lord (1 Corinthians 12:3), even though it is not explicitly trinitarian.

"The theologoumenon of the Trinity may well be indispensable in express Christian teaching but it has only conditional value for the appropriation of salvation in faith" (M. Kähler, *op. cit.,* p. 316). It is thus dispensable as far as concerns the rise and confirmation of justifying faith in individuals. For salvation and not the disclosed essence of God constitutes the essential content of revelation (*ibid.,* pp. 318f.).

Even the trinitarian formulae of the liturgy, which the individual Christian will accept, may remain in a state of incubation for him, and have no intellectual relevance, without the faith of the believer losing any of its saving significance. In popular terms one might say that no one is excluded from the communion of saints because he can make little or nothing of the Trinity and may even regard it as merely a concern of theologians. (It is, of course, conceivable that the Christian who has rather deeper theological insight might find a kind of implicit trinitarian belief in the one who naively trusts in Christ as his Savior and does not find the basis of his assurance in his own psychological world.)[6]

---

[4] To use the term of W. Herrmann in his *Ges. Aufsätze,* ed. F. W. Schmidt (1923), p. 293.

[5] The distinctiveness does not relate to all dogmatized doctrines. Thus the virgin birth is a dogma but it does not have the same rank as the doctrine of the Trinity. Theologically it is an exposition of conception by the Spirit, but one might ask how necessary it is as such. Could we not believe in the conception, i.e., the uniqueness of Christ's origins, without it? Opinions might vary on this as in spite of every nuance they cannot do in respect of the doctrine of the Trinity. For further discussion cf. Part II and the author's *Between Heaven and Earth* (E.T. 1965).

[6] I am consciously alluding here to implicit faith; cf. A. Ritschl, *Fides implicita* (1890).

Second, if one does reflect on the belief in God, the only option for Christian faith is a trinitarian development of the belief. The individual Christian can get along without this explanation, but the church in its totality cannot renounce it. Its office as teacher and watchman compels it to consider all the dimensions of belief and hence to keep in view the multiplicity of possible assaults. For this reason it cannot let go of the doctrine of the Trinity.[7] To this extent dogmatic examination of the doctrine of the Trinity is justified as reflection which stands in a constitutive relation to faith.

This significance of the doctrine of the Trinity finds negative confirmation in the fact that whenever it is fundamentally and not just naively regarded as dispensable, or whenever it is modified not just in nuances but in its essential features, an unmistakable departure from the biblical basis of faith takes place.

Hegel's trinitarian philosophy is an example of the latter case (cf. the chapter on Hegel in Volume I). As a representative of the former one might refer to R. Rothe, who argues that he knows of nothing that might kindle an interest in developing a trinitarian concept of God, since our Christian faith in no way engenders any such interest (*Ethik,* 2nd ed. [1867], § 37, p. 143). In his *Dogmatik* (1870), p. 70, Rothe objects that the doctrine is a very natural and indeed unavoidable product, not of the distinctively Christian God-consciousness, but of philosophical reflection upon this God-consciousness. His position oscillates between outright rejection of trinitarian theology and its Hegelian reinterpretation.

To sum up our findings, we have touched on some of the difficulties in the doctrine of the Trinity (no more!) as these arise in discussion of revelation as the Word that posits history. The question of God's self-disclosure is in fact the thematically decisive question from which all the lines that lead to the doctrine of the Trinity radiate. Since this question has to do with the self-disclosure which is fulfilled and present in Christ, it is a query within the sphere of revelation. Already confronted by the event of salvation, it asks: "Where did this come from, and why?"[8] It does not ask, then, within the framework of a natural theology. It does not inquire speculatively into the being of God in himself. It begins with the God with us who has entered into a history with us in the incarnate Logos, summoned us into this history of his by the Holy Spirit, and made this history our present,[9] always remaining one and the same God at every stage and in every form of this self-disclosure. Hence the triunity of God tells us how God goes his way to us and with us. It tells us about an event. It tells us

---

[7] This is what Kähler meant when he called the doctrine "indispensable in express Christian teaching," *op. cit.,* p. 317.

[8] Cf. P. F. Hiller's hymn: "Mir ist Erbarmung widerfahren" ("Mercy has come upon me").

[9] Cf. Volume I, Chapter IX, and Kierkegaard's concept of contemporaneity.

about God in becoming.[10] Being overtaken by this event, or, better, drawn into it, necessarily raises the question of the being of God, the being in which this event, this self-distinction of God in the various acts and forms of his manifestation, is grounded. The question posed herewith leads us to the insight that the being of God is determined by the sovereign freedom of his grace.[11] He is the one who resolves upon his condescension, upon his history with us, and hence he is always more than his self-disclosure and is never absorbed into it.[12]

This leads us to a final thought which might seem to be a correction of what has been said hitherto. In fact, however, it will simply serve as a knob to bring the picture we have achieved into sharper focus.

We have stated that the doctrine of the Trinity is not itself the object of faith (or revelation) but the reflection of faith on its object.[13] Even in saying this, however, we recognize the difficulties and ambivalences of thought that confront us here. For it has become clear that what is meant in the doctrine of the Trinity, and what cannot be stated in any other way, is revelation, and hence the object of faith, insofar as we can have God as this object, i.e., believe in him, only because he is our God in the Son and in the Holy Spirit. We are thus encircled by the Trinity when we believe. If we define faith from the standpoint of the Trinity, we can say only that believing means laying hold of God as our salvation in Christ (John 4:9; 5:9-12) and learning by the testimony of the Holy Spirit that we have been laid hold of by God (Philippians 3:12), so that strictly we do not have God as object but God has us as his object. For what is imparted to us here has not entered any man's heart and therefore cannot proceed from it. It is "prepared" (1 Corinthians 2:9) for those who love him. And even this love of ours does not take the initiative and set things in train. It, too, is prepared and set in train. For it corresponds to the fact that God has loved us, that he *is* love (1 John 4:10, 16, 19), and that our love is thus a response.

The distinction, then, between the object of faith and reflection on this object demands a final refinement of our statement. We shall present it in three parts.

First, the Trinity is (still) revelation, and therefore an object of faith, insofar as we are encircled by it when we believe. We implicitly confess it when we confess Christ as him in whom God is *our* God, and when we

---

[10] So Jüngel, *op. cit.* The term is a delicate one in view of its philosophical overtones; we use it here in the sense established by Jüngel.

[11] In spite of John 10:30 this seems to be suggested by the sayings in the Gospels which speak of the limitation of the Son as compared with the Father; cf. Mark 10:18; 13:32; Luke 22:42; John 5:30; 6:38, etc.

[12] Volume I, pp. 292ff.

[13] Attentive readers will note that in making this statement we part company both with Barth, who in the *Church Dogmatics* seems not to distinguish between kerygma and reflection, and also with Brunner, who links them only "optionally" and hence tends to separate them (*Dogmatics*, I [E.T. 1959], pp. 226ff., 236ff.).

confess of the Holy Spirit that he makes God's being in Christ present to us. Thus the doctrine of the Trinity has the rank of revelation in respect of its doctrinal aim or intention, i.e., to the extent to which it expresses the way in which God as Father, Son, and Holy Spirit is "our God."

Second, however, the doctrine of the Trinity does not have the rank of revelation but of reflection on it insofar as it represents the dogmatic form of revelation. For in this doctrine we develop in the systematic figures of our thinking what the triune God is as the subject of his self-disclosure and in the mode of his self-disclosure. We do this with the intention of confessing him as one and the same in his history with us, of protecting him against the autonomous attacks of our thinking, and of thus reverencing the mystery of his deity.

Third, although the doctrinal form of the trinitarian statements does not have the rank of revelation (and is thus subject to variation in the different schools), its basic section, namely, the statement about the triunity as such, has still the quality of dogma. For when faith engages in reflection—as the faith of the church has to do for the reasons given—the statement of its thinking can be made only within this schema.

In the last analysis, then, the doctrine of the Trinity is a doxology using the means of thought. It praises God for his majesty, which condescends to our depths and yet remains the same. For this reason the liturgical formula of "Glory be to the Father . . ." is both formally and materially the most fitting form of the trinitarian confession: "Glory be to the Father, and to the Son, and to the Holy Ghost, As it was in the beginning, is now, and ever shall be, World without end. Amen."

This formula expresses the threefold form of God's self-disclosure as Creator, Redeemer, and Holy Spirit. It confesses God's entry into history with the sequence of the times: the once of beginning and the eternal now of ongoing re-presentation. At the same time it confesses that God is one and the same through all the aeons, which he both embraces and shelters in himself. At this point knowledge derives from worship.

The thinking based on worship is no less penetrating, no less critical, and no less sublime. But it is immunized against speculative roaming and the desire for mastery. It is not "free" thought with no presuppositions. Its presuppositions are not self-discovered or ideologically posited axioms. They are a "pre-" by which all else is posited, including thought itself and its very possibility. To this "pre-" which stands over against the finite spirit —with some relish we adopt a Hegelian formula—thought stands in the relation of a recipient; it receives itself from what is presupposed for it.

The doctrine of the Trinity is, then, the classical and paradigmatic instance of thinking on the basis of faith. For the "pre-" by which it is posited and from which it receives itself is not itself the product of thought. The mode in which it achieves self-awareness and expression is that of faith and worship.

This is why in the strict sense trinitarian thought confesses God rather than knows God. The confession is made with the tools of thought and knowledge, but this is only for two reasons. First, when God apprehends us and sets us in his salvation event he wants us with all that we have and are, and this means also as bearers of *nous,* as rational beings. Second, this confession or expression of worship must use the tools of thought in order that it may oppose the autonomy of our thinking and stop this thinking from integrating God into its schemata.

Thus the thinking with whose help the doctrine of the Trinity is worked out is apprehended thinking which does not simply relate itself to the theological "object" of triunity but is already embraced by the Trinity. For the depths of deity to which this reflection is directed are opened up by the Pneuma, by the third person of the Holy Trinity (1 Corinthians 2:10). Trinitarian thinking is possible only in subordination to the Trinity, whether implicitly with the naivety of the simple children of God, or explicitly with the conceptual endowment found among devotees of theology.

Since the doctrine of the Trinity is bound up in this way with the self-disclosing God, we may find hints, traces, and intimations of it wherever we read of what God says and does. The instinct of the fathers was right when they interpreted the OT allegorically in this regard and took from it trinitarian statements which we could no longer do in the same way today.[14] The task itself remains and still awaits proper fulfilment.

In conclusion we might indicate the direction in which the task points if it is pursued within the present understanding of the doctrine of the Trinity.

An excellent passage by which to fix this orientation is the account of the call of Isaiah in Isaiah 6:5-9.

The "Woe is me! for I am undone" describes the dread of the prophet when he encounters God in his majesty. The glowing coal with which the seraph touches his lips to rid them of uncleanness prefigures the event of atonement in the incarnate Word. The sending of the prophet, his task of proclamation, points to the witness of the Holy Spirit by which God opens his Word and makes it present. But God opens his Word in such a way that it still remains his and does not come under the control of its hearers. When the Spirit does not elucidate it, they hear and do not understand, they see and do not perceive (Isaiah 6:9; cf. Matthew 13:11ff.).

The fact that God remains one and the same, as the trinitarian doxology maintains, manifests itself as follows. Although the doctrine of the Trinity develops only in connection with Christology, nevertheless the God who is present in Christ is the same yesterday, today, and forever. It was the Father of Jesus Christ that appeared to Isaiah. We may thus understand why the later statements about the Trinity from the NT onward are not an absolute innovation fallen down from heaven. They come within an existing framework which they do not have to break out of but which they fit into.

---

[14] Cf. W. Vischer, *Das Christuszeugnis des AT* (1934); E.T. *The Witness of the OT to Christ* (1949); H. Hellbardt, "Die Auslegung des AT als theol. Disziplin," ThBl (1937), pp. 129ff.; also "Abrahams Lüge," ThEx, No. 42.

This is a shadow of things to come, just as the covenant and the law are shadows in relation to the new thing which comes with Christ (Colossians 2:17; Hebrews 10:1).

Excursus I: The Essential Trinity and the Economic Trinity and the True Concern of Faith in this Issue

The author realizes that his thesis that the Trinity describes God in his self-disclosure or relation to man might suggest that in spite of every safeguard he is close to the modalist or Sabellian view of the Trinity and inclines to the economic understanding. Further support for this interpretation might be found in our placing of the doctrine of the Trinity, not in the chapter on the question of God, but in a discussion of revelation as the Word that posits history. The decisive point, however, is that our systematic arrangement of the doctrine is determined by the noetic principle which applies in this field. For the task of knowledge in relation to the triune being of God can be both posed and also fulfilled only within the framework of the divine self-disclosure. It is as God enters into a history with us in Christ and the Spirit that the question arises how the revealer relates to what is revealed and to the act of revealing. Only here does the trinitarian problem present itself. Only here do we have the noetic principle. It is here, then, that we are to find the ontic principle too. This can, of course, give rise to the suspicion that the triune being of God is simply an attribute of our relation of knowledge, just as Schleiermacher argues that the qualities of God tell us nothing about his ontic being but only something about the relation of our consciousness to him, i.e., the special way of relating the feeling of absolute dependence to him (*The Christian Faith,* § 50). If this is so, however, we are again close to Sabellius. To clear up this matter, the following remarks are appended.

The so-called essential Trinity means that God's triunity is grounded in God himself and is thus independent of the relation of our consciousness to him. Although it seems dreadful to put it in this way, for the sake of clarity one might say that what the essential Trinity implies is that the triunity describes the immanent ontic structure of the being of God.

In contrast the economic Trinity or Trinity of revelation is a term used for the thesis championed by Sabellius and the modalists and then adopted and modified by Schleiermacher,[15] namely, that triunity relates only to various operational acts and spheres of the deity, which in its general overruling of finite being is the Father, in its work of redemption in the person of Christ is the Son, and in the totality and unity of believers is the Spirit. In contrast the orthodox doctrine of the essential Trinity maintains that the Trinity is immanent and original in God apart from his work, and that

---

[15] Cf. O. Weber, *Grundlagen der Dogmatik,* I, 3rd ed. (1964), pp. 429ff.; Weber also cites J. A. Urlsperger (1728-1806) as a proponent of the economic Trinity.

the deity is eternally Father, Son, and Spirit in itself before ever creating anything, entering into union with the individual, or dwelling in the fellowship of believers.[16] In the view of Schleiermacher it is in any case a mistake to charge Sabellius with irreligion (*loc. cit.*).

In Schleiermacher's arguments for his Sabellian view it is noticeable that his adoption of the consciousness as a starting-point involves a prejudgment of the theme of theology. Attention focuses exclusively on the act and moment of appropriation or the transition to inwardness. The principle of knowledge (which is here a good deal more than reflection) comes to have, then, a dominating influence on the subject matter of theology. The very word "father" in the doctrine of the Trinity implies that the deity can become this first person (or *prosopon*) only in relation to the world in which it operates. Hence the deity *becomes* Father; it *is* not in itself Father.[17]

If the economic understanding of the Trinity has enjoyed a new vogue since Schleiermacher,[18] there is a positive and a negative reason for this. The positive we have mentioned already. It is that the relation to our consciousness, and especially the appropriation of revelation by this consciousness of ours, has decisively determined and also restricted the subject matter of theology (cf. Theology A in Volume I). The negative reason is that for post-Kantian thought statements about the immanent essence of the Godhead, defined independently of the world and consciousness, come under the verdict of dogmatic metaphysics and therefore of epistemological impossibility. In other words, Kant's distinction between the thing in itself and its appearance (the thing for us) is applied to God too. Theology can thus present God only phenomenologically. Necessarily then—and again under the influence of Kant's doctrine of the forms and categories—there arises the question as to the part played by the consciousness in the formation of the concept of God (and therewith also of the Trinity).

An illegitimate change into another genus obviously seems to take place here. God cannot be treated in analogy to objects of our experience. We cannot handle him in terms of our own categories and criteria. He himself in the testimony of the Holy Spirit gives us the categories and criteria by means of which he makes himself known (1 Corinthians 2:10-12; cf. Volume I, pp. 138-173) and calls us into the truth of existence out of which we hear his voice (John 18:37). God is not a possible object of our judgment; we ourselves receive the judgment of God. What the doctrine of the

---

[16] Cf. Schleiermacher's 1822 essay on the difference between the Sabellian and Athanasian views of the Trinity, *Ges. Werke*, II, p. 564; cf. M. Tetz, *F. Schleiermacher und die Trinitätslehre*, pp. 87f.

[17] Cf. Tetz, *op. cit.*, p. 81. The Cappadocian Fathers (Basil, Gregory of Nazianzus, and Gregory of Nyssa) are resisting this view when they speak of *trópoi tês hypárxeōs*, i.e., of divine hypostases which belong to the essence of God apart from the world, and not of mere *trópoi tês apokalýpseōs*, i.e., mere modes of self-disclosure or of relation to our consciousness or to the world in general.

[18] Naturally not in Karl Barth and his school.

Trinity tells us about the third person of the Trinity, the Holy Spirit, it withholds from our grasp. It thus rules out the consciousness as a co-constituting partner. It anticipates the consciousness and constitutes it as the consciousness of the new creature.

Relevant here once again is the fact that the Word whose subject is the triune God is not an interpretative word conditioned by the consciousness. It is a creative act-word. We do not help to constitute either this Word or the underlying concept of God. God constitutes us and in so doing enters into our possibilities of understanding.[19]

The weakness of the economic doctrine of the Trinity is the weakness of a theology (Theology A) which begins, not with God, but with the partnership of God and the world or God and the consciousness, and which in so doing makes the naturally knowable structures of the world and consciousness into premises which determine the being of God. The noetic principle constitutes in this way the ontic principle and the very essence of God himself.

In contrast it is significant that the essential Trinity speaks of the *homoousios* of the Son—"begotten, not made." This reference to the pretemporal begetting of the Son and his consubstantiality with the Father—the same applies to the Spirit, especially in view of the *Filioque*—contains a clear rejection of a purely economic or revelational Trinity. For the trinitarian being of God is not tied to his revelation in the world, or the timebound relations of God and the world or God and the consciousness. The *homoousios* of the Son and Spirit with the Father lifts the Trinity out of the relation to the world. It is before the world and its temporality.

If one says only this, however, the uneasy feeling is left that traditions are simply being repeated and the airy fields of dogmatic metaphysics are being entered. It is thus important that we should bore deeper and raise the question what is faith's interest in the *homoousios* and whether there is any theologically justifiable interest at all.

We offer two arguments in reply.

First, the *homoousios,* the doctrine of the generation of the Son before all worlds or time, even while it might create a mythological impression, expresses in fact the basic relation of God to the world which has always characterized Christian theology. The classical doctrine enshrining this relation is that of creation out of nothing.[20] This stands in unmistakable opposition to mythical cosmogonies. In these God as the demiurge, as in Plato, is tied by pre-existing cosmic matter, which is usually viewed as burdened with a curse. The divine demiurge cannot make out of this matter more than is in it. He has to stand by helplessly when the forces of evil immanent in it become virulent and impose on impotent man his destiny. Hence cosmogonic myths present an eternal partnership, which God does not

---

[19] Cf. the distinction between actualization and accommodation in Volume I, pp. 26f., and also the discussion of the problem of contact, pp. 139ff.
[20] Cf. ThE, I, Index.

transcend, between God and the world or matter. God himself is tied to the time in which he fashions the world. The matter which he shapes works with him. It does not let him be a true Creator but only a co-operating operator.

The doctrine of creation out of nothing protests against this. It presents God as the pre-temporal being who creates time and holds it in his hands (Psalm 31:15). It does not grant to matter the dignity of co-operation. It sees it, too, as coming into being through the divine Fiat. It denies that God is tied to the world or to co-creating consciousness. Thus the saying "before all worlds" is no mere speculation about what happens before time —this immediately raises questions since it involves an element of temporality. The statement has an essentially and exclusively theological intention. The point is that the being of God should not be absorbed in God's relation to the world. Confessed here is the majesty of God which in free sovereignty resolves upon the creation of the world and thus creates for itself a counterpart and a Thou as a partner. In other words, God is not Father because, as Schleiermacher thinks, there is a world in relation to which he can be fatherly. He wills to be Father, the God of grace and condescension, and for this reason he posits the world.

Only in connection with this doctrine does concern about the *homoousios* of Son and Spirit make sense. The negative argument in favor of this interest might be stated as follows. If God is the Father who creates the world, the Son who redeems it, and the Spirit who makes himself present to it, this is not due to the world and its state. God resolves upon this turning to another in eternity and before all worlds. He creates the object of this turning. Thus the doctrine of the Trinity presents God as always one and the same. If he is the triune God, this cannot be regarded as a subsequent matter. It is not brought into being by the world. It antedates the world. As Creator and Redeemer he is more than Co-operator. Since man's consciousness is part of the world, it cannot be regarded as a magnitude which co-operatively determines the being of God, his trinitarian being in the present context. The consciousness to which he discloses himself is also created by him and influenced by his Spirit. He discloses himself to the new creature. This consciousness has its origin in the new being in truth which is the work of the Spirit.

The understanding of the love of God also points to God's trinitarian sovereignty in relation to the world. Eros as the human form of love needs the other to inflame and provoke it. It needs the other for its own completion.[21] God's *agape,* however, is fundamentally different. It needs neither provocation nor completion. Hence it does not have to depend upon the partnership of the man who is able to respond in love. It does not come to itself only by means of this partnership. God *is* love. This "is" means that God loves before all ages and before all worlds. He loves as the triune God. He does not have to come to love. Human love arises only when a counter-

---

[21] Cf. the myth in Plato's *Symposium.*

part is already there. God, however, creates what he loves. As love in eternity he precedes what he loves. No one has put this more precisely or profoundly than Luther in Thesis 28 of the Heidelberg Disputation, when he says that God's love creates its object whereas man's love is created by it.[22]

Second, it may be argued in favor of the essential Trinity that God as the one who reveals himself cannot be other than the one he is in himself. In giving his only-begotten Son (John 3:16) he gives himself. Otherwise there would be in God a dark margin from which perdition might come instead of salvation. We should be exposed to the intolerable question: Which God, or what in God, is pertinent to us?[23]

If God loses his unity in this way, what he says and promises also becomes ambiguous and uncertain. He loses the reliability of the Thou which is identical with what it says and does and purports to be for me. God's resultant loss of identity means that the dark margin as well as the brightness of the self-revealing Immanuel becomes a cipher for something else: the dark margin a cipher for the inscrutability of the incalculable powers of fate and the ray that shines without choice, and Immanuel the cipher for the reference-point of the feeling of absolute dependence (Schleiermacher), or the whence of my drivenness (H. Braun), or the unconditionality of moral imperatives (Kant), or unity with the ground of being in which I think I am enclosed.

The understanding of God as a mere cipher is thus a sign of his being stripped of Thou-ness and personality. (It is no wonder that in Volume I we found this process in Theology A and the so-called theology of the death of God.) This despoiling of God is a result of, or may be one of the reasons for, the fact that an essence of God in himself and a God for us are separated from one another, so that God is not the same as he reveals himself to be and is for us in Christ, since he does not pour out himself fully and is not wholly and entirely present in this God.

If the economic doctrine of the Trinity is not just describing our noetic contact with God but also seeks to express God's ontic being, it opens the door to this fatal misunderstanding. As we have seen, a distinctive aspect of this depersonalizing and dedeifying of God is that acceptance of the economic view from the time of Schleiermacher implicitly or explicitly adopts Kant's distinction between the noumenal and the phenomenal, and that in so doing it bears dramatic witness to the loss of God's Thouness. God is present only phenomenally. Contesting of the personal God who transcends immanence is almost inevitably the next step.[24] In contrast the trinitarian insistence on the consubstantiality of the Son and the Spirit expresses the identity of God in his self-revelation with God as he is in

---

[22] WA, 1, 354, 35. On this cf. also E. Brunner, *Dogmatics,* I, pp. 227f.

[23] Luther's doctrine of the hidden God is not to be taken in this sense; cf. W. von Loewenich, *Luthers theologia crucis,* 2nd ed. (1933), pp. 21ff.

[24] In the doctrine of God we have shown more fully why the word "God" can never express anything but itself and why it can never, then, be a cipher for something else.

himself. In the temporality of the salvation event there reveals himself the one who loves in eternity and before all time, and who is always one and the same. God for us is no other than God himself.

In espousing the essential Trinity, and regarding its theological intentions as indispensable in any Christian doctrine of God, we do not, of course, believe that the essential Trinity and the revelational Trinity have to be set in total antithesis. The economic Trinity becomes a heretical alternative only when it integrates and completely absorbs the being of God into the event of revelation. When it does this, it does violence to the divine sovereignty, makes the world and consciousness co-operators with God, and reduces God's being to its phenomenal aspect. Even the traditional doctrine of the Trinity can be distorted in Sabellian fashion when this is done. The three persons of the Trinity become masks in a phenomenal drama.

But this does not have to happen. The economic aspect may be regarded merely as one element in the doctrine of the Trinity and not its heart and center.

As one element it has a rightful place insofar as it describes the noetic principle in a Christian doctrine of God. Our knowledge of God does in fact derive from a divine self-disclosure in time, from the fact that God makes himself known as Father, Son, and Holy Spirit. The only question is whether God is absorbed into the revelation event, whether he does not just enter into history but becomes history, whether he not only sets up the relation to the world and man but is this relation. If he sets it up, he is himself more than the relation. He transcends the temporality in which it is set up and revealed to us. Hence he not only appears to be the triune God; he is the triune God.

To treat the essential Trinity and the economic Trinity as full alternatives is thus a misunderstanding which arises when the economically oriented Trinity is made into an ontic principle instead of a noetic principle, when its understanding of God is thus necessarily defined in terms of the categories and criteria of our consciousness, when the world is made a partner of God, and when the Trinity is viewed as a mere phenomenon or even as a mime. Here, as so often in the most difficult questions of theology, everything depends on making a clear distinction between the noetic and ontic aspects and not allowing them uncritically to merge into one another.

Excursus II: The Significance of the Doctrine of the Trinity in Basic Decisions in Church History

A glance at the historical relevance of the *Filioque* will give us some impression of the way in which trinitarian differences which may seem abstruse to the casual observer can have important historical effects or may be linked with very practical decisions. The *Filioque* is an accepted abbreviation for the trinitarian tenet that the Spirit proceeds, not from the Father alone, but from both the Father and the Son: *processio spiritus ex patre filioque*.

The *Filioque* was not expressly debated in the early church. Some Greek fathers, e.g., Cyril of Alexandria, used the formula, although it was never put in any official creed. The influence of the theology of Augustine promoted it in the West. Only in the eighth century did it give rise to serious controversy. Charlemagne championed it at the Synod of Aachen, and Pope Leo III confessed it but did not seek any alteration of the creed on its behalf. Between the eighth and eleventh centuries it finally became a point of contention between East and West. Since the great schism of 1054 it has constantly played a basic, although by no means exclusive, role in the conflict between East and West and in attempts at reunion.

It must be admitted that Eastern opposition to the *Filioque* was originally generated not so much by material reasons as by a traditionalistic disinclination to alter inherited creeds. It must also be admitted that rejection of the *Filioque* relates originally to intratrinitarian relations and not explicitly to God's historical movement out of himself, although the question naturally arises whether the controversy can in fact be confined to the ghetto of intratrinitarian differences.

Having made these concessions, however, we can see from what happened in church history that the *Filioque* is no mere strife of words, as Harnack claims. Its content has enormous historical implications, e.g., in respect of the style of piety, the constitution of the church, and its relation to history. Along these lines Karl Barth says in CD, I, 1, 2nd ed. (1974), p. 481: "Yet we cannot avoid asking whether, if that denial (sc. of the *Filioque*), the exclusive *ex Patre,* is to obtain as an eternal truth, it is not inevitable that the relation of God to man will be understood decisively from the standpoint of Creator and creature, and that it will thus acquire a more or less developed naturalistic and unethical character, so that the Mediator of revelation, the Son or Word, will be set aside as the basis and origin of the relation, and it will take on the nature of a direct and immediate relation, a mystical union with the *principium et fons Deitatis*."

In the denial of the *Filioque,* then, one might see a structural element in the thought and life of Greek Christianity which concretely manifests itself in other areas of thought and life as well. The direct relation between Father and Spirit, no longer mediated by Son, leads positively to a mystical immediacy which may sometimes have a pantheistic tinge. A thrust toward mysticism and cosmic piety is unmistakable in the Eastern church. Negatively, the direct reference which results from exclusion of the Son leads to neglect of historical revelation and therefore of history in general. In keeping with this is the backward looking attitude of the Eastern church and its rejection of historical renewal.

The opposite relation prevails in the West. The *Filioque* is a background force in historico-critical investigation, the quest of the historical Jesus, and the general regard for history. One might also put it the other way round. The *Filioque* is adopted because there is this openness to history.

No matter what the right sequence may be, however, there is an obvious correlation between the trinitarian statement and a specific manner of relating to the world, namely, the historical relation. History and the theological consideration of history bring into theology an element of tension, dialectical contradiction, and distrust of conceptual harmony.

Through not accepting the *Filioque* the Eastern church lacks this tension. The lack has broad ramifications. The most significant is that church and state are seen as a unity (caesaro-papalism). The cross is no longer a clear sign of judgment standing over the state—and naturally the church as well. The conflict between kings and popes which began in the eleventh century, the time of the great schism, is a purely Western affair. Only here do we find separation of church and state, a two-kingdoms doctrine, and other expressions of the tension, whereas in the Russian church the possibility of opposition to the state is hardly realized even when an actively atheistic regime is established. The dialectical element which is brought into the doctrine of the Trinity by the *Filioque* may thus be equated with the possibility of concrete historical contradiction which the West alone discovered.

Naturally we are not arguing that the whole complex of Eastern life and thought is a direct consequence of the rejection of the *Filioque*. This would be to attach undue importance to the formula and to distort the historical situation. One can speak only of a structural relation between the doctrine of the Trinity and the other theological *loci,* of a kind of pre-established harmony between the various expressions of Eastern life and thought. The intellectual as well as the practical form of faith has its source in the common fount of piety. The two forms then influence this source in return. In spite of the danger of speculative aberration, it is thus essential that there be an existential or realistic interpretation of even the most abstract and remote of intratrinitarian formulae.

XIV

The Word of God as Law and Gospel

Bibliography: P. Althaus, "Gottes Gottheit als Sinn der Rechtfertigungslehre Luthers," *Theologische Aufsätze*, II (1935), pp. 1-30; also *Paulus und Luther über den Menschen* (1938); K. Barth, CD, I, 1, 2nd ed. (1974), also "Evangelium und Gesetz," ThEx, No. 32 (E.T. "Gospel and Law" in *God, Grace and Gospel* [1959]); Ragnar Bring, "Der Mittler und das Gesetz. Zu Gal. 3:20," KD (1966), pp. 292ff.; O. Cullmann, *Heil als Geschichte* (1965); E.T. *Salvation in History* (1965); G. Ebeling, "Erwägungen zur Lehre vom Gesetz," *Wort und Glaube*, I (1960), pp. 255ff.; E.T. *Word and Faith* (1963), pp. 247ff.; W. Elert, *Zwischen Gnade und Ungnade* (1948), pp. 132ff.; F. Gogarten, "Theologie und Geschichte," ZThK (1953), 3; W. Gutbrod, Art. "Nomos," TDNT, IV, pp. 1022ff.; C. Haufe, "Die Stellung des Paulus zum Gesetz," ThLZ (1966), pp. 171ff.; R. Hermann, *Luthers These "Gerecht und Sünder zugleich"* (1930); also *Zum Streit um die Überwindung des Gesetzes* (1958); E. Hirsch, *Das AT und die Predigt des Evangeliums* (1936); H. Iwand, "Jenseits von Gesetz und Evangelium?" ThBl, 3/4 (1935), pp. 65ff.; also *Gesetz und Evangelium*, Werke, IV; W. Joest, *Gesetz und Freiheit*, 3rd ed. (1961); also "Paulus und das Luthersche Simul Justus et Peccator," KD (1965), pp. 269ff.; also *Ontologie der Person bei Luther* (1967); H. J. Kraus, *Die biblische Theologie. Ihre Geschichte und Problematik* (1970); W. Pannenberg, "Heilsgeschehen und Geschichte," *Grundfragen systematischer Theologie* (1967), pp. 22ff.; E.T. *Basic Questions in Theology*, I (1970/71), pp. 14ff.; W. Zimmerli, "Lit.-Übersicht," ThLZ (1960), 7. Cf. also the author's own discussion in ThE, I, pp. 79-244; E.T. I, pp. 51-146.

THE CONNECTION WITH THE PROBLEM

The Analogy between the Doctrine of the Trinity and the Doctrine of Law and Gospel

To put the reader in the picture three observations may be made, first on why a distinction is to be seen between law and gospel, second on why this theme arises in a chapter on revelation as the Word that posits history, and why it is thus to be given a dogmatic place alongside the doctrine of the Trinity, and third on what material and problems will occupy us as we take up this theme of law and gospel.

1. We turn first, then, to the question why a distinction is, to be seen between law and gospel.

Goethe once wrote to K. L. von Knebel:[1] ". . . As regards the good heart . . . I will say only that we truly act aright only when we know ourselves; obscurity about ourselves does not permit us easily to do justice to the good, and this amounts to the good not being good. Darkness leads us undoubtedly to the bad, and if it is unconditional to evil." This quotation forms a secular prolegomenon to our theme. The fact that a man can do good only if he knows himself is theologically interesting only because of the argument that Goethe uses, namely, that he who has no clarity about himself falls into evil because he falls victim to darkness and self-deception and thus becomes a hypocrite in the basic NT sense. For such a man views his deeds in isolation and does not take the heart into account in interpreting them. He thus contradicts Luther's dictum that the person does the deeds, i.e., that works are qualified by the one who does them. The man that Goethe has in mind does not know this person of his. He thus falls into an obscurity in which he overestimates what he is able to do in the form of externally righteous and faultless acts.

If self-knowledge and the state of the I which is brought to light thereby are central questions in ethics and anthropology, our reference to them can open up for us an approach to the doctrine of law and gospel. For both law and gospel give me self-knowledge. Indeed, the gospel not only gives me self-knowledge. It also makes me what I am in the eyes of God.

To speak in general terms, the law gives me self-knowledge by disclosing the gulf between what I ought to be according to my God-given destiny and what I am in fact. Every "ought"—especially although not exclusively that of the Decalog[2]—has a negative side too: You ought not to be what you are. The "ought" is a protest against the existing state of the one it claims. It is thus a sign of the alienation of human existence, the rift between destiny and being. In this respect the "ought" is a reminder of the fall. Human freedom, which is presupposed along with the claim of the "ought," may well signify the privilege and dignity of humanity, but it also stands under the sign of an ultimate betrayal. The story of the fall tells us that man uses his freedom to sabotage his original determination as the image of God (Genesis 1:26f.) and to grasp after a hybrid equality with God ("ye shall be as gods"). When man has to look at himself against the background of the "ought" and freedom, and when he acquires self-knowledge from the law of God, the darkness is dispelled and turned into its opposite.

The gospel, too, gives self-knowledge, although in a very different way

---

[1] April 8, 1812.
[2] Cf. ThE, I, § 2162ff.; E.T. I, pp. 440ff.

and with a very different result. By raising me up and letting me see myself as justified, it gives me final information about myself. I am the one who is right with God, whom the Reconciler has reconciled to God. But this is too weak because it is incomplete. For the gospel is not just an indicatory or interpretative Word which tells me this above all else. It is an efficacious Word which calls into being and puts into effect what is *not,* namely, the absent peace with God.[3] Because the basis of this reconciling peace does not lie in me but in what is done on me by the sacrifice of Christ; because the effected new being is not my altered attitude to God but God's new attitude to me, the gospel, in distinction from the law, does not lead to self-monitoring, introspection, or fixation on my own state. This self-knowledge of mine is relativized, and it becomes incidental. The law shows me how questionable I am, but I turn aside from this as from something which another has overcome. I know the No of God under which I must stand, but I flee to his Yes. I know that I am unrighteous, but I believe God's assurance that I am righteous, for the one who alone is righteous makes me his brother. I ought to be written off, but my name is written in the book of life.[4] To take up the saying of Goethe, I know myself, my state, and my questionability. But what I thus know through the law is no longer the real truth about me. The real truth is that I am known to God as one who is righteous before him (2 Corinthians 6:9).

According to the reformation understanding the point of the justification of the sinner achieved in the gospel is that its basis lies outside me. Grace never becomes a habitual quality. It is, as it were, *God's* habit in relation to me. It is the favor of God. It is the Yes which God has spoken. "Nevertheless I am continually with thee" (Psalm 73:23). This is said by God to me. This is why Melanchthon and Luther (cf. A. Peters, "Reformatorische Rechtfertigungsbotschaft zwischen trid. Rechtfertigungslehre und gegenwärtigen Verständnis der Rechtfertigungslehre," *Luther-Jahrbuch* [1964], pp. 110, 115ff., 127) protest so strongly against the scholastic attempt to make grace a quality of man rather than a quality of God and to expound it as an infused attribute and faculty of the soul; cf. Melanchthon's *Loci communes* of 1521 (*Melanchthons Werke* [1951], II, 1, p. 85).

Since the alteration which the gospel accomplishes, and in virtue of which I am now in reconciled peace with God, comes about only as I trust God's promise and believe the work of reconciliation,[5] it does not depend on my own concrete state. It is not affected by the fact that I am a sinner. On the contrary, where sin abounds, grace superabounds (Romans 5:20; 2 Corinthians 12:9). Since my present state no longer stands between God and me, since the Mediator has filled the gap, I can know myself quite freely, to use the phrase of Goethe again. Self-knowledge is no longer dangerous;

---

[3] Cf. Volume I, pp. 155ff.

[4] Luke 10:20; Philippians 4:3; Revelation 3:5; 17:8; 20:15.

[5] These statements necessarily anticipate essential elements in what can be fully developed only in the section on Christology.

I need not repress it.[6] I do not have to fall into illusions about myself. I no longer need the darkness. Hence the gospel gives me knowledge of myself with a final depth that the law could never achieve. From the safety of the shore of deliverance on which I am set by grace, I can observe the elements which still rage in me but which can no longer drag me under, and whose power over me is broken.

The first result of our deliberations, then, is that the Word of God reaches us in the twofold form of law and gospel. We may sum up this duality in the words of Luther in his 1519 *Commentary on Galatians:*[7] "Gospel and law are rightly distinguished insofar as the law tells us what to do and not to do, or rather what has already been done and not done, and what cannot be done or not done, so that it simply brings the knowledge of sins, whereas the gospel tells us that sin is forgiven and that everything has already been fulfilled and done. Hence the law says: 'Pay what thou owest' (Matthew 18:28), but the gospel says: 'Thy sins are forgiven thee' (Matthew 9:2)."

2. Our second question is why the doctrine of law and gospel has a place alongside the doctrine of the Trinity in the problem of the Word that posits history.

The answer to this question may be given in two trains of thought.

First, the doctrine of the Trinity has shown us why we may not inquire into a God in himself beyond the God who has disclosed himself as Father, Son, and Holy Spirit. God *is* the one he reveals himself to be. If we ask about a God in himself, the triunity of his self-revelation becomes a (modalistic) masquerade apart from his true being, or a result of the refraction of his being in the medium of our consciousness.

Just as we cannot inquire into a God in himself, so we cannot inquire into a Word of God in itself, i.e., a Word of God beyond law and gospel. What the Word of God means is decided by whether I hear it in terms of Christ or without him and outside him. If I take God seriously, not making him the invention of my wishes or my own projected *alter ego,* I learn to know his Word as death and judgment if I experience it without Christ and apart from him. In this case I cannot give myself back to him as I have received myself from him. I want myself, not him. If, however, I hear the Word in Christ, the rift between saint and sinner, the eternal and the transitory, while it is still not nothing, is abolished and negated. It no longer controls my relation to God. Christ stands in the gap, or, in the words of Colossians 2:14, my bill of indebtedness is affixed to the cross. It is now a mere scrap of paper. Like a banknote which is not covered, it has lost all value. The value represented has been cancelled. Another value has taken its place. This is the Yes which God has spoken to me and which is covered by the passion and death and resurrection of Christ.

When I hear God's Word as it is meant to be heard, i.e., in Christ, then

---

6 Cf. the *en adikía katéchein* of Romans 1:18.
7 On Galatians 1:11f., WA, 2, 466f. There are many similar references.

I have to hear at one and the same time both death and life, both judgment and grace. I come from death and judgment, even though it be cancelled death and judgment. I come from the fact that a gulf yawns between what God wills of me and what I am. It is the function of law to make known this gulf, to keep it open as gauze keeps a wound from superficial healing and thus protects against the illusion of restoration to health. The Nevertheless of God, which he speaks to me in the gospel, and with which he acknowledges me in spite of everything, is to be known for what it is only against this background. Only here is it the miracle that cannot be postulated, the grace of freedom, the thing that contradicts all the logic of guilt and expiation, the reality that cannot be integrated into any schema or system, not even the logic of a view of God which is based on God's own self-declaration as the author of the law. No teleological principle can bind both experiences together and bring out a discernible connection between them. Any connection of this kind would shatter the contingency of freedom in which God turns to me.

What takes place here can be put only in personal categories—this explains our interest in the personal God. We have to use such terms as resolve, free address, and mercy. A sign that personal categories are unavoidable is that the Bible is not afraid even of anthropomorphic associations in its attempt to describe the miracle of God's Nevertheless in his turning to us. Thus we read that God "repents" of delivering up the sinner or the sinful people to judgment, and hence to the logic of guilt and expiation, e.g., Exodus 32:14; Jeremiah 18:8; 26:13; Joel 2:13; Amos 7:3, 6.[8]

In this regard it is again apparent that the gospel is deed-word, event, surprise. It does not just tell us something about a general nature of God. It is experience of God's Yes. It is really God's Yes over against his judgment. It is an act of mercy. In it God is no longer against me. He is no longer the one as whom I must see him outside Christ.[9] The gospel is the wonder of this turning in God. It is the achievement of this turning. It cannot be seen, then, without the background of the law with which it stands in contrast. Without the author of the law I cannot see the author of the gospel as him he wills to be for me, as Immanuel, who establishes his Yes to the sinner in face of himself and his own claim, who "overcomes" himself and "repents."

This is why one cannot possibly inquire into the essence of the Word

---

[8] In the chapter on "The Second Biography of Iphigeneia" in his extraordinary book *Sprung von des Tigers Rücken* (1970), Gerhard Nebel shows that for the Greeks the Furies occupy something of the place that we see the law occupying as the counterpart of the gospel. Apart from the force of judgment liberation becomes a static state of liberatedness, a nontranscendental condition of man. "Man is impure and cannot bear the Furies, and yet he needs them, since, in terms of tragedy, he is guilty, or, in Christian terms, he is sinful" (p. 39).

[9] If there are intimations of this in the OT, as in the idea of God's "repenting," this shows that the God of the old covenant is the Father of Jesus Christ and that the old covenant has a prophetic character.

of God in itself or into the Word beyond law and gospel. Doing this brings about the same results as are brought about by a Sabellian or modalist understanding of the Trinity. The way in which God encounters me through his Word, and which displays him to be the author of both law and gospel for me, no longer sets forth God himself according to this view. We no longer see in it God's own being, freedom, and self-overcoming. Law and gospel are a mere mode of appearance, a drama or mime, like the three persons in modalism. God's Word is thus understood as a monistic substance which when it comes into contact with me is broken up in the medium of my consciousness and takes the separate forms of law and gospel. The prism of my consciousness thus plays a part in the rise of law and gospel by splitting up the beam of the one Word into this spectrum. Insofar as the consciousness is that of the natural man who takes God seriously, God *appears* to me as the author of the law, while insofar as it is consciousness of the man redeemed in Christ he *appears* to me as the author of the gospel.

The truth is, however, that in both modes of authorship God is one and the same and that he remains so for the Christian. If the Christian can understand the gospel only as the event of the miracle of God's Yes to me, then there is a history in God himself, the act of his "repenting," so that God *is* the author of both law and gospel and does not simply *appear* to be so.

For Luther this identity of God's being in both modes of his being was the reason why he clung to the doctrine of the communication of the attributes. When we speak of God's deity, and hence of his majesty as Judge, and hence of him before whose claim I am confounded, we speak at the same time of the God who in the self-offering of his Son, and the Son's solidarity with the sinner, draws near to me, affirms me, and takes me up into his peace. Expressed thus the unity of God implies also the unity of the person of Christ and comes to expression in what seems to be formally the hazardous doctrine of the communication of the attributes. "When you set God before me, you also set his humanity before me. They cannot be separated from one another. He is person, and his humanity cannot be parted from him as Master Hans takes off his coat when he goes to sleep."[10] The coat here represents that which can be put off and which is not a constituent part of the person. It is a kind of "mask" in my appearance to others. This analogy will not do. God is one and the same when he is consuming majesty and when he is a human, brotherly Thou, when he is remote and when he is near, taking me up into his peace. Similarly Christ is one and the same in his deity and his humanity. Finally, the Christian is one and the same when God encounters him as author of law and gospel. Law and gospel are not for two different classes of men, law for the unredeemed and gospel for the redeemed. They are not for two different periods of life, law for the time before encounter with Christ and gospel for the time after salvation. No, even for the Christian, God is still present in both forms. The

---

[10] *Bekenntnis vom Abendmahl Christi,* Cl, III, 397, 29.

redeemed knows that he is constantly and even daily snatched away from judgment. When he says: "God be merciful to me, a sinner" (Luke 18:13), he describes both what he is snatched from and also what he is going to. Expressed here is not a timeless state but a history with God. He continually has to look back and ask from what judgment he was taken and how this is possible. He continually has to understand what has taken place as a miracle, as an event in God.

When, therefore, P. F. Hiller asks how this took place and why, the only answer is that it is mercy and nothing more.[11] This tautology transcends all logic. It simply says that the event of mercy is grounded in mercy. This is the only way we can speak at this point. I do not have in God a personified essence of mercy. He is not a timeless "good Lord." If he were, my relation to him would be a static and timeless one that could never be called in question. Hence when Hiller has to put the astonished question how this took place, he is expressing the fact that mercy is not self-evident but is a surprising event. It is surprising simply because I know that I deserve only wrath. The tautology that it is mercy and nothing more is thus an indication that we cannot get behind the miracle of God's turning to us as the author of the gospel. This is self-grounded in God's history with me. No other ground can be found for it. The final stratum which we reach with our question is the freedom of the grace of God.

It is clear, then, why the doctrinal situation is the same in relation to the doctrine of law and gospel as it is in relation to the doctrine of the Trinity. Here again we obviously are not to ask about God's Word in itself, about a Word beyond law and gospel. The two modes in which the Word reveals itself are the same. The Word of God *is* what it *reveals* itself to be in law and gospel, just as God in the doctrine of the Trinity *is* what he *reveals* himself to be. In the distinction of form he is identical with himself.

The analogy has another aspect as well. Just as the trinity of God can give offense by seeming to impugn the unity and to engender tritheism, so the doctrine of law and gospel can raise the question whether different Gods are not taught whose basis of unity is neither discernible nor indeed credible.

In some of his attacks on Lutheranism Barth clearly suggests that a doctrine of two Gods is implicit in the duality of law and gospel; cf. *Die evangelische Kirche in Deutschland nach dem Zusammenbruch des Dritten Reiches* (1946), and H. Diem, *Karl Barths Kritik am deutschen Luthertum* (1947). As Barth sees it, Lutheranism could find no place for politics in Christian responsibility. It puts it in a field of special responsibility detached at a deep level from the Christian world. This is why it could adopt in relation to National Socialism the unhappy slogan: "Theologically no but politically yes" (Barth, *op. cit.*, pp. 26ff.). In contrast to the God of the gospel, Barth argues, there is in Lutheranism another God, the God of the law in its political use, and since these Gods have nothing to do with one

---

[11] Evangelical Church Hymn Book, 277, v. 2: "Wo kam dies her, warum geschicht's? Erbarmung ist's und weiter nichts."

another we have in fact—although Barth does not put it so sharply—two Gods. As the unity of God is broken in this way, the pathological dualism of law and gospel produces in man too a cleavage of consciousness which isolates the spiritual world from the secular world and threatens man, i.e., the Christian, in his identity.

Barth is undoubtedly right in his castigation of a false understanding of the distinction between law and gospel. But in attacking the distinction itself he commits a similar error to attacking the doctrine of the Trinity for fear of tritheism. The fact that Barth attacks the doctrine itself as well as the misunderstanding has its source in his relaxing of the tension between law and gospel and his swallowing up of the former in the latter. The monistic thrust of his theology may be seen at this point; cf. the analysis in ThE, I, § 596a-x; E.T. I, pp. 108ff., and Iwand, ThBl, *art. cit.*

An extreme form in which the duality of law and gospel degenerates into a doctrine of two Gods may be found in the Christian Socialist F. Naumann. It occurs here within a two kingdoms doctrine which is distorted out of all recognition. (Possibly Barth did not know Naumann, for he would have found in him the best material for his attacks.) In Naumann the law is normative for the secular sphere, the kingdom on the left hand, while the gospel rules in the religious sphere and the zone of direct fellow-humanity. There is, however, a yawning gulf between the two. Naumann can see no way to overcome this. He uses no cheap tricks to disguise the situation. He frankly confesses his helplessness. In a direct I-Thou relation the individual may be committed to patient love but the struggle for existence has taught the nations to be armored beasts.[12] Thus far we simply have the problem of a double morality which arises in every political ethics and with which the two kingdoms doctrine is also wrestling.[13] But Naumann then finds himself pressured into the seductive idea that two Gods stand behind the political use of the law on the one side and the gospel on the other. Following the god of the world produces the morality of the struggle for existence, while service of the Father of Jesus Christ produces the morality of mercy. If he resists this incipient ditheism it is not so much with arguments as with defiant confession: "Yet there are not two Gods but one; in some way their arms embrace" (*op. cit.*, p. 72).

In relation to politics, and especially the problem of double morality and a possible rift between the God of iron and the Father of Jesus Christ, we again perceive the formal similarity between the problems of the doctrine of the Trinity and those of the doctrine of law and gospel. We tread a narrow ridge in both cases.

On the one side is the abyss of an abstract and monistic unity of God or his Word. The trinitarian confession, or the understanding of the Word as both law and gospel, guards against this. But if the significance of God's self-revelation is lost, there is on the other side the abyss of the impossibility

---

[12] *Briefe über Religion* (1903), p. 81.
[13] Cf. ThE, II, 2, § 554ff.; E.T. II, p. 95.

of viewing God as one and the same, or of viewing his Word as one and the same, so that a doctrine of three Gods or two Words arises. This is why we must think out the doctrine in terms of the threats to it.

We are still dealing with the question how far the doctrine of law and gospel has a place alongside the doctrine of the Trinity in the problem of the Word that posits history. Our first train of thought has shown us why in fact we cannot inquire into a being of either God in himself (beyond his trinitarian unfolding) or the Word in itself (beyond law and gospel). This consideration must now be given greater depth from another standpoint.

The second train of thought is as follows.

Only where God is understood and confessed as the author of law and gospel does he retain present actuosity and is he the God who acts with us in history, i.e., the God who here and now does afresh what was done once and for all (*eph'apax*) in the birth, crucifixion, and resurrection of the Lord. Only as God is the author of law and gospel does grace here and now step forth for right, does God speak his Nevertheless to me, and does he offer himself as the Reconciler between whom and myself nothing and no one can come (Romans 8:31-34, 38f.). Only as God is the author of law and gospel am I here and now set in this history with God, appropriating in faith that which has been done to me (the indicative of the gospel), and bearing witness to the new life in my conduct (the imperative of the gospel): "For ye are dead . . . mortify therefore your members" (Colossians 3:2,5); "Ye be dead with Christ, seek therefore those things which are above" (Colossians 3:1).[14]

The significance of the duality of God's Word as law and gospel for the retention of this actuosity or historical correlation of God and man may be seen very clearly if we put the counter-question: What happens (or does not happen) if the tension of law and gospel is removed? This counter-question may be put in three stages. In the present context we shall simply give a systematic development and refrain from giving historical examples of the positions developed, apart from a few references, e.g., to Karl Barth.

(1) If God is absolutized as the author of the law, he becomes the epitome of the numinous. He is thus the symbol of human questionability and vanity, insofar as persuasion of this does not suffice and a suitable projection of it is thus made in the concept of God. On this view God is not the active God who enters into a history with me. He is the whence of the consciousness which sets me in question. He is the timeless principle of this questioning.

(2) If God is absolutized as the author of the gospel and not also of the law, then, as we have seen, the gospel is robbed of its point. It no longer encounters me as active liberation. It is no longer an astonishing act. It is no longer the miracle of the Nevertheless which God speaks to me through the crucified and risen Lord. From being the God who acts upon me and

---

[14] For a fuller discussion of the indicative and imperative in Paul cf. ThE, I, § 315-689; E.T. I, pp. 74ff.

against me God becomes again a timeless principle. This time he is the principle of love, of the "good Lord,"[15] or, as in Abelard, he is a suprapolar principle of indifference as all-embracing love.

(3) If law and gospel are no longer radically differentiated but fused, two results may follow.

(a) The law is understood as gospel too and not as the counterpart to which God speaks his Nevertheless and in face of which he sets forth the gospel as his mighty act. In this case the law is no other than the necessary form of the gospel whose content is grace.[16] As its necessary form the law is no longer in tension with the gospel. It is not that which accuses us, which destroys us, and before which we cannot stand. Instead of accusing us it takes over the function of the gospel. It becomes restoration and promise. Instead of saying: "Thou shalt not kill, for thou art a murderer,"[17] it replaces the accusatory "Thou shalt" with the "Thou shalt" of promise: "Thou shalt be what I demand."[18] Barth in his reinterpretation of the law along these lines can even go so far as to say that the mere fact of God's speaking with us at all is always grace.[19] Is it really true, however, that God's No, wrath, and judgment is grace, or that what is confessed when God is called the author of the law is grace? Is it grace when Adam is asked: "Where art thou?" Is it grace when Jeremiah is told not to pray any more for the people (Jeremiah 7:16; 14:11)? Only against this background of judgment is the salvation wrought in Christ a real miracle. A logical correlating of law and gospel as form and content, and hence as two sides of the same coin, makes it impossible to understand the gospel as an act or event of this kind. Grace becomes a timeless state from all eternity. God does nothing new. There is no "new testament." He simply unfolds his gracious being, upon which he freely resolved from all eternity, in constantly new variations on this identity of his.[20]

God's Word, then, for Barth, is properly and finally grace, free and sovereign grace, God's grace, which can also signify judgment, death, and hell, but which is grace and nothing else.[21] What kind of a grace is this, however, that can also be hell? Do not all these terms lose their specific sense on this view? What are hell and judgment if they are only a form of the promise, a Hegelian transition, leading to salvation as a happy ending? What

---

[15] Cf. A. Ritschl, who in connection with God as the author of the law dismisses the concept of God's wrath as a homeless and formless theologoumenon, *Rechtfertigung und Versöhnung,* II, 2nd ed. (1882), p. 154.

[16] K. Barth, "Gospel and Law," p. 10.

[17] ThE, I, § 2163ff.; E.T. I, pp. 440ff.

[18] Barth, *art. cit.,* pp. 9, 12.

[19] *Ibid.,* p. 4.

[20] This is why Barth's Christology, unlike that of the NT, begins with the pre-existent Christ rather than the incarnation. We see here the influence of the Reformed doctrine of the eternal decrees. Similarly the NT is fundamentally only an explication of the OT. Cf. G. Gloege, "Zur Prädestinationslehre K. Barths," KD (1956), pp. 193ff., esp. 209ff.; ThE, I, § 596; E.T. I, pp. 108ff.

[21] Barth, *loc. cit.*

kind of a gospel is it which simply ratifies this point of the law? Does not all this again make of God's love a nonhistorical habit? Does it not rule out God's "repenting," the miracle of his condescension, and his doing of something new?

Obviously Barth does not want to go this far, just as he shrinks from the universalism which his monism seems logically to imply. In fact, he assures a place for the actuosity of the divine action and resolve with his doctrine of the freedom of God. Nevertheless, do we not still have here a pre-temporal and predestinating resolve? By denying the tension of law and gospel does not Barth rob himself of the possibility of finding a place for the work of God in time, for the character of God's Word as a Word that posits history, and hence for the new thing of the new testament?

At this point we are again threatened by the nonhistoricity of a God in himself and by the dominion of a principle which stands in antithesis to the Word that posits history. This Word can be confessed as an active Word only when the tension of law and gospel is respected. (The author has too deep a respect for Barth, and owes him too much, to be able to think that the foregoing criticism applies to the whole of Barth's theology. Since Barth was above all things a biblical theologian and exegete, adequate correctives were placed at his disposal by the Bible, so that what we are forced to call a dangerous systematic principle and a monistic tendency did not really gain control over his thought and work. Barth's theology amounts to much more, and has a greater fulness, than his systematic approach could ever offer.)

(b) If, as the example of Barth shows, the law can be made into the gospel, the opposite is also possible: the gospel can be made into the law. This can happen when Christ is regarded as an example and the essential and perhaps even the only point of the gospel is imitating him. In support of this the thesis might be advanced that the purpose of redemption is to make it possible for us to fulfil the law of God. Christ gives us the power to do what we are unable to do with our own resources. Redemption is thus the means to an ethical end.[22]

This legalizing of the gospel, which again fuses law and gospel and ends the tension between them, is fraught with many serious consequences.

(1) Imitation piety no longer views Christ as the one who redeems us from the curse of the law and who represents the divine repenting; it makes Christ himself into the law.

(2) The gospel ceases to be a power of giving and becomes instead a power of commanding. If its aim is to give strength to fulfil the law, this

---

[22] Cf. W. Herrmann's statement that men receive through Christ the power to do the good: *Ethik,* 5th ed. (1913), p. 153. For an extreme example cf. A. A. van Ruler's *Christian Church and the OT* (1955; E.T. 1971), where it is argued that we are not men that we might be Christians but Christians that we might be men (p. 68). Thus reconciliation with God is not an end in itself but a means to the greater end of sanctification, the ability to make the earth a site for the kingdom of God. In criticism cf. ThE, II, 2, § 4275ff.; E.T. II, pp. 604ff.

endowment is no longer a gift which is unconditional, free, surprising, and contrary to all our deserts. It is tied to conditions which must be met if the gift is to come into effect. I have to achieve a minimal approximation to the normative model of the figure of Christ.

(3) Above all the gospel ceases to be comfort in trial. It no longer causes me to hear God's Nevertheless. It ceases to refer me to the fact that absolutely everything pertaining to my salvation has been done already in the being and work of Christ. Instead it links my salvation to my achievement in imitating Christ and using the power granted to me in redemption. Thus the gospel itself becomes a source of assault. Instead of being our consolation it brings us into judgment.

The result is that all the familiar problems of legal piety are given new vigor. Constant self-monitoring is needed. How much progress have we made in the imitation of Christ? In what respect are we lagging behind? The balance will undoubtedly be on the negative side. Attention is directed all the time on the self instead of on the salvation event outside the self which Christ has accomplished on and to us. We can no longer sing with Paul Gerhardt that our eyes are fixed on him. We are looking at ourselves. We measure the level of our discipleship. We are condemned to a new curving in on ourselves.

A new form of legalism arises in consequence. This is even worse than the earlier Mosaic legalism, for Christ as an example of legal obligation offers an extreme radicalization of the law of Moses. If along these lines the Sermon on the Mount is no longer understood in terms of the "Blessed are ye . . ." but regarded as a legal expression of the obligation of imitation, then it plunges us into extreme weakness, resignation, and despair.

This is why Luther, who made the differentiation of law and gospel perhaps the most normative theme in his theology, attacked with particular vigor the perversion of the gospel into a new law and the transformation of Christ into a new Moses. His point is that Christ is not example but exemplar, not model but prototype.[23] The significance of Christ as such has a twofold dimension.[24]

(1) Christ is the representation (or exemplar) of the mercy of God, who accepts me and causes me to be righteous. He *is* the active righteousness of God; he does not merely teach it. If I have him, I have Immanuel himself.[25] (2) Christ is eternally actual human faith (Thimme), representing the faith that receives justification. To use the terminology of the two-

---

[23] Luther's concept of Christ as prototype should not be confused with that of Schleiermacher; cf. ThE, I, § 918-920; E.T. I, 186, n. 9.

[24] Cf. on this H. Thimme, *Christi Bedeutung für Luthers Glauben* (1933); E. Wolf, *Jesus Christus im Zeugnis des heiligen Geistes und der Kirche* (1936), pp. 214f.

[25] Harnack, in contrast, presents Christ as the prophet who proclaims the loving Father and not as himself this love and therewith an essential part of the gospel; cf. *What Is Christianity?* (1902), p. 154.

natures doctrine,[26] he is exemplary unity with God and exemplary unity with man. This is the content of the gospel.

Hence he *is* our peace (Ephesians 2:14). In him, by the mere fact that he is, we are rescued from the accusation of the law and the lack of peace it brings. As Christ goes before us, this peace of his precedes our dispute with the law. Hence there are no conditions of peace which have to be met first. This peace precedes all conditions. Above all it is not itself a condition in the sense of being a mere means to make possible the fulfilment of the law and acts that are pleasing to God. The exact opposite is true: because we receive the peace of God in Christ, and his prevenient love makes possible our response of love (1 John 4:19), we attain to a new spontaneity of love in virtue of which we do what is pleasing to God and are freed for a new obedience.

This is why, for Luther, accepting Christ as exemplar of the righteousness of God precedes all else. Only when I orientate myself in faith to Christ as exemplar, only when I see God's mercy and my own new being given in him as exemplar, can I begin to imitate his example. This is the true place for the imitation of Christ. Here alone it is gospel and no longer law.[27]

We may sum up by saying that no matter how the distinction of law and gospel is erased, in all the instances that we have systematically tabulated and examined the result is the same. If God is no longer understood as the author of both law and gospel, he can no longer be understood as the sovereign initiator of the history with us or as the Lord of his free grace and condescension. He is instead depersonalized as a nonhistorical principle. Beyond law and gospel there is no longer any Word that posits history. As is inevitable with a timeless principle, there is only a statement about that which is timelessly valid.

The relation of man to God changes accordingly. If the law already contains the gospel within itself, man becomes the initiator of his history with God. According to the degrees of his fulfilment of the law he can bring about the corresponding reactions in God. The man who acts uprightly and in accordance with the law can lay claim to a reward. He can insist that God be gracious. He can control that which in truth belongs to the free grace of God granted to him in the gospel. This is how there arises the confusion in the relation to God which constitutes the negative impulse in the story of Job. This is how there also arises the sublime hubris of the Pharisee. If on the other hand the gospel is interpreted as law, as imitation of Christ, I as a believer no longer enter truly into the history of God with me but remain captive to curving in on, and controversy with, myself. Understood

---

[26] Cf. Part Two on Christology.

[27] "No one becomes righteous by doing what is right, but he who has become righteous does what is right. Righteousness and the fulfilment of the law come through him who fulfils them as exemplar (Matthew 5:17) before any works are done. Works then flow from this" (the 1519 *Commentary on Galatians* on 2:16f., WA, 2, 492-494).

thus the gospel opens the door to temptation and assault rather than removing them.

In all its aspects, then, our counter-question shows how the doctrine of law and gospel, like the doctrine of the Trinity, protects the Word of God in its character as that which posits history. What is found beyond law and gospel is not the personal God but the speechlessness of a principle or symbol.

There is profound significance, then, in the fact that Luther so radically emphasizes the duality of law and gospel that he will not accept any teleological connection between them, nor any other connection that might be discerned or constructed. Any conceivable relation would eliminate the contingency of the gospel and its basis in the freedom of grace. Since such a connection would be a necessary one, it would be the antithesis and contradiction of the sovereignty of free resolve and the miracle of divine repenting. To put it in other words, and very pointedly, we cannot try to find a basis for the connection between law and gospel. This does not imply agnostic flight, for we can give reasons, and have in fact done so, why no basis can be given.

"No man alive on earth," says Luther, "knows how to distinguish between law and gospel." ("Distinguish" here does not mean differentiate, for differentiation is possible and for Luther it is in fact a condition of all theological thinking. By distinguishing Luther means finding a basis of relationship.) "We think that when we hear them preached we understand, but we do not. Only the Holy Ghost understands this art. Even the man Christ did not understand on the Mount of Olives, so that an angel had to comfort him. He was a doctor from heaven and yet he was comforted by an angel. I might think that I myself could do it since I have written so much and so long on the matter, but I see how much I have failed. God alone must be our most holy master here" (WA Tischreden, 2, No. 1234).

When Luther says that only the Holy Spirit understands the art of seeing the connection between law and gospel, this means that their relationship is kept and concealed in God himself. It is the mystery of his freedom. When in faith I let this freedom work on me and trust God's Nevertheless, I base my life on the fact that the connection exists. But I do not understand it, not wanting to be as God and thereby to rob him of his deity.

3. We ask finally what material and problems will occupy us when we take up the theme of law and gospel.

We have already discussed the fundamental problems which are posed by the relation of law and gospel. Our present concern is to consider in what specific theological themes the difference between the two finds actualization and takes on determinative significance. If we bear in mind our initial thesis, namely, that the duality of law and gospel safeguards the Word of God in its character as that which posits history, two themes especially suggest themselves for exploration.

(a) It must be shown that the duality of law and gospel is of fundamental significance in defining salvation history, and especially the relation between the OT and the NT. Without the distinction of law and gospel, as we shall see, the new thing in the NT cannot be established. The NT becomes merely an expounding and perfecting of the OT. We then have confirmation of the fact that this type of understanding betrays the actuosity or contingent historicity of God's self-revelation. Pursuing the question of law and gospel along these lines, we are led to consider salvation as history, to use Cullman's phrase. Our most immediate task, then, is to throw light on the movement from the OT to the NT from this angle.

(b) The distinction of law and gospel must also be considered in its relevance for the salvation event in the individual Christian. (As compared to the macrocosmic aspect of the salvation event in the OT and NT this is, as it were, the microcosmic aspect.) Some of the questions which arise in this regard are as follows: How do *I* live between the judgment of the law and restoration by the gospel? Is the old thing of the law done away? As a justified man, whom God in his free grace causes to be just before him, do I no longer need the law, or is it still present and in force even for the new being of the redeemed? If it is, does it have the same meaning as before (or as it has for pagans, Romans 2:14f.), or does it now have altered value?[28]

We shall here press our investigation of law and gospel a little further than was done in the discussion in ThE, I, § 79-244; E.T. I, pp. 94ff. We shall also ignore many of the questions and materials that were used there, e.g., the problem of the indicative and imperative in Paul (§ 315ff.; E.T. pp. 74ff.), the question of the uses of the law (§ 624ff., 680ff., 1232ff.; E.T. pp. 126ff., 144ff., 447ff.), the connection between the two kingdoms and law and gospel (§ 1783ff. [and Index "Zwei Reiche" in II, 2]; E.T. pp. 359ff.), the debate with Barth's monism (§ 596; E.T. pp. 108ff.), and the relation of law to natural law (§ 1852ff.; 2010ff.; E.T. pp. 383ff., 400ff.). We shall simply refer to the discussions in ThE or give brief summaries. It is the author's concern that although various aspects are presented the doctrine of law and gospel should be viewed as a totality.

---

[28] The theological issue here is that of the so-called third use of the law; cf. ThE, I, § 552-689; E.T. I, pp. 126ff.

XV

The Distinction between Law and Gospel in its Relevance for the Movement of Salvation History from the Old Testament to the New

THE OLD AND PROPHETIC ELEMENT IN THE OT[1]

A common misunderstanding which might be suggested by the title of this chapter must be set aside at once. It is not possible to understand the movement from OT to NT as though the former represented the law and the latter the gospel. The matter is essentially much more complicated. The OT, in view of its many facets, cannot be reduced to such a simplistic formula. Two points may be made here which will be supported in what follows.

First, the OT itself contains prophetic forms of both law and gospel. The law is set here within God's covenant with Israel. The covenant is not to be regarded as a partnership between two parties with equal rights. It is not a contract between equals. It is a "foundation" and owes its origin to Yahweh's initiative. It does not rest on any special quality in Israel. It is grounded exclusively in the freely electing love of God (Deuteronomy 7:7f.).[2] One might say, then, that the covenant is a measure of gracious condescension and bears intimations of the gospel; cf. Hosea 2:15f. The function of the law is simply to establish normative ways of obedience by which Israel for its part fulfils and ratifies the covenant. Promise (gospel) and claim (law) are thus combined in the OT. (The nature of this relationship will be investigated in the present chapter.) Judgment and grace are linked at all the great turning-points in Israel's history.[3]

---

[1] For a survey of the relationship of the OT and NT cf. H. J. Kraus, *Die biblische Theologie* (1970), pp. 193-305. In distinction from us Kraus does not strictly view the relationship from the standpoint of law and gospel.

[2] This is why the LXX renders the Hebrew *berith* by *diathēkē*, not *synthēkē*; cf. O. Procksch, *Theologie des AT* (1950), p. 92.

[3] K. Koch points out that the linking of promise and claim or grace and judgment at the historical level differentiates Israel's faith from all other oriental religions; "Der Tod des Religionsstifters," KD (1962), 2, p. 103, esp. n. 12.

Second, the terms law and gospel cannot be related to specific groups of OT texts. Every word or act of God may be either the judgment that condemns or the gospel that restores. This is why Luther regarded the first commandment as gospel even though it comes in the law. It is God's assurance that he will be "my" God.[4] On the other hand the gospel can also be law and judgment. God's address, when not accepted, hands us over to judgment;[5] and the blood of Golgotha, which brings atonement, can involve very serious rejection (Matthew 27:25). Similarly the Lord's Supper may be received to condemnation (1 Corinthians 11:29). Events brought about by God are marked by the profound ambivalence that they effect either salvation or destruction. They may come into force as either law or gospel. Thus Amos can issue a warning about the Day of the Lord even though this ought to be a day of fulfilment and joy: "Woe unto you that desire the day of the Lord! To what end is it for you? The day of the Lord is darkness, and not light" (Amos 5:18f.).

For this reason alone, on account of this ambivalence, the OT cannot be regarded as merely law nor the NT as merely gospel. This confirms what we said earlier. Just as we cannot find a Word of God in itself beyond law and gospel, so we cannot reduce the Word of God to either one of its two forms, to either law on the one side or gospel on the other.

Before we inquire into the interrelation of law and gospel or promise and claim in the OT, we must first ask what is meant by the law anyway. This task is a complicated one, for it not only entangles us in the many aspects of the OT but also brings us into lively debate with OT scholars. In tackling the problem we shall begin with this controversy.

THE CONTROVERSY BETWEEN PAUL AND OT SCHOLARS ABOUT THE UNDERSTANDING OF THE LAW

Influential representatives of OT scholarship—G. von Rad and H. J. Kraus may be mentioned as examples—take the view that the "Thou shalt" of the law is to be seen more as a future than an imperative. Kraus stresses whenever he can[6] the joy of the righteous in the law. The magnifying of the law which is found in a piece like Psalm 119 would hardly be possible, however, if the law had for the righteous in the OT the same significance as is ascribed to it in Paul and later, with even greater emphasis, in Luther, namely, the significance of a counterpart of the gospel expressing accusation and judgment. Paul especially perceives the more negative character of the law. When sin is in a state of incubation, the law makes it virulent. It thus

---

[4] Cf. Althaus, *Theologische Aufsätze,* II, pp. 1-30.
[5] Cf. Matthew 13:11-15; John 12:40; Isaiah 6:9f.; Acts 28:26f.
[6] Cf. his exposition of Psalms 1 and 119 in his commentary on the Psalms, or *Die Königsherrschaft Gottes im AT* (1951), or *Der Gottesdienst in Israel,* 1st ed. (1954), pp. 43ff. (Here the locus of the law is found in the amphictyonic feast of the renewal of the covenant, so that it shares the evangelical character of the covenant.)

has the function of a starting impulse (*aphormê*, Romans 7:5, 8). For Luther the true and proper use of the law, its real office, is that by the law sin should grow and become great, and that man should thus be shown his sins, weakness, blindness, death, hell, and judgment before God. Hence the law is hell, the thunder and lightning of God's wrath.[7]

This raises the question whether we do not find in Paul and Luther a different view of the law from that of the OT itself. To put it bluntly, did Paul understand the OT properly or did he miss the point and present a caricature of the law which cannot be substantiated from the Bible itself but is simply a theologoumenon of Paul's own invention? If a little drollery may be permitted, the question might be posed as follows: Who really understands the law, Paul or modern OT scholars?

THE CONTROVERSY BETWEEN LUTHERANISM AND CALVINISM

The importance of the question is evident. Either answer has momentous consequences. Involved is not merely my understanding of the two Testaments and consequently of salvation history but also my approach to the two great Protestant confessions, Lutheranism and Calvinism. The two issues are closely related. In the Reformed as distinct from the Lutheran tradition the law is seen less in its significance as judgment and more in its positive significance as promise and gospel. Hence the gospel can never invalidate the law. It is complementary to it. It bears witness to the fact that the new covenant set up by the gospel cannot be different from that set up by the law. God's aim is that he should establish (*sanciret*) forever the covenant made at the first with his people.[8] Calvin certainly speaks many times of the fact that the law judges while the gospel restores. But he always adds that the antithesis does not mean disparagement of the function of the law. It does not mean that the work of the law is purely negative and brings forth no real fruits. Even in the OT it produces a disquietude of conscience which drives men to the gospel. It thus has a part in salvation and is teleologically related to the gospel. It effects a positive disposition for the gospel. Hence the difference between law and gospel is to be viewed as relative and not unconditional. Only by way of comparison is it presented as the polar antithesis of death and life. This is the only method by which the affluence of grace in comparison with the law can be clearly described. Law and gospel together represent the totality of grace, whereas law alone is only one part of grace which needs to be complemented. The relation between the two is one of quantitative supplementation. There is no basic or teleologically insoluble tension.[9]

---

[7] Cf. the 1531 *Commentary on Galatians*, WA, 40, I, pp. 479ff.

[8] *Comm. on the Harmony of the Gospels* (1555) on Matthew 5:17, *Corpus Reformatorum*, 74, 107f. For supplementary discussions cf. ThE, I, § 614ff.; E.T. I, pp. 120ff.; and II, 2, § 4038-4233; E.T. II, pp. 571-598.

[9] Cf. Inst., II, 11, 7.

Since the law for Calvin already implies the gospel, the new thing in the NT is no real advance which overcomes and leaves behind earlier determination by the law. Instead, it is an expansion of the salvation already given into fulness and completeness. More accurately, it is a disclosure of the fulness of what was previously known only in part and shadow. One might also put it in this way. There is here no ontic movement of the salvation event to a new thing which is given in the NT gospel. There is only the noetic act of making explicit something which was already there implicitly. Even more pointedly, we do not have here a history of the acts of God advancing to something new but merely a history of disclosure in which what happened once and for all is divinely unveiled to our noesis.[10] In the NT a letter which was still sealed in the OT is opened. Nevertheless, this sealed letter of the law contains the whole truth.[11] Both Testaments have one and the same content. The only difference is one of presentation and administration.[12]

We thus maintain that since in the Calvinist tradition the gospel is contained in the OT law as in an envelope, and since it causes this law to participate in itself, it can no longer be understood as a throwing off of the law. For the dominion of law from which the gospel is supposed to free us never actually existed.

Hence we can no longer present the relation between the OT and the NT as a movement in the sense of the Word that posits history. We are rather to use the timeless comparison of the two concentric circles which constitute a narrower and broader sphere of disclosure around the primal decree of God to be our God. On this view the way of salvation does not lead us beyond the OT but leads us merely to an exposition of its understanding. It opens up the OT.

Two things characterize this understanding of the way of salvation. First, there has developed in the Reformed world an extreme and even allegorical christological interpretation of the OT as in the works of W. Vischer and H. Hellbardt (ThE, I, § 573ff.; E.T. I, pp. 100ff.). If the relationship of the OT and NT means an identity of their substance, we naturally have to seek Christ's presence in the OT. Christ does not shake off or transcend the OT but is contained in it. The impression of an unhistorical *eisegesis* is left by the *de facto* elimination of history and of the Word in its character as that which posits history. Secondly, there can obviously develop in terms of this Reformed understanding a view like that of A. A. van Ruler which even goes to the extreme limit of integrating the NT into the OT.

This cursory survey of the Reformed tradition shows us to what extent a specific understanding of law and gospel can entail a corresponding view of

---

[10] The doctrine of the decrees lurks behind the "what happened once and for all"; cf. ThE, II, 2, § 4039ff.

[11] Inst., II, 10f.

[12] Inst., II, 10, 2.

the relations of the OT and the NT. In simplified form one might describe the matter as follows.

Paul understands the new situation under gospel and justification by faith in such a way that he (necessarily) sets it in antithesis to the law (and Moses). The transition from the one aeon to the other implies a change in lordship, or is seen as a transition from bondage to sonship (Galatians 4:1-7), from the death-dealing service of the letter to the living spontaneity of the spirit (2 Corinthians 3:6f.). We have here, not an evolutionary development of the old, but the historical leap into something absolutely new. Equally radical, then, is the difference between the OT and NT. Since God as the author of law and gospel, and also of OT and NT, works in freedom and posits history, his identity cannot be established by a logical conjoining of his very different works. I can only *believe* in him as the one who in every variation on his work is one and the same, the one who was, and is, and will be.

The Reformed view as we have just described it takes the different course of seeing law and gospel as two aspects of the same thing and thus relating them in discernible complementarity. To this extent there is no movement from the one to the other, only cognitive progress of insight into their relationship.

Similarly OT and NT are variations on the one identical message of salvation. The variations arise out of the differing states of those who receive this message. For this reason they are variations in the administration rather than the substance of salvation.

In this formulation a certain analogy to Modalism might be described. The one identical God, and the one identical Word of God, only "pass off" themselves as different. The difference, however, is not in God himself and the free act of his self-disclosure. It lies neither in God's trinitarian self-distinction nor in his duality as Judge and Redeemer, as author of law and gospel or OT and NT.

To avoid misunderstanding we must stress that although the differences between Calvinism and Lutheranism are important in this area they are no reason for schism but are simply theological differences. The above criticism of Calvinism is decisively relativized (so that there can be no rejection of Calvinism as a heresy) by the fact that in Calvin's *Institutes* the inter-relating of law and gospel does not become a systematic principle any more than the doctrine of predestination does (on the latter cf. ThE, II, 2, § 4039, n. 1; E.T. II, pp. 571f.). Since Calvin is above all a biblical theologian, every principle is continually shattered by the fulness of holy scripture. In this sense his theology can never be brought under a principle. That it is still necessary to analyze principles hardly needs to be shown, especially as they are historically important and trigger a legalistic tendency.

Our own inclination within the Lutheran-Reformed controversy is to ascribe incisive significance to the new thing in the NT[13] and in so doing to

---

[13] Cf. our understanding of the Word that posits history.

accept what we regard as Paul's understanding of the law.[14] For this reason, however, it is all the more urgent that we should ask whether Paul does in fact follow the OT understanding of the law, or whether, to be blunt, he does not really understand the OT as it understands itself. If in fact Paul does not offer an authentic reading of the OT, the consequences are incalculable. For if the OT law does not have the negative function that it is given in Paul, if it is not the counterpart of the gospel but a form of the gospel, as Barth puts it, then it must be asked in all seriousness whether the NT can ever be more than a living development of the fixed form of the OT or if it can ever bring a new here and now (Luke 1:48; 22:69; John 12:31; 1 John 3:2, etc.).

We must now turn to this question. In so doing we believe we can show that the question whether Paul has a right understanding of the OT law cannot be answered with a single Yes or No, since the issues are very complex. To give some indication of the lines of our own answer, it may be stated that in our view it is wrong to say that Paul adopts an attitude to *the* OT law. This is unlikely because there is no such thing as *the* OT view of the law. Instead we find many rich nuances in understanding. There is the Deuteronomic view, the prophetic view, the priestly view, the later rabbinic view. The multiplicity of interpretation should help us to see along what lines Paul is speaking with his antithesis of law and gospel. For in each nuance in the understanding of the law there is expressed the fact that Israel had a history with the law and that in this history are reflected very different encounters of Israel with God and of God with his people. Perhaps, then, Paul does not have *the* law in view when he attacks its dominion but rather specific stages in this history of Israel with the law, or possibly the final stage in this history at the moment when the gospel breaks into the history of the law with its "But now. . . ."

This is one of the questions that we must tackle.

THE CONTROVERSY ABOUT THE UNDERSTANDING OF THE LAW IN ROMANS 7

Another question arises as follows. Modern NT scholars are more or less agreed that in Romans 7 Paul is describing his own history with the law, even though he is looking back on this history with Christian eyes. He is seeing it as one who has been liberated from the law and hence not as one who is still within its sphere.[15] In retrospect he understands his being under the law better than he could do so when under its dominion.[16]

---

[14] We put this tentatively, since Calvin and Barth are obviously offering an interpretation of Paul in their view of the law.

[15] A. Nygren in his *Commentary on Romans* (E.T. 1949) dissents from the common view. He does not think that Paul is looking back on the law, but finds a simultaneity of law and gospel which along the lines of Luther's exposition of the chapter determines the present situation of the Christian.

[16] For this interpretation of Romans 7 cf. A. Schlatter, "Luthers Deutung des Römerbriefs," *Beiträge zur Förderung Christlicher Theologie* (1917); P. Althaus,

If this is so, it means that Paul has no real historical interest when he looks back on his being under the law. That is, he is not concerned to analyze the self-understanding of the man who is under the law's dominion. He is interested neither in the self-understanding of the righteous of the OT nor in his own life "before Christ." He wants to get beyond the state of consciousness of the man who sees his relation to God as it is determined by the law. In viewing the situation under the law and its yoke from the standpoint of the situation of liberation and adult sonship (Galatians 4:1ff.), Paul does not have to argue if someone claims that OT man extolled the law, regarded it as gracious, and experienced it as a form of the gospel. He might even concede that subjectively man did not have to feel his being under the law as bondage (*douleía*), although he emphasizes this aspect of the law in relation to his own past. Such subjective interpretations are not his concern. His answer to them would be that the freedom which man might experience in his being under the law (the freedom to force upon God specific reactions in the form of rewards, as Job did), and the extolling of the law which this might bring with it, are seen in fact to be bondage the moment we learn to know true freedom in Christ. This is why, when he looks back, he regards determination by the law as loss and refuse (Philippians 3:8).

The subjective way in which we live out a situation is not a good criterion for true assessment. This may be seen in many other areas of life as well. Thus it might be argued that natural man, not least in the modern variation, is dominated by anxiety. Those who have achieved mastery over anxiety[17] may then study it either by looking back on their own lives or by diagnosing their contemporaries. A subjective experience of actual anxiety is not necessary for this purpose. Anxiety can take many forms. It may be experienced as oppression. It may lead us to take refuge in work. It may even have a productive function, so that it becomes a basis of achievement and the driving force of action. C. Morgenstern in his verses can go so far as to see spirit engendered by it. Existentially, then, anxiety does not have to give an authentic expression of itself. It can put itself in code. It can disguise itself as its opposite. It can take the form of activity rather than paralysis, onward flight rather than resignation, heroism rather than cowardice. Only redemption from anxiety imparts objectivity in relation to it and therewith makes possible its unbiased diagnosis.

In Paul, too, we find this distinction between the true state and the psychological reflection. Thus the pagans depicted in Romans 1:18ff. can hardly have construed their abandonment to various perversions as an out-

---

Paulus und Luther über den Menschen (1938); R. Bultmann, "Röm. 7 und die Anthropologie des Paulus," *Imago Dei, Festschrift G. Krüger* (1952), pp. 53ff.; also "Christus des Gesetzes Ende," Beiträge zur ETh, 1 (1940), pp. 3ff.; W. G. Kümmel, *Röm. 7 und die Bekehrung des Paulus* (1929); W. Joest, "Paulus und Luther. Simul Justus et Peccator," KD (1955), pp. 269ff.

[17] Cf. John 16:33. In our use of the term anxiety the distinction which Heidegger makes between anxiety and fear is essential; cf. ThE, I, § 701; E.T. I, p. 151.

pouring of the penal wrath of God. They found pleasure in these perversions. They constructed a view of the world in which their confused licentiousness could be interpreted, not as destruction, but as the breaking of constrictive taboos and advance to the free unfolding of personality. (We are obviously viewing these pagans in modern categories in this regard, but believe it is legitimate to do so.) Only when they look back as believers is the hardening overcome and the vision freed to see that all this was in fact anxiety and alienation.

The same antithesis between the true state and the psychological reflection may be found in what Jesus says about hypocrisy in, e.g., Matthew 5:23-26; 7-5; Luke 6:42. Here again the reference is not to a subjectively planned dissimulation which is experienced as such. It is to an objective self-contradiction in man of which he may not be aware and which has in fact to be pointed out to him. Through a kind of schizophrenia in the consciousness, the contradiction between correct cultic action and neglect of the neighbor, between the beam in our own eye and the splinter in that of others, becomes "normal" conduct. Its pathological character as self-contradiction comes to light only when man in faith finds himself confronted by the judgment and the grace of God.[18]

These observations are perhaps adapted to shed new light on Romans 7 and the understanding of the OT involved therein. As Paul surveys his past under the dominion of the law, he offers an interpretation of himself in his OT epoch. If the law is thus presented as an enslaving force, this does not have to mean, in relation to the OT, that the OT law was experienced as such, or that the men controlled by it lived in fear of the law. It might mean that Paul could concede that the law was extolled in the epoch of the law. The criteria available in the OT epoch certainly made this understanding possible and might even have demanded it. But all this changes when the new Christ-aeon posits new criteria and when with its transvaluation of all values the crisis character of the law comes to the fore.

We have now worked out the decisive questions at issue. They may be summed up as follows.

First, is Paul perhaps referring to a specific stage in the relation to the law rather than to the OT law as such?

Second, is he perhaps viewing being under the law as non-freedom because he comes to know what freedom and non-freedom really are only in the light of the freedom which he has experienced as the gift of Christ?

The first of these two questions echoes a historical problem. It can be answered only as we present the complex relations of Israel to the law and then ask whether Paul's understanding of the law is especially close to one of these aspects. The second question, however, is a strictly theological one and historical verification is fundamentally impossible in the answer we must give it. The preceding discussion has indicated the lines which our

---

[18] This type of hypocrisy is finely illustrated in the parable of the wicked servant in Matthew 18:21-35.

answer will follow, namely, that Paul understands the OT law better than it understands itself.

THE STAGES IN THE OT UNDERSTANDING OF THE LAW. THE VARIED RELATION OF COVENANT AND LAW

We shall now tackle the first question and consider the stages through which the OT understanding of the law passed.

In this regard it is important that we find a theological standpoint from which to take our bearings in surveying the confusing mass of material, which can only be sketched in the present context. Two things call for attention.

On the one hand—we recall an earlier formulation—it is our task to bring to light the new thing in the NT. This implies that the old covenant is transcended in Christ so that it can now be better understood than it understands itself. The gospel manifested in Christ sets the law in a different light. Compared with this gospel, all that preceded it is judgment. The new thing in the NT consists in that we are rescued from this judgment, that we leave it behind.

On the other hand it must be remembered that the God of the old covenant is the Father of Jesus Christ. This prevents us from seeing only the author of the law at work in the OT or from seeing only an antithesis between the covenants. The conjoining personal union of God himself points to promise as well as judgment in the old covenant, to covenant as well as law, to the offer of God as well as the claim of God. This means, as we have seen, that the old covenant, too, contains a foreshadowing of the dialectic of law and gospel. This means again that the relation between the OT and the NT is one of promise and fulfilment.

If, then, the old thing in determination by the law is despised as refuse, and if there must be no relapse into the bondage that has been overcome (Galatians 3:1ff.; 5:1ff.), this cannot mean that the old covenant has become a negligible quantity. It is relativized only by the gospel. Only in this light does it become shadow. Only in comparison with this light does what was clear day for the fathers become the half-light leading on to a new day.

Only when we keep both these aspects in view can we appreciate the mixture of continuity and discontinuity which characterizes both the relation of individual understandings of the law in the old covenant and also the relation between the old covenant and the new.

We do best to begin by exposing ourselves for a moment to the Psalm which has achieved the rank of a classical representation of the extolling of the law. In Psalm 119 we find the direct opposite of what Paul has in mind when he says that the law accuses and judges. This Psalm speaks of the divine acts to which the law points us (v. 27). It tells us how the consolation or the faithful promise of the law leads us on to obedience, for when God comforts our hearts, we tread the way of his commandments. Yet the opposite is also true. To have a stronghold in God's law is consolation in the time of trouble (v. 92). There is no need to fear God's commands: they are rather to be sought. Far from being the power of destruction, the law is a lamp on the path by night (v. 105). In sentence after sentence the Psalm describes that side of the law which establishes and comforts—its giving and evangelical side.

OT scholars are undecided whether this Psalm is the prayer of a scribe or a teacher of wisdom, whether it originated in Deuteronomistic circles during the exile, or whether it is a collection of individual utterances of post-exilic Torah piety made up of elements of scribal study, Deuteronomistic theology, cultic instruction in the Torah, and the impulses of wisdom teaching (H. J. Kraus, *Psalmen* [1960], II, p. 823; cf. the bibliography, pp. 820ff.). We need not enter into this controversy here. We may simply recall that the Psalm occupies a special place in the OT history of the understanding of the law. Only on this presupposition can one ask whether, apart from its specific historical framework, it contains within it elements which point to general and persistent tendencies in the OT understanding of the law.

In trying to characterize the Psalm, we may say with Kraus[19] that it is one long magnifying of the gracious revelation of the will of Yahweh. The author prays more than once that he might be blessed with God's Word. The Word of God and the declaration of his will are demonstrations of grace. To put it epigrammatically, far from being the counterpart of the gospel, they are the gospel. Like the gospel they work wonders and give life. They are thus extolled in every verse as saving power. Deissler[20] is on the right track when he says that this is not a nomistic Psalm. Transcending the legal aspect, it contains a glorifying of the whole Word of God in its all-embracing significance. The law here is a part representing the whole. Hence the revelation of the will of Yahweh which the Psalm extols is to be regarded as an utterance comprising all God's outward action, not merely what he does in giving the tables of the law, but his miracles in the gracious liberation out of the house of bondage in Egypt, his guidance through the wilderness, the general demonstration of his power in history, and also his promises.

If we view the matter thus—and it is hard to see how else it can be viewed—then it is highly significant that the law is homogeneously included in all the work of Yahweh. It is not seen as an alien work. It does not constitute a foil for his true work. It is not a "schoolmaster" (Galatians 3:24f.). It does not "enter" (Romans 5:20). It is not a foreign body which is simply designed to make the alienation (*paráptōma*) of man from God virulent. The law is so homogeneous with the totality of the salvation event that it can serve as its representative. Here, then, the righteous man is directly and unbrokenly, not dialectically and indirectly, committed to the statutes of Yahweh in delight and love, waiting and looking for God's mighty Word.

We stated earlier that in the light of Christ Paul understood the law better than it was understood even by the righteous of the old covenant. In face of

---

[19] Cf. *ibid.*, p. 829.   [20] Cited *ibid.*

this Psalm, however, the question arises whether Paul's understanding of the law is in any way applicable to it. Can the law which is extolled in this way, when it is set in the light of the gospel, be interpreted only as judgment, challenge, and accusation, as a mere counterpart of the gospel? We simply put the question; it is obviously a rhetorical one.

The problem which the Psalm raises is whether this interpretation of the law is an exceptional one or whether there are other places in the OT in which the law is homogeneously brought into the total context of the word and work of Yahweh.

Now undoubtedly homogeneous incorporation into the total nexus of the revelation of Yahweh is a feature which may be seen over long stretches of the literature of the OT. It is grounded in the relation between the covenant and the law. The first commandment, in which Yahweh speaks to Israel as its Lord and God,[21] shows that the law forms part of the covenant, of a gracious address to Israel.

Implicitly or explicitly the law constantly makes backward reference to the covenant which is its basis. This finds expression even in its formal structure, e.g., the negative form of the Decalog.

1. We have already pointed out that the covenant of Yahweh is not a contract between partners with equal rights. It is a divine institution, a *diatheke* and not a *syntheke*. Yahweh chose Israel as his own possession, not because of its special qualifications, but in spite of the fact that it was the smallest of all people (Deuteronomy 7:6f.).

The understanding of the law necessarily derives from this covenant and the supremacy of Yahweh in it. The law cannot be viewed as instructions given prior to the covenant, as though Israel's obedience to it would qualify it to become the covenant-partner of Yahweh. If this were so, the covenant would lose its character as the one-sided institution of Yahweh. It would be merited and the initiative would pass to man. In reality the direct opposite is the case. The law has to do with the conduct of those who are already under the covenant and who are already the covenant people. In God's covenant statement the indicative precedes the imperative.

We have here one of the elements[22] which underlie the negative structure of the Decalog. The Decalog does not tell us positively what might bring about membership in the covenant, for this is in force already through the decree of Yahweh. It tells us what this membership excludes.

There can be no doubt at all that this side of the OT understanding of the law is taken up in Paul. How Paul accepted this covenant-shaped structure of the law may be seen at various points.

It may be seen first in the indicative-imperative structure of his exhortations. The moral commandments which he lays down for Christians are not designed to produce a status which will dispose them for the grace of justifi-

---

[21] Cf. Althaus, *op. cit.*, and also K. Holl, *Gesammelte Aufsätze*, I, 6th ed. (1932), pp. 9ff.
[22] For others, cf. ThE, I, § 2163ff.; E.T. I, pp. 440ff.

cation. Grace has already been imparted in Christ, just as institution of the covenant preceded the law. The imperatives serve to remind Christians of the implications of God's covenant of grace for their conduct.[23]

Again, the reason which we have given for the negative structure of the Decalog applies equally in Paul. For him, too, there are modes of conduct which are completely incompatible with the new covenant of grace concluded in Christ. Among these is *porneia,* for membership in the body of a harlot cannot be reconciled with membership in the body of Christ. Denial of Christ is also ruled out.[24] In their negativity these injunctions, like the commandments, do not tell us what brings about membership in the covenant but what this membership excludes. They refer to what is prohibited and prevented.

2. Connected also with the relation between covenant and law is the apodictic or unconditional character of the law. If the covenant is supreme, the commandments all carry with them the alternative of remaining in the covenant or departing from it. This alternative, rather than quantitative perfection, is the point of the law. If, as in the ethics of Kant, the goal were that I should achieve my destiny and actualize my humanity by fulfilment of the imperative, then immediately we should have the idea of quantitative approximation. (This has, of course, nothing whatever to do with the categorical and in its own way apodictic character of the ethical imperative; if a quantitative standpoint is adopted, this is connected with the posited relation between the imperative and being.)

Now Paul's imperatives, too, have an apodictic character which finds no place for quantitative grades of obedience. In Paul, too, we either act out of faith or we do not (Romans 14:23; cf. Titus 1:15). We either operate on the basis of the covenant set up in Christ or we do not. This is the only pertinent question.

The alternative may be put in many different ways. Thus I either act out of love or I do not. If all things are lawful, choice within this freedom must be according to the love of self (seeking my own things) or love of others (seeking the things of others, 1 Corinthians 10:23f.; cf. the debate with Gogarten on this point in Volume I, pp. 326ff.). The reference to love of others is also a reminder of the covenant of grace set up in Christ. For my love of others is based on the fact that Christ died for them (Romans 14:15; 1 Corinthians 8:11) and that they, too, are bought with a price (1 Corinthians 6:20; 7:23).

The law has the same apodictic character, and again poses an alternative, in Luther. As Luther sees it, obedience and disobedience are decided by whether I act in faith or not, by whether or not I act on the basis of justification by faith alone. "As nothing justifies but faith, so nothing sins but unbelief. . . . If adultery could take place in faith, it would not be sin. . . . If

---

[23] Cf. ThE, I, § 315ff.; E.T. pp. 74ff.
[24] 1 Corinthians 6:9ff.; Ephesians 5:5. On the structure of these Pauline exhortations cf. ThE, I, § 333ff., 356ff.; E.T. I, pp. 87, 92.

you try to worship God in unbelief, you simply commit an act of idolatry" (Theses on Whether Works Contribute to Grace, 1520, WA, 7, 231f.: Theses 1, 10, 11).

3. The character of the law as the posing of an alternative on the basis of the covenant may be seen in other aspects too.

First, it may be seen in the way in which capital punishment occurs in the OT. If we today find it strange that the death penalty could be meted out for offenses like the mistreatment and cursing of parents (Exodus 21:15,17), copulation with animals (Exodus 22:19), adultery (Leviticus 20:10), incest (20:11ff.), or sabbath-breaking (Exodus 31:15), this is because the punishment does not seem to fit the crime. But they obviously did not see it this way in ancient Israel. These offenses were viewed as a form of disobedience which excludes from the covenant people and which is thus an alternative to entry into the covenant. Hence ethical and penal criteria are not appropriate in evaluating the offenses. These offenses are serious solely because they are directed against Yahweh as the Lord of the covenant: "Against thee, thee only, have I sinned . . ." (Psalm 51:4). The self-exclusion of the disobedient from the covenant is a banishment to nothingness and non-being. It amounts to self-extermination. The death sentence simply ratifies what has already been done in fact by leaving the covenant.

Again, the fact that the law can be a future promise as well as a pure command[25] is also connected with standing within the covenant. Thou *shalt* not kill so long as thou dost remain in the covenant and live by it. If the imperatives of Paul are correctly understood as reminders of the indicative of the promise of grace which is the basis of the new being, then one may see a future element in them too. As you live by this indicative, you will act thus and thus. If the future element of promise is given an imperative form, this is because it is an admonitory reminder: Remember that this conduct befits your calling into the covenant of justification, and that conduct does not.

The need for this reminder is related to what we said above about hypocrisy as objective self-contradiction. Man may indeed affirm God's covenant with his heart and yet the renewed heart may not be pumping blood into every member. Man may not have seen that standing in God's covenant is relevant to his relation to money, sex, business, and every other dimension of life. Hence he can exist in self-contradiction. He can be a hypocrite, and leave the outward impression of being this too.

If the imperatives are understood thus, then in their quality as a reminder they point back to that which precedes all my own action, namely, the divine Yes which is pronounced to me in Christ, in the new covenant. Yet in so doing they also point forward to what I am promised: Thou shalt act thus

---

[25] A. Alt seems to have been the first to note this in his essay "Die Ursprünge des israelitischen Rechts," *Sächsischen Akademie des Wissenschaften, Phil-hist. Kl.* (1934), pp. 37ff. It becomes almost the sole sense in H. J. Kraus.

and thus, and no longer thus and thus, if thou rememberest, and abidest within, thy being in the new covenant.

This future aspect of the law may be seen in Luther. We need only remember his expositions of the Decalog in the Small Catechism. These all begin with the formula: We should fear and love God, that. . . . The "that" is probably to be construed here in a consecutive rather than a final sense; cf. ThE, I, § 312ff.; E.T. I, pp. 60ff. If so, the commandments mean that so long as we fear and love God, appealing to his covenant with us and living in terms of it, we *shall* go the way of his commandments.

THE PAULINE AND THE OT UNDERSTANDING OF THE LAW

These observations indicate that Paul, and Luther after him, accepted the relation between covenant and law or law and gospel, and did not set the two only in antithesis. We have to ask, then, whether Paul, when he speaks of the antithesis of law and gospel, is really speaking of *the* law—he can hardly be doing this, since exhortations are part of the gospel and cannot be seen merely as its opposite—and is not referring only to a specific role or use or aspect of the law. If so, the revelation of God's will acquires its accusatory and condemnatory significance, and comes into tension with the gospel, by reason of my own particular relation to it. But what is this? It is a relation in which I do not see that the covenant precedes the law, that the gracious God has the first word and not God the Judge. Hence the law is for me only an unconditional demand. It is only the radical imperative of him who can claim me completely for himself. If the Sermon on the Mount were to be read without the preamble of the Beatitudes, it would be an extreme expression of this unconditional demand and it would call me radically in question. It would not just call me personally in question. It would call in question the structures of this aeon which oppose the fulfilment of the radical demand and which can never themselves produce any such fulfilment.[26]

Possibly Paul is engaging in speculation here. Possibly he is postulating a relation to the unconditional demand of God which never existed historically in ancient Israel. Possibly there never was an actual confrontation with the God of the commandments apart from the covenant into which the commandments were introduced. (For my own part, I doubt whether we should abandon the historicity of this relation too lightly. The Pentateuch and the prophets constantly ask the people to remember the covenant of Yahweh and his gracious acts and this seems to show that there was a continual temptation to forget the author of the covenant. This could only mean that the people would have dealings simply with the author of the law, unless they forgot him too.)

Even if we have only a postulate, however, it is theologically important, for it makes it plain what our position is by nature if God is not the one who turns to us in free grace, if he is not the author of the covenant, if in contrast

---

[26] Cf. Volume I, pp. 142ff.

he stands on his rights and his demand for a reckoning. As Paul in 1 Corinthians 15:13-19 considers what the situation would be if Christ were not risen, so here, perhaps, his doctrine of the law is triggered by the experimental question how it would be if God were not the author of the gospel, if he were not the Lord of the covenant, if he were not the Father of Jesus Christ. In fact, of course, he is. God's covenant turning to us is no postulate. It is grounded in the freedom of his grace. We can only take note of it in astonishment. The point of Paul's presentation, however, is to show how we should stand in relation to God by nature, i.e., apart from the old covenant and the new. In this case we should be confronted only with his demand and this would be fatal (Romans 7:11; 2 Corinthians 3:6). When Paul says that this is not so, that we can in fact inquire into God's will on the basis of his turning to us, he is thus extolling free and unfathomable grace.

In favor of this thesis that Paul is advancing a conceptual construct with no intention of referring historically to the OT understanding of the law, one might adduce the way in which he speaks of the relation to the law in Romans 7:14: "We know that the law is spiritual: but I am carnal, sold under sin." Here the law has the same rank as the gospel, as the spiritual rock Christ (1 Corinthians 10:4). In it we have to do with the Pneuma of God himself. If it has for me the force of questioning and a divine No, this is because I am carnal. In Paul the flesh does not denote something about man, like his *physis*. It is a manner of his total existence, the orientation of his life without God, determination of his life by what is at hand,[27] a deliberate desire for self-being. This is how I am by nature subsequent to the fall. This is how Paul sees himself and all men in confrontation with God's naked majesty apart from grace. All that is left is consuming and death-dealing contradiction. Grace can be magnified only when the message sounds forth that redemption has been given from the body of this death (Romans 7:24f.).

These considerations lead us to think that Paul does not simply have the law of the old covenant in view when he speaks of its accusatory, condemnatory, and questioning character. When he sees the revelation of God's will in the light of the gospel, we find astonishing analogies to the OT relation of covenant and law. The law becomes the exhortation that follows the gospel. It is a consecutive "that." It is no longer a mere imperative but also a future promise. When the law is the counterpart of the gospel, a specific relation to the law is in view, namely, the relation which arises when we do not stand on the ground of the new covenant, nor ask after the will of God in terms of the gospel, and are thus confronted with its consuming penal force.

This aspect, however, is not the one which the author of Psalm 119 has in mind. For him, as we have seen, the law represents the whole of God's self-disclosure in gracious word and gracious deed. The question arises,

---

[27] Cf. Bultmann, Art. "Paulus," RGG[2], IV, 1034f.

then, whether the different relation to the law solves the riddle which is set by the discrepancy between Paul's understanding of the law and that of Psalm 119.

Finally, the fading of the thought of reward is connected with the relation between covenant and law. It is so at least in the special sense of a particular honoring of obedience to the law outside the promise given with the covenant, and of achievement for the sake of this honoring. Instead of the forward look to a future in which obedience will be rewarded, we find a backward look to the past, namely, to what Yahweh has done on and to his people and the specific mode of conduct that results therefrom. This mode of conduct consists, and finds its reward (if this terminology be used), in the fact of perseverance in the covenant and participation in its blessings.[28] Nothing new will be won by obedience to the law. The decisive reward is already there. It precedes all obedience. This reward, which is participation in God's covenant faithfulness, will simply come to expression in obedience. Obedience is man's counter-signature to God's signature with which he seals his covenant faithfulness.[29]

Since, then, the law is embedded in the covenant and calls for the counter-signature of obedience, it describes the covenant itself and thus becomes a magnifying of God's gracious turning to us, although naturally from a special angle.

When God is spoken of "directly," statements are made about what he does for the people of his choice. When the law is spoken of, statements are made about how this experience of God's action works itself out in man. Since man is not a passive object but a personal counterpart of God, this outworking cannot parallel the manipulations of things or animals, as in the felling of a tree or the slaughtering of cattle. A thing simply stands there. I act "on" it. When God acts on his people or man, however, the objects do not stand still. They become involved. They are taken up into God's work. They are claimed personally. In contrast to trees, stars, or whales, man after his creation has to consider a claim which necessitates decision and opens up the possibility of failure (Genesis 2:16ff.).

Thus the covenant action of God, when it is seen from the standpoint of its outworking in man, always has the character of a claim and cannot be depicted without imperative features.

The structure of claim recurs in the NT, as the exhortations show. On the one hand man's action within the new covenant is described in biological metaphors, so that it seems to have the character of (automatic) natural necessity; cf. the good tree and its fruits in Matthew 7:16ff., the vine in John 15:4f., 16, and the grain of wheat that dies in John 12:24. Nevertheless, when man is addressed by God he does not act merely by natural necessity. The gospel which sets him in these processes is also a claim. It is a call for decision. It demands a particular line of conduct (cf. ThE, I, § 254-266,

---

[28] Cf. the promise annexed to the fifth commandment.
[29] On the NT concept of rewards cf. ThE, III, § 1195ff.

304-310 for a fuller exposition; E.T. I, pp. 56ff., 69ff.). Similarly Luther and the confessions view human conduct from the twofold aspect of bringing forth good fruit and obeying God's will (ThE, I, § 267-303, 311-314; E.T. I, pp. 60ff., 72ff.).

Covenant and law are thus two aspects of the same thing. They are the Word of God, which always remains the same and simply presents different sides of itself.

THE PROPHETIC AND POST-EXILIC RELATION TO THE LAW

In this context we may pass over nuances in the relation to the covenant and the law as they may be seen in Deuteronomy and the Priestly Code. We must be content to concentrate on variations in the understanding of the law which obviously form the background against which Paul's doctrine of the law is to be seen.

The first variation (systematically rather than chronologically) is the understanding of the law in the post-exilic period.

During the exile the threats of the prophets were fulfilled. Israel's disobedience brought down historical punishment. On the return it does not seem that there was any primary return to the covenant or any radical purifying of the disrupted relation to God. We find instead a focusing on the symptoms of the disruption and the disobedience which resulted therefrom. This meant that observing the law became the dominating concern.

This did not entail, of course, a total theological shift in the sense that the law obscured the divine covenant and the author of the law (and the covenant) was lost in his law. Both the Chronicler and Ezra continue to insist that the basis of the existence of Israel is contingent and unmerited election by Yahweh.[30] Nevertheless, the shift of accent is unmistakable. The law acquires in the consciousness a more important rank in the relation to God. A certain movement toward the position which develops later may be seen in the fact that the law becomes almost an end in itself and the Thou of the divine author of the law disappears behind its casuistical rulings. In places, then, the law is praised in and for itself. It is an instrument by which the grace of Yahweh may be secured. We still find, of course, an awareness that this instrument is placed at our disposal by grace; cf. Psalm 19.

Gutbrod (TDNT, IV, p. 1043) points out that this change may be seen especially in the Deuteronomic depiction of history and that of the Chronicler. In both a legal standard applies. Saul is rejected because he transgresses God's command. The judgment of the law overtakes all the kings of Israel. The throne of David is guaranteed by the divine promise, but concretely everything depends on fulfilment of the law (2 Chronicles 27f.). In the understanding of history in Judges we find a characteristic scheme: the sin of the people, God's punishment, an appeal to God in distress, God's help

---

[30] Cf. the penitential prayer of Ezra 9:6-15 which recalls the mercy of Yahweh.

through a divinely sent judge, and the fresh sin of the people (Judges 2:11ff.).

In simplified form, and with due allowance for exceptions, one might establish it as a rule that when the author of the law is obscured by his law, such great motifs are also obscured as God's grace in the making of the covenant and the controlling significance of the covenant itself. The heart of God ceases to be the thematic center of the worship of God. This development reaches its culmination in rabbinic Judaism, which is undeniably marked by an exclusive concentration on the law and its casuistical refinement, even though there are still references to the covenant background and theoretically at least this is not contested.[31] This stage in the development of the relation to the law has also to be borne in mind. For along with factors to which we have already pointed it certainly influenced Paul's distinction between law and gospel. At this stage we have a plain example of the fact that the law can separate from God, that it can become an alienating force, and that it can make servants out of adult sons in the father's house.

The second variation in the understanding of the law to which we wish to refer is the prophetic one. In a simplified form which will serve to orient us this might be described as follows.

Whereas in the post-exilic period and then in rabbinic Judaism the crisis of the law arose because it became an end in itself and removed the Lord of the law from the scene, the reverse is true in the prophets. Here the crisis of the law is that they perceive this danger, warn against it, and make the Lord of grace and judgment the thematic center of their proclamation. Hence the formulated law with its casuistry is relativized. Its misuse becomes the target of prophetic chiding. In the midst of a disobedient people, or a people that is obedient only with servility and formality, going through a cultic routine, the prophets are so smitten with the presence of God himself that they become acutely aware of the contrast between God's majesty and pious or ungodly activity. For them, therefore, God protests not only against the sins of the people but also against its worship. Yet he is also the one whose promises are still in force and who proclaims his readiness to thaw out again the frozen covenant.

This encounter with God shapes the prophetic relation to the law. This relation is both conservative and revolutionary. It is conservative inasmuch as the prophets do not proclaim a new law but refer back to that which is already given. In understanding it as the revelation of *God's* will, however, they also actualize the covenant in which it is set and from which it receives its significance in salvation history. They recall the law as they scourge its transgression (Jeremiah 9:8f.; Hosea 4:1f.; 5:7, 10; 8:11-14; Amos 5:7; 5:10-12, 21-26, etc.). They appeal to the covenant which is its basis as they repeat and modify the ancient principle that God has instituted the covenant on his own initiative and not because of any quality in Israel (Isaiah 1:2;

---

[31] Cf. TDNT, IV, p. 1054.

Hosea 8:13f.; Amos 2:9; 3:2). Along with this conservative recollection of the law, however, we also find a revolutionary trait. What will later be done with extreme radicalism in the Sermon on the Mount is already foreshadowed in the prophetic criticism of legalism. Obedience to the wording or letter of the law can be disobedience to its true sense and intention. Its real point is union with the will of God himself.

The law, then, can be entangled in an elementary self-contradiction. Acceptance of it can go hand in hand with rejection of him who seeks to relate us to himself through the law. There can thus arise the basic form of hypocrisy and (possibly unintentional) role-playing whose unmasking we saw earlier in Jesus' attacks on the Pharisees, who "make clean the outside of the cup and of the platter, but within they are full of extortion and excess" (Matthew 23:25), who "are like unto whited sepulchres, which indeed appear beautiful outwardly, but are within full of dead men's bones, and of all uncleanness" (v. 27). An appeal to the law and outward compliance can be a rejection of true obedience and incur the guilt of lack of love for one's neighbor (Jeremiah 8:8; Amos 2:6; 8:4-8).

This situational analysis by the prophets, this indication of possible objective self-contradiction, forms the basis of the critical attitude to the cultus too. For the cultus and its exact observance can be a way of getting God in our own hands instead of putting ourselves in his hands, of manipulating him magically instead of awaiting a call from him, and of thus concealing personal disobedience by the ritual of obedience. When cultic ceremonies are carried out in faithfulness to the law, the heart, which the law really has in mind (Jeremiah 31:33), may be far from the cultus, may offer sacrifices as a substitute, and may thus bring about a degeneration of worship into empty formalism. This is why the prophets inveigh against cultic acts, against burnt offerings and meal offerings which are not pleasing to God, and against the intoning of sacred hymns which he will not hear (Amos 5:32f.; Jeremiah 2:8; 7:11; Hosea 4:6). Sometimes they even attack the cultus itself on the ground that God did not command it but lays claim only to the heart of man (Isaiah 1:12; Jeremiah 7:21ff.). Israel's hurt cannot be healed merely by cultic reforms. These do not get at the root of the matter any more than an intensification of casuistic legalism. On the contrary, these things simply stabilize the wrong attitude to God which is consuming the people.

The crisis of the law to which the prophets point means, then, that the majesty of God penetrates the religious or irreligious fog and becomes present in burning immediacy. The author of the law becomes the judgment of the law which in men's hands is no longer the sign of the covenant, of the presence of God and the tokens of his grace, but has instead come between God and his people, and is indeed a means whereby to escape the divine address and the divine claim.

This diagnosis of the crisis also indicates the therapeutic way on which alone there can be radical change. If legalism and cultic formalism cannot be cured, and threaten indeed to harden and disguise the alienation from God, then healing is not to be expected from this quarter. It can come only as

Israel learns once again to know the salvation of God as this came to it at the first. The salvation event which overtook it was grounded in the initiative of God when he made the covenant of grace. Hence renewal in head and members can come only when God takes the initiative in a new miracle of self-attestation and Israel accepts this creative renewal of the covenant. This new covenant which Jeremiah promises in the name of Yahweh will carry with it a new relation to the law. The altered form of the law will enter the heart of man and rule out any possibility of the heart absenting itself or offering a substitute in formal acts of external obedience. God will put his law in the inward parts and write it in the heart. When it is set within in this way, no external command will be needed: "Know the Lord." For they will know him already through what is set in the heart (Jeremiah 31:31-34).

Healing by this newly coming salvation takes place, then, by the law becoming inner impulse rather than outward compulsion. This takes place when God works a new miracle of presence, when he comes to his people in a new act of condescension, and when he displays his might in the heart by his Spirit. When this occurs the self-contradiction ends and the sublime withdrawal of the heart ceases, for the whole heart now turns to him and lives with the spontaneity of new self-giving.

Even if the law, as we have seen, seeks to be understood as the other side of the covenant and therewith as the revelation of God's gracious will, even if it signifies a demand to accept God's offer and ratify his covenant, it still contains elements which can make God the enemy of man and man the enemy of God. God is experienced as an enemy and destroyer, before whom we perish, when we see him in abstraction from his covenant and regard him as only the author of the law. This does not happen frequently, of course, for the man who knows nothing of God's grace usually drives out all thought of God and holds down his truth in unrighteousness (Romans 1:18ff.). In so doing, he annuls his awareness of God as Judge and of God's wrath. Paul is the great exception because this is precisely what he did not do. As we have seen, he knew God in his unconditional and annihilating demand, or conceptually at least he set up this view as the background of the gospel. The legalistic Jews of the post-exilic period, for whom the covenant was less prominent than the law, possibly sensed the fear which is caused by the unconditional claim of God and which makes God appear to be a menacing enemy. Flight into an increasingly lofty casuistry signifies the attempt to achieve new forms of armistice, without ever achieving peace, by constant legal refinement.

Not just God's enmity, however, could arise out of the law in the form of fear. Man's enmity against God could also arise out of it. Man could evade, despise, and ignore the law even when meeting its literal commands, as in the case of a modern labor dispute where an employer is opposed by working to agreed rule.

The path of law is thus a dead end street. One might say that it bears no necessary or constitutive relation to the law, for the law has its basis in the covenant and thus has the rank of a sign of grace. Hence it is not the fault of the law—the law is spiritual—if it is made into a dead end street. It is the fault of man, who constantly repeats the fall in new acts of emancipation and alienation. In so doing he can use even the law.

The fact that the path of law leads into a dead end street has a purpose in salvation history, for it shows that the miracle of God's new turning to man, the creative act of the outpouring of the Spirit "on all flesh," and the raising up of children "of these stones" (Matthew 3:9; Luke 3:8), really is a miracle. God again pronounces his unexpected Nevertheless in face of those who withdraw from him, using the capital of the law to leave their father's house and go to live in a far country.

WHAT IS NEW AND WHAT IS BACKWARD-LOOKING IN THE NT

The New Orientation in Comparison with the OT Relation of Covenant and Law

The new situation is present in the NT and is worked out most consistently and systematically in Paul.[32]

It is understandable that the question of the law should have to be put in a wholly new way after the crucifixion and resurrection of Christ. There are both historical reasons for this and reasons of principle.

1. First, there are reasons of principle. The old relation between covenant and law is given a radically new form. The concept of the covenant in its significance for the understanding of the law already presents a problem through the mere fact that the new situation set up by Christ is not simply identical with the old covenant, nor can it be integrated with it, but represents something completely new. Hence the question necessarily arises whether in the new situation the law can be understood any longer as man's counter-signature ratifying the covenant, as it was in the OT. Has not the new covenant, justification by faith alone without the works of the law (Romans 3:28), taken on such total and unconditional significance that it cannot be brought into force by human obedience or fidelity to the law?

This possibility of a radical reorientation becomes a problem only when the Christ event is seen as something radically new, i.e., as a movement beyond the OT and not as its development. When this is not so, as in Calvin and Barth, when the whole of salvation is found implicitly in the epistle of the OT and this epistle is simply opened and its contents are brought to light, then the question of a revision of the law cannot be put in so radical a way. Nor has it been, in this branch of the tradition. This is why the law has been kept in force and applied among Calvinists in a much more undisputed and conservative manner.

---

[32] On the terms "new" and "old" in this connection cf. E. Wolf, *Peregrinatio*, II (1965), pp. 139ff.; H. J. Kraus, *Die biblische Theologie*, pp. 341ff.

2. Second, there are also historical reasons why the problem of a necessary reorientation in the understanding of the law arises. We have seen that the law increasingly interposed itself between man and the author of the law. If a new immediacy to God comes in Christ and the promise of Jeremiah comes to fulfilment in him (Jeremiah 31:31ff.), the distorted and destructive law which makes the relation to God indirect is felt to be especially intolerable.

This crisis in the understanding of the law can be seen already in the primitive community. A brief survey may be given by way of transition to Paul.

The outward occasion for a new actualization of the question of the law was provided by the expansion of the preaching of Christ into the Gentile world; cf. the apostolic council in Acts 15:1-34; Galatians 2:11-21. Without going into the background of what is said about the law here, we may summarize as follows.

A decision is reached not to impose the burden of the law on the uncircumcised. For the way of law cannot lead to salvation. When regarded as such, it proves to be a false path, since it does not have the grace which alone can save. As James puts it (Acts 15:18-20), and as the written decree states (15:23, 29), only the basic rule remains that Gentiles should abstain from idol meats, the blood of things strangled, and fornication. We thus have certain prohibited things which are incompatible with the life of the believer in the new covenant and are on this account to be avoided (cf. ThE, I, § 355ff.; E.T. I, pp. 92f.).

In the present context only one point is significant. This is that the only portions of the law to be retained in these prohibitions are those that cannot lead to the misunderstanding that their observance will lead to salvation or produce legal righteousness. Only modes of conduct that might stand in the way of salvation are at issue. Nor do these modes of conduct stand in the way of salvation because certain letters of the law are not fulfilled and the required level of perfection is not achieved. They do so because adopting them involves another lordship. By sitting at the table of demons one comes within their sphere. Hence one cannot sit also at the table of the Lord who has rescued one from this sphere (1 Corinthians 10:21). Similarly fornication makes the members of Christ into members of a harlot and thus transfers us again to a sphere of alien dominion (1 Corinthians 6:15). The two lordships are mutually exclusive.

The letter of the law is thus robbed of its sharpness and casuistry is tossed overboard. The letter is no help at the decisive point—quite the contrary. Hence it need not, and cannot, burden us any longer with anxiety whether we can keep it or not. The only point is that we must be on the watch for modes of conduct that might subject us to a power which is alien to Christ.

This is why the thought arises—at a first glance the very shocking thought—that the law itself might become for us a power of this kind if in our status under Christ we revitalize it and use it as a pseudo-way of salvation, a false back door to deliverance. If we do this—and it is one of the factors in Paul's understanding of the law—two things follow.

First, I am confounded by the law. On my own I cannot satisfy the will of God or reach the goal of righteousness by this path (Romans 3:28; 11:6; Galatians 2:16). Being confounded by the law, which is the familiar "before Christ" situation, is especially fateful for the Christian inasmuch as he knows the saving act of Christ and thus disgraces Christ himself by his failure (Galatians 2:17).

Second, I make myself a transgressor of the law (2:18) by the mere fact of my re-entry into this sphere. For the law has point only as an expression of God's holy will. But now God wills that I reach the goal of being righteous before him, not by achievements and the fulfilment of demands, but by faith in Christ (Galatians 4:4-6). I confessed this when I annulled the way of the law with my confession of Christ and his justification (2:18). Thus the very attempt to re-enter the sphere of what has been overcome, and to build up what has been broken down, is a transgression.

A surprising thing here is that with the changed understanding of the law there is also a mutation in the concept of sin. Sin or transgression is no longer acting contrary to the law and violating its precepts. It is acting contrary to the gospel by sabotaging the grace of justification which it offers and causing Christ to have died in vain (Galatians 2:21; cf. 5:2, 4).

One of the possibilities of acting contrary to the law in this way consists in correct observance of the law. This occurs when I use such observance as a means to win salvation, so that I live by the principle of achievement. To put oneself on the plane of the law is to go "by" the gospel (the strict sense of *parábasis*). Paul's criticism, then, does not relate to the perfection of possible fulfilment of the law but to the sign before the bracket in which the sum of these acts of obedience stands. This sign can denote that one is foolishly seeking by the law that which the gospel alone can accomplish. One's own initiative is thus being essayed in that wherein God has reserved the initiative for himself. A fresh attempt is made to be as God.

None of this rules out the possibility that in love and missionary concern Paul might practice conformity among Jewish Christians who grew up under the law and whose spiritual growth had not yet reached the freedom conferred in the gospel. Different attitudes may thus be adopted to the law in relation to Jews on the one side and non-Jews on the other (1 Corinthians 9:19-22). Paul can be free and elastic in this way, however, only because he is no longer under the dominion of the law. Instead of the law having mastery over him, he himself can exercise free judgment in relation to it: *toís hypó nómon, hós hypó nómon, mě ǒn autós hypó nómon* (9:20). M. Kähler is surely right when in this regard he points out that Paul also does not become subject to the law of accommodation. While Paul was ready and anxious to be all things to all men, there were two exceptions. He would not be a miracle-worker to the Jews or a cultural Christian to the Hellenes.[33]

---

[33] Anna Kähler, *Martin Kähler, Theologe und Christ* (1926), p. 315.

The freedom of "all things being lawful" (1 Corinthians 6:12; 10:23) includes freedom to live under the law, or, better, to live with it. (The only obligation is avoidance of what is prohibited.) If I live with it in this way, my relation to it is that of regulative use rather than normative use.

This discussion has already brought us into the sphere of the new questions that Paul has to put to the law. In our survey of the stages in the OT understanding of the law we were attempting to trace lines leading up to Paul's theology and to consider the relation of continuity and discontinuity in which Paul stands to the law of the old covenant. Hence the essential point in his understanding of law and gospel has already been made. All that remains is to summarize Paul's position systematically, to expand it, and to round it off. To do this we need to study Paul's usage in relation to the *nomos* concept. Many nuances can be found in his employment of the term, although when it is used without specific attributes it normally denotes the OT law in the broadest sense.

The Decalog is often used as *pars pro toto*. When this is so, it represents the revelation of God's will in the old covenant in general (Romans 2:17-23; 7:7; 13:9). P. Feine[34] points out that there is no difference between use with or without the definite article, although much has been read into this from Origen right up to J. C. K. von Hofmann and B. Weiss. Nor does it seem to have any special significance when Paul adds an explanatory genitive, e.g., the law of God in Romans 7:22, 25; 8:7, or the law of Moses, 1 Corinthians 9:9. Such additions are put in only for the sake of antithesis or to indicate slight nuances. A more important point is that *nomos* is always singular in Paul. In his assessment the law does not break up into various material spheres, e.g., the categorical imperative, national *nomoi*, and other groups. We have in it the one will of the one God. The form of usage thus points to the one author of the law who shows himself to be always one and the same, and always present, in the many commands of the Word of his will. In the law I have to do with God himself, just as in God's trinitarian self-disclosure I have to do with one and the same God in the various forms.

The fact that in the singular *nomos* always denotes sovereign will may be seen also where it is used in a symbolically extended sense and even where it denotes the law of a lordship that is hostile to God. Thus the law of faith can be set in antithesis to that of works (Romans 3:27). Similarly the law of sin (the ungodly will forced on me by sin, Romans 7:25; 8:2) can be opposed to the law of the Spirit who quickens us in Christ (Romans 8:2; Galatians 6:2). Finally there is reference to the law in my members which causes me to remonstrate against the will of God (Romans 7:21-23). (Here the term means much the same as Kant's natural necessity.) It is particularly noteworthy that Paul sticks to the singular even in relation to these forms of anti-nomos.

Obviously he is not interested in the neutral phenomenology of normative magnitudes such as might be listed by a sociological statistician or a religious

---

[34] *Theologie des NT*, 4th ed. (1910), p. 208.

philosopher trying to enumerate the various forces that bind us. The plural would be more likely in such efforts. Paul, however, speaks most emphatically as a theologian who even stylistically remains true to his intention of relating constraints to the one will of God, so that he does not merely list their appearance phenomenologically but interprets them theologically even in the way he mentions them. They thus become either variations on the one will of God (e.g., the law of Moses) or different forms of the one opposing will, of the one tendency to oppose the freedom of grace, to reject God's unconditional claim, or at least to evade it by a special arrangement (cf. the law in my members which reserves for itself zones that are outside the will of God). Cf. the antithesis between the Yes of the *ésō ánthrōpos* to God's commandment and the evasive *nómos ho ōn en toís mélesin mou* (Romans 7:22f.).

After what has been said, there can be little doubt why Paul has to put the question of the law in a wholly new way when he puts it in terms of the new covenant after the crucifixion and resurrection of Christ. The resultant relation of law and gospel differs from the earlier relation of law and (old) covenant. The new question is posed by the new thing in the NT. It arises out of the movement of salvation history from the OT to the NT. This movement is not the development of that which is earlier. It is a new positing by a creative act of God. History did not produce the messianic appearance of Christ: "God sent forth his Son" (Galatians 4:4). But the God who sent forth his Son and did the new thing is the God who is already Lord of the old covenant. The two facts (1) that God is one and the same, that he is identical with himself, in the old covenant and the new, and (2) that in the freedom of his turning to us he does something radically new and in the incarnate Son comes to the side of alienated man—these two facts carry with them the ambivalence of continuity and discontinuity which characterizes the relation of Paul to the OT and its law.

We must now elucidate this ambivalence.

PAUL'S STRUGGLE WITH THE LAW, THE SPIRITUAL MAN AND THE CARNAL MAN, AND THE PHENOMENOLOGY OF HATRED OF GOD

First (1), in order to understand that Paul, even though he attacks legalism, i.e., the determination of our relation to God by the law, does not in any sense regard the *nomos* merely as a hostile threat, we must remember a point that we made incidentally above, namely, that the real antithesis for Paul is not between law and man but between *nomos* and *sarx* (Romans 7:14; 8:7). Just because the law is the good will of God (Romans 7:12) and to that extent is spiritual (7:14), we ourselves are hostile to it. Those who live after the flesh, who are oriented to the transitory, and who rest in false security, see themselves threatened by it. But Christians, says Paul, are determined not by the *sarx* but by the *Pneuma* (Romans 8:4, 9). Being dead to what was against God (6:2), they are no longer in enmity with him

(8:7). They have thus died to the law—an astonishing phrase (7:6). It no longer affects them, just as a dead man is no longer reached by a command.

If we are no longer there for the law, if it has been relegated to a zone of complete irrelevance as far as we are concerned, this obviously does not refer to the law insofar as it expresses the pure will of God but only to a relation in which we stand to this law. This relation is our fault, not that of the law. It is determined by the fact that as those who live after the *sarx* we regard the law as an attack on us and thus let ourselves be brought under bondage to it. In this way, according to Luther's development of the thought, we come to hate that which enslaves us and in so doing we also come to hate the author of the law.

We shall now try to carry what Paul says a step further. Nor shall we ignore certain modern experiences which have been gleaned from the ongoing history of man and the law.

Hatred of the law and of God is not to be understood psychologically. It is not to be thought that there has to be concrete evidence of the psychological state of emotional aversion to God and his law. On this view Paul's understanding would seem to be alien and unreal. For there is no evidence to support it except perhaps in extreme pathological cases. What, then, is the point?

Hatred of God, which is for Luther the final result of legalism, is something existential rather than a psychological state. In explanation of this we may recall our discussion of anxiety. As we have seen, this existential reality does not have to be an emotional state. It does not have to take the form of panic with a high pulse rate. Long before it can assume the form of a psychological state it has already undergone transformation. It can be a forward flight in the form of activism, business, even creative processes, or heroism. Only when anxiety has been mastered by the faith which overcomes the world (1 John 5:4) can a backward glance diagnose the basic impulse of the active life as anxiety. The diagnosis is thus an ontological statement rather than a psychological one. Anxiety is not a matter of concrete emotions. It is rather existential.

The same is true of the hatred of God which is a result of legalism. This hatred is not an emotional act in which we shake our fist at heaven. Where should we ever find such pathetic gestures? Who has ever seen or experienced the like? Hatred of God is again something existential which is encountered, not as a discernible psychological state, but in a transformation. Only when we have been redeemed can we diagnose it in retrospect as hatred of God.

No man can stand hatred of God, just as no man can stand anxiety. This inability to stand the two is why they are transformed, sublimated, and subjected to mutations. We have already seen what this implies in the case of anxiety. We must now ask what it implies in the case of hatred of God and hostility to his law.

We try to come to terms with the law and its author, or, to use an unsympathetic but appropriate term, we try to change their function, before the corresponding emotions can become virulent. To come to terms with the law and its author means viewing them in such a way as to seem to do justice to them. This appearance can be achieved in various ways. Numerous examples are provided not only by the conduct of Israel but also by history old and new, including recent history.

This self-securing by the law and its author may, for instance, be sought by reducing the law to its letter. In this case I simply give God his due in punctilious outward conduct but deny him my heart. Castrated thus, the law can be no more the object of my aversion than its author can. Neither really concerns me.

Israel castrates the law in similar fashion when it forces the whole law into a list of cultic rules and ignores, represses, and holds down in unrighteousness the true and serious claim of the commandment, namely, love of God with all one's heart and soul and mind, and love of neighbor as oneself (Deuteronomy 6:5; Leviticus 19:18; Matthew 22:37f.). It may thus happen that I write my image of God and the commandment on my body, that I adjust them to myself, that I make God in my own image, and that in so doing I simply make him innocuous.

This is the point of idolatry, in which "the glory of the uncorruptible God is changed into an image made like to corruptible man, and to birds, and four-footed beasts, and creeping things" (Romans 1:23). For I am no longer confronted with my creatureliness and sinfulness. I can hold out. There is no need for panic. The golden calf, which apostate Israel made out of the earrings of the women, does not represent the same threat as the tablets of the law which Moses received from Yahweh on Mt. Sinai (Exodus 19:20ff.; 32:1ff.). The God who is near to us and who resembles us can be a friend, but the God who is remote and inaccessible is a hostile God who provokes a reaction of hostility in us.

The history of exposition of the Sermon on the Mount[35] is one long illustration of the concern to make God's claim less radical either by making it a harmless code or by restricting it to the elite as counsel rather than precept.[36] Even Kant's attempt to limit the "ought" to the radius of the "can" ("You can and therefore you should") is a similar deradicalizing which leads to compromise between the claim of the demand and the competence of freedom, so that all threat is removed.[37]

Many more examples and illustrations could be given. But these instances, selected at random, all go to show that hatred of God and cursing of the law do not take open form any more than anxiety does, except in extreme cases. Israel makes no threatening gestures against smoking Sinai where Yahweh's severity holds sway. Before terror at God's majesty and dread of his total claim can come to expression, the instinct of self-preservation pro-

---

35 ThE, I, § 1691ff.; E.T. I, pp. 332ff.
36 ThE, I, § 1719ff.; E.T. I, pp. 340ff.
37 Volume I, pp. 140ff.

vides relief. Smoking Sinai is viewed as a harmless hill basking in the sun. The consuming radiance of the sun of God's glory is reduced to pallid moonlight. The divine judgments which smite me are transformed into a neutral fate which does not smite me specifically but overtakes me at random. To use the terminology of Luther, the heart has come forward as a witness for the defense between the accusing God and me. Its strategy of defense is not to try to show by arguments how far the *nomos* has in fact been fulfilled or what excuses or extenuating circumstances there are for its nonfulfillment. What the defense wants to demonstrate is that God is not the same as the author of the law, that he is much less terrible, and that the commandment which I claim, instead of being claimed by it, is also different from, and much more harmless than, the law of God. The true Prometheus, seeing himself threatened by the gods, does not threaten them in return. His potential for reaction does not take the form of explosions of Promethean defiance: such gestures are only mythology. It takes the form of a reinterpretation of the gods.

For this reason hatred of God and panic about the law are existential things which as the impulse behind conduct, reactions, and moods lie deep within the objectifiable layer of psychological processes. The reality of these things, the possible diagnosis that idolatry and the taming of the law are in fact grounded in hatred of God and anxiety about the law, comes to light, however, only when the hatred and anxiety are overcome and man is redeemed for objectivity in relation to himself. Before this, self-diagnosis is hampered by the self-interest of the heart that tries to defend itself. (Objectivity can hardly be expected from an advocate, especially when a man is his own advocate.) The one who is troubled about the law and incensed with hatred of God cannot see the beam in his own eye, for this would mean surrender and would seem to be against his interests. He has to draw attention to the mote in the other's eye, since this helps to give him self-assurance (Matthew 7:3). He cannot accept God, but is forced to hold down the truth about him in unrighteousness (Romans 1:18, 21). To do this to God is to do it to self-knowledge too. Such knowledge cannot be attained by argument or by Socratic extraction. The wish that God not be as he is becomes the father of all the thoughts that necessarily get in the way of all such argument or extraction. The word "necessarily," which constantly recurs in this context, expresses the power to which those existential things subject me and which defies all argument.

I have to be rescued from this power if I am to know my hatred of God and anxiety about the law, if I am thus to know my true condition, if I am to become objective to myself. This is possible only as I am redeemed. Only when I am at peace with the one who previously seemed to be my foe can I see my earlier conflict with him and the contradiction of my thoughts (Romans 2:15). When God suddenly takes my side in the form of Jesus Christ and justifies me in relation to his own claim, I am encircled by this peace and liberated from the power which forced me to make of the threatening God a harmless *alter ego* of myself. All relations are then reversed.

My heart no longer defends me against God's accusation. Instead God protects me against my own conscience. Awakened, redeemed, and granted objectivity, my conscience now takes over the role of unmasking and accusing. As Luther puts it, God is now the counsel for the defense rather than the prosecution, and the heart is now the counsel for the prosecution rather than the defense.[38]

After this digression, which should elucidate man's controversy with God and the claim of his law, and show how unredeemed and carnal man is pushed into a basic hatred of God and panic about the law, we may return to the express statements of Paul on the subject of the law.

We may now say that what Paul has discovered in contrast to OT joy in the law and extolling of it is not a new quality of the law itself but the quality of a specific relation in which one can stand vis-à-vis the law. He has in mind especially the relation which is characterized by my determination by the *sarx*. The alternative to this can no longer flourish on the way of the law no matter how far I traverse it. The basic fault of determination by the *sarx* can only be intensified thereby. The negative side before the bracket of acts of obedience robs them of their value and all the greater emphasis is thus given to the rejection of God. This way leads to death (Romans 7:11; 2 Corinthians 3:6f.). The opposite way is a new and gracious endowment with the Spirit of God, a new mode of his presence, in virtue of which God takes my side in Jesus Christ and protects me against myself.

Paul has this destructive, *sarx*-determined relation to the law in view when he speaks of some of the great historical decisions of Israel. Man, or Israel, has had a specific history with the law. In the course of this history it has been shown that the carnal relation to the law, and therefore the death-dealing character of the law, can take over. For all my punctilious observance of the letter I may depart from obedience in the inner man (*eso anthropos*), so that the hypocrisy of which we have spoken, the dichotomy of the consciousness, comes into play. If suddenly I see, not the letter, but the law itself, the will of its author and his consuming majesty, I suffer a dreadful shock in which it becomes clear to me that in my external obedience and its apparent conformity to the law I have in fact been maneuvered into drastic antithesis to the law and have thus come under its threat. I suddenly realize that my existence is torn by the antagonism of *nomos* and *sarx,* that by nature, prior to my redemption, I "am" carnal (Romans 7:14; 1 Corinthians 3:3f.). This is the new dimension of the law which Paul brings out when he looks back on it in the light of the gospel and as one whose eyes have been opened by the gospel.

This discovery does not liquidate what the OT says about the law. Hence Paul does not oppose the OT. He simply enters a new phase of the history with the law. Seeing man under the law from the standpoint of liberated being under the gospel, he has the vision of a demand without grace, of a

---

[38] *Commentary on Romans,* Ficker ed., II, p. 44, 3.

justice of God without justification, of law without the sign of the institution of the covenant. This vision links up with actual circumstances. For natural men, represented by the Gentiles (Romans 1 and 2), there is only law without the encompassing covenant of grace. In the Pharisaism of later Judaism, too, there is only law, for the covenant of grace has been betrayed and the nature and will of God are lost behind the letter.

THE SPIRITUAL LAW AND THE SPIRITUAL MAN: THE NEW OBEDIENCE

Having worked out the antithesis between law and flesh, we now turn (2) to the positive side, namely, the relation between law and spirit.

The OT prophecy of the outpouring of the Spirit (Jeremiah 31:31ff.) has shown us already that impartation of the Spirit of God will make impelling imperatives unnecessary. The demand will no longer go forth: "Know the Lord," for the Spirit has put his image and presence in our hearts. Hence the law is superfluous. What had once to be demanded will now be done in the spontaneity of the heart which is freshly oriented to the renewed covenant of God. What happens now can no longer result in what Paul calls the contradiction between the spiritual law and the carnal side of man. For when God pours forth his Spirit, men are determined by him and no longer by the *sarx* (Joel 2:28ff.; cf. Isaiah 44:3; Ezekiel 39:29). The imparted Spirit of God sets up a new conformity to God. Man can now will what God wills. He no longer needs to be driven by law.[39] Previously the law simply exposed its own total weakness. It also had the paradoxical function of prodding the dead and talking to their deaf ears and lifeless stare. Its commands could not be heard on the field of dead bones that Israel had become. But now the Spirit of God moves over the dry bones and calls afresh to what is not, that it may be (Ezekiel 37:1ff.; Romans 4:17).

By effecting in man a new and spontaneous conformity to God, the outpouring of the Spirit both renews the situation of man in creation before the fall and also points forward to what takes place in Christ. Luther points out that the law is a kind of interim emergency measure between the first estate that has been lost and the redemption that has not yet come. By the letter which commands, and therefore in alien form, it reminds us of what was once done by the spontaneity of the heart and what will be again in the state of redemption. Cf. WA, 39, 1, 454, 4.

The ability to will what God wills in the power of the Spirit comes through the possibility of love that Christ has given us afresh. When we are told that God has first loved us (1 John 4:19), a response of love is evoked. Love does not first have to be demanded from us. It is simply the reverse side of the fact that God is for us a lovable object.[40] One might almost say

---

[39] Schiller grasped this liberation from the law surprisingly well and linked it to his concept of the beautiful soul; cf. his letter to Goethe, August 17, 1795 (*Schiller-Goethe-Briefwechsel, Deutsche Bibl.,* I, pp. 86f.).
[40] Apol. CA, III, 5-8.

that God as lovable object and man as loving subject are interchangeable concepts. There is here an underlying tautology. No place is left for intervention by the impelling law and its demand for love. I want to love. I want what he whom I love wants. It does not have to be commanded. It simply arises. It is fruit. As such it can only be affirmed. The fruit of the Spirit is love, joy, peace, longsuffering and so forth (Galatians 5:22).

The fate of the elder brother in the parable of the Prodigal—we have referred to this already—is that he does not will what his father wills nor find joy in what gives joy to his father. He has to be ordered: "Rejoice with me" (Luke 15:32). But here again the law cannot achieve what the spontaneity of the heart withholds.

An important point here is that the new existence in faith, and consequently the new relation to the law, have a christological basis. Typical in this respect is 2 Corinthians 2:12ff. Israel, like Moses, has a veil over its face (Exodus 34:33, 35), so that the children of Israel should not be blinded by the radiance which encounter with Yahweh has put on the face of Moses. The author of the law met the children of Israel indirectly or mediately through the law. The veil, says Paul, is still on today. When Israel is converted to the Lord (2 Corinthians 3:16), i.e., when it achieves immediacy to God such as Moses had when he went in before Yahweh (Exodus 34:34), the veil will be taken away.

This situation arises in Christ. In him the Lord is present directly and makes unconditional fellowship possible. For the Lord is the Spirit who imparts himself to us (2 Corinthians 3:17) and shines a bright light in our hearts, the reflection of the radiance of God in the face of Jesus Christ (2 Corinthians 4:6). In our darkness, as on creation morn, the word goes forth: Let there be light! When we have received the Spirit, we are no longer pushed by the law in the darkness. Light is kindled in us to light up the way. There develops within us the spontaneity to will what God wills and to steer for the goal that he has set. When we have received the Spirit, we, too, are "spiritual." We are thus in conformity. Reflected in us is the radiance of the Lord as Spirit (2 Corinthians 3:18).

Undoubtedly the relation to the law is radically and fundamentally changed herewith. We must now be more explicit about this mutation.

First and above all the rule of the Spirit means that freedom rules (2 Corinthians 3:17). Freedom here is release from commands and leading-strings: Do this and not that. I am now to do as I will. I have not to will what the law forces on me as its will (Romans 7:15), so that it can only be another law (*heteros nomos*) to my carnal existence.

In isolation the statement that I am now to do as I will might sound as though emancipated autonomy were being advocated. Hence everything depends on who or what is meant by the I. Emancipated autonomy arises only if the I is the old man, the subject of willing to be the carnal self. In reality, however, the reference now is to the spiritual I, the man who is determined by the Lord as Pneuma, the new creature (2 Corinthians 5:17), the I awakened to the spontaneity of love. In short, the I at issue is the changed self which can say of itself: I live, yet not I, but Christ liveth in me (Galatians 2:20; cf. Romans 6:4; Philippians 1:21; Colossians 3:3).

If this new identity of the I is kept in view, there is no need to be afraid of such audacious statements as that I am no longer subject to God's law as another law (*heteros nomos*) but am now truly autonomous. For the Spirit of God who constitutes my new identity impels me (Romans 8:14), so that I am the subject of my actions in a spontaneous way.[41] In fact, then, I may very well speak of autonomy so long as I realize that the *autos* is the changed self, the new creature, the spiritual I.[42] When I do God's will it is my own will in the sense of this "converted" autonomy.

NT EXHORTATIONS IN THEIR RELATION TO THE LAW

From this angle the law undergoes a profound change. To define this, we shall no longer consider the law as the judicial law, which is always in the background to show us what the change into a new creature really is, namely, a creative act of divine condescension which rescues me from judgment, and therefore a miracle which cannot be postulated but which we owe to the free grace of God alone. Instead, we shall now ask what the ordering, guiding, and directing command is seeking, and what is its significance, in the new situation.[43] If something is still commanded, as in Paul's exhortations, there is now no coercion contrary to my own inclination.[44] We have instead regulative aids to show me the way on which to practice obedience. Obedience, then, is not demanded as such. Spontaneous readiness for it is already present in the new creature. Instructions are simply given about the manner of obedience.[45] I am reminded how the will of God is to be done in the many phases of life, social, sexual, political, and congregational, and how the new creature will come to expression in these very different fields.

That these exhortations are reminders rather than rules, counsels rather than precepts, may be seen clearly from the way in which love of God is linked to love of neighbor, e.g., Romans 13:8-10. In a bold but plain formulation it might be said that we are not told to love our neighbor, but given to understand that we cannot fail to love him when we know that he was bought with a price and that Christ died for him (Romans 14:15;

---

[41] We shall discuss later whether the old I or Adam is also at work in opposition to spontaneity.

[42] Augustine has this I in view when he suggests that love of self is implied with love of neighbor.

[43] We refer to what is traditionally called the third use of the law; cf. ThE, I, § 624ff.; E.T. I, pp. 126ff.

[44] As Luther puts it (*Von den guten Werken*, 1520, WA, 6, 213f.), believers (according to 1 Timothy 1:9) do willingly what they know and can, marked only by their sure confidence that God's favor and good pleasure rests over them.

[45] Cf. the contested saying of Luther (ThE, I, § 652, n. 1; E.T. I, p. 134, n. 7) in the *Second Disputation against the Antinomians*, WA, 39, I, 485, 22; 7, 34, 12.

1 Corinthians 8:11). In Christ we are offered a new image of the neighbor and then asked why we should not act in correspondence with it, and why we should not view this corresponding action as a consequence of the new being. This question—in the strict sense it is not an imperative—has to be put to us because the old man still lies in wait and wants to drag us back into the defeated allegiance to the *sarx*.

Wherever the new creation is relevant to my action, this reminder is needed to keep me from being betrayed into the self-contradiction of hypocrisy which threatened man under the law.

To put it metaphorically, the outer works may be occupied by the enemy when I am safe in God's mighty fortress. The center of my existence can live in faith and yet the periphery can be threatened and may even live in contradiction to this faith. Without perceiving the contradiction I may stand in a dubious relation to money, sex, competitors, and so forth. The exhortations thus serve as a reminder by portraying the spiritual man in all his relations and thereby warning him not to let the enemy in by a side door or let him move in from the periphery to the center.

Luther depicts this threat from the periphery very graphically: "The man who believes in Christ is by God's reckoning righteous and holy. He is already in heaven, surrounded by the heaven of mercy. But while we are being carried to the Father's bosom clothed in the best robe, our feet peep out under the robe. And Satan, as he alone can, tries to bite them. Then the child kicks and screams and feels that it still has flesh and blood and the devil is still there. . . . We are holy and free, but in the spirit, not the flesh. . . . The feet still have to be washed, for they are unclean. This is why Satan can still bite them until they are clean. You must put your little feet under the robe or else you will have no peace" (*Third Disputation against the Antinomians,* 1538, WA, 39, I, 519).

The point of the exhortations is well brought out here. The feet are the outermost periphery of the I. I have not yet related them to the center of justification or brought them under the beautiful robe of honor. The law in its new form of exhortation issues a reminder: Have you thought of your feet? The conclusion of the quotation is especially significant as regards the function of exhortation. If this were the old law, I should be commanded to take active precautions against Satan's bite, to counter it with all my force, to "work" against it. But Luther says that instead of doing this I must put my little feet under the robe. I must remember that justification covers the extremities too, that these constitute the new being just as much as the heart does. Exhortation is thus a reminder. Its imperatives tell me to be in all life's dimensions what I am indicatively: a justified man living now by justification.

Exhortation is needed because I am still becoming. God has entered into a history with me which has opened but not yet ended. It is an ongoing history. The question whether and how far the redeemed man does not need the law must be given a quantitative answer: To the extent that he is a redeemed man (Luther, *op. cit.,* WA, 39, I, 528, 11ff.). As a redeemed man, however, he is still in process of becoming. He must learn to apply justification to every sphere of his life. There may still be unredeemed areas in him. His feet may not yet be under the robe. This is why a quantitative answer has to be given: To the degree that. . . .

This does not mean that he can grow out of his state of redemption and justification. It means only that he constantly learns to refer back to it or to grow into it. Entry into the new being already includes the whole. The beginning of justification does not carry with it the condition that it applies only when all the extremities are hidden under the robe. From the very first it is granted totally and unconditionally. My growth, progress, and becoming take place as I constantly go back to the beginning. As Luther puts it, progressing is simply a constant beginning. Beginning without progressing is regressing (*Exposition of Psalm 91,* WA, 4, 350, 14f.).

Although Calvin makes this third use of the law the chief one, and in this regard differs from Luther, he follows the same lines regarding the relation of indicative and imperative. For him, too, exhortation does not push us as an alien law (*heteros nomos*). It simply tells believers what is the will of the Lord they seek, confirming what they already know about this will. They need this guidance and confirmation because none has yet attained such a measure of wisdom that he cannot through instruction in the law make new progress toward purer knowledge of the divine will (Inst., II, 7, 6ff.).

The point of exhortation, then, is not to correct by legal demands the straying, inconsistent, and backsliding Christian (Galatians 2:17) who is living at odds with himself. Nor is it to lead such a Christian beyond himself. The decisive point is to refer him back to the starting-point of the new existence where he can begin again. It is to bring him to the indicative which God's new address assures me has already taken place. "Reckon ye also yourselves (*logízesthe*) to be dead indeed unto sin, but alive unto God through Jesus Christ our Lord" (Romans 6:11).

This new relation to the law, which is determined by the Spirit and fulfilled in promptitude and spontaneity, leads, then, to what seem to be conflicting statements, at any rate when viewed from outside. On the one hand we are told that in the new liberty we are free from the law, while on the other hand the assurance is given that we do not abolish the law but establish it (Romans 3:31). Seen from within, however, from the standpoint of the promptitude and the new autonomy of faith, the two statements are complementary.

To be free from the law means to be freed from its bondage and to shake off its enslaving aspect as an alien law. Establishing the law means willing what the law wills. In other words, the law is abolished to the extent that it is against us and seeks to judge or coerce us, for we are now spiritual and are lifted out of the antithesis of flesh and spirit. (This does not mean that we cease to be flesh and become docetically spiritual beings, but that we stand under forgiveness and therefore the carnal element no longer determines our existence before God, since his turning to us brings about our turning to him.) On the other hand, to the degree that the law represents the pure will of God, we establish it, validate it, and confess it. For we now will what God wills—we will it so long as and to the extent that we confess God's turning to us (we are *hypó chárin*) and therewith stand in the new obedience unto righteousness (*hypakoḗ eis dikaiosýnēn,* Romans 6:15f.).

Once again, then, we cannot simply say that Paul understands the law as such differently than the OT. Instead he proclaims that through the appearing of Jesus Christ a new phase in God's history with men has begun and a fresh step has been taken in salvation history. For in Christ we see— without a veil—the immediacy of God, his heart. In response to the love of God thus revealed and enacted, our counter-love is possible as an act of spontaneity and hence as a fulfilling of the law (Romans 13:10). Thus the law retains its validity. But we have a different relation to it.

As Paul's controversy with the "foolish Galatians" (Galatians 3:1ff.) shows, I may fall back into the old relation. Paul regards this relapse as the dreadful possibility of trying to win existence before God on one's own. The distortion in this orientation of life can be seen only when Christ is present and we learn through him what immediacy to God is. Insight into the darkness of the error is thus a true possibility only after the birth, death, and resurrection of Christ. This is why the dark side of the law cannot be seen in the OT, not even when, as in the prophets, the corruption of external observance and servile fear is brought to light. No questioning of the whole way of law as such may be found. Only when we are brought to the goal in another way, by the change of aeons and the fact of Christ, can we look back and see how mistaken was the way of law. As Hamann says, unbelief in the true historical sense is the only sin against the spirit of true religion. The secret of Christian beatitude does not lie in services, offerings, and vows which God requires of man but in promises, fulfil- ments, and sacrifices which God has given and done on man's behalf; not in the first and greatest commandment which he has enjoined but in the supreme kindness which he has bestowed (J. G. Hamann, *Golgotha und Scheblimini, Sammlung Dieterich,* 10, p. 274). Hence it is part of the one sin of unbelief if I leave again the conferred sphere of promises, fulfilments, and sacrifices, and return to the transcended sphere of services, offerings, and vows.

XVI

The Distinction between Law and Gospel in its Relevance for the New Being of the Christian

DISCUSSION OF CONTROVERSIAL INTERPRETATIONS OF ROMANS 7

If Paul has constantly to speak of the possibility of a relapse into legalism (e.g., Galatians 4:8ff.; 5:1ff.), this is not only because acute crises provoke him (*mḗ génoito*) to polemics but also because of basic connections between law and gospel which are made manifest, and brought to expression, only by these crises. Paul's reflections on the relapse into legalism are characterized by a twofold tendency.

First, we find in the background the same style of argument by opposites as in 1 Corinthians 15:12ff.: "What if Christ were not risen?"—the answer being that we should still be shut up in sin and death and the only imperative would be to eat and drink, since tomorrow we die (v. 32).[1] In the same vein he nows asks what the situation would be if Christ had not died for us. In this case we should still be in the hostile relation of flesh and Spirit, not the redemptive relation of Christ and Spirit (Galatians 5:16ff.). What appeared to be twilight, or even light, before the light was seen, is now darkness when measured by the true light (Philippians 3:8).

Second, reflection arises on the constant threat of legalism because Paul is combatting a false understanding of salvation history. This false understanding suggests that there was first a period of law but that with the change of aeons effected by Christ this has now been definitively annulled and *de facto* eliminated. Although Paul does not expressly mention this understanding, it is obviously there in the background. This may be seen from the fact that Paul refers to the constant threat that legalism might come to life again or that the man in Christ might allow the law to regain power over him and place himself anew under its vanquished control. This means that from the standpoint of the initiator of salvation history, i.e.,

---

[1] Jean Paul uses the same type of argument (based on 1 Corinthians 15:14ff.) in his atheistic vision; cf. Volume I, p. 236.

God, the law has been abolished and grace and favor rule. Thus a radical alternative to the dominion of the law has been set up. On man's side, however, there is always the possibility of relapse, unbelief, and unfaithfulness, so that from this standpoint by no means is the rule of law over with no chance at all of restoration.

In this light the debated anthropology of Romans 7ff. seems to open up an unexpected possibility of interpretation. Does not Paul understand himself here as one who, as a Christian, is harassed by this possibility of the rule of law, and harassed to such an extent that he looks back on his own past? Is he not guided by the question what the situation would be if Christ were not there, or if, like the foolish Galatians, I would not let him be there for me, if my faith in him were not the thing that exclusively determines me? Then, and only then, should I realize that I do not do what I will but what I hate, that I will the good but do not perform it (7:15). Certainly my new identity is characterized by the fact that I live, yet not I, but Christ lives in me (Galatians 2:20). But this is not an indelible character which is to be construed ontologically and which has become a static and immovable quality. This identity is imparted to me in faith. Its achievement, however, is linked not merely to past decisions but also to decisions that have constantly to be made afresh. These decisions might be negative and retrogressive. Departure from faith would mean the questioning of my identity: Who is this one who leaves his being in Christ or Christ's being in him? Is this even possible if this being is his new identity? Is he not sustained by this new being in a way that cannot be altered by conduct or work, even the work of faith?[2] Who or what, then, is the I which leaves faith, which enters again the way of law, and which comes to grief on this way?

The only answer Paul can give is that in this article of faith a basic shift in identity takes place. Whereas the believer can say: I live, yet not I, but Christ lives in me, loss of identity changes this into: I live, yet not I, but sin lives in me.[3] In neither case is the I a neutral theater for either the rule of Christ or that of the law. The I is different in the two cases, for its identity depends on that by which it is ruled. If this is the sin that dwells in me (7:17, 20), my identity is characterized by the carnal element where I began and which in the believer was replaced by spiritual existence.

That Paul, in conjuring up his past, has in mind the threatened present and the possibility of a loss of identity, is decisively shown by the final question: "Who shall deliver me from the body of this death?" (7:24). Who *shall*? The final deliverance, the definitive vanquishing of this possi-

---

[2] This is a rhetorical question for A. and T. Schlatter, who regard the new being as ontic and definitive and who thus attack Luther's understanding of Paul, especially the idea of being righteous and sinner at the same time. Cf. A. Schlatter, *Luthers Deutung des Römerbriefs* (1917); and *Erlebtes* (1924), pp. 138f.; T. Schlatter, "Für Gott lebendig in Christi Kraft, Eine Studie zu den Selbstaussagen des Paulus," *Jahrbuch d. Theol. Schule Bethel*, 1 (1930); and "Tot für die Sünde, lebendig für Gott," *ibid.*, 3 (1932).

[3] *Hē emoí hamartía* (Romans 7:20).

bility, is eschatologically ahead of me, for Christ is the Lord of the eschaton. The now of the interim is characterized by orientation to the law of God in the spirit but to the law of sin in the flesh (7:25). The now is the time of decision in which two forms of identity snatch after me and one is won and the other rejected in faith.

If, then, Romans 7 is to be interpreted not as a mere reference back to Paul's pre-Christian days but as a consideration of the dark possibility of becoming pre-Christian again and living as though Christ were not in his life,[4] then in spite of the Schlatters we come up here against something that struck Luther when he spoke of the abiding antithesis of law and gospel.[5] Might it not be that Luther has a more accurate and penetrating understanding of Romans 7 than most modern exegetes? In spite of differences in detail, did not both Paul and Luther find the same end for the abiding antithesis of law and gospel, namely, that the grace promised in the gospel and mediated by faith should never become a static thing that one may take for granted but that it should always be a new miracle of divine self-disclosure, that it should thus correspond to the openness and readiness of man but should also take into account man's possible refusal and rejection as well?

There are many indications that this is what Paul had in view, so that what he wanted to say was that Christ's presence does not mean the final ruling out of the law as a possibility or its consignment simply to the past. Formulated negatively, the statement that Christ is the end of the law and serves as righteousness to every believer (Romans 10:4) means that, while the dominion of law is ended in Christ, this does not imply that *eo ipso* its rule is ended for me. The possibility of this ending for me depends on whether I confess in faith the effected end of all legal righteousness. To set oneself outside this faith is so to set oneself outside the death of Christ and dying with him. It is thus to remain in bondage to the world and under the rod of the law (Colossians 2:20).[6] This is the impossible possibility to which I may fall victim. I can exist outside Christ's death, as though it had never happened, even though I may acknowledge it nominally. Nominal

---

[4] We take issue in this regard with G. Ebeling, who sees only a total change in situation, a definitively old and definitively new. This is partly right, for the annulment of the old is certainly definitive from God's standpoint. It is not so definitive, however, from man's standpoint. The difference between the divine and human standpoint seems to us to be the crux in the interpretation of Romans 7. Cf. G. Ebeling, "Erwägungen zur Lehre vom Gesetz," *Wort und Glaube,* I (1960), p. 270; E.T. *Word and Faith* (1963), pp. 260f.

[5] We thus oppose any basic distinction between Paul and Luther here as, e.g., in Althaus. Our position is closest to that of A. Nygren, *Commentary on Romans* (E.T. 1949), esp. pp. 265ff., and G. Dehn, "Der neue Mensch," *Theologia viatorum* (1939), pp. 67ff.

[6] Cf. Gutbrod, TDNT, IV, p. 1076, who observes that the parting of the law and Christ takes place, not in temporal history or religious history, but in salvation history, the law being done away only for him who in faith appropriates the righteousness of God in Christ.

acknowledgment was not withheld either by the Galatians, the Colossians, or the Sophists whom Luther castigated.[7] But what good is it? Acknowledgment of Christ enters my life creatively and brings about a change of lordship only when I live by the death and resurrection of Christ, relating them to me and letting my existence be determined by them, as takes place in faith. I must die and rise again with Christ. I must come to share in the Christ event. I must be drawn into it, and in so doing die to the law and acquire the new life after the law (Romans 7:1-4; Galatians 2:19; Colossians 2:20). Simply regarding as true in the sense of formal acknowledgment is not enough. It can leave me outside Christ crucified and risen. For me to be outside can be even more disastrous than it is for the heathen to be outside, for my remaining aloof takes place under the cover of Christian concepts and even perhaps of dogmatic orthodoxy.

To end the rule of the law in me, therefore, the objective fact that Christ has come and ended it is not enough, nor is mere acknowledgment of this objective fact. What is also needed is that I should accept Christ as having died for me and that I should live by appeal to this death of his for me. I appeal to it, however, only inasmuch as I enter this death of his with my whole existence, in my own dying with him. If someone is dead—Paul has said this earlier—the law has no more power over him.[8] Legal requirements no longer affect him. No matter how loud the command may be, he is silent. He no longer hears it. It does not apply to him. He is no longer under contract to it (Romans 7:1ff.). This is not Yogi insensitivity or Stoic detachment. It is a particular form of dying, i.e., dying with Christ, which protects me from the death-dealing claim of the law and sets me in a form of life in which nothing can separate me from the love of God (Romans 8:39), not even the accusing heart which serves as an advocate for the complaint of the law. Entry into the death of Christ and death to the law take place in the true faith (as distinct from that of the Sophists) which focuses on the death of Christ, claims it as that which saves, and thus ratifies the new covenant and sets it in force.[9]

WHAT DOES IT MEAN TO DIE TO THE LAW?

We must be dead to the law in Christ. Better, we must be removed from the plane where our relation to God is determined by demands. We must be changed from a relation of carnal resistance to God's will to the conformity of the spiritual man.

---

[7] Cf. the theses De fide, Drews, Disp., I, pp. 9ff. The acquired faith of the Sophists and true faith make a completely different use of the passion and resurrection of Christ. The Sophists acknowledge these formally and speculate about them, but true faith lives by them and sees them as having taken place for it, i.e., for me.

[8] For a fine interpretation of Galatians 2:19 cf. H. Asmussen's little-known commentary on Galatians.

[9] Here again we must express our dissatisfaction with Barth's emphasis on the fact that the world is reconciled in Christ, so that no ratification is needed; on the theological background of this view cf. ThE, I, § 696k ff.; E.T. I, pp. 111f.

From whom am I thus removed? To whom do I die? The insensitivity and detachment at issue may be described in two different ways.

First, I am dead and insensitive to the grasp of the law. I am referred to a dimension in which no challenge, accusation, or subsumption under the principle of achievement can any longer separate me from God. It is important, of course, that I be aware of the challenge and accusation. These are the inalienable negative constituents of faith, for faith, as we have seen, is never just faith in something but also faith against something to which it stands in the relation of a Nevertheless. Only the constant claim of the law can show me from what I have been rescued. Only when I see this can I understand the range of faith and the sphere of new freedom which it opens up. Only thus can I sense the presence of the miracle that God says to the unjust, to the man who is called in question by the law: Thou art just before me.

Having constantly before me my standing under the law is in fact one of the constituents of faith. Without this, faith would not be faith, for the one in whom it is placed would not be the God of the gospel and of gracious condescension. Instead of being the one who turns to us in miracle he would be the static figure of the good Lord. What would then correspond to him on man's side would not be the faith and trust of a Nevertheless; it would be a philosophical hypothesis, no more.

This is why Luther regarded it as a kind of spiritual exercise constantly to be aware of the claim of the law in order to keep in mind the freedom of God's grace and the miracle of the manifestation of Christ. This end was served by phrases which express the tension of law and gospel, e.g., "righteous and sinner at one and the same time," or "sinner in fact and righteous in hope."[10] The exercise is to set together the two aspects of law and gospel which our own existence bears. If I look at my actual state, my carnal condition, I cannot stand. But if I look at the cross, I am saved from the threat and am dead to the attack of the law, for another stands in the place where its searchlight would strike me, and God himself has reconciled me to himself (2 Corinthians 5:18f.; Ephesians 2:16; Colossians 1:20).

To be dead to the claim of the law is not to have forgotten it. It is not to dismiss it as unimportant. The claim remains but it no longer has any power over me if I appeal to what has happened to me, to what I am told and promised, in the death and resurrection of Christ. I am now covered. I am sheltered from the storm. But I cannot measure the fulness of the shelter if I no longer hear the raging of the storm (cf. J. Franck's hymn: Jesus My Joy).

Hostile powers are still there, but I am saved from them. Satan still accuses me; like a prosecuting attorney (Job 1:6ff.) he sets out to show that these powers have a claim on me. But their claim is denied, for Christ, and in Christ God himself, intercedes for me. The accusing law is like a

---

[10] Cf. the classic study of R. Hermann, *Luthers These "Gerecht und Sünder zugleich"* (1930).

snake whose fang has been removed. Or, to use another simile of Luther's, it is like the sloughed off skin of a snake, which looks like a living snake but cannot harm me. The reason why we have to remember the storm is that under Christ the world has not simply been rendered innocuous. There are still abysses and dangers. Only when I realize this do I see clearly that the gracious condescension of God is a historical act and that my faith is also a constantly repeated act which brings me into shelter. Dying to the law is something that must be done again and again if I am to escape the threats that are in fact always there.

Second, I am dead to the claim of the law when I am removed from its level. In our survey of the history of the relation to the law we have seen that law ends with an attack on God. The author of the law is lost in the law itself. The framework of the covenant in which the law is set is thus forgotten. Obedience to the law is misunderstood as a way of laying hold of God. By observance and formal obedience I think I can bring about specific reactions in God (e.g., rewards). I think I can use the law to gain control over events. The Satanic accuser detected something of this in the righteous Job. A popular but revealing saying: Do the right and fear no one, plainly echoes the pseudo-religious idea that God himself can be brought over to our side by our works.

This is the great illusion at the end of the way of law. I am now dead, insensitive, and immune to this illusion. I no longer need it. For I know that God's grace will take better care of me than I can do of myself—better than when I try to make God's reactions dependent on my own actions. If God is on my side, I do not need to bring him over to my side. He represents my interests more loyally than I could ever do (Matthew 6:8).

The illusion of being able to get control of God, the illusion which stimulates the law in emancipation from the covenant, the illusion from which I am now rescued, is man's primal sin in the old and new covenants.

This finds illustration in the story of the fall. When man wants to be as God and to seize the knowledge of good and evil that God has withheld from him (Genesis 3:5), he wants to manipulate God. He thus makes the prototypical attempt which is copied whenever man fashions God in his own image, makes him a function of his own wishes, and integrates him into his philosophical systems. We may also recall the way in which Yahweh counters this primal sin, man's bid for control, by refusing to give his name. When he declares himself to be "I am who I will be" (Exodus 3:14), he does not give a name. He simply says that he will be faithful to himself. In the flux of events and the contradictions of history he will always be the same. This provokes the question: Who art thou then that thou dost remain constant in thy faithfulness? In answer to this question, however, no name is given to distinguish God from other gods (but in so doing to reduce him to their level). The designation "Yahweh" simply says: My acts will show who I am, and you will be near me when you trustingly remain on the track of my acts.

Yahweh's refusal to give a name is an indication that God stays clear of man's primal sin. Magical power is attained by learning a name. If I know God's name I rob him of his inaccessibility and put him at my disposal. What can be done, however, with a magical misuse of the name of God can also be done by misunderstanding the law of God. I can come to think that I am the one who really acts. The initiative in relation to God is mine, whether this be along the lines of a primitive idea of gaining merit or along the lines of refined speculations which make God the function of social (and therefore human) situations, the product of psychogenic processes,[11] or the postulate of human reason.

The true God shatters these attempts to master him, whether by refusing his name or by transcending the resultant ideas of him. When he destroys them, the question of theodicy always arises. Job is confused because he has built his piety on an attempt at control in the form of a doctrine of correspondence between sin and penalty and merit and reward. When God does not conform to the correspondence posited by this all too human postulate, when he does what seems to be completely meaningless, absurd, and contrary to justice, the incongruence between a manipulated idea of God and his true being is brought to light. Job's new beginning consists in the corresponding insight, namely, penitent confession that we cannot control God but he controls us.

Paul's doctrine of justification answers the same question. Behind his "by faith alone" and his protest against "works" as a means of salvation there lies as a sustaining motif the thought that due honor is done to God's glory only if the temptation is resisted to make of God a mere function of the will of man. This is why the Pauline doctrine of justification restores *mutatis mutandis* the ancient sequence of covenant and law. My salvation lies in the prevenient grace of God which encounters me in Jesus Christ. In the resultant spontaneity of the new obedience I do not accomplish the act of grace; I respond to it. In the new covenant, however, there is an unheard of radicalization on both sides.

What was promise in the old covenant—that the law of God would be written in our hearts and God's Spirit imparted to us—has now become an event. For now Christ gives us righteousness and bears our sins.[12] The law, too, undergoes radicalization in the new covenant. The Sermon on the Mount has paradigmatic significance in this regard. It now tells us what it means to be wholly God's and to live in conformity with him.

This radicalizing of the law, and its profound mutation as compared with what law means prior to Christ, may be better appreciated when we remember that there were already similar attempts at radicalization of the Mosaic *nomos* in rabbinic Judaism. Here, too, the strictness of the law is applied

---

[11] So Feuerbach; cf. Volume I, Index.

[12] If God makes his righteousness mine, I am righteous with his righteousness. God is greater than our heart. The one who defends is greater than the one who accuses. . . . God is counsel for the defense, the heart counsel for the prosecution (Luther, *Comm. on Romans*, II, p. 44).

to the stratum underlying external action, i.e., the thoughts. But the content of radicalization differs sharply. Rabbinism produces a casuistical sharpening of the law by means of a concentration on the letter which leads to the obscuring or obliterating of the author of the law. On this view I become one who gains control over God by an excess of achievement, who wrings favor from God, and who is thus conscious of the claim of his own righteousness (*kauchásthai*, 1 Corinthians 1:29; Romans 3:27). In Jesus, however, the radicalization is quite different even though the formulae often sound deceptively similar.

This comes out in the fact that Jesus does not present sharper implications of the law which are on the same level as the commandments themselves. Instead his radicalization with its "I say unto you" (Matthew 5:28-44; 6:25, 29) means removal from the level of the law altogether. For the "I say unto you" means: Now that the kingdom of God is among you (Luke 17:21), now that God gives himself wholly to you, you should give yourself wholly to God. I, Jesus, do not demand more from you quantitatively than Moses did. I expect from you what Moses' law could seek only imperfectly and in a shadow, namely, your total dedication to him who totally dedicates himself to you in me.

There thus arises a distinctive ambivalence in the term "to fulfil."[13] On the one hand Jesus fulfils what the law of Moses has in view. On the other hand he destroys the whole structure of the law and leads us into a new sphere of existence before God. Between the law of Moses and its radicalization, between this law and the hour of the Sermon on the Mount, there lies the break of the change in aeons, the new situation which has come into being in Christ.

Related to this is a final point. The directness to God that is given in Christ, the new freedom and elevation above the service of the letter, is so unconditional that I can now do justice to the law. Previously this was impossible, at any rate when one looked back on the total claim immanent in the demands of God. Because it was impossible, my instinct of self-preservation, or my elemental need for self-esteem, necessarily led me to weaken the law.[14] For this type of weakening a rich spectrum of possibilities offers itself, ranging from the way in which the rabbis deal with the law to the way in which Kant limits the claim of the "thou shalt."[15]

The rabbinic weakening is very refined. It does not relax God's demands but in a sense tightens them. Yet it also weakens them to the extent that the law is no longer understood in terms of its author. If it were, the point would

---

[13] *Plērôsai*, Matthew 5:17.

[14] Gutbrod, TDNT, IV, p. 1076.

[15] I.e., by distinguishing between the immobile part of man, his constitution, for which he cannot be held responsible, and the mobile part, the area of freedom, in which ethical responsibility arises (cf. the author's *Geschichte und Existenz*, 2nd ed. [1964], pp. 68ff.).

be clear that God wants me totally.[16] Above all, he wants my heart and not just conformity to the letter. He wants my obedience, not as meritorious achievement, but as thanksgiving for, and ratification of, all that he has done for me as Lord of the covenant.

Now, however, I can survive without weakening the law. I can confess God totally. I have become objective in my estimation of the law. More accurately, I can now achieve objectivity. Objectivity is attainable only when there is no threat. A doctor threatened by cancer finds it hard to make an objective self-diagnosis. I can be objective in relation to the law only when it can do no more against me. The sentence of condemnation implicit in it, however, has already been carried out. It no longer applies to me. It has been carried out on him who represented me. I am free from the curse of the law, for another has become the curse on my behalf (Galatians 3:13; cf. 2 Corinthians 5:21).

The cross of Christ, then, is both a fulfilment of the obedience which the law demands (Romans 3:25; Philippians 2:5ff.) and also the demonstration of a love which acknowledges us even though we are "man in contradiction" (Romans 8:33ff.). Both these things were the aim of the law when seen against the background of the covenant (Deuteronomy 10:12; Romans 3:21b). It is thus disobedience to the law to want to have it except in this fulfilment.[17]

I can have it in this fulfilment, however, because it is no longer a threat, because Christ who has fulfilled it in my place is here, because he has borne its judgment in my stead. Hence the doxology of Romans 8:31-39 can contain both a Yes and also a No to the law: a Yes to what it truly intends, although I myself could not intend this prior to Christ, and a No to it as an intermediary power (Romans 5:20; Galatians 3:19) which requires of me a conformity to God that I can have only when it is given to me and not demanded from me; or, to state this ambivalence in more directly Pauline terms, a Yes to the law insofar as its true significance is known and established only through the new covenant (Romans 3:31), and a No to it to the degree that Christ is its end and has abolished it, so that it can no longer determine my relation to God (Romans 10:4).

The promise of faith which is normative for our relation to God (Galatians 3:6-16) is superior to the law in age (Galatians 3:17) and also in origin, for the law comes only through mediating angels (3:19) and is simply an interim between creation and redemption (Romans 5:20) which has come to an end in Christ.

---

[16] Luther was led to see this by the first commandment. He could never get past this, and consequently keeping the other commandments could never satisfy him. All the commandments are contained in the first. Hence the truth is, not I can because I should, but I should but will not. I do not want the one who puts me under this "should"; cf. H. Iwand, *Glaubensgerechtigkeit* (1941), p. 38.

[17] Gutbrod, *loc. cit.*

XVII

The Law in its Social Dimension
The Problem of Coercion and Autonomy

In our discussion thus far we have viewed the law as the law of God, or, with reference to the OT, as the Mosaic law. In this respect the difference between law and gospel means tension in God's own will. Coming to us as the author of the gospel, God sets himself in opposition to his claim as the author of the law. Unity and harmony cannot be restored by any suprapolar principle or teleological reference. God's coming to us in the gospel is to be proclaimed simply as an expression of his freedom and therefore as a historical act by which the Redeemer replaces the Lord of judgment.

The question arises, however, whether we have really exhausted what is meant by the law. Are there not, perhaps, other dimensions of the law, and, if so, can we not derive from them new insights into the relation of law and gospel?

These other dimensions are often mentioned by Paul. For although Paul uses *nomos* mainly for the Mosaic law, he does not do so exclusively. *Nomos* can also denote coercive forces which press in upon us in human life. "I find then a law, that, when I would do good, evil is present with me."[1] At issue is the "law in my members" which withstands the law in my mind and motives and thus takes me captive. We also learn of a "law of sin" which subjects me to specific forces of coercion (Romans 7:23). Hence the word *nomos* can denote other things besides God's law. It can be synonymous with any norm, force, or attachment to the degree that this determines the structural form of my existence and manifests itself phenomenologically.

Although Bultmann believes that we have here a play on the term *nomos*,[2] so that it is not used in a strict sense, it is still worth noting, even if we accept Bultmann's view, that the term *nomos*, normally used for God's law, suggests itself to Paul when he wants to describe the forces in life which bind, coerce, and enslave us.

Now the present question is whether the relation of law and gospel is

---

[1] *Parákeitai,* Romans 7:21.
[2] *Theologie des NT* (1953), p. 255; E.T. I (1951), p. 259.

relevant also to this law of coercion. In relation to this law, too, is the gospel the victory, liberation, and new covenant that releases me from bondage to the old Adam? Is the analogy between the different meanings of law so broad that an analogous significance and function of the gospel can be expected, too?

In an age which, like our own, is very conscious of coercive forces in society, and often seems to suffer from psychopathic fixation on them, referring constantly to the pressures of consumption, competition, structure, and achievement, and also to frustration, and singing songs of protest against them, this whole question obviously has a particular urgency.

We certainly do not do justice to it if we hastily lump all the different senses of the law together. Hence our first task must be that of achieving conceptual precision. This can be done only as we first differentiate between the law of God and the law of pressure or coercion.

The first distinction is that the law of coercion resists the law of God and blocks readiness for obedience by raising doubts as to its attainability.[3] This is true even when the law of coercion is found in contradictory impulses,[4] as in such autonomous suprapersonal structures as competition, consumption, and so forth. The common point is that the competence of God's law in various dimensions of reality is called in question. In these areas it merely raises a pretense of validity and can only take the form of heteronomous repression.

Second, whereas the law of God has a questioning and accusatory function (*usus elenchticus*), the law of coercion has an exculpatory function. When I am the subject of freedom, I affirm God's law and want to do it,[5] but I am hindered from without. My constitutional inclinations stand in the way of my ethical intentions. The autonomy of economics forces me into competition, so that I cannot treat my rivals according to the norm of *agape* but only according to the norm of conflict. The autonomy of politics forces the statesman to accept the law of the friend-foe relation and the sacred egoism of nation or race in the sense of Machiavelli, so that assertiveness and force have to be taken into account. I cannot rule the world with either the law of God or the Sermon on the Mount.[6]

It thus seems that I have to act according to the law of coercion. The intervention of God's law in this whole sphere is illusory. Nor does it make any difference whether the law of coercion acts as an inner necessity of my constitution or takes the form of the external pressure of the structures that affect me.[7]

---

[3] *Antistratenómenon*, Romans 7:23.   [4] *Nómos en toís mélesin.*

[5] Cf. the *ésō ánthrōpos* of Romans 7:22.

[6] C. Schmitt, *Der Begriff des Politischen* (1932); Max Weber, *Wirtschaft und Gesellschaft*, I (1921); also "Politik als Beruf," *Ges. Aufsätze zur Religionssoziologie* (1921/22), esp. pp. 536f.; ThE, II, 2, § 3600ff.; E.T. II, pp. 511ff.; J. Burckhardt, *Weltgeschichtliche Betrachtungen*, Kröner Bd. 55, esp. pp. 36f.

[7] Necessity and coercion are the two ways in which the bondage of the will finds realization according to Luther, WA, 18, 634; cf. ThE, I, § 1438; E.T. I, p. 297.

The law of coercion seems, then, to discharge the function of destiny. Against my own will it leads me where I do not want to go. To the extent that it plays this role, it exculpates me. For according to the intensity with which I am determined I am unable to act as a responsible subject. I am delivered up to it as an object. I thus find myself in an autonomously material sphere without values and consequently with no ethical relevance.[8] Hence it is not really I who evade and even resist God's law. The law of God and the law of coercion are two suprapersonal forces which fight it out in me and which drag me into their conflict as an innocent victim. In distinction from God's law, the law of coercion seems to acquit me. I am not guilty, for the law of coercion has no values and hence it makes the concept of guilt completely inappropriate. It leaves me no place to decide between good and evil.

Even in Paul there seems to be an echo of the principle of exculpation in Romans 7 when he speaks of the sin that dwells in me (7:17) and of the sin in my members (7:23), for this seems to be a fate, a non-I, another man than the self, a superior force of non-identity. Is it I myself that resist the divine commandment? Do I not will the good? Is it not an alien power that opposes my will? Is it not fate?

To be sure, this is only an interlude in Paul's train of thinking. It is only a kind of trial balloon which is quickly hauled down again. For having passingly referred to an alien power and to frustration from outside, Paul at once relates this to the self again. He will not let his own role be reduced to that of a function or plaything. He is subject in everything he wills and does. He is thus responsible. He is guilty in face of God's law. I—wretched man—who will deliver me from the body of this death? (Romans 7:24).

With what right, however, does he make this equation? With what right does he refuse to view the law of coercion as a power of the non-I? We must now tackle these questions.

We have already pointed out that the law of coercion and autonomy is an urgent issue in our own generation. Since this aspect has already been treated more fully in ThE, I, § 10-35, 136-181, 1783-1851; II, § 870ff., 1102ff.; E.T. I, pp. 6ff., 359ff.; II, pp. 173ff., a few general references must suffice in the present context. If theological ethics deals with social as well as individual conduct, the problem of autonomy becomes a cardinal theme. Protestant ethics has perhaps been politically and socially ineffectual because it has failed to perceive this problem and has thus confined itself very largely to a discussion of individual virtues.

F. Naumann in his *Briefen über die Religion* (1903) was one of the first to note the problem, but he does not think it out theologically and offers no solution. G. Ritter, *Die Dämonie der Macht* (1947), gives us a phenomenological depiction. The problem is taken up theologically in the *Christliche Ethik* of N. H. Søe (1949), pp. 166ff., 330ff. The immanent autonomy of other spheres is examined philosophically by F. X. Landmesser, *Die Eigen-*

---

[8] Cf. M. Weber, "Der Sinn der Wertfreiheit in den soziol. und ökonom. Wissenschaften," *Ges. Aufsätze zur Wissenschaftslehre* (1922); ThE, II, § 423ff.

gesetzlichkeit der Kultursachgebiete (1926); F. Karrenberg, *Verheissung und Verantwortung in der Wirtschaft* (1954); F. Brunstäd, *Eigengesetzlichkeit des Wirtschaftslebens* (1925); Leonore Kühn, "Das Problem der ästhetischen Autonomie," *Zeitschrift f. Ästhetik u. all. Kunstwissenschaft,* 4 (1909), pp. 16ff.; F. Kreis, *Die Autonomie des Ästhetischen in der neueren Philosophie* (1922); H. Thielicke, *Das Verhältnis zwischen dem Ethischen und dem Ästhetischen* (1932).

It is in fact astounding that Paul does not treat the law of coercion as an alien heteronomous force but ascribes to the self that which is done under compulsion. This course has not always been taken in the history of theology, especially when the law of coercion takes the form of autonomy in the fields of politics, economics, and aesthetics. In this regard we are constantly inclined to interpret the law of coercion as an alien power of fate which is immanent in the world, which comes upon us from without, and which we have to accept, since there is nothing we can do about it. The way in which modern Lutheranism has adopted and distorted the doctrine of the two kingdoms may be cited in illustration.[9]

The obvious temptation is to argue that God's law is not competent in the left-hand kingdom, since this kingdom has its own structurally determinative autonomies. Politics, economics, etc. have their own immanent norms in relation to which God's law represents a heteronomizing. The commandment to love one's neighbor and even one's enemy can have no validity when confronted by the laws of conflict and competition which may be seen in nature and history. This commandment has validity only in the kingdom on the right hand. Its proper sphere is that of piety, worship, and personal life. The final outcome of the principle of assertiveness and competition is war, which arises almost automatically, just as electricity in the atmosphere produces a thunderstorm. Why should we not agitate for the abolition of thunderstorms before we agitate for the abolition of war (D. F. Strauss)?

Acceptance of the autonomies of the secular kingdom gives rise to the following chain reaction of consequences.

First, as Christians we can only let the world run its course and acknowledge its immanent laws.

Second, we must hold aloof from it and emigrate into inner piety.

Third, since the coercive forces operate according to material laws, we must allow experts to deal with them. These are political and economic professionals. We must leave the running of the world to them.

Fourth, the commandments of God cannot force us into responsible political action, let alone resistance or revolution, since their intervention (and ours in their name) is out of place.[10]

Fifth, the church becomes quietistic and escapist. Thus a Hitler claims

---

[9] Cf. ThE, I, § 1783-1851; II, 2, § 3071-3128; E.T. I, pp. 359ff.; II, pp. 443ff., and also the Index under "Autonomy" and "Two Kingdoms."
[10] Even today a serious theologian like Künneth can argue along these lines; ThE, II, 2, § 2489ff.; E.T. II, pp. 363ff.

complete autonomy in the political sphere and protest is made only when he meddles in the kingdom on the right hand, i.e., the church.

From these consequences one may see how momentous a step is taken when forces of fate are found in the law of coercion or autonomies, when these are distinguished from the I as an alien power, and when I understand myself as an object in relation to them. Theologically we can counter the consequences only by understanding action under the coercive forces as our own action and by regarding ourselves as responsible subjects in relation to it. This is what Paul does in Romans 7:24.

We thus take up again the question which we temporarily left an open one. How is this identification possible? How can the transformation of guilt into fate be prevented.[11]

Identification of man with the law of coercion is possible only when it is seen that man is totally and unreservedly guilty before God. This in turn is possible only if God is understood as the Creator in the sense of creation out of nothing.[12] We have already drawn attention to the decisive point in this connection. If God is viewed as the Platonic demiurge who makes the world out of existing matter already laden with its own curse, then the potential curse in the world works itself out historically as the relation of guilt and fate, as in Attic tragedy. The tragic hero cannot be morally guilty in the strict sense, for he does not decide for evil as a free and responsible subject. What is worked out in him is *moira*. He is helpless in the hands of *moira*. Guilt, then, is fate. Only when I realize, in terms of creation out of nothing, that I come wholly from the hands of the Creator, and that nothing exists besides him, can I cease excusing my guilt by appealing to a cosmic matter which has overpowered me and for which I bear no responsibility.

This leads to a completely new relation between cosmology and anthropology. The created and fallen world can no longer be understood as a sphere apart from man with its own significance. It forms man's macrocosmic sphere which bears the marks of its original in every area. Thus Adam is the exemplary and representative prototype of this aeon, just as Christ is the prototype of the new aeon. I am this world, including its structures and orders. It is the macrocosmic representation of my heart, just as my heart is the microcosmic representation of the world.[13] Hence I do not stand in relation to my world as another. Its secularity is my form of being.

The Sermon on the Mount adopts and imparts this view. Its radicalizing of the Mosaic *nomos* makes sense only if the identity of the I with its world and with the structures of its world is perceived.

If I do not kill but hate my neighbor (Matthew 5:21ff.), if I do not commit adultery but lust after a woman (5:28), I cannot say that this is my

---

[11] In this context we can offer only a brief answer to this question. For a more systematic and extensive treatment cf. ThE, I, § 2144; E.T. I, pp. 434ff.

[12] ThE, I, § 712ff., 1330ff.

[13] Francis Thompson's poem *The Heart:* "And all man's Babylons strive but to impart / The grandeurs of his Babylonian heart."

constitutional disposition or impulse and that this is no part of the inner man, with which alone I am identical. I have to say that this sphere, too, is my I. I can no more isolate my impulses than I can isolate the world. (This is not an abstract principle. It finds expression in ethical experience. An envious person, if he is self-critical, can act with friendliness toward the one he envies even though dislike burns behind the external facade. Self-critically he cannot say: I am my friendliness and the dislike is a power of the non-I which fills me in spite of myself. He has to say: I am envious. He notes this identification to his shame.)

Again, as a politician or businessman I may pander to the sacred egoism demanded by the principle of competition. But if I do, I cannot argue as follows: On the one side is the I of the inward man and this I wills Christian love, seeking the things of others rather than self, while on the other side is the evil world with the autonomy of its economic and political structures to which I must conform and which prevents me from doing what I really want to do. The evil world as the sphere of the non-I hampers the development of the true I.

When I come face to face with the divine requirement it is clear to me that I cannot make this distinction between the I and the world. My own heart objectifies itself in secular structures and their autonomous pressure. The world is the structurally shaped essence of my heart. I cannot view even war as a fate which comes upon me from the outside world with no contribution at all on my part. I cannot do this even when I regard the war as a just war and see myself summoned to resist aggression. Even when I believe it is my duty to take part in a war of defense, as a Christian I learn (or ought to learn) that God does not want war, that it is a phenomenon of the fallen world, and that the ambivalence and discord manifested in it are the signature of my own heart (Romans 2:15).

Thus the harsh and apparently alien aspect of the Sermon on the Mount is its true point. It makes its demands with no regard for constitutional factors such as the impulses or for the limitations imposed on my personal will by autonomous structures. To that extent it seems to be remote from the world and alien to it. It claims me totally, with the sphere of impulse and the substructure of the world as well. It does not claim me merely in a sphere of personal freedom. It thus compels me to identify myself with my total I. Hence I have to see in the world, not merely the creation of God, but also the structural form of human sin, i.e., its suprapersonal form, the "fallen" world. When I am forced to speak of the fallen world in this way, I cannot say that the world out there has fallen and that it now draws me into its fallenness. I have to confess that I myself have fallen, and that what I see out there is the structural objectification of my fall.

There thus arise the radical demands of the Sermon on the Mount. These have rightly been described as eschatological. They still address me as though I were in the original state and they already address me as though I were in God's kingdom rather than this aeon. This means that I have to identify myself now with this aeon and its structures.

A central intention behind my "Political Ethics" (ThE, II, 2) was to bring out the significance of this identification in the field of political ethics. This might be summarized in the three theses that follow.

(1) It is impossible on this view to idealize secular structures or to make them normative as in the idea of the totalitarian state or the vision of perfect social orders. The fallen world rules out the achievement of utopias. Perception of its ambiguity is the best antidote to fanaticism.

(2) It is also impossible on this view to entertain the illusion that the world can be brought to perfection by improving its structures and creating conditions in which will be no domination, egoism, or frustration. The ambiguity of the structures of the world is grounded in the human heart. Hence they cannot be corrected in isolation. Possibly this is why the NT proclaims no social program. It does not deal with symptoms. It deals radically with the human heart. Thus the Epistle to Philemon does not directly attack the structure of slavery. It sets up the relation of love, and in so doing accomplishes a reorientation of the heart which affects social structures, e.g., by undermining slavery (ThE, II, 1, § 2060ff.; E.T. II, pp. 642ff.). Political preaching is important insofar as it draws attention to certain political and social goals and then, instead of merely announcing a program, goes on to tackle the human heart as the root of all conditions; cf. the author's "Können sich Strukturen bekhren) Zu einem Grundproblem aktueller Sitialethik," ZThK (1969), 1, pp. 98-114, and *Christentum und Gesellschaft,* ed. W. Lohff and B. Lohse (1969), pp. 248ff.

(3) It is finally impossible on this view to adopt a *laissez-faire* attitude to the autonomies, as though they had the ineluctability of fate and as though this excused us. Realizing that the destiny of man is at issue, and well aware of the ambiguity of the autonomies, I cannot make a virtue out of the necessity of these coercive forces. I must wrestle with them, trying to detect chinks in their armor and to find places where I can make my own decisions.

We thus come up again against the central question which was raised at the outset: Is the relation of law and gospel relevant even when by law we do not have in view the Mosaic form of God's law but the law of coercion with its very different characteristics? In other words, is the gospel a power which liberates us also from bondage to the autonomies, and, if so, how far?

Three considerations incline us to answer this question in the affirmative.

Our first consideration is that the promise of the gospel imparts the certainty that nothing—and this includes the alienating and commandeering structures of the fallen world—can separate us from the love of God which is in Christ Jesus our Lord (Romans 8:38f.). There is spiritual armor against the forces of this aeon which seek to rule over us (Ephesians 6:12ff.). Promised shelter from their threat also offers us the chance of clear vision undistorted by imprisonment. Pressures force us to be defensive and assertive. Unrestricted vision means that we are no longer subject to blocks which prevent us from identifying ourselves with the secular structures and autonomies. We can admit (and confess) not only what we have done but also what we are. Confessing that we cry out of the depths (Psalm 130:1), we have in mind not only individual depths but also the depths of the world. As we say to God: "Thou hast searched me and known me" (Psalm 139:1), what is in view is not just emancipated individuality but also the I as the representative of the world and its total state, as the representative of this aeon and its condition.

Part of the freedom of the gospel is the freedom to see, or, as one might call it, the freedom of objectivity in which I confront myself and can perceive and confess my structural entanglement. Seeing autonomies and coercive pressures compels me not to view them as fate which seizes me but which I can then use as an excuse. It compels me not to limit my guilt to the sphere of individual freedom.

The second consideration is that the gospel teaches me not to regard the proffered chance of love merely in such a way that I acquire a new relation to the immediate Thou of my neighbor but also in such a way that I see this neighbor in his structural involvement and thus realize that the task of loving him is a much bigger one. If I see how my neighbor is exposed to structural pressures, how he is exploited by capitalists, how he is subjected to the forces of a consumer society, how he is brought under the unheard of pressure of competition, or how he is understood as the bearer of a utilizable power of productivity, then I see how he is thereby threatened with self-alienation and can be damaged not merely in his physical existence but also in his "soul." Against the inclination to direct moral appeals merely to conscience and personality the objection might be raised that food comes first and morality second.

Identification of man with his structural entanglements can never be made generally and indiscriminately. In this area there are levels of guilt. Different people undoubtedly bear different degrees of responsibility for a social structure which alienates man. Dependents and those on fixed incomes who are reduced to poverty are far less to blame than the powerful class of politicians and managers. It is far too big a simplification to speak of man in the mass in this context. It is not just man in general who is forced by the Sermon of the Mount to identify himself with the autonomies and pressures of this aeon. Such a simplification might itself become a means of evasion. For the identification might come to be regarded as a kind of fate. C'est l'homme! C'est le monde! Instead of this we are called upon to fight sin, including the sin of structures, and sinning against men and groups of men, whom we see subjected to unjust and alienating structures.

To this extent love of neighbor does not simply mean being there for the individual man whom one encounters. It also means averting from him as far as possible that which threatens him structurally. What this implies is that the sphere of love also carries with it suprapersonal tasks, e.g., those of a political, economic, or social nature.

We have to admit that although Marx had another purpose and used a different terminology, it was he who drew attention to this dimension of love. Marx did not interpret poverty as an individual phenomenon which could be alleviated by individual means, e.g., free meals and financial help. He viewed poverty as the inevitable result of a particular social system. By owning the means of production the capitalist class enjoys monopolistic power, which expropriates the proletarian masses and degrades men to the level of bearers of a marketable power of work.

The validity of the diagnoses and prognoses of Marx is not our present concern. More important is the new thematic intention of his thinking. Concern for man poses above all the task of changing the structures which oppress and devalue him, and which finally warp his personality. If the fault lies in the system, help can come only by altering the system. This insight should lead Christians to the point where love takes up the task of working at the system.

This is (1) a task of reflection. It has to be shown—reason has also to be at work in love—whether and how far hurt is done to the neighbor through faulty structures which can be changed.

Then (2) the question of therapy arises. How can help be given? Can it come from within the system by revision or reform? Or does there have to be a revolutionary and perhaps even a violent overthrow of the system? What is now unhappily called the theology of revolution[14] is in no way compromised by the belief that revolution itself can be a task of *agape,* but in the last resort simply by the fact that *agape* and its theological basis are less important than a messianic and utopian institutional perfectionism.[15]

Maximal efficiency of love (3) is important in the one who loves and who wants to help in love. This cannot be achieved simply by dealing with symptoms in individuals in a kind of patch-up job. It can be achieved only by the rationalization which comes about with the alteration of systems and structures.

Finally (4) the love which truly helps does not consist merely in extending aid when disaster has struck but also in warding off threatening disaster. This preventive action can be effective, however, only if the system which tends to bring disaster is changed.

Along these lines new dimensions of love are demanded of an age which has achieved wholly new insights into the way in which man is conditioned by social structures.

This means that some of the points made in the parable of the Good Samaritan have to be developed (Luke 10:25ff.). While the intention of the parable must not be distorted, a new focus is needed. Let us suppose that the Samaritan had some public office, e.g., that he was mayor of his town. It would then have been his duty to consider what steps could be taken to prevent travellers being molested in the same way in the future.

---

[14] The pioneer was Richard Shaull, *Encounter with Revolution* (1955). The literature is now enormous.

[15] Cf. the author's "Können sich Strukturen bekehren?" *art. cit.,* pp. 103ff.

Police would have had to be set up to patrol the road. Arrested robbers would have had to be asked why they had taken to a life of crime. Possibly hunger and poverty would have been brought to light as contributory causes and then the Samaritan would have had the chance to deal with crime at its root, i.e., at the level of the system.

Our third and final consideration is that when the gospel brings to light these new and, from the traditional standpoint, unusual aspects of *agape*,[16] it is distinguished from secular messianic and utopian theories of revolution by its constantly keeping before us the reason why we have to work at changing the structures. This reason is love. And love itself is grounded in the new view of man which is mediated by the gospel. To love another man is to see him in relation to God. It is thus to realize that he is bought with a price (1 Corinthians 6:20; 7:23), that God is concerned about him. *Agape* is not motivated by pragmatic interests, by the usability or social productivity of the neighbor. It is motivated by his alien dignity, by what he means for God.

What does it imply concretely that this new view of man which we are given by the gospel is the true point of orientation for our work on the structures?

At this point a momentous mistake might be made—and there are good reasons for saying this. We might be inclined to argue that, since this is how matters stand with man, the only thing that counts is to tell him that he is loved by God, that he has been bought with a price, that God's love embraces and upolds him in spite of his present misery, and that because we as Christians have also experienced this love of God, we love him too. We might then press this dubious argument further and say that if the man who is told this accepts it, he is changed or converted. A change is thus brought about at the center of the world, namely, the human heart. Since his heart, as we have seen, is a microcosmic image of the world, and since the structures of the world, including their pressures and autonomies, are simply a superstructure and objectification of the heart, the change in the heart will also find structural expression. Or, to put it more simply and impressively: change men and the world will change itself. If the Babylonian heart is converted the great Babylon of the world will undergo a similar conversion.

I have described this as a momentous mistake. But why? Are we not led to a conclusion of this type if we take seriously the analogy between the structure of the heart and the structure of the world, between the law of egoism in our members and the autonomy of sacred egoism in politics?

The conclusion seems to be a natural one but it is wrong all the same. We have already pointed out that man is alienated and can be warped by unjust and exploitative structures. There is thus the possibility of deafness to every message of love. Or, better, the message of love may lack credi-

---

[16] On the newness of these dimensions cf. ThE, II, 2, § 1924-2193; E.T. II, pp. 289-317.

bility. If it is proclaimed by those who represent a loveless world of exploitation and who do nothing to promote change, the idea might be (and is in fact) conveyed to the recipient that he must be reconciled to his fate, that he must be quiescent, that he must soothe his anger with the opium of religion. Behind the message of love there is thus seen the ulterior motive of stabilizing the status quo. Instead of leading to this kind of reflection, perverted structures might even drive alienated and distorted man into crime and a confusion of all values, so that we are finally confronted by pure inhumanity, by human bestiality.

This shows us how wrong it can be to begin with a message of love in a loveless world which is left unchanged, and to entertain the illusion that a disordered world will soon be set to rights once the human heart is affected and changed by this message. Some situations and structures can in fact block the message. Hence many young Christians are right when they say that before preaching we must remove the obstacle by doing something to change the world, and that before speaking about righteousness by faith we must first make the world more righteous. Otherwise the injustice of the world and our own passivity in face of it will rob what we proclaim of any credibility. Before we preach to the rock and drug world we must first draw alongside the people of this world as brothers and set up a fellowship with them which will counteract their innate impulse for perversions of this kind. Only in this way, if at all, can we win a hearing for our proclamation.

Here, however, a new problem arises. A switch can take place which will lead to a new error. Where once it was held that changing the human heart can change the world and its structures, the opposite illusion will be entertained, namely, that changing the world can change the human heart.

A Hamburg pastor has said this in the clearest possible terms: "Theology thus far has sought to change man in order to change the world; we are seeking to change the world in order to change man" (*Hamburg Abendblatt* [1968], 300, IV). Theologically speaking this is a new form of the righteousness of works. The righteousness of works has always had its source in the illusion that man can achieve self-fulfilment by his own action. Today this illusion has simply been transferred from the individual sphere to the collective sphere. It now runs as follows: Since man is the product of social relations he actualizes himself by manipulation of the relevant relations. To the extent that he achieves perfection in the relations he himself becomes perfect, so that in the end even crime and the impulse of aggression will be extinguished (so Herbert Marcuse; cf. my book *Kulturkritik der studentischen Rebellion* [1969], pp. 40ff.; R. Havemann, *Dialektik ohne Dogma?* [1964]).

In consequence of this passion for changing the world even Christian theologians can reach the point where they simply draw up and carry out programs of practical action, where they fill up their time with statistical analyses and revolutionary activity, and where they do not accord any recognizable role to the message of love as the generative impulse and standard of every change. We thus finish up with utopian dreaming and a preoccupation with the future, which no longer understands God's kingdom as that which encompasses us transcendentally but understands it simply as a goal of future actualization. But even if it were attainable, what kind of a world would this be which is envisioned, and whose attainment is sought, according to a model of institutional perfection? Might it not be a world in whose smooth functioning man would freeze to death in spite of every attempt at acclimatization? Might it not be a world of contented lemurs which, well fed and superbly adjusted to an ingenious social apparatus, would proceed from cradle to grave with neither risk nor conflict? What are these utopias which are being dreamed up here?

As is surely plain by now, we must avoid both mistakes. The question whether the heart must be changed to change the world, or the world must be changed to change the heart, poses a false alternative. Is there, then, a third option?

The third option is that the motive of love should direct every concept of world change and every attempt to correct the structures of the world. Negatively this means that such concepts and attempts are not to be formed or undertaken merely for the sake of structural perfection. I must not think that I can reverse the fall or that I can produce a new man with the help of new relations. I must not fall victim to the illusion that the correspondence between the structure of the world and that of the heart can be abolished and that a newly fashioned world can be the *cause* of a changed man. (We have shown already how inhuman a world might result from the desire for perfection and for a smoothly functioning apparatus.)

The question, then, is that of our motives and intentions in working for the changing of the world. Do I do this work for the sake of man? Do I do it, then, because I have discovered the structural dimension of *agape*?

If *agape,* and the view of man influenced by it, is the impulse and goal behind my program for the alteration of the world and what I seek to accomplish by it, then this is not limited to the inner sphere of subjectivity or mere motivation. It also comes to exercise a determinative influence both on the material content of my goals and also on the methods by which I seek to achieve them.

With this compass in my hand I am safe against the tendency to view the desired order of things as an end in itself, i.e., in perfectionist terms, and thus to ascribe to man a purely dependent and functional role. I realize that the Sabbath—or an achieved shaping of the world—is made for man and not man for the Sabbath (Mark 2:27). I will thus seek arrangements which make possible a just peace in social, racial, and national affairs, and which reduce as much as possible the gap between rich and poor. I will work against the anonymity of institutions and the loneliness of the masses. I will open up the field for personality and communication[17] and try to check the impersonal rule of the collective. I will also be careful

---

[17] Cf. ThE, III, § 203ff. and esp. § 243-671.

not to make freedom an ideological end in itself, not to make the virtue of freedom a necessity which simply makes a monopoly of the superiority of stronger individuals, races, and classes.[18] I will thus seek the establishment of a state which makes no claim to omnipotence but which is also not a mere caretaker state that passively accepts the chaos of egotistical individuals and groups and their conflicting claims for freedom.

These suggestions are not an explicit program. They are simply illustrations of the way in which concepts of world change might develop when they are decisively determined by love and by the view of man influenced by it. Planning informed by this goal will be proof against utopian and perfectionist dreams, for the planner will realize that even at best orders of this type can offer only chances of humanization and the overcoming of alienation. They cannot achieve humanization automatically or prevent alienation automatically. They are still affected by the profound ambivalence which has confronted us in our consideration of the structure of the fallen world. Even a world which comes very close to justice and peace can still give birth to new forms of egoism, selfishness, and excess of freedom. It can produce a sequence of good days which are hard to bear, which can become a source of temptation, and which offer the devil new points of entry. There are no institutional safeguards against the devil. No matter what new form the world might be given it will still remain in the half-light between creation and the fall.

It might well be true, and indeed it is, that we cannot declare the message of love, the gospel, without becoming involved in plans and acts of love, i.e., without trying to organize a form of the world which will help to ward off the miseries of hunger, poverty, and injustice, which will work against the alienation of man and the blocking of his ability to hear, and which will also bring opportunities for humanization. The message of love, the gospel, cannot be brought to man if the world is accepted unchanged. For this involves misuse of the gospel as false consolation in face of the suffering that man has incurred. It means offering the gospel without the law. Our condition and the state of the world cannot be called in question if the gospel alone has force. On its own the gospel becomes no more than the message of the good Lord who is well intentioned toward individuals in their sufferings but unable to generate any will to change things. It becomes the message of the God who is like the impotent old man in Borchert's play *Draussen vor der Tür,* who cries over the misfortunes of men but can do nothing to stop them. Understood thus, the gospel of mere consolation is indeed opium for the people. Its hereafter is a tactically invented paradise which makes men ready to endure passively the miseries of the here and now. It thus becomes a demonic weapon to stabilize the status quo, whereas the message of love that the true gospel proclaims demands the changing of relations and structures.

---

[18] Cf. E. Heimann's criticism of the ideology of freedom in his *Reason and Faith in Modern Society* (1961), pp. 39f.

If the evangelical message of love is impossible without the planning and undertaking of world change, so, too, is the idea that world change must be achieved before preaching of the gospel can begin. There has to be simultaneity here. For those who with a particular sense of political responsibility evolve conceptions of world change, the decisive issue is in whose name they do this, whether they are directed by an ideology, e.g., Marxist-Leninist or Maoist, or by the view of man which is found in the message of love. In the latter case the message is already normatively present in every initiative for the changing of the world; indeed, it is itself the trigger for all movement in this direction.

If this is so, if the gospel is at one and the same time the motive of love and the spur to alteration of the world, this means that simultaneity is not to be replaced by chronological sequence. Hence no changing of the world can be sought or achieved in the name of love unless the motive which is the source of it all is proclaimed at the same time, i.e., unless the gospel is also preached and confessed. How can we possibly fail to refer to a motivating force of this kind? To do this is to deny its determinative role. It is thus to make it completely subordinate to the shaping of the world, as it actually is among many social revolutionaries, critics of society, and utopians with a Christian or theological background. In these circles the message which forms the original motivation is crowded out by postulates, programs, and activities. But how, then, will those whom they address perceive it? They will rightly ask why they should buy such things as psychotherapy (which as an extension of pastoral care is also an expression of Christian love) or pleas for racial harmony in a Christian package when round the corner they can buy the same things in a secular one which seems indeed to be a little more up to date. Perhaps the Christian wrapping appeals to those who are sentimental enough to like the old symbols, but the number of these is melting rapidly under the sun of secularized theology.[19]

Naturally the demand that preaching of the gospel and world change should go hand in hand in indissoluble union does not mean that proclamation must stop when there is no opportunity for world change. For this would imply that the gospel should not be passed on from the weak and suffering to the weak and suffering, as, e.g., in a concentration camp.[20] The love awakened by the gospel can bear witness to itself in solidarity with those who suffer even when nothing can be done to change the world or conditions in it. Sometimes the resolve to change the world which love engenders can display itself only partially, e.g., when the message comes not only as good news to the suffering and oppressed but also as law to rulers, officials, and executioners, as may be seen from the example of Paul Schneider, the preacher of Buchenwald, who not only comforted his fellow-

---

[19] P. L. Berger, *A Rumor of Angels. Modern Society and the Rediscovery of the Supernatural* (1969).

[20] Cf. the autobiographies of H. Grüber (1968) and C. Zuckmayer (1966); Volume I, p. 228, n. 4.

captives, but reproached his tormentors for their sins with loud cries from his cell window.[21]

The worker-priests were trying to do something similar when they associated with their proletarian brethren, and by sharing their political and economic interests and entering the class struggle they also brought injustice to the attention of rulers.[22] Even in situations of special stress under ideological dictatorship the union between the gospel of love and the motive of world change which love inspires can never be completely broken. Apart from direct plans for revolution[23] this can come to expression especially in the admonishing and comforting of the oppressed and in the contribution which the involved church can make to unsettling of the government by castigating it for its misdeeds.[24]

The mere fact that the Christian message, seen from the social and political standpoint, always speaks (or ought to speak) to both sides, rulers and ruled, tormentors and tormented, privileged and deprived, expresses the simultaneity by and in which the message of the word of the gospel is bound to the law that judges. Only the *extent* to which commitment to world change can or cannot lead to far-reaching plans and actions depends upon the situation and its possibilities—which naturally vary in democracies and despotisms based on terror—and upon the influence and gifts of the persons concerned. Only the *extent!* In *principle* the simultaneity of the two tasks always remains.

We may sum up as follows. The initial question was whether the relation of law and gospel retains its significance even when by law we do not mean God's commandments but the pressures and autonomies of material spheres and the restrictive relationships of rule in general. Has the gospel antithetical and liberating significance in regard to these laws as well?

We found the decisive starting-point for an answer in a theological understanding of the coercive pressures and autonomies. These are not a fate which hangs over us, which robs us of responsibility, and which thus exculpates us. They are the macrocosmic and suprapersonal expression of the human heart which here bears witness to itself in its creatureliness and fallenness. They are thus the signature of the fallen world with which I have to identify myself: I am this fallen world.

This means that the promised forgiveness of the gospel extends also to my

---

[21] J. Erb, *Die Wolke der Zeugen,* II (1954), pp. 518ff.

[22] In ruling against the worker-priests the Vatican expressed a justifiable or unjustifiable concern that the message of love was here being made secondary to the social conflict which love demands and that the simultaneity of message and action was thus being dissolved. On the problem of the worker-priests cf. H. Perrin, *Tagebuch eines Arbeiterpriesters* (1955); G. Cesbron, *Die Heiligen gehen in die Hölle* (1953).

[23] E.g., the plot against Hitler on July 20, 1944. For the Christian background of this plot cf. G. Ritter, *Carl Goerdeler und die deutsche Widerstandsbewegung* (1954).

[24] This is how M. Niemöller, the Evangelical bishop T. Wurm, and the Roman Catholic bishop Graf Galen understood their ministry of proclamation under National Socialism.

involvement in the world. This involvement would itself be transposed into fate if I were simply to accept it as given. But this is impossible, for the responsibility and participation of different individuals and groups in relation to world conditions vary enormously. The upper classes and the lower classes have different opportunities to make changes and are victims to varying degrees. Hence the gospel cannot be regarded merely as comfort to the relations that now exist. It also carries with it the demand to change the world in the name of love.

In the name of love means that the direction of world change is not fixed by a utopian state which is understood as an end in itself. The norm is the picture of man that the message of love presents, namely, the picture of one who is bought with a price, whom God calls by name, who is not made for the Sabbath or for institutions. In this sense the proclamation of the gospel and the implied task of working at the structures of the world (love in structures) are bound together in an indissoluble simultaneity.

Thus the tension and interrelation of law and gospel still apply, although in a different way, even when what we understand by law is not the law of Moses and God but the law of structures, forces, and dominions. As we adopt this course, subsuming these different things under the single concept of law, and yet retaining a sense of difference between them, we follow up a line that is already indicated in Paul, for he too, as we have seen, understands by *nomos* not only the law of God that calls us in question and judges us but also coercive forces and ineluctabilities of a very different kind.

Part Two

THE FORM OF REVELATION:
GOD THE SON

Bibliography

1. Questions of Dogmatics and History: R. Slenczka, *Geschichtlichkeit und Personsein Jesu Christi* (1967); H. Braun, "Der Sinn der nt.lichen Christologie," ZThK (1957), 3, pp. 341ff.; G. Ebeling, "Kerygma und historischer Jesus," *Theologie und Verkündigung* (1962), pp. 19ff.; E.T. *Theology and Proclamation* (1966); M. Kähler, *Der sogenannte historische Jesus und der geschichtliche biblische Christus*, 2nd ed. (1928); H. W. Kuhn, "Der irdische Jesus bei Paulus," ZThK (1970), 3, pp. 295ff.
2. Monographs on Jesus: G. Bornkamm, *Jesus von Nazareth* (1956); E.T. 1960; G. Gloege, *Aller Tage Tag. Unsere Zeit im NT* (1960); K. Heim, *Jesus der Herr*, 4th ed. (1953); E.T. *Jesus the Lord* (1959); M. Dibelius, *Jesus* (1939); E.T. 1949; O. Dibelius, *Bericht von Jesus aus Nazareth* (1941); H. Zahrnt, *Es begann mit Jesus von Nazareth* (1960).
3. The Self-Consciousness of Jesus: O. Cullmann, *Heil als Geschichte* (1965), pp. 89ff.; E.T. *Salvation in History* (1965), pp. 107ff.; H. J. Kraus, *Julius Schniewind* (1965), pp. 173ff.; K. Rahner, "Dogmatische Erwägungen über das Wissen und Selbstbewusstsein Christi," *Schriften zur Theologie*, V (1962), pp. 222ff.; E.T. *Theological Investigations*, V (1966), pp. 193ff.; J. Ternus, "Seelen- und Bewusstseinsleben Jesu," *Das Konzil von Chalkedon*, III (1954), pp. 81ff.; A. Vögtle, "Exegetische Erwägungen über das Wissen und Selbstbewusstsein Jesu" in H. Vorgrimler, ed., *Gott in Welt*, I (*Festgabe K. Rahner*, 1964), pp. 608ff.
4. The Death and Resurrection of Christ: P. Althaus, "Das Kreuz Christi," *Theologische Aufsätze*, I (1929), pp. 1ff.; E. Bizer, W. Fürst, J. F. G. Goeters, W. Kreck, W. Schrage, *Das Kreuz Christi als Grund des Heils* (1967); H. von Campenhausen, *Der Ablauf der Osterereignisse und das leere Grab*, SBAW (1952); H. Conzelmann, E. Flesseman-van Leer, E. Haenchen, E. Käsemann, E. Lohse, *Zur Bedeutung des Todes Jesu* (1967); H. G. Geyer, "Die Gegenwart Christi: Die Auferstehung," *Dtsch. Ev. Kirchentag Hannover* (1967); H. Grass, *Ostergeschehen und Osterberichte* (1956); E. Käsemann, "Die Gegenwart Christi: Das Kreuz" (as Geyer, *op. cit.*, pp. 424ff.); G. Koch, *Die Auferstehung Jesu Christi* (1959); W.

Künneth, *Theologie der Auferstehung*, 4th ed. (1951); Richard R. Niebuhr, *The Resurrection and Historical Reason* (1957); U. Wilckens, *Auferstehung* (1970).
5. Monographs on Christology: P. Althaus, "Christologie, dogmatisch," RGG³, I, 1777ff.; O. Cullmann, *Christologie des NT* (1957); E.T. *The Christology of the NT* (1957); G. Ebeling, "Leitsätze zur Christologie," *Theologie und Verkündigung* (1962), pp. 83ff.; E.T. pp. 83ff.; F. Gogarten, *Jesus Christus, Wende der Welt* (1966); M. Kähler, "Die Lehre von der Versöhnung," *Dogmatische Zeitfragen*, II, 2nd ed. (1908); W. Pannenberg, *Grundzüge der Christologie* (1964); E.T. *Jesus God and Man* (1968); K. Rahner, "Probleme der Christologie von heute," *Schriften zur Theologie*, I, 6th ed. (1962), pp. 169ff.; E.T. pp. 149ff.; Also "Auferstehung des Fleisches," *op. cit.*, II, pp. 211ff.; E.T. pp. 203ff.; also "Die ewige Bedeutung der Menschheit Jesu für unser Gottesverhältnis," *op. cit.*, III, pp. 47ff.; E.T. pp. 35ff.; also "Zur Theologie der Menschwerdung," *op. cit.*, IV, pp. 137ff.; E.T. pp. 105ff.; also "Die Christologie innerhalb einer evolutionären Weltanschauung," *op. cit.*, V, pp. 183ff.; E.T. pp. 157ff.; also "Chalkedon — Ende oder Anfang?" *Das Konzil von Chalkedon*, III (1954), pp. 3ff.; K. L. Schmidt, E. Gaugler, R. Bultmann, A. Gilg, E. Wolf, M. Dominicé, *Jesus Christus im Zeugnis der heiligen Schrift und der Kirche*, Beihefte zur ETh, 2 (1936); G. Thomasius, *Christi Person und Werk*, I-IV (1856ff.); H. Vogel, *Christologie*, I (1949); O. Klumpp, F. Mildenberger, G. Ebeling, J. Baur, H. Diem, *Was heisst: Ich glaube an Jesus Christus?* ed. Ev. Landessynode in Württemberg (1968).

XVIII

Preamble: The Systematic Place and Method of Christology

1. THE SYSTEMATIC PLACE

The theological point of what we were working out in Part I on the origin of revelation may be summed up in the thesis that the Creator is never identical with creation, that God is not absorbed and integrated into the process which he initiates. As the one who remains different from his action and work, he is always the same, identical with himself, in this action and work. We thus encounter one and the same God in creation and redemption, in the once of the past, the experience of the present, and expectation of the future. "The same yesterday, today, and for ever" (Hebrews 13:8) applies no less to him who made the world, to him who accompanies it to its end in judgment, grace, and providence, than it does to Christ, in whom he comes into the world in bodily presence, constituting himself a part of it even while he remains distinct from it. Thus the trinitarian division of our doctrine of revelation (Father, Son, and Holy Spirit) points to the fact that we can think of the one God only in the different forms of his self-disclosure.

If, however, there are different forms of this kind—three different forms according to the doctrine of the Trinity—how can we describe Christ as *the* form of revelation? In so doing do we not say both too much and also too little? Do we not say too much inasmuch as Christ is only one among many forms of revelation? Is he not a latecomer in world events? Was there not a long period prior to his birth? Do we not have to describe also as a form of revelation the way in which God revealed himself in creation or made himself known to Abraham, Isaac, and Jacob, to the patriarchs and prophets? Is it not, then, too much to speak of Christ as *the* revelation? On the other hand, is it not also too little? If it is God himself whose seeking, sacrificing, and condescending love is present in Christ, is not the term "form" far too formal and external, and hence wholly inappropriate? If God is *in* Christ, if he *is* in him (2 Corinthians 5:19), what is implied is material identity and not just formal and external manifestation. God comes into the very depths of humanity. As we noted earlier, this is no mere masquerade or shadow play or pedagogically intended symbolism. Is it not saying too little, then, to call Christ merely the "form" of divine revelation?

The first question, whether Christ may rightly be called *the* form of the divine self-disclosure, not just one form, can be answered only with an exposition of Christology itself. Nevertheless, in order not to keep the reader on tenterhooks, the following hints as to the direction we shall take may be given already.

We have spoken of the threefold identity of God. We have also shown why we must do this. If we do, however, Christ is the second form of the Godhead not merely from the time of his historical incarnation but "from the foundation of the world" (Ephesians 1:4; 1 Peter 1:20). The Logos which is in God and which becomes history is already "in the beginning" (John 1:1). The lofty way in which the Johannine Christ speaks of himself also points to this identity: "Before Abraham was, I am" (John 8:58). Particularly to be noted here is the tense—the eternal present. Christ's being in eternity, which is the incommensurable framework of his historical presence from A.D. 1-30, finds formulation in the doctrine of the pre-existence of Christ.

Christ's pre-existence is in fact an inalienable element in any theology with a trinitarian orientation. The problem is not whether pre-existence has to be accepted but how it is to be expressed. Its denial is always connected with an Antiochene Christology which finally leads to an understanding of Christ merely as the most human of men. On the other hand, if it is made the main point of Christology and hence the presupposition of all else that is to be said in this field, the incarnation threatens to become a mere exemplification and illustration of what has always been, so that it loses its character as a contingent act of God.[1] Nevertheless, no matter how we may speak of pre-existence, and no matter how dubious many of our reflections on it may be, the thesis at issue, namely, that Christ's reality is not restricted to his historical existence, but includes the "yesterday, today, and for ever," is still an essential element in Christian theology. To this extent we have to speak of Christ as *the* form of revelation.

As concerns the second question, namely, whether the term "form" says too little, not doing adequate justice to the being of God in Christ, all that is required here is a brief terminological explanation. In the present context we are not using "form" in the modern sense of the reverse of content but after a more Aristotelian fashion, although not in strict dependence on Aristotle. Form (*eidos*) is the principle of shape (*morphe*) which impresses itself on formless matter (*hyle*). Hence, in contrast to modern usage, form is not the external side of something. It is the nature, character, and goal of a thing, living creature, or event. In this sense Christ is the form which determines the nature of revelation, for in virtue of his *homoousia* with

---

[1] Barth's Christology seems to skirt the edge of this danger; cf. ThE, I, § 596a-x; E.T. I, pp. 108ff.

the Father he manifests himself as God condescending from the foundation of the world in a manifestation of love and sacrificial self-giving.

The analogy to the Aristotelian concept of form which we are using here in elucidation has a further aspect as well. Aristotle's metaphysics offers plenty of scope for the use of the concept of form, so that transitions between form and matter are fluid. To take an illustration, a hewn stone which has been prepared for building is form in contrast to its unhewn state. But in relation to the house which is to be built it is itself mere matter or material. Similarly the soul is form in relation to the body but matter in relation to reason, which for Aristotle is supreme form, the form of form (*eidos eidous*).[2] Similarly one might say that the self-declaration of God in the words and deeds of the old covenant is the form of his revelation in contrast to the raw state of nature religions, but is itself matter in relation to what is revealed about him in his self-disclosure in Christ. If we were to use Aristotelian terms, the self-disclosure in Christ would be the form of form. We have to do with one and the same God and one and the same form, but the modes of his self-declaration and the dimensions of his being that are manifested therewith are different, and bring us constantly closer to the heart of his Godhead, until God stands directly before us in the form of Jesus Christ as the form of form.

Now we do not want to adopt the terminology of Aristotle as a framework of thought which fixes our christological deliberations in advance. Certain scholastic developments offer a warning in this respect. Nevertheless, the use of his concept of form seems to be a good one from the terminological standpoint. It is in this sense that we here speak of Christ as the form of revelation. In so doing we express the fact that it is one and the same God who bears witness to himself before and in the incarnation of the Word and who thereby effects a movement into his innermost being (the form of form).

2. THE METHOD

A Historical Survey of Christological Methods

Every Christology faces the difficulty of making appropriate statements about its theme. Even a brief glance at the confused history of Christology, at the conflict over minor nuances, at the unstable and often non-existent balance between the divine and the human character of the figure of Christ, confirms this impression. The implied problem of statement and the methodological attempt to overcome it will occupy us in Chapter XXI. But some initial clarification is necessary. This must be brief; the undergirding will come later.

Part of the tragedy of the history of Christology is that we seem to be forced to choose between an Alexandrian type and an Antiochene type.

In brief the Alexandrian type proceeds deductively from the supernatural

---

[2] Cf. K. Vorländer, *Geschichte der Philosophie,* I, 9th ed. (1949), pp. 175ff.

divine sonship of Christ whereas the Antiochene type proceeds inductively from the man Jesus of Nazareth. This polarization may still be seen in modern theology. Thus Barth is an Alexandrian, while Bultmann adopts the Antiochene approach, as do also death of God theologians and the theologians of humanization in their different ways. In saying this we are ignoring distinctions and nuances. Our task for the moment is simply to indicate basic trends in christological understanding.

The confessions espouse both the deity and the humanity of Christ: very God and very man. Ancient creeds such as the Apostles' Creed, the Nicene Creed, and the Athanasian Creed, which the confessions quote, show already what mental acrobatics are needed to discover a form of thinking in which the two can in fact be stated at one and the same time. One detects uncertainty of thought in face of the danger that Christology might be put off balance on either the divine or the human side (as constantly happened). The doctrine of the communication of attributes, in which theological thought makes a final and supreme effort to conceive of the unity of Christ as both God and man, is a mere wisp of thought, a mental walking on eggs, at least if the statements are taken at face value and it is not considered what they are futilely trying to say in their supra-paradoxical confusion.

Why is it so difficult to make christological statements? Does the difficulty lie in faith and its irrationality or in reflection about faith?

Obviously it does not lie in faith. Unguarded, naive, and cheerful statements are constantly made in hymns about the divine sonship of Christ and his brotherhood with man. It is when reflection gets to work on these that they immediately threaten to become irreconcilable contradictions. Problems of contradiction arise, it seems, only as difficulties of thought. This is especially true in the framework of ontological thinking. It is here that statements about divinity and humanity become entangled in the contradictory antithesis of two different things, so that the union of both in Christ becomes a logical impossibility. Is not God the epitome of omnipotence, infinitude, and majesty, whereas man represents impotence, finitude, and guilt? Is not the thesis of Christ's divine humanity, then, comparable to mere abstractions such as wooden iron or a four-sided circle?

Nevertheless, the difficulty of thought is in no way restricted to the ontological sphere. An existentialist or personalist approach also runs into the difficulty that in Christ one has to think together things that seem to be mutually exclusive: God as the Holy One and man in the brokenness of his existential situation.

Only with a psychological approach, such as we find in Schleiermacher and more recently E. Hirsch, does the difficulty vanish. But the price that has to be paid is the surrender of certain essential elements of divine humanity. Thus the undivided being of God in Christ becomes the constant force of God-consciousness in distinction from other men.[3] Since God is

---

[3] *The Christian Faith,* § 94.

relevant here only insofar as he is reflected in the consciousness, the difference between Jesus and us may be seen only in the different extent to which this God-consciousness fills his psyche. The qualitative difference of God from man ceases to be a theme of study. Instead we have a quantitative difference in consciousness of God. Quantitative distinctions of this kind naturally cause no friction in logic. The question arises, however, whether this kind of approach does not strip away its true secret from what traditional Christology has always had in view. Another question which arises is why the fathers accepted logical friction—surely they might have concealed it—and why they did battle for it against every form of Antiochene Christology that might have resolved the contradiction.

Our finding, then, is that seemingly by necessity Christologies will either have to be Alexandrian or Antiochene.

What will happen, however, if the deity and humanity of Christ are both essential to faith but reflection on faith cannot think together these ontologically related things? A self-critical and epistemologically concerned theology cannot put this question without also feeling some compulsion to explain why they cannot be thought together. Only if it can find some such explanation will the admission of contradiction not be a mere capitulation or a flight into the asylum of ignorance. When the mathematician admits that he cannot square a circle geometrically, this is not epistemological defeatism, for he can show why this particular geometrical task is an impossible one.

In arguing that reflection cannot master the contradiction of the divine and the human in Christ, but faith must believe it all the same, theology might perhaps use an analogy from microphysics. Tiny particles which are the building blocks of matter might be regarded as either waves or corpuscles and very different perspectives will result. This is because the process of observation causes a disturbance in relation to these particles. The behavior of the particles is related to the process of observation. This means that the building blocks of matter, which are originally regarded as final objective reality, can no longer be viewed in themselves. They escape objective rootage in time and space. In the last resort we can make only our knowledge of these particles the object of knowledge.[4] If this analogy be used in Christology, the implication is as follows.

The building blocks of the figure of Christ, if one may put it thus, namely, true God and true man, cannot be known in themselves, since here again the process of observation, or rather reflection, causes a disturbance. For what is meant by both God and man (omnipotence-impotence, infinitude-finitude, etc.) is set in preconceived schemes of thought, so that justice cannot be done to the divine-human reality of Christ. The schemes of thought impinge on this reality and alter it. Hence we do not confront the reality in itself, or, rather, the reality in itself cannot be the object of

---

[4] W. Heisenberg, "Das Naturbild der heutigen Physik," *Die Künste im technischen Zeitalter* (1954), p. 61.

our knowledge and reflection. Only our knowledge of the person of Christ can be this object.

Theologically the knowledge to which Heisenberg refers is faith in Christ. No leap into another dimension, or transfer into another genre, takes place here. We remain within the analogy. For what we call our knowledge of Christ is imparted to us only as we achieve a personal relation of trust in him. (The difference is that the relation is personal and not impersonal as in the case of the particles.) This relation for its part arises only as Christ discloses himself to us and works on us, and only as we let him work on us.

Apt here is Melanchthon's celebrated thesis in the 1521 *Loci* that to know Christ is to know his benefits. When Heisenberg says that our knowledge of the particles and not the particles themselves can be the object of knowledge, the strict theological equivalent is that the object of theology is not Christ in himself as the subject of his work but his history with us, his contact with us, and his effect on us. (The important difference between impersonal and personal reality may be ignored in this connection.) When we encounter the reality of Christ in faith, when we let him work on us, when we follow him and he is our comfort in life and in death, then the reality meets us in undivided form and the qualitative distinction between the divine and the human is not yet in force, just as the difference between a wave and a corpuscle plays no part in everyday dealings with reality in the case of the physicist. Only when the latter with his probing or the theologian with his means of reflection tries to get closer to the material or christological reality in itself does it break up into heterogeneous aspects which form a contradiction on the logical level.

This, then, is the reason why the contradictions and tensions with which every Christology has to wrestle (apart from Antiochene psychological Christology) find their basis, not in faith itself, but in reflection on faith. They constitute a logical scandal so long as reflection "goes it alone." (In this case the doctrine of the communication of attributes is sheer absurdity.) They are reconciled—not dissolved—only when faith is understood as the fixed point around which reflection circles, so that faith and reflection are commentaries the one on the other. To put it simply, the man who is unaffected by faith in Christ will not be able to understand christological reflection. The man who lives by believing contact with Christ will recognize him even in the most paradoxical leaps of reflection, for there is entrusted to him the reality of him who escapes rational comprehension and who thus makes those leaps necessary.

Implications for the Method of Christological Thinking

From what we have just said various inferences may be drawn regarding christological method.

First, I must give up trying to think together what I believe together. If on the one hand Christ is an example of faith, if he is with me under assault, if he must find his way to the same Nevertheless as I do (Luke 22:42); cf. John 5:30; 6:38), but if on the other hand he is also the object of faith, these things which are apparently an irreconcilable contradiction on the intellectual plane cease to be mutually exclusive in faith. This does not mean that faith is, or ought to be, intellectually blind. It can mean only that a different role is assigned to thinking here. In Anselm's phrase, faith seeks understanding in order that it may say and make clear what it means. In relation to Christ as both example and object of faith this implies two things.

Negatively it implies that reason cannot be content merely to assert the immanent exclusiveness of two self-contradictory statements. Positively it means that reason has to show why the contradiction necessarily arises and why what faith has in view cannot be stated without it. An example which suggests itself here is the doctrine of the Trinity. In this we have on the one side the *homoousia* of the Son with the Father (Christ the object of faith), while on the other side we have the loving self-giving of God to solidarity with us in our human situation (Christ as the example of faith). Other antinomies which might be mentioned in relation to the doctrine of God are the contradictions between justice and love, omnipotence and evil, etc. In face of these all that reason can do is to give up, cynically, ironically, or sadly insist on the contradictions, renounce any claims it might have to be a normative criterion (normative use), and instead be ready, or make itself ready, in relation to the object of faith, to think the thoughts of faith after it (organic use).

We are reminded here of the distinction that Quenstedt, Hollaz, and J. Gerhard made between the normative (judicial or material) use and the organic (instrumental or formal) use. The reason which proclaims its normativity is that of the fallen man who in virtue of his reason makes himself the measure of all things. The instrumental reason which thinks "after" is regenerate reason restrained by the Word of God. Reason shares man's destiny. There is no such thing as reason in itself (indifferent transcendental subjectivity), only rebellious reason which makes itself the measure of all things, or receptive reason which thinks the thoughts of faith after it; cf. C. A. Hase, *Hutterus redivivus,* 5th ed. (1842), pp. 66f.

Second, if this role is assigned to reason, including theological reason, one can see which is the best approach to Christology and which has least to commend it. With this formulation we are already pointing out that the approach which is being suggested is not that of an unconditional theological requirement based on confession but that which starts with an evaluative judgment.

We do not commend a theology from above, e.g., one which, as in earlier Calvinism, begins with the decrees or with the doctrine of the two natures. Dogmatic and theological history offers many illustrations of the methodological danger of this approach (although "danger" is not a theological concept). It threatens to open the door to a normative use. Given concepts such as the decrees or the doctrine of the two natures initiate a process of deduction and systematization. For this reason it is best to base Christology on that which wins us to faith. Only along these lines can reason be prevented from anticipating faith with conditions and preconceptions. Only along these lines can it think "after" faith and let faith seek understanding. Faith certainly does not arise through someone telling me that Christ is God's Son and different from you and me. Faith is directed in the first instance to the man Jesus, who wins my trust. It is directed to him who comes to me as the incarnate Word in solidarity with me. Only later does the difference strike me.

This is true, of course, only in relation to conscious personal faith and not the inherited faith of children or implicit faith (cf. Volume I, pp. 124, 155). In the latter cases, and consequently in Christian education, the first stage of faith is obviously reached through the total portrait of Christ which is presented by instruction in the biblical narratives. This portrait implicitly contains all that the figure of Jesus signifies for faith, namely, that he is the Savior, God's Son, who has pity on us and does mighty works. The question hardly arises, then, where faith has its starting-point. No distinction has to be made between "from above" and "from below." Possibly the special place of Christmas and Good Friday in liturgical life carries a hint that adult faith rests on that wherein Christ is in solidarity with us and wherein we see ourselves in him. For all the sentimentality and superficiality associated with these seasons, we may still maintain that what strikes and claims us here, what is pertinent to us, is the humanity of the Redeemer, his humanity as the child in the manger and the one who undergoes suffering and death.

Are we not warned by historical examples, however, that starting with the man Jesus can also be a false approach? Does not this way of putting it sound suspiciously Antiochene? When we say that the man Jesus wins our trust, are we not using an expression which echoes Herrmann and which brings us close to the dubious theologians of Ritschlian Liberalism or reductionist Existentialism?[5] This seems to be so, but it is an illusion. For everything depends on *how* we start with the man Jesus.

Thus Herrmann and Bultmann—to stay with our examples—never get any further than the man Jesus. They never reach the deity that transcends him, or they do so fragmentarily. They never come to grips with the doctrine of the two natures in their Christologies. Nevertheless, their failure in this regard is not due to the fact that they begin with the man Jesus; it is due to the way in which they begin with him. In different ways both these theologians are guided by the question how Jesus relates unconditionally to us, how he reaches our understanding and can be appropriated by it. If Herrmann never gets beyond the inner life of Jesus and Bultmann sees Jesus only as the bearer of the kerygma and its existential interpretation, this is because of the role that is played in their thinking by their initial ques-

---

[5] Cf. Volume I on Herrmann, Bultmann, Braun, *et al.*

tion, valid though this may be in itself. For the question how far something or someone can relate to me unconditionally can surreptitiously achieve normative rank. I may claim to know in advance what a thing has to be to have this unconditional relevance. I already know about it in my pre-understanding. I then ask whether something or someone, e.g., Jesus Christ, fits into my given understanding of what is significant—this understanding being provided by Heidegger's ontology in the case of Bultmann. Anything that cannot be accepted as significant in terms of this understanding, anything that cannot be interpreted existentially, can no longer be the object of a theological statement.[6] This is what we have in mind when we say that the initial question how the man Jesus comes to me and wins my faith can surreptitiously take on a normative function, have a prejudicially restrictive effect on the answer, and obscure in part the figure that encounters us.

Third, the failure of this experiment leads us to the insight that the question of what attracts us to Jesus, with its implication of an approach to Christology by way of the humanity of Jesus, cannot be more than a heuristic and provisional question. We have to be prepared for the fact that the answer which is given in the figure of Jesus might be greater and other than what is expected in the question. It might be that what we regard as pertinent, significant, and unconditionally relevant prior to encounter with Christ pales into a mere shadow when his light arises. It might be that we are not given an answer to our question but are ourselves put to the question by him. When Christ changes us and makes us new creatures, our questions, too, are changed. This has the following implication.

We begin with the man Jesus and his solidarity with us. We may put our imagination to work and vividly portray his joys and sorrows, his fulfilments and disappointments. We may read the Gospels as though they were biographies, taking seriously his solidarity with us and recognizing ourselves in him. Trying to understand him and to see how he touches and affects the questions in our own lives, we may treat him as someone like ourselves, as a man like you and me. Nevertheless, we are always open to the fact that this figure can suddenly transcend all analogies and confront us with the majesty of the Wholly Other. It is then that we know we have reached the real truth. But we want to *discover* this Wholly Other. We want to be aware of this transcending of all analogy. Whether in astonishment, offense, or adoration, we want to achieve personal knowledge of it. For we realize that we have missed the best if this transcending brings no surprise, if we do not receive the solution of the riddle of Jesus as believers, as those who are compelled to believe, if it is imparted to us in advance in the form of a dogma. We want to have our own history with Jesus, a history with his benefits. We do not want to be cheated out of this history by receiving the decisive thing in the form of a dogmatic premise, as though this would be "receiving" in any true or meaningful sense.

---

[6] For a fuller criticism of Bultmann cf. Volume I.

Fourth, this means that we cannot grasp the transcendent element in Jesus in the same way as we grasp the analogous element. What must be said here lies beyond the horizon of what Kant calls "experience" and what he defines as the sphere of competence of *a priori* and *a posteriori* synthetic judgments. Statements have to be made which are not objectifiable and which cannot be verified as historical experience, e.g., statements about the resurrection, ascension, and session. This may be seen from the fact that we have to use the "negative way" here. We have to do this even in relation to the conduct of the man Jesus. For even in the most human parts of his story we already come across the transcendent element. Can we describe the way he loved, for example, except by using the negative way? The unconditional nature of his loving self-sacrifice is brought out by the fact that "when he was reviled, he reviled not again" (1 Peter 2:23) and also by the fact that he commanded us to love even when we are hated (Matthew 5:44, 46). In the very thing in which he is closest to us—the unconditionality of his love—he is also most alien to us, the Wholly Other. How else but negatively can we express this manner of his loving? A love which is no mere echo differs radically from every human form of love. The fact that we have to say that it is "no mere echo" shows even linguistically that we are forced to use the negative way at this point.

We may sum up under three heads.

1. There is obviously good reason to approach Christology from below and not from above. We thus begin with the man Jesus. But we realize in so doing that the initial question has only provisional and heuristic rank, not normative rank. It must always be prepared to be transcended by the figure of Jesus. The element in Jesus which transcends the human transcends also the questions with which we come to him and which we put to him. The dialogs of Jesus recorded in the Gospels are enough to show that he is never a mere answer to pre-existent questions.

2. We are well aware that the biographical element in Jesus lies on a different level from the transcendent element, so that the human and the divine aspects, the this-worldly and the wholly other, cannot be brought together under a comprehensive system. What faith sees and confesses as a unity breaks up into irreconcilable elements for discursive thought, as in the case of the wave and the corpuscle in physics. This is why the negative way is legitimate in our attempts at formulation.

3. Under the guidance of the question how God comes to us in the form of the man Jesus, we turn our attention to the history which he begins with us, and into which he takes us up, through Jesus of Nazareth. This history, and the benefits which come to us in Jesus Christ, are the true theme of Christology. Included in all this is the question who the subject of these benefits is, i.e., the question of the mystery of the person of Jesus. This question raises the difficulties stated under 1. and 2. We cannot master these difficulties in such a way as to be able to co-ordinate the divine and the human aspects (as in a doctrine of the two natures). We can do so

only as we reflect individually on his specific benefits, on his solidarity with us, and on his divine authority, without conceding to theology any competence to think these things together. Faith alone grasps the unity of Jesus; thought does not. Faith should not, of course, believe things that it cannot venture to think, too. Faith always calls for understanding. But the thought that faith demands is thought along the lines of the organic use. It is an exposition of faith with methodical strictness. Methodical strictness means orientation to a principle. This principle is the history of God and his benefits with us, in the light of which the figure of Jesus is to be interpreted.

Before embarking on a Christology of this type, however, we must consider, with the help of the NT, some basic problems which are the subject of heated debate. In so doing we shall be dealing once again, although in relation to broader questions, with many of the matters to which attention has already been drawn in this preamble.

XIX

The Horizon of Christology: The Relation between Faith and History

SCHLEIERMACHER'S CHRISTOLOGY AS AN EXAMPLE OF THE PROBLEM

Someone, possibly Karl Barth, once said that when Schleiermacher moves on from the smooth and very elegant basis of his *Christian Faith* to the theme of Christology, he makes heavy going of it. He has lost his first wind and strains and labors at the task. For, as Barth puts it, Christology is the great stumbling-block in Schleiermacher's doctrine.[1] The figure of Jesus of Nazareth is too big to fit into his projected system. The difficulties Schleiermacher faces here have exemplary significance for every theology, since all theologies have an inevitable drive for systematization either small or great. Just because Schleiermacher is the greatest theological systematizer of the modern period, and meets correspondingly with very acute difficulties in the systematic co-ordination of Jesus Christ, we can profitably study in him the problems of method which confront us all when we try to master the christological task.

What is the nature of these difficulties as we meet them in the test case of Schleiermacher?

In the introduction to his *Christian Faith* Schleiermacher establishes what might be called today an existential standpoint. He begins by developing our general self-consciousness as existing men. Against the background of this general self-consciousness, which need not be expounded here, he finds the consciousness of something comprehensive (to use an apt term suggested by Jaspers). He thus discovers the religious dimension of consciousness. We are pointed to that which comprehends us by the feeling of absolute dependence, which qualitatively transcends all feelings of partial

---

[1] *Die protestantische Theologie* (1947), p. 385; E.T. *Protestant Thought* (1973), pp. 312f.

dependence. The origin of this feeling of absolute dependence is denoted by the term God.[2]

For readers who are not very well acquainted with Schleiermacher, the following explanation may be given. Our self-consciousness is determined by a partial feeling of dependence and a partial feeling of freedom. In immanent relations we are never wholly dependent nor wholly free. Our positive activity, which is mediated by the feeling of freedom, comes up against limits, so that this feeling is restricted and partial. Yet the feeling of dependence has similar limits. We are not just dependent on an immanent magnitude, e.g., fate, or autocratic government. Within limits, however small, we can react. Thus our self-consciousness in relation to the world is a sequence of the partial feeling of freedom and the partial feeling of dependence. In this whole sphere there is no feeling of absolute dependence (i.e., apart from the feeling of freedom) and no absolute feeling of freedom (i.e., apart from the feeling of dependence) (§ 4, 2).

Nevertheless, we have a feeling of absolute dependence. We are thus forced to two conclusions. First, this religious feeling is not located in the sphere of self-consciousness insofar as this is determined by immanent feelings of dependence and freedom, for there is nothing absolute here. The feeling of absolute dependence is the sign which stands in front of all similar feelings of this kind. Even in our conditional feeling of freedom we are aware of being posited from elsewhere (§ 4, 2). Second, and in consequence, the feeling of absolute dependence cannot relate to any immanent object but points to that which transcends the cosmic nexus. The "whence" of our receptive and active being that is posited in this self-consciousness is denoted by the expression God (§ 4, 4).

Modern forms of the problem of identity might serve as an illustration of Schleiermacher's concept of absolute dependence, the self-consciousness of being posited from elsewhere. The way in which I reach my identity, my "I am," like the decision whether I want to be the subject of partial feelings of dependence and freedom, or even whether I want to exist at all, is not under my control. I am never consulted on such matters. I find myself "flung" into being (Heidegger). I am thus absolutely dependent on the fact that I am at all. My identity is a being from elsewhere. It embraces all partial feelings of dependence and freedom.

Augustine experienced this basic dependence as a crisis in the sense of identity. In his Tractate on John (29, 3) he comments on the christological context of John 7:16: "What is so much thine as thyself, and what is so little thine as thyself?"

This analysis of the self-consciousness in its relation to the phenomenal world and the nonphenomenal whence that transcends it is primarily a type or forerunner of existential philosophy, and it leads into a sphere of free speculation in which no sacred books or sources of revelation are

---

[2] *The Christian Faith,* § 4.

needed. Undoubtedly Schleiermacher counted on it that Christians, secular humanists, and the adherents of other religions could all agree with him when he made this kind of analysis. For here he is still moving in the sphere of common humanity which precedes and underlies all philosophical and religious differences.

Nevertheless, this free speculation is not Schleiermacher's final concern. For he is, and wants to be, a Christian theologian. Hence he has to take this sense of absolute dependence, which he has advanced after the manner of religious philosophy, and relate it to the historical figure of Jesus.

Two questions arise here. First, how does he make the connection? Second, why does he take the detour of an analysis of the self-consciousness? In other words, why does he have this involved preamble, or lay down this philosophical foundation, when it will obviously be very hard to erect a concrete NT Christology upon it? Why does he not simply begin with Christ himself? We shall now tackle these questions.

First, how does Schleiermacher relate the religious self-consciousness to Jesus Christ? He does it by seeing in Christ the prototype or model of this self-consciousness. In us the basic consciousness of the relation to God is a broken one. It is constantly crowded out by other things. Christ, however, is completely filled by it. The relation to God is present at every moment and in every dimension of his consciousness. This means that the figure of Jesus has two characteristics.

First, he exists in solidarity with human nature.[3] He is determined by the specifically human self-consciousness and enclosed by the reference of the feeling of absolute dependence back to its whence. Second, there is also difference from all other specimens of the human. For Christ, as we have already said in another connection, is distinguished from all other men by the constant strength of his consciousness of God, which was an undivided being of God in him.[4] This "in-being" of God is fragmentary, partial, vacillating, and weak in the human nature of others. In Christ, however, it is total. It completely fills him and determines him absolutely. The quantity of his God-consciousness surpasses that of others and so completely fills him that there is—if we may venture a bold expression—a change in quality. He is in solidarity with us and at the same time he is wholly other. Yet since he is also an extreme fulfilment of the human, he is the original of man and expresses in a unique and privileged way what human nature ought to be.

This prototype of the human is fully historical and actual in Jesus, so that each of his historical moments is also prototypical.[5] Hence the original is no mere idea; it took historical shape. Although Christ is above time, although we can thus be contemporary with him, not just in Kierkegaard's sense but also Schleiermacher's, and although he takes us up into the

---

[3] § 94.
[4] § 94.
[5] § 93.

strength of his God-consciousness[6] and thus becomes our Redeemer, he is still a specific point in the continuity of the historical process, even though he cannot be explained in terms of this process.[7] The prototype becomes a historical event.

When we look at these theses, we at once get the impression that there is "construction" here, that history, for some reason, is being manipulated. This element of manipulation might be explained in simplified form as follows. Schleiermacher does not begin by asking: Who was Jesus Christ? He does not open his inquiry by going to the shaft of history to look and listen, by analyzing the witness of history, and then asking whether Jesus has something to say to us, whether his person and message are unconditionally relevant to us, or whether his self-consciousness (or inner life) can be adopted by us and can pass over into us. He takes the opposite route, starting with an analysis of general self-consciousness and the states of Christian piety.

To put it metaphorically, he digs a tunnel into the mountain range of Christology from two ends. The one end is the self-consciousness, the zone of the I, anthropology. The other end is history, the zone outside the I, the NT records. As in the building of a tunnel like the St. Bernard, his great aim must be to see to it that the two shafts meet exactly in the middle. But his effort does not seem to succeed. One is left with the impression that the two shafts do not meet. All kinds of emergency cross-cuts have to be made to get from the one tunnel to the other, and even then very difficult scrambling is needed. We thus seem to have here an experiment that has failed.

In plain terms Schleiermacher comes into conflict with history in his christological construction. The Christ of history is not to be found at the point at which he aims with his analysis of self-consciousness and states of Christian piety. The historical is too large to fit into a prefabricated existential framework. If the ardently desired integration is to be achieved, the historical has to be manipulated, altered, and cut down to the right size. Artificial emergency measures have to be undertaken to connect the two tunnels.

This is what we find in Schleiermacher. Christ is seen in terms of total God-consciousness because only thus can any analogy to our consciousness be conceived and quantitative similarity dialectically changed into the qualitative dissimilarity of otherness. But this Christ with an unbroken totality of God-consciousness has hardly anything at all to do with the Christ of the Gospel records. What do we really know about his consciousness, even

---

[6] § 100.

[7] § 93, 3: His spiritual content cannot be explained in terms of that of the circle of human life to which he belonged but only by a creative divine act in which the concept of man as the subject of God-consciousness comes to supreme and absolute fulfilment.

his messianic consciousness, let alone his inner life (Herrmann)?[8] Do we
not do violence to Christology when we concentrate on this side-issue, or,
better, when we let ourselves be forced by an existential preamble into
making this question of the self-consciousness of Jesus the central question?
Can we move on from this to matters like the resurrection and the return
of Christ which no longer have anything to do with this self-consciousness?
(Such things are indeed largely dropped, although, since they are in the
Bible and the tradition of the church, Schleiermacher accepts them and
drags them in somehow, specially in his sermons at Holy Trinity, Berlin,
in which he is not constrained by his system.) The Last Things are thus
introduced very artificially; special emergency shafts are needed for the
purpose. Brunner is not wholly wrong when in his *Mystik und das Wort* he
speaks of the eschatological lacuna in Schleiermacher. In the area of eschatology the kerygma contains elements which are alien to this system and
cannot be absorbed into it. If the main point of the NT is to tell us about
the mighty works of God (Acts 2:11, 22), the systematician Schleiermacher
finds it hard to speak about these works at all, since they bear no relation
to the starting-point of his theology in the consciousness. Christ has a
consciousness which is at one and the same time both different from ours
and yet also in solidarity with it. But he is no longer the subject of acts.
Within the system at least he is no longer the bearer of the active Word
which brings change, healing, and the revolution of the aeons.

UNAVOIDABILITY OF A PRE-UNDERSTANDING

If, however, Schleiermacher's existential preamble brings him into an inevitable tension with history, our second question arises: Why does he adopt it?
Why does he engage in this analysis when it obviously leads nowhere and
blocks rather than opens up access to the mystery of Christ? Why does he
not begin by listening as objectively as possible to the historical accounts
of Christ without letting himself be conditioned by a pre-understanding?

If we make an experiment and imagine what would have happened had
Schleiermacher taken this course, the result might be as follows. He would
have analyzed the historical figure of Jesus with the fullest possible objectivity and tried to discover his original significance. Only then would he
have considered the implication of Jesus for his own self-consciousness and
ours. Only then—after the historical analysis—would he have accorded him
the rank of a guiding image. This would be the exact opposite of the way
Schleiermacher actually took. Why did he not choose it? Why, like later
kerygma theology, did he begin instead with general self-consciousness?

There seem to be three reasons why neither Schleiermacher nor we ourselves can do what seems to be the obvious thing for the believing community and turn to the history first.

1. The first reason is that tackling the history with no presuppositions at

---

[8] Cf. the section on the self-consciousness of Jesus in the bibliography.

all is impossible. Even the pure listener implicitly or explicitly lays down conditions which have to be met if he is to be able to hear and verify the historical accounts.

For example, E. Troeltsch suggests causality, immanence, and analogy as criteria of verifiability. Obviously this involves a pre-understanding of what may be called historical. Every historian—from Hegel and Marx to Spengler and Toynbee, to take very different examples—begins with certain heuristic principles which he finds realized in history and in terms of which he questions history.

To try to know history as it really was—the well-known postulate of Ranke's historical work—is thus extremely naive. In history we are dealing with material that we have already worked over, shaping it in accordance with our criteria, heuristic principles, pre-understandings, and expectations. Expecting and imparting meaning, the historian is also at work. Along Kantian lines one might say that we never see the sequence of historical events "in itself." Part of historical experience is its active fashioning by our own categories, postulates, and approaches. T. Lessing may be exaggerating when he says that the process that we call history is the giving of meaning to what is without meaning, but this is undoubtedly an essential aspect of our encounter with history.

We may thus conclude that even the objective historian is not just a film which passively absorbs light and makes a chemical record of what has happened. The historian always imposes conditions and makes evaluations. He is steered by latent principles and often does unconsciously and implicitly what Schleiermacher with his existential approach does consciously and explicitly. He advances a preamble, or builds an intellectual fortress, from which he may then conduct his forays into history.

2. The second reason is that if we begin by viewing Jesus Christ as a figure of history, like Hannibal or Napoleon, we actually set him at a distance and thereby relativize him. He becomes only one of an endless number of points on the timeline and is set at a historical distance from us, who are also points on this timeline. Under the pressure of the autonomy of historical study, he is put in relation to other points in history and explained in terms of this relation. It thus becomes impossible to think of him as a prototype, to use the term of Schleiermacher. For if he is a prototype he has his own uncaused origin. We thus have to speak of his supernatural derivation. Negatively, this means that he cannot be derived from the nexus of history nor interpreted in terms of his environment. If Jesus Christ as the Lord of time and eternity is the object of our faith, if the times are in his hand (Psalm 31:15; 139:16), then he cannot be reduced to the state where he is simply in time and no more than a particle in temporal processes. This element in him which transcends temporal processes comes to expression theologically in his miraculous birth and his exaltation. In view of all this,

however, the act of historical verification is neither adequate nor indeed appropriate if I want to know the figure of Christ.[9]

Kierkegaard deals with this question in his *Training in Christianity*. Although his thought moves in different circles than that of Schleiermacher, it might be fruitful to illustrate the problem in Schleiermacher by his exposition of the crisis of historical knowledge in relation to Christology.

Kierkegaard's question is this: What can historical investigation attempt or achieve in relation to Christ? The argument is advanced that if we see the results of his life we are led to the conclusion that he must have been God. Faith, however, espouses the opposite thesis, namely, that to begin with this syllogism is to begin with blasphemy (p. 32). Why? Well, purely historical figures can be assessed by their influence and explained in the light of their origins. They can thus be understood in terms of their relation to other historical phenomena. With reference to Christ, however, this is blasphemy. For the imposing historical results which might convince even a professor of history that he was God are not the same thing at all as his return in glory. The blasphemy of the syllogism is that it makes that wherein Christ transcends all history into an element in history, namely, the historical results of his coming, the two thousand years of church history.

Nor is it merely the *parousia*, fatefully equated here with his historical influence, that compels us to regard historical investigation as inappropriate. The ontological structure of his person already brings this inappropriateness to our attention. For the mystery of this person finds expression in the scandal that here a historical individual is God. If, as in Hegel and D. F. Strauss, no more than the union of deity and humanity is seen in him, if abstractions are conjoined in characterizing him, this is a logically possible operation that causes no offense (the same applies to what Schleiermacher does). Scandal arises only when we let the gospel tell us that this individual who appears contingently in history is God. As Kierkegaard sees it, the combination in one figure of human limitation and divine freedom from limitation, of membership in history and lordship over history, is more than ordinary epistemology or categories can stand. It is thus an offense.

This Christ, then, can be encountered only as a paradox, in faith. Faith embraces what is contradictory. It is an elemental personal experience preceding reflection and already possessing that on whose contradictions subsequent reflection founders.

An everyday illustration might help. All personal relations, that of faith included, involve logical contradictions which do not arise in material relations. When I trust someone, this relation is objectively paradoxical. In the strict sense I do not trust this person only when I have objective certainty or proof that he is trustworthy. I cannot advance the syllogism: "This person is objectively such and such a person and therefore I trust him," as objective logic would demand. Trust often has to defy objective appearance or

---

[9] Cf. the fine work by H. J. Rothert, *Gewissheit und Vergewisserung als theologisches Problem* (1963).

evidence: "Even though he is the person he seems to be, and has done this or that, nevertheless I trust him." The personal relation of trust covers what seems to be an irreconcilable contradiction to objective thought. This relation is not a later synthesis of apparent contradictions. It precedes the contradictoriness. I simply trust. Only in the later reflection of objective thought does that which trust holds together break up into antitheses.

Our relation to Jesus is like this. What is paradoxical to later objective (i.e., historical) thought, what breaks up for this into God on the one side and individual man on the other, is held together in the act of faith and is in fact the ground of faith. In the very antithesis faith experiences the fact that Christ in his humanity is alongside us in solidarity and weakness and that Christ in his deity, as Lord of time and its creatures, is at the same time over us.

The problem with the objective or historical relation to Christ is the same as the problem with the ontological thinking that we find in the doctrine of the two natures. Here, too, subsequent reflection makes a contradiction of that which faith accepts as the unity of Christ's person.

This is why historical epistemology is inappropriate in relation to the phenomenon of Jesus Christ even though he is the incarnate Word and hence a phenomenon of history. Kierkegaard has this in view when he says that historical impartation is the impartation of objective knowledge and therefore nothing can be known about Christ from history (p. 26).

Summing up, we may say that the second reason for the impossibility of questioning history directly about Jesus Christ, and therefore for Schleiermacher's existentialist preamble in his approach to Christology, is that Christ is not to be viewed as a mere point on the timeline nor is he to be understood simply in terms of his relation to other points on this timeline. Since God is in him, in a way still to be described, we are told that as the incarnate Word he is both immanent in history and also transcendent over it. Basically, the terms "immanent" and "transcendent," which have their origin in discursive thinking, prove to be inappropriate in this context. They are emergency terms which we cannot avoid using in an intellectual framework that is alien to the matter at issue. They are thus a negative sign that Christ lies outside the normal grasp of history.

3. The third reason why we cannot get at the figure of Christ directly through history is as follows. According to the confession of faith I can speak of Christ only in such a way that he is immediately relevant to me as the basis, goal, and meaning of my existence. But a distant historical phenomenon cannot be relevant to me in this way. If I regard Christ only as the founder of Christianity and a specific form of Western culture, I do, of course, confess that I am under his influence, and that he is one of the forces, especially the cultural forces, that has shaped my morality and·religion and oriented my cultural background. Yet my relation to him is only indirect and mediate, not immediate and direct. Even an author like

G. Szczesny[10] can speak of his influence along these lines. But this cannot be all that I have in view when I speak of him in the framework of the confession of faith. Here historical distance disappears. The temporal space between him and me becomes porous. He is not just David's Son, a distant point in the historical process. He is also David's Lord, and therefore my Lord too, so that I am in direct relation to him with no historical distance (Matthew 22:41-46).

This means, however, that I must relate him directly to myself, that I must let him touch all the dimensions of my being, that I must "appropriate" him. But I can appropriate something only if I know what is proper to me and who I am. How can I relate him to all the dimensions of my being, e.g., my humanity, or sexuality, or self-understanding, or guilt, or finitude, unless I see what these dimensions are and know something about them? How can I know Christ as him who pardons, i.e., how can I appropriate pardon, unless I am first bothered in some way by the problem of my guilt? How can I appropriate the message of the resurrection unless I first bring with me some of the questions that are put to me by my finitude?[11]

If appropriation is possible only as I see what is proper to me, only as I have some knowledge of myself, one may understand why theologians must reflect on the being of man all the more seriously now that a developing historical sense threatens to push the figure of Christ into historical distance. For the more vigorous and determinative the sense of history is, the stronger is the tendency to relativize all historical phenomena and set them in the remote past.

In relation to the figure of Christ there seem to be only two ways of reversing this trend and retaining the contemporaneity which faith confesses.

The first is that of dehistoricization whereby he becomes a timeless idea. This is the way taken by D. F. Strauss, at any rate at one stage in his development. For Strauss Christ has only symbolical significance. He represents the idea of humanity, which is the union of two natures, the child of the visible mother and the invisible father, or spirit and nature, the wonderworker as in the course of human history spirit increasingly masters nature and reduces it to the level of impotent material (*Das Leben Jesu*, 4th ed. [1840], § 151; E.T. 1974 (1892), § 151, pp. 779ff.).

Along these lines Strauss overcomes historical distance, yet only by taking the figure of Christ out of history altogether and setting it in the timeless resting-place of a symbolical reference. Christ becomes the quintessence of that which is timelessly valid. The timeless is immediate in every time, as mathematics shows. Thus the problem of historical distance is solved. But at what a price! The operation of dehistoricizing amputates the message of the incarnation of the Word. It robs this message of its whole point, namely,

---

[10] *Die Zukunft des Unglaubens. Zeitgemässe Betrachtungen eines Nichtchristen* (1958).

[11] From another angle we are again coming up against some of the problems that we dealt with in Volume I in the critical analysis of Theology A (Cartesian theology).

that God is present here in an individual man, and that he has ranged himself alongside us under the pressures of history. The final upshot is the falsifying heresy of Docetism.

The second way of overcoming the distance posited by historical inquiry is that of finding out how the alien and historically remote individual (i.e., Jesus) relates to what we have discovered to be our own self.

Schleiermacher in his hermeneutical writings (cf. J. Wach, *Das Verstehen,* I [1926], pp. 83-167, esp. 95ff., 137ff.) considers the possibility of feeling one's way into another person by "divination" and coming closer to the individuality of this other by comparison. Comparison means starting with the human nature which is common to us all and comparatively noting its differentiation in individual cases. W. Dilthey takes up this basic concept of Schleiermacher in his *Entstehung der Hermeneutik, Ges. Schriften,* V (1924; 3rd ed. 1961), pp. 329f., where he argues that individual distinctions are not finally due to qualitative differences but only to differences of degree. As expositors set themselves in a historical milieu, they may thus momentarily stress some things and repress others, and in this way reconstruct the life of others within themselves. Decisive here is the analogy between the one who understands and the one to be understood.

Historical distance can thus be overcome, and the sense of historical relevance enhanced, to the extent that I discover the relationship between the individuality of others and my own. This presupposes that my own individuality is present in my self-consciousness and that it is already an interpreted individuality. Thus even before Schleiermacher turns to the Gospels to learn about Christ he already knows that the self is determined by the feeling of absolute dependence. When he turns to the Gospels he understands Christ by relating him to this basic determinative feeling. This means that Christ is seen as the one who is entirely filled by the basic religious feeling, whereas I myself have only a partial and fragmentary share of it.

It may thus be seen why Christ is unconditionally relevant to me and can enjoy a direct relation that is not disrupted by historical distance. For he is my own *alter ego,* except that he represents the prototype of the human and is thus an undistorted model of what I ought to be.

Already, of course, the urgent question confronts us which we met in the Prolegomena and will constantly come up again in this christological discussion, namely, whether Christ can in fact be set in the given schema of my self-consciousness, whether he for his part does not basically change my understanding of myself, whether his understanding of me does not differ from my own, whether faith does not mean learning to see and understand with his eyes. If so, my general self-understanding cannot go unaltered when I "integrate" Christ into it. It becomes a new and changed self-understanding, and the old one is set aside like the old Adam. We mention this question here, however, only as a critical interim question. For the moment we shall return to our experiment with Schleiermacher.

Since Cartesian man always begins with his understanding of himself, and since the self seems to have fixed and distinct contours, there is an obvious temptation to give the analogy a helping hand, i.e., to manipulate the alien individuality so as to make it conform to my established model of myself.

Some broad examples may be given by way of illustration. The early Apologists, for instance, saw in man a bearer of the *logos spermatikos,* and hence found in Christ the Logos himself, who represents the fulness of what Greek philosophers could think of only fragmentarily.

Lessing in his *Christianity of Reason* (1754) sees in Christ an image of the universal reason in which I myself have only a limited share.

For the so-called theology of revolution of our own age I am characterized by my frustration by questionable social structures and the consequent pressure toward criticism and revolt. In this regard Christ is analogous to me, for he, too, is the victim and critic of the structures of this aeon, the only difference being that he is unrestricted and radical in his criticism of the world, so that he is a perfect model of the postulate of criticism, whereas I make my criticism only in attenuated, limited, and partial form. Christ can thus serve as my guiding image.

In all these cases it is plain that the way in which I understand myself (and on this basis plan reforms) exercises a normative influence on the image which I form of Christ. This necessarily entails a manipulation of the image.

Solution of the Problem of Analogy by an Understanding of the Spirit as the Positing of Analogy

It is important, and only fair, that consideration should be given to the reason for manipulations of the alien individuality (in this case the figure of Christ). Theologians are tempted to say that any child can see how Christology is here swallowed up by anthropology, how a hybrid self-assertion of man takes place, and how by its attempts at integration this self-assertion simply safeguards itself against having to face the real Christ and the disturbance of the old man by him. This judgment can be wrong, however, even though the swallowing up of Christology by anthropology cannot be denied.

For if this result is unintentional and inadvertent, as in fact it is, then a tragedy is enacted on the stage of thought. Clarity of vision is thus demanded. The initial intention behind this reconstruction of Christology is very different. The aim is to make legitimate appropriation possible. This becomes a serious problem once I know, or think I know, what is proper to me. For on this basis I cannot appropriate anything I want. If I did this quite uncritically, then one of two things would happen. I would either be untrue to myself and would sell out myself. I would become guilty in relation to the self and surrender my human dignity. (This was the concern of men of the Enlightenment like Lessing.) Or else, trying to maintain the self, I would suffer from a cleavage of consciousness. I would hold to be true, and feel committed to, something which stands in no kind of relation to the other contents of my consciousness. Hence I would not do justice to what I appropriate, not even the figure of Christ. Basically I would leave him outside instead of taking him into my life and setting him in living relation to all its dimensions. If I tried to dispense with the analogy at issue, I would thus be on the horns of a dilemma: I would have to deny either myself on the one hand or Christ on the other.

This is true, at least, if I think I know my clearly delineated self, if I thus think along Cartesian lines. Now that the self-consciousness of adult and self-reflexive man has broken loose, I seem to be in serious straits in relation to Christology. Again, therefore, the underlying question arises as to the true rank of this self-consciousness. Is it in fact a fixed point of orientation for all analogies? Or were we right when in our doctrine of the Holy Spirit[12] we pointed out that we have to be made analogous, so that, while we have to be reached in the old self-consciousness, this old self-consciousness has then to be overtaken and baptized into death?[13]

At any rate, when I find myself in the serious situation described, I cannot evade the question as to the relation of the Christ revelation to my self-consciousness. Schleiermacher is trying to deal with this situation when he engages in the religio-philosophical preamble to his *Christian Faith*. In positing an analogy between Christ and the self-consciousness he is simply trying to make plausible a possible appropriation of Christ by this self-consciousness and therewith to avoid what he thinks is the schizophrenia of the traditionalists. In his letters to Lücke[14] Schleiermacher emphasizes that in his existential preamble he has not the slightest wish to level Christianity down, to manipulate it, or to absorb it into general pantheism or into a philosophy or anthropology. If he had, he would be grounding the certainty of his Christianity upon prior certainty about himself and his philosophical pre-understanding. In this case his christological statements would simply be a confirmation of what he already knew in his self-certainty, and Christ would be nothing more than a function of this self-understanding of his. He energetically repudiates any such idea. As he puts it, he could never admit that his faith in Christ rested on learning or philosophy.[15] He could not imagine how dogmatics could ever arise if piety were not there first,[16] if there were not, then, some prior correlation between the religious self-consciousness and other forms of the self-consciousness. This correlation, however, must be a theme of theological reflection. What are called other forms of the self-consciousness include scholarship and intellectual honesty. Religious contents can be appropriated, then, only if they can be harmonized with the criteria of the intellectual consciousness

---

[12] Volume I, Chapters VII-XI.
[13] Volume I, Chapter IX.
[14] Ed. H. Mulert (1908). P. Siefert, *Die Theologie des jungen Schleiermacher* (1960), thinks that this relativization of the philosophical schema of thought applies to his earlier *Speeches* as well.
[15] Second Letter, Mulert, *op. cit.*, p. 38.   [16] First Letter, p. 17.

and do not come into conflict with these. For this reason Schleiermacher is convinced that every dogma, representing an element in the Christian self-consciousness, can be understood in such a way that it does not cause us to tangle with science.[17]

We need to pay careful attention here. If faith is not to come into conflict with science, then I must find it a place in my self-consciousness as a rational creature. Theoretically this might be done in two ways. One might show that the religious contents are rational even though their form might be mythically pre-scientific (Lessing's solution). Or with the help of scientific reflection one might show that the religious contents are outside the sphere of scientific competence, so that no conflict can possibly arise.

This is the route taken by Schleiermacher. For the feeling of absolute dependence which he propounds transcends the subject-object correlation that characterizes the scientific experience. Within that which can be objectified by science there is only a partial sense of freedom and dependence. If religion and faith have to do instead with the sense of absolute dependence, there is obvious distinction in the levels of experience. No rivalry need be feared, then, between science and faith. Religious contents can be appropriated without disruption. If, however, I start positively with the accidental truths of history by which the mighty works of God are attested to me, or with the miracles which supposedly validate the divine sonship of Christ, I have to do battle at once with the historical criteria of verification or with the immanent principle of natural science.

As Schleiermacher says, we do not have to face natural science alone; we are threatened also by historical inquiry and by the criticism which we cannot evade in our profession. Can we know what the latest claim will be about the Pentateuch or the OT canon? (Second Letter, p. 41). Hence we cannot base our faith on the reliability of the historical documents of the Bible. These might be torn apart by scholarship. How can we ground the unconditional certainty of faith on scientifically conditional and therefore destructible certainties? Even the concept of miracle might not be able to continue in its existing form. Are we then to take shelter behind these outer fortifications (which are not even the true fortress of religious certainty) and let ourselves be blockaded by science? Such a blockade, in addition to the total impoverishment which it entails, will force science to raise the standard of unbelief. Christianity will thus come to be equated with barbarism and learning with unbelief (p. 37). The same aim, i.e., that of avoiding tangling with scholarship (and especially history), lies behind the attempt made by W. Herrmann to find a zone for Christology that will be immune from scientific attack. Beginning once again with the self-consciousness, he seeks a dimension of this self-consciousness outside the competence of purely theoretical reason. In distinction from Schleiermacher, however, he turns, not to the religious, but to the ethical dimension, in which practical reason alone is competent. He thus begins

---

[17] Second Letter, p. 40.

with the experience of trust which comes to fulfilment in the "inner life" of Jesus and which cannot, then, be affected by the critical scientific study of Christ as a phenomenon of history.

Schleiermacher's Christology is determined, then, by the fact that he is in constant discussion with the modern consciousness and has an apologetic relation to it. The tragedy of this approach is simply that the modern consciousness, instead of being either ruled out as a hindrance to faith or brought into harmony with it, is surreptitiously and involuntarily accorded normative significance and thus involves the manipulations of Christ which we have depicted.[18]

The difficulty leads us to the decisive problem which we must keep in view in our exposition of Christology.

Since Schleiermacher's approach through the self-consciousness makes good sense in terms of the intellectual situation after Descartes, but proves to be unworkable, the question necessarily arises where, then, we can begin. We certainly cannot do so at a point where the modern consciousness of self and the world is not yet in force, as in older Lutheran orthodoxy. This would be just as absurd as saying that the historico-critical investigation of Scripture has caused us so much theological inconvenience that we should cut it out and begin once again with a noncritical view of Scripture. Why this course cannot be adopted is palpable. If faith is a form of appropriating what is believed, it is not possible without understanding. There can be understanding, however, only within an analogy between him who understands and what is to be understood. This in turn means that in some way a relation has to be demonstrated between Christ as the object of my faith on the one side and my self-consciousness on the other. In no sense can the problem of self-consciousness be evaded. But does not this problem lead us into the vicious circle which we have detected in Schleiermacher's theology of self-consciousness?

As this section draws to a close, then, we again have to face in all seriousness, and with some indication of what seems to us to be the answer, this most delicate of all the questions that confront Christology.

The problem of appropriation, which we have already dealt with at some length, arises out of two elements.

First, appropriating understanding presupposes a necessary analogy. No theological epistemology, no matter from what school it emanates, can disregard this problem.

Second, the two analogous entities are of different structure. On the one side he who is to understand has a self-consciousness which he already brings with him (at least in the case of Cartesian man), so that he is a given and invariable entity. On the other hand, what he is to understand (e.g., the alien individuality) will necessarily have to be crowded and

---

[18] Cf Bultmann's principle that understanding of records of events as God's acts presupposes a prior understanding of what can be called God's acts, ZThK, 47, 1 (1950), p. 66.

altered by this given element, so that it is for him who is to understand a variable entity. Only for this reason is it constantly manipulated. Only for this reason is there, for example, a history of the concept of Christ.

If, however, this entails falsification, i.e., if the Logos is hereby robbed of his historicity and incarnation, then the serious question arises whether the necessary analogy can in fact be achieved only in this violent fashion and under the tyranny of the invariable self-consciousness. In other words, we are forced to ask whether the phenomenon of Jesus does not offer indications that the analogy can be achieved in a very different way and one which is more commensurate with the matter itself.

Such indications do in fact exist and we shall try to find them. To show in which direction they will lead us we may refer to some initial pointers.

Jesus does not disregard what the modern age calls the self-consciousness. He approaches men by way of it. He turns to those who know that they are sick or guilty. His ironical saying that those who are well do not need a physician but those who are sick (Luke 5:31) shows that he has nothing to say to those who have no consciousness of themselves as sinners. He speaks instead to those who are oppressed by this consciousness. His remarks about counting the cost of discipleship are also addressed to the element of calculation in the consciousness (Luke 14:25ff.) which causes us to ask: "What shall we have therefore?" (Matthew 19:27). Finally his use of parables is an indication that Jesus speaks to men on the horizon of their existing concepts. This latching on to what is already there will be developed more fully at a later stage.

In the Gospels, however, existing questions and ideas and the existing self-consciousness are never a fixed and invariable factor resulting in an analogy to Christ. Christ is never the answer to a given question; he does not fit neatly into the intellectual framework of the one who puts the question. He himself is the one who puts the questions, calling the question itself in question.[19] He begins with the existing self-consciousness but does not let himself be integrated into it. He does not leave it as it is; he turns it upside down. When the issue is how he is to be known and appropriated, a completely different form of analogy suddenly comes into play.

This is not a given likeness which binds us to him and enables us to understand him. It is the content of a new creation. We are placed in an analogy which in itself, in terms of our own nature, is not at our disposal at all. Hence in the strict sense what takes place here is more than a change in consciousness, a spiritual opening up of the self. It is a transformation of existence in which a transformation of the consciousness is included. (We are submitting here to some terminological pressure and trying to stay with the modern concept of consciousness which we have used thus far.) We are brought to an existence in the truth which enables us to see him who *is* the truth: "Every one that is of the truth heareth my voice" (John 18:37; cf. 3:21; 14:6).

---

[19] Cf. the question about his authority in Matthew 21:23-27.

There is a similar reference to calling into an analogy of existence in John 7:17: "Only if any man will do the will of him that sent me shall he (be able to) know of the (i.e., my) doctrine, whether it be of God or whether I speak of myself" (cf. 5:44). The question whether Christ is authorized by God or not entails a fundamental decision that must be made concerning him. For this fundamental decision there are no cognitive criteria. It does not come within the competence of our consciousness, whether rational or of any other kind. It is possible only when we stand in a very specific attitude of existence toward God, namely, when we do his will. Only conformity to God's will—to substitute a theological term for the concept of analogy—can open up access to knowledge of the figure of Christ. This attitude of will, however, is unattainable by me. "No man can come unto me, except it were given unto him of my Father" (John 6:65; cf. 6:44). What Jesus says about hardening also shows that I have to be placed in the analogy if I am to understand him (Matthew 13:13ff.). So, too, does the hortatory call: "He that hath ears to hear, let him hear" (Mark 4:9, 23; 7:16, etc.). In Volume I[20] we stated that in Paul only God is analogous to himself. Hence the only adequate knowledge of God is his self-knowledge (1 Corinthians 2:10f.). Knowledge of God is thus imparted to us only insofar as we share in God's self-knowledge, or, better, are summoned to share in God's self-knowledge. This is where there comes into play, as we have seen, the doctrine of the Spirit who sets us in the analogy.

Along lines such as these we think we can overcome the difficulty in Schleiermacher's approach to Christology. We do not propose either to underrate or overrate the given reality of our self-consciousness, especially as modern men. The alternative would be the non-adult acceptance of a servile or implicit faith which does not truly appropriate the object of faith, which therewith denies humanity, and which exposes us to the cleavage in consciousness which was described above and the danger of which was clearly perceived by Schleiermacher. On the other hand, we shall relativize the rank of this consciousness with which God makes contact, disallowing its normative claim and thus preventing the figure of Christ from being manipulated in its name. The mode of relativization that we have in view is placed at our disposal by the new analogy of faith. We are summoned to conformity with him who addresses us in Christ. We are transformed into the new creature which banishes all old things, including the old consciousness (2 Corinthians 5:17).

---

[20] Pp. 195f., 207, 211.

XX

The Historical and Suprahistorical Aspects of Christ's Manifestation

We shall now try to develop the question of the historical figure of Jesus in its systematic dimensions.

The confession "Jesus is Lord" (*Kyrios Christos*) has been from the very first the central confession of the community. Obviously this is more than the confession of an individual figure of history. One cannot confess a historical figure in the sense of relating the basis, goal, and meaning of one's existence to it. All historical figures are in principle of equal rank. Only quantitative differences lie between them. In principle means here that they are of equal rank with reference to the fundamentals of human existence, e.g., guilt and finitude. Qualitative equality of this kind makes it impossible for one figure in history, e.g., myself, to find the ground of its existence in, or to be absolutely dependent on, another figure in history.

One cannot confess a historical figure but only admire, honor, or receive inspiring or deterrent impulses from such a figure. One may indeed "love" a figure of history, although naturally in a transferred sense. But when one confesses Jesus Christ in the doxology *Kyrios Christos,* this expresses something other than respect for a past figure. What is done might be provisionally formulated as follows: By means of the individual element in this figure one is confessing the universal element, or, better, the suprahistorical element, for the debated term "suprahistorical" is surely justifiable in this context.

On this term, M. Kähler especially should be consulted. He uses it in twofold differentiation, first, against the timelessness of a freely roving idea (*Dogmatische Zeitfragen,* II, 2nd ed. [1908], p. 75), and second, against absorption in time (*ibid.,* III [1913], pp. 163f.). The term denotes, then, the presence in the objectifiable historical phenomenon of a transcendent element which escapes objectification. Christ's work and his divine sonship, even in their historicity, are both full of eternal content for subjective receptivity. They are thus suprahistorical even in their historicity (*ibid.,* III, p. 154). Cf. also H. Leipold, *Offenbarung und Geschichte als Problem des Verstehens* (1962), pp. 57ff.; M. Dibelius, *Geschichtliche und über-geschichtliche Religion im Christentum,* 2nd ed. (1929); O. Eissfeldt, *Geschichtliches und Übergeschichtliches im AT* (1947). Instructive, too, is the similar understanding of the humanity of Christ in Luther, although the term "suprahistorical" is not used; cf. E. Wolf, "Die Christusverkündigung bei Luther," *Jesus Christus im Zeugnis der heiligen Schrift und der Kirche,* pp. 207ff.

Confession of the *Kyrios Christos* recognizes a suprahistorical dimension in Christ inasmuch as it makes his individual historical figure, his humanity, transparent for a transcendent element in virtue of which he is not just in history but also embraces history and holds its time in his hands. This means that he is universal as well as individual, and present and future as well as past. Already attention may be drawn to the fact that in this interrelating of the individual-historical and universal aspects we have a modern modification of the ancient doctrine of the two natures.

We shall now give a brief survey and characterization of the two dimensions.

1. THE UNIVERSAL AND COSMOLOGICAL ASPECT

Testimony is borne here to Christ's suprahistoricity to the extent that he embraces the world from creation to the *parousia*. The world was made in him, by him, and to him (Colossians 1:16; Ephesians 3:9; cf. also 1 Corinthians 8:6). Already, then, the creation of the world itself has christological significance; salvation is projected in it. The love which caused God to give his only-begotten Son (John 3:16) does not have its ground in mere spontaneity but is already at work in the plan to create the world. In both creation stories man as the crown and representative of creation is summoned from the very first to partnership with God (Genesis 1:26ff.; 2:15ff.). Related to this universal cosmological thesis is the fact that election to salvation in the world has a christological reference prior to the world: God has chosen us in him (Christ) before the foundation of the world (Ephesians 1:4). The axis of the salvation event does not lie in an individual decision in virtue of which I confess God on my own initiative. It lies in a universal decision of God for us before all worlds, in his confession of us as his creatures and children.

Creation has, then, a theological *telos*; it is with a view to salvation. When this is remembered, creation has a different aspect. This sheds new light on the ancient controversy between the doctrine of creation and science. Underlying this controversy are apparently rival answers to the question how we are to think of the origin of man and the world. Theology replies that they have their origin in a divine act of creation, while science says that they come by a long process of evolution. These answers seem to be mutually exclusive. But if we remember the christological background of creation, it is seen that these are not alternatives and the controversy falls to the ground. For the mystery of creation is not the object of a question as to the Whence; it is the object of a question as to the Whither. (Even if a question as to the Whence is still pursued, the meaning of the Whence in theology differs from its meaning in science; cf. ThE, II, 1, § 1164-1275; E.T. I, pp. 455ff.).

In the light of this universal christological aspect the doctrine of redemption as well as the doctrine of creation takes on a different look. First, it is no longer a mere doctrine of the settling of an incident, the correction of the fall. It relates to the purpose of the whole project of creation. Second, it is not controlled merely by the dualism of belief and acceptance or unbelief and rejection, and therefore by the process of church history. It has a cosmological horizon. Christ is the secret of the world even where there is no knowledge of him and no actualization of the question of decision. He is the cosmic Christ as depicted in Colossians (cf. O. Dilschneider, *Christus Pantokrator* [1962]). Even atheists and the adherents of other religions stand in relation to him. The world cannot be divided into God's supporters on the one side and his enemies on the other, at least not in the sense that God rules only among his supporters. Nebuchadnezzar and Cyrus also come within God's plan for the world and have to play the roles assigned to them (Jeremiah 25:9; 27:6; Ezekiel 26:7; 29:18f., etc.). The rainbow after the flood, which Yahweh arches over the earth as a sign of the covenant with Noah, speaks of salvation to the created world at large (Genesis 9:12ff.). In the NT, too, God causes his rain to fall and his sun to shine on both the good and the bad, the just and the unjust (Matthew 5:45). All who share in creation, not just Christians, live under the promise of salvation, so that our hour has the character of *kairos*. This is why it makes sense to speak of the Christ before Christ or of Christ in the OT, although this is no reason for forced allegorizing after the manner of W. Vischer in his *Christuszeugnis des AT* (1934); E.T. *The Witness of the OT to Christ* (1949), or H. Hellbardt in his article "Abrahams Lüge," ThEx, No. 42.

One might say, perhaps, that the universal or cosmic aspect is a special feature in Paul's theology. This is true to the extent, although only to the extent, that Paul brings it out very clearly with the help of his doctrine of Christ's pre-existence. It is a mistake to think that we have here a gnostically inspired reconstruction which involves addition to an original Christology.[1] Paul's statements are merely an intellectual development of the implicit universalism which is to be found already in the synoptic Jesus.

Jesus does not just *teach* a reference back to creation; he *is* this reference. As the sayings about divorce show (Matthew 5:31; 19:1ff.), in him we have to do with the original will of God valid *ap' archês*. This will takes form and is present in him. His authority consists in the fact that in him we are reached by God's command at creation which transcends all the later legal systems and emergency ordinances of this aeon and which divests them of their usurped absoluteness. In the light of the creation command

---

[1] The view of E. Haenchen in RGG[3], II, 1652f.

they are suddenly seen to be limited. They apply only to the fallen world. In them God comes to grips with our hardness of heart (*sklerokardia*).

In illustration reference might be made to our earlier interpretation of philosophical ethics, especially in Kant. The action demanded by morality is normally restricted by my inclinations. Among other things the axiom: "You can because you should," means that no one can give more, and from no one should more be demanded, than what he has and what is under his control. I can be ethically claimed and held responsible only in respect of will, disposition, and action (which lie within my radius of competence), not in respect of being, constitution, and inclination. The Sermon on the Mount, however, makes a radical claim which demands that I be wholly for God, in inclination as well as action, in heart as well as disposition (Matthew 5:28).

This unconditional claim which in fact I cannot meet makes sense only against the background of the reference to creation. I come whole from the hands of the Creator and must give myself back intact to him. If I cannot do this—and in fact I cannot—then the alienation of my being, and of my being in the world, is displayed. I am called in question in being as well as work, in state as well as act. But the one who authoritatively tells me this himself represents the whole and intact man who stands in harmony with God. His representativeness is here my judgment.

In the first instance, then, the Sermon on the Mount judges me, not because it comes with unconditional demands which radicalize the Mosaic *nomos,* but because the fulfilling of these demands stands before me bodily and in person. He is the one who does not destroy but fulfils (*plērôsai,* Matthew 5:17). As the kingdom of God is present and comes among us in him (Luke 17:21), the circle of the fallen world is transcended—of that world which always tries to reassure itself by reducing the requirements and which makes itself the measure instead of letting itself be measured and evaluated. In him God's aim in creating the world is disclosed. In him, too, the original state in which God's plan is still intact is portrayed and is present in person.

Hence the orders of this world are relativized. Far from being the true and original will of God, they express on the one hand God's patience with our condition while on the other hand they are an institutional objectification of our hardness of heart. The sacred egoism of the structures is simply a macrocosmic reflection of what determines the state of our heart. Thus the Preacher on the Mount still makes demands of us as though we were in the original state as we came from the hands of God, and also as though the kingdom of God were already present in which the will and lordship of God are in force without let or hindrance. This backward reference to creation and forward reference to the eschaton lead to a relativizing of this aeon and its orders. Christ is indeed "in" this aeon and therefore "with " us; but he is not "from" this aeon or "of" us.

One might say that the universal aspect which comes to light here is eschatological, since Christ embraces the beginning and end or basis and goal of the world, and brings our aeon under the measure of these frontiers. The result of this measurement is as follows. Our aeon or world is an interim phenomenon. This world, including the men who dwell in it, has not come out of the hands of God in its present form. It is alien to these hands. Hence it is no longer "creation" in the strict sense. To that extent it does not have a definitive character. It will pass away. (For this reason the concept of orders of creation, apart from marriage, is unsuitable and even misleading.)[2] As it now is, this world has not been from the beginning and similarly it is not the end of God's ways. It is something which will be outdated, which God will end, for this world cannot itself produce the plan of salvation. Utopian ideas of the end of the world and millennial hypotheses indicate this in mythical form. The returning Christ expresses cosmologically the fact that this world is at an end.

Expectation of the future eschaton, which naturally embraces and decisively determines the present,[3] is thus an inalienable part of the universal aspect of Christology. The ground is prepared for this view, at least among some second generation Bultmannians, by the insight not merely that NT eschatological expectation is a temporal form of expression but that eschatology actually loses its point if, instead of proclaiming an aeonic coming and going, it is simply a statement about the present moment of decision, so that what was originally only a deduction—an implication for understanding of the moment—becomes the dominant and exclusive theme.

Thus Käsemann ("Zum Thema der urchristlichen Apokalyptik," ZThK [1962], 3, pp. 278ff., repr. in *Exegetische Versuche und Besinnungen* [1964], II, pp. 105ff.) criticizes realized eschatology when, from Hellenism to Bultmann, it finds in future expectations only apocalyptic relics or (Ebeling) apocalyptic fantasies (ZThK, p. 278). On this view such expectations are a heteronomous and undeveloped element in an anthropology that we can understand and appropriate at all other points. In reality, however, expectation of Christ and his future coming again is a basic element in Pauline thinking. The theology of existence blinds us to one of the finest trains of thought in the apostle and to something which modern proclamation finally needs to recapture (p. 282n.).

The reason for this fatal reduction is that existential theology is mired down in the tradition of the reformation interpretation of Paul. This is characterized by overemphasis on the anti-judaistic element in Paul, so that he is understood only in terms of his attack on nomism and on the resultant error regarding righteousness. This aspect is true enough, but has only partial importance. It is a serious mistake to package the whole of Paul's theology in it. If all his thinking is reduced to the dualism of

---

[2] Cf. ThE, III, Index.

[3] It is a strangely mistaken but common view that a futurist eschatology disavows the here and now. A glance at secularized forms of such an eschatology, as in Marxism, ought to be enough to show clearly to what extent a definite future expectation can characterize and mobilize the present.

law and gospel, inevitably it seems to center exclusively on the self-under-standing of the man who stands under the law and is then rescued from it by grace. There is no real justification for providing Paul's theology with an exclusively noetic theme and then presenting it as anthropology, as the the doctrine of Christian existence.

Naturally the reformers were right enough to stress this aspect of Paul in the contemporary context of their battle against a legalistic church. As we showed in Volume I, various elements in the message are theologically urgent or remote according to changing perspectives.

Nevertheless, the overemphasis is a fatal one in the sense that it produces blindness to other essential elements in Pauline thinking whose careful examination and adoption might have made it much more difficult to slip into a theology of self-understanding and anthropological reductionism. What are these other elements?

Historical research has shown that alongside the battle for justification and the anti-judaistic polemic there is also in Paul a rejection of enthusiasm (ZThK, p. 279). The enthusiasts thought that the eschaton and the final consummation were already present or very close. The promise of recep-tion of the Spirit had already been fulfilled. There was no more need to pray: Veni Creator Spiritus. The essential form of holiness is already pos-sible here and now.

Paul does not fight the enthusiast merely by opposing to this view an apocalyptic future expectation. He does not exalt what will happen at the expense of what has already happened. Instead he binds the Now and the One Day together. This is especially clear in his understanding of baptism. According to Romans 6:4f. this mediates a share in the destiny of the Redeemer and plunges us into Christ's death (p. 279). It already does this now. The baptized gains a share in the heavenly life and is thus empowered for new obedience. The new thing that comes, that is given by baptism into death, is the work of the risen Lord. If, however, baptism denotes our dying and rising again here and now (and not just in the future), it might be inferred that already here and now we participate in the resurrec-tion life of Christ and enjoy this participation as one of the present gifts. "Why should not physical resurrection from the dead be one of the gifts?" seems to be the rhetorical question of the enthusiasts. It is worth noting, however, that Paul does not draw this inference. He certainly links partici-pation in the cross to participation in the resurrection, but with a striking eschatological caveat. Participation in the resurrection (as distinct from the cross) is spoken of in future terms. Baptism prepares us for it and sum-mons us to it but does not confer the gift itself. The Now does not become a fulfilled present. It remains open to the future. It is kept in expectation. Even the new obedience mediated by baptism is not a definitive fulfilment. It is a prophecy of what will be only when we shall be redeemed from the body of this death (Romans 7:24). The resurrection itself is reserved for Christ alone. The Spirit gives us only the pledge or reversion of the future awakening (Romans 8:23; 2 Corinthians 5:2). We are candidates for the resurrection. The new obedience is simply an anticipatory demonstration of what has begun to work in us as something new.

Along the same lines the resurrection of the dead (cf. 1 Corinthians 15:20-28) is not an event which can be fully stated within the confines of anthropology. It is part of a Christology that cannot be integrated into anthropology. As an event accomplished by the second Adam, it is not oriented to our reawakening to life but to the lordship of Christ. "He must reign" (1 Corinthians 15:25) is the heart of the exposition and the basis of assurance as to our own destiny (p. 280).

The doctrine of the resurrection is not competing, then, with that of the immortality of the soul. The latter necessarily means that we are interested only in ourselves. Its orientation is foreign to that of Paul's eschatology. No perspective can be more apocalyptic. Nothing is more alien to Paul than speaking about an end of history which has already come. The end-time has begun to run its course, but the decisive moment is still future. In speaking of the beginning of the end-time, Paul uses certain elements in the realized eschatology of the enthusiasts. But he sets them in a different systematic context and thus gives them new rank. The present is seen in the light of the future. He thus protects present statements against the danger of becoming elements in a packaged anthropology.

In Paul, then, present eschatology is not an alternative to future eschatology; it is a constituent element in it (p. 280). For the future already has a bridgehead in the present. I have been given the pledge of the Spirit. Still to come, however, is the end of the reign of death on earth, which is identical with the end of history (p. 281).

We have included this short excursus on the present and future because it thematically supplements the cosmological aspect of Christ and at the same time indicates that this cannot find appropriate expression within the confines of anthropology alone (including a Christianity which is reduced to mere ethics and fellow-humanity). At the same time, the excursus makes it plain that considering the future lordship of Christ must not divert attention from the here and now of the present. Our glance at the future includes this too. It does not permit any emancipation from the present. According to this universal and cosmological aspect, Christ comprises the proton and the eschaton of the world. All things are from him, by him, and to him. Hence our present is included too.

2. THE INDIVIDUAL AND HISTORICAL ASPECT

In opposition to Hegel, Kierkegaard observed that it is the paradox of Christianity that God is an individual man. This helps us to see that the historical element in Christ is not just the actualizing of an idea. If it were, the form of the historical actualization would be far less important than the idea.[4] For the gospel, however, God's entry into history, the incarna-

---

[4] As it obviously is in D. F. Strauss.

tion of the Word, is itself the point of the salvation event. The history which
culminates in the event of Jesus Christ is no mere container for something;
it is the thing itself. It is not a symbol which is by its very nature improper
and which points away from itself to something else; it points to itself.[5] It
is not the manifestation of something. It is this something in actuality.
"Behold the man" means that God himself has come among you in this
man (John 19:5)—although Pilate himself can hardly have meant this.
As he has come among you, the kingdom of God is among you (Luke
17:21).[6]

The individual and historical aspect of Christ is thus related to the universal and cosmological element and the two together constitute what might
be called the christological melody. As the one who represents the dominion
of God which embraces us from the beginning of history to the end of
history, Christ also comes into the history which lies between this beginning
and this end. He is with us and among us, not just before us and after us.
This is what we mean by the individual and historical aspect.

Christ is not just the one in whom the world was made and who is coming again. He is also the one who has come, who was born in Bethlehem,
who was tempted with us and alongside us, who died with us and alongside
us, who thus bears the pressure of history with us and alongside us, who is
in solidarity with us. He does not march alone in cosmic sovereignty over
the world. He also enters the ship and is with us as it is battered by the
waves (Matthew 8:23-27). He makes himself an object of what happens
in the same way as we are. If he is the Lord of history he is also its member.
Time is in his hands (Psalm 31:15) but he is also in the hands of time. He
grows, achieves maturity and wisdom, is subject to his parents (Luke
2:51f.). He comes under the control of men. If we are to call him Redeemer we must see him under both aspects.

We shall now try to think through the relation between the two aspects.

First, Christ can be our Redeemer only because he himself stands at the
place for which he redeems us, the place of eternal fellowship with the
Father, the place where God's lordship embraces us. As one who stands
thus at the side of the Father he is both the goal and the means of redemption. He is the goal inasmuch as the end of redemption can only be acceptance into his union with the Father and therewith into eternal union with
himself. For he is not just a station on the way which we must pass through
to reach God and then leave behind. If he were, he would have only the
rank of a teacher whose aim is to make himself superfluous. A teacher earns
little thanks if his pupil always remains a pupil.

Along these lines Christ in Lessing is only a stage which must be traversed
on the way to the eternal pure gospel of reason. He is also our elder brother

---

[5] This must be said in opposition even to a lofty view of symbols such as we find
in Tillich; cf. K. D. Nörenberg, *Analogia imaginis* (1966).

[6] The identity of fact and meaning plays an important role in the eucharistic
debate between Luther and Zwingli.

who knows this final stage of history before we do, who anticipates it in his own life, and who thus in principle can be surpassed.

According to the common witness of the NT, however, Christ is himself the goal of redemption. Both in faith and in sight, both now and in the eschaton, Christ is and always will be the one in whom I have the Father. He is not just the way; he is also the truth and the life (John 14:6). He is both the way and the goal. For in addition to being the goal he is also the means or the way. The fact that he is the means to bring us to the goal means that he has authority (*exousia*). He can command the waves. He can say: "Take up thy bed and walk" (Mark 2:9). He can forgive sins. He can accomplish thereby the work of redemption.

It is easy to see that confession of this power, of the significance of Christ as both the way and the goal of redemption, lies behind the dogmatic struggles relating to the *Filioque* (on the *Filioque* cf. also the second excursus on the doctrine of the Trinity). In this controversy, which contributed to the schism between the Eastern and Western churches, the question is whether the creed should add that the Holy Spirit proceeded from the Son as well as the Father ("from the Father and the Son"). What interest can faith have in this hotly contested addition?

The Holy Spirit is the power within the Word to make it a living Word, to actualize it for life and understanding. The Holy Spirit is thus the power of illumination which enables me to know the Word as God's Word—and not just to know it, but also to acknowledge it and thus allow it to be powerful in me. On this understanding of the Holy Spirit the *Filioque* takes on theological relevance. If we were simply to follow the original statement: "I believe in the Holy Ghost, the Lord and Giver of life, proceeding from the Father" (and not also from the Son), this would mean that the true history of salvation would take place in immediacy between the Father and us, and Christ would have only a temporary place in this history with clearly defined and limited functions. He would not be for me the end (*telos*) of the process of salvation history; he would simply be an instrument of it.

What seems at first glance to be a mere conceptual refinement in the sphere of speculative metaphysics leads us on closer inspection to a wholly new conception of the figure of Christ and the event of redemption. Hence it is not primarily a speculative interest which produces the *Filioque* debate. In what seems at first to be a purely speculative problem a momentous question of faith may be discerned.

To appreciate it properly note should be taken of the great change in the style of our thinking. Since the reformation, and especially in the age of the existential or social orientation of theology, the only theological problems normally to catch our attention are those which crop up in the sphere of personal existence or the social nexus. A few examples may be given. For instance, does justification mean passivity in relation to what God does, or are we summoned to cooperation? This kind of question can split churches, as we see from the reformation schisms. Again, does faith in the salvation event imply a specific historical belief too? Have we to accept certain historical events (e.g., the empty tomb and the virgin birth)? Or is it possible, in view of the difficulties for the modern mind, to transplant the salvation event from the plane of history to the direct history which I have here and now with the kerygma? Is salvation history composed, not of that which is alleged to have taken place in the past in Bethlehem, Nazareth, and Jerusalem, but of what happens to me here and now as I die and rise again with Christ? This kind of discussion, as may be seen from the Bultmann controversy, can also lead to the very borders of schism, and it has obvious existential relevance and anthropological significance. Finally, may we not rescue all the problems of faith from the transcendence of theistic definitions and set them in the concrete situations of life, so that they are totally absorbed in these? Is not God incarnated in our fellow-man? Does not theology consist, then, of statements about human communication and the social structures which control it? These questions, too, cause battles of the same intensity and divisive vehemence as marked the christological and trinitarian controversies of the early centuries.

For us theological problems obviously have reality only as they are formulated in terms of their influence on existential situations and only as their anthropological or social significance is demonstrated. The exact structure of Christology, the interpretation of the doctrine of the two natures, its liquidation in favor of other conceptions—these things leave us relatively unconcerned unless their existential implications are plain to see. Things were completely different, however, for the Spanish church which included the *Filioque* in the creed in 589, for the Frankish church which followed suit in 767, and for the Roman church which in 1040 (after some 450 years) adopted the *Filioque* into the cultus. In those days the ontological structure of thinking caused theologians to consider relations of being even down to the remote details of the intratrinitarian relationship, for in these there was anticipated what we today call existential relations. Existential relations were already known in the early stages of potentiality. The passion engendered in the related controversies was not due to the dynamic of a purely speculative interest in formulation. It derived from awareness that the minute differences in trinitarian or christological statements carried implications for the historical being of man and his self-understanding. For this reason we can see the importance of these ancient discussions only if we look beyond the thought-forms which first catch our attention.

After this historical digression we now repeat the decisive statement underlying the first aspect under which we see Christ as the Redeemer. He can be our Redeemer only because he himself stands at the place for which he redeems us, namely, the place of eternal fellowship with the Father. As the truth and the life he is the goal of salvation history. As the bearer of supreme authority he is also the way to this goal.

Second, Christ is our Redeemer only to the extent that in solidarity with us he is our Brother who bears the burden of our guilt and fate and brings us home in love.

In both dimensions of his redeemership what matters first is not what he *does* but what he *is*. We may thus define redemption only if our definitions are predicates in sentences containing ontic statements about his person. We have to declare that the nature and mystery of the person of Jesus Christ have always been at the heart of what Christian doctrine has to say about redemption, justification, reconciliation, forgiveness, new creation, and consummation. The ontic statements of the NT are to be understood along these lines. Thus he is our peace in Ephesians 2:14, the way, the truth, and the life in John 14:6. Characteristically we are not told that he simply brings or provides or teaches these things. No, peace is given and is among us in his being; it is identical with his being.

Since the being of his person (as the Lord who has authority and the Brother who is in solidarity) is always the element which gives meaning to his words and works, these words and works come under severe misunderstanding if they are ever detached from his person. What becomes of the miracles of Jesus if they are severed from his person and thus considered in isolation from that which interprets them? They lose their transparence as signs (*semeia*). They become ambiguous miracles which lead away from faith. They are evaluated by those who benefit from them merely according to the criterion of effectiveness (the satisfaction or healing they bring) (John 6:26).[7] What becomes of the Sermon on the Mount and especially the Beatitudes if they are detached from the one who speaks and causes both the fulfilment of the law and also the promised blessedness to be present in his own person (Matthew 5:17)? They become a legalism which, enhanced with absurd radicalism, disqualifies itself by its harmful significance in actual life. What becomes of the parable of the Prodigal Son (Luke 15:1ff.) if it is read in isolation from the one who tells it and who makes present in his own person the mercy of the Father? It becomes a moving story which is far too beautiful to be true. It we eliminate the person of Christ as a key to the interpretation of his words and works, if we think that only the Father belongs to the gospel and not the Son,[8] the works are obscure and the words simply become the occasion of misunderstanding.

The essence, way, and goal of redemption are to be described simply in terms of the attributes of his person. He is Lord and Brother, King and Companion, Son of God and Son of Man, holding the times in his hands and giving himself up to them. All these terms express in the form of qualities the polarity of his person and also the polar dimensions of the salvation event.

---

[7] Already in the OT one may see how miracles become ambiguous and lose their quality as signs when they are detached from the person and from the context of salvation. Thus the magicians can do before Pharaoh many of the same works as Moses and Aaron (Exodus 7:11, 22; 8:3, 14f.).

[8] A. von Harnack, *What Is Christianity?* (1902), p. 154.

They occur again in the NT predicates of his person and constitute the programmatic statements of a systematic Christology.

Two supporting and supplementary points may be made at this juncture.

First, if Christ's person is the ontic ground of his words and works, and must always be used to interpret them, it would be an illegitimate step from the ontic to the cognitive sphere if this were taken to mean that we must begin with a christological analysis of the mystery of his person if we are to be able to understand his words and works and conduct. Our process of understanding in relation to the gospel has a highly dialectical structure. For we learn who he *is* precisely from his words and works, from what happens to us through him. Melanchthon is right when he says that to know Christ is to know his benefits. How else can we know him? By dogmatic statements about his pre-existence? By the doctrine of the two natures? This is too absurd to require express refutation. His words and works (in relation to us) trigger in us the question who he is. But when they do, the answer that he is Jesus Christ becomes the light in which his words and works appear to us. Only along these lines, within this dialectic, do we assert that the person of Christ is the norm by which to interpret his words and works.

Second, what we have said about the relation of the person to its words and works and conduct applies not only to Christology but also, under the inspiration of Christology, to anthropology. My own salvation is not brought about by what I say or do but by what I *am* as a person, e.g., whether I am in the truth (John 18:37). Nicodemus cannot come to share in salvation merely by listening to Jesus the teacher or receiving new direction from his signs (John 3:2) but only as he is born again, as he becomes personally a new creation (John 3:3ff.), as this renewal is imparted to him by the only-begotten Son (John 3:16). Redemption undoubtedly issues in new words and works. In itself, however, it consists in what causes these new words and works. This is the regeneration of the person. It is the raising again to a new life which is empowered by the risen Lord and is grounded in the union of our person with the person of Christ. Similarly I am not justified in terms of my own words and works which have now become righteous. The factual sinner is still there behind the man he already is in the eyes of God. The verdict of justification applies to my person. *Thou art just before me; I confess thee.*

In analogy to what we find in Christology, all statements about my thoughts and words and works are predicates whose subject is the person. As Luther puts it, the person does the works. The person, then, is the criterion for evaluating the words and works. Now the person is qualified by whether he believes or not, whether he is just before God or not. By the criterion of the person, then, works which are objectively dubious before men can still be just before God, and conversely works which are objectively righteous before men can fall under the judgment of not being pleasing to God. Taking an extreme example, Luther can thus argue that adultery in faith is no sin, while worship of God in unbelief is idolatry (Theses [at the 1520 Disputation] on Whether Works Contribute to Grace, Nos. 10 and

11, WA, 7, 231f.). The analogy between some of the structural features of Christology on the one side and anthropology on the other seems to us to be worth noting.

Implications for Christological Method

Now that we have clarified the dimensions of the reality of Christ (the universal and the individual or historical), we must turn to the urgent question how any statements at all can be made about a figure which appears to us under such diametrically opposing aspects.

The problem is this. Insofar as Christ encounters me as an individual figure in history, he (also) belongs to the sphere of objective historical research. Yet insofar as I have in view his universal significance, which Kähler, as we have seen, describes as suprahistorical, he embraces me and is basically "non-objective"—at least to the extent that he lies outside the sphere of the knowledge which seeks to lay hold of objects. Since, however, the universal and suprahistorical element is present in the individual personal figure and is indeed identical with this figure (John 1:14), it is open to question whether I can make even the individual and personal element the object of inquiry and research with the usual historical methods. When it is said of the Jesus who figures in history and walks on earth that, being reviled, he reviled not again (1 Peter 2:23; cf. Luke 6:22; 1 Corinthians 4:12), do we have here a reference to the individual and personal element or to the universal element? Is this history or suprahistory? It is of the very nature of everything historical that the echo principle applies to it. Here, however, a mode of conduct is described historically which very definitely does not fall under the structural law of history. How so?

We have only to put the question to see at least that negatively the universal and historical or divine and human elements cannot be discursively sundered from one another, that one cannot say where the one begins and the other ends, or that the one can be grasped objectively while the other is not objectifiable. The fact that this sundering is not possible, but founders on the person of Christ, is shown in its own way by the doctrine of the communication of the attributes. (The range of what this is seeking to say with ontological means extends far beyond the original issue, for obviously the critical study of scripture and the question of objectifiability could not be envisaged when the doctrine was formulated.)

The difficulty of trying to separate the historical and suprahistorical elements in Christ may be seen from the constant failure of all attempts in this direction. Most striking in this regard is the fact that the quest of the historical Jesus has proved so spectacularly unsuccessful. The history of the quest is a history of frustration; cf. A. Schweitzer's *Quest of the Historical Jesus* (E.T. 1910). The quest was bound to fail, for the question of the historical Jesus as the original and as yet undistorted basis of the Christian faith can be put only on two conditions.

First, there has to be the underlying assumption that Jesus is a normal if outstanding figure of history whose depiction demands the elimination of anything supernatural, suprahistorical, transcendent, or divine. This elimination is demanded by the premise that what transcends history has to be mythological, having its basis in the theology of the community and necessarily being an exaggeration. Layers of color have to be peeled away, then, in order to bring the original to light, i.e., the historical Jesus. Only when this is done can one call upon Jesus with one's own faith, since previously faith rests on the faith of others, i.e., the primitive community and its additions to the portrait. Unfortunately, however, there is a twofold error in this whole procedure. For one thing, it is thought that the divine and human or suprahistorical and historical elements in Christ can be separated. For another it is thought that only the historical figure who is achieved by elimination of the divine or suprahistorical element is genuinely historical, while the transcendent reality is simply human embellishment.

Second, it has to be assumed that the original figure who is brought to light in this way can be objectified like all other figures of history. Criteria of historical verifiability such as those advanced by Troeltsch (causality, immanence, and analogy) have to be regarded as applicable, and have to be applied, in this case too. But this condition also runs up against what we have called the unity of the figure of Jesus. It fails to take into account the fact that the Jesus who walks on earth is full of traits that transcend the ordinary picture of man, so that the echo principle is overcome here.

Related to this is another reason why the quest of the historical Jesus has failed. This consists in the properties of the texts which have to serve as sources in the quest, namely, the Gospels. These texts confess Jesus as our Lord and Brother. As kerygmatic forms of statement, they are so structured, then, that they presuppose at every point the unity of the two dimensions.

M. Kähler, in his *Der sogenannte historische Jesus und der geschichtliche biblische Christus,* was the first to point out that the texts which bear witness to Christ do not aim to be history or biography. They do not treat Jesus of Nazareth merely as an object to be scrutinized as other figures of history are scrutinized. They are thus poorly adapted to foster this kind of objective relation to Jesus. If we approach them with this in view, we shall investigate them in a very inadequate way, putting questions to them which they do not put and which they are thus unable to answer. Any investigation which runs contrary to the thrust of the text which is being investigated will necessarily lead to purely abstruse answers. How nonsensical the whole procedure is may be clearly discerned from Schweitzer himself. When the last layer has been peeled off, and we tensely await the original, all that is seen is an unreal apocalyptical ghost and not the man whom we sought; cf. F. Holmström, *Das eschatologische Denken der Gegenwart* (1936), pp. 72ff.

There is a good reason why the original texts are kerygmatic rather than historical accounts. The primitive community speaks of Jesus as one who has won its faith. The center of its interest is not a historical individual called Jesus. It is what Kähler calls the historically powerful personality of Christ.

The historical power of a figure may be seen from the effects it has. The effect of Christ is the faith which he causes and the preaching which follows from this faith. The historically powerful work of Christ[9] consists in the fact that he becomes the preached Christ. The gospels themselves are part of the effect, for their writers are "reached" by the Christ of proclamation and only in this light do they deal with the question who he is; cf. my book *Wie modern darf die Theologie sein?* (1967), pp. 31-72; E.T. 1969, pp. 21-59. The idea of being reached is an indication that we have here a reversal of the subject-object relation. The evangelists do not make Christ (and even less so the historical Jesus) the object of their inquiry. As those who have been claimed and reached, they are themselves the object of the preached Christ.

Within our own train of thought we may supplement Kähler's view as follows. The disciples cannot see Jesus of Nazareth as a historical figure, at least after the resurrection, because they have learned to see him in his identity with the exalted Lord. In other words, they have grasped the interrelation of the individual or personal aspect and the universal aspect. In retrospect, then, the one who walks on earth is for them the receptacle of the Logos, the universal pantocrator, whom the universe cannot contain. This enables us to see how doubtful and hopeless is the question of the historical Jesus. If the quest has now been renewed, as in Käsemann, it is in a very different way and with a plainly modified aim. The new goal is no longer the unreal one of trying to achieve a basis of faith which is objectifiable and from which all human embellishments have been eliminated. It is that of achieving a corrective to a purely kerygmatic theology which threatens to rule out historical facticity altogether.

We now return to our initial question: How can we grasp at all a figure which has such heterogeneous aspects?

If we could separate the two aspects—which we cannot—then many things might be said with no particular difficulty. We can think through that which encompasses us non-objectively. Hegel's concept of spirit might be adduced in illustration. The idea of God, the idea of humanity, and even the union of the two (D. F. Strauss) lie in the confines of the possibility of thought. Similarly that which is individually historical can be an object of thought when taken alone. But I cannot combine it with the first group, at least theoretically. That God became an individual man is the absolute paradox, as Kierkegaard would say in opposition to Hegel.

When I pursue theology or Christology, however, I do not make this impossible combination, at any rate in the sense of constructing the figure of Christ out of the two elements by adding them together. Instead, I encounter the figure of Christ in whom the combination meets me with ontic givenness, but in a direct, pre-theoretical way. As W. Herrmann might say,

---

[9] We deliberately restrict Kähler's concept of historical power to a single area. Outside this it seems to us to be dubious and even unfortunate. Kierkegaard would not have liked it.

I come under the "impression" of this figure in whom I find both a strange nearness to me and yet also a strange difference, distance, and remoteness from me, yet not in isolation but as a unity. Only in later reflection when I try to expound this figure and relate it to my general experience of reality does that which is one in immediacy seem to be heterogeneous and conceptually irreconcilable. What is homogeneous in experience breaks apart in the act of reflection and suffers the fate imposed by the discursive structure of human thought.

Our relation to freedom offers a certain analogy to this transition from immediacy to reflection. For Kant the awareness of freedom is an experience which I come to know in the sphere of practical reason. The expression: "You can, for you should," has a direct stringency which cannot be questioned. If, however, I try to grasp the nature of freedom with the methods of theoretical reason, it seems to be a paradoxical contradiction which only by very dialectical detours can be brought into systematic connection with the categories of theoretical reason.[10] If we could conceive of a being which had no ethical experience of freedom but existed in pure intellectuality, Kant's theoretical-dialectical arguments for freedom would seem to him to be absurd somersaults of thought. Freedom can be seen only from within, and only when it is seen from within does the theoretical dialectic of its description become meaningful or intelligible. In contrast, a freedom that is seen only from without necessarily seems to be nonsense. That which determines our personal existence has to be seen from within, from the involvement of the person.

This applies to Christ, too, insofar as he determines our being as persons. He who has not experienced Christ, and who thus sees the intellectual difficulties of a theoretical Christology only from without, will turn away with horror and incomprehension from these paradoxical gymnastics. The doctrine of the two natures and the doctrine of the communication of the attributes will have for him the appearance of monstrosities of thought. But he who has met Christ in person has in his hand the key to the statements. He finds in them attempts to encircle discursively the simple center of the encounter and to fix geometrical points which focus on this center even though the point of intersection itself cannot be grasped intellectually.

Cautiously one might suggest that there is some analogy to this in the way that Schleiermacher speaks of feeling. Feeling for the *universum* is a direct experience which undergoes change into another genus when an attempt is made to speak of it; cf. the second of the *Speeches*. Schleiermacher is not satisfied with talking about it because this makes it unintelligible and he wants to lead people to have the experience themselves. Goethe has the young Werther say something similar when he acknowl-

---

[10] On the dialectic in Kant's understanding of freedom cf. ThE, I, § 1517, and also the author's *Das Verhältnis zwischen dem Ethischen und dem Ästhetischen* (1932), pp. 101ff.

edges that his experience of oneness with the universe cannot be expressed in art or literature.

We have thus developed the problem of method in terms of the figure of Christ himself. In this figure we encounter two dimensions, a universal cosmological dimension on the one side and an individual historical dimension on the other. In the act of faith-encounter the two constitute a unity but in later reflection they fall apart paradoxically. Although reflection cannot comprehend what faith apprehends, it cannot be left out and has to be undertaken. If it were left out, Christ would be left standing at the gate of reason and would not be Lord of every area of life. He would be shut up in the religious department. If we do not want this, we have to engage in reflection, setting him in relation to other contexts of life and thought, and being willing to bear the burden of paradox.

This venture can be meaningfully undertaken only on one condition which our discussion thus far has helped to analyze. The condition is that we realize that pre-theoretical encounter with Christ must be the guide and norm of theoretical Christology. In traditional terminology, faith precedes theology. If theology is not to fall victim to speculative entanglement, it must be informed by the certainty that it is a broken enterprise which follows faith, which always stands in need of forgiveness, and which seeks to include the doxology of reason within the doxology of faith.[11]

We now face the task of considering what way christological reflection must take if it is to meet the condition indicated.

---

[11] On this role of the reason in theology cf. ThE, II, 1, § 1321ff.

XXI

The Basic Problem of Expression and the Unavoidability of Paradox

The rational difficulty with which every Christology is confronted is that of bringing together the universal-suprahistorical aspect of the figure of Christ and the individual-historical aspect. A negative sign of the difficulty, as we have seen, is that constant attempts have been made to isolate the two aspects.

A classical model of this type of separation may be found in K. Jaspers[1] when by contrasting Giordano Bruno and Galileo he discerns two different kinds of truth which are alternatives, i.e., which cannot be integrated. The one kind of truth is that of objectifiable knowledge and the other is that of non-objectifiable faith. The former, represented by Galileo, has the possibility of objective certainty. It can be the mathematical truth of astronomy or even historical truth. In contrast, Bruno's thesis that all the worlds have souls and are entelechies (cf. later Spinoza and Goethe) relates to the truth which encompasses me and which cannot be grasped objectively. It is thus dependent on the conviction of the one who believes it. If the witness denies it, he betrays the truth which depends on his witness. Galileo, however, can calmly deny and retract, for his truth is objectifiable; it does not depend on him; even without him it will prevail in virtue of its general validity. The two forms of truth are thus mutually exclusive. They cannot be integrated even in the figure of Christ. I have to choose under which of the two aspects of truth I wish to see him, whether as an objectifiable figure of history (as a man like ourselves, like Caesar or Gandhi), or as representative of a universal determination of being which escapes objective grasp.

Jaspers' model implies a distinction between faith and knowledge. Bruno believes and Galileo knows. Bruno was ready to recant many things but not the decisive proposition and so he died a martyr's death. Galileo recanted the doctrine of the movement of the earth round the sun. We see

---

[1] *Der philosophische Glaube* (1948), pp. 11f.; E.T. *The Perennial Scope of Philosophy* (1949), pp. 4f.

here the distinction between truth which suffers from recantation and truth which is unaffected by it. The two men did what was appropriate to the truth championed by them. Truth by which I live is truth only as I am identical with it. It is historical in manifestation, does not have general validity in terms of objective statement, but is unconditional. Truth which can be demonstrated exists without me, enjoys general validity, and is nonhistorical and timeless but is not unconditional, since it relates to the presuppositions and methods of knowledge and thus comes within the context of finitude. It is inappropriate to want to die for what can be proved right. But when a thinker cannot recant without harming the truth itself, this is his secret. No general insight can demand that he be a martyr. If he is, like Bruno, this is a mark of true faith, namely, of the certainty of faith, which I cannot demonstrate as I can the scientific knowledge of earthly things; cf. *ibid.,* p. 11 (E.T. p. 4).

On this view the truth "Christ" is truth after the manner of Bruno. Indeed, it offers an exemplary illustration of what is meant by trust in the unconditioned, in the fatherly ground of the world which embraces me. It has for us the same significance as for Bruno when we hear it. It triggers similar acts of trust. Since, however, the point at issue is the fulfilment of a particular idea of trust, of a venture of faith, it seems to make no difference whether the figure in whom the idea first presents itself as a model is Christ or Bruno, or whether it is truly present, and existed historically, or not. Christ and Bruno can have the force of a trigger even if they are only invented figures like Goethe's Faust or Shakespeare's Hamlet. It is inappropriate to want to base non-objective philosophical conviction (a truth of faith and not a truth of knowledge) on objective historical facts which are by nature demonstrable, which enjoy general validity, and which thus enforce recognition. The venture of trust or final conviction is always an individual and, as it were, solitary act which cannot be enforced and which has, therefore, the character of venture and decision. Figures which particularly illumine the event of trust or conviction work in terms of personal demonstration rather than historical facticity, and invented figures are also capable of this.

It thus becomes clear why, when Jaspers tries to understand Christ after the model of Bruno, namely, as the representative of a truth of faith and philosophy, denying him historical and individual facticity in the sense of a truth of knowledge, this attempt is bound to fail, for it cannot achieve the union of the two aspects which is to be found in Christ.

What Christian faith believes in is not the truth of Galileo, which we may deny, since its objective correctness will prevail without us. It is not this kind of truth because the truth at issue in faith cannot be objectified or demonstrated. If it is to be known there has to be a sovereign calling into the truth, the testimony of the Holy Spirit (John 18:37; 1 Corinthians 2:10f.). On the other hand, in opposition to Jaspers, it is not the truth of Bruno, which stands or falls with Bruno because it exists only in his communication with reality, and the spark of illumination shines forth only when there is the unique contact with reality which takes place in **Bruno** or to which a poet gives form with the help of his characters. **Chris**tian faith is not grounded in a general experience of reality. Hence **Schleier**macher's sense of the *universum,* which is close to what we find in Bruno, is not in any sense a description of Christian faith. This faith relates to historical facts, to the mighty acts of God which really took place, even though, in spite of their historical facticity, they are not objectively accessible or comprehensible to all men, as are the contents of Galileo's truth of knowledge.

In other words, faith is dealing with a reality which I cannot prove and yet which exists without me, which enjoys objective givenness and yet which is not accessible to me in an objectifiable way. It is not objectively verifiable and yet it is an objective truth.

In this instance, then, a distinction has to be made between the ontic and the noetic sides.

For Jaspers what is objective ontically (e.g., that the earth goes round the sun or that an event took place) is also objectively accessible noetically. For faith, however, the situation is different. We have something that is ontically given, the salvation event, or the mighty acts of God. But this is not objectively accessible noetically. It has to be made manifest to me. The resurrection of Christ is a fact. As a historical event, however, it cannot be established by historical means. It does not meet the criteria of historical verifiability. This inaccessibility even applies to events which a secular historian will accept as having taken place on the historical time-line, e.g., the death of Jesus. For faith we do not have the objective truth of knowledge even in such cases, for such a truth could include only the actual fact of the crucifixion. The point, however, is whether Christ died for me, whether his death is not just an individual historical event but also has universal redeeming significance, so that to this extent it has a suprahistorical aspect. Knowing this, however, is not under my own control; cf. Luther's exposition of the third article of the creed in the Small Catechism.

Serious consequences follow from this, which show how in Jaspers too the interrelatedness of the two basic dimensions of Christology is shattered and what faith believes is thus misunderstood.

The truth of God, having come into history, is present without me, as in Galileo. But it does not prevail without me, in contrast to Galileo. After what has been said, this is easy enough to understand.

Since the historically objective mighty acts are not objectively accessible, I cannot leave the truth about them to itself, since if I do no one will gain access to it.

The positive implication is that witness must be borne to this truth. Though it is there objectively, I have to act like Bruno. I must confess it and not deny it. If I deny it, I do not destroy it, of course, as Bruno would have done in his case. But I lock it up. I thus crucify Christ afresh. This means, not that I cancel out the death of Christ by my denial, for it is an objective fact, but that I cause Christ to have died in vain. The truth of God is by nature one that has to be passed on. It ties itself to witnesses and to the community. It has to be told, for it is a truth for man which man must experience and appropriate. If I keep silent about it or reject it, I do not reverse it, for Christ finally died and rose again independently of my attitude to these events; I alter its nature. Its nature, as we have said, is to be there *for* man. As denied truth, however, it is truth *against* man; he eats and drinks condemnation to himself (1 Corinthians 11:29). It is always there, but it is there as something else. The unvoiced truth issues loud complaint; the denied truth becomes judgment. This is evident from the fact that God's Word is always either law or gospel; it is never nothing. It does not return empty (Isaiah 55:11) but always brings back its booty with it: the loosed and the bound. Even the Christian who is ordained for blessing can come under accusation; cf. the world judgment in Matthew 25:31ff. and the parable of the wicked servant in Matthew 18:23ff.

We thus have three truths, that of knowledge, that of philosophy, and that of faith. We shall now try to reduce them to a concise formula which will show that the universal dimension and the individual historical dimension, which faith sees in union, fall apart in either Bruno or Galileo.

The Christian says: I stand or fall with my truth; it will become judgment or grace for me; either way it will always be the truth.

Bruno says: My truth stands or falls with me.

Galileo says: I fall, but my truth stands.

Just because the two aspects, the individual historical aspect and the universal suprahistorical aspect, turn out to be so heterogeneous outside the faith-encounter with Christ, they are continually separated in many different ways in the history of dogma and theology. In a somewhat bold formulation one might even say that these movements of isolation and reintegration constitute the history of Christology. The early stages of this history offer us several examples, some of which we might use by way of illustration.

WAYS OF ISOLATING THE UNIVERSAL ASPECT AND THE INDIVIDUAL ASPECT IN EARLY DOGMATIC HISTORY

On the one side the universal and suprahistorical aspect is isolated and given independent validity. Christ is viewed as only a divine being, or, as one might say today, as simply a timeless and nonhistorical idea. Eutyches is an example.[2] He espouses the doctrine of the one nature of Christ which argues that his deified body merely looks like, but is not in fact, a human body. He thus comes close to the classical docetic view which leaves no place for the individual historical existence of the man Jesus, and to that extent for the true incarnation of the Logos.[3]

On the other side stress is laid on the individual historical figure, as in

---

[2] During the Eutychian controversy, A.D. 448-451.

[3] Cf. the treatment of this from another angle in the section on the Trinity.

Theodoret. For Theodoret the Logos adopts, as it were, a perfect man of the lineage of David and makes him the temple of the Logos. As such he remains at all times on the level of holy and God-filled men who are temples in whom the Most Holy dwells. Only a quantitative difference arises at this point. Christ is the most religious man of all. There is, however, no qualitative distinction from other men.[4] This understanding of the figure of Christ as a superlative of the *humanum* is even clearer when one considers the mode of the indwelling of the Logos (*enoikesis*). Theodoret rejects all ontological definitions in terms of a substantial union of the two natures and defines the divine relation of the man Jesus ethically. He is oriented to God in his consciousness. His mind is filled with God. *Hénōsis physikě kat' ousían* is replaced by *hénōsis schetiké,* a manner of attitude and conduct. This alone is the mode of Christ's relation to God. The analogy to other historical men is so complete, and is so stressed, that Jesus the Son of David develops and goes through the same process of becoming as all other men. His ethical divine sonship becomes increasingly intense. Moral development brings him into a union with God which constantly grows and increases in fervor.

Both these one-sided solutions, the docetic on the one hand and the ethical on the other, involve a smoothing down of Christology.

When Christ is understood in docetic and suprahistorical terms as an idea, he can be systematized. Since he cannot be defined historically or objectively, he does not come into conflict with historical statements, nor with the criteria of historicity, nor with logical frictions, nor with the pressures of paradox. Indeed, no serious problem would arise if the historical existence of Jesus were denied altogether and he were relegated to the sphere of pure myth.

The same smoothing down is to be found in the other solution too. When the self-consciousness, the *schésis,* and the inner life of Jesus (Herrmann) are made the object of Christology, some historical controversies certainly arise, and it can even be asked how we know anything about his self-consciousness in any case; but these controversies arise only on the periphery of our certainty. There is no basic conflict with history. There is no conflict between the accidental truths of history and the necessary truths of reason, between the transhistorical dimension of Christology and the historical dimension. Jesus dwells on the normal plane of historical being. There is thus an unequivocal analogy between him and us. The premises of historical verifiability and historical understanding are thus met unconditionally.

Both exaggerations, however, blunt the point of the NT message, namely, that in the historical figure of Jesus God himself has come among us.

It seems to us to be highly significant that we have almost unintentionally slipped into the early Christology of the fifth century, and that we find almost unbroken continuity with modern Christologies from Schleiermacher

---

[4] For a similar view cf. Schleiermacher's Christology in *The Christian Faith,* § 94.

to Herrmann and Hirsch[5] and even the theology of revolution and the death of God, although naturally with a change of terminology. The following implication seems to be clear.

One cannot argue that it was the ontological schema of thought of ancient Christology which led to a constant balancing of the two natures against one another. One cannot argue that the failure to bring the two natures into equilibrium was due to an unsuitable ontological structure of thought. One cannot argue that a one-sided stress on the one at the expense of the other was always bound to arise in these circumstances.[6]

On this view it may be postulated that if only the inadequate ontological schema is abandoned and a modern personalistic structure of thought is substituted for it, the difficulties of the early period will be solved at a stroke.

In fact, however, the ontological structure of thought is not to blame for the constant overemphasis on the one side or the other. This is made apparent by the fact that we run into exactly the same difficulty when we use other modes of thought and work with terms like universality and individuality or suprahistorical and historical.[7] We have to realize, then, that we face here a difficulty which arises no matter what christological terms we use. If we want to avoid manipulating the reality of Christ by our terms and smoothing it down by rational simplification, we are confronted by the same problem of expression whether we cling to the older concept of natures or use such newer concepts as symbol, existence, or self-consciousness.

Our finding, then, is that we constantly face a twofold difficulty. We may elect to smooth over everything and make it comprehensible by activating the normative use of reason. But if we do, we isolate the two poles of Christology and are forced to choose either docetism and pure supernaturalness on the one side or the representative of the religious man, morality, and the consciousness of existence on the other. Or we may elect to make statements about Jesus Christ which fall in the zone of inexpressibility and paradoxical irreconcilability. If we want to say everything, we have to speak paradoxically. We can avoid paradox only at the cost of being able to deal

---

[5] *Jesus Christus der Herr,* 2nd ed. (1929).

[6] This is the line taken by Tillich in his analysis of the vocabulary of the Nicene controversy in *Systematic Theology,* II (1957), p. 143. He accepts the Athanasian concept of redemption but blames the ontological structure of thought for the fact that within this concept Christ's historical manifestation was obscured and he necessarily became a docetic shade.

[7] Tillich himself has to concede this. Thus he can say that the basis of the problem lies, not in the doctrine of the two natures, but in the mystery of Christ, so that the difficulty arises in his own terminology too. The attempt to interpret conceptually the assertion Jesus is Christ "can lead to an actual denial of the Christ-character of Jesus as the Christ; or it can lead to an actual denial of the Jesus-character of Jesus as the Christ. Christology must always find its way on the ridge between these two chasms, and it must know that it will never completely succeed, inasmuch as it touches the divine mystery, which remains mystery even in its manifestation" (*op. cit.,* p. 142).

with only partial aspects. A whole history of Christology might be written in illustration of these two options.

PARADOX AND ANTINOMY AS THOUGHT-MODELS IN CHRISTOLOGY

The epistemological question now arises whether and how far paradox can be a legitimate form of theological expression.

This crucial question is a justifiable one. Paradox as such involves antinomy, contradiction, and nonsense. When do two statements p and p' stand in a contradictory relation to one another? Only when a statement q exists in such a way that it can be shown that p and p' imply both the truth and the falsity of q.[8] If two mutually exclusive statements are made at the same time and both are said to be true, only three explanations are possible: 1. there is an error of thought; 2. the person who makes them is deranged or schizophrenic; 3. the limits of the competence of human reason are passed. Kant deals with the third explanation in his three forms of the conflict of transcendental reason.[9] He does this by presenting a thesis and antithesis. The thesis is that the world has a beginning in time and is limited in space. To this is opposed the antithesis that the world has neither beginning in time nor limit in space, but is infinite in regard to both time and space. Both statements are supported by proofs which are strict in themselves but which lead to a contradiction that reduces them to absurdity. The solution to the contradiction is perceived when it is realized that the world as a whole is beyond the horizon of our experience and hence is not a possible object within the competence of reason. Reason is betrayed into contradiction when it transgresses the boundary of its competence and deals with transcendental ideas as though they were objects of objective experience.

The urgent question is whether the paradoxical statements with which we have to do in Christology fall under the verdict of being antinomies and therefore come under one of the three explanations advanced above. To be forced to accept this means no less than declaring the bankruptcy of Christology. On these terms Christology becomes in the strictest sense a meaningless enterprise.

For the sake of self-critical honesty, and also for heuristic reasons, it is important that we resist the first impression that the paradoxical nature of christological statements involves discrediting antinomies of this kind.

When it is said that Christ is both (infinite) God and (finite) man, or that the Christian is both righteous and sinner at one and the same time, this certainly sounds as though we have an antinomy. What cannot be united is being united and nonsense results.

In the United States and England linguistic analysis in theology and philos-

---

[8] H. Scholz, "Wie ist evangelische Theologie als Wissenschaft möglich?" *Zwischen den Zeiten* (1931), 1.

[9] *Critique of Pure Reason* (E.T. 1929), pp. 384ff.

ophy has focused attention on this problem. Thus R. M. Hare in the falsification debate has noted that religious statements may rightly be criticized
if they are advanced as objective assertions or explanations (*New Essays
in Philosophical Theology* [1955], pp. 99ff.; cf. also the researches of
A. Flew, A. MacIntyre, and F. Ferré, the latter further in *Language, Logic
and God* [1961]). The formal question is raised whether these statements
have any meaning at all. From this formal standpoint the result is usually
negative. What these authors fail to see, of course, is that the negative result is perhaps an indication that the formal approach is inappropriate. This
question will occupy us in what follows.

Careful consideration has thus to be given to the question whether what
is being said will not be challenged because the paradoxical form of expression gives rise to the suspicion that it all belongs to the sphere of antinomies.
In other words, if Christology does not seem to be possible without paradox, may it not be that the whole enterprise is meaningless? Does not the
conclusion suggest itself that the confession of Christ as God and man can
no more be expressed reflectively than the idea of wooden iron or a square
circle? Are not those theologians right who one-sidedly isolate in Christ
either the universal element or the individual, the divine or the human?
Anyone who has a feeling for conceptual sobriety will have to face these
questions.

A first argument against the idea that Christology is antinomy and nonsense is breathtakingly simple. Obvious nonsense usually reduces itself to
absurdity. Through mass hysteria it may prevail for a moment, but over the
long haul of history it can have no force. If psychiatry interprets the idea
of righteous and sinner at one and the same time as schizophrenic, one
might surely ask when schizophrenic nonsense ever made history. Even if
it is suggested that Paul started this erroneous thesis by induction and
brought certain psychologically susceptible people under its spell, can we
seriously believe that this kind of nonsensical induction can exert an influence for two thousand years? This question certainly has to be considered.

Might it not be that the impression of contradictory and schizophrenic
nonsense arises in a very different way? Thus (1) the starting-point might
be an existential and even an exceptional experience. This can be verbalized
only in a halting and contradictory form. But in spite of the inadequacy of
the verbalization anyone who has had the experience can recognize what
is being described. Did not Schleiermacher have a true and decisive insight
when in the *Speeches*, in a different area from Christology, he made a distinction between experience and its verbal expression?

Those who have lived through air raids, for example, are not surprised
that the accounts of them are very contradictory. Some remember what
they saw and others what they heard, as in a thunderstorm. Some prayed
and others cursed. Some were even able to remain indifferent like animals.
It is not surprising, then, that accounts of the same incident are hard to piece

together. Those who have had the experience are well aware that words and concepts can only circle around this kind of event; they cannot depict it adequately. Hence those who did not have the same experience might be inclined to write off the accounts as mere glossolalia.

An ordinary process like walking offers another example. Walking involves a highly complicated act of the brain which stands in grotesque contradiction to the simplicity of the process itself. Any healthy man can put one foot in front of the other, cause his bones to rise and fall, and in so doing keep his balance. But the simplicity vanishes when analysis is made of the physiological processes and physical acts which make walking possible. Everything becomes hopelessly complicated and a scientist is hard put to describe what is really happening (cf. R. Janzen, *Elemente der Neurologie* [1969], pp. 35ff.). Various signals have to go out: Move your foot; not too hard, however, or you will jump; but not too weakly, or you may finish up crawling instead of walking; yet brake hard enough, or you will leap. Thus an ordinary act like walking is seen, on reflection, to involve an incredibly complicated system of reactions which defies adequate description.

Now it is true that we confuse two different spheres if we try to use this example to elucidate christological statements. Nevertheless, the analogy is plain. In Christology, too, we have a very simple experience-process called faith. As Christ is known in faith, there takes place pre-reflectively an event which can be shared by even the most simple and primitive people, and possibly even those who are weak-minded. But once faith takes what is believed, and what takes place in this belief, and sets it in the sphere of reflective statement, a chain of contradictory reactions comes into being. (It would be interesting to study the controversies about the balance and imbalance of the two natures from this standpoint.) A person who had never seen a man walking, or had any experience of walking, but simply read a neurological description of the process, would not only get from this no concrete notion of what walking is, but would be left with an impression of utter absurdity. The same is true of someone who has had no experience of Christ and simply studied christological speculations. (For an earlier discussion of the relation between the theoretical and the pre-theoretical cf. Chapter XIX.)

But (2) the impression of contradictory and schizophrenic nonsense can arise because concepts used in the cognitive sphere relate to the world of objective experience and cannot adequately denote what lies outside this world. This may be seen not only in the theological sphere but also in conceptual descriptions of personal reality.

A classical instance of the problem is to be found in Kant's juxtaposition of natural causality and freedom. Purely theoretical reason, whose border of competence is marked by the horizon of objective experience, implies causality as a category. Hence it cannot descry a-causal freedom in the field of its objects.[10] It thus seems that causal natural necessity and a-causal freedom are in the first instance mutually exclusive, i.e., an antinomy. The possibility of relating them in thought would mean proving the antinomy to be non-existent. But how can that be done? It can be done only by showing that the spheres of necessity and freedom lie on different levels of experience. Necessity rules in the sphere of objective experience while freedom rules in that of personal experience. The latter form of experience is governed by the ethical imperative, whose Thou shalt implies a Thou canst, which in turn implies freedom.[11]

The apparent antinomy of the formula "righteous and sinner at one and the same time" is to be resolved along similar lines. The terms righteous and sinner do not stand on the same plane. If they did they would in fact be mutually exclusive. The two judgments are rendered in the sphere of different relations. I am a sinner when I consider myself before myself in my concrete state. I am righteous when I see myself before God, for within the framework of justification by faith God tells me that for him I am righteous.[12]

Always, then, when paradoxes arise in the personal and christological sphere and they seem to me to be antinomies, I have to put the self-critical question whether this appearance arises because I am thinking within the framework of objectively oriented theoretical reason, and whether the statements which seem to be contradictory do not really belong on different levels.

Kant sums up the problem with the necessary strictness at the end of his *Fundamental Principles of the Metaphysics of Morals* (1785; E.T. 1873). The moral imperative has the character of necessity and general validity. Because of its unconditionality it can thus be described as natural law. Nevertheless, the analogy between the two necessities raises philosophical problems. For natural necessity in the form of the causal nexus can be established and can demonstrate itself *a priori* in my synthetic judgment: my conceptual apparatus, being oriented to objective experience, is in its element here and is wholly competent. This is not the case, however, with the necessity of the moral imperative. For we do not have an objective statement here. We do not find this imperative or the related freedom in the external world. We can find no break in the causal nexus into which freedom can be in-

---

[10] In spite of this Kant does find the idea of freedom even in the sphere of pure reason to the extent that something unconditioned necessarily belongs to every series of conditions, so that there has also to be a wholly self-determining causality. For this reason the postulate of possible freedom is an analytical principle of pure speculative reason; *Critique of Practical Reason* (E.T. 1949), pp. 234ff., and also the preface to the 2nd edition of the *Critique of Pure Reason*. In this case, however, freedom is not one of the objects of pure reason but occurs in reflection on the conditions of its knowledge, i.e., in its self-criticism.

[11] The person is not a "thing" in the world of objective experience but a kind of "thing in itself" which is not subject to the categories of our experience or, then, to natural causality. Cf. the reference under the previous footnote.

[12] Cf. R. Hermann's penetrating study, *Luthers These "Gerecht und Sünder zugleich"* (1930).

serted. We experience moral necessity in the non-objective region of the conscience. Hence we do not comprehend the practical unconditioned necessity of the moral imperative. What we comprehend is its incomprehensibility. This is all that can be fairly asked of a philosophy which pushes to the limit of human reason (*ibid.,* p. 102).

Much the same might be said of the antithetical statements of Christology. We comprehend their incomprehensibility. We can see why an objectively oriented reason cannot reconcile logically the assertion of the true God and true man, why statements such as this necessarily take the form of paradoxes, and why paradoxes of this kind are not antinomies.

The epistemological question which arises in every Christology is as follows. Do we do anything here but comprehend the incomprehensibility of what has to be said? Do we do anything but comprehend the fact, and the reason for the fact, that we encounter a mystery here? Is paradox anything other than a sign of this encounter?

In intellectual responsibility no one can tackle Christology without engaging in a criticism of reason and posing the problem of the possibility of statement. Confrontation with the mystery of Christ, if nothing else, will demand this act of reflection. If it is felt that personal concepts must be used instead of the two-natures schema to describe this mystery, this is a result of the need to criticize reason. The process of thought that began with Kant cannot be reversed. This process challenges the two-natures schema because in naive fashion it thinks objectively and hence is in no position to articulate the different level of reality on which valid statements can be made about the person of Christ.

Having now worked out the presuppositions for the possibility of statements about Christ, we may sum them up as follows.

What is to be stated must have affected experience first. It must have been gone through or lived out. For Kant practical reason could not be depicted or criticized unless there had first been an experience of conscience and freedom. The same is true in Christology. It becomes a possibility only where encounter with Christ has taken place and faith precedes reflection. Only then does the subsequent conceptualization of what has been experienced make sense. As we noted above, the man who has the background of the experience will recognize the unequivocal experienced reality even in the contradictory statements. To use a Platonic expression, anamnesis will take place.

Negatively, however, this means that the experience cannot be demonstrated by concepts to those who have not had it. People of this kind will see only the untenable contradiction; they cannot see beyond it. Christological action cannot trigger the reaction of faith. Faith has its origin, not in theology, but in proclamation. Proclamation has its origin, not in theology, but in proclamation.[13] The pre-theoretical realm of faith is a premise of theological and christological reflection.

Students of Kierkegaard will already have noted that we are indebted to him for our understanding and use of the term paradox. When Kierkegaard calls paradox the passion of thought which involves offense, he is drawing attention to the phenomenon of the cognitive. Thought is kindled to this passion by a reality which it encompasses. It is stimulated by the pre-theoretical experience of faith which it encompasses without being able to find any adequate reflexive form for it. Thought oriented to the world of objective experience comes up against its limit when it tries to express or comprehend this experience, just as the one who falls in love cannot adequately verbalize what is felt. As the word seeks statements which are beyond its grasp it must be ready for offense, pressing on with its statements regardless of the cost, accepting distortion, and paying if necessary with its own destruction. The fact that Kierkegaard uses the difficulty of expressing love as an illustration shows that he has in mind the pre-theoretical personal experience which is analogous to faith and which can find no suitable verbal dress. Paradox is the passion of thought. A thinker without paradox is like a lover without passion. In its supreme form, however, passion is always ready for its own destruction. The supreme passion of the understanding is to be ready for offense even though this turns to its own destruction. For the supreme paradox of thought is wanting to discover what we of ourselves cannot think (*Philosophical Fragments* [1936], p. 29).

In the absence of the pre-theoretical experience on which our theoretical attempt at statement founders, the paradox in what we say will usually seem to be no more than an indication of logical imprecision or intellectual sloth. This is the accusation of Settembrini in Thomas Mann's *Zauberberg:* "Paradox is the poisonous bloom of quietism (intellectual sloth), the vacillation of the lazy mind, the greatest dissoluteness of all" (p. 293).

---

[13] Cf. the author's work *Über die Angst des heutigen Theologiestudenten vor dem geistlichen Amt* (1967), pp. 11ff.

XXII

The Question of the Person of Christ

CRITICAL EVALUATION OF THE CHALCEDONIAN DEFINITION

When we put the question who and what Christ is, and how we are to state this "who" and "what" intellectually, we immediately run into the difficulties described. We have to face them no matter whether we use an ancient or a modern schema of thought.

This becomes plain when instead of using the ontological concept of natures in our description of the figure of Christ we turn instead to the more personal category of the historical. For when we do this Christology sets us the task of taking a historical entity, the figure of Jesus of Nazareth, and treating it as such even though it sustains all history and is yesterday, today, and for ever.

This plunges us at once into paradox. For he who determines and encompasses history, as we have shown, surely cannot himself be history. What is historical is tied to a particular point in the timeline and surely cannot be its beginning and end, or can it?

Two examples which seem to illustrate the impossibility of uniting the two aspects may be given. Thus D. F. Strauss says that it is not the manner of the idea in its self-realization to pour its whole fulness into a single specimen and to be parsimonious with others (*Das Leben Jesu*, II, p. 779; E.T. p. 780). In this context the point is that a single specimen of history cannot stand representatively for its whole fulness and range. Second, Tillich argues that we cannot speak of a personal God, or of God as a person, because God is not a single person but the ground of the personal, the basis of its ontological power (*Systematic Theology*, I, pp. 244ff., esp. p. 245). God is the principle of participation and individualization, but he also creates what he allows to participate in himself. How can he be understood as a person, in the sense of historical individuality, when he is not marked off from other persons, when he is not at a distance from them, when he does not stand in encounter with them, but when he comprehends and sustains all personal life?

Although we face here the logical irreconcilability of two statements, although reason has to make do with paradoxes, although there is no possibility of resolving the contradictions in synthetic judgments, we still have to consider which form of statement is the most appropriate and which is the least suitable.

In spite of the dubious concept of natures, tradition has always regarded the Chalcedonian definition as the most appropriate statement, especially in view of its use of the negative α in its decisive statements. As we are told, the two natures, the suprahistorical and historical aspects, or the universal and individual aspects, are neither confused nor divided. In this negative way the definition thus denotes the sphere in which the mystery of Christ dwells. In the decisive passage we have an indirect statement rather than a supposedly adequate set of definitions. In our own later attempt at a christological formulation, we shall have to adopt the same model of indirectness.

We shall now try to work out the significance of the indirect statements of Chalcedon. We turn first to *asynchýtōs,* "without confusion." If the two natures are are not confused, this means primarily that the one nature is not absorbed by the other, as in Monophysitism and Monothelitism. This is naturally a negative statement, for it does not say how the natures are related nor attempt a relational calculation. It simply tells us how the relation is not to be defined. The one nature is not absorbed by the other.

What happens when the divine nature is absorbed by the human nature may be seen in a series of theologians that runs from Theodoret by way of Abelard to Schleiermacher. Christ as the most religious of men can be an example but not the Mediator. In the main, however, Christian antiquity was in little danger of reducing Christ to simple humanity. It was in greater danger of absorbing the human nature in the divine nature. We must pause to consider the implications of this form of one-sidedness.

It means that Christ is only a form of divine appearance, so that the appearance, as K. Rahner rightly observes, has no reality of its own over against the one who appears.[1] This means in turn that Christ is no longer strictly understood as the Mediator who is our peace in the ontic sense (Ephesians 2:14), and in whom reconciliation is achieved and is present in person. The human nature loses any independence of its own. It is no longer an *autokíneton.* Christ simply represents God. He is no longer our representative before God. The priestly aspect of his mediatorial office, as this is presented in Hebrews (cf. 4:14ff.), drops away when the human nature is seen only as an instrument and function. Christ as Mediator is the person who carries within him the opposed entities of God and man, who himself bears the antithesis, who sacrifices himself to it, and who makes it the content of his history, with all its tensions, between birth, death, and exaltation.

---

[1] "Probleme der Christologie heute," *Schriften zur Theologie,* I, p. 176; E.T. *Theological Investigations,* I, p. 155.

The Chalcedonian definition with its "without confusion" is thus both a negative defense against the emptying out of the human nature and also a positive safeguard for the mediatorship of Christ. Nevertheless, the question arises whether the concept of nature is the proper means of achieving this linguistically. Does it not open the door too easily to one-sidedness? Does not the one nature come to have far too easily a purely functional significance in relation to the other? Can mediatorship be expressed in any other mode than the personal, in which the contradictions within the sphere of the person are manifestly non-objectifiable, in which they cannot be played off against each other, in which one of the two competing forces cannot be surrendered in favor of the other. (By way of elucidation we might refer again to the formally analogous problem of the antithesis between necessity and freedom in Kant, which cannot be objectified because it is grounded in the mystery of the person.)

It is surprising that Rahner, even though he is a Roman Catholic and is thus traditionally more committed to the concept of nature than Reformation theologians, raises very much the same objection. If we speak only of nature, and do so in distinction from the divine person, how, he asks, can we have any clear conception of the originality of the human history of Jesus to God and before God, or of the direct empirical subject of this history? In practice, does not redemption become simply God's act on us and not the act of the messianic Mediator between us and God? Are we not almost unavoidably forced to accept what is undoubtedly the dominant popular view, that of our Lord ($=$ God) still walking the earth with his disciples lowly and unrecognized?

A Christology which fails to check the natural thrust of the concept of nature toward absorption of the human nature into the divine nature comes suspiciously close to mythology. Rahner has a fine definition of what is meant by myth in this connection (*op. cit.,* p. 176, n. 3; E.T. p. 155, n. 3): An understanding of the incarnation is mythological if it views the human element simply as a garment or livery which God uses to denote his presence among us, without this human element achieving its supreme originality and autonomy precisely from the fact that God assumes it. NT Christology, in contrast, is nonmythical because it confesses the full humanity of Jesus Christ, which is distinguished from our unnatural and alienated humanity by the very fact that it is authentic humanity and brings before us the original of the *humànum*. (In this regard Schleiermacher's concept of the prototype is on the right track.)

In endorsing the spiritual concern of the negative definition "without confusion," we are thus forced to confess at the same time that the use of the concept "nature" threatens to run contrary to the true intention.

Along with *asynchýtōs* ("without confusion"), Chalcedon also has *achōrístōs* ("without separation"). The fact that the unity of the figure of Christ might be wrongly presented (i.e., by losing the one nature in the other) should not blind us to the reality of the union of the two natures in Christ. The expression "without separation" expresses the concern for unity.

The question how we are to think of this unity leads to the assertion in various ways that the true question is where it is to be found. The answer is that it is to be found in Christ's work, in his acts, in his benefits, or, more generally, in his activity as the Mediator (Matthew 11:2ff.). Naturally this cannot mean that he is identified with his deeds and absorbed into them. It can mean only that he is to be sought in his deeds and this is where his unity will be found. This unity lies in the history of Jesus Christ with us and consequently in what he does, in his work on us.

This is the christological approach of the Gospels. When it is asked here who Jesus is, his works and conduct always trigger the question. For example, when the rumor goes round that he is John the Baptist risen again, or the returning Elijah, the basis is "all that was done by him" (Luke 9:7f.). Herod's question who he was is similarly motivated (9:9). In face of his authoritative word and the accompanying signs, the question arises: "From whence hath this man these things? and what wisdom is this which is given unto him, that even such mighty works are wrought by his hands?" (Mark 6:2). The disciples' question in the ship is along the same lines: "What manner of man is this, that even the winds and the sea obey him?" (Matthew 8:27). For the chief priests, scribes, and elders, the question as to his person is also posed by his works. They cannot fail to see that something transcending all human possibilities is done in them. To put this in terms of our own problem, they cannot fail to see that here is a man who is in union with suprahuman power. The only question is whether this power is divine or demonic. Does he do his work with the help of God or with the help of Beelzebub? This is why they ask him: "By what authority doest thou these things? and who gave thee this authority to do these things?" (Mark 11:27ff.; cf. Matthew 12:24-27; Luke 11:15-19).

Jesus himself leads his disciples to put the question of his person in such a way that it arises out of his acts and work and has as its point the interpretation of his acts and work in terms of his person (Matthew 16:13ff.). Since Peter, in spite of his confession of Christ (16:16), thinks in isolation from the person of his master, for him the person of Christ is not the key to his work and acts. This is why Peter cannot understand the passion (16:21-23).

Finally, the Christology of Acts also begins with the deeds of Christ: "Jesus of Nazareth, a man approved of God among you by miracles and wonders and signs, which God did by him in the midst of you, as ye yourselves also know" (2:22). Nor does Acts merely begin here; it also shows that there is no other point of access. Access, however, is not the end and goal; it is only the beginning. His mystery is not illumined by mere acquaintance with his acts. He might be understood in different ways. He could be basically on the same level as ancient and modern fakirs and dervishes whose powers are incontestable. Healers like Zaiss, Bruno Göring, Branham, and Tommy Hixt might dare to compete with the "sorcerer" from Galilee (cf. John 8:48).[2]

The deeds and works of Christ, then, are simply the legitimate approach to what then becomes the urgent central question who he is. Only from this angle can this question be posed. From this angle, however, it has to be posed. For only when I have penetrated the mystery of this "who" do I have the key to interpretation of the acts. Only the person opens up the acts for me. Without the person the acts are ambivalent. They might be sorcery.

Here, then, we have an interpretative interrelation. The acts interpret the person, for they are the legitimate approach to the question of the "who." But the person also interprets the acts, for the person makes their meaning unequivocal and rescues them from ambivalence. To ask concerning Christ's person without first studying his acts is to arrive at either a docetic supranatural Christ, a purely human man who is the most religious of all men, or even a sorcerer. In any case the unity of the "without separation" of Chalcedon is broken. On the other hand, to begin with the acts but not to go beyond them to the person who interprets them is to be trapped in the ambivalence of possible interpretations and again to miss the unity.

We have thus reached an important finding. When the christological problem is approached through the acts, conduct, and work of Christ, the unity of his person becomes the object of a question: How is all this possible in a man? but it does not give rise to the questioning which is *a priori* implicit in the concept of "nature." The authoritative word and the authoritative sign may be seen in a self-enclosed unity. They cannot be divided into a normal word of man on the one side and a sign coming down from heaven on the other side. No, it is this one man, "found in fashion as a (normal) man" (Philippians 2:8), who speaks in so extraordinary a way and does such extraordinary things. To put it popularly, he works in personal union as man and more than man. This unity is what calls forth astonishment, alarm, puzzlement, and finally the question who it might be that can speak and act in this way. Only in subsequent reflection is the unity itself called in question, either on the view that he is a docetic supranatural figure, John risen again or Elijah come back again (Mark 9:7-9), or on the view that he is just a man with his place in local history and with nothing extraordinary about him.[3]

Thus even to look first at his works, where the "without separation" of Chalcedon is most evident and the unity of Christ's person is most easily perceived, is not to make the "without separation" immediately perspicuous.

Melanchthon's knowing the benefits is not a christological panacea which takes us out of the realm of paradox and offers a clean slate for reflection and statement. In the profundity of the question which the benefits raise,

---

[2] G. Gloege, *Aller Tage Tag,* p. 208.
[3] He is just the carpenter, the son of Mary and Joseph (Mark 6:3; John 6:42f.); and what good thing can come out of Nazareth (John 1:46), or how can a prophet arise out of Galilee (John 7:52)?

namely, who he is and with what kind of a person we have to do, we still run up against the same basic contradictions and difficulties of expression which meet us on every hand no matter what approach to this figure we take or what conceptual means we use to express the encounter. Here again the unity of this figure (the "without separation") becomes a question. Here again we come up against the contradiction between the universal or divine aspect and the individual or human aspect. Here again we run into the problems with which the doctrine of the two natures wrestles. Even if we are able to throw off the additional liabilities incurred by the concept of nature in christological statements, even if we acquire instead the assets of personal and historical categories, we cannot remove the difficulties nor find immunity against the temptation of one-sided solutions.

The doctrine of the two natures, even if we are unable to accept it, still retains its permanent significance. It is a stern watchman which forces us to face up to the difficulties and not take refuge in smooth and distorting solutions. It demands that our question be focused, not on the intellectual difficulties in the foreground, but on the kerygmatic core, on the person of Christ himself, who wins our faith and who, when reason also enters into discipleship, requires of us the courage to lay claim to paradox.

Excursus: The Controversy between Luther and Zwingli regarding the Person of Christ

For an example of what happens when a theological attempt is made to grasp the person of Christ directly and not through his deeds and work, we may turn to the eucharistic controversy between Luther and Zwingli. (For Luther cf. *Der Sermon vom Sakrament des Leibes und Blutes Christi* [1526]; *Dass die Worte, das ist mein Leib, noch feststehen* [1527]; *Das gr. Bekenntnis vom Abendmahl* [1528]; for Zwingli, *Klare Unterrichtung vom Nachtmal Christi* [1526]; esp. *Das diese Worte, das ist mein Leichnam . . . ewiglich den alten Sinn haben werden* [1527].)

It is beyond question that Luther's Christology has originally a decisive soteriological interest. The person of Christ is seen in the light of his work and is also embedded in this work, in this history wiht me. The exposition of the second article of the Creed in the Small Catechism formulates this with classical pregnancy. It is wholly oriented to the "for me."

It is true that within this conception extreme statements can be made when it is a matter of Christ's unity. The deity cannot be too deeply thrust into the nature and the flesh (On Luke 2:1ff., WA, 10, I, 1, 68). God treads the streets and fetches bread and water and eats and drinks with his mother Mary, even though fetching water, buying bread, and having a mother are attributes of the human nature and not the divine nature (*Von den Konziliis und Kirchen,* WA, 50, 588). Indeed, in expressing the unity of the divine and the human in Christ Luther can even go so far as to say that Mary suckles God at her breasts and bathes, rocks, and lifts God (On John 3:34, WA, 47, 200).

Nevertheless, the concern in these extreme statements is not for an intrinsic ontic unity. Luther is seeking instead to elucidate the miracle of the incarnation. The incarnation is not an end in itself. It is strictly seen from the standpoint of the "for me." It is the work of the divine mercy in which God condescends to me in love, exposes himself to the pressure of history between birth and death, and bears the curse of the law. Far from being an abstract and timeless identification of the divine and the human, the incarnation expresses a living history in God himself. God in his love overcomes his holiness (cf. the earlier discussion of the law and the gospel).

Up to this point, i.e., the incarnation and the "for me," the soteriological concern and the description of Christ's divine humanity in terms of his work are clear. In some parts of his theology, however, Luther does not stop at soteriology but tries to analyze the structure of the incarnate Christ, i.e., his person "in itself." Here the soteriological reference to his work is still in the background, but only as a hidden implication which the perspicacious interpreter alone can see. In itself what he says in this regard seems very distant from the benefits of Christ and, contrary to the initial starting-point, it seems to let itself focus on the naked majesty of the person in itself. The soteriological background against which even these more extravagant statements are to be set is provided by the motive which leads Luther into these dubious fields of speculation. He wants to make it clear, no matter what the rational price may be, that God is not an eternal idea of which we see only a part in the incarnate Word, so that there are obscure tracts of the *Deus absconditus* beyond this, and in himself God might be very different from what he appears to be in this partial aspect. Luther wants to state as strongly as he can that God has poured out himself in all of his fulness, and kept nothing back, in Christ. He really is the one he seems to be. We do not see only the tip of an iceberg whose depth, form, and nature cannot be estimated. In Christ we have God whole and entire. Christ himself is the whole Logos. There is not in addition a hidden non-incarnate Logos.

In motive Luther's christological statements are sound. They are dubious only in relation to the speculative consequences to which he was led by the opposition of Carlstadt and Zwingli. He entangles himself in speculation because he lets the questions of his opponents control his thinking.

The transition to the field of speculation is a fluid one. The relevant point christologically seems to be his concern to safeguard the unity of Christ's person. He thus brackets the deity and the humanity in order to understand the incarnation radically and to prevent it from becoming an empty symbol.

At issue is God's real presence in grace. We Christians have to realize that unless God himself weights the scales we shall go down. If only man died, not God, we are lost. If, however, the death of God is on the scales, he goes down and we rise up. The death of the man Jesus alone could not save us, for then we would not be dealing with God. The solidarity of a man with our guilt, suffering, and death does not help us, only the solidarity of God himself, only his loving condescension. But God could not sit in the scales. He had to become a man for us to be able to speak of his agony, blood, and death. For God in his nature cannot die. God and man, however, are united in one person, so that we can speak of God's death when the man dies who is one thing and one person with God, *Von den Konziliis . . . ,* cf. WA, 50, 390.

The way in which Luther speaks of the death of God (cf. Volume I, Chapters XIII-XVII) may be bold, but it is clear so long as he has the work of redemption in view. It loses this clarity, however, when he takes the next and apparently logical step of reversing things so that not only does God become man but the humanity of Christ becomes God. This takes place when the attributes of the divine nature are communicated to the human nature. The argument may be summed up as follows. If we maintain the unity of Christ's person, we cannot go on to restrict it, e.g., by saying that only the divine element in Christ can command the wind and the waves or call up from the grave. To do this is to make the human nature a mere mode of manifestation, a livery, and thus to betray the incarnation. One has to say that it was Jesus Christ who ordered the wind to cease and smoothed the waves. But when one does this, then in the name of the unity of the person the human nature has to be meant as well. It has to be regarded as having a share in the divine authority.

In letting his original concern of faith lead him so far into speculation, Luther takes a fateful course. For the doctrine of the communication of the attributes suggests itself as a means of ontological expression. Briefly, this doctrine means that every attribute is an attribute of the total person of Christ and is thus shared by each nature. The same applies to every operation. When the implications of this thesis are worked out in pseudo-rational fashion, it necessarily means that the divine nature in Christ communicates its attributes to the human nature and *vice versa.* Hence the divine nature becomes subject to the fate of human existence (the death of God) and the human nature is decked out with divine predicates such as omnipotence and omnipresence. As a final and supremely speculative deduction we have the doctrine of the ubiquity of the body (or human nature) of Christ, which plays so significant a role in the Lutheran doctrine of the real presence of Christ in the Lord's Supper. With this doctrine of ubiquity Luther tried to provide a speculative metaphysical background for his insistence on a literal "This *is* my body" in opposition to Zwingli's more restrictive "This *signifies* my body."

At the very climax of this apparently abstruse speculation, however, a remarkable reversal takes place. Luther returns to his initial soteriological concern, to the evangelical appeal. He does so in two ways.

First, he stresses the comfort in the "This is," in the real presence. By it I have assurance of the gracious bodily presence of the Lord. By eating and drinking he comes into contact with my body. I can be certain, then, that I am not just relating myself symbolically to an idea of reconciliation or merely reminding myself of a past event, but that reconciliation and salvation history are a concrete event here and now. Through this concreteness the unity of God and man in Christ brings it about that my humanity comes into contact with deity and I am included within the unity which obtains in him. Thus Luther's ontological speculation about Christ's person and the eucharistic elements is brought back under the control of what the eucharist accomplishes, of its work. The ontic relations are again subordinated to the act and function.

Second, there is a return to the starting-point because the presence of the body in the Lord's Supper becomes a special presence for me. The body comes down from heaven in order that there might be a personal presence for me. We must expand a little on this understanding of the presence.

Carlstadt, and later Zwingli and Oecolampadius, advanced some plain arguments against Luther's principle of ubiquity and the resultant under-standing of the eucharistic "is" (cf. *Dass die Worte . . .*, WA, 23, 114, 160). The main point is that if Christ sits in heaven at the right hand of the Father, he cannot be bodily present in the sacrament. This is just as speculative as Luther's appeal to the fact that the omnipotence of God can effect different modes of presence; cf. *Gr. Bekenntnis vom Abendmahl,* Cl, III, 389 and 396. In this regard Luther adopts Occam's scholastic distinction between three modes of being and forms of presence: local (normal bodies in space), definitive (spirits and angels not confined to space), and repletive (God in his omnipresence).

These metaphysical theses remind us of the antinomies in Kant, namely, that at the point where reason passes beyond the horizon of experience its statements become irrelevant and wander off into contradictions. In these areas two things may be said: first, Christ is exalted and omnipresent and hence he is also present in the sacrament; second, he is exalted and omni-present and hence his presence cannot be confined in the sacrament. At the level of speculation on the person of Christ the debate reaches a stalemate. No decision can be reached with speculative weapons.

This is why it is significant that at the point of stalemate Luther reverses himself, speaks once again after the manner of direct practical appeal, and returns to his christological and eucharistic starting-point in the work and operation. He suddenly drops the ontological framework and places the whole discussion in the setting of a personal relation to Christ, i.e., of faith. Thus in his work *Dass die Worte . . .* he argues that I do not control Christ's presence when I am present to him. He imparts himself to me only where he has promised in his Word and with the means to which he has tied his presence for us. He sees a distinction between Christ's presence and our grasping it. God's being there is one thing, his being there for us another. He is there for us when he tells us in his Word: You will find me here. If we have the Word, we can assuredly grasp and have him and say: I have thee as thou hast said (WA, 23, 150).

Zwingli found it easy to criticize Luther's doctrine of ubiquity, but his own position seems to fall under the same verdict of being metaphysical speculation. He rightly perceives a docetic shade in the person described in the doctrine of the communication of the attributes. What can be meant by an omnipresent body when the body is ontologically characterized by limitation in space? If divine attributes are allotted in this way to the human nature of Christ, and specifically his body, then quite apart from the logical antinomies one might justly accuse Luther of the theological fault of abandoning the "without confusion" of Chalcedon. The question that Zwingli himself has to face, however, is how one can avoid this error and yet see the unity of the deity and humanity in Christ, maintain both the true God and the true man (as Zwingli does), and always have the unity in view when speaking of the words and acts of Christ. How can one say that one and the same person suffered and died in human fashion and yet was also sustained by divine power in his mighty acts? To say this is to say that Christ, and in Christ both his divine nature and his human nature, must always be the subject of these predicates. Or is it?

Zwingli has no wish to surrender the unity of Christ's person. Nevertheless, he thinks that when Christ is the common subject of divine and human predicates, this personal union has only the character of an *alloiosis,* a figure of speech. If one looks more closely at the reality behind the figure, one has to say that Christ did this in his quality as man and that in his quality as God. He suffered and died in his quality as man while in his quality as God he did mighty works and rose again and ascended. If the qualities are not strictly differentiated, the divine and human merge into one another and we fall victim to docetism and conceptual glossolalia. Deity is enclosed and made finite in humanity while humanity is extended beyond its natural limit and becomes as wide and infinite as deity (*Dass diese Worte . . . ,* Walch, XX, 1491, 1502ff.).

In answer Luther points out that if *alloiosis* means that the humanity alone suffers, then the incarnation breaks down and with it the whole work of salvation. Zwingli severs the person of Christ and leaves us no other Christ than a mere man who died for us and redeemed us. But this overthrows the Christian faith and negates the promised salvation. For he who is redeemed by humanity alone is not redeemed. For this reason Luther issues a warning that *alloiosis* is the devil's mask. If I believe that only the human nature died for me, Christ is a poor Savior for me; indeed, he himself needs a Savior (*Christmas Sermon* of 1533 on Luke 2:10, WA, 52, 41ff.).

The True Significance of the Controversy

If Luther with his communication of the attributes offends against the "without confusion" of Chalcedon, he can argue that materially, if not verbally, Zwingli for his part transgresses the "without separation." By not relating the two natures, and reducing the divine-human unity of the person of Christ to a mere figure of speech, he shakes the saving work of Christ to its foundations.

In simple terms Luther's criticism is that Zwingli does not see the significance of God for the salvation event and leaves him, as it were, on the outside. As Luther sees it, if God is not in full union with the human nature, if the incarnation is not believed to the very limit of our capacity, then there is no history of the heart of God, of the overcoming of God's holiness by his grace, of his movement from claim to promise. God in his eternity remains intact and unaltered while the Jesus drama is being played out on the human historical level.

The lack of any history of God with himself may in fact be inferred from Zwingli's doctrine of the incarnation. Strictly the idea of God's becoming man is inappropriate for him. As Thomasius says (*Christi Person und Werk,* II [1857], p. 310), God cannot become anything. He cannot undergo alteration, e.g., into humanity. Hence the incarnation is simply the assumption of human nature, a uniting of deity with it, and this only to the extent that the unalterability permits.

Zwingli's Christology is thus along the line of thought initiated by Abelard. What is history and mutable does not belong to the sphere of God's being. This sphere does not belong essentially to history; it stands in timeless indifference above it. It lets dramas such as the crucifixion take place and depicts the immutable love of God in mutable events. History does not contain God; it simply gives hints of him. It is in some sense symbolical. Epigrammatically one might put it thus: The real truth is, not that God *is* in the suffering and dying Christ, but that Christ *represents* God, just as the real truth is, not that Christ *is* in the Lord's Supper, but that this *represents* the being of God signalized in Christ.

Zwingli's *alloiosis,* which in its own way is just as absurd as Luther's doctrine of the communication of the attributes, makes it plain that these abstruse speculations have a highly relevant theological content which profoundly affects the word of redemption. For concrete faith it is obviously a very relevant question whether I see in Christ the event of blessing, the self-overcoming of the divine heart, God's "repenting" as act, and therefore the transition from law to gospel, or whether I have to say that the acts are simply a demonstration, whereas the real thing, God's attitude to me, remains frozen in the timelessness of a principle of love and is the suprapolar point of indifference, the point beyond both law and gospel. This means the end of the history whose emphasizing in reflection is the decisive impulse behind Luther's doctrine of law and gospel (cf. our earlier discussion).

Whereas the orientation to the salvation event is evident in Luther here, however, it is obscured in the speculative portions of his Christology. It is only when we come up against his true concerns in the controversy with Zwingli, and necessarily discover that even in the speculations the true issue is that of history, of the salvation event and the work of redemption, that we can again perceive the radical difference in basic theological decisions even in the antinomies and absurdities of the communication of the attributes and the doctrine of *alloiosis.* Again, it is only when we see the fundamental distinction that we can also understand why the controversy between Luther and Zwingli was no sham fight between unreal conceptual shadows. The controversy is not removed by unmasking and chasing away the shadows. In the background of the unreal fencing are granite cliffs which demand decision and force us to ask whether we should go round them to the right or to the left.

We may thus say in conclusion that concentration on an analysis of Christ's person in isolation from his work leads to speculations which in detail can no longer be described as theological. Nevertheless, the confusion is reduced by the fact that even in the jungle of extreme speculation a compass is still carried. In Luther at any rate there is still awareness of the initial soteriological concern, and this finally comes to the fore again. It is pointless, then, to simplify the controversy in such a way as to engage in mere speculation about Christ's person and to try to defend Luther's doctrine of the communication of the attributes. Advance can be made only by going back to the initial concern and making a decision between event and meaning or history and timelessness. (The author confesses that in this regard he sides with Luther, but in so doing would like to add that he does not equate Zwingli's position with that of the Reformed world in general. Even if comparisons are odious in view of the difference in theological conceptions, Calvin is surely closer to Luther than to Zwingli. This is not to say that the same problems with history as we find in Zwingli may not still plague the Reformed churches; cf. our debate with Barth in ThE, I, § 596; E.T. I, pp. 108ff.)

A final observation may be made. We have seen that in Christology Luther and Schleiermacher are poles apart. Speculation on the person of Christ ends in Schleiermacher with the positing of man as absolute (the most religious of men). In contrast, deity is posited as absolute in Luther (the participation of humanity in the attributes of the divine nature). The astonishing thing, however, is that the exaggerations and truncations which are to be noted in the theological speculations of the two men do not occur in their sermons. Even skilled theologians well acquainted with the problems can detect only traces of them here. Why is this? Is it because the abstractions which result when inferences are drawn from the doctrine of the two natures, or when this doctrine is disputed, are too difficult for discussion in the pulpit? This may well be a secondary reason. But the true reason is to be sought elsewhere. Preaching is address. Its task is to bear witness to the mighty acts of God. It is to relate these acts to me. Hence pulpit Christologies are shaped supremely by the benefits of Christ, or they ought to be. In the event of preaching witness is borne to Christ. He is mediated to the people. His presence is in the preaching of the Word (Matthew 18:20).

Naturally, then, preaching offers a corrective to one-sided speculation about Christ's person. Witness is more than theology. Schleiermacher's christological and eschatological witness in the pulpit of Holy Trinity, Berlin, is of incomparably greater fulness than one would expect from the way in which his schema of thought restricts his theological utterances. Preaching takes place within the framework of the initial motifs which are developed in later theological examination but which in the process are exposed to the dangers of reflection.

This does not mean that we shall preach better if we steer clear of these danger zones and remain in the pre-stages of expansive and critical reflection. It means that the preacher, when he has traversed the field of reflection, must return to what we have called the sphere of the initial motifs, as both Luther and Schleiermacher do in their different ways. The preacher must regain the "second naiveté" which Kleist demands in his *Marionettentheater* (cf. ThE, II, 1, § 1627ff.). Having lost the paradise of a direct statement of witness through reflection, and after roaming the world of reflection, he must regain the paradise of immediacy from behind.

Preaching, then, is an exercise in conservation which is indispensable for the theologian. Its correctives keep him close to the heart of the matter and protect him against the ferment of destruction and disintegration which will inevitably be present in reflection when it is not corrected by immediacy.

We have thus been given a decisive clue in our own search. Being direct, preaching is the most appropriate form of christological statement. For preaching proclaims the gospel of the forgiveness of sins, of comfort, of hope, and of the new future. In it the fact of Christ does not have to be established. It is itself the foundation. Christ is the representative of God condescending to us in love. He is also the representative of man, bound to him in solidarity and bearing his burdens.

We can do Christology, then, only as we repeat preaching in the different form of reflection. Preaching, and the administration of the Lord's Supper, consists in the active Word of remission and the promise of new life. It is not a discourse about forgiveness and life. It is the impartation and distribution of forgiveness and life. Preaching is part of the work. It belongs to him who works. It is itself one of Christ's benefits. Being oriented to the unity of person and work, and representing this unity in action, it is an antidote to all speculative dissipation.

The action of the outgoing Word must be described in such a way that Christ is always thought of as the subject and not in the isolation of an "in itself." This is to do Christology.

Since we have used the *Critique of Pure Reason* before for this purpose, we may perhaps try to put all this in Kantian terms. If we do, what is meant is that Christ as person is a mystery that we cannot approach directly. He is a "thing in itself" which I cannot objectify but which affects me by way of my experience. It is in experience that I let his work and action take place in me, that I achieve awareness of him, that I am thus affected by him. The personal statements, very God begotten of the Father in eternity, and very man born of the virgin Mary, are enclosed within the true and comprehensive statement about what he does in me and what he is in doing it, i.e., my Lord who redeemed me, lost and condemned.[4]

---

[4] Cf. Luther's exposition of the second article of the Creed in his Small Catechism.

XXIII

The Approach to Christology through the Mighty Acts of God

The decisive result of our preceding discussion is that in virtue of its two-fold character as historical and individual on the one side and universal and all-embracing on the other, the person of Christ cannot be expressed directly. We can understand it and think of it only indirectly as the subject of its works. We cannot know this figure in the way which is valid with other historical personalities and which finds hermeneutical justification in the principle of analogy. The historical accounts of the Gospels about the Jesus who walked on earth cannot be separated from the witness which sees in the historical Jesus the cosmic, universal, and suprahistorical features of the Christ figure. The historical record and the kerygmatic witness are not alternatives.

"Recollection of the days of his flesh and confession of his eternal significance, and of what we have in him, are inextricably intertwined in the NT. The two types of testimony belong together and offer the presupposition of an estimation of his figure in faith" (M. Kähler, *Der sogenannte historische Jesus* . . . [ed. 1956], pp. 63f.). As Schniewind puts it in his reply to R. Bultmann in KM, pp. 79f., recollection is itself part of my existence as a historical being. There is neither decision, encounter, nor personality without it. Thus the idea that recollection and existence, or historical record and witness of faith, are alternatives is reduced to absurdity. The unique Christ event certainly has a historical character. It is an event in human history. It forms part of the causally linked chain of events. It is passed on by recollection. It can be investigated by the discipline of history. Nevertheless, and paradoxically, this historical event as such is eschatological event, salvation event (*loc. cit.*).

We shall turn first to the NT itself to see how it approaches the historical figure of Christ and leads us to the interrelation of the two basic aspects. In this regard decisive help will be found here in the story of the Baptist's query when he was in prison: "Art thou he that should come, or do we look for another?" (Matthew 11:2ff.).

When John is pressured into asking Jesus: "Who art thou?" he is basically asking how the individual historical aspect and the universal suprahistorical aspect belong together in Jesus. His primary question concerns the individual relation between the one he has proclaimed and the one about whose further story he receives accounts in prison. Is the one whose weakness and lowliness are attested to by my situation in prison really the one whom I heralded as a forerunner?[1] This leads on at once to the second aspect of the question: Is Jesus the Messiah? The Messiah is supposed to bring judgment, to purge the floor and burn up the chaff (Matthew 3:12). In him God himself will come (Malachi 3:1; Zechariah 14:1). Judgment will begin in him. So will the new world of God's forgiveness and presence. He will be the Son of Man of Daniel 7:13. He will be the coming One who brings about the turn of aeons. For John, then, the Messiah is as supraterrestrial (Matthew 3:11f.; Mark 1:7)[2] as God himself or the Son of Man of Daniel. Yet he awaited him on earth and wanted to be his lowliest slave. What John is asking about, then, is the universal and suprahistorical significance of Christ.

This comes to expression in the fact that he asks under temptation. The root of this temptation is that the universal suprahistorical aspect does not find appropriate expression in the objective and objectively analyzable situation of the Baptist. Indeed, it stands in flagrant contradiction with it. For John sees himself as a prisoner in virtue of his witness to the Messiah. The appearance does not tally with the universal suprahistorical significance of Christ. To put it in popular terms, if a man cannot take care of his own people he cannot possibly have a commission for the whole world.

Christ gives only an indirect answer to the Baptist's question. He does not say: "Yes, I am the coming Son of Man. You need not look for another." Instead, he points to his works: "The blind see and the lame walk, the lepers are cleansed and the deaf hear, the dead are raised and the poor have the gospel preached to them . . . " (Matthew 11:5). His works are signs that a new world has come. They show that the change in aeons is taking place.

Does this help us, however, in relation to the question of his person, the "who"? If it is a mistake, as we have seen, to isolate the person of Christ from the works, it is just as much an error to divide the works from the person and to ascribe to them an independent quality. But does not Christ himself do this by pointing to his acts instead of himself? When he simply draws attention to the many miracles and mighty works that those around him have seen and heard, does it not almost seem as if he is using what is objective and perceptible, what can be analyzed, as a legitimate test? But if so, is he not, in a way which is hard to understand, presenting only a partial aspect of his person, viewing himself as recording officials and later historians see him?

---

[1] Cf. A. Schlatter, *Erläuterungen zum NT*, I (1922), p. 113.
[2] Schniewind, *NT Deutsch, ad loc.* (p. 135, 25).

If this is what Jesus means, he reduces both the Baptist and all of us to profound helplessness. For (1) it is epistemologically inconceivable that his comprehensive and universal character could be confined in what is apprehensible in this way.[3] Then (2) those of us who belong to a later time cannot dispute the dictum of Lessing that experiencing miracles ourselves is a different thing from being told by others that they have experienced them. The ambiguity and inappropriateness of testimonies to miracles increases for later generations who have to depend on the witness of others.

For this reason it is important that a reference to word and person is in fact linked to the reference to act and work. Neither is isolated from the other. The saying in which the mighty acts are enumerated culminates in the preaching of the gospel to the poor. This preaching is the key to the miracles. If the miracles are isolated from the word, their point can no longer be seen, their transparency is lost, and their character as signs is obscured. The reply of Jesus, however, rises in a crescendo to the ultimate joy that the real issue is something new and higher than miracles, namely, that the poor receive the glad tidings.[4] This new thing transcends miracles and also gives them their meaning.

The saying in which we are told this, however, depends on the person of the one who utters it. In it Jesus confesses that he is the bearer of glad tidings who proclaims God's kingdom and in whom it is among us (Luke 17:21), present in word and work. In his word, and in him as the bearer of the word, the eternal rule of God, the remission of sins, the peace of the future world, and the presence of God are pronounced to those who have ears to hear.

Thus the word and person of Jesus are indissolubly bound together. Only when a man trusts in him does he pay heed to his word and only when a man follows his sayings does he understand his secret.[5] Only in faith, then, do we have the coincidence of his person and work, of his word and miracles. These interpret one another.

This is why the answer of Jesus is couched in the words of Isaiah 35:5f.: "Then the eyes of the blind shall be opened, and the ears of the deaf shall be unstopped. Then shall the lame man leap as an hart, and the tongue of the dumb sing." The quotation of this prophecy is as such a commentary which integrates the one who uses it, who relates it to his own works, into the salvation event and which sees him indeed as the fulfilment of this event.[6] The promised coming of God is fulfilled in the person of Jesus. Hence this person is always presupposed as the subject of its works. Jesus

---

[3] Jesus' own criticism of miracles points in the same direction (see below).
[4] Schniewind, loc. cit.
[5] Ibid., p. 136.
[6] Cf. the use of Psalm 22:1 to express the dereliction on the cross (Matthew 27:46). By using God's words Jesus does not break away from God but binds himself to him. Hence the dereliction is also integration into the salvation event and its coming fulfilment; cf. Psalm 22:22-28.

makes us think of himself here as the subject of what he does. In relation to the Baptist he does this almost in Socratic fashion. He does not confess the mystery of his person directly. He evokes this confession in John, forcing him to say: Therefore he is the one that should come.

THE PERSON OF JESUS AS THE SUBJECT OF HIS WORKS

The problems are thus taking shape which arise out of this reference of Jesus to his works.

It is evident that there is a valid way and also an invalid way of describing the mystery of the person of Jesus by a reference to his works. The story of the answer to John's question offers us an example of the valid way. We shall now try to sharpen up the contrast between the two.

1 a. We have an invalid appeal to the action and work of Christ when objective certainty is sought. In such cases Jesus rejects the requests for signs (Mark 8:11ff.). Sighing, he says: "There shall no sign be given unto this generation." If we are not ready to subject ourselves to the word, and through the word to the person of him who speaks it, signs lose their transparency and will simply harden us in our wickedness and rebellion (Matthew 12:38-42). We will experience the miracle of feeding (John 6:1ff.) only as a banal satisfying of the demands of the stomach. We will not let it touch the heart and see the bread of life which the miracle denotes and sets before our eyes in person (John 6:26). The mere fact of the miraculous act leaves us blind and without a sign because we do not let ourselves become involved. This involvement comes only by confrontation with the word and person. Hence signs are denied to those who seek after them (Matthew 12:39; 16:4; John 4:48). When isolated from the word, the mighty act is silent.

This is why Satan in the temptations tries to silence Christ by urging him to offer signs (Matthew 4:1-11). If as Redeemer he were to rely on the impression made by his mighty acts he would fail to claim the decision of the heart and therewith the commitment of discipleship. He would thus betray his calling. Miracles begin to speak only as interpreted signs. They are interpreted by him who does them and by the word he speaks (Mark 2:1-12). This is why the mere fact of making bread miraculously is no help. Only understanding of the meaning of the bread brings faith. This meaning, however, depends on the person of Jesus: "I am the bread of life" (John 6:35). Thus the person of Jesus is present in the works inasmuch as it is he who makes himself known in them and who calls men out of a distant observation of signs into personal fellowship with himself. Jesus Christ, then, is to be distinguished from his works—he is more than they are—even though he is not to be had apart from or outside his works.

b. Another aspect of the invalid way of appealing to the action and work of Jesus may be perceived when we note that miracles are in principle ambiguous. The fact that they have taken place may be incontestable. For eyewitnesses this is evident. Nevertheless, this makes all the more equivocal the background of this reality, the sign which stands before the sum of the mighty acts of Jesus. This ambiguity finds expression in the question: "By what authority doest thou these things? and who gave thee this authority?" Does God stand behind them or demonic power? Is heaven at work or hell? Do we have here charisma or magic (Matthew 9:34; 12:24; 21:23, 24, 27)?

The half-light between the divine and the demonic in which the miracles are set may be seen also in modern scepticism with regard to miracles. The problem now is not whether God or Beelzebub is at work. It is that of the relation to natural causality. If miraculous things take place, if a wrongdoer is suddenly punished, is this not due to the intersection of several tightly knit causal sequences in these events? But seeing in the conjunction of such causal sequences the miraculous acts of God cannot be objectified either by observation or deduction. What means certainty for faith is thus uncertain in the objective sense. Miracle, then, lives and moves in a sphere of confusion. The half-light and confusion disappear only for those who relate miracles to the person of Christ and interpret them in terms of this person. The relation to Christ, however, is faith. Thus miracles belong to the sphere of faith. Although the event which the believer calls a miracle can be seen, it is not an event in which faith can give place to sight and thus become superfluous, so that commitment yields to the indifference of a mere spectator. When this is sought, or when Satanic power holds out the enticements of such a course (as in the temptations), Jesus rejects miracles. Hence the word which brings faith and the miracle which can be seen are not alternatives. They are tied to one another and expound one another. The word expounds the miracle as an act of God and a sign of his dawning rule. The miracle for its part expounds the word as an active word, a deed-word. And the person in whom faith believes validates the word.[7]

c. For modern and especially post-Kantian thought the invalid concept of Christ's work has some particular implications. This work is no longer sought in the ontically objective sphere, e.g., in stilling the storm or healing the sick or helping the needy. On ontological, epistemological, and historical grounds the supernatural miracle is no longer a possible object of experience and assertion. The work of Jesus is now sought exclusively in the psychological and ethical realm, in the sphere of experience, consciousness, and will. The plasticity of our inner matter—if one may use so bold a phrase—makes it possible for us to think of a transformation here without running into the intellectual difficulties that we encounter with the idea of external intervention in the self-resting reality which is ruled by natural causality. In the name of this concept of his work the figure of Christ is reduced to a prototype of trust (W. Herrmann), of loyalty to calling (A. Ritschl), or again of trust (G. Ebeling).

---

[7] Cf. the discussion of miracle in the author's *Theologie der Anfechtung* (1949), pp. 94ff.

The objection which has to be brought against this is that it negates the dialectic of Christ's person and work. For along these lines there is no longer a relation of reciprocal exposition. Christ's person is understood expressly and exclusively in terms of his work, the work itself is forced into the Procrustean bed of the modern thought-schema, and its validity is restricted to personalist categories. It is not interpreted in terms of Christ's person. Hence the difference between person and work vanishes; the two are virtually equated. If Christ is in this way only the subject and prototype of faith (or trust, or loyalty to calling, etc.), how can he be the object of faith? Is he not simply the first and exemplary believer? And if Christology is structured in this way, do I not have to believe in the faith of someone else? Is not the subject-object correlation, whose doubtful aspects are rightly castigated in the Bultmann school, so radically shattered here that faith loses its object and in the last resort it becomes only faith in faith itself.[8]

2. After considering the mistaken approach which isolates Christ's work from his person and remains stuck in the ambiguity of miracle or in its own thought-schema, we shall now look at the valid way which leads from Christ's work to the mystery of his person.

Luther's frequently quoted statement that the person does the works can be applied to Christ too. Its implication here is that Christ's word and work are to be understood in the light of his person. The "what" of the work is to be construed in terms of the "who" of him who is at work here. (To this extent the hermeneutical circle is in force.) Negatively, this means that he is not his work (in the sense of ontic equation), but is only in his work (so that the work opens up noetic access for me).

This is how Kähler sees it when he distinguishes between the historical biblical Christ and the so-called historical Jesus. The church and preaching are his work, his historical effect, but he transcends both. Nevertheless, I "have" him only through the church and preaching. I "have" him only as I expose myself to his work, to the preaching which awakens faith. Only he who is of the truth hears his voice (John 18:37). This means that only he who is brought into fellowship with Christ by his life-changing work hears his voice and knows him.

The mere facts of the works which he does in his Father's name, and which bear witness to him, are not enough (cf. John 10:24-30). He who does not belong to the flock is deaf to his word and deed (v. 26). Here it is not just a matter of his work as an objective fact; it is a matter of his work on me through which I am a member of the flock.

Two things must be said: first, that he is more and other than his work, and second, that I cannot have him apart from his work. I "have"

---

[8] Cf. the way in which faith is almost personified in the existential interpretation, O. Rodenberg, *Um die Wahrheit der Hl. Schrift* (1963), p. 46. Faith knows what to say neither about itself (cf. Schniewind, KM, p. 72) nor about him in whom it believes (Rodenberg, *loc. cit.*).

him only insofar as I am an object of his work and I understand him to be its subject.

When I interpret his work in this way, I realize that it cannot be recorded and verified in the same way as "normal" historical facts. It discloses itself to me only in the light of the person who works on me. Whether or not this work wins power over me, whether or not the Lord becomes my Lord through this work, whether or not he is present for me in it, is not under my control. For it is not my own receptive and ready spirit which leads me into this truth; it is the Spirit of God (John 16:13). The result is that I do not control this work; in scientific terms, it is not objectifiable.

This determines the style of statements about it. Objective facts enjoy general validity. A synthetic judgment *a priori* or *a posteriori* forces us to accept them. In relation, however, to what is non-objectifiable, to what is subordinate to the field of force of Christ's person, I can make statements only in the form of confession, of defenseless confession which is always exposed to the possibility of rejection.

A new style of recognition as well as confession is also posited. For in the light of the person from whom the work emanates much seems to be possible which does not correspond to the objectifiable possibilities of ordinary history. He who believes in the *exousia* of the *Kyrios* will include miracle in what he holds to be possible: the lame walking and the blind seeing (Matthew 11:5). As a theologian, i.e., as one who considers his methods, concepts, and epistemological situation, he will have to be aware what kind of statements he is making in this regard. Negatively, he is not engaging in ordinary historical assertion and evaluation. He is not arguing on the basis of records which have to be regarded as reliable either as a whole or at least in part according to the customary methods of historical criticism. If he were, he would be adopting the "therefore" which Kierkegaard criticizes: Since these acts are beyond the power of man, therefore Jesus of Nazareth must have been more than mere man.

This form of argument, which we reject for many reasons, is seen by many modern theologians (e.g., in the school of Bultmann) to be remarkably influential in circles which not only accept the miracle stories of the NT in principle but also regard them as important to faith. These theologians seem to me to be right in their rejection of the supposed proof of miracles and also in their refusal to view the mighty works outside faith as miracles which make faith easier and can even confer noetic certainty. In fact, as we see it, the supposed proof necessarily leads to intellectual dishonesty and a split in consciousness.

On the other hand, it seems to us to be a mistake for theologians of this school to argue that confession of Christ as the bearer of authority and the doer of mighty works is always based merely on the above argument. We for our part do not use that argument and yet we acknowledge the theological relevance of miracles. It is surely clear by now how we can do this. Miracles are not objectifiable facts. In the sphere of objectifiability they fall victim to the criteria of verification laid down by Troeltsch. For me, then, they are possible events only because I first have the person for whom all things are possible (Mark 10:27). This knowledge is not objective; it is personal. To use Kantian terms, although not without some reservations, it lies within the sphere of competence of practical rather than theoretical reason. Theoretical reason does not regard freedom as possible, at least within its own area of experience; it cannot accept any breach in natural causality.[9] The impossibility of objectifying miracles[10] is similar to the impossibility of establishing freedom.

I have just said that I can think of miracles as possible events only because I first have the person. But this is too simplistic. The facts are in truth dialectical. For I have the person only by way of the works. I allow the witness to Christ, the accounts of his words and deeds, to refer me to the person. The records are the spokes of a wheel that lead me to the true axis. I do not see the central point directly. It makes itself known to me through the spokes, i.e., through the works which emanate from it. Only as the one who is thus made known becomes "my Lord"—was not this the way of the eyewitnesses too?—do the works and signs find their validation, whereas previously they lay in the half-light between God and Beelzebub (Matthew 12:24; Luke 11:15-19) and to that extent could not be verified.

It should be noted in passing that the acknowledgment of miracles by faith does not confer a wholesale validation which makes all further historico-critical investigation of scripture unnecessary. If it has sometimes done this, the intention is very different. By considering accounts of the works of the *Kyrios* and the acts of the apostles from the standpoint of their *exousia,* other limits are undoubtedly set for what is possible than those imposed by the criteria of Troeltsch. The boundaries are pushed back. But a critical study has still to be made to see what is fact and what might be legend. Poetic and mythical additions might have been made to the true wonders and signs by the community and its tradition. It has even to be considered whether some such additions might be distortions which part company with reality. For example, might it be that the story of the Gadarene swine in Mark 5:1ff. is not witness but satire on the Jewish refusal to eat swine's flesh? Theologically, it seems to be more satisfactory to view any possible accretions as commentaries on the person and deeds of Jesus, as a kind of poetic doxology in which the community responds to the word and work of its Lord.

On this view faith in the *Kyrios* is no longer threatened by detailed critical distinctions. It does not have to await nervously the approval or disapproval of historians. It is no longer open to constant challenge. For it makes no difference to faith whether the Lord works through accounts

---

[9] Cf. the discussion in Chapter XXI.   [10] Unless, as in Schleiermacher's *Speeches,* miracles are taken up into subjectivity and understood as the religious category of vision; cf. also *The Christian Faith,* § 47. On the whole problem of miracle cf. the author's *Theologie der Anfechtung,* pp. 94ff.

of facts or through responsive doxologies of the type mentioned.

The presupposition of faith's indifference to historical differentiation is that the basic facticity of miracles and signs is accepted. Hence doxological accretions do not basically alter the picture of the *Kyrios* given us in the Gospels. If, however, all the signs and wonders are viewed as projections, the picture of Jesus changes decisively. He becomes the mere place of a speech-event, or the mere prototype of faith, or the mere subject of a call for decision. His works, and with them he himself, are thus spiritualized. As in kerygma-theology, he becomes no more than the trigger of processes of consciousness, e.g., a new self-understanding.

The decisive thing for Christology, then, is that the facticity of the works of Christ should be firmly upheld—just as firmly as it is by all the NT witnesses. In this regard faith would not be basically affected even if we were in a position to view only a single miracle of Jesus as attested in such a way that there can be certainty of its quality as a factual event, and we had to reject all the rest of the records as legendary. The existence of an authentic factual element is what counts.

Summing up all that we have tried to say about the connection between Christ's person and work, we may say that the mighty acts of God are the theme of Christology insofar as they take place in and through the figure of Christ.

What are these mighty acts?

We shall give a provisional answer to this question in a brief thematic survey which will also outline our task. We shall then inquire into the systematic principle which is to be adopted if we are to see the themes in their theological interrelationship.

The thematic survey consists of four points.

1. Included among the mighty acts of God is the incarnation of Christ in which God fulfils his resolve to give his only-begotten Son (John 3:16) and to exalt him through the crucifixion. In this regard the facts of the virgin birth and the empty tomb have of themselves no convincing power in the sense of forcing us to the conclusion: Therefore. That is to say, we cannot argue that because he was born of the virgin, therefore he is the Son of God, or because the tomb was empty on Easter morning, therefore he rose again in the body. The virgin birth and the empty tomb acquire significatory force only insofar as they denote God's coming among us and the equation of this coming with Jesus. Jesus *is* the event of this coming. To this extent he represents an event which makes it impossible to explain him in terms of the continuity of history, e.g., his genealogy, or to view him as enclosed within the nature of this world which is given up to death.

2. Also included among the mighty acts of God is the crucifixion of Christ as the completion of God's condescension in the incarnation and as the depth of God's sacrifice. The passion brings to light the human nature of Christ, which freely resolves upon suffering, which is determined by the situation of temptation (Hebrews 4:15), and which "learned by obedience the things which he suffered" (Hebrews 5:8).

3. Another of the mighty acts of God is the exaltation of Christ, i.e., his raising up from human historical limitation to his universal suprahistorical presence in the form of Easter, Ascension, and Coming Again.

4. The act behind the act in all these things is the removal of that which separates us from the love of God (Romans 8:31-39). It is immediacy to God in the spontaneity of the Spirit and of love (Hebrews 9:10; Jeremiah 31:31-34).

XXIV

The Systematic Principle of Christology:
The Doctrine of the Offices[1]

When we ask what principle suggests itself for the relating of the theme of Christology, i.e., the mighty acts of God, to the person of Christ, and for the understanding of the person of Christ as that of these acts, we come up against one of the oldest problems in the history of Christian doctrine.

We have seen in what difficulties we are involved when we try to move ahead with the help of the doctrine of the two natures. This doctrine focuses on the mystery of Christ's person, and although, as we have seen, the work of Christ is constantly kept in view, although all the conflicts and exaggerations in trying to balance the natures relate to the work of redemption, nevertheless the person is not understood in terms of the works. In other words, the answer of Jesus to the Baptist's question about the "who" of his person (Matthew 11:3; cf. John 10:24f.) is not adopted as a blueprint for Christology. The "who" of the person is not learned from the works. But this is precisely the way that we should try to learn it. This being our goal, we do best to adopt as our systematic principle, not the doctrine of the two natures, but the doctrine of the offices.

Like the predicates of dignity, the offices of Christ, which are traditionally the prophetic, priestly, and kingly offices, are in the first instance functional, not ontic, designations. In this regard they do, of course, point to privileges of the person and consequently to their ontic character. For we cannot think of any other subject for these functions in and through which God does his work and Christ acts in relation to his Father. Only Christ, and no one else, can be the locus of this work and hence the bearer of these offices. To this degree ontic statements are implied, and yet only in such a way that they are made implicitly, and hence indirectly, along with statements about his functions. As it seems to us, however, indirect state-

---

[1] F. Hahn, *Christologische Hoheitstitel* (1963); G. Gloege, *Aller Tage Tag* (1960); O. Cullmann, *Die Christologie des NT* (1957); E.T. 1959; E. Schweizer, *Erniedrigung und Erhöhung bei Jesus und seinen Nachfolgern* (1962).

ments about his person are the most suitable forms of christological definition. We shall try to illustrate this by first considering some of his christological titles.

The way in which an indirect style corresponds to the NT mode of statement may be seen from the use of the title "Son of God."

In pre-Christian Palestine Judaism this concept had not been developed in such a way that it applied to the Messiah or suggested itself as a predicate of dignity for Christ. In the prophets, for example, Israel itself could be called the son of God (Hosea 11:1). An angel or the king could also be the son of God (Psalm 2:9; 89:27). Even in the NT the term "son of God," especially in the plural, does not have to be a designation for Christ; cf. Matthew 5:9. It can also be used for believers. Nevertheless, when this predicate of dignity is used in relation to Christ, especially although not necessarily with the definite article *ho*, it serves to denote an exceptional and privileged role and function.

This uniqueness of his may be seen especially in relation to his authority, which manifests itself in his power over demons (Matthew 8:29; Mark 3:11; 5:7; 8:29) and in his wonders and signs; cf. Peter's confession in Mark 8:29. In the dialog with the tempter in the wilderness (Matthew 4:1ff.) the designation "Son of God" again refers to the privilege of unique authority, although in the answers of Jesus we find an obvious shift of meaning, the title now denoting special conformity to the Father, a harmony which rules out any self-will. To this extent the phrase is not in this instance a title which denotes Christ's own dignity but a reference to the alien dignity which is conferred on him by the Father and which exists only in relation to the Father. Thus he is properly called the Son of God, not when his majesty is expressed, but when what is at issue is his humble submission and subjection to the cross and passion.

This humility of subjection comes to expression when the predicate occurs in the form of a unique statement about himself in which Christ says that not even the Son knows the day and hour when heaven and earth will pass away, since the Father has reserved this knowledge for himself alone (Mark 13:32). This shows that "Son of God" is not a title in the sense of denoting special majesty in relation to men but only in the sense of expressing special conformity to the Father. Only on this basis, and very secondarily, do we have the indication of a privileged position in relation to men. (A negative sign of this is that Jesus never associates himself with other men in his relation to the Father, not even in the Lord's Prayer.)

Once the main point of the term "Son of God" is perceived we find it implicitly in many other sayings, as in Gethsemane when Christ submits himself so unreservedly to the Father's will (Luke 22:42).

This conformity with the Father, which is expressed in so many different ways, especially with the help of the predicate of sonship, is not, of course, a self-contained thesis about the ontic character of his person. Only indirectly does it have the purpose of interpreting his work and function. This happens when the appropriate subject is taken into account along with the work.

The fact that the characterization of Christ as the Son of God is not attempted directly may be seen from the absence of the designation where one would expect it, namely, in the nativity stories in Matthew 1:18-21; Luke 1:26-38. Its omission in these stories shows that physical or ontic concerns are not the primary ones in the use of the title Son of God. It is characteristic that the title occurs first (on God's own lips) on the occasion when Christ is chosen and separated for his work by baptism and when God acknowledges him as the one in whom he is well-pleased. The election recorded in the baptism story cannot possibly denote a mere exaltation and distinction of his person. There is always intent in election. Election is for something, for a work.

The baptism itself is an initial event in the work which is to be done, for in it Christ accepts solidarity with sinners, and the next step along this line comes at once as he exposes himself to temptation. Also related to this work is the recognition of his sonship at the transfiguration: "This is my beloved Son: hear him" (Mark 9:7). Here the predicate of sonship is clearly connected with the fact that he is the subject of the Word, of the Word which comes to fulfilment as the liberating and binding Word. The designation "Son of God," then, is more a designation of goal than of origin. Its point is not supernatural descent, but mission and destiny. Naturally these are not alternatives. They are closely related. It is more a matter of emphasis, of the question as to which is the direct and basic statement and which is the indirect and implicit statement.

Early Christology caught the distinction very well. It saw that ontic statements were implied, and realized that it is not enough to speak merely of Christ's works and benefits. We have seen the results of this type of one-sidedness. Christ becomes no more than the kerygma or its effect. He becomes a mere historical cause. He rises up into history (G. Koch, *Die Auferstehung Jesu Christ* [1959]). The only trouble with the early church, however, was that while seeing the need to differentiate between the person and work, under the pressure of its ontological system it went to the opposite extreme and made the person an independent and almost isolated theme in separation from the work. Nevertheless, it should not be overlooked that in the debates about the definition of Christ's essence the ultimate concern, as we have seen, was whether this or that definition might truncate or distort the work of salvation. To this extent there is never an absolute separation between person and work.

Establishment of the error should not hinder us from recognizing the concern of faith which led to ontological statements about the person. Negatively, the concern means a desire to confess that Christ is not made what he is by his task or work. He is not in himself a mere anybody who comes to be qualified as the Christ in virtue of his mission, as in the saying that when God gives someone an office he also gives understanding. The very reverse is true. Because he is Christ ontically and by nature, he is given his commission. His special relation to the Father is the presupposition of his office and task, not its consequence. He can fulfil his office of bringing the kingdom of God and the change in aeons only because he stands as the privileged Son at the side of the Father. This is why the Nicenes contend for *gennēthénta* ("begotten") instead of the Arian *poiēthénta* ("made"), quoting in support the saying in Psalm 2:7, which is so important in the Easter understanding of the primitive community (Acts 13:33).

It should be noted—and we want to stress this—how these ontological statements are to be interpreted. They describe a person who is to be defined in terms of his commission. This description can vary according to the linguistic resources available. The doctrine of the two natures is only one among many possible modes of expression. It carried with it, as we have seen, the danger of one-sided concentration on the personal nature of Christ and can easily lead to hopeless controversies about the balancing of the natures. The passion engendered in these controversies would be hard to understand if we did not see behind the extreme esotericism of the metaphysical distinctions the concern to express the event of redemption without truncation and hence to achieve a proper understanding of the subject of the work. In our view better justice can be done to this concern if we work out Christology in terms of the offices. For this means that the relation between office and person will have to be a constant and explicit theme.

THE TITLE MESSIAH AS A CONFESSION OF FAITH

By way of preface to the doctrine of the offices it might be as well to try to see from another title whether this approach seems to be justified. The most obvious title to take is naturally the title Messiah or Christ.

It is a familiar fact that Jesus never calls himself Christ except perhaps in the dialog with the Pharisees in Luke 22:67-71. Gloege constructs for heuristic reasons a declaratory sermon in which Jesus calls himself the Messiah so that against this background he may show how different is the spirit of the NT sayings: "I am the Christ, the Messiah. Believe that I am. Woe to you if you do not believe."[2] In contrast, Jesus is most reserved even when others ascribe this title to him. He does not want the story of his exorcisms (Mark 1:44f.; 3:12; 5:43; 7:36), or Peter's confession (Mark 8:30), or the transfiguration (Mark 9:9) to be spread abroad. This is why W. Wrede speaks of the messianic secret in Mark[3] and why M. Dibelius calls Mark the book of secret epiphanies.[4] The reserve in relation to the

---

[2] *Op. cit.,* p. 216.

[3] *Das Messiasgeheimnis in den Evangelien* (1901); E.T. *The Messianic Secret* (1971).

[4] *Die Formgeschichte des Evangeliums* (1919); E.T. *From Tradition to Gospel* (1935).

title Messiah is all the more strange in view of the fact that the post-Easter community unanimously ascribes it to Jesus.

What is the reason for the reserve? If we are right, there is both a foreground reason and a background reason.

1. As concerns the foreground reason there was undoubtedly great difficulty in fitting the person of Jesus into the messianic tradition of Judaism. The difficulty is similar to that of integrating the phenomenon of Jesus into the Logos tradition and characterizing it in terms of the Logos concept. The problem as we have seen it in relation to the latter is as follows: Who or what is defined by whom or what? Does Christ define the Logos concept as in the Prologue to John or is he controlled by the concept as in the Apologists? The same problem arises in relation to the Messiah concept. Can Christ be defined in terms of the Messiah title as already shaped by the tradition or does that which is called Messiah after his appearance have to be filled out materially by his person?

Now in relation to this question the situation before Easter differs from the situation after Easter. After Easter the risen one is proclaimed as the unique Lord, so that there can be no question of fitting him into an existing schema and relativizing his uniqueness by the principle of analogy. He who brings the change in the aeons and is Lord of the coming kingdom of God cannot be defined by the schemata of the old world. He himself becomes the standard and criterion, the hermeneutical principle, for the way in which God's Word in the old covenant, and representative figures in this Word, are to be understood. As the fulfilment of all the promises he is also their corrective. These take their measure from him. We have only to look at Paul's christological understanding of the OT[5] or at the unique priesthood of Christ in Hebrews, which transcends all the cultic rules of the OT (5:4ff.; 7:11-28; 9:11-28; 10:11-18, etc.), to see that on the one side Christ stands at the end of the salvation history of the OT and that on the other side he transcends and transvaluates this history.

Before Easter, however, the situation is radically different. When Jesus first came to walk the earth, it was unavoidable that claiming the title of Messiah would mean definition by this title, so that he would be caught in the schema of expectation and would be understood as a symbolical exponent of this expectation. If Jesus had allowed himself to be defined by the traditional messianic title he would have been seen as the end-time king who would liberate his people from Roman oppression. The reaction of Jesus to Peter's confession at Caesarea Philippi shows plainly how he steers clear of this understanding. He rejects the title of Messiah, at least in Peter's sense, and points to his suffering. He is not the one that Peter had in mind with his messianic doxology (Matthew 16:16, 21-23). For the same reason, i.e., because the traditional title does not fit him, he withdraws from the crowd when he notes, according to John's account, that they want to proclaim him king (John 6:15).

---

[5] E.g., in Galatians 4:21-31.

The difficulty posed by the traditional title increases when it is recalled that the messianic expectation of contemporary Judaism distinguished between different messianic figures. Thus some were waiting for both a royal and a priestly Messiah while according to the Qumran texts the Essene community expected first the prophet (Deuteronomy 18:15), then the Aaronic Messiah as the end-time high priest, and finally the eschatological king of the tribe of Judah and the house of David, the priestly Messiah taking precedence of the eschatological king. If Jesus had wanted to confess himself as Messiah, which of the two or three would it have been? And if he had left this an open question, would he not have seemed to be a vacillating and ambivalent or even trivalent figure?

The later doctrine of the offices, which takes its cue from Christ rather than identifying him as this or that traditional figure, shows much greater freedom in this whole field even though there is an astonishing similarity to the Qumran texts when it refers to Christ's prophetic, priestly, and kingly office. For it make it plain that equation with only one of these messianic concepts would be an intolerable restriction of Christ's person and work and would develop Christology along erroneous lines. Certainly it would have been a liability for Christ to have tied himself down to the messianic tradition. We can thus understand why he not only avoided any self-predication as the Messiah but held aloof from any such predications on the part of those around him.

2. The background reason for rejection of the title of Messiah is, of course, to be sought elsewhere. In this regard the author will venture a suggestion for which he cannot rely on help from his NT colleagues but which seems to have certain factors in its favor.

In some of the dialogs which are adduced in support of the messianic secret the title of Messiah seems to run up against the mystery of his person without being expressly repudiated. Instead, it is left open in the form of a question which acts as a spur and a trigger.

Of the texts in question we may mention again the accounts of exorcisms. When the possessed and the sick find in Christ the superior force which threatens them, they achieve a better diagnosis than the secure and indifferent Pharisees, and break forth involuntarily into Christ doxologies. Jesus then forbids them to tell others what has happened, but he does not in fact reject the Christ predicate or withdraw into an esoteric messianic secret. From Wrede to Bultmann his attitude, or recorded attitude, has usually been taken to mean that the life of Jesus was wholly nonmessianic[6] and that later this was not understood, so that Jesus was made into the Messiah who takes refuge in a secret and who thus produces the failure of the disciples to understand him. The alienation which a real nonmessianic life of Jesus would have caused was skilfully avoided, then, by the argument that in reality he was not nonmessianic but merely appeared to be, or, more accurately, gave the appearance of being, or, even more accu-

---

[6] Bultmann, *Theologie des NT* (1953), p. 32; E.T. 1951, pp. 31f.

rately, Mark made him appear to be. For the messianic secret has its seat in the redactional statements of the evangelist and not in the primitive tradition.[7] To put it more crudely, it is a literary device.

Dibelius (*op. cit.*, pp. 225f., 231f.; E.T. pp. 223, 229f.) takes a similar view. The messianic secret is Mark's answer to the question why Jesus was not recognized. He was God's Son but he did not reveal what he was to the people. This is why he was not recognized and could be brought to the cross (p. 231; E.T. pp. 229f.).

For our part we resist strongly the attempt to explain texts from outside—in this case by the sophisticated pragmatism of Mark[8]—until every possibility of expounding them in terms of the matter itself has been exhausted. What, then, do we learn from the matter itself?

It should be noted that in face of the doxologies of those he heals Jesus never says expressly: "You are wrong. I am not the one you call me." He does not contest his messiahship. He simply asks them not to speak about it to others.

But why does he do this? It should cause us to take notice that he asks for silence not merely when the messianic title is used but also when what is not to be spoken about is simply the miracle itself (Mark 1:40-45, etc.). Obviously the silence does not relate specifically to the title but to something much more general which includes the title. Since miracles are part of the more general thing which is set under the discipline of silence, the attitude of Jesus to miracles might well be a pointer to the solution of the puzzle of the messianic secret.

In fact miracles are anticipatory manifestations of his glory. The eschatological Son of Man (Daniel 7:13; Revelation 1:13) already gives proleptic signs of his power (Mark 2:10). Understood in this sense miracles are, like the Spirit, a deposit or pledge (*arrabón*) or anticipation of what is to come (2 Corinthians 1:22; 5:5; Romans 8:23; Galatians 5:5). As we have seen, however,[9] miracles do not go beyond the Word in the sense that the Word demands faith while miracles offer sight and yield eyewitness proof. Miracles are subject to the same ambivalence as the Word and are equally defenseless. They stand in the half-light between God and Beelzebub (Matthew 12:24). As acts of demonic power they might be a refutation of every messianic claim.

Jesus does not substitute clarity for ambivalence. The name in which he exercises his power is not displayed but is kept in the uncertainty of which Kierkegaard says that it mobilizes the infinite passion of inwardness, whereas objective certainty lulls to sleep. "Neither tell I you by what authority I do these things" (Matthew 21:27). Jesus can even keep silent about his miracles when it is obvious that these are being used as a way of evading faith, i.e., of evading a direct commitment of trust to his person.

---

[7] *Ibid.*
[8] Dibelius, *op. cit.*, p. 225; E.T. p. 223.
[9] Chapter XXIII.

In this respect the struggle with the tempter is again instructive. All the latter's cunning attacks use the argument that if you do this or that—some spectacular miracle—they will believe in you. In reality, however, the aim of the tempter is to obstruct faith. If men were overpowered by the impression made by the miracles of Christ, this would not be faith in the strict sense. It would emphatically not cause them to give themselves in trust to his person and message but would simply bring them under the power of sensory impressions and suggestions. No involvement would result from this type of miracle. It would not lead to discipleship. It would lead past it. This is why Jesus upbraids those who seek after a sign (Matthew 12:38f.; 16:4; Luke 11:29f.). People of this kind want to look on as astonished spectators. They do not want to be committed to discipleship. They are evading the venture of faith.

Accounts of miracles as well as miracles themselves can produce the same psychological overpowering which wrongly avoids commitment. When Lessing says that it is one thing to experience miracles and another to hear about others experiencing them, we find in this statement not merely scepticism about historical truth, and the actual occurrence of supernatural miracles, but also an aversion to coming under the claim of an act of power. What really claims me, what comes home to me with unconditional force, cannot be mediated by a sensory demonstration or an impressive account, but for a man of the Enlightenment like Lessing it must come by way of reason and conscience. This aspect of Lessing's objection should not be overlooked. In this regard his position is not wholly unlike Jesus' own reserved attitude toward miracles.

Keeping silence about miracles, then, might be designed to guard men against thinking that they have to accept a visible, sensory demonstration of power. For this kind of acceptance might work against the very different acceptance of Christ's person and mission—the acceptance which can come only in discipleship, only in confession of his word and work, only in faith and obedience. What Jesus is saying, then, is that I want men to confront *me* and not your stories of miracles. I want the decision to be made in relation to my person. I want men to understand the miracles in terms of my person. This is the only valid way.

What it means to take this way *via* the person we learn from the Johannine Christ: "If any man will do the will of him that sent me, he shall know of the (my) doctrine, whether it be of God, or whether I speak of myself" (John 7:17). The mystery of his person, then, is disclosed only in the obedience of discipleship, only in commitment. It is not disclosed to those who learn about miracles as mere onlookers.

If this interpretation is correct, it sheds light on the injunction to keep the messiahship secret. The discretion recommended here is simply one aspect of the larger silence. For the title "Messiah" has the same type of effect as miracles. It nourishes the same type of rumors among the people. Certainty as to the equation of Jesus and the Messiah means having a black and white definition of Christ. This involves an objective mistake, for in fact Christ is not this Messiah. It also involves a failure to face up to his claim. Objective certainty—we are again alluding to Kierkegaard's concept of the incognito—obviously means noninvolvement.

It might be allowed that the possessed meant more by their hailing of Christ than was contained in the traditional messianic title. This seems to be so, since Jesus obviously finds himself discovered rather than misunderstood when he is greeted thus. Nevertheless, the productive moment of discovery would still be falsified by merely talking about it. For the autonomy of the traditional title "Messiah" would affect the telling which is triggered by the situation of discovery. (The history of Protestantism knows a development which in virtue of its formal similarity might provide an illustration. When Luther's doctrine of the freedom of a Christian man is detached from its doctrinal basis and we are simply told about the moment of its discovery, the freedom is distorted into a Protestant principle and a protesting liberalism that knows no commitment.) The messianic title itself becomes an attraction. It exercises a superficial power of persuasion. But it leaves the core of personhood intact. Only the "nerves," only the thirst for sensations and political expectations and desires, are mobilized.

Fundamentally this danger threatens all Christian proclamation and not just miracles or the messianic title. Mere telling which does not lead to involved confrontation with the center of the message engenders empty dogmatic formulae and the pseudo-faith which is conventionally called a purely historical faith or *fides quae creditur* in distinction from *fides qua creditur*, i.e., belief in distinction from faith.

All this might well be the reason why Jesus, although he does not deny that he is the Messiah or that he works miracles, still does not want to see himself proclaimed on this level. As we see it, his concern is not to repudiate the actual title. It is to repudiate the way by which confession of his messiahship is reached if this confession is merely suggested by the title or by accounts of his miracles. The legitimate way to confession of his messiahship—and this confirms our thesis—is the exact opposite. Men come to confess him as they encounter him, as they come to trust in him and to follow him. Confession of his messiahship is the result or final act of this encounter and not its presupposition.

The relation of the messianic title to discipleship is much the same, then, as that of dogma to faith. Dogma is not a premise which has to be accepted by way of presupposition before faith can arise. It is faith in the subsequent form of reflection. This is of great significance for the way of man to faith. Being a Christian does not begin when we first manage to recognize Jesus of Nazareth as the Christ, the Son of God, and a supernatural figure. When Jesus perceives faith in men and women, e.g., the Capernaum centurion in Luke 7:1-10, the Canaanite woman in Matthew 15:28, or the woman with the flux in Luke 8:43-48,[10] these may well be people who know little or

---

[10] Cf. the author's *Und wenn Gott wäre . . .* (1970), pp. 59ff., 89ff.; E.T. *How To Believe Again* (1972), pp. 51ff., 77ff.

nothing about the title "Messiah," but they have come to trust in the person of Christ and later perhaps—we do not know—they find their way to confession of Christ. Faith grows into the Christ dogma but does not grow out of it. Dogma is the result and not the premise. When the reverse is true and theology wins primacy over faith, everything becomes sterile and orthodox and there is no commitment. This is why, in evangelistic preaching, we ought, perhaps, to be less lavish in our use of the title "Christ" and even in our use of the word "God."

The title "Messiah" is legitimately used, then, when it is the confession of a preceding faith. It must not be misused as a way of evading faith and commitment. Only when it arises out of faith do we have the situation in which the title is defined by the person of Jesus, as the title "Logos" is in John 1, and not the opposite situation in which Jesus is defined by the title.

This sheds an instructive light on the incident at Caesarea Philippi in Matthew 16:13ff.[11] Here Peter seems to confess Jesus as the Christ on the basis of faith. He is thus defining the title "Messiah" in terms of the person. Nevertheless, the very next moment, when Jesus expounds his person and mission in terms of the prediction of his passion, we see that this is not entirely so. For it is obvious that Peter is still influenced by the traditional concept of the Messiah and radically misunderstands his Lord under the pressure of this concept. According to the prophecy of the passion, which transcends this concept, the person and mission of Jesus are even more mysterious. Jesus does not issue any command not to tell about this secret. For the secret of his passion is in no danger of being misunderstood under the influence of the traditional concept. In fact, it is not understood at all. He guards this secret, not by stopping any mention of it, for it can and should be told, but by preventing the spreading of false reports, e.g., the extolling of his miracles, which might give the impression of magic or satanic arts, or premature proclamation as the Messiah, which might expose him to misinterpretation as liberator king.

This conception of the messianic secret is supported by the observation that Jesus does not use the title "Messiah" or "Christ" to define his person and mission but handles it socratically, leaving it ambiguous and thus maieutically triggering the question of his person. This may be seen in the pericope about Jesus as David's Son and Lord in Mark 12:35-37; cf. Psalm 110:1. The point of the story is a question which is left open and which might be formulated as follows: How can he be both at one and the same time? How can he be the descendant of David, who is later in time, and yet also the Lord of David, who embraces all times? Here, then, the predicate "Messiah," which may not be mentioned but is indubitably implied (David's Lord of the house of David from whom the Messiah comes), is not a definition which answers the question of his person but is itself a statement which forces us to ask about his secret and thus points us to himself and

---

[11] *Ibid.*, pp. 44ff.

his mission. He himself maintains the incognito which constantly provokes this question.

The same applies fundamentally in the examination of Jesus according to the various accounts. According to Mark 14:61, when the high priest asks: "Art thou the Christ, the Son of the Blessed?" Jesus seems to give a direct answer and therefore to break the messianic secret which he has kept thus far: "I am: and ye shall see the Son of man sitting at the right hand of power, and coming in the clouds of heaven" (v. 62). Why do we say that this only seems to be a direct answer? Does it not have all the clarity that might be desired? All the terms used are familiar: Messiah, Son of God, Son of Man, heavenly Judge. Nevertheless, one cannot speak of a direct Christ-confession even here. It is striking that Jesus uses these predicates of majesty only when he is being delivered up to death, exposed to humiliation, and plunged into the passion, so that the confession of his messiahship can no longer give a wrong impression of loftiness nor lead to a theology of glory, but engulfs us in the depths of his destiny. For here the question of his messiahship is a catch question; if he answers it in the affirmative, this will justify his condemnation.

One might ask, then, whether the predicate which Jesus accepts is really the same as it was when people wanted to proclaim him the Messiah in the boom period? Is the messianic title a true answer to the high priest's question in the direct sense? Is it not instead a monstrous provocation which unmistakably leaves the mystery of his person an open question? For what is finally a Messiah who is delivered up into the hands of men and exposed to ultimate humiliation? What is a figure that proclaims itself the Lord of those who hold it captive, so that it cannot deny its supreme lowliness and yet still asserts its eschatological majesty?

Thus the answer of Jesus, for all its apparent directness, does not contain a self-definition of his person but simply presents the question of his nature and mission, his person and function. Far from being an answer, the title "Messiah" is simply a means of posing the question.

Here again we see clearly that the truth is bound to the situation. The statement: "Jesus is the Christ," does not lie outside time and space. In one case it can express the truth while in another it may lead into untruth. If it is simply passed on it can become an empty husk which has lost the kernel of truth. In an alien situation it withers and decays.

The intention of Jesus is even clearer in the Lucan version, which still has the "I am" (Luke 22:70), but which shows earlier why this answer does not have the character of a directness that would reveal the secret but has instead an indirectness (cf. the parables in Matthew 13:10-15) that keeps the secret and makes the impotent Messiah an enigma. For when Jesus is asked in v. 67: "Art thou the Christ? tell us," he answers: "If I tell you, ye will not believe." For this reason—this is the point—he can in fact tell them. In this situation his apparent answer is simply a tremendous challenge and demand. It is a testimony against them (Luke 9:5; 10:11).

Jesus speaks, then, along the lines of an implicit Christology (cf. Luke 12:44-50).

Our finding may be summed up as follows. When titles are used of Jesus they never serve as definitions to describe his person. Their task is to trigger questions. When these questions are blocked they lose their relevance and are withdrawn from circulation. The person of Jesus must not become an independent theme. It acquires urgency only in encounter with his task, work, and mission. "He that believeth on me, believeth not on me, but on him that sent me" (John 12:44). We recall the question which John the Baptist asked from prison. He was not sure about his Lord. He wanted to know whether he was the expected Christ or not. But Jesus' answer did not consist in a definition of his person. It consisted in a reference to his mission and work. I am, said Jesus, the subject of whom it is heard and seen that the lame walk, the blind see and so forth. We also recall the question of authority, which with reference to his work asks concerning the divine or satanic power which is in operation (Mark 11:18).

All this serves to strengthen us in our resolve to approach Christology through the doctrine of the offices, since here as nowhere else we find his person and work so closely tied together.

Excursus on the Self-Consciousness of Jesus and his Statements about Himself

A word should be said here about the self-consciousness of Jesus, for the christological titles raise the question whether they are simply ascribed to him or whether they may be regarded as self-descriptions expressing his own awareness of himself. Our aim, of course, is not to attempt exegetical investigations of our own in competition with NT scholars. Irrespective of the differing conclusions of the experts, we are simply interested in the systematic position regarding this question of the self-consciousness of Jesus.

That the question is not a matter of indifference in the present context is obvious. When we ask: "Who is Jesus Christ?" is it not natural to suppose that the best answer will be found if we consult Jesus himself and ask what witness he bears about himself? But what bearing does it have on this matter that according to many exegetes the messianic self-consciousness of Jesus and his words concerning the matter do not derive from the historical Jesus himself but from the post-Easter community, so that what we have is in fact the response of this community to the appearances of the risen Christ? What bearing does it have if in fact we do not have any historical accounts of the self-consciousness of Jesus? This is the question which concerns us.

Unquestionably the men of the NT did not have the consuming interest in psychology and the processes of the consciousness which has characterized more recent times, especially from the Romantic age.[12] On the other hand, the question of the self-consciousness of Jesus (quite apart from varying historical interests) always has fundamental relevance. It has to have, for the hypostatic union is a real ontological determination of the human nature, and hence this union is necessarily a datum in this nature's consciousness of itself.[13] To put it more simply, if Christ is one in substance with God, he has to share in the self-consciousness and omniscience of God. So the argument has constantly run.[14] Nevertheless, it is open to objection both historically and in principle.

a. Historically, does not Jesus himself refer to the limitation of his knowledge when he says that of the day and hour when heaven and earth shall pass away "knoweth no man, no, not the angels which are in heaven, neither the Son, but the Father" (Mark 13:32)? He "suffers" from the prophetic foreshortening of time perspective and says that the end is going to come immediately: "This generation shall not pass away, till all these things be done" (Mark 13:30; cf. Matthew 24:34).

b. In principle, omniscience destroys the true humanity of Jesus.[15] If anything, freedom and the ability to decide are constitutive human elements. These are possible, however, only if things are open and uncertain. God in veiled form (not God as man) would be in no position to act. Human communication, too, is possible only when we do not know what others are thinking or what they will say. If mental and emotional reactions, and their verbal expression, are known in advance (as in many old and threadbare marriages), communication stops, and so, too, does speech. Confession of Jesus Christ as man means implicitly confession of the limitation of his objective self-consciousness as this relates to history and ranges over past and future.

This does not imply, however, that the self-consciousness of Jesus, and inquiry into it, are now irrelevant. If to make of Christ a concealed omniscient God is to rob him of his humanity, to ascribe no significance to his self-consciousness, or even to deny it to him altogether, is also to rob him of his humanity. For self-consciousness is also an inalienable part of being human, not in the intellectual sense, as though everybody had to be a mini-philosopher, but in the sense that I must lay hold of myself and plan my destiny. I cannot simply drift. I cannot surrender to the working of my impulses. I have to become someone and something. I have to relate my acts and conduct to myself. This is a historical process. It is a development. Jesus, too, "increased in wisdom and age . . ." (Luke 2:52). If this seems to be a self-evident and almost banal statement, nevertheless it is a con-

---

[12] Theologically Schleiermacher is the turning-point. For the orientation of Christology to the consciousness of Jesus cf. W. Herrmann with his idea of the inner life of Jesus.

[13] Rahner, *Das Konzil von Chalkedon*, III, p. 22.

[14] Pannenberg, *Grundzüge der Christologie*, pp. 337ff.; E.T. *Jesus God and Man*, pp. 333f.

[15] Rahner, *Theological Investigations*, V, pp. 201ff.

fession of his humanity and hence of something which is by no means self-evident. If we take the humanity of Jesus seriously, the question of his self-consciousness necessarily arises.

Even if we leave it an open question whether he was aware of and spoke about his messiahship and divine sonship, we do violence to the very foundations of his mission if we say that he was unaffected in his self-consciousness by his mission and that his place in salvation history made no impression at all on his self-consciousness.

In raising this question of the self-consciousness of Jesus, however, are we not indulging in mere speculation? In the last analysis we surely have no data on the subject.

The difficulty is more apparent than real. To prove this we must return to the matter of the messianic secret. We have already pointed out why Jesus' statements about himself had to be indirect. We have spoken of the "implicit Christology" of these statements. They had the aim of a Socratic appeal. They were meant to provoke us and not just to be simple teaching. At this point, then, we may claim that his self-consciousness, too, manifests itself indirectly. Two examples may be given.

The "I say unto you" of the Sermon on the Mount (Matthew 5:22, 28, 34, 39, 44) proclaims the end of the earlier aeon which was based on the law of Moses. There has now come the age of joy which Christ not only announces but also himself brings. To be sure, he does not say directly: "I bring the change in aeons." But with his authoritative "I say unto you" he brings it implicitly, signifying the authority in virtue of which he accomplishes the change.

The parable of the wicked husbandmen (Mark 12:1-12) offers our second example. These workers mistreat the messengers of the owner, just as Israel did God's servants the prophets. They finally seize and kill the son and heir whom the owner sends in the mistaken belief that these rebels will respect the son (12:6). In identifying himself with this son, or hinting at such an identification, Jesus gives himself a place in the process of salvation history to which the OT bears witness. He is sent by God, like the prophets, and he shares their fate. Nevertheless, he differs from them, and has unique privileges, as the "Son."

Thus the self-consciousness of Jesus, and his statements about himself, fit into his general kerygmatic style. He does not use stereotyped titles or conventional slogans to express what he is. Neither the concept of the Logos nor that of the Messiah can swallow him up. In shunning all such concepts, he calls for a direct relation to his person, for discipleship, and for the experiment of faith.

When, impressed by his figure, men cry out: "Thou art the Messiah," or: "Thou art the incarnate Logos," or when they put statements to this effect on his lips, these descriptions do not in any sense confine him. Instead, two things take place.

First, the concepts are reshaped by him. Logos and Messiah take on new meanings when they become predicates of which he is the subject.

They are baptized and die to their former content. As we said earlier, the concepts do not define Jesus; Jesus defines the concepts. The figure has to precede if the terms are to be adequately understood. The figure interprets the terms. We might say, not merely that the person does the works, but also that the person defines the titles.

Second, the words Christ and Logos, and all other titles, are simply emergency terms, mere stutterings, which the contemporary vocabulary suggests. They do, of course, have a certain dignity inasmuch as they come from the traditional terminology of salvation history. For this reason we can never dispense with them. But if we take seriously the indirect Socratic style of NT Christology, this means that we have also constantly to express encounter with this figure in our own terms. A purely mechanical and unmodified adoption of the ancient terms and titles might well denote the decay and death of true faith.

When Lessing called Christ "world reason," he was no doubt compressing him, and forcing him into the schema of rationality, in typical Enlightenment fashion. Nevertheless, he was perhaps "not far from the kingdom of God" (Mark 12:34), for he was at least trying to integrate Christ into his own thinking and vocabulary, and hence making a serious effort to appropriate him. He used his own words to describe him. Not without truth, he thought he could see objectifying withdrawal, and therefore traces of death, in the mechanical way in which orthodoxy was simply repeating sacrosanct shibboleths like "Christ" or "Son of God" or "Savior." Along the same lines, we have to take the shocking step of paying tribute to the theology of revolution. Dubious though this enterprise is in itself, it does at least center on the thesis that Christ is shaking this aeon to its foundations and is thus challenging all its structures. Now we recognize that, although there is truth in this, a Christology which focuses on this one point will inevitably be one-sided and restrictive. Nevertheless, this concept has the advantage of responding to the figure of Christ with personal appropriation and commitment and of relating him to what is thought to be the urgent problem of changing the world.

Individual encounter with Christ will always be critical of tradition. It will try to leap over every traditional mediation back to the beginnings. It will make the figure of Christ the test of the tradition through which encounter comes. It will not just be content with the traditional terms but will try to express the encounter in its own words.

During the days of Hitler, if someone at a congress of "German Christians" meeting in the Sports Palace in Berlin had shouted out the confession: "Christ is the Messiah," this would have met with incomprehension and would have been ignored. But if he had put the confession in his own words and made it relevant to the current situation, saying: "Christ is the only Lord and *Führer,* and anyone who plays the redeemer in his place is no *Führer* but a seducer of our age," a commotion would have been caused. For in this case the traditional words would have been given a contemporary interpretation. When this is done legitimately, and not in opportunistic accommodation (cf. Volume I, pp. 27ff.), the presentation of Christ to our age does not offer a simplistic possibility of faith but demands decision and division, with cries of "Hosanna" on the one side and cries of "Crucify him" on the other. Without this attempt at contemporary application the most startling things can be said in the traditional jargon, e.g., that Christ is risen, and not the slightest ripple will be caused in the pond of the world. The Theological Declaration of Barmen in 1934 is a final instance in Protestantism in which such an application of Christology has achieved confessional rank (cf. on this whole problem Volume I, pp. 119-128). It has been said that keeping tradition alive (instead of just conserving it) is like guarding the flame, not preserving the ashes. A mark of this flame is that older concepts can always be forged anew in its glow.

To be sure contemporary application means entering open country and leaving the protected area of the standard vocabulary which guarantees orthodoxy. But following Jesus demands that kerygmatic risks of this kind be taken. We naturally have to draw attention to the failures and reductions and impoverishments which can result when the venture is made. But for all our criticisms and reservations we have to respect the impulse behind it. It derives from what we have called the response of the community. Often heresies may have to be risked to get at the truth. There can be courage for the venture only where there is confidence in the power of truth to prevail in spite of all that we distort or eliminate (Acts 5:38f.; 2 Corinthians 13:8).

In this sense it is theologically important that we cannot agree upon any hard and fast self-statements or self-consciousness, that we should be confronted instead by an implicit Christology, and that we should let ourselves be challenged by this to respond in our own words. The post-Easter community accepted this challenge when in its own word it bore witness to Jesus of Nazareth as the Christ.

XXV

The Offices of Christ in the Schema of Prophecy and Fulfilment

Apart from the fact that the doctrine of the offices classically interrelates the person and the work, there is another good reason for choosing this christological approach. The tradition ascribes to Christ the three mandates of prophet, priest, and king. In the OT these figures are the representative office-bearers of God. We have shown already that they recur in the three messianic figures of Qumran. It is self-evident, then, that when the christological tradition uses these three predicates for the office and mission of Christ, it has in mind the prophecy of the old covenant, and regards Christ as the fulfilment of this prophecy. The doctrine of the offices is thus well adapted to offer a localization of Christ in salvation history and at the same time to bring to light both his continuity and also his discontinuity with the history of Yahweh with his chosen people Israel. To this extent the schema of prophecy and fulfilment is an important one in Christology.

The doctrine of the offices, then, raises the question of continuity and discontinuity with the OT. If we turn to this for a moment, we quickly see that when Christ is called prophet, priest, and king OT themes are both adopted and yet at the same time transcended. This is drawn to our attention by the fact that the three figures are separate from one another in the OT. In Qumran they are even distinguished hierarchically. In Christ, however, the three coincide and are brought into personal union. Hereby the OT schema of the offices is transcended. This fact, and the resultant discontinuity, may be seen in two other ways as well.

First, the threefold designation of Christ is not to be understood as an adding up of the three offices or an accumulation of offices. One may see this from the fact that in the OT the prophet, priest, and king are not harmoniously co-ordinated into an integrated whole. Instead, the three offices are often in tension and may even be in competition.

For the prophets, especially Amos but also Isaiah and Jeremiah, the priestly office is a dubious institutionalizing of the relation to God. The liturgical element, if one may put it thus, constantly threatens to suppress prophetic preaching. The noise of songs and the playing of stringed instruments (Isaiah 1:11-17; Amos 5:21-27) take the place of obedience to the prophetic Word. Instead of opening the way to righteousness and love, they obstruct it. Like the law, they claim the self only partially and fail to bring other regions of the self under obligation (Matthew 23:25-33; Romans 7:14-23). This tension between cultus and prophecy still finds an echo in the command in the Sermon on the Mount which will not let ministry at the altar be a substitute for what God demands directly, namely, reconciliation with one's brother (Matthew 5:23f.).

Nor does kingship fit smoothly into this triumvirate of offices. Although later it receives sacral validation,[1] an ambivalence very close to disqualification rests over its initiation. When the elders came to the prophet Samuel at Ramah with their request that he give Israel a monarchical constitution, he prayed to Yahweh and received from him an answer to the petition. When Yahweh told him to grant the request, his approval took the form of a word of judgment, for Yahweh takes the ground which man has arrogantly occupied and as the Lord he thrusts on him the consequences of his action:[2] "They have not rejected thee (Samuel), but they have rejected me (Yahweh), that I should not be king over them," and: "Hearken unto their voice" (1 Samuel 8:7). It is another matter that what is meant for evil will later be turned by Yahweh for good (Genesis 50:20) and will thus find sacral validation. In the beginning the setting up of a king is an act of disobedience and it stands in conflict with the will of God to which the prophets bear witness.

One may thus say that the three offices not only are ill-adapted for their integration in Christ, but also in addition to being fragmentary they contain dubious features which show that they are not simply mandates of God but also, like all the orders,[3] manifestations of human self-will. They are also heterogeneous. Thus one might well argue that they are not "prophetic" in an unequivocal sense. They do not constitute geometric places which either individually or in concert point forward to Christ. When Christ really comes and unites the three offices of prophet, priest, and king in himself, these lines which point to him only very conditionally are undoubtedly deflected.

The same discontinuity between prophecy and fulfilment is plain from another angle.

Second, apart from the empirical ambiguity which constantly falls over the offices, their basic and immanent meaning is not simply adopted and "purely" represented by Christ. Their proper meaning is altered too. Thus Christ does not have the office of a prophet who simply proclaims the will of God. He *is* this will of God, as we shall show later.

---

[1] G. von Rad, *Theologie des AT,* 5th ed. (1968), I, pp. 48ff.; E.T. I (1962), pp. 39ff.
[2] Cf. the *parédōken* of Romans 1:24.
[3] Cf. ThE, I, § 2144ff.; E.T. I, pp. 434ff.

As priest, too, he transcends the analogy of the OT cultic minister. Hebrews makes the analogy and discontinuity with the Levitical priesthood its main theme. Three relevant aspects may be noted.

a. In contrast to what we find in the earlier cultus, Christ is victim as well as priest (Hebrews 9:14). For this reason he can stand in solidarity with us and know genuine sympathy (5:15f.).

b. He sets aside the curtain in front of the holy of holies and unlike the OT priest opens up direct access to God (9:8ff.).

c. Whereas the older priest has to make continual offerings, Christ as priest and victim, i.e., as the one who offers himself, has achieved reconciliation once and for all (9:26).

Finally, the kingship of Christ does not have the ambivalence which rested over the monarchy in Israel. He who chooses Christ does not reject God; he *is* in the truth which God wills. Even the sacral quality of the later monarchy is only a figure of what the king with the crown and the sickle will be (Revelation 14:14).

The fulfilment is always more than the prophecy. This means that the fulfilment can never be constructed out of the prophecy.[4] The prophecy can be known and understood only in the light of the fulfilment, i.e., as the Bible is read backward.

Discussions with contemporary Judaism offer an illustration of this. There is no compelling way from prophecy (i.e., the OT) to the fulfilment in Christ.[5] The way is ambiguous because it may end, as it has done historically, in either the NT or the Talmud. Similarly, we cannot construct the figure of Christ out of a combination of the three offices of prophet, priest, and king. When this figure appears, it is a surprise. It is hidden from the wise and prudent (Luke 10:21), and the scribes and Pharisees, who have the prophecies, do not recognize it (1 Corinthians 1:18-25). Thus Christ takes up what has been prophesied in the offices and also breaks it. He both fulfils and transcends it. He radicalizes what was there (i.e., goes back to its roots) and also sets himself in antithesis to it: "But I say unto you."

---

[4] The same applies to secular prophecies such as those of de Tocqueville, Burckhardt, and Spengler.

[5] Cf. the *plērōsai* of Matthew 5:17.

XXVI

The Prophetic Office

In our methodological discussion of the doctrine of the offices attention has already been drawn to the essential marks of the prophetic office. It remains only to fill out and round off what has been said.

As the kerygma uses traditional concepts but baptizes them, so Christ in representing the traditional offices also relativizes them.

In his first appearance he is taken for a prophet (Matthew 16:14) or a rabbi expounding scripture in Capernaum (Mark 1:21; Luke 4:31). From the very outset, however, it is apparent that the person transcends the office. The truth is not that Christ is what he is through the office conferred on him. It is the reverse: What he already is gives meaning—new meaning—to the office. Three things show this.

1. Negatively, Jesus never uses the prophetic formula of validation: "Thus saith the Lord." This formula implies the extinction of the prophet's own person and the preeminence of his commission. The person of the prophet is a pure transparency. It is subordinate both to him who speaks through it and also to what is said. The person of Jesus, however, is identical with his Word. Thus the Prologue to John, which presents the Word as incarnate and identical with the person, is repeated in many different forms. The authoritative self-testimonies show this. Here the person is subject: "I am come . . ."; "I say unto you." If we still find the prophetic transparency in the Christ of John,[1] it does not simply point through him but to him. In his humanity, in the incarnate Word, we find God.

2. Along the same lines, his Word is not just didactic like that of the prophets. The teacher does not retire behind his teaching and make himself superfluous. His Word is active. For this reason it is related always to him who speaks it. He is the one who brings the change in the aeons and bears witness to it by powerful signs. In him the kingdom of God is "among

---

[1] "He that believeth on me, believeth not on me, but on him that sent me" (John 12:44).

you" (Luke 17:21). Even the evangelical saying which is the thematic heart of the parable of the prodigal son would be empty without his presence and the parable would be a noncommittal story. That a father would freely accept in mercy his alienated son would be "too good to be true." Hence, even when Jesus says nothing about himself, even when he simply seems to be telling a story, he is more than a narrator, herald, or messenger who is of no importance in relation to what he has to tell. No, that he is who he is constitutes the validity of what he tells us. If in Jesus Christ the incarnate Word were not among us who hear the parable, if he did not represent the Father and were not the guarantor of his mercy, the parable would lose its kerygmatic rank.

3. Jesus, then, does not continue the prophetic line; he breaks it off. Here is more than a prophet (Matthew 11:9) and indeed more than John the Baptist. For the Baptist was the last of the old covenant, not the first of the new covenant. He was among the prophets who prophesied until now (Matthew 11:13).[2] "Many prophets and righteous men have desired to see those things which ye see, and have not seen them; and to hear those things which ye hear, and have not heard them" (Matthew 13:17; cf. 12:39). In the parable of the wicked husbandmen, as we have seen, Jesus clearly differentiates himself from the prophets. These were servants whom the lord of the vineyard sent first. But he is not another servant or even a foreman. He is the son. In him God himself comes and sets himself in the scales.

The sharpest distinction from the prophets, however, comes when he constantly relates all that he proclaims and does to himself and what God does in him, even when he does not say anything explicit about himself. The question of his self-consciousness and of direct statements about himself is of little relevance compared to this, as we have already noted in another context.[3]

The faulty construction of liberal Christology, as in Harnack, is basically due to a failure to see the hermeneutical significance of the person of Jesus for his word and conduct. The stress is thus shifted from the being and work of Jesus to his message, and he remains imprisoned within the traditional schema of the prophetic office. Only the Father and not the Son belongs to the gospel as Jesus proclaimed it.[4] This famous thesis of Harnack makes the only possible deduction from the premise that Jesus was simply a prophetic teacher. To that extent, even though Harnack can speak very impressively of his uniqueness, Jesus does not speak a

---

[2] Christ is more than a prophet just as he is more than a priest; cf. the "how much more" of, e.g., Hebrews 9:14.

[3] Cf. E. Brunner, *Dogmatik*, II (1950), p. 324; E.T. II (1962), p. 277, who points out that none of the statements of Jesus, unlike timeless truths, rests upon itself but all stand in relation to him the speaker. The "I say unto you" is always an essential presupposition of proper understanding. Cf. on this E. Schweizer, *Ego eimi* (1939).

[4] *What is Christianity?* (1902), p. 154.

word of fulfilment which is related to him and to him alone. He simply unveils a new picture of God. Basically, then, Harnack sees only one theme "about" which Jesus spoke. It is the middle of three thematic circles and consists of the fatherhood of God and the infinite value of the human soul.

The infinite value of the human soul, which the Father recognizes, is the basic existential element which is the impulse behind Harnack as it was behind his teacher Ritschl. For the latter the question of existence was the force that generated his theology. As he saw it, the essential thing about Jesus was not that he performed miracles or intervened with power either in world history or in the transformation and reconstruction of individual life, i.e., existence. The essential thing was that he answered the decisive question whether we are helplessly caught up in bitter necessity (in natural causality or the autonomy of social and economic occurrence) or whether there is a God who sits on the throne and whose power over nature is to be sought and experienced. In such a God, as every religion shows, the claims and independence of the personal spirit will be upheld and confirmed against the constraints of nature or the natural operations of human society. Here believers are assured of spiritual dominion over the world and they are guaranteed the position in the world which overcomes its constraints; A. Ritschl, *The Christian Doctrine of Justification and Reconciliation* (E.T. 1900), pp. 17, 212, 326, *passim.* Essentially Jesus is no more than the prophetic teacher who comforts, refreshes, and establishes us by teaching us about the correlation between the basic existential question and the picture of God, thus supplying an answer to the question.

In contrast, we note in Jesus both the fulfilment of the prophetic predicate and also the crisis which overtakes it.

The fulfilment is that under the aspect of the prophetic office he is seen as the one who (a) stands at God's side and stands over against man in God's name, (b) tells reason what it cannot find out for itself, and (c) brings into history what history cannot bring out of itself. As the bearer of the prophetic office he is sharply differentiated from men. He is wholly other. John's Gospel puts this in mythically spatial terms by saying that we are from below and he is from above (John 8:23; 3:31; 19:11).

Other forms of expression might easily be substituted. To put it more clumsily and less plastically, for example, he belongs to the center and we to the periphery, or he has his identity in relation to the Father and thus enjoys authentic existence whereas we live in alienation, or (cf. Tillich) he represents the ground of being and we the mere surface.

The prophet too—and this is the point of comparison—is not from below. He does not grow out of his time. He is not its proponent. If he were, he would be a false prophet opportunistically backing his time and saying what it wants to hear (Jeremiah 5:31). The true prophet, however, is an alien in his time. He has to speak a message which does not come from his time but which is against it and which is aimed against its common sense. This is why the prophets are felt to be a scandal and are persecuted

(Matthew 5:12; 23:29). To this extent Jesus suffers the fate of a prophet from his very birth. There is no room for him in the inn of the age. This is why he is crucified and hurried out of the world. He does not support the world. He is within it an alien body and has to be removed. To integrate him too easily into the world, to make use of him sacrally as at baptisms, weddings, and funerals, is to mar his face and put him in the gallery of false prophets who simply give us their support. There may well be a trace of this attack on the figure of Christ in the modern theology of revolution.

The crisis which overtakes the prophetic office in Jesus is that the analogy to the prophet is transcended and denounced as no more than a stammering form of speech. For now the aim is not merely to silence the alien word, as in the case of the prophets. In Christ it is especially the alien person which shakes up the world. The prophetic antithesis to the world is completely intolerable when the alien word is identical with the person who speaks it, when the word of this person is not just a verbal protest against the state of the world and of man within it but when this person, by its very existence, violently shakes the structure of the world to its foundations, and when it takes the first steps of the great dismantlement and ushers in the new aeon by the power of its being.

This shows us why Christ is more than a prophet, why the picture of Christ as a prophet begins to falter, why it is no longer adequate christologically. Christ does not stand in antithesis to the world simply because he speaks the Word of God but because God "is in Christ" (2 Corinthians 5:19). He does not simply pronounce God's peace over the world; he is this peace (Ephesians 2:14). Where he is, there is peace among men. Where he is, there is the kingdom of God among us (Luke 17:21).

We thus see that the doctrine of the office leads us on to the person. It involves statements about the person. These statements are the same as those made ontologically by the doctrine of the two natures. Thus, when the Chalcedonian Definition says that the two natures are without separation or confusion, the point is that he who is among us in human form does not merely bear witness to God's antithesis to us but is himself this antithesis. That he is God's being among us is also, as we have seen, what the prophetic office tells is. Ontic statements are thus made, as they have to be when what is expressed is the mystery of Christ's person and not just the status of his words and teaching. The ontic statements themselves, then, are not what distinguishes the doctrine of the offices from that of the two natures. The distinction consists solely in the systematic place from which the being of Christ's person is viewed. Within an ontological schema the structure of this being becomes an independent theme. Since this being is a mystery, however, it resists this thematic approach, finds its mystery negated thereby, and raises impossible frictions and difficulties for overextended and even presumptuous reflection. In the doctrine of the offices, by contrast, the being of Christ's person is seen in terms of its determination, its task, and the fulfilment of its task. It is understood as the mighty act of God within which Christ does his own work. Hence the being of the person is in fact seen in the light of the benefits whose subject is the Kyrios Christ.

XXVII

The Priestly Office

1. THE PROBLEM OF THE HUMANITY

The core of what is expressed by the prophetic office is clearly that at this point Christ, who brings the change in aeons, who controls the active Word of judgment and grace, is on the side of God. He is God's representative and thus far stands over against men.

In contrast the priestly office expresses the fact that Christ is on the side of man, that in solidarity with him he lets himself come under the pressure of history, its guilt, its oppression (*thlípsis*), and its finitude. Here then, being true man, he is man's representative and in this capacity stands over against God.

The term "priest" suggests itself for this dimension because the priest represents the people before God. He can do this only because he comes from the people and performs the rite of atonement in its name.

Hebrews lays special stress on this representation which is based on solidarity. For the priest "ought, as for the people, so also for himself, to offer for sins" (5:3). He joins the ranks of those whom he represents. He is one of them. As he accepts the guilt of those represented by him, he also shares other spheres of their existence and destiny. He faces temptation (4:15). He is subject to finitude and the anxiety it brings. Therefore "in the days of his flesh he offered up prayers and supplications with strong crying and tears unto him that was able to save him from death" (5:7). Hence his priestly solidarity gave him compassion and endowed him with mercy (2:17; 4:15).

The priestly category is also apt because, to break the analogy, Christ does not merely offer but is himself the offering. Here again, then, we see the transition from a functional statement to an ontic statement, to what he *is* as person.

If the priestly office bears witness in this way to his humanity, one should remember that, apart from various docetics, all theologians and confessions have accepted the "very man," including both Alexandrians and Antiochenes, both Schleiermacher and Barth, and even, or precisely, Harnack.[1]

This virtual consensus on the humanity shows that the true problem is the manner of the humanity rather than the fact. The christological controversies have all been about the manner. They are governed by the question what it means that God himself has come among us in this one man. Is he a superlative man, e.g., the most religious of men, or do we have here the condescension of God? Are we dealing with the ascent of man or the descent of God? Is there a transcending of the human or divine incarnation? Does Christ represent the upstretched hand of man or the downstretched hand of God?

This was and is the question. There naturally depends on our answer to it our understanding of redemption and the way of salvation. In spite of all the speculation about the natures, then, the question is not just ontological but existential and soteriological. This confirms that the ancient Christologies are rightly understood only when this question is discerned and the metaphysical shadow fighting does not obscure it.

The question of the humanity seems to arise in a very simple way. We see with some astonishment that an authentic human life was lived out by Jesus, including joy at the marriage feast at Cana (John 2:1ff.), anger at the desecration of the temple by the money-changers (Mark 11:15), tears over Jerusalem (Luke 19:41), the temptations of life, and fear of suffering and death. But just when we see here an ordinary human life, as a non-Christian might do in reading the Gospels for the first time, and when we are tempted to feel our way into it and explain it psychologically, as in the case of Egmont or Antigone, we note that it slips through our fingers and transcends all analogy with our own lives. When this happens, when the life and conduct of Jesus become a question for us, we are really at grips with the heart of the matter. This impression of fellow-humanity and yet also of elusiveness and psychological incomprehensibility may be provisionally formulated in the saying of Rahner that he is not a man as I am (*Theological Investigations,* I, p. 176). In what sense is this so?

The question of the manner of Christ's humanity is the question of its closeness to and distance from my own humanity. It is especially the question of the difference. I find myself in my humanity, I am thrown into existence (Heidegger). In it, to use a Fichtean phrase, I find the material of the fulfilment of my duties. That is, I see myself under obligation to make something of this fact of my existence. I understand it as an opportunity. I see it as my destiny to become what I am (Schiller, Herder). When I *find* myself in my humanity this means that I am not asked whether I want to be what I am. I have not chosen myself. Or, more precisely, my freedom does not consist in my having chosen myself as the one I am.

---

[1] This interest in the humanity of Christ lies behind the doctrine of the virgin birth (although many modern interpreters fail to see this); cf. H. von Campenhausen, *Die Jungfrauengeburt in der Theologie der alten Kirche,* SBAW (1962); E.T. 1964.

My freedom of choice arises only on the level of this givenness.

Christ, however—and this is the difference—*is* asked whether he will be who he is. For him humanity is the content of a resolve, namely, of readiness for self-emptying. As the hymn in Philippians 2 puts it: "He emptied himself, he humbled himself, and became obedient unto death, even the death of the cross. Wherefore God also hath highly exalted him" (vv. 7ff.). The depth of his humanity is his dignity. For he was not thrown into it; it was chosen by him. Roman Catholic crucifixes express this by providing the humbled man with a crown even in the very depths.

This is the true reason why it is wrong to see in Christ the ideal or prototype of humanity, as though there were fulfilled in him that which is only broken and corrupted by sin in us (Schleiermacher). If this is done, the figure of Christ is projected in terms of the existing idea of man. His existence is constructed from below as a self-transcending of the human, as an ascent of man to divine likeness and essential identity with God. In contrast the real message based on the fact of his existence is that we have here the descent of God to humanity, i.e., a movement in the very opposite direction.

The ascent can be stated only with the help of the concept of the disposition (*schésis*).[2] When this is done, the mystery may still be respected but it is another mystery than that which is proclaimed here. We thus sympathize with the Alexandrians in their dislike for disposition theology and their linguistic interest in the concept of "nature," which negatively and polemically seems well adapted to rule out the understanding of Christ's deity as a mere ascent. The *genitum* ("begotten") of the Nicene Creed serves a similar purpose, as we shall show later. For the danger of *factum* ("made"), which Adoptionists of various kinds espouse, is that when Christ is understood as a creature, he can only ascend to divine likeness and the message of the incarnate Word is thus betrayed.

By way of illustration we might refer to a problem of missionary theology which surfaces in certain christological debates in Japanese Christianity. The Japanese internist Nobuo Odagiri founded The Research Fellowship for Christological Studies in Japan in 1957. His crucial theses were stated in a work called *Who Do You Say that I Am?* (1958), which has been published in many languages.

Odagiri's concern is with the problem that the gospel does not portray the ascent of Jesus of Nazareth to deity but the descent of God to human form and a solidarity of love. Since this is a common theme in the history of theology, it might seem that there is nothing to be gained by considering this special instance. We mention Odagiri's essay, however, because the particular religious situation in Japan to which he speaks leads to an interesting variation on the doctrine of descent, and shows in a basic way how

---

[2] This comprehensive term can have many nuances, e.g., God-consciousness (Schleiermacher), fidelity to calling (Ritschl), the inner life (Herrmann), or exemplariness of faith and conduct (Ebeling and Fuchs).

the statement of Christian doctrine can be influenced by the situation and how problems arise in consequence when we transplant these doctrines into another culture.

Odagiri, although a believing and evangelistic Christian, thinks he must oppose especially the dogma that Christ is God. He ran up against the dogma in 1950 in the form of the Y.M.C.A. confession of Jesus Christ as God and Savior (p. 2). It is remarkable to see how a Japanese Christian, who as a nontheologian has not studied the details of theological history, reproduces in his personal history the dogmatic positions which played a role in the historical processes of christological development.

He attacks especially two christological concepts. The first is that of Docetism. A man who is predicated as God can die only a sham death. But this robs the cross of its point. It does the same with Easter, for the miracle of reawakening becomes a mere consequence of the divine nature. The whole thing is mere theater (p. 3). It is an unreal figment of poetic imagination. The second concept that he opposes is the opposite error of the Antiochenes, namely, the divinizing of the human.

Odagiri's conclusion is that true man is not God and true God is not man (p. 14). It is thus heretical to call Jesus Christ true God and true man (p. 14). But since Christ is confessed as Savior, a special and even a supernatural element cannot be denied. Odagiri can even speak of his pre- and post-existence (p. 6). The only thing is that he will not predicate deity. He tries to solve the problem by speaking only of the Logos that became flesh and not the God that became man. Viewing these as mutually exclusive, he is naturally forced to distinguish the Logos strictly from God and hence to attack the Gnosis which confounds them.

Odagiri's view leads to considerable difficulties. On the one side it sets the incarnation of Christ at the heart of the event of redemption (p. 14) and thereby confesses the true humanity of Christ. On the other hand, the incarnation has soteriological significance only if in some way it expresses the divine love in solidarity with man. (What does it finally mean that a "man" declares solidarity with me and shares my destiny? This may be consoling, as we know in everyday experience, but it does not redeem.) Odagiri finds it impossible to put the two things together. He is prevented from doing so because he does not understand what the doctrine of the Trinity means for Christology in this connection. For in the form of three relations of God to man this doctrine tells us that the true God comes down to true man in the form of Christ's true humanity and draws true man to himself. Odagiri cannot even consider this connection of the doctrine of the Trinity with his problems, for this doctrine is for him a docetic theologoumenon with no biblical basis.

Interesting though all this is, there should be no occasion to mention it were it not that the motive behind the presentation is so alarming. The motive arises out of the Japanese situation of the author. Odagiri tells us (p. 2) that in Japan and other East Asian countries it seems to cause no offense to ascribe deity to a particularly pious or righteous man. In Japan with its polytheism, in which the pious can be immediately divinized after death, the confession of Christ as God is thus very dangerous (p. 4). Odagiri fears that the safeguards of Western theology against the docetic misunderstanding are not strong enough in the Japanese situation with its deified men. The dominant categories of understanding will automatically mean a misunderstanding of the deity of Christ, and the boundaries between deity and humanity will be blurred whether in a docetic or an Antiochene sense. If we make Christ God (p. 3), this will give rise to a definite idea in the average Japanese. He will assume that Christ was a very pious man who after death was venerated as God. This docetic misunderstanding, which is almost a reflex in Japan, became clear to the author when after his sermons non-Christian hearers constantly asked him whether Christianity was a religion which worshipped the foreign holy man, Jesus Christ, as God (p. 4).

Odagiri's discussion shows clearly that theological problems do not arise in a vacuum. They always stand in relation to definite situations. They are historical. Theoretically it is thus conceivable that a christological thesis which describes the content of our faith in a suitable reflective form might be a heresy somewhere else. For this reason theology cannot be exported and imported as it stands. It is possible that Christianity is doing so poorly in Japan and other lands because in its reflective form it is regarded as a foreign import and has not been adequately transposed into the local system of intellectual co-ordinates. In turn there might be historical reasons for this, e.g., the late acquaintance of Japan with the religious and cultural heritage of the West and the need for catching up which overhastily adopted the reflective structures along with the kerygmatic content. If appearances do not deceive, independent thinking is now beginning, at least in relation to the reception of alien thought, including theological reflection on the Christian message.

As regards the theological side of reinterpretation, it obviously occurs in the non-church movement. Odagiri's work is an important sign of this. It displays independent wrestling with Christology, at least to the extent that the structures of Western thinking are boldly set aside and Christology is directed to his own "antennae." This remarkable process is probably more important than obvious defects such as the ignoring of the doctrine of the Trinity. One might hope that this defect will be made good in further thinking, although it can be safely assumed that the theologoumenon will be given another form than that which it has been given in our own tradition.

What stands out in all this is the inexhaustibility of the figure of Christ. This is tied to no specific concepts or traditional (e.g., Western) modes of thought. Encounter with Christ constantly produces new forms of reflection. New schemas of thought are adopted to convey the incarnation into the intellectual world. The act of catching up continually takes new forms. The task of understanding is to see one and the same Lord in new intellectual forms and not to attack the new structure in the name of existing (accidental) structures. For Christology can employ very different structures of thought.

At the same time there has to be a definite missionary theology which serves the transposition from one system of co-ordinates to another, which is thus opposed to the mere exporting of Christianity in a Western package, and which leads to the independent appropriation and packaging of the kerygma. This damps down the superficial activism which pushes technical religious man into the forefront. It demands the humility of standing back and confidently letting the kerygma create its own new forms of theological reflection. We should no longer try to hold the younger churches in tutelage but cut them loose. Love is also needed, however—the love which takes the Christians of other cultures seriously and allows them to find their own forms of appropriation, church structure, worship, and so forth.

After this excursus we now resume our train of thought. We have said that the priestly office accentuates the human side of Christ. Christ stands at man's side as his representative before God. For all his solidarity with us, however, this cannot mean that Christ is just man as you and I are.

In approaching the priestly office of Christ, then, we run into the same situation as we did with the prophetic office. In regard to the latter we said that the prophetic concept is both fulfilled and also transcended in Christ. Here is a prophet and more than a prophet. The same applies to Christ as man. He is on the one hand the fulfilment of humanity. For he is wholly and utterly man. In dogmatic terms, he is the incarnate Logos. Yet he is also the crisis of humanity. For he comes into it; he is not thrown into it. He does not follow a given plan; he himself is the plan.

Nowhere is his function as both the fulfilment and the crisis of humanity so pregnantly portrayed as in Hebrews. Here temptation is a sign of humanity and this shows Christ's solidarity with us. Yet he was tempted without (*chōris*) sin (4:15). This "without" points to the elusive aspect. (We shall return to this.) In the very depths in which he is so close to us that we are delivered from our sufferings in virtue of his pain and anguish, he is also distant from us in uncompromising majesty and remoteness.[3] His bitter cry from the depths: "My God, my God, why hast thou forsaken me?" (Matthew 27:46) bears witness that the very thing which plunges him into these depths of humanity and distance from God is also the sign of his most intimate relation to the Father: he is not complaining *about* God but speaking *to* God, so that even in his dereliction God is the Thou with whom he communicates. He also expresses his complaint about dereliction in the form of a quotation from the Word of God, Psalm 22:1. The current is not cut off; it is blocked.

This characterizes his humanity. What exceeds and transcends it is not something supernatural. It is not a docetic extra beyond the existence which he shares with us. The transcendent element may be seen in the very ground

---

[3] Cf. Nicholas of Cusa, *De docta ignorantia,* III, 6.

of his humanity. This is why the humanity of Christ escapes us at the very point where it seems closest to us. Faith can address him only in worship; it can say no more about him. If we are already speaking about him, we can more easily say what he is not than what he is. The alpha privative of the Chalcedonian adverbs is of symbolical significance in this regard.

2. THE FORM OF THE HUMANITY

The figure of the humanity of Christ manifests itself in three spheres: (1) in the depth of his condescension which has the form of service; (2) in the union of his mission with naturalness of act and speech; and (3) in his temptation.

a. The Depth of His Condescension

His humanity comes to realization in the sacrificial ministry to sinners of him who has no sin. "The Son of man came not to be ministered unto, but to minister, and to give his life a ransom for many" (Matthew 20:28). He thus opposes the establishment, and in the parable in Luke 22:24ff. he makes it clear that he is among those who serve and not those who sit at table. The Fourth Evangelist bears witness to the unity of his life and death in service in his depiction of the foot-washing (John 13:4ff.). Peter is shocked at this, but only those who let Jesus serve them with this humility can have a part in him (v. 8). God is now to be found in the depths and not in the heights.

The picture of the Good Shepherd points in the same direction. The shepherd is superior to the sheep. He tends them, leads them to pasture, and protects them against threats. Jesus has this in mind when he calls himself the Good Shepherd. He it is who spots the wolf when the sheep are quietly grazing. He it is who can find and bring back the lost sheep. But the very thing that exalts him above the sheep is also the thing that makes him less than the least of them. For he sets his own life below that of his flock. In this parable the interrelation of majesty and lowliness is presented with a dialectical clarity that the confusing concept of nature can never achieve. What exalts the shepherd above the sheep grants him a possibility which animals do not have, i.e., that of self-sacrifice (John 10:15). By self-sacrifice the Good Shepherd lowers himself below his sheep. He makes them more than he himself seeks to be by saving their lives at the expense of his own and making them ends in whose service he uses himself as a means. He thus engages the wolf even though he perishes in so doing (10:12ff.). In defiance of all rational calculation he goes after the sheep that has gone astray (Luke 15:4ff.; Matthew 18:12ff.). The majesty of the Good Shepherd is thus his lowliness, paradoxical though this may sound. The paradox is the reason why the sheep have a part in him and his voice is trusted by them. For his majesty is not the basis of their trust and participation. The basis is that they receive this service from him, that they know that they are safe with him, that he is thus there for them and hence is not a hireling who is willing to surrender them to save his own skin (John 10:1ff.).

The analogies to faith hinted at in this parable do not arise in virtue of the ontic qualities of the Shepherd. In other words, the faith statements are not based on ontological statements about Christ, e.g., that he is depicted as the bearer of both a divine and a human nature. They rest on the reference to the fact that he is there for me in service and sacrifice, not that he is this or that "in himself." What he is in himself is included, just as implicitly in himself the Good Shepherd is more than the sheep, being a man who is gifted with reason, who can make provision and use implements, and who is thus far superior to animals. This is not, however, the essence of the Good Shepherd. It is simply the material presupposition of the fact that he can become what he is, namely, the Lord who serves and loves and gives himself.

Our criticism of the doctrine of the two natures, then, is that it never speaks of more than the presuppositions which enable Christ to discharge his function as the Good Shepherd. In contrast we venture to take the opposite path, speaking of the act of service and self-sacrifice and merely implying what is to be said about the presupposition of his ministry and its subject. We thus say: Therefore he is thus and thus, or better, along the lines of the Chalcedonian alpha privative: Therefore he is as we are and yet again he is not as we are.

Part of this service, of this supreme condescension of his majesty, is that he declares his solidarity with publicans and sinners and censures Pharisaism (Matthew 21:23; Luke 18:10ff.). He does not attack the Pharisees because they are inferior to characterless and a-social opportunists who are slaves of the libido. Naturally they are superior to such people. They are respectable folk and we cannot accept the popular caricature of the Pharisee. The issue is not the ontic being of the Pharisee any more than it is the ontic being of the Good Shepherd as one who is endowed with reason and can use implements. What matters is that the Pharisees do not use their superiority to understand love and hence to accept solidarity with the despised and to draw near to them in service. Because the one who is truly superior acts differently in this respect, or, better, because he is different, the publicans and sinners are not the opponents of Jesus but the Pharisees. Being only superior, they represent the exact and strict antithesis of the friend of sinners. The self-righteous become the foes of him who makes others righteous, who serves them by making them righteous, and who sets them right with God.

His majesty is such, then, that he is closer to the lowly than the lofty. Only those who will accept his service win a part in him. This is why the spiritually poor and those whose hands are empty are called blessed (Matthew 5:3). They are by nature close to him whose majesty is loving service, whereas the healthy, who do not need a physician, are far from him (Luke 5:31).

His solidarity manifests itself finally in that he does not command as he might. He obeys. He learns obedience in the ministry of suffering (Hebrews 5:8). He is subject to his parents (Luke 2:51) even though no human authority corresponds to him. He goes down to baptism along with sinners even though he does not need it (Luke 3:21).

b. The Union of His Mission with Naturalness of Act and Speech

When we look for a moment at this side of his humanity, it would make no sense apart from what has just been said. We should simply see a man who displays sensitivity and even genius in the use of words, parables, proverbs, and popular wisdom. Taken alone as in a literary approach, this would signify at best only a summit of human attainment and would be completely inadequate to his true reality. In conjunction with what we have called his majesty in lowliness, however, it takes on theological meaning. It has the significance of a demonstration. It is to be regarded as the style and expression of his lowliness.

His parables and popular wisdom do not disdain an appeal to reason. The situation here is the same as with the messianic secret. Familiar titles are presented as a basis on which to discover what escapes normal understanding.

The relation of pupil to teacher or slave to master (Matthew 10:24) might belong to a wisdom writing. But who is this teacher and master to whom the figure is applied? Does he not transcend the relation? "No man can serve two masters" (Matthew 6:24). "The life is more than meat, and the body than raiment" (6:25). "Where your treasure is, there will your heart be also" (6:21). Who could say more illuminating things or things more spontaneously understood and accepted? Yet the secret is manifested only when one begins to get an inkling of the true relations which the sayings and parables serve.

The topical reporting and its ironical glosses are designed to stress the foreground aspects (cf. the similar procedure in Dürrenmatt's *Besuch der alten Dame* [1956], pp. 101f.). Jesus, for the sake of the messianic secret, can play on this. Luke 14:28-33 offers an example. It is obviously a well-known fact that there is somewhere a tower which is only half-finished because the builder ran out of money. How ridiculous and shameful! Or a ruler thought he could defeat a well-equipped enemy with an inadequate force and had to give in tamely. How stupid and absurd! But this is how it will be with those who do not pay the price of discipleship, who want cheap grace (Bonhoeffer), who will not sell all that they have for the pearl of great price (Matthew 13:45), who are not ready to watch painfully like the wise virgins (Matthew 25:1ff.), who do not want discipline, and who look back when they have put their hand to the plow (Luke 9:62). Not being ready to give up all things, they will be tepid in their Christianity (Revelation 3:16). This is a sure sign that they do not realize for whom and against whom they are contending. The result is that they collapse.

They are indeed worse than they were before, for the evil spirit returns to them sevenfold (Matthew 12:45; cf. 2 Peter 2:20).

In the story of the foolish builder or ruler the crowd smiles understandingly and takes comfort: "Such things could not happen to me." But could they not? The story suddenly and unexpectedly leads them into backgrounds they did not originally think of.[4] The more clearly I see what discipleship involves, the more serious is the problem of counting the cost. For in these parables discipleship is not just an enhancement and enrichment of life as it is. It is something which has to be paid for with this life. I am promised abundance of houses, brothers, sisters, etc. (Matthew 19:29; Mark 10:29), but I am given certainty as to this only as I make the experiment and undertake discipleship. Unlike the unlucky builder or ruler, I cannot work out my objective assets in advance and strike a balance. The assets in discipleship are unknown; they are only promised. I can count on them only in the venture of trust, of trust in him who summons me to discipleship. But how can I learn to know him and trust him unless I make the venture, test him out, and thus enter his fellowship? I cannot discover his being from outside.

The image of foreground calculation is thus transcended. Sound common sense, which the hearer thinks he has and which causes him to say with a smile: "Such things could not happen to me," can weigh up only formal things like income and expenditure, profit and loss. But this type of calculation is suddenly changed when it has to be applied to the true theme of the sayings of Jesus, i.e., discipleship and its cost.

How human is all this, and yet how it transcends the human! The mysteries are not located in a spiritual and mystical sphere above the human. They do not belong to a world of ideas to which one must ascend. They take us to the workaday world of tables and accounts and the question of profitability (Matthew 19:27). But suddenly in the midst of everyday reactions and reflections the gears of natural thinking come to a halt and the familiar game is interrupted. This world can offer only comparisons that do not fit. At the point where they do not fit, where we thought we were in the normal sphere and traversing only too human territory, there stands the Son of Man who is the Son of God.

If this is not an innoculation against Docetism, it is hard to see what can be. The concept of nature is also a common human concept, at least for scholars. It is also obvious that it must be dealt with in the same way as we deal with the much simpler proverbs and stories. What it tries to say and understand escapes it. The concept no longer covers the matter. The foreground merges again into a deeper background. We thought something

---

[4] Nathan uses the same technique with David in 2 Samuel 12:1ff. He tells a banal, sentimental, and shallow story about a rich man who is so avaricious that he will not use an animal from his own large herds to feed a guest but takes the one cherished sheep of a poor man. David needs considerable help from the prophet to get through the foreground anecdote and recognize himself in the wealthy man.

familiar was being said—being said a little better than we could say it—
but then suddenly we heard something not at all familiar: "But I say unto
you." Even the familiar commandments of Moses were quoted and heard.
But as he spoke them they were suddenly changed and radicalized. In the
familiar statements stands a new subject who had previously been overlooked. He does not add anything. He seems to have nothing new or additional to say. He is so human that his Logos took the flesh of these familiar
statements. Within them—not above them—he finds a place for himself.
What was once understood as a general statement suddenly becomes the
sphere of thought and the proclamation of his lordship.

c. His Temptation[5]

In tackling this question we come up against what is perhaps the ultimate
problem of Christology and one which makes heavy demands on our mental
resources. Nevertheless, for all the intellectual difficulties the fact itself is
basically simple, namely, that Christ is our Lord and Brother, our King
and Companion. The joy of working at Christology (if we may put it thus)
is that we can rediscover this simple fact in the most profound problem-
areas.

For Hebrews, as we have seen, being tempted as we are is the true mark
of Christ's humanity. Christ entered the sphere between God and Satan.
He faced the possible failure of his mission and the fall of the Messiah.

If this is not just a theatrical demonstration (Abelard), he confronts
the real possibility of being unfaithful to his mission and himself, or concretely, of grasping at equality with God (Philippians 2:6). He might
choose the solution of Dostoievski's Grand Inquisitor. For all three temptations focus on the attractive possibility of usurping divine power without
serving, suffering, loving, or obeying. Such snatched power, however, stands
under its own impetus and is forced to deny the ends of God. It will not
be used to bind men's hearts to God or to call into his kingdom. It involves
(the first temptation) a mere appeal to opportunism. To make bread out
of stones, as Satan suggests, is to count on the cheap eudaemonism of the
masses, which will sing the song of him whose bread they eat. Again, to
throw oneself off the pinnacle of the temple without suffering hurt (the
second temptation) is to play on the nerves of men, to treat them as a
bundle of nerves, to establish authority without claiming the heart. Finally,
to receive the kingdoms and the countries from Satan (the third temptation)
is to appeal to men's susceptibility to power, to their confidence that Chris-
tianization can be easily achieved under the protection of arms and the
banners of an obvious authority.

That Christ stands on this threatened frontier on which he is exposed
to the tempting possibility of becoming a demonic alter ego of God, of

---

[5] Cf. the author's book *Zwischen Gott und Satan. Die Versuchung Jesu und die
Versuchlichkeit des Menschen*; E.T. *Between God and Satan* (1958).

becoming as God, without taking the path of self-emptying and humility (Philippians 2:7f.); that he takes the middle position between God and Satan means that he truly becomes flesh and is our brother.

But how are we to think of this temptation of Jesus when Hebrews adds the strange restriction that he was tempted apart from (*chōrís*) sin, in complete isolation from it? Does this not mean a break with human solidarity, with the sympathy which is supposed to be manifested by his temptation? Temptation is surely possible only when there is openness to it, i.e., when the tempter already has a bridgehead in the heart of man. Temptation is the possibility of setting a potential energy of evil in motion, of actualizing it, of breaking the dams against it. Is temptation to adultery possible unless these is already the libido which prompts looking on a woman to lust after her (Matthew 5:28)? Can there be any temptation to murder unless there is already present the aggressive impulse which envies or wants to oppress, i.e., something which only needs to be brought out of the state of incubation (Matthew 5:21f.)? It is possible to think of temptation without sin, i.e., without susceptibility to temptation? Is not this essential to the concept? Without it, does not that which is meant to bear witness to humanity oppose its own intention and become an argument for Docetism? In logical terms, is not temptation without sin a contradiction in terms, an antinomy?

Some eminent theologians contest this. They try to define temptation in such a way that the implication of Docetism is ruled out and no logical friction is caused. Among such theologians are Schleiermacher, Schlatter, and K. Bornhäuser.[6]

Schleiermacher sees in the temptation of Jesus only a neutral and nonsinful conflict between desire and nondesire (*The Christian Faith,* § 98, 1). Schlatter in *Das christliche Dogma* (1923), p. 314, takes a similar view. The choice in which Jesus achieved and maintained purity of will shows no susceptibility to sin, since the necessity of choice is not posed merely by the presence of evil desire, i.e., sin, but by the manifoldness of the longings which we have the power, and which it is our duty, to control. The conflict arises because a human desire, which is legitimate in itself, has to be subjected obediently to the will of God. What has to be resolved is a cleavage in the will between the rejection of suffering as an evil according to a healthy instinct of self-preservation and the acceptance of the divine will and union with it.

That the temptation on this view takes place so smoothly is enough to arouse our suspicions. Is it not a trivializing of Satan's attacks to see at issue only the instinct of self-preservation and divinely willed avoidance of suffering, such as we might all experience in a bank holdup or when firedamp threatens in a mine? Surely the assault of Satan does not amount to

---

[6] For a discussion of the issue cf. also K. Heim, *Jesus der Weltvollender;* E.T. *Jesus the World's Perfecter* (1961).

much if the same effect might be achieved by waving a gun. Did not even the martyrs undergo much more than fear of physical annihilation? Did they not experience the much deeper temptation of seeing the foundation of faith threatened by the adversary and of being offered the fascinating possibility of a new view of life?

If Schlatter's view were right, we should not have any real temptation. Choice between two goods, which is what Schlatter sees, would not implicate any values. In fact, however, Christ faces a basic decision of existence which is then repeated in his summons to us to decide. Should he claim equality with God as booty instead of finding it in the depths of suffering? Should he denaturalize his mission to spare himself, not with a view to mere self-preservation, but with a view to God's greater glory and the more effective and comprehensive fulfilment of his messianic mission along the lines of the Satanic tempter? This was the demonic background of the attack in the wilderness. He should yield, not in antithesis to his messianic calling, but in the name of it, thinking that he was doing God service (John 16:2). Is not the law of least resistance a divinely established law, a principle of economy, with whose help maximum results can be obtained with a minimum of opposition?

The bloody sweat of Gethsemane (Luke 22:44) shows that Christ is not just choosing between two goods or making the kind of evaluation that a computer might make. He is under assault by demonic thoughts (thoughts!) and in this situation chooses God and rejects himself.

Thus something threatens to arise in him which will serve as a bridgehead in his own soul for the cunning stratagems of the tempter. If he had not been horrified and shaken by the power of temptation, there would have been no temptation.

What we have to think would be inconceivable if Christ had been basically unassailed and if he had been sheltered from the sphere where demonic power is deployed and where we live our lives. Is the "without sin" of Hebrews really to be understood in this way? Does it bear witness to the unreality of his humanity? Does it revoke his priestly sympathy? Is it a testimony to Docetism?

We thus seem to be up against an insoluble problem.

On the one hand we can take the temptation of Jesus radically, not seeing in it merely the peripheral act of rejecting a tempting possibility. To see it thus would create no difficulty, since it is something we meet with every day in ethics. We ourselves constantly know both victory and defeat in temptation. But in the last resort we have here much more than the peripheral act. Radically understood, temptation is a problem because it presupposes susceptibility to it. On this side, then, we view Jesus as open to temptation. We construe his humanity so unconditionally and uncompromisingly that only his solidarity with us is seen and not his difference from us. He is with us, as it were, in the same condemnation. He offers the comfort of solidarity, but not superiority over a situation from which he can free us, and in which he can act as the Redeemer. He does not have the redemptive authority of deity.

On the other hand, we could choose not to go so far. But then we deprive him of the central core of susceptibility to temptation and consequently of his humanity. We thus have a mythical redeemer figure who belongs to heaven but not to earth and flesh, not sharing our existence at the decisive point.

Some analogy might be seen in Tolstoy, who according to his diaries put himself on the same social footing as his serfs and shared their primitive life-style to show the seriousness of his solidarity and love. But when he told them this, and asked if they understood and accepted it, he received the astonishing answer that for them it was all a show and what he was doing had no credibility. No matter what he did, the decisive thing needed for true solidarity was missing, for he was free at any time to stop working and go back home, whereas they were held by an oppressive fate which they could not alter. For all the similarity of life-style, the acceptance of poverty and lowliness, and fellowship in joy and sorrow, the decisive lack of community in destiny meant that there was nothing like any real solidarity. In this sense Christ is not man in solidarity if he does not share the basic condition of man, his susceptibility to temptation.

We will now take two steps in an attempt to deal with the problem of the *chōrís* (without sin) in the temptation of Jesus, well aware that we are circling around a mystery which basically is not objectifiable but whose ineffability we need to examine.

In the first step we shall explore further the reason why the real temptation of Jesus is a matter of theological concern.

In so doing we again come up against a basic problem with which the doctrine of the two natures also wrestled and which Karl Rahner has summed up for us. On the one side we may say only that he has come to us, that he wept, that he died, that he is flesh, that he is the emptiness whose immeasurability is its hollowness. The Redeemer is thus among us but is also trapped among us, and what use is he if he is merely what we are, if his human nature simply means solidarity with us? On the other side we may say that he is eternally the same, impassible, immutable, and we say this not merely because we are under the rule of a metaphysics of pure, infinite and flawless being but because we need someone different from us in order to be redeemed in what we are (*Theological Investigations*, I, p. 178 ["Current Problems in Christology"]). If, however, he is only different from us, then there is one element which resists the union of incarnation and redemption as the gospel proclaims it.

This is why the doctrine of the two natures has to say both these things together. As we do today, it saw a greater temptation in thinking of Christ as purely divine and hence as immune to temptation and death. If he is merely a phenomenal form of God—God in earthly clothing—he is no longer the Mediator between God and man. He is simply the mediator to himself.[7] He is a transpolar point of indifference or a pantheistic spirit embracing all antitheses. Christology, however, says something different. It confesses and points out that Christ is man and Mediator to the extent that he exposes himself to the pressure of history, that he adopts the schema of sin, that he bears the reality of humanity. This is why in the teaching of the early church the human nature of the Logos has to have a genuine, free, spontaneous, spiritual center of action, a human self-consciousness, which as a creature confronts the Word in the truly human attitude of worship, obedience, and the most radical creaturely feeling.[8]. Only because he is thus does he stand at our side and become the bridge between our existence (which he shares) and God's existence (which he also shares).

The church's concern in insisting on this is not that of ontological speculation on his person but a concern to present his mediatorship. Christ is not just a phenomenal form of God. He manifests the majesty of God on his path of lowliness by becoming other than God in spite of his being in the form of God (Philippians 2:6), by bearing this otherness and distance in himself, and by being exalted therein. The majesty of the exalted one is that of him who is not overcome by the depths and who thus becomes a bridge between those who have fallen into the depths and the height where God dwells.[9] If, however, this mediation between below and above belongs to his calling as Mediator, if the human person belongs to it as the center of action,[10] then the reality of the susceptibility to temptation is the test point. It is no sham fight. It involves engagement and danger.

As Luther puts it, we should not be persuaded by those who think of Christ as an unfeeling block. We must believe that as a true and mere man he must have been subject to every temptation (Op. in Psalms, WA, 5, 387). Luther is even bolder in a sermon on Psalm 8 in 1537. He says that the humanity was on its own and the devil had free access to Christ. The deity withdrew its power and left the humanity to fight for itself. Hence the righteous and innocent man had to tremble and quake and feel God's wrath and judgment against sin in his tender and innocent heart (WA, 45, 239; cf. T. Harnack, *Luthers Theologie* [ed. 1927], II, p. 174).

Here, then, Christ's majesty is a ministering majesty and his temptation is a ministering act of compassion by which we gain a share in him and receive him as Mediator.

At this point, however, a second step is required. If, as Luther says, the deity has lifted the drawbridge, if for our sake the man Jesus in his priestly office has given himself up to susceptibility to temptation, how are we to understand the *chōris hamartias* ("yet without sin") without losing again the soteriological thrust and being entangled in an absurd antinomy?

---

[7] Rahner, *op. cit.,* p. 157.

[8] *Ibid.*

[9] On this "height" cf. Luke 1:78; 2:14; Psalm 93:4; 148:1; Isaiah 33:5; Jeremiah 25:30.

[10] *Autokíneton,* as Rahner calls its, *op. cit.,* p. 157.

From all that has been said there seems to be a possibility of understanding in two directions.

First, it was on his own initiative that Christ came under the burden that we bear constitutionally as the burden of human existence. In this regard the basis is the *egeneto* (the Word was made flesh) which denotes his entry into humanity. He is man, not as he finds himself thrown in, but as he goes into the depths himself. Thus the miracle of Christmas stands at the commencement (even though the account be regarded as an interpretation of the real event). In this regard it is no accident that the appearing of the Word in the flesh can be denoted only by active verbs (not ontic nouns). God "sent" or "gave" the Son. The Son "came" to his own. He "became" like other men and was found in fashion as a man.

A self-giving to humanity is thus implied which also expresses a remoteness that cannot be misinterpreted docetically. The very thing which makes him adopt the schema of sin, of the existential burden of susceptibility to temptation, is also the very thing which mysteriously sets him at a remove from this schema, namely, the impelling motive of a more than human love. At this point we run up against the extreme paradox that it is the very opposite of sin which drives him to the form of sin.

We do not refer to a suprahuman docetic margin which lies above his humanity and enables him always to keep one foot in the saving sphere of heaven.[11] The point is that he lays hold of the depths of solidarity; he is not thrown into it. For this reason the solidarity cannot lay hold of him and integrate him into itself.[12]

Second, a further active basis of the *chōris* is that Christ overcomes the situation of susceptibility to temptation in prayer, clinging to the one from whom the tempter seeks to separate him. In prayer he yields to God and thus stands above his inclinations just as the man who cries: "I believe! help thou mine unbelief," stands above his unbelief.[13] When he says: "Not my will, but thine be done," the cup of suffering which exposes him to the temptation of fear loses its force.

It is not as though we could understand all this. Here, too, there is no answer to the question which Nicodemus asked regarding the new birth: "How can these things be?" (John 3:9). In principle this question, which Jesus refused to answer, is the same as ours. The point of comparison is that both questions are asking about the connection of a divine event with the level of empirical reality. What Nicodemus wants to know is how the new creation wrought by the Spirit can be harmonized with the fact that we men have an irreversible history, that we cannot return to the mother's womb (3:4) to receive a new and different form of life, that we cannot undo determination by our past, that we cannot project our future afresh

---

[11] The equivalent of Tolstoy's position.

[12] This is what the *extra Calvinisticum* is designed to safeguard, Volume I, pp. 292ff.; 374f.

[13] F. Büchsel, *Die Christologie des Hebräerbriefes* (1922), p. 38.

and unhampered as an open sphere of freedom. How can the event which gives us eternity in the Spirit be reconciled with the laws of time and its ineluctable flow? The answer of Jesus ignores the question and simply states that God has so loved us (3:16). He does not say anything about the How but simply charges us to reckon on the fact in face of which the question of the miraculous How is God's affair and not a proper subject of investigation by us. The same applies to the relation between Jesus' susceptibility to temptation and his actual sinlessness. Here again the ontic connection between the two dimensions cannot be presented in terms of the How. Hence it cannot be investigated. The answer is simply given that in fact we are loved to the deepest depth of solidarity and that the one who loves thus is more and other than him whom he loves. For this reason the Redeemer has the power to be the Redeemer even in the impotence of his love. He is not trapped in solidarity. Even in achieving it he is more than solidarity. This is the point.

When we see that the question of the How, of the ontic structure of the temptation, is an inappropriate one, it is also plain that the biblical treatment of the mystery does not serve an analysis of the person but again proclaims the blessing (*beneficium*), namely, that love and power are at work for us here, the love which meets us in solidarity and the power which brings us to our goal.

In saying this we adduce a new irreconcilability that cannot be explained. In our experience love and power are at odds with one another. "He who loves most is always subject," says Thomas Mann in *Tonio Kroeger*. He accepts defenselessness. He renounces force and self-assertion. But here love and power are at one. We have to confess this unity to be able to describe the miracle of the blessing imparted to us. For if we are met in the situation of our existential burden, we are also taken out of this situation. One and the same man is both with us in the situation and also above it.

As already expounded, we have to think of Christ in connection with this blessing and we thus refer to the personal traits implied by it. Without this subject anything we might say about this theme belongs merely to existential philosophy.[14] If, however, we isolate the subject and describe it in and for itself, we slip into hopeless speculation about the natures. This explains our approach through the priestly office. We have simply tried to describe the solidarity of Jesus as the event of redemption and to think of the Redeemer himself only in this connection—no more. But this is all we need; it is all that faith needs. The need of faith is the boundary of theology. When the theological supply outruns the demand of faith, theology becomes speculation. This principle applies in exemplary fashion to the temptation of Jesus.

---

[14] Cf. parallel materials in Sartre and Anouilh.

3. THE DEPTH OF THE HUMANITY: THE CROSS

In giving to the doctrine of the cross of Christ the title "The Depth of the Humanity," we have in mind the saying of Mann already quoted: "He who loves most is always subject." Christ is subject because he gives himself wholly and unreservedly, because he holds nothing back and leaves no way out, whether in the form of twelve legions of angels (Matthew 26:53), or of a supranatural docetic margin which sees to it that he escapes the final solidarity of suffering, that this touches only the human livery and not the body itself (Job 2:4f.). This is why we are concerned to lay constant stress on the non-docetic aspect of Christology (and in the last resort the temptation). Christ is the one who intervenes totally and casts himself wholly in the scales. This is why he is subject. What makes him subject is the unrestrictedness of his love. Paradoxically this unrestrictedness is what causes him to accept restriction.

He is also subject in the sense that by thus restricting himself he exposes himself to mutability. What makes him unique—the unreservedness of his love—also makes him like us all. He is in the incognito of everyman, for to all appearances he can be subsumed under any general concept, e.g., that of the rabbi, the martyr, the bankrupt, and, of course, the founder of a religion. What makes him seem to be a normal phenomenon of religious or general history—at best only quantitatively higher than the average and at worst below—is that wherein he transcends this history and manifests himself as the wholly other, i.e., the condescension of divine being to humanity out of the motive of love.

He remains subject in each new generation. Those who try to free him from this by trying to explain his uniqueness, e.g., by describing him as God in human livery, or exalting him as the idea of humanity (Strauss), or presenting him as the climax of human possibilities, can do so only by eliminating the point of his becoming man, falsifying him by depriving him of both his majesty and his lowliness. For what we have here is an attempt to see him without that which constitutes his true being, namely, his love.

The way of solidarity reaches both its high point and also its low point in the cross. In the light of the cross, the whole of his earthly pilgrimage is seen to be one long way of suffering. Even at his birth there is no room for him in the inn (Luke 2:7). Men reject him. His cradle is among the beasts. Crib and cross are of the same wood.

He is also a stranger on earth with neither home nor shelter—with nowhere to lay his head (Luke 9:58). If he is hailed with hosannahs and shouts of joy, this is all a mistake, a wrong interpretation, like that of Peter's confession at Caesarea Philippi. Once it is seen that he is not what he was thought to be, the hosannahs change into "Crucify him." He weeps over Jerusalem, which does not know the day of its visitation (Luke 19:41). "How often would I have gathered thy children together, even as a hen gathereth her chickens under her wings, and ye would not" (Matthew 23:37). His suffering is that he is a knowing witness to the way in which those he loves rush unsuspectingly to destruction, ignoring all warnings and rejecting the offered anchor of deliverance. Nietzsche says in his *Zarathustra:* "You do not yet suffer enough, for you do not yet suffer from man." Here, however, we do find suffering from man.

It is true, of course, that this type of pain does not indicate the true depth of his suffering. It is no more than its foreground. Part of the humanity of Christ, however, is that this human side of his suffering, like the thirst and agony of his crucifixion, has also to be taken into account if we are not to fall into involuntary Docetism through sheer dogmatic profundity. There is here suffering from man, whether from supposed superiority, as in the case of the Pharisees, or from baser motives, from sadism, cruelty, a lust for destruction, as in the case of the spectators and the executioners, or scorn and contempt.

Even in this human element, however, a specific depth may already be seen. For suffering from man grows immeasurably if I love those who make me suffer. This is what Nietzsche means when he has Zarathustra say: "Love of man is God's hell." Here someone goes through this hell.

Finally he is afflicted with an ultimate loneliness which also has a human aspect, for those who had been his companions left him (Mark 14:50). When Socrates drank the hemlock he was surrounded by his friends and engaged in a final philosophical discussion with them. But Christ hangs between two thieves, and the uninvolved soldiers cast lots for his garment (Matthew 27:35). Even the sorrowing women miss the real point. They are grieved by his smitten hands and the pain of his death struggle. They do not weep about the true event, namely, that he is suffering the ultimate torment of his and their dereliction.

One might almost read the story as though it were a tragedy, in which the hero wants the absolute but for this reason he is rejected by society as an alien body and comes to grief on the relativities of this world. This is a familiar curve of destiny. Many of those who see the Oberammergau passion play or hear Bach's Passions with only a literary or musical interest do in fact fall victim to this appearance of tragedy and in so doing again miss the true point.

This can be grasped only when we ask wherein his suffering properly consists.

In trying to plumb its true depth we will start again with our earlier formula that he suffered because he loved as he did. When someone loves another, he wants to share everything with him. This is why Christ does not remain in the safety of his eternal radiance, in his Logos home, when those whom he calls his brothers stand on the front of historicity. Because he loves actively and sacrificially, we can believe his love. It is easy enough to be socially concerned, to play the philanthropist, and to send tax-deductible checks. To call all this a sacrifice is a mere euphemism, for it does not really hurt. Jesus, however, does not transfer money. He transfers himself from the shelter of his Logos home to the abyss of guilt, pain, and death.

When someone gives himself in this way, transferring his own being and not just money, he is close to the one for whom he does it. The need of this other affects him as though it were his own.

Here, then, to love is not just to be overwhelmed by emotions. These are there, but they are not the true theme, and so they receive little mention in the Gospels. Loving here is a state of being, or, better, a movement of being. It simply means being there for the other, entering into his situation, not keeping anything back. It means transferring oneself. This is how Jesus loved.

The opposite is finely depicted in the elder brother of the prodigal (Luke 15:25ff.). The guilt of this brother is that he cannot love. Apart from this he is morally blameless. He has served his father faithfully, never gone astray, and remained pharisaically upright. But he cannot enter into the pity of his father for his estranged younger brother. He remains cold. He feels no surge of love. He is even jealous. He knows nothing of the depths of life. The temptations of his wild and restless brother are alien to him. He is secure in a life in which is no moral risk. Self-centered thus, however, he does not love. He is there only for himself and not for another. Being unable to love, he cannot imagine how lost a man can be in murder, robbery, and licentiousness. He certainly cannot feel solidarity with those who fall victim to these sins. Without love, he cannot see beneath the surface. He does not see the "tigerish disposition" (Stifter) which lurks in himself even though it has not broken out as it has in others. Because he is so terribly upright and so totally without love, at the decisive moment his heart is not in tune with his father's. Cutting himself off from his brother— the representative of his fellow-men—he also cuts himself off from his father, whom basically he does not love either, since he is not there for his father and turns from the one to whom his father turns.

With underlying irony the point of the parable thus turns into its opposite. In a secret way, which is only now brought to light, the elder brother is the prodigal. He has gone into a far country from which there is this time no return. For lovelessness knows no sorrow, and where there is no sorrow there can be no repentance and no longing for home. The loveless do not find their way back. In contrast, the homesick who are racked by unhappy love and driven by hunger for righteousness (Matthew 5:6) can come back. Which of the two, then, is in fact the prodigal son?

Thus far we can to some extent understand the suffering of Christ. For with the help of analogies we have considered only its human side. We recognize why this side is important. It is an antidote to every form of Docetism.

This is the side which moves most people at Good Friday services even if they find the core of his vicarious expiatory work alien to them. There is a law of consolation which is fairly close to the principle of homeopathy. Our own suffering is softened by seeing the similar suffering of others. This is one reason why the poet says that wounds must heal wounds. Theologians and preachers should not despise this aspect of Christ's passion. We often have a fatal tendency to present the Christian message in the negative form of demarcations: God is not our dear Father above the starry universe; Christ does not suffer as the martyr does or as we do; his suffering is on a completely different plane. Now we are denying that there are these other dimensions. What we are saying is that even these other dimensions have become as it were incarnate. They include the enigmatic suffering of Job. They include the suffering of Socrates, who is punished for something which he must regard as the determinative factor in his life. They include the anguish of the schizophrenic. They include the suffering of the oppressed and of the old and lonely. All these find their own suffering in what is suffered on Golgotha. Hence we are not to rob them of their comfort by constantly shattering the analogy with a "Yes, but. . . ." If we do, if we allow only that Christ bore vicariously the wrathful judgment of God, that a collective world judgment was focused on him, and that he bore the great burden of the world's weight (Paul Gerhardt), the very exclusiveness of this dogmatic standpoint opens the door again to Docetism. The physical pain of him who hung thirsty under a tropical sun, the associated torment of waiting, and the final disillusionment with humanity, become only a theatrical symbolism. In fact, however, the sufferings of the Lamb that taketh away the sin of the world find embodiment in these authentically human physical and mental pains. At this point, too, we cannot go too deeply into the flesh. The Roman Catholic Church shows wisdom in this regard by setting up the stations of the cross. The Protestant need not fear that in adopting them he will also have to adopt the associated schema of the analogy of nature and grace.

Concentration on the human and psychological aspect is certainly less to be feared than a cold and uninvolved docetic dogmatism. This was what finally caused Lessing and Schleiermacher to attack the orthodoxy of their day. The stiffness of its doctrines of suffering and atonement was offensive to them, not so much for its content as for the fact that it ignored the human dimension of Jesus' existence or dismissed it prematurely. They thus felt that their own humanity was not affected. In this connection it is worth asking whether the increasing transformation of theology into anthropology[15] is not a reaction to the nonhuman character of orthodox Christology. Although many factors in intellectual history after Descartes were at work—we analyzed them in Volume I—this weakness in the church's Christology prepared favorable soil for anthropological overcompensation.

Our plea, then, is that men should be led to the suffering creature called Jesus. Meditating on his creaturely suffering will itself disclose a dimension of this suffering which eludes the criteria of the creaturely and thus leads us to the true heart of the matter. Beyond the threshold of what we can understand—but only beyond this threshold—we can learn something very different, namely, that this man Jesus did not suffer merely at men's hands. He did not suffer merely because a unique, exemplary, and unconditioned

---

[15] As in Theology A (Cartesian theology); cf. Volume I.

man could no longer be tolerated, but was rejected, by the world between the fall and judgment.

In this regard already we have every right to ask whether we do not have more than human suffering, analogous to our own, when a man comes to a terribly painful death just because he is the exemplary man—the kind of man that we as men in contradiction are not. Schleiermacher was trying to express this more than human element when he called Christ a prototype (*The Christian Faith,* § 93) and marked him off from empirical man. The fact that he is whole man as a prototype and model undoubtedly distinguishes him from us, who are only partial and unnatural men. Thus someone who is destroyed as whole man will suffer differently and more fully than we do. Different frequencies of sensitivity will be in play. Even in ordinary life we can see something of this. The more highly organized a man is and the more sublime his constitution in mind and soul, the more sensitive he will be and the broader his capacity for suffering. Manfred Hausmann meditates on this aspect of the suffering of Christ in his book *Einer muss wachen.* Those who read the accounts of his suffering as wholly human accounts will undoubtedly stumble on this dimension which is far beyond what we suffer.

His true suffering, however, is not that he just suffers at men's hands but that in a mysterious way he suffers at God's hands. The older dogmatic tradition has this in view when it says that he bore and suffered the wrath and judgment of God in our place. We shall now try to see what this means.

The passion hymns express both aspects. They say first that Christ suffered at my hands and with me. He suffered at the hands of men and I was among the crowd that shouted "Crucify him." "I, I and my sins" have done it to him.[16] "Whence come these sorrows, whence this mortal anguish? It is my sins for which thou, Lord, must languish; Yea, all the wrath, the woe, thou didst inherit, This I do merit."[17] But then they say that he suffered vicariously at God's hands, bearing the divine penalty. He bore all the burden of my sin on the sacred cross.[18] "Thy grief and bitter passion, Were all for sinners' gain; Mine, mine was the transgression, but Thine the deadly pain."[19]

Just because there is so much here to affect us at the human level, and even the vicarious bearing of judgment has the human trait of solidarity with us (how else could we sing about it?), the question arises: Why is there transition from this aspect to the true core? Or, more precisely: Why has this humanly so impressive and obvious aspect been fitted into what seems to be an alien dogmatic framework? Why is there all the talk about expiation, substitution, and judgment? A more popular form of the same question

---

[16] P. Gerhardt.
[17] J. Heermann.
[18] J. Gesenius.
[19] P. Gerhardt.

might be as follows: Once the heart is engaged, once unselfish love has made its impact, why does reason have to ward off at once something that it finds alien, something that suggests mythology, something that threatens to take from us what is so close at the human level?

We must discuss for a moment these objections against what seems to be an alien intrusion. We shall focus on their theological rather than their psychological aspect. For in many circles they give rise to theological arguments in self-justification.

A specific exegesis of the parable of the prodigal son, for example, is often used to tie Jesus down to the purely human zone and to dedogmatize all theories of atonement and vicarious suffering. In this parable the central theme is the divine pardon. This does not demand any expiation. No concept of an equivalent arises such as one finds developed by Anselm in his *Cur deus homo?* God is simply compared to an earthly father. Forgiveness springs out of a wholly human love. This love is so spontaneous, natural, and overflowing that it overcomes the breach and welcomes back the prodigal.

There are—and have been—theological movements which have tried to free the figure of Jesus from dogmatic ballast along these lines.[20] But what is left of Christology when this is attempted? Do we have anything more than the bearer of a prophetic office who brings illumination to our existence?

We might refer to H. Braun once again in this connection (cf. Volume I, pp. 160ff.). We might also refer to the theological line from Herrmann to Ebeling, which regards Jesus as an example of the believer and sees in the cross the acid test of faithfulness.

When this dedogmatizing, this reduction to the prophetic office takes place, it may be noted time and again that the prophet surreptitiously becomes the teacher—the teacher of faith and love—and that he thus makes himself superfluous. He has only an explicitly interim function. When I have learned the idea of faith, or the I should or I may, when I have claimed it through the mediation of Jesus of Nazareth, I am autarchous and stand on my own feet.[21] The next step might then very well be an independent and purely secular existentialism which need hardly remind us of its Christian origin.

Another obstacle, however, also bars access to the background of Christ's passion as this comes to expression in the doctrines of expiation and sub-

---

[20] Christian Geyer, the great Nuremberg preacher and representative of theological liberalism, tells us in his book *Erlebtes Christentum* (1913) what a great liberation it was for him when H. R. von Frank, his teacher at Erlangen, presented a Christology which stresses the humanity of Christ and his forgiveness without wrapping it up in the theologoumenon of expiation. (Whether he *fully* understood Frank is another matter.)

[21] Ebeling is forced to admit that he has to mobilize all his resources to resist this conclusion.

stitution. So long as this is not dealt with, all such doctrines remain unintelligible.

If the cross of Christ is to be a sign of atonement, this sign must obviously presuppose a conflict between God and man which has to be overcome. This brings us up short, for it might be asked rhetorically which of us or our contemporaries has experienced God as an enemy ·or opponent. Who can take to himself the saying of Peter: "Depart from me; for I am a sinful man, O Lord" (Luke 5:8)?[22]

How is it that we do not seem to experience God in this way, at least when we are influenced by the common sense and normal religious outlook of our day?

Some indication of the answer to this question might be given by recent religious surveys. These give evidence of belief in a higher being or a God of nature. But this God does not call us in question. He is so lofty that he is above our private lives with their guilt and conflict. Just as recreation enables us to get away from the complications and frictions of everyday life, so this God helps us by providing a higher observation post to relativize things. For the average man today the function of religion and the concept of God is to lift us up above the everyday. The official acts of the church, i.e., baptism, marriage, and burial, are part of this. Those are not the worst pastors who in this regard either resist popular clamor and ecclesiastically sanctioned assurances or—which is better—use such occasions to proclaim the very different God, even though they risk giving offense in so doing.

At this level of average religion, in which God hardly challenges or opposes us, the word of reconciliation, or of Christ's reconciling death, obviously finds no correlation in existential experience and thus appears to be pure absurdity.

Even polytheism, e.g., in the form of Greek mythology, cannot integrate Golgotha as a reconciling event into the system of coordinates of modern thought. To be sure, it finds a place for antitheses, polarities, and breaks, as in Homer's religion. But these do not imply an absolute breach between the gods and men. The gods cannot become a true source of dread. The antitheses in being are projected into the gods themselves. The gods divide into Olympian parties. In the Trojan War Hera represents marital faithfulness in opposition to Aphrodite who represents erotic love. The basic conflict in values takes on symbolical form in the Olympian struggle for power.[23] Hence the world of the gods does not stand in antithesis to man and his alienation. The polarities of man's being have counterparts among

---

[22] Cf. also the dialog between Yahweh and Moses in Exodus 33:18-23, and the saying of Isaiah at his call: "Woe is me! . . . because I am a man of unclean lips" (Isaiah 6:5).

[23] W. F. Otto, *Die Götter Griechenlands,* 2nd ed. (1934); E.T. *The Homeric Gods* (1954); G. Nebel, *Homer* (1959), pp. 292ff.; J. Sellmair, *Der Mensch in der Tragik,* 2nd ed. (1941), pp. 7ff.

the gods. Face to face with Moira both gods and men are in the same condemnation.

Pantheism especially is unable to adapt any form of the theology of the cross. In it the difference between God and man has become a different aspect of identity. One may see this in the philosophical secularization of pantheism, as in Hegel.[24]

In opposition to this we maintain that the gulf or antithesis which has developed between God and man as expressed in the story of the fall is in fact the *terminus a quo* from which alone one may view the reconciling event of the cross.

This brings us to one of the most basic and most delicate problems in preaching.

If as a preacher I constantly ground my proclamation of the gospel on the presupposition that man is alienated from God and that God is thus a threat and danger to him, I am exposed to the peril of beginning by preaching the law. I have to struggle against the inclination to show the rottenness of everything, to bring out the emptiness of technology and the welfare state, to emphasize the injustice of both individual and global structures. I have to resist the temptation to use a kerygma of doom as a means of stirring in my hearers a sense of the general lostness of man and his need of redemption. Preaching of this type divides the message into two different parts, and in the first of these it paints a dark and accusing picture. It is of the truth and art of authentic preaching, however, to avoid this danger. While critical analysis will find a place, it will be secondary to the main theme of the gospel. This is not just a matter of rhetorical craft, although this aspect is not to be disregarded. It rests on a theological foundation and is connected with the relation between law and gospel. The law does not precede the gospel chronologically when it proclaims judgment. Authentic judgment does not come to expression in the pre-evangelical stage. If it did it might be deflected and engender either a despair or an assurance which does not stand in relation to God. The depth of judgment may be seen only in the light of the gospel, i.e., when I realize what price was paid, and what price had to be paid, to rescue me from my alienation. The depth of judgment is perceived, not from the demand and claim of God which I resist, but from the love and sacrifice of God which I reject (John 15:22-25).

Preaching, then, cannot introduce too soon the positive side of the evangelical message. It can assume that hearers themselves will relate it to the failures of life, so that only a few references are needed and no broad canvas will have to be painted. The right effect can be achieved only if the preacher himself is aware of the problem of alienation in all its range, and can impart something of his awareness. Luther in the *Second Disputation against the Antinomians* (WA, 39, I, 445) has shown us why the law

---

[24] Cf. Volume I, pp. 259-262.

itself cannot give us any knowledge of sin but needs the help of the Holy Spirit, i.e., of the gospel; cf. ThE, I, § 598ff.; E.T. I, pp. 117ff.

Our next step will be to try to expound the NT metaphors for what took place at the crucifixion. Among these are the concepts of the priest and victim which we find in connection with the priestly office. We shall see that there are in fact various groups of metaphors which are taken from different spheres of life, e.g., that of civil and criminal law, that of the cultus, and that of the army. Each metaphor stresses one aspect of the meaning of Christ's passion. Taken alone they have only limited significance and may even be misleading. They express the totality only when they are taken together and are seen to be complementary. They have to be brought into association. They can then present a multi-colored picture which, when the goal of the statement is considered and not just the fragmentary achievement, will bring to light the original color of the event.

XXVIII

The Metaphors of the Atonement within the Priestly Office

1. THE CULTIC METAPHOR

The cultic metaphor is a kind of ellipse with the priest and victim as the two foci. Along with its illustrative force this metaphor is particularly significant because it enables us to locate the death of Jesus within the process of salvation history. It connects it with the sacrificial ministry of the OT and thus establishes the continuity of prophecy and fulfilment, of the old covenant and the new. It also stresses the diastasis between the two. The OT cultus is only an "example and shadow" (*hypódeigma* and *skiá*) of the heavenly cultus (Hebrews 8:5) and of what has been enacted in Christ the eternal high priest. That he has fulfilled what was promised means here that the atoning death of Christ follows the line indicated by the earlier cultus.

To what extent Christ fulfils the priesthood we have already seen. He both fulfils and also transcends the priestly function. He fulfils it by standing over against God, like the priest and unlike the prophet. He stands over against God by taking his place alongside man and representing him before God with his expiatory sacrifice. In Hebrews the stress in the priestly office is that Christ is one of us, that he is in the same depths as we are, that he lets himself be tempted like us, and that he can thus have sympathy. But there is also seen in all this something that transcends everything priestly. Although he stands in solidarity with us like the OT priest, although, like the OT priest, he is called to his office and has not usurped it (Hebrews 5:4), he differs from the OT priest at a crucial point. The OT priest is a man like those whom he represents and hence he has to make an offering first for his own sins (5:3). But Christ does not. He is solitary and sinless among sinners. He offers only for others. His being different, his nonconformity to this aeon, is what makes him victim as well as priest, "the Lamb of God, which taketh away the sin of the world" (John 1:29; 1 Corinthians 5:7f.; cf. also 1 Peter 1:19; Romans 3:25; Ephesians 5:2; 1 John 2:2).

The fact that Christ is sacrificial lamb as well as priest undoubtedly stands behind the Last Supper. In this regard the difficult historical question whether this was the passover or not makes no difference. The associations of the passover and the Lord's Supper in both symbolism and significance were undoubtedly in view.

According to the synoptic accounts Jesus seems to have celebrated the passover and died on the feast day. If John (19:14) associates the condemnation of Jesus with the day of preparation when the lambs were slain, this was in order to emphasize that he himself is the paschal lamb and that he fulfils the point of the celebration in his crucifixion (cf. 1 Corinthians 5:7).

It has been suggested that in its oldest form the passover was an apotropaic blood-ritual.[1] With the spring the nomads from the steppes would come back from the winter pastures and drive their flocks to summer feeding near more inhabited country. This was a laborious and dangerous business. The time for the change, namely, the first full moon of spring, would suggest a connection between human and cosmic processes and—to use more modern and perhaps romantic terminology—give rise to a feeling of metaphysical awe. In any case ritual safeguards were ordained for the change, which in the life of the nomads marked the decisive break in the yearly rhythm. The tent-doors were smeared with sacrificial blood to ward off demonic powers of destruction from both man and beast.

Apart from the aim of warding off harm, the passover was marked by two further elements which with a new meaning are still found in the Lord's Supper. First was the fellowship meal, in which the roasted victim was eaten with unleavened bread, and second was the readiness to depart. The fact that the meal was a ceremony of departure was what gave it a special affinity to the event which was so vital a part of salvation history, namely, the exodus from Egypt—the great change of pasture for Israel— and the entry into the divinely appointed land (Exodus 12:21ff.). Modern Judaism still observes the passover ritual in remembrance of Yahweh's great act of deliverance at the exodust from Egypt (Exodus 12:14; Deuteronomy 16:1).

Since the NT sets the sacrificial death of Jesus in parallelism with the slaying of the passover lamb and thus finds correspondence between the Last Supper and the feast of the passover, it is incumbent on us to interpret the crucifixion of Jesus with the help of the concepts found in the passover ritual.[2] We shall simply list here the analogous elements.

1. The blood of the lamb of Golgotha protects us against threats. The threats which the ancient Israelite nomads feared on the nights of the full moon are naturally only an inadequate symbol for the threatening forces which Paul has in view when he enumerates that which stands destructively and disruptively between the love of God and us but which can no longer

---

[1] H. J. Kraus, *Gottesdienst in Israel,* 2nd ed. (1962), pp. 61ff.; E.T. *Worship in Israel* (1966), pp. 45ff.

[2] Cf. on this G. von Rad, *Theologie des AT,* I, pp. 249ff.; E.T. I, pp. 250ff.

do its work now that the love of God has been manifested in Christ: "What shall separate us from the love of God? shall tribulation, or distress, or persecution, or famine, or nakedness, or peril, or sword?" (Romans 8:35). As the passover once sealed the covenant of God with his people, so the Lord's Supper, with its reference to the sacrifice of Christ, seals the new covenant. This sacrifice offers us protection. We are set under the patronage of a covenant in which no alien or divisive force can overpower us.

2. The sacrifice has an expiatory function.[3] A vicarious bearing of judgment makes atonement for the breaking of the covenant and the breach of fellowship with God (Isaiah 53; Hebrews 9:22). Obviously an expiatory offering of this kind can make sense only in connection with a very definite view of God as the God who calls his people into personal fellowship and claims personal attitudes of faithfulness, gratitude, and trust. Only on this view can there be a breach of fellowship. The later a-personal idea of God as a transpolar principle of indifference, or as a concept of love which embraces antithesis, and hence cannot be disturbed by it and need not take it tragically, is still distant here. Within such a principle of indifference an expiatory offering would be meaningless as it would be also in a pragmatic partnership which is undertaken merely for the purpose of cooperation, as in politics. Since the idea of indifference and the concept of a pragmatic alliance are increasingly influential today, it is hardly surprising that the concept of an expiatory offering seems more and more to be an archaic alien body on the modern scene. How childish and anthropomorphic, we feel, that a lamb should have to be offered to an angry God in sacrifice!

Yet a different picture emerges if—to adopt a thought of Anselm's—we see that fellowship with the majesty of God is at issue. For this majesty is marked by two features. First, we are totally indebted to it, so that we have no way of making satisfaction in ourselves. All that we have is already God's. We cannot dedicate it to him. Second, this majesty manifests itself by freely summoning us into the covenant, so that we have no rights as partners. The covenant is no treaty between equals. It is a matter of God's sovereign choice and institution.[4] Hence breaking the covenant involves loss, as the analogy of human relations shows. We need only think of the reaction to shattered trust: "Things can never be the same again"; "If for practical reasons I overlook it and let things be as they were, I shall lose my self-respect."

To the extent that we are insensitive to the personal element we lose our understanding of the loss—our understanding of the fact that God's majesty does not permit a cool and unaffected overlooking of things, as might be possible in the case of a principle of indifference. This is why Anselm, for all the criticisms that might be brought against his doctrine of the atonement and especially his idea of satisfaction, surely grasped something very

---

[3] *Ibid.*, p. 253; E.T. pp. 254f.

[4] The LXX makes this plain by using *diatheke,* not *syntheke;* cf. O. Procksch, *Theologie des AT* (1950), p. 92.

true and important when he argued that the majesty of God has something owing to it, that a loss has to be made good.

We do not have enough information[5] to say for sure whether ancient man really thought that the lamb was in fact a substitute and made a real atonement or offered equivalent payment, or whether he viewed the lamb as a sign that he recognized the need for expiation, that he was ready to make it, that this would not be a cheap thing for him, and that he could not regard the restoration of broken fellowship as a mere matter of course. Although one may suspect that no very clear differentiation was made conceptually, nevertheless it seems that the latter view is the more likely. The fact that the best is offered and is not to be put to any other practical use symbolizes renunciation and the acceptance of loss, so that the offering "signifies" more than it "is." Perhaps the prayer for divine acceptance which accompanies the sacrifice (Wisdom 3:6; 1 Maccabees 1:12, 46; 2 Maccabees 1:26) is also an indication that it is not just a payment and can never be a full equivalent but that God reckons it as such in grace. If, then, he who is guilty does not include himself within the sacrifice, but tries to get off cheaply by external payment and cultic formalism, God can refuse acceptance (1 Samuel 3:14; Amos 5:21ff.; Matthew 5:23).

The offering is not, then, a way of getting around God. It cannot be used to negotiate with him. It does not constitute a claim. It has to be accepted in grace. Hence it is God himself who sacrifices something and leaps into the scales (Luther). In the sacrifice which man brings to God there lurks an underlying inversion. God himself is the one who sacrifices; he offers himself to man.

This inversion brings out an element for which the cultic metaphor of sacrifice is not adequate, so that it has to be transcended by new content. (The same applies to Anselm's presentation.) Christ does not simply offer himself to God in the name of man, so that God is the object of atonement (as in Anselm). He also offers himself to man in the name of God and as God's sacrifice (John 3:16; Romans 8:32; cf. also Romans 5:8; 1 John 4:9).

3. The passover ritual also contributes to the interpretation of the crucifixion of Christ the idea of table-fellowship or communion. The reconciled who stand in the covenant are one body (1 Corinthians 10:16ff.). Perhaps the passover analogy brings out the fellowship of the altar more clearly on the negative side (10:18). He who is related to the Kyrios by the body and blood of Christ's offering separates himself from idols and from the threatening forces of disruption (10:14ff.). Fellowship is characterized by inclusion but also by exclusion, by the non-admittance of certain things. He who is bought with the price of Christ's sacrifice (1 Corinthians 6:20; 7:23) can no longer belong to the powers of temptation but is related to those who with him have been bought as members of this body.

4. The final passover analogy has been almost completely ignored in

---

[5] Or the author at least has not been able to find it.

our eucharistic theology. It is that of readiness for departure. The fellow-ship of the meal tells us to break camp and march out. For the nomads of ancient Israel this involved the risky movement to the spring pastures. For us, as the charge of Jesus shows with its use of the simile of the sacrificial lamb (Matthew 10:16), it means going forth as sheep in the midst of wolves. It means being the salt of the earth and delivering the message of reconciliation (2 Corinthians 5:20; Ephesians 2:16; Colossians 1:20).

It seems to us to have been a fateful mistake that the Lord's Supper has been increasingly celebration as a cultic action of the core commmunity, so that it has been understood as the true goal and climax of worship, or, more sharply, as a liturgical end in itself. In truth, its inner intention is the very opposite. It makes us ready to march out. It is a meal of missionary sending. It strengthens our readiness to offer ourselves in our own follow-ing of the sacrifice of the cross. It is a summons to venture the dangerous change in pasture, to go forth in exodus, and thus to do, not what is cultic, but what is wholly and entirely secular, moving out to the world over which all power has been given to the Lord of the Supper (Matthew 28:18).

The Lord's Supper, then, is not a cultic end in itself. It is a preparation for departure to proclaim the Lord's death until he comes (1 Corinthians 11:26). The Supper is an initiatory rite for going into the world; it is not a cultic center constituting the goal of world evangelization. We have to learn that the Lord's Supper is also to be interpreted theologically in such a way that it is seen in relation to the secularity of Christianity.

While the OT offering is an indication and prophetic sign of what takes place in Christ's death on the cross, it is also relativized. We find here the same process as in the earlier chapters on Christology. Christ as fulfilment transcends the prophecy. He is prophet and more than prophet, Messiah and more than Messiah.

That wherein he breaks continuity with the OT sacrifice may be seen under two aspects.

First, we recall how Hebrews speaks of the transcending of the OT ritual and the diastasis in relation to it. It refers to the incompleteness of the OT covenant and its need for fulfilment (8:6). The deficiency in the old covenant is that the offering has to be repeated daily and yearly. No definitive order is set up nor definitive peace with God achieved (7:27; 9:7). That which breaks fellowship with God constantly renews its strength. The shedding of the blood and burning of the ashes of animals never brings any true peace (9:9, 13f.; 10:14).

One might say that Christ fulfils *de facto* what the ancient sacrifice can only signify. The sign is meant to signify the self-offering of him who makes the offering. This is why it is futile if this self-offering is lacking. In reality, however, the one who makes the offering does not present himself but is (more or less) represented by his sacrifice. He simply gives a sign. Here, however, the eternal high priest brings himself as the offering. This cannot be repeated. It is once and for all (*eph' hapax*). Hence definitive peace is set up with God. There is now access to the holy of holies, and all that divides is set aside (9:6ff.; 10:20). The temple curtain is torn in two (Matthew 27:51). A solid basis is established for Paul's hymnal affirmation that nothing can separate us from the love of God.

Second, the OT concept of sacrifice is transcended from another angle too. This echoes something we said earlier. Anselm is wrong when he takes over the original concept unchanged. He is wrong when he says that in the sacrifice of Christ an equivalent is offered to God and a payment is made which no creature but only the God-man can pay.[6] In the NT God is not the object of the atoning work of Christ. He is always the subject: "God was in Christ reconciling the world to himself" (2 Corinthians 5:19). The OT concept of sacrifice is thus inverted, as we put it earlier. Man does not bring God an offering; God brings man an offering, he brings himself. To forgive means entering the breach and taking up the burden of loss. Golgotha means pain in God.

The change in the meaning of sacrifice here is the same as may be seen in the dissolving of the glory of the law into the glory of the gospel. The OT offering stands under the sign of the law, for it is an action toward God, even though on the basis and within the framework of God's covenant initiative. In the crucifixion of Christ, however, God is exclusively the one who gives himself, who bears the cost, and who himself suffers in Christ. The change from law to gospel is thus radical and complete.

Luther made this change a decisive point in his thinking. He issued a warning against a recurrent danger in theological history that if the change is overlooked it will not be perceived that there is manifested here a revolutionary resolve of God and therefore a personal event. This alone blocks the broad way which leads to the idea of God as a timeless principle of love and consequently to theological monism. (Cf. the relevant discussion of Barth's doctrine of law and gospel in ThE, I, § 596 a-x; E.T. I, pp. 108ff.).

We might say that the law constantly forces the believer in Christ to remember the incongruence between what we already are in the eyes of God (reaccepted sons) and what we are in fact (people who lag behind this calling at every conceivable point) (Philippians 3:12).

The gospel, however, tells us that the dubious relic of our existence does not have to be cleansed first. We can place it under the forgiveness of God. As Luther puts it in his *Third Disputation against the Antinomians* (WA, 39, I, 519ff.), a man who believes in Christ is just and holy by God's reckoning. He lives and is already in heaven. But even though we are in the Father's bosom and are wrapped in the best robe, our feet peep out under the mantle and Satan tries to nip them. Then we cry out and realize that we are only flesh and blood and that the devil is still there. We are indeed holy and free, but in the spirit, not the flesh. The feet have still to be washed, for they are unclean. We must pull our feet under the mantle or else we shall have no peace. This passage gives classical expression to

---

[6] For the same dubious concept cf. CA, III, which speaks of the reconciliation of the Father to us as the goal of the incarnation of Christ.

the overcoming of the law. The washing of the feet, as an action for God's sake and in relation to him, is not a presupposition of entering into peace. We have only to draw our feet under the mantle. We have only to accept and claim the reconciling work which is God's alone.

2. THE PENAL METAPHOR — THE VICARIOUS ASPECT

This metaphor is an obvious one, for the model of Isaiah 53 suggests that Christ's passion be understood as the suffering of a vicarious penalty. The imagery is influenced by the fact that the term penalty or punishment belongs to the legal world rather than the cultic world. Underlying the use of the term is the idea that man is exposed to the consequences of a fault which merits death. In a chain of ever new revolts which are only variations on the original fall, man has sinned against the Lord to whom he belongs with all that he is and has.

The gravity of the fault is also marked qualitatively by the fact that there is not only sin against God's commandments but also despising of the love which God continually attests to man afresh. The covenant is broken which God made with man in the free initiative of this love of his. Complaint is thus made against man's ingratitude as well as his disobedience when Jesus says that Jerusalem slew the prophets of God and stoned the messengers of the covenant of grace (Luke 11:47-49).

The weight of man's offense against God, and the related theme of substitution, cannot be understood if the guilt is not seen which cannot be fixed legally and which transcends the whole sphere of law. It has to be realized that man resists not only the commandments of God but also the heart of God. He sins not just against the order of God but against God himself.

It is natural and permissible at this point to escape the abstraction of the legal schema by using human illustrations.

1. If someone with whom I am personally involved and whom I am prepared to love treats me disdainfully either by being indifferent or by imputing wrong motives, I can be very much hurt. The wound is not just peripheral and partial. It does not affect merely my "quality" as a driver with the right of way or my "quality" as a political being whose property or prestige is challenged. When my readiness of heart is questioned, the center of my person is wounded. I was prepared to give myself. Hence I am not hurt in mere details but in my true self. My involvement is rejected.

Man's sin, then, is not merely that he rejects the law of God but that he despises the gospel. He does not merely resist the will of God but sabotages his heart. The true depth of the crucifixion is perceived when one understands it as the guilt of those who were ready to let the blood of Christ be on them and their children (Matthew 27:25). This depth is not just that of a dubious trial and a breach of legal procedure. It is not just that of treating Jesus as a member of the legal society. The dreadful thing about the crucifixion is that it entails the repulse of one who gives himself totally in love.

This is why Luther does not expound the divine commandments merely in terms of juristic or moral casuistry nor interpret obedience as mere conformity to law. In the preamble to his exposition of the Decalog in the Small Catechism he says that we must fear and love God (so) that we. . . . The possibility of this total commitment of the self in love is grounded in the fact that we are loved first and that we respond to the voice of the heart of God (1 John 4:19). He who breaks the commandments offends against God and not just an order. He does not love. And he does not love because he does not let himself be loved, because he repulses the one who runs toward him (Luke 15:20). The repulse may take the form of breaking the commandments. It may also take the form of keeping them in the pharisaic security of self-righteousness. Only thus can one explain why sinners against the law, why publicans and harlots, are treated mildly in the sayings of Jesus—they are people with empty hands who are ready to receive God's self-giving bounty—whereas those who trumpet forth their uprightness fall under his condemnation. With their empty self-righteousness the latter have resisted God's proffered love and rejected his involvement.

2. This leads on to a further illustration of the gravity of man's fault. The law touches and claims only half the heart.[7] I endorse it only partially, while partially I protest against it. Hence the law entangles me in a conflict against myself which I can understand as a battle between flesh and spirit (Romans 7:4-24) or will and impulse (Kant). Only when I am freed for the ability to love is there a total movement of the self.

Nor is it that only the one claimed by the law is not total (but only partial) in his obedience. The fact is that the author of the law, too, is not total in his law. At any rate this is how it seems to be when he is viewed solely under the aspect of law. To put this concretely, one might think of the absolute king of the feudal epoch giving laws to his state with the idea of establishing order. This function of his laws is completely independent of his personal attitude or motives, e.g., whether he issues the laws in the name of God or in the name of self-glorification or for purely pragmatic reasons, or whether he is a philanthropist or misanthropist. Again, he invests himself only partially in his laws. His heart does not have to be invested in them. For this reason, so long as he is seen only in the mirror of his laws, breaking of the laws cannot be a personal violation of the majesty of the king.

This is where the analogy between the laws of a king and the commandments of God breaks down. For God's commandments are manifestations of his heart. They are means whereby he upholds his covenant and therefore makes Israel and all mankind the object of his love (Deuteronomy 4:40; 5:21; Psalms 119:92, 165, etc.). Just because he gives himself in

---

[7] Cf. Chapter XV.

his commandments, the man who disregards them offends against God himself, so that he has to confess: "Against thee, thee only, have I sinned" (Psalm 51:4).

What does it mean that Christ represents us in the penal judgment which is passed on this particular aspect of sin, on the "against thee, thee only, have I sinned"?

If we note first the fact of this representation, it means, according to Isaiah 53, that he bears the punishment instead of us, that he has adopted the *schēma tēs hamartías,* that he has turned the judgment on himself. This has almost a mythological ring and we must now examine it more closely. Even the concept of the Suffering Servant[8] is in the first instance only a metaphor and it awaits elucidation. When we try to understand it, however, we come up everywhere against elements which transcend the penal schema. We shall restrict ourselves here to only two of these elements.

First, the penal schema is transcended especially by the fact that God does not come as a plaintiff to the judgment with the claim that a wrong against him has to be righted and that damages have to be paid. Although Christ acts as an atoning priest in relation to God, the crucial point is that it is God himself who rights the wrong and enters the breach. Now it is right, as we have seen, that Christ should not be viewed merely as a function of the divine action. For the sake of his humanity and the incarnation, he is to be understood as his own center of action (*autokineton*) and hence as one who acts on God and over against God. Otherwise his temptation would be a mock struggle and his humanity would be a docetic masquerade. Nevertheless, even though we have to regard the earthly personhood of Christ as an active agent in this way, we should not fail to see that God is at work in him, nor should we miss the manner of this action. For everything that Christ does and suffers is included in God's initiative whereby he gives his only-begotten Son and makes Golgotha his own pain.

God as the one who turns to us in love cannot be explained in terms of the legal schema. But in order that this transcendent element may be manifested, there is need to begin with this schema. For only thus can it be seen that God himself meets the claims which he brings and that in Christ he is himself our representative and advocate.

Second, the penal schema is transcended because Christ's vicarious action cannot be taken to mean merely that he does something for me, in my place, and that he pays a price I ought to have paid. Coming to the aid of others is certainly possible in law, at least in civil law. One man may take over the indebtedness of another. But we perceive at once that this analogy does not fit the relation of Christ to us. For this type of vicarious action leaves me, as the one for whom it takes place, untouched. It might take place over my head without involving any personal claim at all, as

---

[8] "The chastisement of our peace was upon him" (Isaiah 53:5; cf Romans 8:1f.).

in some cases of compensation.[9] If this false schema is applied to Christ, it might be said by way of caricature that I am a hardened sinner, and God can take little pleasure in me; but between A.D. 1-30 someone put this straight, and so it no longer affects me, and I can still enjoy my sins without much concern.

When we put it thus, it is at once apparent that a decisive element is missing in this view of Christ's vicarious work. What is missing is that it does not claim me.

We are reminded in this connection that the NT sayings which speak of Christ as our representative also speak of claim and commitment. His death and resurrection draw us into death and resurrection with him (Colossians 3:1-4).[10] With his indicative reference to what has taken place in Christ Paul links an imperative: We are to lay hold of what has happened and work it out in our lives (Colossians 3:5ff.; Ephesians 5:1ff.). This process of putting on Christ can sometimes be presented as a completed act (in the perfect), as in Galatians 3:27, but sometimes it is an ongoing ethical task in the Christian life (Romans 13:14). Promise and claim are so closely related that they seem to be two sides of the same coin. Since what was done in Christ, including his vicarious work, can never be detached from involvement, Paul firmly resists the false inference that because Christ intervened for me I can continue in sin that grace may the more abound (Romans 6:1f., 15ff.). "God forbid" that I should be uncommitted or that I should not be led by his death to my own dying with him.

For this reason we obviously have here a concept of vicarious action which cannot be fitted into the categories of civil law.

In fact the form of substitution in everyday life is and has to be exclusive.[11] It presupposes the inequality of men. Because all cannot be equal, a system of sharing our tasks had arisen. The engineer drives a train for the passengers. The canner acts for the housewife in food-preserving. The workman does things for me that I cannot do myself. The rich, or society, act for the poor in emergencies. All these forms of substitute action follow rules which do not demand co-operation on the part of those represented but in fact forbid it. To this extent they are exclusive.

In distinction from the functional mechanism of the social system of representation, personal representation is definitely inclusive. It takes up the one who is represented into its action. When we sacrifice ourselves for others, whether by giving our lives or wearing ourselves out in service on their behalf, we claim them. The point of the action is that they experience

---

[9] Thus arrangements might be made which are simply taken for granted, or are even in the interests of human relations and business promotion, so that no loyalty or gratitude is felt.

[10] W. T. Hahn, *Das Mitsterben und Mitauferstehen bei Paulus* (1937).

[11] Cf. on this problem the essay by P. Althaus, "Das Kreuz Christi," *Theol. Aufsätze,* I (1929), pp. 36ff.

and accept obligation. When we aid released prisoners, for example, we do not want to leave them in a freedom which carries no sense of obligation; we want to lead them to a sense of obligation which no moral appeals could ever inculcate. The theologian who vicariously undertakes the labor of profound and critical thinking on behalf of the community is not excluding the laity from this work but trying to involve them in it. The teacher who at first has substitute learning for the student is trying to nurse him into this learning and hence regards his substitution as purely transitory.

In this sense, the vicarious work of Christ obviously has also an inclusive character. His death leads us to dying with him and his rising again leads us to rising again with him. The end of the old life and the beginning of the new life of the redeemed are both demanded. What has taken place in him requires that we apprehend that wherein Christ has already apprehended us (Philippians 3:12). The indicative proclamation of his vicarious action is also an imperative summons to go where he is, to believe as he believed, and to love as he loved us (1 John 2:19).

Nevertheless, we do not adequately describe the inclusive character of this substitution if we locate the element of inclusion merely in the fact that Christ's saving act carries an imperative summons and imposes an obligation. The inclusive element is to be found already in the indicative of the address. In his doctrine of justification Luther laid decisive emphasis on this.[12] The righteousness of God which is imparted to us in the cross of Christ is not for him a passive righteousness which distributes reward and punishment according to a schedule. This would simply be the distributive justice of the law according to which God is a just judge who gives to each his own. In the gospel, however, we have an active righteousness. That is to say, God does not give to each his own. He gives himself. This self-giving finds expression in that he lays the sin of man on his Son and gives man the righteousness of his Son. He reckons to man what is not his (imputation), i.e., alien righteousness, and does not reckon to him what is his, i.e., his own sin (non-imputation).[13] For this reason the alien righteousness of Christ is not something that lies in a remote "outside me." It is imparted to me. It is also my righteousness. It includes me.

This inclusiveness is, of course, an absurdity, and seems to be pure dogmatism, unless one appreciates the total theological and anthropological understanding which underlies it. This is characterized by the fact that God and man are seen within a constitutive relation, or, more precisely, within a schema which is not determined in Aristotelian fashion by a timeless ontology but which is posited by God. What God posits is that he does not will to be God in himself but God for us. He wills to be Immanuel, the covenant God, the God who reveals himself. Hence God is what he is, not for himself, but for us. He includes us in what he is. He is God in action

---

[12] On what follows cf. especially H. Iwand, *Glaubensgerechtigkeit nach Luthers Lehre* (1941), pp. 56ff.
[13] *Op. cit.*, p. 57; cf. the 1519 *Commentary on Galatians*, WA, 2, 504, 4.

encountering us in his works. One cannot speak of his might in itself but only of his might as he imparts it to us and makes things possible thereby. Nor can one speak of his wisdom in itself but only in such sort as we are wise in fellowship with him.[14]

Similarly man is not determined in his ontic "in himself." He, too, is constitutively characterized by the fact that he is a being in relation. He is from God and to him. The true mark of his existence is his relation to God, or, better, his attitude to God's dealings with him.[15] His personality depends on the fact that God addresses him as a Thou and makes him his partner and image (Genesis 1:27f.; 2:16).[16] It stands always in relation to its abandonment to judgment and its goal of calling out of servanthood into sonship (John 15:15; Galatians 4:1-7).

This correlation of God and man leads necessarily (and one might even say logically) to the fact that all statements about God's being, acts, and conduct imply statements about man's act and conduct and *vice versa*. There is thus no substance in the much debated theological question[17] whether through justification man acquires a new ontic quality, an actual being righteous (*justus esse in re*) or whether God simply treats him as though he were.[18] Such an approach, Luther would say, can be taken only within an (e.g., Aristotelian) ontology in which God and man are regarded as qualitatively independent beings. The question of a possible "as though" does not arise, however, when the relation between God and man is seen as constitutive for human existence. For on this view the statement that God intervenes for man and grants him his righteousness means that man *is* righteous and accepted. When it is a matter of being in relation, the alteration in relation which takes place in justification means also an alteration in being as thus understood. This is why Iwand, even though he does not accept the relational system, is correct when he says that in the light of Christ no one can say that God is righteous and holy while he himself is not. The divine righteousness manifested to the world in Jesus Christ does not exclude the sinner but includes him.[19]

What we have called the vicarious work of Christ is thus a special kind. The position here is the same as with the Logos concept. Just as the Stoic idea of the Logos cannot tell us who Christ is as the incarnate Logos, so the normal idea of substitution cannot tell us who Christ is as our representative and substitute. These terms do not define Christ. He is not absorbed by them. They are just temporary bridges. Christ himself defines them. Since his vicarious work includes us rather than excluding us we

---

[14] Luther, Preface to the Latin Works, 1545, WA, 54, 186.
[15] G. Jacob has worked this out in his *Der Gewissensbegriff in der Theologie Luthers* (1929). He argues that conscience is always conscience in relation to either law or gospel, so that it is always despairing, assured, or comforted.
[16] On the image cf. ThE, I, § 763, 834; E.T. I, pp. 152ff., 171ff.
[17] Cf. ThE, I, § 482ff.; E.T. I, pp. 78ff.
[18] Cf. A. Ritschl, *Justification and Reconciliation*, pp. 78ff.
[19] *Op. cit.*, p. 56.

cannot understand it simply in terms of civil law. The new being of the justified is a being in Christ our representative and substitute.[20]

This, then, is what Christ's vicarious work implies. When he takes our place, when he sheds his blood a ransom for many (Matthew 26:28; 1 Peter 1:1, 8), when he "blots out the handwriting of ordinances that was against us . . . nailing it to his cross" (Colossians 2:14), we are not left in a freedom in which he need mean no more to us. This is not just an external transaction in which our own involvement is superfluous. We have here the personal address of a love which brings readiness for a response of love, for discipleship, for entry into the covenant. For "know ye not, that to whom ye yield yourselves servants to obey, his servants ye are to whom ye obey?" (Romans 6:16). This kind of vicarious action takes into service. It is inclusive place-taking.

Luther expresses this side of it sometimes in his concept of the exemplar (cf. his *Commentary on Romans*, II, 204). The exemplar is the prototype in contrast to the example as a model or legal norm (cf. E. Wolf, *Jesus Christus im Zeugnis der heiligen Schrift und der Kirche* [1936], pp. 214f.). For Luther Christ is the prototype in a double sense: first, as he represents God's saving work, and second, as he represents man's state of salvation. He represents the Father to me and me to the Father. He is my relation to the Father.

Thus all the statements that I make about him apply also to me. H. Thimme makes this point in his *Christi Bedeutung für Luthers Glauben* (1933), pp. 214f. As he puts it, faith finds exemplarily in Christ's life, in his incarnation, cross, and exaltation, a representation both of the saving work of God and also of the saved reality of man. It thus identifies the historical Jesus with the eternally present work of God and reality of salvation. Thus the once-for-all Jesus as an exemplar of the righteousness of God in all its aspects can be called the cause, content, and theme of saving faith. This is why it may be said that Christ is our righteousness and effects our righteousness. This means three things: 1. Christ reveals the righteousness of faith in his historical life; 2. Christ is the eternally active power of divine grace in virtue of his exemplary unity with God; 3. Christ is eternally real human faith in virtue of his exemplary unity with us.

3. THE POLITICAL AND MILITARY METAPHOR AND A HOMILETICAL SUMMARY

The final metaphor for Christ's redeeming and vicarious work makes use of analogous elements in the sphere of power-conflicts. We have shown already why power and love are one in Christ, so that what are at odds in this aeon are united in him. His love means not only his solidarity with man

---

[20] On Christ in us and our being in Christ cf. E. Lohmeyer, *Grundlagen paulinischer Theologie* (1929), pp. 139ff.; A. Deissmann, *Paulus,* 2nd ed. (1925); E.T. 1926; F. Neugebauer, *In Christus* (1961); and the NT theologies.

but also his power to alter man's state. When he comes, the power of Satan must yield.[21] The powers of darkness cannot remain where he is. Hence those who believe in him can no longer have any part in darkness. They cannot be at one and the same time members of Christ and members of a harlot (1 Corinthians 6:15ff.). They cannot sit at the table of the Lord and the table of demons (10:21). They cannot be both servants of God and servants of mammon (Matthew 6:24). Christ's exemplary unity with the Father is also exemplary exclusiveness in relation to the demonic world which enchants and captivates us.

For this reason his vicarious action means that he stands fast against the powers of darkness and rescues us from them. He "delivers us from the power of darkness" and translates us into his kingdom (Colossians 1:13). He has "spoiled principalities and powers" and "made a show of them openly, triumphing over them" (2:15).

There is thus a change in lordship in which we are not, of course, mere objects of conflict whom the stronger snatches from the weak, but which decisively involves our own Yes and in which we have a part in the struggle. There is no liberation from the dominion of darkness without commitment to the new lordship. The freedom for which we are freed is not the opposite of commitment. It is entry into new commitment. It is not just freedom *from* something. It is also freedom *for* allegiance to the victor.[22]

We need to conclude this chapter on the priestly office with a homiletical summary, since proclamation is very much at issue here and it will bring reflection back to its starting-point.[23]

Gottfried Benn quotes somewhere a profound if very pagan saying from *The Psychology of Art* by André Malraux. This is to the effect that on the day of judgment the statues of humanity and not the forms of life will appear before the gods. Malraux is saying that when the last judgment comes man will need a representative, since he cannot stand alone. The gods will not look on man himself with mercy in view of his murdering, theft, and pettiness. But perhaps they will look on his statues in which he presents his nature without spot or failure.

Along these lines one might say that Jesus is the statue (exemplar) of authentic man. In him, who has bound his destiny to mine, God will look on me when I have to appear at the last judgment. When the eternal judge calls my name and the hour strikes when I must give account, he will ask me: "Who art thou?" Before I can answer the accuser will say in my stead: "Who is this man? He is the one who has done this and that. He was a servant of ambition and has shown miserably little love. He was always himself his neighbor. He disregarded the numerous cries for help on all

---

[21] Cf. the exorcisms.

[22] Cf. P. Gerhardt's Easter hymn which speaks of our accompanying Christ through the world, sin, death, and hell.

[23] In what follows an actual sermon is used. Cf. my book *Ich glaube* (1965), pp. 145ff.

sides. He was much too selfish either to notice them or to do anything about them."

As the accuser says this, my past will rise up before me and I will have to admit that he is right. For I am my past. Whenever I want to know who someone is, I always ask about what is behind him. A man is what he has behind him: his achievements and failures, what he has done and what he has not done. When appointments are made, a dossier is consulted, for what the person has been thus far is what he is. And if I am serious about what is behind me—as I have to be before the eternal Judge—there can be no escape. I am at the end. I cannot evade this identity with my past.

But then my advocate and representative steps forth. Christ speaks: "All that you have said, accuser, is true. And yet it is also false. For what this man has behind him, and it is really behind him, he no longer is. I have cancelled it and taken it as a burden on myself" (Colossians 2:14). He then turns to the judgment throne: "If thou dost ask, Father and Judge, who this man is, I answer: He is the one for whom I died and with and in whom I suffered. He has become my brother and has let himself be taken up by me. He knew his hands were empty. He knew his conscience was stained. He knew his wretchedness which he could not escape. And he was ready to let me say to him: Be clean. He was ready to accept my offer to bear everything for him and with him. He has taken his place under my cross, saying: I will stand here by thee, do not despise me. So then, Father, he is thy and my possession and I bring him to thee. As he looks with faith on me, so do thou regard him as my brother and let him stay with me in thy peace and glory."

This, then, is the miracle of change. I am no longer identical with my past. I live, yet not I (Galatians 2:20). I am the friend of Christ and I thus acquire a new identity. My true nature and essence is to be included in his vicarious work.

XXIX

Excursus on the Metaphors of the Atonement: The Virgin Birth and the Descent into Hell

1. THE VIRGIN BIRTH

Bibliography: P. Althaus, *Die christliche Wahrheit*, II (1948), pp. 215ff.; K. Barth, *Credo* (1935), pp. 62ff.; also E.T. 1962, pp. 69ff.; also CD, I, 2. pp. 185ff.; H. Braun, "Der Sinn der neutestamentlichen Christologie," ZThK, 54 (1957), pp. 341ff., esp. 335ff.; H. von Campenhausen, *Die Jungfrauenge-burt in der Theologie der alten Kirche* (1962); E.T. *The Virgin Birth in the Theology of the Ancient Church* (1964); M. Dibelius, "Jungfrauensohn und Krippenkind," *Botschaft und Geschichte, Ges. Aufsätze*, I (1953), pp. 1-78; F. Hahn, *Christologische Hoheitstitel* (1963), pp. 273-279, 304-308; O. Michel-O. Betz, "Von Gott gezeugt," *Judentum, Urchristentum, Kirche* (1960), pp. 3-23; E. Norden, *Die Geburt des Kindes* (1924); W. Pannenberg, *Grundzüge der Christologie* (1964), pp. 140ff.; E.T. *Jesus God and Man* (1968), pp. 141ff.

With the dogma of the conception by the Holy Spirit, the dogma of the virgin birth opens the christological section of the Apostles' Creed. It also plays a notable part in the doctrinal tradition of the church, being closely related to Mariology in Roman Catholicism. Nevertheless, its basis in the NT is obviously slight. John's Gospel never speaks of it. Nor does Paul. In Matthew and Luke it is mentioned only once in each case and then the subject is closed. There is not even an indirect indication of its having any serious christological significance.

Since the question of the historical facticity of the virgin birth is irrelevant, the dogma can be approached only in terms of its christological teaching. Does it harmonize with the basic trend of NT Christology? Or does its isolated mention mean that it is merely a side issue? No matter what our answer may be, the kerygma of the virgin birth seems in any case to be a theologoumenon, an interpretation of the coming of Christ, a statement about the manner of his becoming man.

In Matthew 1:18 the reference to the virgin birth is connected with the genealogy of Christ: "She was found with child of the Holy Ghost." In

Luke we find it in the annunciation but not the nativity story itself. In both accounts there is a specific point in the reference (von Campenhausen, *Virgin Birth*, pp. 25ff.). Luke is characterizing the child. He will not be conceived like other children but will be born by the overshadowing of the Holy Spirit and will thus be called the Son of God (Luke 1:35). The special and miraculous power of God at his coming into life finds expression in the transcending and suspension of the natural processes of generation. With God all things are possible (1:36f.). He can give Elizabeth a child in her old age. He can also accomplish the even greater act of sending his Son into this world without male agency.

Matthew's approach is different. He is not interested so much in the ontological implications of the virgin birth for the Son of God. He is more concerned about the context of salvation history. Prophecy is coming to fulfilment here. By birth and birthplace Jesus is the expected Messiah. He is the Son of David (1:20). He is Immanuel (1:23, 25). He comes from Bethlehem (2:6). He is called out of Egypt (2:15). He is a Nazarene (2:23). (On these points cf. von Campenhausen, *op. cit.,* p. 26.) Similarly the prediction of Isaiah 7:14 LXX is fulfilled. There is an apologetic nuance here. The verse is quoted to quell the doubts of Joseph and thereby to meet the attacks of unbelieving Jews.

If the interest of Luke is christological, that of Matthew is apologetic. Matthew is using fulfilled prophecies to combat scepticism.

Since Mark omits the earlier history of Jesus, there is no place for the virgin birth in his work. It begins with the account of John the Baptist (1:1ff.). What precedes is irrelevant from the standpoint of this Gospel. It is assumed to be known. The birth and family relations of Jesus seem to be normal and are common knowledge. This very fact raises doubts as to his extraordinary mission: "Is not this the carpenter, the son of Mary, the brother of James, and Joses, and of Juda, and Simeon? and are not his sisters here with us?" (6:3). The very openness and normality of everything means that the prophet has no honor in his own country and among his own kin and in his own house (6:4). No mystery of time and space and transfiguration surrounds him. There is thus no place for the concept of the virgin birth as a sign of transcendence.

In John the concept is even more remote. In the conversation between Philip and Nathanael the one of whom Moses wrote is Jesus of Nazareth, the son of Joseph. Furthermore, the Christology of this Gospel is along different lines from those suggested by the virgin birth. There is no point in defining the nature of Jesus, since decision in relation to him is based exclusively on encounter with his person and message. Again, his manifestation is externally equivocal, as the ambivalence of the signs displays. There is constant reference to the lowliness which veils him and which is an offense to the Jews because it does not meet their demand for validation. He does not measure up to the criteria which should make it clear that he is the Messiah, namely, the criteria of Davidic descent and birth at Bethlehem (John 7:42). And how could his parents be known if he really came down from heaven (6:42)? John does not just stress the earthly descent of Jesus; he also lays emphasis on his humble origins. Generation without a father, which would demonstrate a supernatural origin, obviously does not fit in with this presentation. (We are not convinced, however, by Pannenberg's argument that the doctrine of the pre-existence of the Son of God, found in both John and Paul, also stands in contradiction with the depiction in John; cf. Pannenberg, *op. cit.,* p. 142; E.T. p. 143; and also F. Hahn, *op. cit.,* pp. 306f.).

Paul, too, does not refer to the virgin birth. In itself, since the development of his Christology is complicated, this might be explained by the argument from silence. The main problem, however, is that the virgin birth does not fit in very well with his christological thinking. In the introduction to Romans, in which Christ's coming is presented in terms of the polarity of flesh and Spirit, mention of the virgin birth might have been appropriate if he had known of it and upheld it. But the birth is seen here simply from the standpoint of the flesh ("made of the seed of David according to the flesh"), and there is not even a trace of the conception by the Spirit. In Paul Jesus is not made the Son of God by his birth; he is it from the very beginning (Romans 3:8; Galatians 4:4; Philippians 2:5-11). The Spirit is mentioned in relation to the resurrection, not the birth ("declared to be the Son of God with power, according to the spirit of holiness, by the resurrection from the dead," Romans 1:3f.). This act of exaltation by the Spirit stands in the strictest contrast to that of humiliation by human birth; cf. also 2 Corinthians 13:4. Here he is still the Son in his alienation and not yet in power and immediacy. Similarly in Galatians 4:4 the birth is the sign of self-emptying. The point of the statement is that the one who is born of woman—not the virgin—and subject to the law is in full solidarity with those whom he redeems. If we were to read "born of a virgin" the point would be blunted (Dibelius, *op. cit.,* p. 29).

From the standpoint of the NT data,[1] then, the message of the virgin birth is very isolated and marginal. It is mentioned only in Matthew and Luke, and the other writers seem not to have any systematic "place" for it. It would be a foreign body in their work. If we need not go so far as von Campenhausen, who says that we have in Matthew and Luke "tendentious legends,"[2] our survey undoubtedly shows—to put it cautiously—that some NT Christologies carry no reference to the virgin birth. This has two implications.

First, the virgin birth is not fundamental to Christology. One does not have to accept it to have faith in Christ. There can be faith in Christ even when this doctrine, which is not christologically constitutive, is eliminated theologically.[3] The dogmatic rank of the article is best expressed in the

---

[1] The problem of the genealogies need not be discussed here; cf. the commentaries and Althaus, *op. cit.,* pp. 217f.

[2] *Op. cit.,* p. 15.

[3] Cf. E. Brunner, *Dogmatics,* II (E.T. 1962), pp. 353ff., in contrast to Barth, who sees in the virgin birth a sign that is not to be surrendered.

words of W. Herrmann, who would call it, not a ground of faith, but a concept of faith, i.e., an attempt by the Easter community to project back its knowledge of the exalted Lord into his origin, or, more sharply, to interpret Christmas in the light of Easter.

The second implication is related to the first. We are given the task of testing whether the interpretation of Christ's being and nature which comes to expression in the virgin birth is materially appropriate, whether it has worth as a theological symbol, whether this concept of faith is an apt explication of the ground of faith. In the last resort, then, one has to ask what should be the attitude of the Christian, including the troubled Christian, to the statements of the Apostles' Creed.

What is in fact the ground of faith which can serve as a criterion for the legitimacy or unsuitability of the virgin birth? Perhaps it can be formulated best in the statements of the Johannine Christ about himself: "Ye are from beneath; I am from above; ye are of this world; I am not of this world" (John 8:23). As we have already noted, e.g., in connection with the temptation story, this brings out clearly the central affirmation of the incarnation. In distinction from us, Christ is not "thrown" into existence. He does not just find himself in it. He has come into this existence of ours from another dimension.

Adoptionism is thus ruled out. The man Jesus does not become the Son of God; the Son of God becomes the man Jesus. He does not come forth from the sequence of human generations; he moves into it. Hence those who interpret him in terms of his earthly origin ("Is not this the carpenter of Nazareth?"), and who thus assume that he has proceeded from it instead of entering into it, are in total error.

If the eternal, pre-existent Logos (John 1:1-3) incarnates himself thus in Jesus of Nazareth, this naturally includes a statement about his origin, and this statement will obviously have a negative accent, namely, that his genesis is different from ours and hence he cannot be understood in normal genetic and genealogical categories. There can be no doubt that the conception by the Holy Spirit as this is taught by the Apostles' Creed corresponds in this regard to the genesis of Jesus Christ and carries with it an exclusion of Adoptionism.

What is signified by it can be seen from analogous statements about believers. For in keeping with what is said about the Kyrios the spiritual existence of believers is also posited from above and involves a break with all natural continuities. "But as many as received him, to them gave he the power to become the sons of God, even to them that believe on his name, which were born, not of blood, nor of the will of the flesh, nor of the will of man, but of God" (John 1:12f.). Believers who receive him do not proceed, then, from the flesh, from the dimension of what is finite, corruptible, and alienated. They belong to the physical realm according to the flesh but they are not characterized thereby in their true and proper being. The spiritual mark they bear excludes and contradicts their carnal genesis. This characterization from above, however, does not eliminate their carnal genesis. It co-exists with it, taking place in its sphere.

The same problem occurs in the nocturnal discussion between Jesus and Nicodemus (John 3:1-13). Here again we read of a new begetting and birth from above, of the Spirit. The basis of this new being does not allow of continuity with natural being and becoming. The new being cannot be a result of this. It comes into it. This is for Nicodemus a problem on which the discussion almost founders: "How can a man be born when he is old? Can he enter the second time into his mother's womb, and be born?" (3:4). Does not physical birth mean endowment with a specific identity which I do not control but which determines me? Does not the new being in regeneration (3:3), which will bring a transformation of my identity, carry with it the postulate that physical birth, which gives me my identity, will have to be repeated? How can there be this radical change within my previous (physical) existence which remains the same?

The miracle of birth of the Spirit is precisely that it is accomplished in our present being and existence. That it is a divinely performed miracle may be seen in the futility of the question as to the How of the relation between the basis of the new being and the established nature of the old being. How can the act of God be measured by the categories of the old aeon? How can it be objectified within the sphere of the experience of the flesh? "The wind bloweth where it listeth, and thou hearest the sound thereof, but canst not tell whence it cometh, and whither it goeth: so is every one that is born of the Spirit" (3:8). Thus the birth from above, the creative act of the Spirit, can take place within the nexus of the generations and yet in such a way that it is grounded in grace and hence eludes the question of the How.

Finally a similar situation arises in the meeting between Jesus and his mother and brethren in Mark 3:31ff. and parallels. He and all who do the will of God are united in the relationship of mother, brothers, and sisters. Their true being is governed not by the relationship *kata sarka,* but by determination by God's will within their natural existence. Thus the natural constitution of existence, the nexus of generations, descent, and physical identity, is relativized, although not eliminated, by the creative intervention of the miracle and calling of the Spirit. "As natural Abrahamic sonship does not rule out the possibility that the children of Abraham might be called children of the devil (John 8:44), so believers, notwithstanding their natural conception and birth from earthly fathers and mothers, are to be regarded as pure 'children of God,' virgin born like God's only-begotten Son, who nevertheless has Joseph as his father" (von Campenhausen, *op. cit.,* pp. 16f.).

It might be said, then, that the "conceived of the Holy Ghost" in the Apostles' Creed points in the direction indicated. It confesses that, while Jesus Christ comes in the nexus of the generations, and has a genealogy, his identity is not determined thereby. It is determined by the fact that he is from above and that his existence is grounded in the creative miracle of the Spirit. The question which arises is whether what is true of believers, namely, that their new being is established within natural continuity, is not also true of the Son of God himself. Can he be the son of both Mary and Joseph and still be "wholly other"?

The Question of the Obligatory Significance of the Doctrine of the Virgin Birth

Our intention in posing the problem of the virgin birth is thus theological. By locating it in this particular context of thought we can achieve a criterion by which to test the doctrine.

If the "conceived of the Holy Ghost" speaks to the christological basis of faith, the "born of the Virgin Mary" is a concept of faith which interprets the basis. It does so by expressing the fact that here the analogy to believers is broken to the extent that one does not just say of Christ that the miracle of the Spirit works itself out in him within the nexus of nature. At one point, if at one point alone, it breaks this nexus. It rules out an earthly father and has Jesus born of a virgin. We have seen the reasons for this teaching in Matthew and Luke. They express it by means of very different concepts of faith. Our task is to consider whether their interpretations are justified. On this will depend our judgment whether the clause in the Apostles' Creed can be a legitimate confessional statement.

Our deliberations thus far have suggested that it is wrong to pose the alternative of legitimacy and truth on the one side and illegitimacy and error on the other. The real question is this: What concept of faith is meant to be confessed by the doctrine of the virgin birth? If the question is put in this way, it is presupposed that the doctrine can be filled out with different (and even erroneous) contents. It is also conceivable that orthodox correctness might be expressing something very erroneous whereas rejection of the virgin birth on christological grounds might be accompanied by true confession of Christ.

What all this amounts to is that the doctrine of the virgin birth as such does not have any necessary implication for *koinonia* with Christ, since it might involve either confession or denial. Hence we have to put more precisely the question whether the virgin birth is an apt and appropriate interpretation of the conception by the Spirit. What is meant by this interpretation and what can it not mean if it is to be a legitimate christological confession?

We shall tackle the problem by listing some negative and positive theses. The negative theses are as follows.

1. The thesis of the virgin birth is theologically insupportable if it is meant to be a biological explanation or even buttressing of the creative work of the Spirit at Christmas. Since the explanation would involve a fresh inexplicable factor, this would be absurd. It would also contradict the underived nature of the work of the Spirit, and of all miracle, as this is taught in the Nicodemus incident.

2. Similarly it is hard to think that the point of the virgin birth is that the exclusion of the male as the designated bearer of humanity can alone make possible man's receptivity for God's word and work.

Karl Barth argues along these lines when he says that man in the sovereignty of his willing and doing and achieving is not free for God's Word, that he is free for this only when that is excluded which since the fall, not creation, distinguishes the male as the bearer of humanity, and that the judgment on the male means that Joseph is not permitted to be the physical father of Jesus (*Credo*, pp. 64f.; E.T. p. 71; cf. CD, I, 2, pp. 193f.). Some obvious difficulties spring to mind. Surely a metaphysics of the sexes, and the attributing of different roles to men and women in the history of salvation, is alien to the NT. Does not the distinction of the sexes disappear in Christ (Galatians 3:28)? Can we say that the fall gives rise to it? In the fall story does not the initiative lie with Eve, even though this does not allow us either to ascribe greater weakness to the woman or to engage in speculation on the sexes?

If in the virgin birth Mary is purely receptive, placing herself in the service of God's promise (Luke 1:38), this is surely not meant to be an allusion to her nature as a woman. Women can be obstinate and pseudo-sovereign as well as receptive; the different roles of Eve and Mary show this. Mary is rescued by her calling from the curving in on self (Luther) which characterizes man, whether man or woman, after the fall. Only thus does she come to represent the new humanity which in faith is opened up to God.

To the degree that later docetic trends view Christ exclusively as God and not as the priestly representative of man, the figure of Mary fills the resultant vacuum. Mary rather than Christ becomes the representative of believing man who is open to God. Mistaken ideas of the virgin birth have undoubtedly formed the presupposition for the competitive relation between Jesus and Mary to which certain mariological speculations constantly lead. The added dogmas of the immaculate conception and the assumption are in line with this train of thought. Cf. on this A. Dhalenne, "Widerchristliche Mariologie," *Luther. Rundblatt*, 11, 1 (1954), pp. 170ff.; G. Ebeling, "Zur Frage nach dem Sinn des mariologischen Dogmas," ZThK (1950), 3, p. 383; E. Wolf, "Ekklesiologie und Mariologie nach dem II. Vaticanum," *Materialdienst* (1967), 2, pp. 21f.; W. Pannenberg, *op. cit.*, pp. 144ff.; E.T. pp. 144f.

3. The doctrine of the virgin birth is finally misunderstood if it is construed docetically and taken to mean that Jesus is not a whole man, that the Logos did not become completely incarnate, and that he touched the circle of humanity only tangentially. Thus the Valentinians argued that quite apart from the absence of a human father Christ received nothing earthly even from Mary, merely passing through her as water through a pipe or canal (*quasi aquam per tubum*).[4] Here the virgin birth is used as

---

[4] According to Irenaeus; cf. von Campenhausen, *op. cit.*, p. 23; and cf. also H. J. Schoeps, *Vom himmlischen Fleisch Christi* (1951), p. 6.

a witness against the incarnation. The doctrine of the immaculate conceptions of Mary seems to be close to this, since it seeks to dam up at an earlier stage the flow of heredity which is Christ's according to the flesh.[5]

We now turn to the positive theses.

1. The virgin birth is interpreted legitimately, i.e., in line with the total christological witness of the NT, when there is derived from it the confession that Jesus Christ is not just a religious man who qualifies himself for the role of a prophet and for particular closeness to God and who by way of this development grows into the status of divine sonship. To the extent that an anti-adoptionist stress is found in the virgin birth it agrees with the consensus of NT testimonies that do not include any reference to it. It also pushes into the background the docetic tendency which the Valentinians found in it. For the anti-adoptionist emphasis means that Christ is Son of God from all eternity. The man Jesus did not become the Son of God. The Son of God became man.[6] Thus the full incarnation is not called in question. Witness is indeed borne to it. At issue is not the self-emulation of a man, even with God's help, but the condescension of God. The virgin birth is thus regarded as a sign which bears witness to the miracle of union. Only thus is this sign an interpretation of the conception by the Spirit in a figure—a figure which bears witness to a special concept of faith and which is hallowed by the faith of the fathers.

2. As a figure, of course, it expresses what is to be said only in broken fashion. It is thus open to misunderstandings which very quickly arise and can be seen even to our own day. Furthermore, it permits what is intended to be put in other forms without any loss of christological fulness as in John's Gospel or the Pauline Epistles.

To sum up, one may say that the doctrine of the virgin birth is an optional rather than an obligatory confession in Christology. It is possible and legitimate when one realizes what is meant and what is not meant by it. This realization is at any rate necessary at certain stages of reflection, e.g., in question and answer dialogs relating to the dogma.

Hence the confession can and should have a place in Christian worship. It makes sense to confess ecumenicity in time as well as space by using the words of the fathers to the extent that the present-day community finds its own heritage of faith in them. Whether it does so, and whether this confession is thus seen to be legitimate, depends on how it is interpreted in teaching and preaching. Without accompanying proclamation the Apostles' Creed is open to question not only at this point but at all points, for without interpretation it might give the impression of being a summary of things that have to be regarded as true (*credenda*) and hence of being a dubious advocate of *fides quae creditur*.

---

[5] Ignatus of Antioch, the first and for a long time the only witness to the virgin birth after Luke and Matthew, opposes docetic implications of this kind; cf. von Campenhausen, *op. cit.*, pp. 29f.

[6] Connected herewith is the significance of Christ as the mediator of creation; cf. Pannenberg, *op. cit.*, pp. 169ff.; E.T. pp. 168f.

Those who cannot recite the article about the virgin birth because of erroneous ideas relating to it do best to keep silence. Since the article is not the basis of Christology, but is simply one of many ways of expressing faith in Christ, tolerance is required here. The question whether it can become part of my own confession of faith depends on what I confess therewith. Simply reciting it, or reciting the Apostles' Creed as a whole, has no confessional rank in and of itself.

In stressing that the "born of the Virgin Mary" needs interpretation, we do not mean that faith begins with a certain degree of intellectualization and bypasses completely the stage of implicit faith. As academic theologians, especially those of the existentialist persuasion, may easily forget, it is possible to adopt a truth by way of the figure of it, i.e., to "have" the truth in the figure. A child can grasp the great mystery of godliness (1 Timothy 3:16), namely, that God was manifest in the flesh, simply by hearing the Christmas story. Hence Christianity should respect the important traditional images.

This respect, and the tendency to conserve, i.e., conservatism as defined in Volume I, do not, of course, rule out the fact that the open mystery of Jesus Christ can be expressed in new confessions as well as in traditional formulations. It bodes well for the vitality of such new confessions if in them, as in the NT itself, the mystery can be stated both with the help of the virgin birth and also without it, as an indication that both forms of statement have a place in the confessing church of Jesus Christ. If the "conceived of the Holy Ghost" has to be left intact as the basis of faith, the "born of the Virgin Mary" as a concept of faith may be omitted without risk to the actual substance of faith.

The church should not merely accustom itself to this type of pluralism and learn to tolerate it. It should be prepared to welcome it in the freedom of the children of God. For ultimately it does not believe in propositions. It believes in the Lord whom propositions can describe only lispingly and in relation to whom no images are adequate. It might even be a form of confession to see the Lord exalted above every confession. It might be a sign of humility to realize that in our words and images we are simply aiming at his truth and can never capture it in this medium of the flesh. There has to be room for this kind of pluralism in other areas too, e.g., in the co-existence of adult and infant baptism.

2. THE DESCENT INTO HELL

Bibliography: P. Althaus, "Niedergefahren zur Hölle," *Zeitschrift für systematische Theologie* (1942), pp. 365ff.; also "Calvins Kampf um seine Lehre vom Leiden Christi," ThBl (1942), 132ff.; W. Bieder, *Die Vorstellung von der Höllenfahrt Christi* (1949); G. Friedrich, TDNT, III, p. 707; A. Grillmeier, LThK, 2nd ed., V, p. 453; H. Heppe, *Reformed Dogmatics* (E.T. 1950), pp. 490ff.; E. Kähler, *Studien z. Te Deum und z. Geschichte d. 24. Ps. in d. alten Kirche* (1958); M. Lauterburg, Art. "Höllenfahrt," RE; B. Reicke,

Art. "Höllenfahrt," RGG³, III, 408ff.; E. Vogelsang, *Der angefochtene Christus bei Luther* (1932); "Weltbild und Kreuzestheologie in der Höllenfahrtsstreitigkeiten der Reformationszeit," *Archiv für Ref.-Gesch.* (1941), 1/2, pp. 90ff.

The question regarding the place of the doctrine of the descent of Christ in dogmatics is hard to answer, the more so as there is such a broad band of possibilities of interpretation. The descent of Christ is sometimes depicted as the low point of his humiliation and the culmination of his passion. But it can also be seen as a symbol of his triumphant exaltation, as his victory over hell and death. Between these two extremes all kinds of variations are possible. There is thus some reason to deal with the doctrine on the border between humiliation and exaltation. Material affinity to the virgin birth may be seen to the extent that we have in the statement about the descent an interpretative figure in exposition of a different event, namely, the death of Jesus. Bultmann says incorrectly that the resurrection of Christ is not a historical event but the mere interpretation of a different historical event, i.e., the death of Jesus. What is untrue of the resurrection is true of the descent. As an interpretative figure or concept of faith it has a similar degree of obligatoriness to the virgin birth. Unlike the resurrection, it cannot be the object of historical investigation. It is an expository idea or image which has come down to us in the tradition. As with the virgin birth, we have to inquire into its legitimacy as such, and the basis of faith must be our criterion. Within it both legitimate and illegitimate things may develop, and have in fact developed, together. One of the errors is that of trying to understand the descent into hell, not as a mere exposition of Christ's death, but as factual information. Since we can know nothing about the inner dimension of Christ's death and passion, nor about the state between Good Friday and Easter Day, from this angle the dogma of the descent becomes the stage for wild speculations which are not subject to any theological control.

Before discussing the differences in exposition, we need to ask first what the word "hell" means in this context. The fact that the term can have various meanings has played an important role in the varying interpretations of the descent.

Hell can simply mean the realm of the dead, like the Hebrew *sheol* and the Greek *hades*. Since the later Judaism of the age of Jesus thought that the righteous went to paradise after death, the realm of the dead came to be used for the place of those who were consigned to shadow and darkness, i.e., Gehenna, the sphere of the damned. In accordance with these two possibilities the descent into hell, as we have seen, can mean either that Christ worked in the realm of the dead, preaching the message of the change of aeons there in exercise of his prophetic office, or that in final fulfilment of his solidarity with sinners he took upon himself the dereliction of the damned in exercise of his priestly office. A third interpretation of the descent is that, as in his fight with demons, he triumphantly defeated the powers of the abyss in exercise of his kingly office.

When we thus link the descent with the different concepts of hell and also with the three offices, although these associations are rare in the tradition, we get some impression of the rich variety of the ideas that have clustered around this dogma.

An added complication is that Gehenna as the place of the damned (Dante) is a general term which in reality covers a whole range of meanings.

As final exclusion from fellowship with God (Luke 16:23ff.) hell is not just a place where the damned are assembled after death. According to Luther it does not have to be any particular place prior to the last judgment. Each man carries his own hell with him wherever he is so long as he feels the final pangs of death and the wrath of God.[7] Hell is thus the torment of banishment from God and imprisonment in nothingness. It is the human aspect of death as distinct from biological termination.[8] Human death is eternal exclusion from the eternal life of God and carries with it the anamnesis that that which snatches away from God's eternity lowers the boom of finitude and signifies for man that he is only man (Genesis 3:22f.), that he is only grass that perishes (Psalm 103:5). If he has thus to go from hence like the beasts (Psalm 49:12; Ecclesiastes 3:19), the *phobos* of this end is precisely that he is not like the beasts, that he is destined for a share in the life of God, and that death cuts this short.

The death of Christ on the cross shares the fate of human finitude, the *schema hamartias*. At the same time there is an even deeper depth of suffering in the cross. Man can hide from himself the mystery of his death. The fact that death is exclusion from his true destiny, that it is a final alienation of existence, that notwithstanding the naturalness of birth and death it is contrary to man's authentic nature, that it disrupts the communications of divine and human love—all this can be clearly seen and therefore suffered only by those who have experienced life from God and the new quality of human life in faith. Those who have no part in this can never know the experience of death in all the wealth of its forms, or, rather, they can conceal this from themselves. They can always take refuge in the provisional and the immediate. A vegetative death corresponds to a vegetative life. With the loss of human existence human death loses its specific significance and can become a trivial extinction which is concealed even from the one who suffers it—what Rilke calls "little death."

The profoundity of the crucifixion of Jesus is that the triviality of death, which is achieved and snatched so cunningly, is remote from this one life. Jesus comes from the side of God. He has eternal life. To be thrust out of this, to be thrown into the nothingness of human death, and to have to suffer final dereliction (Matthew 27:46), is hell. We have here the pains of death felt by Christ as he died on the cross and perished and came under

---

[7] *Exposition of Jonah* (1526), WA, 19, 225; cf. Brecht and Sartre.
[8] Cf. the author's *Tod und Leben*, 2nd ed. (1946); E.T. *Death and Life* (1970).

the power of God.[9] For Luther, then, the descent into hell begins with the crucifixion. This is not a hell into which he descends. It is a hell which he experiences in himself, which he takes upon himself. To be sure, this is only one aspect of the matter in Luther. Yet it is perhaps the most basic.

As in the case of the virgin birth, NT references are few. It is doubtful whether many of the passages quoted are relevant, e.g., Matthew 12:40; Acts 2:24, 27, 31; Romans 10:7; Ephesians 4:8f.[10] Revelation 1:18 says that Christ has the keys of hell and of death. It is presupposed here that the exalted Lord who lives from eternity to eternity has victoriously withstood the conflict. The *loci classici* for the descent in the NT are 1 Peter 3:19 and 4:6. The reference here is to proclamation of the gospel to the dead who lived before the birth and crucifixion of Christ, especially the flood generation, or, as some think, the sons of God who in Genesis 6:2 took wives of the daughters of earth and brought forth "giants in the earth." These verses show strikingly that the doctrine of the descent into hell is a theological interpretation of the crucifixion of Christ, particularly as regards its universal significance. Two elements especially support this universal aspect.

First, it presupposes a specific anti-adoptionist Christology, or, more positively, it implies the thesis that in Jesus Christ the eternal and pre-existent Logos became flesh. If Christ is "from the beginning" (John 8:58), and if we are "chosen in him before the foundation of the world" (Ephesians 1:4; 1 Peter 1:20), this means that his saving work cannot be restricted to the limited historical periods of the post-Christ era. He embraces all ages. No generation is not related to him. Embracing all times, he also embraces all places. He has access to those who are not reached spatially by the message of his salvation.

Second, the universality of his saving work takes on its most profound dimension by reason of its being tied to his passion and lowliness. The eternity of the Logos as such is not in these sayings the reason why Christ's work of redemption extends to all ages and places. This role belongs to his passion and death. This is denoted by the symbolical chronological placing of his preaching to the dead. It takes place between the crucifixion and the resurrection. Hence the descent into hell carries with it the thought that Christ suffers with us the final consequence of death as separation from God. This address to all men takes place at the lowest point on his way of suffering.

Declared here is the fact that even in the depths of his humiliation he is already exalted. He moves through the realm of the dead as Victor. The dead hear him. He no longer leaves them in the power of the abyss. What is symbolized here is the same as that which is denoted when Christ is portrayed as him who bears a crown even on the cross.

In his very crucifixion he thus fulfils his destiny and *is* the exalted

---

[9] Luther, *loc. cit.*
[10] Reicke, *art. cit.*, p. 409.

Lord (Philippians 2:8f.). In a somewhat bold phrase one might say that the doctrine of the descent into hell presents the incarnation of Christ in an extreme form as subcarnation. Precisely with this zone below the flesh it links the universality of the salvation which he achieved by his sacrifice.

The meaning and content of all Christian mission is also set forth herewith. With his victory in the realm of the dead Christ as universal Lord has set his hand on all men in the universe. What is done by way of mission cannot stand under the sign of an activism which imagines that it can of itself carry the message across the globe and bring Christ to the nations. The arm of Christ has already been stretched over the earth, and all missionary work is done only under the shadow of this stretched out arm. While the slogan "demythologization" does no doubt give rise to serious questions in other areas, here the figurative statement demands an unveiling of its conceptual content. For the descent, unlike the resurrection, does not have the facticity of a concrete salvation event. It is the figurative garb for kerygmatic statements which for their part are not tied to the image, since they are grounded in the facts of salvation, namely, in the cross and resurrection, and may thus be made in nonfigurative form as well.

Perhaps one might say, then, that an obligatory statement of faith— the extolling of the universal act of salvation accomplished at the cross, of the incarnation and the subcarnation of Christ—is linked here with an optional metaphor. Since the metaphor has the dignity of a long tradition, it does, of course, express communion of faith with the fathers. Hence the word "optional" does not mean that it can be lightly discarded. The point is rather that, as a way of expressing theological ideas, it calls out with particular urgency for interpretation.

It is understandable that the wealth of theological associations evoked by this figure has made the choice of interpretation especially difficult, so that the descent, as already indicated, can symbolize extreme humiliation on the one side (as solidarity in death and dereliction), and also supreme exaltation on the other side (as victory over death and hell). It would be a mistake, however, to regard these alternative understandings as mutually exclusive, as though one had to choose between them. Humiliation and exaltation (the *status exinanitionis* and the *status exaltationis*) are undoubtedly stages in the salvation event and may thus be developed apart. Nevertheless, they constitute a unity (Philippians 2:8-11) and thus compel us to see each in the other.

The two interpretations are linked in Luther, although with the greater emphasis on the thought of triumph over hell. On the one side Christ partakes of death and dereliction and goes to hell with us and for us (*Sermon on Preparation for Death* [1519], WA, 2, 690; cf. also on Psalm 22:1, WA, 5, 604 and 606, 13ff.). His is, however, a triumphant weakness (cf. the passages in Althaus, *op. cit.*, p. 372). By the very fact that he does his work of redemption in final humiliation, in subcarnation, he becomes the victor and waves his banner as a hero.

In depicting the victory over hell Luther can go to extreme lengths and he is not even afraid of mythological deception theories (E. Seeberg, *Luthers Theologie* [1940], p. 99) in his grimly humorous attempts to make the matter plain. The devil, greedily devouring the tender meats of sin, fails to notice that the one unspotted Son of God falls victim to his cannibalistic lusts. The purity of the Son makes him ill and so turns his stomach that he spews him out again, and with him he spews out sinners who had previously been to his taste. (We are here conflating images from various sources, e.g., Sermon on Matthew 27:57ff. [1525], WA, 17, I, 78f.; for a collection cf. T. Harnack, *Luthers Theologie*, II [1927], pp. 308ff.) In the Torgau Sermon of 1533 (WA, 37, 35ff.) the same concept of triumph is expressed with similar intensity although not quite so crudely. Neither monkery nor worldly might can quench even a spark of hell fire. But this man does it when he comes down with his banner. The devils run and flee as before their death and poison, and all hell with its fire is put out, so that no Christian need ever fear it.

Calvin's exposition is similar, although we do not find the same flights of fancy in him. He lays emphasis mainly on the suffering of dereliction in death, on the divine judgment which the one righteous man suffers for sinners. The triumph of this man over hell and death is a triumph in suffering. To turn aside the severity of divine judgment he had to engage in personal combat with the powers of hell and the terrors of eternal death (Inst., II, 16, 10).

In the Reformed tradition the descent into hell came to be seen increasingly from the standpoint of penalty, of the dereliction of the "Eli, eli, lama sabachthani," and of extreme humiliation, as in J. Altingius, P. van Mastricht, J. Marckius, and J. Cocceius. The Heidelberg Catechism finds the saving significance of this final suffering in solidarity, and hence we catch again the note of victory in the descent. Question 44 asks why we read that he descended into hell, and the answer is that he did so in order that in my severest trials I might rest assured that my Lord Christ has redeemed me from hellish anxiety and anguish by the indescribable torment, pain, and terror which he suffered in soul on the cross and earlier.

XXX

The Kingly Office

Bibliography: P. Althaus, *Die letzten Dinge*, 6th ed. (1956); K. Bornhäuser, *Die Leidens- und Auferstehungsgeschichte Jesu* (1947); E. Brunner, *Das Ewige als Zukunft und Gegenwart* (1953), ch. 15; H. G. Geyer, "Die Gegenwart Christi: Die Auferstehung," *Dtsch. Ev. Kirchentag Hannover* (1967), pp. 463ff.; H. Grass, *Ostergeschehen und Osterberichte* (1956); G. Koch, *Die Auferstehung Jesu Christi* (1959); W. Künneth, *Theologie der Auferstehung*, 4th ed. (1951); R. R. Niebuhr, *Resurrection and Historical Reason* (1957); C. Stange, *Das Ende aller Dinge* (1960); U. Wilckens, *Auferstehung* (1970).

1. SURVEY OF THE PROBLEMS

What is denoted by the kingly office of Christ is his being and work in his exaltation, his lordship over this world and the next. What is graphically depicted already in the descent into hell, his triumph in all space and time, now becomes the theme of the confession that he is exalted at the right hand of God and that all power is given to him in heaven and earth (Matthew 28:18; 1 Corinthians 15:24; Ephesians 1:20f.). The initial act in this exaltation is his resurrection from the dead, his anticipatory victory over the last enemy (1 Corinthians 15:26). The glory of the one who is exalted thus does not erase or cancel humanity, suffering, and lowliness. As it was the basis of his secret majesty in the time of his earthly being and his humility, as crown and cross belonged together here, as he "reigned in weakness" (Luther), so as the exalted one he is still he whose love impelled him to become man and to enter into the solidarity of the most profound humiliation. Even as the risen Lord he still bears the nailmarks of the crucifixion (John 20:24ff.). Even as the Lord who returns in glory he will do again what he has done on earth, namely, gird himself and serve his people. His service is his glory. It is the hallmark of his lordship (Luke 12:37).[1]

Hence the doctrine of Christ's royal office can never be *theologia gloriae*.

---

[1] Käsemann, *Dtsch. Ev. Kirchentag* (1967), p. 430.

It is always part of the *theologia crucis*. The one who rules is the one who serves, the one who suffers in love, the one who suffers with us. We recall again the saying of Thomas Mann that he who loves most is always subject. This is true of him who is exalted to world supremacy. God has made it the destiny of himself and his Son to be subject. Hence Christ's exaltation is not ascent into a mythically supernatural transcendence, into a divine beyond. It maintains identity with the Incarnate and the Crucified.

It is concern for this identity of the crucified Jesus and the exalted Christ which in the sphere of the doctrine of the two natures forces us to say that Christ's human nature shares the royal dignity of the exalted Lord. This might seem at first glance to be barren speculation, but on closer inspection it proves to be a statement which belongs necessarily to the schema of the two natures. We see in it the soteriological determination not to accept any *theologia gloriae* or docetic concept of a cosmocrator but to confess the Savior as one and the same, whether humbled or exalted. To express this there has to be reference to the majesty of the human nature. (The doctrine of the communication of the attributes is an extreme form of this line of thought.) A fine statement of this may be found in J. A. Quenstedt's *Theologia didactico-polemica* (1685), III, 261, where it is pointed out that although the glory is the same, the mode varies, since it belongs to the divine nature from all eternity but to the human nature by and on account of the personal union (cf. H. Schmid, *Dogmatik*, p. 268).

Christ is "the same yesterday, and today, and forever" (Hebrews 13:8). He rules in serving and serves in ruling even though the salvation event divides into phases, of which one manifests the self-emptying of majesty and the other claims and fulfils it.

Within Lutheran orthodoxy the kingly office manifests itself in three forms of lordship. First is the kingdom of power, in virtue of which Christ exercises his divine might in the governing and sustaining of the world and is thus the Lord of history in all its dimensions. Second comes the kingdom of grace, in which Christ is the Redeemer, the Head of his community, and the Lord of the church. Finally we find the kingdom of glory, which as the end of history and the full incursion of the kingdom of God will manifest his secret lordship, so that faith may see what it has believed, what it has previously seen only under the veil of the cross, and unbelief will have to see what it has not believed.

This theological schema is well adapted to set before us the intellectual tasks with which the royal office confronts us. They can only be enumerated here; we cannot tackle them all in the present context.

First, it is a matter of the act of exaltation itself, of the resurrection on the third day. What does this event mean? How far is it an event and not just the symbolical interpretation of another event, namely, the cross? How can a suprahistorical fact take place in the form of a historical process? These are only some of the questions that arise here. We shall deal with them in the next section.

Second, it is a matter of understanding how the kingdom of power and the kingdom of grace are related to one another in the lordship of Christ. What is meant by the personal union between the Lord of the world and the Lord of the community? This brings us to a problem which is thematized in the doctrine of the two kingdoms and which has not only divided the main Protestant confessions[2] but has also led eventually to hotly contested revisions of the doctrine within Lutheranism itself.[3] These issues have been extensively discussed in Volume I of the *Theological Ethics,* and we need not go into them again in this context.[4]

Third, our task is to develop what is meant by the lordship of Christ in the kingdom of glory. This question is part of the theme of eschatology and will be dealt with in that context. We shall thus close our Christology in the narrower sense with the subject of the resurrection.

2. THE RESURRECTION OF CHRIST

Bibliography: The following works have been chosen out of the vast body of literature either because they are particularly relevant to this chapter or because they supplement it: G. Bertram, "Die Himmelfahrt Jesu vom Kreuz und der Glaube an seine Auferstehung," *Festschrift Deissmann* (1927); E. Bickermann, "Das leere Grab," ZNW, 23 (1924), pp. 281ff.; H. von Campenhausen, *Der Ablauf der Osterereignisse und das leere Grab, Sitzungsberichte der Heidelb. Akademie der Wissenchaften* (1952); H. Conzelmann, "Jesus von Nazareth und der Glaube an den Auferstandenen" in H. Ristow and K. Matthiae, *Der historische Jesus und der kerygmatische Christus* (1960); G. Friedrich, "Die Auferweckung Jesu, eine Tat Gottes oder ein Interpretament der Jünger," KD (1971), 3, pp. 153-187; E. Hirsch, *Die Auferstehungsgeschichte und der christliche Glaube* (1940); G. Kittel, "Die Auferstehung Jesu," *Dtsch. Theol.* (1937), 4, pp. 133-168; K. Lehmann, "Auferweckt am 3. Tage nach der Schrift," *Quaestiones disputatae,* 38 (1968); W. Marxsen, *Die Auferstehung Jesu als historisches und als theologisches Problem* (1964); also *Die Auferstehung Jesu von Nazareth* (1968); W. Michaelis, *Die Erscheinungen des Auferstandenen* (1944); F. Mussner, *Die Auferstehung Jesu* (1969); K. H. Rengstorf, *Die Auferstehung Jesu,* 5th ed. (1967); K. Schubert, "Das Problem der Auferstehungshoffnung in den Qumrantexten und in der frührabbinischen Literatur," *Wiener Zeitschrift für die Kunde des Morgenlandes,* 56 (1960), 154ff.

A preliminary note on the following chapter seems to be needed.

No theologian can deal with the resurrection of Christ without becoming involved in innumerable debates. These are both historical and theological in origin.

---

[2] Cf. Barth's attack on the doctrine.
[3] Cf. the debate between J. Heckel ("Im Irrgarten der Zwei-Reiche-Lehre," ThEx, 50 [1957] and P. Althaus ("Luthers Lehre von den beiden Reichen im Feuer der Kritik," *Luth.-Jahrb.* [1957], pp. 40ff.; "Die beiden Regimente bei Luther. Zu J. Heckels 'Lex charitatis,' " ThLZ [1956], 3, pp. 129ff.).
[4] Cf. esp. ThE, I, § 1783ff.; E.T. I, pp. 359ff. On the debate between Lutherans and Reformed (Barth, Kuyper, and van Ruler) cf. ThE, II, § 4000ff.; E.T. II, pp. 565ff.

They are historical inasmuch as modern secular empiricism, which starts with the axiom of self-resting finitude, finds it absurd that a supranatural event should occur within historical processes or should be recorded in historical reports of concrete happenings. They are theological to the extent that the NT narratives raise the claim that this event, which breaks the immanent continuity of occurrence and is predicated as a historical fact, is the very axis of the Christian faith.

The conjoining of the historical and the suprahistorical dimensions poses problems which set much more delicate tasks for critical reflection than the dogmas of the virgin birth and the descent into hell.[5] For whereas the descent might be regarded as the symbolical expositions of very different events, namely, the events of Good Friday and Easter Day, so that there does not have to be a direct uniting of history and suprahistory, the very heart of the Christian faith is assailed if we try to see the resurrection of Christ as no more than the symbolical interpretation of a different event, namely, as an expression of the significance of the cross (Bultmann). To question the facticity of the Easter event is to contradict the very point of the Easter witness of the NT. On the other hand, if one rejects the task of seriously investigating the epistemological and ontological problems which are raised by the conjoining of historical and suprahistorical events, this is to give the appearance of evading the claim of the modern understanding of reality and of parting company with the contemporary world.

It is undoubtedly connected with the difficulty which modern immanentism finds in the NT accounts that recourse is had to a purely psychological—the vision hypothesis—or existential interpretation. Such theories avoid the ontological problem posed by the recording of non-objectifiable events as historical. They regard the Eastern stories as being of the same literary genre as the accounts of the virgin birth, the descent into hell, and the ascension. In contrast, our own concern will be to indicate and establish a fundamental difference.

We can thus write our chapter on the resurrection only in constant dialog with opposing scholars and especially in debate with the Bultmann school. We have thus to take up once again the controversy with Bultmann which occupied us in Volume I (Chapters III and IV). The resurrection kerygma provides us with a decisive model in this area.

a. The Significance of the Resurrection for Faith

The central significance of the fact that Christ rose from the dead and became the first-fruits (*aparché*) of those that slept (1 Corinthians 15:20) is beyond question in the NT writings. The resurrection has this significance here as an event which took place in time and space even if it cannot be explained in terms of time and space. The declaration of this transub-

---

[5] Cf. also the doctrine of the ascension.

jective "event-ness" is at the heart of the argument in 1 Corinthians 15, some twenty-five years after the death of Jesus.

The emphasis in this distinctly theological argument does not lie on the historical indications of the event-ness nor on the multiple testimony to the resurrection appearances. The "proofs," which even externally are localized as introductory observations (vv. 1-8), simply serve as a preamble to the true argument. As a prolegomenon they have a double purpose. First they testify to the good historical conscience of the community. Second, along with the historical proof they safeguard the transubjective nature of the event and serve as a prophylactic against spiritualizing, i.e., against interpretations which depict the event as purely subjective, e.g., in psychogenic terms.

The historical demonstration, however, is not itself theological. Although the introduction in vv. 1-2 shows how important the story is for faith, we are not shown by the references how momentous this (transubjective) event is for the existence of the Christian.

The importance of the event is brought out from v. 12 onward, and here Paul argues from its opposite. His leading question is this: What if Christ had not risen? Then everything else contained in evangelical and apostolic proclamation would be incomplete, like an "i" without the dot. Indeed, it would be futile and meaningless. Preaching would be without point, even the preaching of the words and deeds of Jesus. Faith in the preached word would collapse, even faith that he was wounded for our transgressions and bruised for our iniquities (Isaiah 53:5). We (i.e., the apostles) should be unmasked as false witnesses. What we proclaim concerning the death of Christ would have no cogency. In describing it as an atoning death we should be reading too much into it and ascribing to it a rank and effect that it does not really have. All this would be entailed if Christ were not risen. We should still be in our sins. We should be locked in our finitude (vv. 14-19). The dead who in their last hour confessed him as their only comfort in life and in death would have staked everything on the wrong card and been shown up as fools.

Paul conjures up this apocalyptic vision in order to show that everything depends on the fact of the resurrection. Jean Paul takes a similar tack when in his "Sermon of the Dead Christ" he declares that there is no God[6] and works out what it would finally mean if Christ were mistaken and we were orphans. In this way the positive message of the existence of God is contrasted with its absurd opposite and its credibility is thereby strengthened.

Paul, of course, is not just saying that the resurrection kerygma *brings out* the meaning of the birth, life, suffering, and death of Jesus. Both in his didactic listing of the witnesses and also in his apocalyptic depiction of what no resurrection would imply, he is stating that the resurrection *effects* and *establishes* this meaning by its ontic facticity within the historical process.

---

[6] Cf. Volume I, pp. 236-242.

If the resurrection kerygma were simply disclosing meaning noetically, the life and death of Jesus would be effective even without this disclosure. The lack of noetic evidence would simply mean that they would not be effective for me.

Paul, however, is saying the direct opposite. Without the resurrection the life, suffering, and death of Jesus would be robbed of all saving significance. Jesus would lose his calling as Savior. Indeed, he would never have had it.

For Paul then, the point of the resurrection is not that it discloses and demonstrates but that it puts in force. It does not merely shed light on an event that would otherwise be obscure; it makes this event ontically what it is, namely, a series of salvation happenings. It grants to the event of the life of Jesus a privilege which makes it more than the subject of just another biography. In other words, the resurrection has ontic as well as noetic significance.[7]

All references to the meaning of the resurrection are thus designed to solidify its ontological historicity. Christ *is* risen. Existential interpretation has its place as a means of appropriation. It is preceded, however, by the ontic decree.

As Paul makes heuristic use of the negation of the resurrection, the positive aspects might be put to similar use. G. Wingren offers an example of this in his *Die Predigt* (1955), p. 156: "If we accept the resurrection of Christ with all that it includes, his exaltation, his judicial authority, his lifegiving power, his right to grant eternal remission of sins, then we have in this fact of the resurrection adequate grounds for preaching the gospel to every generation and every people on earth. The hitherto unstated presupposition of every attack on Christianity is the conviction, frequently taken for granted, that Christ never did rise from the dead. . . ."

b. The Problem of Facticity

Herewith the problem of the facticity of the Easter event is posed—the question of fact. Kerygma theology undoubtedly underestimates this aspect in consequence of its premises. We thus need to ask why it does this, and we shall discover the real problem of facticity by removing this obstacle of its premises.

Why does the problem of facticity play so minor a role in it? If we are right, various reasons may be advanced.

The first has to do with the relation between fact and meaning.

The question of the significance of the event replaces that of its facticity. The ontic question as to the being and character of the event itself pales before that of its meaning.

Bultmann's approach makes this clear.

---

[7] Cf. ThE, I, § 596; E.T. I, pp. 108ff. (on K. Barth).

1. According to Bultmann, for well-known reasons which we may now omit, the work of God cannot take place in objective experience. Its presentation thus is a mark of myth, which is to be taken seriously as a mode of expression and is by no means to be eliminated. What it expresses, of course, can be achieved only by interpretation, i.e., by stripping off the mythical form. If one asks what is the purpose of the mythical form, the only possible answer is that these texts seek to change my self-understanding in the sense of making me contemporary, so that I no longer fix on the past or anxiously project myself into the future, but achieve the present.[8]

Only as the texts are thus interpreted with reference to my self-understanding can two results be achieved.

The first is a detachment of the mythical statement from its time-relatedness, e.g., from the cosmological vesture in which the earth is viewed as a disk. This enables me to see that the cosmological system of co-ordinates within which the kerygmatic statement is made does not have to be believed as well. The time-related ciphers of statements of faith are not themselves legitimate objects of faith. Consequently I am not tied to ideas current when the statements were formulated. I can believe as a modern man.

The second result is positive. If time-relatedness is negated, relevance is achieved. I can interpret the kerygmatic statement *ad hominem,* i.e., in relation to my self-understanding. This relevance is a fruit of the insight that in this kerygma which comes home to me we have themes of existential knowledge which I was already aware of, which already applied to me, and which are simply appropriated here, e.g., the themes of righteousness and guilt. What I already knew about such things in the form of pre-understanding is actualized by proclamation and fashioned into a new understanding.

Along these lines, one cannot recognize a historical event of revelation in time in the sense of a fact, a miracle, which invades and changes reality, even the reality outside man. This would be a mythological understanding. Bultmann can recognize an event of revelation only in the sense that it brings and releases self-understanding—the self-understanding which I could never produce on my own. What takes place is not a reality outside man; it is consciousness. The predicate in the statement in the Prologue to John: "The word was made flesh," does not denote a historical fact in the manger at Bethlehem. It denotes the act of change in my own self-understanding which comes from this historical site. To put it pointedly, what is reported as historical in the NT is not itself event. It is the prolegomenon of an event, namely, the event of my own change of consciousness.

When, therefore, Bultmann seems to stress very sharply the event character of the kerygma in contrast to Liberal theology, we should be under no illusions as to the rank of this event. Our impression is—and we shall try to support this in what follows—that the event has as it were the rank of a

---

[8] Cf. G. Ebeling, *Theologie und Verkündigung* (1962), p. 88; E.T. *Theology and Proclamation* (1966), p. 88.

postulate. It is an inference from the Christian self-consciousness or the existential self-understanding.

What this means is that the new existential relation is only made possible by the Christ event in the background. But this event itself is no more phenomenological than the postulate of God in Kant. The men of the NT, and we with them, are sitting in Plato's cave, or so it seems to me, and simply seeing the shadows of our consciousness which then permit the inference of a background reality that gives rise to them. When Bultmann speaks about the supramythological element in the core event which lies behind the Christian self-understanding, he simply makes the negative point that the story of Jesus, his cross, should not be investigated historically, since its significance arises out of what God wants to say to me through it. The meaning of the figure of Jesus is not to be grasped in terms of its immanent context. Put mythologically, Jesus is not of natural or human origin; his derivation is eternal.[9] Eternity denotes the fact that the incarnate Logos involves a self-understanding which cannot be grasped in terms of the objective phenomenology of immanent reality. Strictly, the key sentence in Bultmann ought to run: "The Word was not made of flesh."

In arguing that according to Bultmann the only event is consciousness, we obviously do not mean that consciousness is autogenetic, that it is self-producing in a Socratic or any other sense. An event is needed to trigger it. It has to be set going deistically. This is the basically negative and indirect statement about the event background of the NT kerygma, and of the self-understanding mediated thereby, which we think we detect in Bultmann.

2. As regards the resurrection this means that there is no further interest in its facticity. What matters is the way in which it contributes to my understanding of Christ, irrespective of what may lie behind it ontically. In this connection Bultmann maintains that *what is said* about the resurrection can only be an *expression* of the significance of the cross.[10] Note that Bultmann refers only to words ("what is said," "expression"). When a change in self-understanding is at issue, there is in fact no need to reflect about an event. This self-understanding is influenced by words, by poetic figures, by philosophizing, by the message of writers. In introverted fashion, the whole focus is on the event in existence and the immanent processes of consciousness. All interest in the ontological quality of that which triggers the change is extinguished.

The word of the resurrection is important to me only to the extent that I find out from it how the primitive community understood the cross, namely, as judgment on the world and liberating judgment on man.[11] This means that the death of Jesus was regarded as more and other than a martyrdom. It was fraught with significance which passed unnoticed at the

---

[9] KM, p. 35.
[10] KM, p. 38.
[11] KM, p. 37.

time it took place but which struck the disciples later under the influence of visionary impulses.

With this interpretation Bultmann avoids the offense that the assumed facticity of the resurrection gives to the historical consciousness when it tries to conceive of something as having happened even though it lies outside the framework of ordinary historical events like birth, suffering, and death, and is in principle nonverifiable.

It seems, then, that many advantages are gained at a single stroke. Categories of the NT age such as myth, magic, and cosmology, which might be obstacles to faith, are removed by interpreting them as mere forms of expression for faith. Relevance is achieved for the past to the extent that my present self-understanding is affected.

This whole approach has fundamental implications for theological epistemology. The most important of these is what is usually called the removal of the subject-object correlation. If normative rank is accorded to the existential interpretation, the emphasis shifts from the past event to my momentary present, to the change in my self-understanding, to what might be called the event of faith.

What takes place in salvation history is thus reduced to a present result, namely, dying and rising again with Christ. What the NT tells us about the past death and resurrection of Christ is not a chain of events that can be detached from this. The underlying reality of what is narrated cannot be a condition for the dying and rising again with Christ. These can be grounded in the mere word of the resurrection, in what may be just a figurative word, and they can be achieved through this "word" along the lines of "perish and become."

Only in this sense are the kerygmatic account of the past and the kerygmatic promise for the present indissolubly related. Only he who now fulfils salvation history for himself as perishing and becoming can understand the past. This past is no longer important in virtue of its character as ontic event. It is important only in terms of what it triggers now. As noted, it can exercise this function as a trigger simply as kerygma, i.e., as "what is said about" or "an account of. . . ."

To this extent what is reported, spoken of, and proclaimed can remain an X ontologically. The present can claim equal rights with, if not priority over, what is usually called the salvation history of the years A.D. 1-30.

This is best expressed in the equal ranking of the past of salvation history with the present of salvation history in the Tübingen work *Für und wider die Theologie Bultmanns* (1952), p. 32:

> We are accustomed to distinguish between the objective content of faith and the subjective act of faith. The more this way of putting it pretends to be the only appropriate one, the more it runs the danger of radically misunderstanding what the Bible and the reformation call faith. For it gives the impression that the divine act of salvation which constitutes the content of faith stands over against the act of man which subjectively appropriates in

faith that which is divinely objective. In this way the essence of faith is turned into its opposite. In the NT faith is the work of God in which God makes an event here and now of what he did once and for all in Jesus Christ. In saying: "I believe," the believer confesses at the same time: "I live, yet not I, but Christ lives in me" (Galatians 2:20). That faith is the same work of God, now taking place in me, as the work done for me once and for all in Jesus Christ is one of the basic insights of the reformation and only in this very close union of faith and salvation event can one say that the justification of the sinner takes place through faith alone. This means exactly the same as confession of justification through Christ alone, since God's act in Christ cannot be isolated from faith as the becoming present of this act. Conversely faith can as little be detached from that act of God in Christ.

The result to which we are led by this train of thought may be summed up as follows. That in which faith believes, to the extent that it is a past event or can be reported as such, can no longer be separated from the present fulfilment of faith. To this extent the subject-object relation is eliminated.

Thus the new thing in the rise of Easter faith is not a new object of faith but the rise, the kindling, the coming to life of faith itself (G. Ebeling, *Das Wesen des christlichen Glaubens* [1959], p. 72; E.T. *The Nature of Faith* [1961], p. 62). Even verbally faith acquires an almost autonomous subject-role as that which takes place in existence now. The table of contents of Ebeling's book shows this, for the nature of Christian faith is dealt with exclusively in terms of faith as subject ("The History of Faith," "The Basis of Faith," "The I of Faith," etc.) This can be carried to the point where faith seems to be a constitutive element in the salvation event and even in the Easter event itself, so that one is reminded of the saying of Angelus Silesius that God can live no Now without me. Faith even has a share in the resurrection of the crucified Lord, since it confesses Jesus publicly as Lord (Romans 10:9f.) (E. Fuchs, "Die Spannung im neu-testamentlichen Christusglauben," ZThK [1962], 1, 42). Christ is risen if this confession is a statement of love (*ibid.,* p. 43).

c. The Relation between Faith and Historical Knowledge

If this elimination of the subject-object correlation is a consequence of the theological approach at issue, it can also appeal to other arguments which we must now consider and critically evaluate. (They are already intimated in the long quotation on the previous page.)

The elimination of the subject-object correlation rests also on the serious concern that its retention would lead to the following epistemological situation.

Quite apart from faith, e.g., by philological and historical analysis, a specific event, in this case the resurrection, might be established as an objective event, or, better, as a miracle that has really taken place. On the basis of this demonstration the possibility of belief in this historically verifiable miracle might then be shown. Belief in this case would be subsequent subjective assent to what is first known objectively in proof of the credibility of what is to be believed. But all this is soteriologically as well as epistemologically impossible, for it would equate faith, not with confidence, but with the certainty of sight, and in addition it would make it a function of human cooperation.

The only question is whether this impossible procedure can be avoided only by eliminating the subject-object relation itself and consequently by making the ontological character of the Easter event a matter of indifference. Bultmann and his disciples (especially Ebeling) are right at least when they point out that historical knowledge and faith cannot be separated in the manner described. They are closely related. Faith is not subsequent assent to what is first to be known apart from faith. In relation to Easter, knowledge itself is already bound up with faith.

This is true because knowledge, insofar as it concerns things and events affecting our existence, is a work which is determined by the state of the acting and knowing person.[12] The one who is captive to finitude and the existing situation cannot know that which transcends them. Only he whose existence itself is taken up by the witness and act of the Spirit[13] into the death and resurrection of the Lord is placed in the situation of analogy from which the resurrection can be a possible object of knowledge. There can thus be no question of a knowledge by which faith relates itself to its own object.

Only the believer perceives this event. Only he who is in the truth, who exists in believing death and resurrection with and after Jesus, hears the voice of the empty tomb. Apart from this situation of faith Easter is not in fact verifiable.

d. The Ontological Singularity of the Easter Event as Illustrated by the Problem of the Empty Tomb

What has been said applies especially to the Easter event. Ontologically this is hard to put on the same plane as historically objectifiable events like the "suffered under Pontius Pilate, crucified, dead and buried." The non-objectifiability of the resurrection, however, is to be differentiated sharply from the question whether it did in fact take place transubjectively, i.e., really, in the external world, and is not just to be attributed to visionary experiences of the disciples. To this objectivity the NT bears very definite witness with every possible argument.

The noetic problem, however, concerns objectifiability. How far is it possible to establish the event of the resurrection neutrally and apart from faith? No less unambiguously the NT returns a negative answer to this question of objectifiability. (If it causes some surprise that objectivity, with its

---

[12] Luther, WA, 18, 709.
[13] Cf. Volume I, Chapters IX and X.

freight of epistemological tradition, is affirmed, this is because it is usually understood as the presupposition of a possible objectifiability; hence some might prefer to speak of transubjectivity rather than objectivity. At any rate, this is the sense in which we are using it here.)

That the NT witness does in fact deny the objectifiability of the Easter event may be seen already from the fact that only those who had been in touch with the earthly Jesus witnessed the resurrection. No others, Jews or Gentiles, are brought forward as witnesses. To make the testimony more convincing, and to meet the objection of prejudice on the part of believers and disciples, there would surely have been great interest in neutral witnesses "outside faith" if objectifiability had been regarded as legitimate or possible. But sufficient instruction had been given by him who walked on earth to make it clear that miracle is in principle non-objectifiable even though it may be perceived by the senses as in the case of the feedings and healings. Important here is a point that we made earlier, namely, that miracle is in principle ambivalent. In relation to what it is meant to attest, and to its nature as a *semeion*, faith cannot be replaced by sight. Miracle demands faith and withholds itself from objectifying knowledge.

Reserve in respect of a possible objectifiability of the miracle of Easter also finds expression in the NT to the extent that categorical attestation of the fact of the resurrection almost completely crowds out the question of its manner. There is a sharp antithesis here to apocryphal accounts. When hints are given of an apparently objectifiable process, the imagination seems to have been at work.[14] When men are totally apprehended, it is only natural that the imagination should also bear interpretative witness.

It is at these points especially that apparent discrepancies appear in the accounts. These are instructive—if one might put it thus—inasmuch as they show that our categories become crossed when even the slightest attempt is made to objectify miracle.[15]

An analogy from the field of physiology might help us here. J. Müller (1801-58) has shown that a blow in the face affects sight and hearing even though the appropriate nerves receive no direct message. The senses feel that they are involved and they thus produce impressions, not on their own initiative, but in reaction to something outside which bears witness to itself in these effects. But because there is nothing the eye can see or the ear hear, because there is no transposition of a reality appropriate to ear and eye, the indirectness of the impression means that the reality perceived seems to be contradictory and inadequate, various noises being heard and phenomena seen. The analogy is in many ways a poor one, but if the point of comparison is kept in mind it will help us to understand what happens

---

[14] In the canonical Gospels cf. Matthew 28:4ff.; Mark 16:5; Luke 24:4; John 20:1ff.

[15] Cf. the story of the conversion of Paul (Acts 9:1ff.; 1 Corinthians 15:8).

when the suprasensory event of the resurrection is transposed into the dimension of sensory perception.

The NT witnesses, with their love of truth, do not even try to harmonize the resultant stories. They let them stand even though they seem to be contradictory. They thus offer us an illustration of the non-objectifiability to which we have referred. Even if the NT authors were unaware of the noetic situation, and certainly could not describe it in strict epistemological terms, by letting the apparent discrepancies stand they bore unintentional witness to it with what one might call the instinct of the children of God.

We thus maintain that the non-objectifiability of the resurrection is to be strictly differentiated from its ontic character as a transubjective event. Its non-objectifiability comes to expression in the NT in the almost complete absence of statements about the manner of the resurrection. Its transubjectivity comes to expression in the solid testimony that is given to the fact of it.

When Ebeling insists on an indissoluble connection between knowledge of the resurrection and faith in the resurrected Lord, he rightly quotes Luther's exposition of the second article of the Creed. But he appeals to Luther illegitimately when he makes faith the real focus of the salvation events, so that the "then" of the christological event becomes fundamentally a function of the "now" of faith.

To clarify the epistemological situation as thus envisaged, one might adduce Kantian transcendentalism, to which Bultmann, unwittingly perhaps, has a vital connection by way of his teacher W. Herrmann. Here what is real is the world of my experience, in which an ontic X, the "thing in itself," plays a part, since it affects my forms and categories of perception, but which is essentially constituted by my own contribution, my forms of consciousness. The original ontic element can no longer be apprehended. What really happens takes place in the Now of my act of experience. One has only to put faith for act of experience and the events of A.D. 1-30 for the "thing in itself" and the analogy is complete. Religious objects, to speak unguardedly, do not exist apart from me, apart from the structure of my consciousness, apart from my appropriation, apart from the change in my self-understanding. They exist only in their significance. But this is the product of my active apprehension, i.e., of my interpretation. The self-consciousness which is affected by an ontic X constitutes the world of experience of faith. This leads to the mystical position already mentioned, namely, that God can live no Now apart from me. Christological events can live no Now apart from me, apart from my faith, because they depend on this faith, they are oriented to it, and they thus lose their ontic independence and therewith their ontic character.

As we have seen, Wobbermin was thinking along the same lines when he liked to quote Luther's saying that faith and God are part of the same heap. What Luther meant, of course, was that without faith we can make no statements about God. Wobbermin, however, draws the false inference that faith constitutes God in his being in encounter with me. This is opposed to Luther. In Luther's ontology of the Word of God it is decisive that this Word is a real transubjective event, an event which takes place even when man does not receive the Word, or misunderstands it, or contests it. (Cf. in this connection the Lutheran doctrine that the wicked, too, feed on the body of Christ.)

A further observation might be made in confirmation. Eschatology is affected as well when the ontic event-character of the Then apart from faith is denied. For the word "eschatological" denotes in this case a mere aspect under which I see past events and records. They are not just historical, i.e., important in their own time and place. They are important for every possible self-understanding. Eschatology, then, is no longer the doctrine of things to come or events whose real manifestation—the *parousia*—I await. It is simply a term for the significance of messages whose ontic background escapes our field of vision. As Wingren puts it in *Predigt*, p. 168, faith cannot basically be expectation of events if it does not rest basically on events. The awaited second coming is replaced by the eternal present of eschatology, the "moment" of Kierkegaard. The Christ who has already come is the end of history (E. Fuchs); we do not watch and wait for this end. From this standpoint history is singularly deprived of its reality. (E. Käsemann seems to have made a significant break with this nonfuturist eschatology of the Bultmann school; cf. his essay "Zum Thema der urchristlichen Apokalyptik," ZThK [1962], 3, pp. 257ff.)

How, then, can we legitimately maintain facticity?

In our approach to facticity we need the help of history, i.e., an analysis of the texts. The controlling questions in this investigation are as follows: (1) to what degree are the texts trying to express a transubjective event which has taken place in time and space? and (2) what theological importance do they attach to this transubjective-ontic element? Answering these questions is a task for NT scholarship. In this context we must be content simply to say that notwithstanding individual differences both questions may be answered positively. The systematic theologian has here a different task from that of the NT scholar. He has to say something about the basic rank of such analyses of the texts when the issue is whether and how far they can help faith to confidence respecting the facticity of its object.

This investigation is methodologically important. From what has been said already, we may state that it is a mistake to give this analysis of the texts the task of furnishing faith with indisputable historical data and thus changing the assurance of faith into objectifying historical certainty as to the fact of the resurrection, e.g., by arguing that this is the best attested fact in the history of antiquity. It has already been pointed out that for good reasons the NT does not offer a neutral and noninvolved affirmation of the resurrection events. Those who have no relation to the risen Lord—and this relation can only be one of faith—cannot accept the resurrection as either possible or factual. The risen Lord is Lord not only of death but also of the resurrection itself.

Historical proof does not precede faith as the ground of its possibility or as its condition. The role of the empty tomb makes this plain in exemplary fashion. Even if one agrees with H. von Campenhausen[16] that unprejudiced historical analysis leads to the conclusion that the tomb was with a very high degree of probability empty, this finding does not mean that we have a miracle which makes faith easier or possible. There are three reasons for this.

a. The first is theological. Faith tied to miraculous preconditions would no longer be faith. It would be replaced by sight and would thus be superfluous. But this is seeking after signs.

b. The second is empirical. Other reasons (some criminal) can be found for the disappearance of the body of Jesus. A certain ambivalence marks the disappearance. This is not just an empirical statement. It also contains a theological appraisal of the empirical element. All miracle is ambivalent. Faith cannot be replaced by objective sight.

c. The third is ontological. The resurrection stories bear witness to the identity of the risen Lord with the earthly Jesus. They do so by referring to the wounds of the cross borne by the Resurrected (John 20:25ff.). Nevertheless, they also indicate discontinuity in the mode of physical existence (1 Corinthians 15:45ff.). The earthly Jesus and the risen Lord have a different bodily quality analogous to the difference in modes of being between the first Adam (*psychḗ zôsa*) and the second Adam (*pneúma zōopoioún*) (15:45). Hence belief in the resurrection is not tied to the fact of the empty tomb, since the latter, while it can make a statement, ambivalent though it is, about the fate of the old body, lacks any competence to make a statement about the difference between the old and the new corporeality.

The empty tomb is not the thing that makes faith possible. On the contrary, it can provoke the reaction: "They have taken away my Lord, and I know not where they have laid him" (John 20:13). Only in relation to the resurrection appearance is the question of the empty tomb significant. Its significance is obviously this. The emptiness of the tomb confirms already existing faith in the risen Lord. It thus becomes a witness to the background reality, and consequently the nonsubjectivity, of the encounters with the risen Lord.

e. The Rank of the Question of Historical Truth

Since that which can be established historically cannot be a basis of faith, the question arises as to the place, if any, of the question of historical truth. In these circumstances is it not enough to adopt the kerygma as we have it in the Gospels without engaging in any historico-critical investigation? If, however, this is not enough, if the kerygma of the resurrection has also to be the object of research into its historical truth and facticity, will not

---

[16] *Der Ablauf der Osterereignisse und das leere Grab* (1952).

this have to be for a very different reason than that of proving or even buttressing faith? And if so, what?

The following arguments may be advanced for not abandoning historico-critical study and at the same time for according it theological rank.

(1) Historical reason cannot be suppressed. If it were, faith would not be that of the whole man. Some sectors of the I would be shut out. Faith would then be reduced to a partial religious province.

A psychological manifestation of this degeneration of faith would be that the believer would have to suppress some aspects of the question of truth, i.e., the historical. The subject of faith, however, cannot be divided, i.e., into a religious and rational ego, any more than the truth can be divided. There can be no cleavage between the truth of faith and salvation and the truth of reason and history. The differently oriented questions of truth have to bear with one another. This is one reason why we have to put the historical question as to the facticity of the object of faith.

(2) The second reason is that only as we put the objectifying historical question does the frontier emerge which separates it from the relation of faith to its historical object. Whereas the first reason made it plain that historical work serves faith by testifying to its indivisibility, we see from this second reason that faith has significance for the personal knowledge of what is known historically. In elucidation we may refer to the observation in 1 Corinthians 15:17:[17] "If Christ be not risen . . . ye are yet in your sins."

This tells us first that if Christ remained dead and has no death-defeating presence, he cannot forgive sins.

It then tells us—and this is the decisive point—that if and so long as we are still in our sins, not having died to sins but being still their captive, we cannot grasp or accept the news of the resurrection. For our concern is still to remain autonomous. We do not want Christ to have power over us. When we want to be our own lords, we cannot tolerate any other lord. Hence the news that Christ is Lord in virtue of his resurrection is unacceptable to us. This is why Wingren can say that in the facticity at issue here is enclosed the facticity of our captivity.[18] Noetically this captivity takes the form of prejudice.

What happens here, then, is not that the historian is made aware of the epistemological difficulty which consists in the fact that he is supposed to verify an event like the resurrection for which there is no cause, analogy, or immanent condition. The historian knows this difficulty already. He has already publicized it. It results from contemporary philosophical theories in the noetic field. The historian is confronted here with a difficulty of a different kind which he himself cannot diagnose since it belongs already to the sphere of objects of faith. This difficulty consists in our being captives without Christ. We are captives in mind too. Existential factors—self-

---

[17] Cf. Wingren, *op. cit.*, p. 159.
[18] *Ibid.*

assertion, anthropocentricity, and supposed autonomy—prevent us from recognizing in history the realities which threaten these basic existential attitudes. In this regard Paul in Romans 1:18ff. points out the connection between knowledge and sin.

Knowledge, as we have shown elsewhere, is not just a matter of reason and the critique of reason, as Kant thought. It is a matter of existence, by whose hopes and fears reason is also affected. Thomistically, the existential condition of reason has to be considered as well as its nature.[19]

The situation at issue, which can be described only dialectically, is as follows.

First thesis: Only the fact that Jesus Christ is risen from the dead makes it possible for me to die with him (to die to sin and escape its bondage) and also to rise again with him, and thus to walk in newness of life and to be in the truth.

Second thesis: Only when I am in the truth do I hear his voice; only when I die and rise again with Christ can I appropriate noetically his death and resurrection.

In terms of the second thesis, then, faith must acknowledge historical work on its objects in order to show the historian his limit and his possibility: his limit to the extent that he might be bound and prejudiced and therefore hampered in a manner that he could not even suspect without faith; his possibility to the extent that as a believer he can find his way to certainty, validly asking about the facticity of the basis of his new being, even though this facticity cannot be objectified with the immanent criteria of historical research.

(3) The third and in this context the decisive reason for the necessity of historical work is the indispensability of counter-criticism.[20] If historical work cannot be regarded as the critical survey of a territory where faith might settle, it does have the task of discovering whether the results of historical criticism are or are not in contradiction with Easter faith. For obviously something which is demonstrably nonfactual cannot be an object of faith. In this case it would violate our postulate under (1) that truth is indivisible. Easter faith would be possible only in virtue of a split in consciousness. This is intolerable.

The point of historical work in relation to Easter faith, then, is not critical preparation but counter-criticism, i.e., contending against historico-critical presentations that might rob Easter faith of its historical basis. In an incidental way this struggle will entail much detailed analysis; but its primary concern will be whether the historicism against which it does battle does not rest on a defect in epistemological approach, i.e., on what we have called the captivity or prejudice which results in certain methodo-

---

[19] Cf. J. Maritain, *Christian Philosophy* (1955), esp. pp. 62ff., and the section on the theology of reason in ThE, II, 1, § 1321ff.

[20] Cf. Althaus, *Die christliche Wahrheit*, II, p. 269.

logical axioms such as the criteria of historical verifiability laid down by Troeltsch.

The task of counter-criticism carries with it the implication that the facts of history which can be established with exactitude will not be in contradiction with Easter faith. If an incontestable psychological explanation of the resurrection experiences could be achieved, the disciples would be unmasked as deceivers or deceived. If the resurrection accounts could all be shown to be legends, Easter faith would collapse. Our thesis is no less than this, even if some respect might remain for the meaning with which those who have come later have filled out the illusion.

The counter-critical task brings us up against NT themes such as the question of the historical Jesus. Since Martin Kähler it has been clear to us why the historical Jesus who is investigated by objectifying science cannot be the object that is proposed for faith. We need not go into that again. Nevertheless, this does not eliminate the task of objectifying science or the question of the historical Jesus. The same principle applies here as in relation to historical work on Easter. Insofar as it is done by theologians, this work has the task of counter-criticism.

In this regard Ebeling rightly points out that reference to (the historical) Jesus is constitutive for Christology (i.e., the statement who Jesus is). Hence Jesus is the criterion of Christology. If it could be shown that Christology has no foothold in the historical Jesus but is a misinterpretation of Jesus, Christology would be at an end.[21]

More is involved, then, than simply making it possible to believe in Christ with a good conscience. At issue is a penetration, found elsewhere as well in the Bultmann school, beyond the mere Christ kerygma, beyond the mere "account of," to the attested reality itself. Initial points have to be indicated which work against a de-actualizing of history and anchorage in the sphere of consciousness alone. The question is raised concerning the ontic event which as the change in aeons summons us not merely to a new consciousness but also into a new being.[22]

f. Counter-Criticism of the Vision Hypothesis

The only serious target of counter-criticism is the vision hypothesis which historians often advance in relation to the resurrection story. This hypothesis, which is usually given the status of a thesis, is to the effect that the kerygma of the resurrection can be adequately explained in terms of subjective experiences on the part of the disciples. Real encounters in the objective world are not needed on this view.

Now it may be conceded that the hypothesis cannot be totally refuted. If it could, this would be tantamount to proof of the resurrection, for all

---

[21] *Word and Faith* (E.T. 1963), pp. 288f.
[22] In this regard cf. esp. E. Käsemann, *Exegetische Versuche und Besinnungen* (1964), I, pp. 187ff.; II, pp. 31ff.

other possibilities of explanation would be ruled out and it would have to be concluded that a supernatural event took place. In addition to the epistemological problems that such a negative proof would involve, one must also say that it is theologically untenable. For it would entail an objectifying of miracle, and this would be in contradiction with the nature of miracle as attested in the NT. It would divest it of its ambivalence, whether the noetic ambivalence that explanations in terms of natural causality are always possible (a mere appearance of death in raisings from the dead, or psychosomatic factors in healing, etc.), or the theological ambivalence that the devil can be driven out by Beelzebub as well as by the Spirit of God (Matthew 9:34).

In virtue of this ambivalence, counter-criticism cannot set itself the task of demonstrating the non-ambivalence of a supernatural intervention on the third day by completely eliminating all other explanations, e.g., that of visions. The only possible task of counter-criticism is this. In the name of theological awareness of ambivalence, of lasting ambivalence in principle, it must undermine the illegitimate non-ambivalence which a secular historian might accord to the hallucination thesis. For this historico-critical non-ambivalence is just as false as the pseudo-theological non-ambivalence with which a certain type of orthodoxy seeks either positively or negatively to establish the fact of the resurrection.

Thus it is not the task of counter-criticism to refute the vision hypothesis as such, which in any case it cannot do. Its task is to oppose the rank which this hypothesis assumes, i.e., the rank of non-ambivalence, of a thesis which can be proved.

What form will such counter-criticism take?

We begin by asking how the vision hypothesis arises. We may then survey some typical examples of it.

Now even extreme scepticism can hardly deny that something must have happened between the crucifixion of Jesus and the faith of the primitive community in the risen Lord. For Golgotha reduced the disciples of Jesus to despair and resignation. They were scattered helplessly to the winds. Nevertheless, in a very short span, which hardly leaves time for psychologically explicable restoration, they are together again, worshipping the failure on the cross as their Lord. Obviously something must have happened in the interval.

Since, however, in virtue of his categorical commitment, the historian not only regards a supernatural fact as non-objectifiable but contests such a fact in principle, his only remaining option is to locate the intervening event in the subjectivity of the disciples and to speak of a visionary experience, or a hallucination. His explanation will thus resemble that of D. F. Strauss, namely, that the impression made by Jesus of Nazareth on his disciples was so profound that they could not think of him as swallowed up by death but began to think of him as still alive. This psychogenic faith was then projected into objectivity and led to the hallucination that the risen Lord met them. In this way the story of the resurrection is radically de-objectified and reduced to the inner psychological sphere.[23]

Bultmann's vision hypothesis does not go quite so far as this. In it one may still see the margin of reality which he always tries to keep and which is meant to maintain the relation between consciousness and history even if the historical component is the non-objectifiable X to which we referred earlier. In intention at least Bultmann wants to avoid the absolute immanence of a mere process of consciousness. He thus opposes a purely psychogenic or hallucinatory understanding of faith in the resurrection.

A vision, he can say, is never a wholly inward process. It carries its basis within itself as a present reality. The encounter which precedes it comes to ripeness in it. It becomes itself a new encounter. Thus in a dream our eyes can be opened to ourselves. Our sleeping conscience can be awakened. It is foolish to take the psychological view that dreams and visions are the product of their subject. Real forces are met in them. The disciples' vision was imaginary to the extent that they projected its object into the spatial and sensory world, but the object itself was not imaginary. My faith, awakened by the Word, is not a purely inward or human process any more than is the love I have for a friend. It has its target, its object. If this is not "alongside" or "behind" it, nevertheless it works as a reality in it (KM, p. 152).

Bultmann's answer confirms what we have been trying to show. First, he is plainly concerned to avoid slipping into a philosophy of immanent consciousness. He wishes to maintain the historicity of the kerygma. But second, he cannot guarantee the historical basis on his plan of operation. For in fact faith for him does not depend on the fact of the resurrection. Instead, the resurrection depends on the faith kindled by encounter with Christ, with the Jesus of Nazareth who walked on earth. Hence the resurrection is in no sense an event. It is simply the result of an encounter and is to be taken figuratively.

Clearly the scientific conviction that the supernatural not only is non-objectifiable, but also cannot exist, comes into conflict here with the self-understanding of the NT authors. Hence considerable portions of the resurrection kerygma fall away, including not only facticity in time and space but also some of the broader intentions of the NT statement. Bultmann still accepts, and has to do so, some working of Jesus Christ on his disciples. But this is simply an indirect working in the form of posthumous influence. He can no longer accept a work of God on Jesus Christ which takes place irrespective of our receiving subjectivity, namely, the work of resurrection, the miracle of the third day, God's confession of his Son.

---

[23] We thus have what Strauss calls an evangelical myth, i.e., a story, directly or indirectly related to Jesus, which is not the impress of a fact but the deposit of an idea of the first disciples; cf. *Das Leben Jesu,* 4th ed. (1840), p. 98; E.T. 1974, p. 86; and § 151. An even clearer form of the same thesis is naturally to be found in Feuerbach.

What Bultmann can still accept relates to a postulate which he who has been with the earthly Jesus finds himself forced to make. This postulate is that Jesus of Nazareth cannot remain dead. This possibly subconscious postulate—there are good reasons for using the terminology of psycho-analysis in this regard—comes to expression at the imaginative level, manifests itself as vision, and in some cases, as in that of Paul, may rise to the dimension of theological reflection.

The NT witnesses, however, present the event of the third day as the act of God. Witness to this act does not take place merely as the advancing of a thesis. It is impressively indirect. Reference is made to the despair of those who were left behind. No spiritual or psychological potential was available, then, for the making of the postulate mentioned above. Encounter with the risen Lord takes place in opposition to all postulates. It has the shock of the absolutely unexpected, of what was regarded as impossible. It is this situation in particular which bears witness to God's act on his Son. This act is not at all in line with our postulates. It is contingent in relation to them. It has all the surprise of the will of God and of those higher thoughts of his which cut right across our thoughts.

The vision hypothesis allows for the relation between Christ and man but not for the relation between God and Christ. It is thus in conflict with the essential theologoumenon that the point of the Easter story lies in God's act on his Son. Its understanding leaves no place for an act in this dimension. Only when this is realized does its inadequacy appear. It is forced to resist the facticity of the resurrection, its character as an event in time and space. It lives by the thesis that what is not objectifiable does not exist objectively or ontically. God's act on his Son and the facticity of the event are indissolubly connected. The former can be expressed only when resurrection is implied as its effect and its reality is included.

As stated, historico-critical inquiry cannot prove this. It can simply do two things as counter-criticism. First, it can resist the attempt to advance the vision hypothesis as an adequate explanation of what intervened after the death of Jesus. The claim that such an explanation is non-ambivalent can easily be challenged. It leaves far too many questions open, e.g., the question how there can be so swift a change from deep despair to the joy of Easter faith. Second, counter-criticism can show that the vision hypothesis omits whole sections of the Easter faith, especially the belief that quite apart from any later experience of ours God acted on Jesus Christ, so that in this faith there is expressed not only the relation of Jesus Christ with us but also the relation between God the Father and God the Son, and to this extent—to put it dogmatically—an intratrinitarian dimension is involved.

This argument has considerable counter-critical force. For it is absolutely impossible to say that to assume an event of this kind between God and his Son is to arrive at the postulate that God had to raise him again. At this point it is perfectly clear that the very opposite is the case. The astonishing encounter with the risen Lord itself gave rise to the theological thesis that God is to be praised for his acts because he has in fact performed an act (Acts 2:24-28).

g. Basis of Faith or Concept of Faith?[24]

Only now can we see why the biblical witnesses stress the event character of the resurrection so strongly and in so many ways. Even though they differ in detail and may even seem to be contradictory, their common intention is to confess one thing with many voices and to reflect on the fundamental significance of this one thing.

To say this is to take sides in a debate which has occupied theology from the turn of the century, which was a particular concern of W. Herrmann, and in relation to which Schleiermacher played the role of a forerunner with a very similar conception. We have in mind the distinction, to which frequent allusion has already been made, between that which is the basis and direct object of faith and that in which faith forms doctrines that simply reflect faith, or expound it in figurative conceptions, and thus follow it. This distinction takes on enhanced significance in Christology and at this point actualizes itself especially in the resurrection kerygma.[25]

We have a certain anticipation of the hermeneutical problem posed by existentialist interpretation when Herrmann distinguishes along these lines between basis of faith and concept of faith. (Even historically there is a connection between Herrmann and Bultmann in this regard.) A basis of faith is here a reality which imparts certainty of faith, so that it cannot be called in question or destroyed by any reflection. Concepts of faith, in contrast, are ideas and reflections in which the believer elucidates the evidence with the intellectual resources at his disposal.[26]

Concepts of faith are thus subsequent to the basis of faith and they are also variable. For naturally the resources of ideas and concepts are subject to historical change. To pursue the analogy with Bultmann, they may be the resources of myth, logos, and cosmological ideas. Such concepts are relative, whereas the basis of faith is absolute.

This distinction between basis and concept of faith poses the task of categorizing every locus of dogmatics as either basis or concept. Is the resurrection, for example, to be classified as part of the basis of faith? Or is it simply a later form or figurative expression of the true basis? Herrmann takes the latter view and his answer calls for rapid survey.

Like the champions of existentialist exegesis, Herrmann is bothered by

---

[24] For an earlier discussion of this problem in connection with the doctrine of the Trinity cf. Chapter XIII.

[25] Cf. Schleiermacher, *The Christian Faith,* § 99 and 100, 1: "The facts of the resurrection and ascension . . . cannot be regarded as a true part of the doctrine of his person."

[26] *Gesammelte Aufsätze,* ed. F. W. Schmidt (1923), p. 293; *Der Verkehr des Christen mit Gott,* 7th ed. (1921), p. 11; E.T. *Communion with God,* 2nd ed. (1906), pp. 10f.

the fact that the contents of proclamation transcend the sphere of our experience and are not, therefore, verifiable. There can be no crossing the frontier of objective, universally valid, and verifiable experience which the epistemology of Kant has uncovered. This is a serious problem, for faith constantly relates to facts of this kind. It is thus in the position of having to suppress the concept of the true imposed upon the theoretical conscience by Kant, and of having to surrender therewith its intellectual honesty.

Nor do epistemological considerations alone make it doubtful whether faith can be founded on facts which are supposed to belong to the objective world. Herrmann is very conscious of the increasing historical criticism which is carried out in the name of this epistemological theory and which undermines historical confidence in the facts which are the basis of faith. He is thus faced by the question where solid evidence can be found which can be neither challenged nor eroded.

As a disciple of Kant Herrmann can only say that such evidence is not to be found in objective reality but only in the sphere which Kant puts under the competence of practical reason. This sphere is the experience of personal, human reality, or, as we would say today, of human existence. I must interpret the objects of doctrine in orientation to this experience.

But where do I find this sphere in the world of the NT and its message? I find it in encounter with the person of Jesus. We have here evidence which Herrmann calls the inner life of Jesus. As I encounter this inner life, I experience an intellectual and moral force in contact with which I am aware of being elevated to a true and inwardly independent life of my own.[27]

This experience of personal awakening is the criterion of whether or not I come up against something indisputable. This is the only possible place of certainty. By it I learn that the power of redemption touches me here. Dogmatics says, then, that the power of Jesus Christ to save us can mean only that the reality of his person as it is now experienced by us can convince us as nothing else can that God will accept us.[28]

In interpretation of this statement it is important that the reality of the person of Jesus, that which makes it the basis of our faith, comes to manifestation in the possibility of its presence and immediacy to my experiences today.

The relationship of Jesus with God is exemplary for my relationship with God. It can be repeated. I experience it when through encounter with Jesus Christ I am led to my own encounter with God.[29]

As Jesus Christ is thus the living representation and guarantee of the love of God, he cannot belong only to the past. He is the revelation of this love disclosing itself to me. Hence the inner life of Jesus, which is in har-

---

[27] *Gesammelte Aufsätze*, p. 325 (cf. also pp. 318ff.); *Dogmatik* (1925), p. 83; *Ethik*, 5th ed. (1921), § 20, etc.

[28] *Ethik*, § 45.

[29] Cf. *Dogmatik*, p. 84.

mony with the Father, is a present and not a past factor. For the same reason it is not just a form of revelation; it is *the* revelation.

In all this we have been describing the basis of faith as Herrmann sees it. For him it has, then, a personal quality.

Only on this basis can there be concepts of faith. Those who try to put these first, i.e., to achieve them before being reached by the basis of faith, begin at the wrong end. They seek the consequences without first having the premises. Thus those who talk of divine sonship and vicarious suffering without starting with personal experience of the inner life of Jesus are guilty of rashness and fall victim to the temptation of occupying themselves with their own speculative notions.[30] Only when we have had the initial experience and come to know the basic evidence do we discover the lines that lead to concepts of faith, even if we may then formulate these very differently, as Herrmann essentially does with all the loci of dogmatics in relation to their traditional form.

All this has particular relevance for faith in the resurrection. For Herrmann this cannot be the basis of faith, for it cannot be verified as regards its character as supernatural event. Furthermore, in relation to the accompanying historical facts, there can be no saying in detail what really took place at Easter according to the biblical accounts.

But this is not a disaster. For those who have experienced the inner life of Jesus as the basis of faith have been given the certainty that Jesus is alive and present. Hence the disciples would have had to say that even without the appearances what they had received earlier from their encounter with Jesus and his inner life would have given them the certainty that for Jesus death was the consummation and not the destruction of his obedience.[31]

Here it is plain that concepts of faith are only inferences from the basis of faith, that they can be drawn from within the self, and that in principle there is no need at all for a historically manifested confirmation such as the Easter event. On the basis of its own autarchous experience faith finds itself led to the certainty that Jesus was not held by death.

On the other hand faith is constantly threatened notwithstanding its basis. It may hesitate in face of the inferences that it should draw. The concepts of faith may not come. For Herrmann, then, the appearances of the risen Lord are helps in drawing the inferences.[32]

Like the disciples, we, too, need such helps. Instead of the appearances we have the proposition that the Christian community is grounded in those experiences of the exalted and present Lord. This is a kind of divine aid

---

[30] *Ges. Aufsätze*, p. 293; *Verkehr*, p. 11; E.T. pp. 10f.

[31] G. Koch, *Die Auferstehung Jesu Christi*, p. 95.

[32] Cf. Lessing's position in *The Education of the Human Race*. Reason (not faith) could reach by itself all the truths imparted in revelation, but revelation has served as a pacemaker to speed up the development of rational knowledge. Cf. the author's *Offenbarung, Vernunft und Existenz. Studien zur Religionsphilosophie Lessings*, 5th ed. (1967).

granted to us when we form concepts of faith. In spite of this divine co-operation, however, the resurrection kerygma is subordinate to the primary experience which is linked to encounter with the inner life of Jesus and which mediates to us the evidence of faith and its later forms of reflection.

This may seem to be an attractive view. In it faith avoids conflict with epistemological theory and thus escapes collision with theoretical reason and historical experience. An apparently clear path is marked to the veri-fiability of the ground of faith. This ground is no longer a foreign super-natural body in the objective world of history. It is a personal thing which can be experienced, namely, the "existence" of Jesus. All else belongs to the sphere of concepts of faith which can be relativized and demythol-ogized.

Of course, the question arises at once whether this separation and later reuniting of the ground of faith and the concepts of faith can be upheld.

Undoubtedly the NT witnesses, if they had been confronted with this choice between ground of faith and concept of faith, would have placed the resurrection event on the side of the ontological basis. Their encounter with the inner life of Jesus—it is only with a bad conscience that we can use this modern psychological term—and even their encounter with the authority which enabled him to perform miracles and signs and to speak the word of fulfilment, had ended in the darkness of despair at Golgotha. In the strict sense the history of Jesus with his disciples had come to an end there. It continued only in virtue of the fact that a history between God and the Son took place. The resurrection was the light which in spite of every postulate and all logic broke into the darkness.

Undoubtedly, too, the event of the resurrection was not regarded by the disciples as a divine aid to their thinking—always assuming that the first Christian witnesses could be asked about the choice in question. For the disciples did not experience the event of the resurrection as a clarification of what was previously obscure nor as the completion of knowledge that had hitherto been fragmentary and vacillating. For them it was a shock which cut right across all their psychological dispositions.

What is even more important, they did not experience the event of the third day as a noetic event which helped them to understand with full clarity what they had thus far only suspected. They understood it as an ontic event which gave meaning to the outer and inner life of Jesus, not just subjectively as an enlightening of the understanding, but objectively. To put it in Kantian terms, as Herrmann might do, one could say that for the disciples the statement that Jesus lives was not an analytic judgment, a tautology of higher order which simply maintained what encounter with the earthly Jesus had already expressed or at least implied and potentially included. It was a synthetic judgment, which carried with it the new factor of the Easter event and thus drew a conclusion both from the encounter with the earthly Jesus, which only the witnesses of the resurrection had enjoyed, and also from the resurrection itself.

If we adopt Herrmann's thesis that the new, true, and independent life which is found in me guarantees the spiritual power of Jesus to bring this into being, we must also add that the true criterion which the believer has for the resurrection of Jesus Christ is the experience that there is dying and rising again with him. But this is more and other than what Herrmann means with his experience of inner independence and new personal existence.

Does this mean that the relation between ground of faith and concepts of faith falls to the ground completely? The relation is much too complicated for us to be able to give a simple answer to this question.

Perhaps one might say that the relation is false when it is structured along the lines of Herrmann, that is, when concepts of faith to which the resurrection kerygma is ordered occur simply in an analytic judgment. For when this is done the relation robs the resurrection of the facticity which for good reasons is all-important to the NT witnesses.

The relation is not wholly wrong, however—to put it cautiously—if it is meant to describe the noetic way which leads to confirmation of the resurrection event. For this way begins with a basis which is laid by encounter with the life, suffering, and death of Christ and also by encounter with the so-called inner life of Jesus. All the witnesses of the resurrection start here. None of them begins the way of faith to Christ with the Easter experience. This is their common testimony. Hence the way which starts at the basis in the life of Jesus and leads on to the empty tomb must be described as prototypical.

The point is that we too, as later witnesses of the risen Lord, are in the position that our faith does not begin with the resurrection kerygma. The way of our faith begins with the earthly Jesus, with his nativity, his teaching, his acts and accomplishments, and finally his death and passion.

Faith always has its beginning with what takes place on earth. For the Word was made flesh and must be sought in the flesh. One cannot drag God too deeply into the flesh. It is also essential for our faith, of course, that the history of the earthly Jesus should be seen and described and understood already in the light of its end, of the resurrection. This means that the resurrection kerygma will come as a shock to him who considers the death and passion of the earthly Jesus, even though this is hard to grasp psychologically and cannot be compared psychologically to the shock of the disciples. (Apart from all else, this is so because within the framework of Christian education we have known the message of the resurrection from youth up, and because the light of the resurrection in which the history of Jesus is seen and described prepares us for the event of the third day.) Nevertheless, even within the tradition there is a moment—not necessarily one that can be fixed chronologically—when we are unavoidably struck by the break between the earthly history of Jesus and his Easter exaltation, and when the resurrection narratives confront us with the question whether we are to worship or whether we are to draw back, to draw back either in the form of denial—this cannot be true—or in the form of reinterpretation to make verifiability possible, as in the vision or hallucination hypothesis.

The very question whether the Easter message is true is a symptom of this existential shock, for the question points to the realization of a break between the life of the earthly Jesus and the status of the risen Lord. The shock of having to put the question is caused by relationship with the Jesus of the Gospels. This Jesus forces us to inquire whether the one who goes through the land, does and proclaims acts of power, and finally perishes on the cross, can be identical with the exalted figure whom we meet in the Easter stories.

At this point the analogy between today and yesterday is so strong that it is still true for us who come later that if we do not encounter the earthly Jesus we can feel no shock. In this case, when we are told that the cult hero of Christians is alive again, we treat it either as an incontestable legend or as the mythical garment of an idea along the lines of D. F. Strauss. Either way there can be no shock, for reason is untouched by the former, and the idea behind the latter can actually be produced by reason, so that there is no shock of antithesis to science.

This confirms the fact that the beginning of the disciples' history of faith with the earthly Jesus is of prototypical significance for us. We, too, can feel the discontinuity between the earthly life and the exaltation—even if it be in the form of doubt as to the truth of the resurrection kerygma— only if we start at the earthly Jesus.

h. Continuity and Discontinuity between the Earthly Jesus and the Risen Christ

Everything depends, then, on the sense of discontinuity and the exposure to shock which this entails. If we bypass this, and do not experience in our own history of faith the subjective break corresponding to the ontic discontinuity, we are not confronted with the facticity of the resurrection. More accurately, we do not stand over against the act of God on his Son which as God's act, as the history enacted by him, bears always the mark of the contingent and is thus surprising, cutting right across all our expectations, programs, and postulates.

This cutting across is in keeping with the style of the divine action.

When men count on salvation, like the false prophets, God's judgment falls. When men count on a calculable relation between guilt and punishment and merit and reward, like Job, God does the incalculable and brings this pseudo-faith under severe assault. When men count on a Messiah who as a king will overthrow the world order, like the Israelites, God sends the despised and rejected and is concealed under his opposite.

The inference to be drawn from this is that so long as we do not experience the shock of astonishment we are not yet facing God's contingent act, the brute fact of his resolves, or the facticity of his work. Thinking that we can believe without that break, we are still moving along the lines of our own postulates.

In our view this applies to the strict form of the existential interpretation. So long as Easter is for me only a commentary on Golgotha, there is no break, for a good commentary is in unbroken consensus with the text on which it comments. Characteristic here is the fact that this understanding can speak only of the Easter kerygma and not of the facticity of an event. It can speak only of what happens to us.

The same applies to the hallucination or vision hypotheses. Visions can only confirm what has already been experienced. What happens in a vision is in unbroken continuity with what happened earlier. I simply recapitulate this in my dream. I take it up into my subconscious imagination. Visions are dotted continuations of lines on which I have moved in the real encounters of conscious daily life. In the resurrection event, however, we do not have confirmatory "visions" but "revisions" of what human reason can postulate. These postulates could end only in hopeless attempts to seek the living among the dead. He was, in fact, sought there. The women at the tomb were postulating women who experienced a shock (Luke 24:1-5).

Nevertheless, we do not have here pure and abstractly understood discontinuity. Obviously our pre-formed ideas, which relate to phenomenological reality, are not adequate when it is a matter of grasping the occurrence of this kind of reality. What has been long since realized in respect of the subject-object relation, namely, that it is inadequate vis-à-vis the facts of salvation history, must also be realized in respect of the terms continuity and discontinuity. These are not to be taken in pure form. If Herrmann and the whole Bultmann school are wrong in postulating continuity between the earthly Jesus and the risen Christ, i.e., along the lines of an unbroken relation between the basis of faith and the concepts of faith, Althaus is also on dubious ground when he speaks of pure discontinuity. The two are in fact interrelated.

An example which clarifies the form of this interrelationship is the connection between prophecy and fulfilment. It seems to us that we have here an excellent model of the union and distinction, the continuity and discontinuity, between the earthly Jesus and the risen Christ. All fulfilments of prophecy are different from the prophecies themselves. They transcend them.

In the OT predictions of Christ which are quoted in the Advent and Christmas stories, it is plain that Christmas brings with it something new which both transcends and modifies. We need not expound this in detail here. It is familiar territory. The same applies to the prophetic references to the Suffering Servant, e.g., in Isaiah 53.

If the ordinary Christian with no theological training does not see this, it is because he does without thinking what the church does consciously when it adopts the quotations and builds them into the church's year, reading the Bible backwards, i.e., reading the OT in the light of the NT. There thus seems to be unbroken continuity.

In contrast, the theologian, representing the intellectually adult community, suffers a shock of astonishment when he sees in the fulfilments the new elements which transcend and modify the prophecies. This shock can go to the point of breaking the schema of prophecy and fulfilment for him. To put it abstractly, he can get the impression of full-scale discontinuity which shatters the schema. On the other hand, the fact that the OT can be read in the light of the NT, that there is the possibility of that naive understanding of ongoing and unbroken salvation history, simplistic though it may be—this fact is a sign that the line of prophecy does point to fulfilment when seen retrospectively.

Here, of course, the metaphor from geometry immediately breaks down, for if we were to follow that line alone we should not land up in the manger at Bethlehem or the empty tomb. This is shown by Jewish exegesis, e.g., that of Martin Buber. Only when, advancing on that line, we are confronted with *new* events and new *events,* only when we follow a new history, do we find in retrospect that this history has a pre-history and that the fulfilment has a prophecy.

The new thing is not just new, nor is the otherness of the fulfilment wholly other. But he who stands in the light of the fulfilment knows more than the prophet who knew the fulfilment only in the form of the prophecy.

Everything depends, then, on one's place in the salvation event if the schema of prophecy and fulfilment is to be upheld. Continuity can be seen only in retrospect.

The same applies to eschatology. As Josef Wittig has finely put it, a man's biography can be written only when he is dead. Similarly, the world's biography can be written only after its end, the eschaton. Looking back from the Last Day we shall see continuities which escape us now. We shall perceive the line running straight from the fall to the judgment whereas now we see only the breaks of meaninglessness, or of what seems to be meaningless.

One of the decisive differences between faith and sight is that faith believes in spite of the breaks, clinging to the non-objectifiable consistency of God, whereas sight will be able to perceive the continuity of God's faithfulness in the continuity of phenomena, as it views the panorama of history from the height of the Last Day.

Thus fulfilment through the status of resurrection differs from the prophetic life of Jesus as he walked on earth. This status is a new thing. It is a transcendent happening. It sets the earthly life in a different light. It offers a new commentary on it. The element of discontinuity finds expression here. The ascension then provides an additional interpretation.

At the same time the disciples recognize the validity of the prophecy in the light of resurrection. The identity of the earthly Jesus and the risen Christ becomes plain to them.

The ontic background of the continuity between the two states comes to expression in that the risen Lord bears the marks of the nails (John 20:20) and recapitulates the supper with his disciples (Luke 24:30). The noetic background may be seen in that he opens the *nous* of his disciples and causes them to recognize that there is agreement between this event and the scriptures (*graphai*), so that this fulfilment does not lie outside the range of the prophecies (Luke 24:45; 24:25).

The model for this dialectic of continuity and discontinuity is to be found in the NT itself, namely, in the story of the conversation between the risen Lord and the two disciples on the Emmaus road (Luke 24:13-35).

Here both factors occur. First is the experience of discontinuity. Their eyes are held and they do not recognize him (v. 16). They do not recognize him, i.e., they cannot identify him as the risen Lord, because they are thinking in terms of their own hopes and postulates. They have been hoping that he would be the one to deliver Israel (v. 21). The risen Lord points them to the continuity with scripture: Did he not have to suffer? (v. 26). But this "necessity" is not one that can be calculated in the form of postulates. It is clear only when they later meet the one who has moved through suffering to his exaltation. Only the self-disclosure of the risen Lord brings it to light.

In this light alone is it clear that the Lord's Supper was not a parting meal but had its own prophetic significance as it pointed to coming fellowship with the exalted Lord. This continuity is first made evident when the exalted Lord breaks bread.

A psychological indication of the relation between continuity and discontinuity in experience may also be found in the Emmaus story. After their encounter with the risen Lord the disciples say to one another: "Did not our hearts burn within us. . . ?" (v. 32). This reference to the *kardia kaiomene*, the burning heart, shows us that even at the first stage encounter with the risen Lord was not just a negation of our hopes. Even as wholly other the risen Lord did not stay outside the system of co-ordinates of our thinking, feeling, and willing. He entered into it. He did not just cut across the line of our expectation; he was also on this line. The point is that our schemata, being tied to "normal" history and psychology, could not locate him on it and identify him with the help of it. We simply noted that our hearts burned. This was an indication that he entered our psyche with its hopes and fears.

But this symptom of burning, this slight movement of our geiger counter, could not point us to its source. We heard bells ringing but did not know where they were. Our encounter with the prophecies of scripture and the prophetic life of Jesus could not enable us to perceive the fulfilment. The colon behind the prophecies left us helpless. We could not construct for ourselves the text of the fulfilled reality. If we tried, i.e., in the form of giving concreteness to the hopes nourished by prophecy, we were led in the wrong direction. Only when the risen Lord revealed himself as the text of fulfilment and put in the period did we grasp the context and hence the continuity of the full sentence. Only then did we begin to see that the colon in the middle had both separating and also uniting significance.

By now it has become sufficiently clear why we have to lay stress on the fact that the resurrection kerygma does not just contain an idea of faith deriving from the true basis of faith, namely, encounter with the earthly

Jesus, and to that extent standing in continuity with this basis. We can see from the model of prophecy and fulfilment in what sense and to what degree the resurrection of Christ is a new happening which only by the fact of its presence, its coming as the risen Lord came into the room where his disciples were, transcends the old prophecy, in this instance the prophetic life of Jesus, and yet at the same time elucidates it, both moving beyond it on the one hand and moving toward it on the other.

Those who begin their history of faith with Jesus Christ as indicated above, namely, with the earthly Jesus, the incarnate Logos, will also be conscious of a burning of the heart. We hope that readers will not take this sentimentally. What is meant is this. If we take the incarnation of Jesus Christ seriously, we will read the life of Jesus as a biography, as one biography among others, with at most a belief that we have before us the supreme example of homo sapiens, an example which few atheists, anti-Christians, or other rebels have ever attacked no matter how violently they have opposed the church and Christianity. Even if, however, prejudice in favor of Jesus has been stirred up by such experiences, it cannot prevent the reader of the life of Jesus from understanding him in analogy to other men. The reader will try to penetrate to his inner life and to relate the love he showed to what he himself has experienced and bestowed of love. He will also raise psychological questions.

In so doing, and in ruling out anything supernatural, from the virgin birth to the ascension, he will let Jesus be a whole man, as he should. But when this is done, as it ought to be, the reader will come up against an inexplicable element for which there is no analogy.

His experience will perhaps be like that of Albert Schweitzer, who in his account of the search for the historical Jesus tells of the attempt to find the historical Jesus by stripping away the dogmatic trappings and getting to the true historical core, but then shows that what was finally found behind the wrappings was not a man like ourselves but an apocalyptic phantom, alien and alienating, and completely unable to bind us to himself in faith.

Precisely when we find that there is no analogy, however, we reach the heart of the matter, namely, the prophecy of this life which found its fulfilment on the third day.

In this knowing-unknowing encounter with the heart of the matter our hearts burn within us as did those of the disciples on the road to Emmaus. The burning heart is not a torch which can show us the way from the prophecy to the fulfilment. If the risen Lord had not kindled his light on the way to Emmaus, the torch of the heart could have lit up only the ruins of buried hopes, and he who walked on earth would have taken on ghostly features in retrospect.

The burning of the heart and movement of the geiger counter, which point to new and unknown radiations, are not enough to give us orientation. Schweitzer was not led by this burning to the empty tomb. He tried to deal in other ways with the alien apparition of the historical Jesus.

The prophecy imparted to us with the experience that there is no analogy for Jesus remains mute if it is not given words by the risen Lord and if it does not then in retrospect become a stage on the way of life. Prophecy alone becomes a wrong road or dead end. Only when I find myself on the other side of the gulf do I see, looking back, that I have been led over a bridge, namely, the bridge of prophecy. Nor would I be there were he not really there, even though I could not count on his being there or on the fact that he went there on the third day.

XXXI

Postscript on Christology and the Witness of the Spirit

In the preceding chapters we have referred repeatedly to the implicit Christology of the Gospels. The mystery of the person of Jesus is not stated directly by Jesus himself; it is set forth indirectly, veiled in enigmatic sayings. The "objective uncertainty" of which Kierkegaard speaks, the confusing antithesis of the claim to majesty and the form of humility, is the very thing that demands faith and confronts us with the alternative of all or nothing—the all of fulfilment or the nothing of charlatanry and meaninglessness.

Along the same lines one might say of Christology (as in our own work) that it contains an implicit doctrine of the Holy Spirit, and indeed that the testimony of the Holy Spirit is in a special way an "enveloped" witness which is always present under this cover.

Already in Volume I[1] we have discussed the hermeneutical significance of the Spirit and shown how we are summoned by the Spirit to participation in the self-knowledge of God (1 Corinthians 2:10f.). Because God himself is present in Christ, the same may also be said of the Son of God. If we are not touched by his Spirit, we are closed to him and he to us. "If any man have not the Spirit of Christ, he is none of his" (Romans 8:9). "No man can say that Jesus is the Lord, but by the Holy Ghost" (1 Corinthians 12:3).

There can be no reaching him by human initiative, whether it be intellectual apprehension, religious receptivity or affinity, or the activism of imitation of Christ.[2] Even though Jesus dispels the thin air of abstraction by the vivid imagery of the parables and moves deeply into the sphere of worldly wisdom (1 Corinthians 1:18ff.), where he touches the most elementary strata, there is still no natural bridging of the gulf which separates

---

[1] Chapter XI, pp. 193ff.
[2] Cf. Luther's exposition of the third article in his Small Catechism: "I believe that I cannot of my own understanding and strength believe in or come to Jesus Christ, but that the Holy Ghost has called me by the gospel. . . ."

man from the mystery of God. Human eyes do not see here nor human ears hear, even when eternal truth is put in teaching form and given didactically (Matthew 13:13). On the contrary, in this extreme proximity the shock of something alien is felt and eternal truth is not recognized in the lofty steepness of its *totaliter-aliter*. When the parables are unveiled, it is to those to whom it is given by him who speaks them (Matthew 13:11).

If, then, Christ makes God's truth present by his own presence, it is not just by speaking it. The fact that he lives it out in his words and conduct does not in itself make it powerful unless its power be seen also in its ability to provoke hardening, resistance, and offense (Matthew 13:14f.; cf. 6:9f.). No, beyond the whole content of what is said God's truth is present only as hearts are opened to appropriate it. This is why we have said that the Word of God is not just indicatory or interpretative. It does not merely set the truth before us and point to it. It has the force of an active Word which changes and discloses.

What makes this action possible and therefore causes it to be an active Word is the Holy Spirit. The testimony of the Holy Spirit means, not that *we* grasp the truth that is set before us, but that it is *disclosed* to us by the Spirit-witness with which it is furnished. We do not know him who is the truth (John 14:6); we come to be known by him (1 Corinthians 13:12) and our eyes are opened so that we for our part know this being known.

This is what the Parting Discourses in John have in view when they show how the mystery of Christ is unveiled. Who he is may be known only in the light of his resurrection and exaltation. The Paraclete, whom he will send after this exaltation of his, who "proceeds" from him, will disclose his truth to us and unfold it in its fulness (John 16:5ff.). This is why it makes no difference to the apostle whether he says "God's Spirit dwells in you" or "Christ is in you" or "he who has the Spirit of Christ. . . ."[3] For this Spirit of his gives life (Romans 8:2), guides into the truth (John 15:26), and calls as the community those who are in the truth and who hear his voice.

What the Spirit reveals about him, what the Spirit unfolds concerning his truth, will, of course, always be his truth. What is promised in the Parting Discourses will always apply to this activity of the Spirit: "He shall receive of mine" (John 16:14).

Hence the Spirit does not lead away from him to emancipation nor past him to new and "higher" revelations. His exaltation and his presence by the Spirit are simply developments of what took place in the miracle of the incarnation of the Logos, of what became event in the earthly Jesus, of what was expressed in his being, word and work, and of what was reported about this.[4] The risen Lord still bears the marks of the nails, as

---

[3] M. Kähler, "Das schriftgemässe Bekenntnis zum Geiste Christi," *Dogmatische Zeitfragen,* I (1898), p. 145.

[4] In this respect too, although he said it in a different context, Ebeling is right when he points out that Christology must have a foothold in Jesus himself ("Jesus

we have said. He is the same, the one who is, and was, and is to come (Revelation 1:4; cf. 4:8). He is the same, Jesus of Nazareth, the exalted Christ, and the present Spirit.

Jesus, as the form of God's condescension, is thus the norm for confession of Christ. Only Christ, however, reveals who this Jesus "is." And who Christ "is," is disclosed only by his Spirit in whom he has promised his presence.

To be drawn into this dialectic is to believe. Prophecy unveils itself only in its fulfilment. This applies also to the prophetic life of Jesus of Nazareth. The book of the great acts of God has to be read backward. For the Spirit of Jesus Christ transcends the past-ness of the past; he is present and future (Matthew 18:20; John 16:13). He is the end where the power of revelation is at work and where the Spirit as interpreter causes blind eyes to see and deaf ears to hear.

Thus the very architecture of the Apostles' Creed has its own message when in the third article it sets the final future under the confessional theme: "I believe in the Holy Ghost," and when it thereby brings to bear upon all that has just been said about God the Father and God the Son the new light of this Spirit-witness.

---

und Glaube," *Wort und Glaube,* I, p. 208; E.T. "Jesus and Faith," *Word and Faith,* p. 205).

Indexes

1. SUBJECTS

Absoluteness of Christianity   6, 10
Absurdity, *see* Experience
Achievement, Principle of   92ff., 238f.
Actuosity of God   6f., 192
Adoptionism   141ff.
Aeons, Change of   355, 361, 366
Agape   251f., 254; *see also* Love
Aletheia, *see* Truth
Alienation   25, 35, 169, 185, 219, 363
   from God   208, 216
   from self   208, 216
Alloiosis (Zwingli)   328
Alteration of Structures   48ff.
Amphictyony   200
Ancient Symbols   265
Analogy   19, 70, 78, 270, 283, 284ff.
   of being   34
   of faith   34, 289
Ansbacher Ratschlag (1934)   27
Anthropology-Christology   284, 301
Anthropomorphism   103
Anticriticism and Resurrection   437ff.
Antinomy   268, 284ff., 315, 327
Anxiety   201, 224f.
Apokatastasis   193f.
Apologetics (nineteenth century)   66ff.
Apology (Schleiermacher)   287
Ascension of Christ   349
Atheism   99
   Christian   122
   scientific   65, 75
Author of Covenant   212
Author of Law   212
Autonomy (of Man)   169, 230
   sense of   75

of thought and things   242ff.

Baptism   344
Baptism of Concepts   27, 98, 356
Barah   124
Barmen, Theological Declaration of   357
Beautiful Soul (Schiller)   228
Being   163
Being, Diminution of   162
Bios   27

Caesaro-papalism (Unity of Church and
   State)   183
Cartesian Theology   118
Category of the Personal   105, 163
Category of the Quantitative   125
Cause
   efficient and final   55
   formal and material   51, 55
Certainty   36, 431
Chalcedonian Definition   320ff., 364
   alpha privativum   372ff.
Christ   227ff., 342, 345
   as exemplar   404
   as exemplum   194ff.
   as form of revelation   262ff.
   as hermeneutical principle   346ff.
   as high-priest   360, 366ff.
   as idea of man   282
   as kyrios   290ff., 365
   as logos   85f., 133ff., 139, 159, 263, 284
   as man in solidarity   379, 381ff.
   as mediator   133, 320ff., 380
   as messiah   333, 345ff.

457

2. NAMES

Abelard 193, 320, 329, 376
Acton, C. 46
Alt, A. 211
Althaus, P. 21, 25, 26, 27, 33, 39, 72, 105, 126, 129, 184, 200, 204, 209, 236, 261, 262, 401, 407, 409, 415, 419, 421, 423, 437, 448
Altheim, F. 107
Altingius, J. 420
Altizer, J. 62
Andresen, C. 129
Angelus Silesius 430
Anouilh 382
Anselm 95, 269, 388, 394, 395, 397
Antigone 367
Antweiler, A. 61
Apollonios of Tyana 162
Arberry, A. J. 10
Aristotle 55, 156, 264, 265
Arius 141, 158
Asmussen, H. 237
Augustine 162, 166, 167, 182, 230, 275

Barth, K. 10, 17, 34, 45, 61, 68, 72, 76, 102, 104, 105, 110, 127, 129, 173, 177, 182, 184, 190, 191, 192, 193, 194, 198, 204, 219, 237, 264, 266, 274,

330, 367, 397, 407, 409, 413, 423, 426
Barth, M. 36
Basil 177
Baumgärtel, F. 37
Baur, F. C. 129
Baur, J. 262
Beck, M. D. 129
Benn, G. 32, 405
Benz, E. 17
Berger, P. L. 256
Bertram, G. 423
Betz, O. 407
Beza 3
Bibra, O. S. von 59
Bickermann, E. 423
Bieder, W. 415
Biedermann, A. E. 103
Bizer, E. 261
Blanke, F. 126
Bloch, E. 45, 64, 75, 76, 100
Bloy, L. 77
Bock, J. C. 61
Boehner, P. 120
Bollnow, O. F. 70
Bonhoeffer, D. 17, 65, 66, 68, 100, 167, 374
Borchert, W. 255
Bornhäuser, K. 377, 421
Bornkamm, G. 40, 261
Brandi, A. 66
Branham 322
Braun, H. 15, 61, 63, 99,

107, 180, 261, 270, 388, 407
Braunfels, W. 129
Brecht 417
Breuning, W. 129
Bring, R. 184
Brockes, B. H. 66
Brunner, E. 25, 44, 61, 68, 72, 129, 151, 165, 173, 180, 278, 362, 409, 421
Brunner-Traut, E. 150
Bruno, G. 307, 308, 309, 310
Brunstäd, F. 246
Buber, M. 17, 106, 449
Büchsel, F. 381
Bultmann, R. 5, 7, 12, 16, 17, 23, 45, 61, 69, 70, 72, 116, 151, 205, 213, 243, 262, 265, 270, 271, 287, 294, 299, 332, 337, 347, 416, 424, 426, 427, 428, 429, 431, 433, 434, 438, 440, 441, 442, 448
Burckhardt, J. 224, 360
Buren, P. M. van 62, 99

Caesar 307
Calov 74
Calvin, J. 106, 201, 202, 203, 204, 219, 232, 330, 420

465

3. SCRIPTURE REFERENCES

Genesis

1:1   67
1:2   67, 124
1:26   164
1:26f.   81, 185
1:26ff.   291
1:27ff.   403
1:28   28
1:28f.   54, 81
2:7   94, 124
2:15ff.   291
2:16   54, 403
2:16ff.   28, 214
3:3   81
3:5   52, 89, 239
3:9   81, 97
3:19b   29
3:22   29
3:22f.   417
6:2   418
9:12ff.   292
11:1-9   45
17:5   108
17:15   108
32:29   111
50:20   359

Exodus

2   12
3:13ff.   83
3:14   12, 109, 239
3:14f.   35
3:15   12
6:2   12
7:11   300
7:22   300
8:3   300
8:14f.   300
12   12
12:14   393
12:21ff.   393
12:26   115
13:14   115
14   12
15:11   109, 113
18:11   113
19:20ff.   225
20:2   12
20:5   45
20:12   45
21:15   211
21:17   211
22:19   211
23:13   109
31:15   211
32:1ff.   225
32:14   141, 188
33:12ff.   83
33:18-23   389
33:23   114
34:33   229
34:34   229
34:35   229

Leviticus

19:18   225
20:10   211
20:11ff.   211

Numbers

19:2   97
19:4   97
19:10   97
19:14   97
19:18   97

Deuteronomy

4:29   93f.
4:40   399
5:21   399
6:4   12, 89
6:5   225
6:20   115
7:6f.   209
7:7f.   199
10:12   242
13:2-4   37
16:1   393
18:15   347
31:18   106
32:29   113

Joshua

10:12   67

Judges

2:11ff.   216
13:17f.   111

Ruth

1:20   108

1 Samuel

2:35   127
3:14   395
8:7   359